Contemporary Authors®
Autobiography Series

ISSN 0748-0636

Contemporary

Authors

Autobiography Series

Joyce Nakamura
Editor

Shelly Andrews
Motoko Fujishiro Huthwaite
Associate Editors

Marilyn O'Connell Allen
Editorial Associate

volume **18**

Gale Research Inc. • *DETROIT* • *WASHINGTON, D.C.* • *LONDON*

EDITORIAL STAFF

Joyce Nakamura, *Editor*

Shelly Andrews and Motoko Fujishiro Huthwaite, *Associate Editors*
Linda R. Fischer and Michael J. Tyrkus, *Assistant Editors*
Marilyn O'Connell Allen, *Editorial Associate*
Laurie Collier, Heidi J. Hagen, Carolyn C. March, and Vida Petronis, *Contributing Copyeditors*

Victoria B. Cariappa, *Research Manager*
Mary Rose Bonk, *Research Supervisor, Biography Division*
Reginald A. Carlton, Clare Collins, Andrew Guy Malonis, and Norma Sawaya, *Editorial Associates*
Rachel A. Dixon, Eva Marie Felts, Shirley Gates, and Sharon McGilvray, *Editorial Assistants*

Peter M. Gareffa, *Senior Editor*

Mary Beth Trimper, *Production Director*
Shanna Philpott Heilveil, *Production Assistant*

Cynthia Baldwin, *Art Director*
C. J. Jonik, *Keyliner*
Willie Mathis, *Camera Operator*

David Jay Trotter, *Index Programmer*

Library of Congress Catalog Card Number 86-641293
ISBN 0-8103-4515-3
ISSN 0748-0636

Printed in the United States of America

Published simultaneously in the United Kingdom
by Gale Research International Limited
(An affiliated company of Gale Research Inc.)

The trademark ITP is used under license.

10 9 8 7 6 5 4 3 2 1

Contents

Preface

A Unique Collection of Essays

Each volume in the *Contemporary Authors Autobiography Series (CAAS)* presents an original collection of autobiographical essays written especially for the series by noted writers.

CA Autobiography Series is designed to be a meeting place for writers and readers—a place where writers can present themselves, on their own terms, to their audience; and a place where general readers, students of contemporary literature, teachers and librarians, even aspiring writers can become better acquainted with familiar authors and meet others for the first time.

This is an opportunity for writers who may never write a full-length autobiography to let their readers know how they see themselves and their work, what brought them to this time and place.

Even for those authors who have already published full-length autobiographies, there is the opportunity in *CAAS* to bring their readers "up to date" or perhaps to take a different approach in the essay format. In some instances, previously published material may be reprinted or expanded upon; this fact is always noted at the end of such an essay. Individually, the essays in this series can enhance the reader's understanding of a writer's work; collectively, they are lessons in the creative process and in the discovery of its roots.

CAAS makes no attempt to give a comprehensive overview of authors and their works. That outlook is already well represented in biographies, reviews, and critiques published in a wide variety of sources. Instead, *CAAS* complements that perspective and presents what no other ongoing reference source does: the view of contemporary writers that is shaped by their own choice of materials and their own manner of storytelling.

Who Is Covered?

Like its parent series, *Contemporary Authors,* the *CA Autobiography Series* sets out to meet the needs and interests of a wide range of readers. Each volume includes essays by writers in all genres whose work is being read today. We consider it extraordinary that so many busy authors from throughout the world are able to interrupt their existing writing, teaching, speaking, traveling, and other schedules to converge on a given deadline for any one volume. So it is not always possible that all genres can be equally and uniformly represented from volume to volume, although we strive to include writers working in a variety of categories, including fiction, nonfiction, and poetry. As only a few writers specialize in a single area, the breadth of writings by authors in this volume also encompasses drama, translation, and criticism as well as work for movies, television, radio, newspapers, and journals.

What Each Essay Includes

Authors who contribute to *CAAS* are invited to write a "mini-autobiography" of approximately 10,000 words. In order to give the writer's imagination free rein, we suggest no guidelines or pattern for the essay.

We only ask that each writer tell his or her story in the manner and to the extent that feels most natural and appropriate. In addition, writers are asked to supply a selection of personal photographs showing themselves at various ages, as well as important people and special moments in their lives. Our contributors have responded generously, sharing with us some of their most treasured mementoes. The result is a special blend of text and photographs that will attract even the casual browser. Other features include:

Bibliography at the end of each essay, listing book-length works in chronological order of publication. Each bibliography in this volume was compiled by members of the *CAAS* editorial staff and submitted to the author for review.

Cumulative index in each volume, which cites all the essayists in the series as well as the subjects presented in the essays: personal names, titles of works, geographical names, schools of writing, etc. To ensure ease of use for these cumulating references, the name of the essayist is given before the volume and page number(s) for every reference that appears in more than one essay. In the following example, the entry in the index allows the user to identify the essay writers by name:

> Auden, W.H.
>   Allen **6:**18, 24
>   Ashby **6:**36, 39
>   Bowles **1:**86
>   etc.

For references that appear in only one essay, the volume and page number(s) are given but the name of the essayist is omitted. For example:

> Stieglitz, Alfred **1:**104, 109, 110

CAAS is something more than the sum of its individual essays. At many points the essays touch common ground, and from these intersections emerge new patterns of information and impressions. The index is an important guide to these interconnections.

For Additional Information

For detailed information on awards won, adaptations of works, critical reviews of works, and more, readers are encouraged to consult Gale's *Contemporary Authors* cumulative index for authors' listings in other Gale sources. These include, among others, *Contemporary Authors, Contemporary Authors New Revision Series, Dictionary of Literary Biography,* and *Contemporary Literary Criticism.*

Special Thanks

We wish to acknowledge our special gratitude to each of the authors in this volume. They all have been most kind and cooperative in contributing not only their talents but their enthusiasm and encouragement to this project.

A Brief Sampler

Each essay in the series has a special character and point of view that sets it apart from its companions. A small sampler of anecdotes and musings from the essays in this volume hint at the unique perspective of these life stories.

Matt Cohen, haunted by a man in a picture: "I was looking through some photographs I'd accumulated during the writing of *Nadine* and included amongst them was one of a group of Jews being boarded on a train destined for Auschwitz. It was late in the war, and there was no doubt that the prisoners knew where they were going and the fate that awaited them. One man, as he was climbing onto the train, had turned his head to look at the camera. At the particular moment I was re-inspecting this photograph, it occurred to me that this man, a man whose name I could never know, was aware both that he was looking at a camera and that, by looking at the camera, he was looking at someone—like myself—who would one day look back at him. There he was, going off to his death while I, forty years later and comfortably ensconced in my office, was watching."

Howard Fast with his brother maintained the family as best they could after their mother died: "We didn't complain, Jerry and I, and in a sense the challenge of keeping the family alive was a game we played. We lived in two worlds, the wretched world of reality and the marvelous, endlessly exciting world of the books we read. In those days, bread, milk, and cheese were delivered very early in the morning to the doors of the prosperous. When we had no food, we'd be up at six in the morning to find bread and milk and cheese that would keep us alive. We did not consider it stealing; we never questioned our right to remain alive. Once, we appropriated—a better word—an entire stalk of bananas from a truck. Some we kept for ourselves, eating bananas until we could not face another. The rest we sold for a nickel a hand. When we were utterly penniless and my father was unemployed, we scoured the neighborhood for milk bottles, a nickel for each returned. We knew the back way into every house in the area; we knew the rooftops."

William Matthews, remembering Spot: "But the best thing my newspaperboy days brought me was Spot, the dumpy dog. 'Vaguely beagle,' as I described her in a poem, she followed me one morning for the whole length of my route. She was waiting for me the next morning, and I was like some inexplicable canine Pied Piper, for dog after dog joined us as I covered my route. Dogs love me, I thought, but in fact, as my parents explained to me, Spot was in heat. We took her in and slowly the blood-stirred males dispersed. She lived fifteen more years, with her faint, persistent smell, in all seasons, of leaf mold and her peculiar way of cocking her head as if someone only she could hear had made an especially apt comment. My parents let me name her, I hardly need to say, and praised me for giving her the best possible name. But one day I found my mother shooing the dog out the back door from the kitchen and murmuring to herself, with a pleased smile, 'Out, out, damn Spot.' "

Harold Norse, a friend to many writers in their humble beginnings: "I moved to a tiny room in Greenwich Village on Horatio Street, near a slaughterhouse, and plunged into Village life. One dark glacial dawn in the winter of 1943, as I was about to enter a cafeteria on Fourteenth Street with a friend called Harry Herschkowitz, a protégé of Henry Miller, we ran into a small, thin, black youth shivering in a sweater full of holes and a navy watchcap pulled down over his ears. His eyes bugged out and he looked desperate. Harry introduced me to James Baldwin, age nineteen. Auden would surely have told him to forget writing—he had less of a future than I, was also illegitimate, with a violent father who was a Baptist minister, and a squalid, poverty-stricken home life in Harlem. Staring into mirrors he'd moan, 'What's going to become of me? I'm poor, black, ugly, and queer!' His father knew the answer: he wanted him to be a saint! . . . Mutually protective, we solaced and supported each other. I read the manuscript of *Crying Holy*, his first novel that would take ten more years of revision before it was published as *Go Tell It on the Mountain*. He visited me often and we sat huddled in the cold before the little fireplace, discussing books, racism, being gay."

Jane Rule, considering morals: "Moving from New Jersey to California, from California to Illinois and then Missouri taught me at a younger age than a child growing up in one place that values are clearly relative. In California I went to school with black, Japanese and Chinese children, with children of migrant workers. In Missouri, schools were segregated as were movie houses and country clubs. My father came from the South, and, while he didn't approve of segregation, he was used to it. If there clearly isn't one right way of doing things, any community's values are not a matter for moral commitment so much as a matter of social survival. You pull up your socks when other people do. You roll them down when other people do. You don't much mind about the socks. You do get tired of how entirely right people think they are."

These brief examples only suggest what lies ahead in this volume. The essays will speak differently to different readers; but they are certain to speak best, and most eloquently, for themselves.

Acknowledgments

Grateful acknowledgment is made to those publishers, photographers, and artists whose works appear with these authors' essays.

Photographs/Art

Michael Anthony: p. 21, John Griffiths.

Philip Appleman: p. 25, Thomas Victor © 1981.

Ben Bova: Cover from *Colony,* written by Ben Bova. Copyright © 1978 by Ben Bova. Jacket design by Joe Curcio. Cover from *The Kinsman Saga,* written by Ben Bova. Copyright © 1987 by Ben Bova. Jacket art by Pat Rawlings. Jacket design by Joe Curcio. Cover from *Cyberbooks,* written by Ben Bova. Copyright © 1989 by Ben Bova. Jacket art by Boris Vallejo. Jacket design by Carol Russo. All reproduced with permission of Tor Books/Tom Doherty Associates, Inc./ Jacket illustration from *Mars,* by Ben Bova. Copyright © 1992 by Ben Bova. Jacket illustration copyright © 1992 by Pamela Lee. Jacket design by Jamie S. Warren Youll. Reprinted with permission of Bantam Books, a division of Bantam Doubleday Dell Publishing Group.

Howard Fast: p. 173, Julius Lazarus; p. 177, M. H. Rosenman; p. 182, Maxine C. Gomberg.

Laura Furman: p. 189, Sally Gall; pp. 194, 195, Sylvan Furman; p. 196, Charles Stein; pp. 200, 202, Laura Furman; p. 201, Marcia Leath; p. 203, Hester Magnuson.

Josephine Jacobsen: p. 205, David W. Harp.

Charles Johnson: p. 225, 20th Century Studio; p. 243, Robin Platzer, Twin Images.

Frederick Manfred: p. 245, Larry Risser; p. 259, George H. Spies.

William Matthews: pp. 263, 272, Judith Taylor.

Harold Norse: p. 281, Marcus Blechman; p. 286, Marthe Rocher; p. 288, Michael Kellner; p. 290, © 1991 Michelle Maria Boleyn.

Jane Rule: p. 309, Alex Waterhouse-Hayward; pp. 310, 312, A. R. Rule; p. 313, Leon Tuey; pp. 317, 319, Betty Fairbank; p. 320, Judy Baca; p. 321, John S. Edgar; p. 324, Daphne McKeen.

Pamela Sargent: p. 327, Deborah Martin; p. 337, Michael Orgill.

Text

Contemporary Authors®
Autobiography Series

Michael Anthony

1930-

"When I was down beside the sea . . ."

Michael Anthony on "a visit to the Sealey house in 1991, after fifty years and shortly before its demolition"; he based his novel The Year in San Fernando *on his experiences there*

One of the earliest poems I read had a special attraction for me. It began:

> When I was down beside the sea
> A little spade they gave to me
> to dig the sandy shore . . .

I read this in my first primer when I was five. I had just started school. The fact that I found myself beside the sea made me feel, in a strange sort of way, that this poem was speaking to me personally. True, I never had a little spade to dig the sandy shore, for my parents were as poor as the proverbial church mice, yet I loved the poem very much and I read it so often that I soon knew it by heart.

The place where in 1930 I opened my eyes to find myself beside the sea was Mayaro. At that time it was one of the most remote villages in Trinidad and one of the most beautiful. It is still charming

1

and scenic, but it can no longer be considered remote, and, regrettably, no longer unspoilt. Lying in the far southeastern corner of Trinidad, it was one of the last areas to receive the ordinary amenities. For instance, it was only in 1929, the year before I was born, that proper roads were established, linking it to other towns and villages. Before that, to get to the capital, Port-of-Spain, or to the second town, San Fernando—both on the western coast—one had to take the round-island steamer. This proved a very expensive way of travel for an island less than two thousand square miles in area, and in the 1920s the government embarked on a program of laying down roads to connect remote seaside villages.

I am not clear if it was the idyllic beauty of this village which made me like the little poem or if it was the poem that drew my attention to this beautiful place. But what I was conscious of was that I liked the picture the poem drew, and I felt there was something magical in the way the words were strung together.

Of course, being five I would not have been able to put my thoughts into words. But I think that if I had been asked at that time what I would like to do above all else, I might have answered: "Write a poem like that." Or maybe just: "Write a poem."

Possibly one can say the love of writing was deep inside and spurred on by a poem. This could be true. But I am sure it is also true that even then I had a special feeling for that seaside place and wanted to sing of it.

If the love of writing was deep inside then I do not know how it got there. For there is nothing even faintly literary in my background. My mother was a domestic servant who worked for nearby estate-managing French Creoles, and my father, when he was not ailing, was a drain-digger.

I emphasize *when he was not ailing* because I can hardly remember him being in good health. This was mainly the reason, I think, why my mother, a very home-loving person, was forced to look for a job.

Not that there was the sense of any hardship in our happy home. The struggle to "make ends meet" was never apparent to us three children. My brother Sonny, four years older than me, and my sister Annie, two years older, were always cheerful and happy. Yet it could not have been easy. We moved from that house where I was born, when I was barely two years old, and went to live in estate barracks, and the children kept laughing and playing. Our move was to only about a mile-and-a-

half "down the beach"—that is, southwards—beneath the tall coconut palms that fringe the Mayaro shore, and, like before, it was only a few yards from the sea. As small as I was I did not think any place could be more pleasant.

From this new place, Panchoo Barracks at St Ann's Estate, school was only about half a mile away and, as I said, when I was five I entered school. In the infant department we spent the day playing with beads on frames to learn to count, drawing with coloured pencils, making shapes with plasticine, playing ring games, reciting nursery rhymes, and singing nursery songs. Usually it was a din, but emerging clearly from the din are the nursery rhymes I remember.

And so it was quite easy for me to tell what was going to be my favourite subject. Those were still the days when teachers insisted that to spare the rod was to spoil the child and it seemed to me that what children received the rod most for, and mercilessly, was "not knowing their poetry." I often breathed a sigh of relief that I could recite the poems from top to bottom.

We left Panchoo Barracks at St Ann's in 1936. My mother had just had a fourth child. I had become quite attached to the St Ann's setting, but when one is so young, change is always exciting, and I remember looking forward to the new house.

So far as the house itself was concerned, there was nothing much to look forward to. True, it was a single house by itself, not barracks, but it was hardly more spacious than where we had been. It was a little thatched house, on an incline, next door to the post office. It was the part of Mayaro called Pierreville, or Quarters, though this last name has entirely disappeared. We were just a little west of the centre of Quarters, and Quarters was the "town" of Mayaro. In a quarter-mile radius from the centre you could reach the police station, the hospital, the district medical officer's quarters, the government school, the warden's office, the post office, the government bus garage, the public works department, and, there in the centre of all these, all the shops and stores. I grew to love Quarters, and love it very much, but the truth was that Quarters was nowhere as beautiful as St Ann's, or Lagon Mahaut, where I was born, and I was never again to live in such an idyllic setting as when I was down beside the sea.

Our new home was, as the crow flies, about a mile from the one we left, maybe about three quarters of a mile inland and one quarter mile to the north. Quarters was not flat, sandy terrain as at the seaside, and unlike the strip of Mayaro coast it was not covered by coconut trees. It was on the edge of virile, thick virgin forests and its rich brown earth flourished with things that did not grow by the seaside, like bananas, cassava and other vegetables, and one of the main crops of Mayaro in that day, cocoa. The terrain was gentle, and so were the people.

When I left the seaside I was six and only just becoming aware of Mayaro seaside life, which in the main was a life of fishing. The sea was always filled with boats with seines piled high at their sterns, and on the beach there were always lines of fishermen pulling in seines. And the picture that is most vivid in my mind would be of throbbing heaps of fish brought ashore in the nets.

Apart from fishing the other main activity by the seaside was the picking of coconuts. The coconut industry was a big one, and you could hardly walk along the sand path underneath the palms without being aware of some coconut picker dropping coconuts. At various points under the

coconut trees would be coconuts heaped up for cracking, and very often if the coconut picker was not on the tree he would be on the ground "slamblaying." That was the patois word we used for describing the gathering of the coconuts in a heap, and much later I realised that the word came from the French *assembler,* meaning "to gather." (Mayaro was first settled by French planters and their slaves and for a long time French patois was the language spoken in Mayaro.)

My parents seemed to have made a very clean break with "down the beach," for I cannot ever remember hearing them talk of St Ann's, or Panchoo Barracks, or even of their friends beside the sea. I had no intention of making so clean a break. Although Quarters had the Mayaro Government School, considered the premier school in the district, I insisted on continuing at Mayaro Roman Catholic School, which to me was the best school of all—naturally, because I had all my friends there, and I didn't intend to lose them. My brother, who was about ten, also continued there.

"A typical scene in Mayaro, early morning"

Mayaro Roman Catholic School, at St Ann's, 1970

So we let our sister Annie go to the government school while we walked the mile and a quarter to the Roman Catholic school.

I believe my real introduction to literature came when I got to the third standard, round about age ten. Those were the times when we began letter-writing exercises. The teacher would call on us to do some such thing as "Write a letter to your aunt telling her what is happening at home and saying you would like to come and spend Christmas with her. Ask her what is happening in the village."

I am sure I did not write better letters than the other pupils but I am also sure very few of them enjoyed these exercises more than I did. And as I wrote the letters, possibilities were aroused in my mind. Although there was always the temptation to embellish on the situation at home for the sake of writing a better letter, I always tried to stick to the truth. If I wanted to write about home, the truth was dull. Nothing much was going on at home, and there was nothing exciting to talk about. Our house on Post Office Hill was a two-roomed, tumbling-down thatched house, always leaking when the rains came down. My parents, whom I have already described as "poor as church mice," could not afford much and so there was hardly any furniture in the house. My mother, who had worked for French Creole estate owners when we were living "down the beach," now got a similar sort of job at the post office next door. Only it appeared that she worked harder there, doing everything: cooking, washing, starching, ironing, housework, etc. Could I write about that? My father, who dug drains for the estates, and who had been frequently ailing, now seemed to be ailing even more. He was barely able to work now, and the doctor said he had "water under the heart." In my whole life I have never met a second person with water under the heart, but it just had to happen to him! Anyway, he could not work. So there was more pressure on my mother and perhaps more of the need for one of the three bigger children to go to my aunt's and not only spend Christmas but a much longer time. So without anything thrilling to write about from my old Mayaro home, my imagination resorted to something outside the home, something romantic or adventuresome, like what might be happening in my aunt's village. Here there was bound to be a story.

Came the year 1938 and something happened that in itself was perhaps an exciting story, only that it was not at all exciting for any of us children. My sister, the only girl in the house, was sent to live with a lady telephone operator at Usine Ste Madeleine. I suppose this stemmed from the post mistress, who was the lady's friend—a lady called Myra Taylor. I remember the name well because it was the only thing I liked about this person. None of us children took kindly to the idea and I believe that when my sister was gone even my mother regretted the move, for she missed my sister very much. However, after a period of eight or nine months my sister, who was ten at the time, came home on a visit, and happily she never went back. Even now I remember the day she turned up. It was as if Christmas had come.

My father constantly had to go to the Colonial Hospital in Port-of-Spain to be rid of the water that had gathered under his heart. When he returned, his belly got big in a few months and he had to go again. Then once he went and he never came back. When a few months after his departure my mother asked the district nurse what had happened, the district nurse telephoned Port-of-Spain only to hear that my father had died. We were told that since no one had claimed him he was buried as a pauper in Port-of-Spain. When the news came to us there was much desolation, tears, and gnashing of teeth.

This happened in 1940, and the pressure on my mother was almost more than she could take. She had a boy of fourteen, and he certainly had to look for work. She had my sister, who was twelve, and next was a ten-year-old, who was me. After me was the one who was born just as we left St Ann's. He was now four. She had had another baby in 1939 but this child was so ill at birth that she only survived ten months. The baby was born ill because of the awful hard work my mother had to do at the post office.

Shortly afterwards there came another change and this one influenced my whole life. I am sure the culprit was Post Mistress Olga Cuffie. The change was this: during Christmas of 1940, a guest at the post office by the name of Sealey, no doubt hearing of my mother's plight and either wanting to lighten her burden or take advantage of the situation, asked if I could go to San Fernando with him to be a companion and help to his old mother. My mother might not have wanted to part with a child after the first experience but at the same time she felt she could not let the opportunity pass. On New Year's Day, 1941, when the visitor was leaving, I left with my belongings for San Fernando.

How did I feel? Did I want to go? I would be dishonest if I gave an outright no. I loved Mayaro but the keenness to know what lay beyond always tugged at me. It was a bittersweet occasion. I was

not anxious to leave home, but the bright and exciting colours in which San Fernando was painted certainly influenced me.

I spent exactly a year in San Fernando—as was said, I left home on New Year's Day, 1941, and I returned for the purpose of spending that Christmas at home. Like my sister a few years before, once I arrived home wild horses could not get me away again. True enough during that year, 1941, I saw a lot of new things, and had grown much wiser, but despite this—and although I had made a lot of new friends, and had encountered things I had not known to exist, such as electric lights and water in pipes—I simply did not want to go back.

What of the year in San Fernando? It haunted me from the moment I got back to Mayaro and all through my adolescent years. Was I ill-treated by these strangers, or was it that I was so sensitive and nostalgic that being back in my safe haven, all that had happened seemed wrong and cruel?

I was happy to be in the beautiful coastal village again, around home and friends, and I was anxious to resume school at Mayaro Roman Catholic. No sooner had I got back to school, my schoolmates, my teachers, and I myself felt the difference of my having been away for a year in San Fernando. I had attended the San Fernando Government School, where I was cordially received as a country bumpkin and, to start, was the cause of much mirth. But I quickly lost my country accent and country ways, and was soon "one of the class." The teacher became quite surprised that a boy from the distant wilds could contend with her other pupils, sometimes on even terms. I did not consider myself "bright," but the teacher had her doubts. Now, back in Mayaro RC, it looked as if the brightness of the really bright San Fernando children had rubbed off on me. I would not have remembered this but for a remark by one of my favourite Mayaro teachers, Arthur Julien. It must have been midyear and I was comfortably back in the Mayaro world. One day "Teacher Arthur" asked me a question and I stared at him blankly. He moaned: "A bright boy becoming dull." Those words still ring in my ears.

Sometime in that year, 1942, the post mistress, having heard that I read well and even liked books, decided to put it to the test. One day she called me and said: "I hear you can read. Can you read storybooks?" I said yes. "Well now," she said, "I can lend you a few books, but when you read them I want you to explain the story to me. Tell me what happened. Okay? I'm too busy to read them myself."

I was excited but I was not so silly as to believe that she had not read them. She wanted proof that I could read.

Anyway, that was the start of a great season of adventure through reading. She lent me most of the children's classics like *Tom Brown's Schooldays, Alice in Wonderland, The Wind in the Willows, David Copperfield,* etc.; and other books not so well-known but equally delightful, such as *The Atma* and *Lives of the Saints.* I guess it was the first time I felt gratitude to the post mistress. She had introduced me to such beautiful stories, at the same time opening up such a wide window on the world.

Another pleasant thing that happened to me around that time also had to do with the matter of books. I became aware that one of the bookshelves on the school stage was supposed to be the school library and that it contained about half-a-dozen books. How those books got there and who decided it was the library I cannot tell. One of the books contained a Shakespeare play, and another was a thin volume of poems called *Songs of the World Unborn.*

Songs of the World Unborn contained several poems, all on the theme of the unborn world. The title poem began somewhat like this:

Songs of the world unborn
Swelling within me a shoot from the heart of
    Spring
As I trudge the busy streets
This sullen and misty morn,
What is it to me you sing?

Then towards the end of that long, disturbing, and vibrant poem came these words:

Oh houses erect and vast,
Oh steeples proud,
You are but dust.
I shall come with the winds and blow
And you will crumble,
Oh phantoms fair!

I was fascinated by the power of those words. I could see in my mind's eyes the erect and vast houses of the unborn world, the proud steeples, and I could imagine what the great and frightening passage of time would do to these "phantoms fair."

It was at this period that I really felt the desire to write. I thought if I could paint a picture of life and give the feeling that what I was portraying was

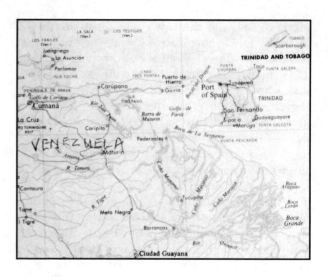

really happening, something like what Thomas Arnold did in *Tom Brown's Schooldays,* or like what Charles Dickens did in *David Copperfield,* this to me would be the most satisfying achievement in the world. I felt if I could get the force of simple words to move the reader, like in *Songs of the World Unborn,* I would not want anything else.

But the interesting thing was that I had no desire to imitate a *David Copperfield* or a *Tom Brown's Schooldays.* I knew at once that I wanted to tell my own story, in my own setting. What *David Copperfield* did, apart from telling me a very moving and credible story, was to show what England was like at the time its author, Charles Dickens, was writing, or the time he was writing about.

The fact that there were no Caribbean versions of these books did not worry me in the very least. Why should it? To me all that a person would need in order to produce something was a pen, some paper, and a story to tell.

I started taking more interest in compositions. When I had resumed school at Mayaro in 1942 there was a new schoolmaster. He had come from the urban areas around Port-of-Spain and it was the first time the education authorities had sent him into such deep countryside as Mayaro. At first he looked upon it as a punishment, but having decided he could do nothing about it he set out to learn as much as he could about Mayaro.

My chief reason for remembering this schoolmaster was his great interest in our compositions. I don't know if it was because he was getting so much information about Mayaro through these compositions, but he really came to life when this was the subject. I found him extremely encouraging and he always tended to overpraise my work. He kept on stressing the value of reading, and said that whenever we encountered a beautiful phrase we should use it in our compositions. Just around that time I came upon a description of a walk in a tropical forest and the writer used the words: "Wild nature, itself, was luxuriantly beautiful." I was thrilled at this exciting phrase. I never thought mere bush could have been described so richly. In my next composition I, too, had taken a walk in a forest and I declared: "Wild nature, itself, was luxuriantly beautiful."

The schoolmaster seemed even more thrilled than I was, and expressed such delight and surprise

that I remember the occasion as a sort of turning point. Because, in describing the phrase as a jewel he said that my selecting it meant that I had what it took to be a writer. I sat in class, in a way embarrassed, but overflowing with quiet joy. I am sure this was the occasion that made me decide I was "going for it."

Of course, in hindsight I ask myself: how could taking phrases from another's work and putting them into one's own composition be a fine thing? Yet, without such encouragement as I received, I do not think I would have written.

This incident happened in 1942 or 1943. Came 1944 and very early in the year Mayaro RC School received an invitation from a certain Reverend F. J. F. Streetly to send boys to participate in an examination to be held in San Fernando. The

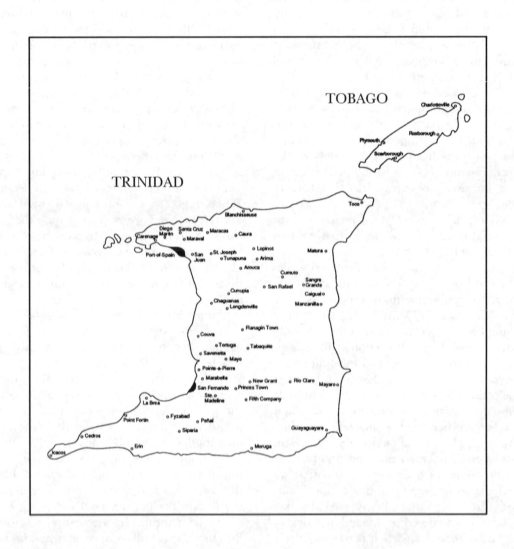

Reverend Streetly was a minister of the Church of England, and I later learned he had come to Trinidad in 1925 to serve as a priest in the Anglican ministry, but before that had graduated as an engineer. Fond of engineering just as he was fond of his chosen field, he joined the Board of Industrial Training in Port-of-Spain and set out to see what contribution he could make. But the Board of Industrial Training, formed in 1906, did little more than train girls in the finer points of needlework and help boys to learn a little carpentry. The Reverend Streetly wanted to prepare young Trinidadians leaving school for the industrial world, which he knew lay ahead. He began giving lessons in workshop practise. In 1939 he was transferred from Port-of-Spain to St Paul's Church in San Fernando and it was around that time that his pleas to the Board of Industrial Training to set up a technical school to train boys in engineering met with a positive response. But it did not mean that the Reverend Streetly did not have to set up the school himself! He managed to get half of a rambling old house at a nominal rent and there he opened the Junior Technical School. The school was situated at the bottom of San Fernando's High Street, and it opened its doors in January 1943.

He opened it with fifteen boys from schools in and around San Fernando, but by 1944 he was reassured enough to cast his net far and wide and invited participation from several schools in the south of the island. As was seen, his invitation reached as far as an obscure little village forty miles away.

Our schoolmaster accepted the invitation with great enthusiasm and set about preparing two boys—myself and a classmate.

The examination took place sometime in April 1944 and I remember the occasion distinctly. Having to get to San Fernando by nine o'clock, we caught the first bus at Mayaro at five in the morning, but because the bus was not mechanically too sound, we missed our connection at Rio Claro. If we had waited for the other bus we would have arrived well in time, but my mother felt it was best to take the train. The train left Rio Claro and went "all around the world," as one would say, and arrived at San Fernando at a quarter past nine. The Reverend Streetly, a strict disciplinarian, forbade us to enter for the exam and it must have been only my mother's tears and the fact that we had come from so far away that made him relent. Also, I had fallen ill with a heavy cold the day before. I felt so bewildered and jaded and sick in the examination room that when it was all over I could not even tell how I did. My mother was very disconsolate.

That day we had no intention of going back to the train. As we left San Fernando by bus to return along the Princes Town–Rio Claro route, the village of Ste Madeleine lay just ahead. Here was where my aunt lived, the one I had to write to, asking what was happening in her village. Also, this was where I had been in 1934 when I was four. I hardly remembered these things now, being so ill, but my mother, although she wanted to reach home as fast as possible, thought it wise to pass to see my aunt, tell her what was happening, and ask her if I could stay there in case I passed the exam for the Junior Technical School.

So we stopped off at Ste Madeleine first, before continuing on to Mayaro.

April was long past, and in fact it must have been high June when one midday, during the stamping of letters after the mail bus had arrived, Miss Cuffie came to the window and cried, "Sonnyboy there? Come Sonnyboy, come, a letter for you."

(Sonnyboy was what they called me at home.)

I ran over to the post office.

Olga Cuffie's excitement arose not simply because of the fact that never before in her life had she come across a letter for the little boy next door, but also because she saw the letter postmarked "San Fernando" and she knew that I had gone to San Fernando to take an examination. When I got to the post office there was much excitement among few staff. I took the letter and ran over to our house. My mother, who was Miss Cuffie's cook, ran over too, and I can't remember about the rest of the family. In the yard of our house I stood up and with trembling fingers I tore the envelope open. There was the letter, headed: "Junior Technical School." It began: "We wish to inform you that you have passed the entrance examination to the Junior Technical School and will be eligible for entry next term."

Then it went on to say that the Junior Technical School was charging $2.50 a term for the special exercise books the students were going to use. According to the letter the term was to start on Monday, September 11, 1944.

It could well be that this was the most exciting day of my teen years. I did not spare a thought for the fact that I had wanted to be a writer and that the Junior Technical School was going to prepare me to be a mechanic, a technical sort of person. Because, first of all, it never dawned on me that I could ever make a career of writing, and secondly, even if I had thought this possible, it was obvious there had to be something else to sustain me until then because I could not become a writer overnight.

For me, as much as I loved Mayaro I knew being able to leave was a wonderful opportunity to learn a line of trade and fit into a niche. I had never contemplated the oil industry, let alone finding employment in the oil refinery after six terms at the Junior Technical School. All I knew of oil was that somewhere in Guayaguayare, a village just south of Mayaro, there was an oil field with the exotic and historic name of Abyssinia. Even I had heard about Haile Selassie, Emperor of Abyssinia, Lion of Judah, and King of Kings. There was oil at our Abyssinia and I had often seen pipelines alongside the road, passing through Quarters, black oil oozing from their joints. After technical school, if I was lucky, I would be going to work in an oil refinery, doing *what* I did not know, but I had the vague idea that it was the place where they made gasoline and products of that sort.

Came the Saturday, September 9, 1944, that armed with a suitcase, and all or most of my belongings, I left Mayaro, with my mother, to enter this new phase of my life. Having no one in San Fernando with whom I could stay in order to go to school, my mother took up the offer my aunt had made earlier, that I could stay there and walk the three miles to San Fernando in the morning and the same homeward in the evening. No arrangement was made for paying, for my aunt had said I would just fit in with my cousins and eat what they ate. My aunt's husband had enthusiastically approved.

So, installed at Ste Madeleine, I plunged into my new life as one standing on the bank of a boisterous river might do. This river proved as boisterous as it was unfamiliar. At Mayaro RC School we learned English grammar and composition, history, arithmetic, hygiene, and nature study. At the Junior Technical School in San Fernando the subjects were English language, English literature, history, geography, mathematics, physics, chemistry, mechanics, mechanical drawing, metalwork theory and practise, and woodwork theory and practise.

It took a great deal of application to enable me to "keep my head above water" during the two-year course. The course was extremely intense and some of the subjects were much too complicated for my sort of brain to keep up with. I could only work hard at subjects I liked. I was therefore very

conscientious about English language and literature as well as composition writing, and I was also enthusiastic about history and geography. But it was a technical school and the subjects which were regarded as the most important were subjects most closely associated with the technical life. It was much more important to understand Boyle's law on the expansion of steam, and Archimedes's principle concerning a body when partly or wholly immersed in water, than to know what were the hallmarks of beautiful writing. There was no doubt that I was a misfit. There was a teacher who was a misfit too, Norman Girwar, the professor of English language. He really came to life when we were discussing William Shakespeare or reading one of the classics, and he quickly saw in me a kindred spirit, and we sympathized with each other. The main difference between us both, though, was that while I was there to take in a technical education and was going to be measured by how well or ill I grasped the subjects, he was being paid simply to teach us English language and literature, as well as geography, and history, and he did not have to care what happened or did not happen to the technical subjects.

However, it was interesting and instructive to see the attitude of the arch-technical man and Junior Technical School founder, the Reverend Streetly. He was deeply earnest when holding forth on any branch of engineering and reacted as though it were the rock of his very life. He also seemed gripped with what he was doing when he had us in the workshop for practise, and that was where we glimpsed his amazing aptitude. But strangely enough it was when he taught us literature that he seemed to come most to life. Especially if the book was *The Splendid Spur,* set in his native Bath, in Wiltshire, England. I can still picture him going into ecstasies on reading the first lines of the book: "He that hath jilted the Muse, forsaking her gentle pipes to follow the drum and the trumpet, shall fruitlessly beseech her again when the time comes for him to sit down and write of his adventures."

The Reverend Streetly was that rare combination of a man of letters, a top engineer, and a man of the factory floor.

At Junior Technical School the main subjects were clearly physics, mechanics, chemistry, mathematics, and mechanical drawing, and during the two years of my tuition I noticed over and over again how fortunate the Reverend Streetly and the Board of Industrial Training were to have attracted boys who were remarkably adept at those subjects. There were very, very few misfits. Indeed, the only complete misfit that I ever knew at the school was myself.

Under ordinary circumstances I would have been dreadfully unhappy, but quite early on—in fact, it was Friday of the first week—Mr Norman Girwar touched a chord in me when he asked each student to write a poem for homework "and bring it in on Monday."

I wrote a poem about the Naparima-Mayaro Road—the road which linked Mayaro to San Fernando—and Mr Girwar, extremely pleased with my work, took a special interest in me from that day onward. He was even more excited when I told him that I wanted to become a writer.

I kept on middling in the two-year course, trying not to make a complete mess of it. Middling is the right word to use here, because I usually obtained middle marks in most subjects and at the end of the terms, middle results. There were a few subjects that pulled me down badly, like mathematics, which I could never do, and physics, and mechanics, which in a way were closely related to mathematics, having a great deal of calculations; mechanical drawing, which I had no aptitude for at all, and which, it appeared to me, one had to be born to do; and workshop practise, which again was for the apt—people who could make things out of wood or metal. This was not a subject for the clumsy.

On the other hand there were subjects which boosted my marks, such as English language and literature, history, and geography. These subjects rescued my performance at the Junior Technical School, but they could not rescue me from the opinion that I was not the material from which engineers are made.

But notwithstanding these things, my technical school days were happy, happy days. I made lifelong friends there, and was up to so many pranks that it is hard to think all these things took place within a period of two years.

I had remained at Ste Madeleine only for the first term, September to December 1944. When I went home for Christmas and spoke of the weary walk to school and back, my mother, anxious that I should have some time for study, managed to get a family in San Fernando to put me up.

This was arranged by the district nurse of Mayaro who had two children staying in San Fernando to go to school and suggested that I join them. It was a successful arrangement and I remained there until my spell at the Junior Techni-

cal School came to an end. When this event took place in 1946, I was duly sent to the oil refinery at Pointe-à-Pierre as an apprentice, as expected, but I cannot say it was generally expected that I would do well there.

I myself was eager but not optimistic because I knew my limitations. In any case I did not like workshop affairs and could not bring myself to strive to make a success of it. But it was a job, something to live by. Apart from that, I was now sixteen and my mother was as eager as I was that I should begin to "hold my own."

With the rest of my classmates—apart from two or three boys who went elsewhere, and a few boys who came from other places—I entered the Trade Shop at Pointe-à-Pierre in September 1946. The Trade Shop as such was nonexistent, except for a large room. Simply physical space. We were the first boys who were going to use this shop and so we had to make all of the workbenches and install, by directions, all the machines sent from other sections of the company. There was a lathe, a

*Apprentices department photo, 1946–47
(Anthony in front row, at far left)*

milling machine, blacksmith equipment, carpenter's equipment, and so on. I have always boasted that I helped to build and set up that Trade Shop.

However, my mind was stubbornly inclined to the literary life. That was what I liked, although I did not see any way of my becoming a writer, and I personally knew of no one who had ever done so, and of course I knew no writers. But that was what I liked—the world of writing. And I continued to live in this dream world.

But perhaps I was not living in a world entirely made of dreams. For while at Junior Technical School I had started writing. My chosen field was poetry, ever since Mr Girwar had praised my poem, and I had continued trying my hand at poetry. In fact, as I have shown, I have loved poetry since my infant days.

In the Trade Shop at Pointe-à-Pierre it became clearer and clearer to me that I was in the wrong niche in life, and secretly I became more determined to become a writer. Mainly I was hoping to emerge as a poet, but could anybody live on poetry? Most of my friends to whom I confided these dreams laughed at me. Poet? First of all, there were no established poets in Trinidad and none of my friends felt that a poor country boy like me could ever achieve that goal. This was the main sentiment. They did not even see it worthwhile to consider whether I could ever live on poetry, they felt so sure I could never become a poet.

But they all knew I loved writing and I felt that they secretly admired me for it, seeing I was so hopeless in the practical world.

We apprentices were to spend one year in the Trade Shop, after which we were to be sent out to our chosen fields, or those recommended by our instructors. The purpose in having us in the Trade Shop for a year was to notice where we excelled. On entry, each boy was asked his preference, but seeing none had any practical experience of any trade it was thought prudent to regard their preferences only as guidelines. And a good thing too, for there were certain "glamour" trades that most boys asked for and yet had not the slightest knowledge of, nor aptitude in. I, for example, chose being an electrician simply because being an electrician was what most of the young men wanted at that time. I am glad they were not so crazy as to give it to me.

At the end of the year in the Trade Shop about half of the boys got the trades they had asked for at the beginning, and almost all the rest were given other jobs, but not too different from what they had wanted. A few got jobs that were

not represented in the Trade Shop at all. I remember that at the Junior Technical School one of the students, Errol Dwarika, always startled us by his amazing talent in mechanical drawing. His work could often be mistaken as that of the instructors. The record of each boy at the Junior Technical School was communicated to the authorities at Pointe-à-Pierre, and Dwarika and, I believe, Hugh Gibbs, another one proficient in mechanical drawing, received tests at the drawing office. They immediately became draughtsmen.

I was one of the apprentices who was offered a job not represented in the Trade Shop, but not under as happy auspices as that of the two young draughtsmen. At the end of the year, and just after I had an unfortunate accident—the mark of which I still bear—I was offered the opportunity of either going home or accepting a job in the company's foundry.

First of all, the accident: I was in the woodwork department and the test piece we were making had to do with mortise and tenon. This called for a great deal of chiseling. The instructor, Dad Hinds, could not look at everyone and I took to holding the chisel, not with the blade away from me, as I should, but chiseling with the blade towards my wrist. Inevitably, pressure caused the blade to slip and it went straight into my left wrist. I received the most horrible cut and I never like to think about that day because a little more pressure might have proved fatal, or at best I would have escaped but without the use of my left hand.

This, and my previous record at the Trade Shop and the Junior Technical School could not have endeared me to the authorities, and one feels grateful to Clinton Cater, the then superintendent in charge of apprentices, for even offering to keep me on in the refinery. Having to choose between going to the foundry and going back to Mayaro, I went to the foundry.

Maybe everybody knows what foundry work entails, but I suspect modern methods are gradually making this type of activity obsolete. Even in the 1940s it occurred to me that it was the most old-fashioned job I had ever known or heard of, and I was not in the least bit surprised that no young apprentice wanted to go to the foundry. At the oil company's foundry the typical job was to make the heavy equipment, which had to be out of cast iron, and from Monday to Thursday we were engaged in preparing to do this. First there had to be a wooden pattern of the equipment to be made, and this pattern would be moulded in sand so that the shape of the equipment would be in the sand when the pattern was drawn out, and then all one had to do was to pour molten cast iron into the space or mould. There were several fine points to moulding but it was an extremely dirty job and amazingly primitive. Friday, casting day, was usually the most difficult of all. Having various boxes with moulds prepared earlier in the week, this was the day we would "cast" or pour molten metal into the moulds. Scraps of cast iron as well as "pig iron" (iron smelted from ores) would be put into a furnace and heated until the iron was melted. The heat would make the foundry almost unbearable. But we had to put up with it. When this molten metal was ready, we had to pour it into ladles and then into the moulds. No matter how successful the casting, the foundry men would end up dizzy and exhausted.

I never knew how happy I had been until I went to the foundry, and yet in a way my relationship with my colleagues during the seven years I spent there made this period one of the most cherished of my life. But more than that it was the period that shaped my future, for I disliked the work so much that I took certain positive steps that ended up in making me a writer.

When I went to the Trade Shop in 1946, I decided to live at Marabella, which is just a short distance from Pointe-à-Pierre. I was very fond of sports and one of the biggest events of the Trinidad sporting calendar was the Southern Games, held on Pointe-à-Pierre's Guaracara Park. From the time I got into the Trade Shop, and after I went to the foundry, the Southern Games and the preparation leading to it were the only things which made my life tolerable.

I recall the first time I actually became overwhelmed by the Southern Games. The year was 1948, when the Olympic Games were held in London. Trinidad Leaseholds Limited had a sports club, the Leaseholds Amateur Sports Club, renowned throughout Trinidad simply as LASC. The LASC athletic coach, Albert Browne, had been chosen to go to London as a member of the official delegation accompanying the athletes and when he returned he could hardly contain his enthusiasm. He was extremely impressed with the Olympic Games and decided to make the Southern Games a true Trinidad version of them. He decided that no longer would we run distances in yards but metres, as they did in the Olympic Games, and it was the first time distances like 100 metres and 200 metres were run in this country. He organised the Southern Games of 1949 in Olympic style, introducing events like hurdles,

discus, throwing the javelin, putting the shot, etc., events seldom seen in Trinidad before. He had the lanes marked out in the fashion he had seen in the London Olympics so that the 200 metres, for instance, would be run on a curve, with a final straight stretch, but the 400 metres would be one lap of the athletic track. Milers had to forget the mile because what they were going to do from henceforth was 1,500 metres (a little longer than the 1,760 yards). He arranged for the games to open with all the flags of the participating clubs flying in the wind, just as at the Olympic Games there were the flags of the various nations. But for me one of the most impressive things he introduced was a reproduction of the Olympic opening ceremony, complete with the parade of athletes and the public swearing of the Olympic oath on behalf of all the athletes.

Even today I can see the opening ceremony of Southern Games 1949. From that year on every Southern Games had an opening ceremony, but it was that first one that moved me the most. I could see the athletes led by the police band filing out of the estate constable's quarters: the dazzling colours, the standard bearers, the flags flying. As they took the track the police band bore right, and the athletes made their way onto the track, stepping high and proud. Each standard bearer wore the name of the club his team represented: Arima Sports Club, Saddle Boys, Whizz Wheelers, about fifty clubs in all. The host club, LASC, came last, just as the host nation in the Olympic Games did. As they marched along the track, the leader of the police band carried out his fantastic drill, throwing up his mace and catching it as it fell, all in time with the music. The music itself was as beautiful as it was appropriate. The band was playing the haunting "Whate'er we try to do we try to do it well." As the parade reached the pavilion, close to the podium, the leader of the police band goose-stepped into the inner track, and with the last athletes still leaving the estate constable's quarters, those nearest the band filed in formation until, at the end of the parade, the athletes lined up into a neat symmetrical pattern in front of the podium. At that point one of the prominent athletes was directed to the podium to take the oath. It was the same Olympic oath put into a Trinidad context.

The games themselves, staged over two weekends, were very efficiently run and exciting beyond any telling of it. Roars of joy and groans of anguish shattered those four thrilling days—especially during the last event—and it was no surprise that the noise was heard in San Fernando, four miles away. The occasion ended with another impressive performance of the police band. On that sunlit and solemn final afternoon, with the reddened rays of the sun seeming to spill over from the Gulf and wash the twilight, the police band rendered "The Last Post," and I stood there with a heavy heart. It was the memory of those games that inspired me to attempt my first novel, *The Games Were Coming*.

The day after those 1949 games were over I went to Coach Browne and asked if I could join LASC.

That was the beginning of golden days. The rest of my Pointe-à-Pierre period was anything but boring or difficult to bear. I had athletics. Athletics did not make me dislike foundry work less, but it gave me something to look forward to. I lived through most days at the foundry just waiting to hear the 4:00 P.M. refinery whistle, then I would hasten away to Guaracara Park to train. (Four o'clock marked the end of the workday.) There was always some sports meeting to go to somewhere, and so one was always in training. LASC's bus would take the club's athletes to all the major sports meetings, most of which would follow Southern Games. These games almost always took place in February. It was wonderful going with a bus full of athletes to these sports meetings—there was such camaraderie and entertainment that the actual sport itself seemed to take second place. Many of the athletes and myself became close friends and this was to prove useful to my writing in later years.

Those years of apprenticeship, through pleasant relationships at the foundry and truly happy camaraderie with the athletes, very much influenced what lay ahead in my future. The two together caused me to take my most decisive step towards becoming a writer.

One of the persons I admired most at the foundry was Joe Henry Blackwell. He came to the foundry as a young man of about twenty-three in 1951, and we immediately became friends. For we saw at once that we both liked the same things. He in particular was very fond of learning and always seemed to want to show how much he knew. Maybe I was the same way, but unlike him I didn't know very much. However, from the time Joe discovered I liked writing he became very interested and he was one of the few of my friends who did not think me a joke for dreaming of becoming a writer. In fact, he was keen to encourage me along

that line and was most delighted when, after a few months of merely talking about writing, I had a poem published in the newspaper.

I had once again become intensely interested in poetry and this was partly due to the fact that the newspapers used to publish a poem now and again on its "Voice of the People" page, and I had wanted to prove to myself and to my friend that I was capable of joining these budding writers. When that first poem was published, Joe was filled with admiration, and although he was just a year or two older than I was, he became my mentor.

At that time also I became member of the Southern Writers Association, a group of writing hopefuls who met quite informally in San Fernando to read each other's works. This was no society for saying nice things; there was burning but honest criticism for those who could take it. I probably learned more at meetings of this group than anywhere else.

Regarding the influence of my athletic friends, my mind goes in particular to a running companion, Canute Thomas. Canute was a friend from Junior Technical School days who, seeing how hopelessly ill-fitted I was for the technical life, and knowing that I loved writing, was extremely keen on seeing me find some sort of way into the writing world.

Canute, who was also an apprentice, joined LASC just a little before me and in a quick time became top junior sprinter, over the 200 metres.

This successful junior sprinter was also extremely successful in the workshop. He was made an outstanding apprentice in the instrument engineering department and in 1952 was awarded a Trinidad Leaseholds scholarship to study his profession in England. After he left for England (around September 1953) we began corresponding, and it was typical of him that in an early letter he should say something like this: "You've always talked about writing and you say you want to make it a career. Look, if you want to write, this is the place to be. I mean to say, there are all sorts of magazines and all sorts of publishers here in London. Why don't you try to come up?"

It was now about mid-1954 and from that moment on my mind was set on going to England. Not that I had not thought of it before. Even before Canute Thomas went to England I had considered the idea of one day emigrating to England. It is probably the dream of everyone brought up in the colonial days where from the cradle one gets a healthy respect for the "mother country." It might have been in one's mother's milk. For one's parents are moulded by it through their education, and from the time one begins school the message is reinforced: "All that is best is in Britain." For the writer this message is even more compelling. It is the country of Shakespeare and Milton, Keats and Shelley, Charles Dickens and all the lofty models of English literature you were made to love—perhaps not without justice. These were the writers one met from infancy, and their adept strokes of the pen painted the picture of England. Apart from the "When I was down beside the sea" poem quoted earlier, there were the famed poems like "Rule, Britannia!" "Ye Mariners of England," and a number of such works which always tended to whip up "patriotic" fervour among the people like us. And whipping up even greater fervour perhaps were patriotic English school songs which we sang with great feeling. The one we loved best was "Land of Our Birth We Pledge to Thee." Land of our birth indeed!

What was there to counteract this excessive and insane desire to reach out to the metropole? Very little or nothing. At least nothing for the young writer. Most beginning authors need inspiration and strength from what has gone on around them before, but during this period the West Indian would find next to nothing written by a West Indian in a schoolbook, or anywhere, and one grew up with the vague and upsetting feeling that no writers could come from these parts, that in order to write one had to go to England. There was no logic in it whatsoever, but the feeling was there anyway, in the subconscious mind, and I am not ashamed to say that such a feeling was part of me. I wanted to go to England to become a writer.

So as soon as my friend urged me to make the trip I began planning. Then one day a simple incident caused me to spring into action. It was disappointment in love. Someone I loved dearly appeared to change course and choose somebody else. This was in fact not so at all, but that was how I saw it. I felt shattered, and I thought the best thing to do was to finalize my plans as quickly as possible and leave my woes behind me. I went to work next morning and, as crazy as it seems to me now, I resigned forthwith. The date was November 4, 1954. First of all I went and told my workmates what I was going to do. Nobody believed me; Joe thought I was joking. I then went to the office and resigned. With the money due to me from the oil company I went up to Port-of-Spain and bought a ticket for England.

Those were still the days when all but the wealthy travelled by ship. I had noticed, from the newspapers, that the Booth Line vessel SS *Hildebrande* was calling at Trinidad on its way from Manaus, Brazil, to Liverpool, England. I managed to get a passage on that liner, and on December 13, 1954, I sailed from Port-of-Spain. I arrived in England on Boxing Day, December 26, 1954.

Boxing Day was of course a public holiday and we found out that English dockers were not working so there was no chance of our landing. Also when a public holiday falls on a Sunday it is celebrated the next day so we had to wait until Tuesday to land.

Just before I left Trinidad, Canute Thomas had written saying there'd be a message for me when I arrived at Liverpool, and sure enough I got this as soon as I landed: I was to take the boat train and come straight to London.

The feeling of being in England was so overwhelming that it seemed even the cold and fog were welcoming me. The *Hildebrande* docked in Liverpool and I caught the train from there to London, and all the way down, travelling those two hundred miles, I kept looking out of the window at the drab houses with their chimneys, grey and dank, with the sky like slate, and rejoicing in my mind that I was at last in this great historic country, and remembering the lines of Browning's poem: "Oh to be in England now that Spring is here." Yes, Spring in December, for heaven's sake!

However, politically, I felt very differently about England. The "Mother Country" was also the mother of a lot of our ills in Trinidad and the wider Caribbean, in Africa, and in the other colonies, and as a black man the chief of these ills for me was colour prejudice and racial discrimination. I could never forgive England for this, no matter how much I admired its great writers. Also, some days before arriving there were conversations among the black passengers aboard touching on the severe racial discrimination in England. This subdued my enthusiasm but I was not unduly fearful. Canute Thomas and I had discussed this at length, and he had given me a good idea of what I was going to meet. He had by now spent a year there and he had dealt with it in his way, and lived with it, and achieved. We knew that I too would be able to do the same thing.

Although there was nothing remarkable about the train journey to London, everything was new in a strange sort of way. It was uncanny. I was seeing England for the first time, yet there was something remarkably familiar about it. The grey, misty landscape, the square, stone-white houses with smoking chimneys, the winter-coated shivering people in the streets, the vegetation, the sheep in the meadow, the odd haystacks and farmhouses—I had seen them all before. Where? Why, in Charles Dickens, of course, and in Charles Kingsley, in the Brontës, in Keats, Browning, Shelley, Byron, even in Lewis Carroll and Thomas Arnold.

By the time we got to London it was already dark. Yet the train could not have taken more than three hours and we had left at just about noon. This was my first confrontation with the difference in climate and latitude, and neither Kingsley nor Browning nor Shelley nor Sir Walter Scott had prepared me for it. I soon was to realise that while in Trinidad it never got dark before six o'clock, during the winter months in England four o'clock could look like night.

The great and happy thing for me on getting down onto the railway platform in London was to see my friend Canute Thomas. He had a winter coat in his hands, waiting to receive me. Following our warm reunion we went around in what seemed to be a maze in this great city until we arrived at the home of a mutual friend, Leslie Lewis. This was journey's end for me—at least temporarily. This friend, whom I had known at Pointe-à-Pierre, but who had travelled to England earlier in 1954, had agreed to have me stay at his home until I could find somewhere else. (Canute was staying with a family.) This friend received me with great warmth, and in his typically subdued but generous way, he said: "You can stay here as long as you wish, until you find a better place."

And before he left that night, Canute Thomas said to me: "Now, Tony, you are here in England. And you know what you are here for. So you know you just have to write. Just try your best. I hope you make it."

Grass was not going to grow under my feet! The first thing to do was to find a job and only three days afterwards I found a job in a nearby factory. And although my friend was quite comfortable with me in his home and was quite content for me to eat and drink to my satisfaction, without any payment whatsoever, I did not wish to be a guest for long. Also, if I had to write, I had to be on my own, and I had to have my peace of mind. Shortly afterwards I heard of a vacant room across the road, not far from us, and I went there.

On one of Canute Thomas's early visits to my place he saw that I was writing and he said, "How can you write without a typewriter?" I made some excuse about not being ready to get one yet, and that I'd soon get one. He did not pay me any mind but made an appointment for us to go to Regent Street together sometime that week. There in Regent Street he walked into Remington's and bought me one of their latest typewriters. He said, "Look, you need this. I don't mind when you pay me back. Pay me back when things are comfortable."

I have never possessed a nicer, hardier typewriter. It went with me to the half dozen or so places I moved to in London, and later to quite a few distant parts. Round about 1977 in Trinidad it began to fall into disrepair—I worked it hard and I cannot say I treated it well. I am not a careful person. I took it to a repairer and I do not know what he did to the lubrication but its springiness was completely gone. It was never the same again. Reluctantly, I got another typewriter. But I still have this old typewriter in my storeroom and will never get rid of it.

Up to the time I left Trinidad I had been writing poems and these were published mainly in the *Trinidad Guardian.* By the time I sailed away in 1954 I believe I must have been regarded as a budding poet. But I had also wanted to write prose. As early as 1951 I joined the group of hopefuls I referred to earlier. There were many extremely promising writers in the group, a few of whom had the distinction of having been published by *BIM,* the reputable Barbados literary magazine. Perhaps even more notable was a member who had gotten his work broadcast on a prestigious BBC overseas program, "Caribbean Voices."

No sooner had I settled down in London—I think it was in February 1955—I mailed this BBC Caribbean program a few poems and some freshly written short stories. About two weeks later I got a letter from the program producer, who was a young Trinidadian newly graduated from Oxford University. He asked me to come in and see him. His name was V. S. Naipaul, and I remember asking him if he was related to Seepersad Naipaul, who used to have some exquisitely mystic short stories published in the *Trinidad Guardian.* Seepersad was his father, he said. The interesting thing about that meeting was what he told me about my writing. He said, "Michael Anthony, do you know why I asked you to come to see me? I received your poems and your short story. What I want you to do for me is to stop writing poetry. Keep trying at short stories. Your story is promising. Stick to that. Forget poetry." This may not be word-for-word what he said, but he was as blunt as that.

I don't know how faithfully I followed his advice but I know I never sent the BBC any more poems, even after he himself had left. But I was inspired by the fact that he liked my short stories and I put a lot of energy into writing these. By April 1955 I had a story accepted for broadcast and with the excitement of this success I wrote furiously. But the drawback was that it took at least three months between the acceptance of a story and the broadcasting of it, and however furiously you wrote you could not get very far. At least not very fast. But as I look back now I can see how contentedly I took this. I had a great sense of achievement and success, and had something extremely illogical not happened I probably would have been content to stay in that groove and remain a short-story writer.

What happened was that shortly after the Federation of the English-speaking West Indies in 1958, the BBC decided that having a "Caribbean Voices" type of program broadcast to the West Indies showed a lack of respect, and the program was stopped. I could not, and still cannot, see the logic of their argument, and strongly suspect the program was scheduled to cease anyway. I was dejected but determined to keep going. What made me even more determined was that I now had more people to please—I had a family. I had recently married and my wife, Yvette, was as keen as I was to see a little success come my way. We soon had two other close well-wishers. In 1957 my daughter Jennifer was born, and three years later we had a son, Keith.

Anyway, after "Caribbean Voices" stopped, I thought the next best thing was to try to get a collection of my short stories published. I mentioned this to the then producer of the program, Andrew Salkey, and he told me that the publisher Hutchinson had a new division called New Authors Limited for which they were inviting fiction, poetry, and plays from new authors. He, in fact, was going to be the first person to have a book published under the scheme and he pressed me to try them. He did not have to press very hard. I believe I got my stories together the same night and sent them to Hutchinson the next morning.

After about two weeks, the editor of New Authors Limited, Raleigh Trevelyan, wrote saying that the stories were interesting but that New Authors could not embark on publishing them because short stories don't sell, and would I not consider writing a novel. He said after my novel

The author's family: (in front) daughter Sandra and son Carlos; (middle) son Keith and wife, Yvette; (back) Michael Anthony, mother-in-law, Eugenia, and daughter Jennifer, 1975

was accepted they could then look at my short stories again.

It was one of those letters calculated to make you burst with excitement if you are one of those writing hopefuls who gets excited easily. And if you are not very easily discouraged and are always ready to take up a challenge. Although I had earlier seen myself as a budding poet, and later was content just to write short stories, I did, deep in me, always want to write a novel. I remember, for instance, that in late 1953 or early 1954, a dear friend, Marjorie Daniel, asked me in one of her letters: "Michael, do you see being a poet your goal in life?" To which I had replied, in part: "One of the things I want to do is to try my hand at a novel."

Anyway, at this point, 1959, the burning desire in me was to write a novel and send it to

Raleigh Trevelyan of New Authors Limited, and I began to think about a theme I might use. Very few of my short stories were built around plot, but instead came out of my nostalgia for Mayaro and from childhood memories. What I had tried to do was to create atmosphere and emotion and a sense of place, and I knew this was the sort of writer I was and that if I was to handle a successful novel I had to go back in time to some incident of my life, something that I felt deeply about, and try to tell the story faithfully, yet creatively, painting the picture of a real world and genuine people.

It was then that a phase in my life that I had always thought of came dramatically to the centre of my mind. It was about the year I had spent in San Fernando in 1941. I felt this was the theme I should write about, for apart from attempting a novel I would revisit that strange year and, seeing it from a child's point of view, would have a good idea of what really happened.

I immediately headed my story "The Year in San Fernando" and started to write. It would have been fine if I had done what I had planned: create character and atmosphere and tell a story. But the force of the memories made me write the tale exactly as it unfolded in 1941. Apart from a little embellishment, I had written autobiography.

I clearly remember Raleigh Trevelyan's letter to me after keeping the manuscript for about six weeks. He said, in part: "I was very interested in reading 'The Year in San Fernando.' It sounds to me as if all these things you wrote about actually happened. There are many fine things but we must remember that not everything that happens to us is important. I think what you need to do is to forget what has happened to you directly and tell a story. What I would suggest is, put down the book for two or three months, and then come back to it, and you'll probably see just what is wrong."

I felt very disheartened having the book returned and I did not really want to see anything of it so I just dashed it aside. However, having written something as long as that—in other words, having gone the distance—I was keen to go the distance again. I began thinking of themes again, but this time I felt the plot had to be a key part because I tended to let memories lead me astray. I knew that plot would keep me in check. I also felt I wanted something bright and fast-moving as opposed to the solemn drift of what one would tend to associate with a boy spending a year in a strange household, far from home and friends. And what was it that came to mind? One of the fastest-moving and brightest parts of my life was what

unfolded at Pointe-à-Pierre's Guaracara Park every April when the Southern Games were coming.

At that time, no sooner would the Pointe-à-Pierre whistle blow than I would be out of the foundry like a bullet and down the road to Guaracara Park, where both the LASC and the refinery flag would be flying; where hordes of cyclists, club members, and outsiders would be whizzing round and round the track, their cycling garb glittering in the sun; where the runners—and I was quick to join them—would be on the grassy inner track practising starts, and upon which dozens of athletes and cyclists would be reclining on the grass and chatting. There would be runners and cyclists in the stands nervously talking and being massaged with embrocation, the air permeated with liniment smell.

A bright and colourful scene, rivalled only by scenes of Carnival, which at that point would have been just past. Yes, the Carnival. The Southern Games and the Carnival. Here was the recipe for a sparkling novel.

I am sure I have not written that sparkling novel but in 1962 I did write a novel with the backcloth being the Southern Games and the Carnival—a book called *The Games Were Coming*, published in 1963. Shortly after this book was published I felt sufficient peace of mind to look again at the manuscript of "The Year in San Fernando," and on going through the first few pages, I was shocked and taken aback. It was so bad I could hardly read it. It wasn't a novel at all, it was autobiography, and telling of one incident to the next in a manner that seemed to be begging the reader to say: "So what!" Raleigh Trevelyan's words came back to me: "It sounds to me as if all these things you wrote about actually happened. There are many fine things but we must remember that not everything that happens to us is important."

Right away I decided to scrap that version of the book and begin anew. I again headed the page "The Year in San Fernando" and set to work. To write this novel I would have to deal with the same material and the same general incident, but the big difference would be that I would have to forget the historical truth of what happened to me in San Fernando and just write a story of a little boy under the same set of circumstances in a strange town. In 1965 this novel was published, and although I may not have adequately captured the feeling of nostalgia, and the sense of strangeness the little fellow must have felt, nevertheless this is much more like what I wanted to do. Yet the irony is that this version seems to carry more of the essential truth of the year I spent in San Fernando than the "autobiography" I had written before.

In 1966, having at this time published two novels, I felt that I wanted to tackle something I had always dreamed of doing. That is, pay tribute to the village I really loved by bringing it into the limelight. When I was growing up Mayaro was still very remote, and untouched, as in the days of my infancy. When I left Trinidad in 1954 it had not even gotten running water yet, neither had it the blessing of electricity. The only current is in the sea, as one disgruntled villager said. Indeed it was not until several years afterwards that it received water and electric power.

But Mayaro always had charm. Also, it was one of the most beautiful villages in Trinidad. But it was very much unknown. In reference to it people in the towns often talked about "Mayaro bush," and it was often described as being "behind God's back." It was formerly settled by French planters and their slaves, and it was famous for patois (French Creole), as well as for the *soucouyant,* a nonexistent female werewolf in French-Caribbean folklore. I was very much aware that in people's minds Mayaro was very much obscure and unknown, and I felt I wanted to set a novel there, showing it as it truly was: normal, green, bushy, scenic, tranquil, majestic, and full of really lively and interesting people, ordinary people, and where the youngsters plan and hope and dance and sing and fall in love. Beyond that, I wanted to show what a fine place Mayaro was to be in and to belong to.

On another plane, I wanted to capture Mayaro at a certain juncture of time—say 1950—so that someone visiting Mayaro fifty years later, or maybe a century or more would be able to say, "God, this place has changed!" or "God, this place hasn't changed!" as the case may be, and at least can renew acquaintance with the layout and topographical features that they saw in the book.

I also wanted to give a feeling of the two geographical aspects of Mayaro—the seaside Mayaro with the blue Atlantic indented like a big C, the broad sandy beach, the shore fringed by coconut palms, the various settlements (with their typically thatched houses) stretched out along the ten miles of coast; this and the virile, forested inner Mayaro, the life and soul of which was Quarters, the commercial centre. The focus of the story was going to be a little estate or "garden" beside the big river of Mayaro, the Ortoire.

That year, 1966, I wrote *Green Days by the River.* In order to get the feeling in myself that the story was really true—to believe that what was taking place in the book was really happening—I drew all the characters from people I had known in real life. Perhaps this is why *Green Days by the River* has a special meaning for me. Oddly enough, it is as close to autobiography as a book can get, yet no one has said, "It seems to me that all these things actually happened to you."

The next year, 1967, I was hit by a serious illness—meningitis. I nearly did not make it back to health. When I was on the mend my doctors advised me to try and return to tropical climes.

I sought a job in Trinidad but could meet with no success. Just around that period, I made friends with some young Brazilians in London and took to going with them to their cultural house, Casa do Brasil. Brazil had long been a favourite country of mine. As an adolescent I had always heard of Brazil as a country without any racial prejudice, and as a black man this strongly attracted me. Yet this description of Brazil was only hearsay, until accidentally I thought I found some proof. One day in 1950 I was in the LASC clubhouse at Pointe-à-Pierre, and while leafing through a recent edition of the English magazine *World Sport* I noticed a photograph of Brazil's World Cup soccer team on its way to the World Soccer games in Sweden. About half of the players were black. I was greatly impressed.

So hence my interest in frequenting Casa do Brasil. One of my Brazilian friends, hearing that I was advised to seek a job in a warmer clime said, "Why don't you go to Brazil? It would be so easy to get a job there. Everybody wants to learn English."

I was extremely keen on this idea but was told I would first have to go to Brazil and get a job offer before I could get a visa to stay in that country any length of time. I made preparations and in February 1968 I left for Brazil to see if I would have any luck.

True enough, it was very easy to get a job offer to teach English in Brazil, and I returned to England, got my visa, and then I left London to settle in Brazil. I could not take my family with me at the time as we were expecting our third child, so while the wife and the children were waiting in London I went to prepare the way for them to follow as soon as they could.

From the time I had seen Brazil that February it was love at first sight. The language did not pose a great problem, for I had been so keen on learning the language since I started going to Casa do Brasil that I could have gotten by with what I already knew.

My first impressions of Brazil were very favourable indeed, despite the fact that I had arrived in Rio de Janeiro on the most tumultuous day of a most tumultuous period. It was a time of great student unrest. Ideologically, the National Students Union (Uniao Naçional dos Estudantes—UNE) had taken on the government full tilt. And the government had also taken them on full tilt. The result was chaos in the streets. There was no shooting but the soldiers used canisters of teargas most copiously, and all along the main thorough-fares as I came from the immigration building, there were scores of red-eyed people and the air was blue. I at once realised there was unrest from the soldiers and army transport about, but I had not seen teargas before and it was not until I began to feel the sharp burning in my eyes that I realised what was floating in the air. It was really scary. And yet, otherwise it was so much like home that I felt more comfortable there in a few hours than I had felt after fourteen years in England.

The unrest died down and everything re-turned to normal after about a week. I loved Rio de Janeiro for its tidy streets, its patterned pave-ments, its colourful, frequent, and efficient buses, for its warm-spirited and friendly people, and for the cosmopolitan nature of its population. There were black, brown, and white faces everywhere. Of course, the story about Brazil, being free of racial discrimination, was nothing more than a popular fairy tale, but the discrimination is so quiet and subtle that one took a little while to notice it. But being what I was, when I went into the banks to do any business I looked around for black faces, just as I did when I went around to big firms and offices of distinction. I did not see any there—or perhaps I should say many. Yet they seemed in equal numbers on the streets and they predominat-ed at Carnival. A number of black people assured me there was no racial discrimination in Brazil. Because they wanted to believe it. I begged them not to tell me that but to tell that to the marines! Yet Brazil is the most enjoyable place I have ever lived.

Maybe the happiest moment I experienced during the first few months was when my wife and our three children arrived in Rio de Janeiro that October. The youngest, my son Carlos, was born in London that July, and having left in May I had not seen him. It was an indescribable reunion with the family.

After teaching English for seven months, I happened to meet, in the Bank of London and South America, a Trinidadian, Dr Harry Major. It was the very last day of 1968. A few months before, I heard on the air that the state of Trinidad and Tobago was planning to open an embassy in Rio de Janeiro, and I had written to the prime minister of Trinidad and Tobago offering my services as a Trinidadian who spoke Portu-guese. When Dr Harry Major realised that I was Trinidadian he said he had a message for Michael Anthony and did I know him. Naturally I did. He was thrilled to meet the person he had been trying to contact for some days. He was the councillor, or chargé d'affaires, sent to open the new embassy, and he said the prime minister had asked him to give me a job.

I began working at the embassy early that January as an interpreter and translator, as well as cultural attaché.

In the meantime Jennifer, now twelve, and Keith, now nine, began to go to school. We three were fluent in Portuguese but Yvette, my wife, could not speak a word of it and she did not try hard to learn. We enjoyed Brazil greatly and it is still our favourite country, but I could not help feeling uneasy that I was unable to continue my literary career. There seemed to be no good reason why not, but I just could not concentrate on writing. By the end of 1969 a number of little factors had conspired to make us feel very uncom-fortable. Inflation had increased enormously and my salary was thereby reduced to a pittance, and there seemed no hope of getting an increase of pay. Then the rent for houses in Rio de Janeiro went up about 100 percent. I did not know what to do. It was no good going back to teaching English, and as a non-Brazilian my chances of getting any other job were extremely limited. Around that time, having contact with Trinidad through the newspapers at the embassy, and seeing that my children were beginning to forget English (my little one, Carlos, had Portuguese as his first language while learning to speak), I began to think homewards. One of the only kinds of writing I did at this time was for the *Trinidad Guardian*, describ-ing sporting and other events in Brazil. Towards the very end of 1969 I wrote to the editor of this newspaper, Len Chongsing, saying I was coming back home and asking if it would be possible to get a job in his establishment. He wrote back saying they could not offer me a specific job as they had no vacancies, but if I were to turn up at the

Trinidad Guardian they could not in good conscience turn me back.

So I prepared to pack my bags. At this point, the end of 1969, my wife was pregnant, and the travelling plans we were making had to take into account a little baby. Just before the baby was born, very disquieting news of Trinidad came to us at the embassy. There was an uprising in Trinidad, the news said, and the country was in chaos. There was mutiny in the army and law and order was in shambles. The government was facing a coup and the country was on the brink of anarchy. We all but held our breaths for news of further development but nothing I heard shook my plans. Trinidad was home and I was going there.

My daughter Sandra was born in March. Because of her birth we delayed our plans a little, and on June 24, 1968, we set off. It was still the days of passenger liners. Trinidad was in the grip of a state of emergency and no ships could call there. Our trip was to take us by bus to the town of Fortaleza—about a thousand miles to the northeast of Rio de Janeiro—and from there we were to catch a Booth Line ship for the island of Barbados. By the time we arrived in Barbados, we figured, the state of emergency would be lifted and we would fly to Trinidad.

Incidentally, the day we left Rio de Janeiro, Wednesday, June 24, 1970, was the very day the victorious Brazilian soccer team was returning from their campaign in Mexico, and to say that they were returning to heroes' welcome is understating the fact. The players were not expected before noon but by 8:00 A.M. Rio de Janeiro was jampacked with people and completely dislocated.

But we managed to get out of Rio de Janeiro before the jam-session reached its peak, and after four days and nights we arrived at Fortaleza. At Fortaleza we waited for the SS *Clement,* which had a very imprecise schedule but was due "any time," we were told, and when the ship arrived, after three days of waiting, we were glad to board right away, so bad were hotel conditions. We left there the next day and arrived in Barbados at the end of June.

I was excited to be in Barbados for the first time. I had had a long literary association with this island, but apart from this, Barbados, for its tiny size, was about the biggest little island in the Caribbean. It was big in education—we had always heard so much of its Lodge School and its Combermere High School; it was big in politics, mainly through its renowned statesman Grantley Adams; and it was big in cricket, the most popular game in

the English-speaking Caribbean through figures like Frank Worrell and Clyde Walcott. The exciting thing was that it was also the home of *BIM* and *BIM*'s editor, Frank Collymore, and none of the hundreds of its achievements was to me bigger than this fact.

I had wired Frank Collymore saying that I was coming and no sooner had I arrived than Frank Collymore collected my family and me and accommodated us in one of the houses on the university campus. I believe he was some official of the university. Not only did he accommodate us but stocked our refrigerator with foodstuffs, and showed us dozens of other courtesies. The only criticism of *BIM* among some Caribbean writers of that time was the fact that *BIM* either did not pay or paid so little as to make no difference. With me, it had always been enough to get into *BIM* and I never cared whether I was paid or not. It seemed heavenly justice, therefore, that owing to my association with *BIM,* I was richly rewarded and royally treated during my stay in Barbados.

We flew out of Barbados after about a week. After I arrived in Trinidad I turned up at the *Trinidad Guardian* and sure enough the editor, Len Chongsing, offered me a job. I was to be a subeditor on the night desk, working from 4:00 P.M. to 11:00 P.M. He said, "We'd have liked to offer you something better than this, but we can't. See what you can do, and in the meantime if you get anything better, please feel free to take it."

I was with the *Trinidad Guardian* only a few weeks when I received a call from the Pointe-à-Pierre oil refinery where I'd worked in the foundry years before. The company there was now Texaco and they asked me if I would like to work on the company's newspaper, the *Texaco Star.* I accepted the offer, and that September (1970) I started working at Pointe-à-Pierre again, this time in the company's administration building which housed the office of the *Texaco Star.*

But although the job was quite different, there were similarities with my foundry life. When I went to the foundry twenty-three years before, I did not like what I called the hot, dirty, laborious job, and I thought this would in no way help me to be a writer. Now the present job was nice and clean, and anyone would say that it had everything to do with writing, but it was the first time I discovered that journalism and the editing of a house journal had nothing to do with creative writing. Being a writer hardly prepared me for this job. One had to have the knack and the flair for producing house journals to be able to cope with

Daughter Sandra, Michael Anthony, wife, Yvette, and son Carlos, 1986

this. The previous editor, whom I was succeeding, was an excellent newspaperman who did not claim to be a writer at all. Yet bringing out this journal was for him so simple, it was like doing nothing. He did very little original writing, except the writing of captions, and was always aided by a great pile of photographs of employees at work and play, long-service ceremonies, people who were "moving up" in the company, and that sort of thing. Then there was the company director's editorial to be inserted, and if the photographer was truly worth his salt there would be some big picture of one of the company's installations that would take up more than half of one page. The former editor would just slap these items in place while laughing and joking with me. And presto! He would be ready for the printers. However, when I took over the job I was like a cat on a hot tin roof.

Firstly, I never liked the role of public relations, having to sing the praise of the firm under all circumstances. But having naively accepted the job, I had to wrestle with it. Secondly, and maybe more importantly, I had no flair for this sort of work. What took the former editor, Don Scofield, one hour to do, took me about four hours, and not half as expertly. I struggled with that job throughout the rest of 1970, through 1971, and most of 1972. In mid-1972 I was feeling as frustrated as I had been with foundry work some two decades before. In 1971 the prime minister of Trinidad

and Tobago had set up a National Cultural Council and the chairman of this body, Dr J. D. Elder, asked for a writer of books for children. I applied, and as both *The Year in San Fernando* and *Green Days by the River* were being used as literature in schools, I thought I had a good chance of success. But no one paid me any mind. In 1972 the Public Library asked me to contribute to a newspaper supplement intended to mark International Book Year. I was to contribute an article entitled "Writing for the Younger Ones."

On the day the supplement was published, Sunday, October 22, 1972, the prime minister telephoned Dr Elder and said: "You said you want a writer of children's books. This guy in the supplement wrote as if he knows about it. Why don't you call him up immediately and offer him a job."

The chairman, who previously paid me no mind, called me up the next day. I started to work with the National Cultural Council just the week following, on Monday, October 30 in that year.

My employment with the National Cultural Council was to mark the most satisfying period of my literary life. I stayed with the council for sixteen years, until my retirement in 1988, and the fact that I have only produced five books for this organisation was because, always strapped for money, it was not able to publish them fast enough. But my time was constantly taken up with such matters as organising literary competitions, holding seminars and workshops, and carrying out research on various things.

Between my arrival in Trinidad in 1970 and my departure from Pointe-à-Pierre, I had done no creative writing of consequence. In fact, from the time I had left England for Brazil in 1968 up to November 1972 all I had published was a chapter called "In a South-Eastern Village" for a book on Trinidad published in 1972. So now, I began to think of continuing my literary career while I served the National Cultural Council. By the outset of 1973 I had signed a contract with André Deutsch, my publisher, to bring out a collection of my stories (the BBC stories), and this book appeared in the summer of 1973. At the same time I had undertaken a book of historical essays for the National Cultural Council, a book called *Glimpses of Trinidad and Tobago,* and the National Cultural Council published this book in 1974. In 1974 I also published a history of Trinidad, *Profile Trinidad,* through the English publisher Macmillan. I began thinking of attempting another novel, and Brazil, having such a tremendous influence on my life and then still so fresh in the mind, provided the backcloth. I thought of that first day on the streets of Rio de Janeiro, with soldiers and students confronting each other and with teargas saturating the atmosphere, and I wrote the novel *Streets of Conflict,* which was published in 1976. In that year, I undertook to produce nine folk stories of Trinidad. They were going to be stories based on our folk legends, and one or two of them would be fantasies. This little book, called *Folk Tales and Fantasies,* was published for the National Cultural Council in 1977.

That year, I was busily thinking of another book for the National Cultural Council. In 1975, for the first time, I had gotten into free-lance radio work, broadcasting, then a long historical series on Port-of-Spain. Just before that, I had done the same thing by way of some articles on the newspaper. Now in 1977 I was taking another look at the articles and at the scripts used in the broadcast and in 1978 I produced a book called *The Making of Port-of-Spain.* I continued several historical series on the radio, awaiting my chance to do something purely literary again. The chance came when Thomas Nelson and Sons, the publishers, invited me to write a small novel for schools. I wrote a story of Carnival, published under the title *King of the Masquerade.*

The years 1980 and 1981 were filled with literary competition affairs and seminars but again I thought it was time to turn to another novel. I wanted to return to the familiar world of my childhood and see from some other perspective life as it was carried on there. I knew it was going to be autobiographical, but what I wanted to do was to write a love story observed by a schoolboy and I wanted to superimpose on this story the feeling of tension and suspense. The resulting novel, *All That Glitters,* was published in 1982. Always mindful that it was as a writer that I was employed by the National Cultural Council, I sought to publish another book under its auspices. Throughout 1983 I worked on producing, as a result of intensive research, a book that told the story of the war years in Trinidad, especially with the entry of the United States soldiers. This book was published in 1984, as *Port-of-Spain: In a World at War.*

Just a little before this I had published a school novel for Thomas Nelson based on Sir Walter Raleigh's exploits on his search for El Dorado and the impact of the intrusion of Europeans on Amerindian life in Trinidad. The title of this book was *Bright Road to El Dorado,* published in 1983.

Between 1985 and 1989 I decided to bring out, under my own imprint, what I felt to be much-needed historical information on Trinidad. I wanted to do it myself as it did not make much sense engaging a publisher here—I would have to pay for production in any case—and I could not interest my English publishers in books that would be focussed entirely on Trinidad. In 1985 I published *First in Trinidad;* in 1986, *Heroes of the People of Trinidad and Tobago;* in 1987, *Towns and Villages of Trinidad and Tobago;* in 1988, a constitutional history called *A Better and Brighter Day;* and in 1989 I published *Parade of the Carnivals of Trinidad, 1839–1989,* to mark the 150th anniversary of Carnival of the Streets.

The year 1988 was the end of a fruitful period with the National Cultural Council. I retired that year.

In 1990 I began work on a historical dictionary of Trinidad and Tobago, which was commissioned by the Scarecrow Press of New Jersey, USA. At the end of 1991 I went to the United States to teach for a semester, and while at the University of Richmond, Virginia, teaching Caribbean literature and creative writing, I wrote a book of short stories, all of them based on actual historical incidents that have taken place in Trinidad. In 1991 also, I was finishing a book that I had written on the four voyages of Columbus with a view of publishing it to mark the 500th anniversary of Columbus's first voyage. This book, *The Golden Quest,* was published in 1992. The volume of historical short stories are scheduled to be published in June 1993, and the historical dictionary of Trinidad and Tobago is expected to be out in 1994.

After I had returned to Trinidad in 1970 I had temporarily lived at my wife's relatives at Tunapuna, a little town just about six miles east of Port-of-Spain. The invitation to work as an editor at Pointe-à-Pierre came so shortly after I had settled down at the *Trinidad Guardian* that from Tunapuna I moved directly to one of the villages adjoining Pointe-à-Pierre, a place known as Marabella. Here I rented a house which was just a few streets away from the address at which I lived during the years when I used to be an apprentice, and in many ways it was a kind of homecoming. I lived here from the end of 1970 until July 1973, which was shortly after I assumed the job with the National Cultural Council of Port-of-Spain.

At the time when I went to work with the National Cultural Council, a fine building project was started at a place called Chaguanas, which lay midway between Pointe-à-Pierre and Port-of-Spain, on the Western or Gulf Coast. I thought if the family went to live at Chaguanas we could maintain contact with our Pointe-à-Pierre and San Fernando friends, on the one hand; and with Port-of-Spain, my new workplace, on the other. Port-of-Spain, the capital, would be especially important to me now, for of course it was Trinidad's cultural center, and due to my new job I would need to frequent its libraries and archives. Chaguanas was one of the fastest growing places in the Trinidad of that time and was a delightful little district. It was regarded as a vegetable garden centre, and its commercial area was very busy, yet it was very rural for the most part. Just as Mayaro was known for its coconut palms, Chaguanas was known for its fields of waving sugarcane. It was a fascinating area and I grew to love it, especially the countryside atmosphere, but I did not stay long enough to enjoy much of this. The main highway link between Port-of-Spain and San Fernando was so

"Two handsome devils"—Michael Anthony with Canadian critic Doug Rollins, 1989

cluttered up between Chaguanas and Port-of-Spain during the rush hours that within months I decided something had to be done. I came to the conclusion that too much of my life was being spent on the road between Chaguanas and the National Cultural Council where I worked. My children of school age, then thirteen and ten years old (the other two were four and two), were attending colleges in Port-of-Spain, and after I took them to school on mornings all I needed to do was to go to the library to do research for my various National Cultural Council projects. I felt that if I lived in Port-of-Spain I could use a lot more productively those hours which I normally spent travelling.

In May 1974 I acquired this house, 99 Long Circular Road, and this place has proved a home, a haven, and a base. My children, now grown men and women, were raised here, and since 1974, everything that I have written has come from here. From this vantage point in the historic Port-of-Spain suburb of St James, one can see the blue Gulf of Paria, just about half a mile away, as the crow flies. True, the Gulf of Paria is not the rolling Atlantic and does not cater to those who love turbulent, frothy waters, pounding on sandy beaches. It is like a great inland lake, separating Trinidad from the mainland of South America. The setting and the sea is very different from the scene where I first opened my eyes, but this is home too, and it has been for eighteen years. I find it very pleasant here, and here is where I expect I shall produce my last book. I often go to Mayaro to my mother's house, which is now mine as I acquired it after her death in 1985. For Mayaro is home, too, and I am afraid it never ceased being that. I shall always want to spend some time at Quarters, and to walk down to Plaisance, and to Lagon Mahaut, and to St Ann's, although I shall not see my old RC School, for it was demolished in 1977. And I shall want to watch that turbulent sea, the lagoons, and the River Ortoire, as well as the green coconut palms, for they will always remind of green days, and this writer will always be grateful for having sprung from such an idyllic setting.

BIBLIOGRAPHY

Fiction:

The Games Were Coming, Deutsch (London), 1963, Houghton (Boston), 1968, expanded edition, Heinemann Educational, 1977.

The Year in San Fernando, Deutsch, 1965, revised edition, Heinemann Educational, 1970.

Green Days by the River, Deutsch, 1967, Houghton, 1967.

Michael Anthony's Tales for Young and Old, Stockwell, 1967.

King of the Masquerade, Thomas Nelson, 1974.

Streets of Conflict, Deutsch, 1976.

All That Glitters, Deutsch, 1982.

Bright Road to El Dorado, Thomas Nelson, 1983.

Short-story collections:

Cricket in the Road, Deutsch, 1973.

Sandra Street and Other Stories (illustrated by Richard Kennedy), Heinemann Educational, 1973.

Folk Tales and Fantasies (illustrated by Pat Chu Foon), Columbus (Port-of-Spain), 1977.

The Chieftain's Carnival, Longmans, Green, 1993.

Nonfiction:

Glimpses of Trinidad and Tobago with a Glance at the West Indies (essays), Deutsch, 1974.

Profile Trinidad: A Historical Survey from the Discovery to 1900, Macmillan (London), 1974.

(Editor with Andrew Carr) *David Frost Introduces Trinidad and Tobago*, Deutsch, 1975.

The Making of Port-of-Spain, 1757–1939, Key Caribbean, 1978.

Port-of-Spain: In a World at War, National Cultural Council, 1984.

First in Trinidad, Circle Press (Port-of-Spain), 1985.

Heroes of the People of Trinidad and Tobago, Circle Press, 1986.

(Editor) Gaylord Kelshall, *The History of Aviation in Trinidad and Tobago, 1913–1962* (by the Airports Authority of Trinidad and Tobago), Paria, 1987.

Towns and Villages of Trinidad and Tobago, Circle Press, 1987.

A Better and Brighter Day, Circle Press, 1988.

Parade of the Carnivals of Trinidad, 1839–1989, Circle Press, 1989.

The Golden Quest: The Four Voyages of Christopher Columbus, Macmillan Caribbean (London), 1992.

Philip Appleman

1926-

I was four years old when I first saw the fierce-looking sword and its black leather scabbard. My maternal great-grandfather, Charles Collins, fought with the 129th Regiment of the Indiana Volunteer Infantry at Kennesaw Mountain, Georgia; at Nashville, Tennessee; and in eleven other battles in 1864 and 1865; was promoted from private to sergeant to second lieutenant in the field; and by the end of the war, had lost all four of his brothers, killed in action and buried in the South. Sixty years after discovering the sword, I found, among my Aunt Helen's keepsakes, their letters home: terse, dignified, slightly misspelled, heartbreaking. It was the first time the Civil War had ever made me cry.

Contemplating our lives, we have to ponder connections. My father, William Russell Appleman, was an orphan, his real parents unknown, though he had his hunches about them; only one generation of adopted history on that side, but it gave us our family name. On the other side, my mother, Gertrude Collins Keller, came from a family that was grandly treated by a genealogical service that, I was told, had traced the Scotch-Irish Collinses back beyond my great-grandfather, all the way to the Mayflower. I always considered that pedigree an unusual triumph of aspiration over skepticism—until my wife and I, in Europe as students in 1952, went to war-ravaged Darmstadt, Germany, to trace her paternal antecedents and found one branch of the family in possession of a handsome genealogical chart that put them in a direct and continuous line from "Carlus Magnus."

Someone having roots as deep as Charlemagne (even as a pious fiction) is pretty impressive to a young man from Indiana, where, at my birth, all of local history was no longer than the overlapping lives of two octogenarians. But if we seriously wonder just who we are and where we came from, we have to think back well before Charlemagne, to those Mediterranean forebears who originated Western history in the first place; and even past them, to the Neolithic hunter-gatherers whose beautiful flint arrowheads stud not only the fields around Darmstadt but also the cornfield behind

Philip Appleman, 1981

my family's rented house in Kendallville, Indiana, where my brother Jack and I followed the plow in the spring and picked them up, one by one—finely wrought, keen edged, delicate—artifacts not only of skill, but of intelligence and civilization. Having now spent many years studying the works of Charles Darwin, I would even propose that, to be thorough, we would have to think still further back, twenty-two thousand years, to the capable hands that carved, in mammoth ivory, the small human head, an exact replica of which is now on my desk: the beautiful (female) face of Cro-Magnon, our ancestor. And back even further, fifty thousand more years, to the clever woman or man who chipped and flaked the hand ax my wife and I brought home long ago from Petra, Jordan, and that now sits beside the Cro-Magnon head. This is not fantasy: we humans have been around for a long time, and if Darwin taught us anything, it is the value of context. I'll come back to that thought later.

A lot depends, of course, on when you were born, and where. Having been born in 1926 meant that my active memory began in 1929, just in time for the stock market crash and the ensuing twelve harsh years of depression; and it meant that I was of military age in time for World War II. Growing up among the hardships of the Great Depression and the Great War wouldn't be any reasonable person's first choice, but there were compensations. Families pinched by hard times often developed a defensive toughness, and just as often demonstrated the compassion that comes from being "all in the same boat." And the war, terrible as it was, had a positive, unifying effect on a country that had become, in its long economic distress, a house divided.

My family had its share of mixed blessings. We were, on the one hand, shabby-genteel, but on the other hand, upwardly aspiring: wonderful things were always, supposedly, just around the corner. My father, who was brought up on the farm of his adoptive parents, and after his marriage variously employed, usually as a salesman, eventually developed his own business, manufacturing and selling, single-handedly, an insecticide called Banol. Unfortunately, it never made him rich, as he perpetually hoped. My mother, long-suffering and cheerful throughout the depression, managed, in spite of formidable odds, to come up with good, nutritious meals and a wealth of moral support—until, at age forty-five, she was stricken (and often thereafter bedridden) with rheumatoid arthritis, which tormented her, and worried her family, for the rest of her life. Of their six children, my parents lost their eldest, Jack, to a streptococcus infection in 1936 (when he was twelve and I was ten), and a newborn son, Charles, about a year later. But my three sisters, Barbara (born 1928), Ann (born 1932), and Sara (born 1940), and I grew up in a sheltered and nurturing household, where not only our parents but also our nearby maternal grandmother and two aunts were constantly encouraging us to do well, and to do good.

In 1993, as I write this, those years before World War II seem distant not only in time but in spirit. At the beginning of my novel, *Apes and Angels,* I tried to conjure up some of the flavor of that period:

Imagine.

Not the dark avenues of cities, the long files of traffic lights going green in unison, the throb of the all-night bus at its terminal stop, the lonely cruising taxi; but the moonshadows of maple leaves on quiet sidewalks, the sounds of birds that never sleep, sending their liquid keening into a honeysuckle midnight, and a time, only yesterday, but before television, before jet planes or astronauts, before civil rights, transistors, Xerox, AIDS, the Pill, or the Bomb . . .

Summers lasted longer in those days, and were a lot hotter. The only air-conditioned refuge in town was the Strand Theater, where grown-ups surrendered a hard-earned quarter, kids a dime, and sat through a double feature and the Movietone News and two short subjects and Merrie Melodies and maybe a chinaware lottery or Bank Night or a sing-along, just to get out of the heat. There was no such cool comfort in the churches, and on Sundays in summer, pious men's suit coats peeled off like scalded tomato skins, and cardboard fans from a local undertaker, featuring a beatific blue-eyed Jesus, fluttered through the congregation like busy butterflies.

In poetry, I recorded the contrast between that time and the present somewhat differently. This is the first poem in my book, *Open Doorways:*

Memo to the 21st Century

It was like this once: sprinklers mixed
our marigolds with someone else's phlox,
and the sidewalks under maple trees
were lacy with August shade,
and whistles called at eight and fathers walked
to work, and when they blew again,
men in tired blue shirts followed
their shadows home to grass.
That is how it was in Indiana.

Towns fingered out to country once,
where brown-eyed daisies waved a fringe on
    orchards
and cattle munched at clover, and
fishermen sat in rowboats and were silent,
and on gravel roads, boys and girls
stopped their cars and felt the moon and touched,
and the quiet moments ringed and focused
lakes   moon   flowers.
That is how it was
in Indiana.

But we are moving out now,
scraping the world smooth where apples
    blossomed,

paving it over for cars. In the spring
before the clover goes purple,
we mean to scrape the hayfield, and
next year the hickory woods:
we are pushing on, our giant diesels snarling,
and I think of you, the billions of you, wrapped
in your twenty-first century concrete,
and I want to call to you, to let you know
that if you dig down,
down past wires and pipes
and sewers and subways, you will find
a crumbly stuff called earth. Listen:
in Indiana once, things grew in it.

G rowing up in a little midwestern town in the
1930s was, as I now see it, rather more like
living in the nineteenth century than in the fast-
approaching twenty-first. The schoolhouse we
attended was in fact built in the nineteenth century, and we walked to it all year, rain or snow, and
then walked home for lunch (no buses or school
cafeterias in those days) and then back and forth
again. In summer we walked and played in those
same streets barefoot, toes prodding the pudgy hot
tar in the pavement cracks; or in August spent our
carefully hoarded nickels at the Noble County Fair
out at the edge of town, where the 4-H kids
exhibited their prize sheep and pigs; or followed
the iceman's truck or the horse cart of the fruit-
and-vegetable man or the hominy-and-horseradish
man; or hung around at the New York Central
station, where the Twentieth Century Limited
roared through Kendallville without slowing
down; but the coal-burning locomotives of the
local trains stopped, hissing out clouds of steam,
while oilers clanged at the huge wheels and
passengers and conductors and baggage men bus-
tled around until the piercing whistle and the "All
aboard." Or we rode our bikes to the town tennis
courts for long, hot, intense, and exhausting (if
uninstructed) games; then down to the town's
popular Bixler Lake beach, where, in the prim
Hays Office thirties, even the men were required
to wear swim-suit tops, and where we all swam and
dived so long that our skin would shrivel and turn
bluish: that was an almost daily routine. When I
was seventeen and the older men were all at war, I
was the sole lifeguard at that beach, and on one
crowded Sunday afternoon, while hundreds of hot,
picnicking visitors jammed the sand and the water,
a little boy drowned. Given that big crowd of
splashing bodies and bobbing heads, no lifeguard
could have prevented such an accident, and nobody ever blamed me; nevertheless, I felt responsible, and the grief stayed with me. Eventually I

wrote a poem about it, which begins with Socrates'
last words.

A Word to Socrates

> "Crito, we ought to offer
> a cock to Asclepius."

And is death, then, old man,
the purest Idea of all,
the cure for life?

I have seen only one face
return from that gray world
you welcomed: a boy who, at
a beach beyond your strange
geography—a beach
I guarded—slipped away
and drowned. We dragged for him
in the yellowing Sunday sun
and caught him on our hook,
snagged at the elbow. His
hand broke water first
and held there for a moment,
reaching out of that clammy
death to snatch at the low
daylight—a reaching out
that caught no life but mine
who lost him.

Old man, I would not since
that hour exchange the song
of one brown bird at sunset
for the purest Idea in all
eternity.

(From *Summer Love and Surf*)

A lot of us seventh graders joined one of the
town's two Boy Scout troops and proceeded from
Tenderfoot to Second to First Class Scout. My best
friend, Charles Ralihan, two years older than I and
one rank ahead, somehow impressed me with the
urgency of doing well in scouting, so we both
applied ourselves avidly, progressing merit badge
by merit badge to Star, Life, and Eagle Scout, all
before I was fourteen. Then we kept on, in a kind
of manic chase, Charlie always a few badges ahead,
to Bronze and Gold Palm. By the time we reached
Silver Palm, I had finally caught up with him, and
we were accorded that highest honor together.
Charlie, with the same diligence, became valedictorian of the Kendallville High School class of 1942,
and was soon drafted and killed by a Japanese
sniper on Okinawa.

Some people think it clever to belittle scouting, but at that time and place, it was, for me at
least, an immeasurably important activity, making

me aware of the world as a place to be learned, to be examined piece by piece, subject by subject, until whole areas of experience had been illuminated, if not mastered; none of that was available in any other way. (The current problem of Christian zealots expelling scouts who come from nonreligious families didn't exist then; we were a strictly secular group.) And there was a rare opportunity for pride in being the best tent riggers in the county and one of the best first-aid teams in the Midwest, demonstrating our skills in the grand ballroom of the Hilton Hotel in Chicago. But it was the outdoor experience that was always at the center of things: the long hikes; the overnight camping out in the woods, building twig cooking fires as neat and controlled as gas jets; the intimate knowledge of all the local trees by leaf, bark, and grain; the silent communion with birds and small animals. In 1993, amid high-rise buildings as I write this, it really does sound nineteenth century. And yet, it was after an overnight camp-out in the woods near Kendallville in 1939 that I came back early in the morning to find the local newsboy biking around town with the only local "extra" edition I can remember from those days, and the headline: "Hitler Bombs Warsaw"; the ineluctable future was taking shape around us.

In our moderately large extended family, we celebrated all of our birthdays with inexpensive but carefully considered gifts, and it was obligatory that each one be accompanied by a little poem. (Sometimes, during the depression, the poem was more impressive than the gift.) The family masters of this fine art were my mother, my maternal grandmother, Minnie May Keller, and my aunt, Helen Keller, all of them turners of neat phrases. Of course, no one made any grand claims for those occasional pieces (a lot of them extant in various old scrapbooks), though some are pretty good light verse. But the important thing, for me, was that the whole family took poetry to be a natural mode of expression, something that, for all its casualness, was expected to be both amusing and affecting.

Before Indiana consolidated most of its public schools in the 1960s, every little town had its own high school, and Kendallville, with five thousand inhabitants, was the biggest town in Noble County, and therefore had the biggest high school. I graduated in the class of 1944 with fifty-eight others, all of us friends, or anyway friendly, most of whom still attend (as I do) our class reunions—and I was, and am, convinced that we had a solid secondary education. I don't remember taking IQ

tests or SATs as students now routinely do, so the first time I learned how well I had been taught was when my army General Classification Test score turned out to be not only the highest in my company of Aviation Cadets but so high that it caused a stir among the examiners. What our teachers had given us was a strong sense of the importance of doing a job well. I have clear memories of some of the specific things I learned in grade school from Miss Erie, Miss Ryder, Miss Sawyer, Miss Habegger, Miss Jordan, Miss Campen, and Miss Coplin; and clearer memories of what I was taught in high school by Miss Power, Mr. Tritch, Mr. Howerton, Miss Will, Miss Page, and Miss Stevens. Most of my early self-discipline, though, I owed to Miss Eva L. Robertson, one of our high-school English teachers, who was especially demanding, and therefore, to many of us who remember her fondly, especially valuable.

Why were there so many "Misses" among our teachers, and virtually no "Mrs."? It was because, during the depression, jobs were so scarce that it was considered unfair for a married woman, who had a husband to provide for her, to "take a job away" from a "head of family." So if a single (female) teacher got married, as sometimes happened, she had to resign. Most, however, stayed single, and were, in a way, married to their jobs. Few would try, in this more enlightened time, to justify that old logic; no male teachers were ever fired if their wives happened to work. But one of the side effects of that policy was a teaching staff of women who were highly focused on their jobs.

All of the teachers, for their munificent salaries of about nine hundred dollars a year, had extracurricular duties, including such humiliations as taking tickets at basketball games. But Miss Robertson's extracurricular duties were her main interest: as adviser to the "Wig and Paint" dramatic club and director of all the class plays. I enjoyed dramatics, and since it was a small school, I was able to participate often, taking the male lead in a number of plays and becoming president of Wig and Paint.

Some of the women who taught grade school also taught Sunday school, a few of them in the church my family attended, the First Christian Church of Kendallville, also called the Disciples of Christ. That denomination is undeniably fundamentalist ("No creed but the Christ, no book but the Bible"), but in our congregation, doctrine was fairly relaxed. On one occasion, I even remember the minister grudgingly conceding that Christians whose baptism was by sprinkling rather than immersion might *possibly* be "saved"—but that if you were smart, you wouldn't gamble on it; you'd opt for total immersion.

As in most churches, an important part of the services was music. I attended choir practice on Thursday nights and sang the standard hymns on Sunday mornings, in a group that had more spirit than talent. I can still sing most of those songs with a kind of perverse pleasure, vestiges of my years as a young believer.

I enjoyed all kinds of music. I remember my innocent presumption, at about age thirteen, when I announced to Miss Love, the school music teacher, that I had definitely decided my favorite composer was Mozart. "Well," she allowed, "he *was* a good one." My parents had somehow managed to shell out weekly quarters for four years of piano lessons, three years of violin, and three years of voice; so I ended up singing in the a cappella choir and playing violin (and, at various times, bass viol) in the high-school orchestra and (having taught myself the brass instruments) the sousaphone and baritone horn in the marching band. Small schools have their compensations, one of which is abundant opportunity for minor talents.

"Pomp and Circumstance" in the high-school gym sent us out into the world in 1944, and for boys, in those days, that meant into the military. I enlisted in the U.S. Army Air Corps, in the Aviation Cadet program, but at that stage of World War II, the army already had more pilots than it could use. So my whole generation of Aviation Cadets was put on hold, on temporary duty as "on-the-line trainees" (which meant airplane windshield washing more than anything else), and then as clerks, typists, whatever. I spent the last year of the war as a physical training instructor, including a long stint leading mass calisthenics at an air base in the mangrove swamps west of the fabled Boca Raton Club. Boca in those days looked rather like a little west-Texas town of modest one-story bungalows. And the whole Florida east coast, from Lauderdale to West Palm, was largely "undeveloped," as the real-estate people put it—that is, it was unspoiled, wild, and beautiful. It would have surprised me to know that the alligator-circled tarpaper barracks of the Boca Raton Army Air Base would one day be superseded by a big university campus.

It was at Boca that I got the totally unexpected news of the destruction of a then unheard-of Japanese city by a then unheard-of kind of bomb reported to have the incredible force of twenty

With his aunt, Helen Keller, in Kendallville, Indiana, 1944

thousand tons of TNT. Because of that new bomb, the war soon ended, and around the country, millions of young men who had been expecting years more of military service were suddenly faced with the happy prospect of returning to civilian life. No wonder so few of us had second thoughts until later on about the morality of using the atomic bomb.

I came out of the army at an awkward time—in November, 1945—too late for fall-semester college courses, and especially for the course I most wanted: the new and very special "B.A. Program" at Northwestern University, which admitted freshmen only in September. I decided to wait until the following autumn, and having heard from some army buddies about the merchant marine, proceeded to join up. I soon got my Coast Guard Ordinary Seaman's papers and my National Maritime Union card in Chicago, but wanted a little time at home, so I spent a couple of strenuous and bitterly cold months as a gandy dancer, laying rail (by hand, the old-fashioned way), on the frozen New York Central Railroad tracks near Kendallville. Finally, at the beginning of February, 1946, I said goodbye to family and friends and took the train, over the tracks I had just been laying, to New York.

The end of the war had meant a steep decline in American shipping, so in 1946, the National Maritime Union hiring hall in New York was full of seamen waiting for their numbers to come up; some of them had been waiting for months. I registered at the hiring hall, but realized that it would be a long time before I could bid for a coveted ship to Europe (the longer runs meant more pay), so I compromised on a United Fruit ship bound for Honduras, Guatemala, and Cuba, carrying general cargo. By great good luck (for me), that ship developed a generator problem after the crew had signed on, so we got paid while we worked on deck and waited for repairs, at the now extinct Pier 9, North River—currently the site of Battery Park City and the World Trade Center, but in those days one of the busiest parts of a noisy, bustling port. The working piers ran every block from the Battery to Midtown, and below the roaring West Side Highway (not then a ruin), the trucks and carts and taxis and passengers and general hustle were exhilarating: crossroads of the world. For seven wonderful weeks, I chipped rust and painted bulkheads on the MV *Rolling Hitch* by day, and by night explored the magic of that great city.

Finally they got the defective generator out and the new one in, and we were away. The sea was just what I'd hoped for—something out of Joseph Conrad: I was twenty, and the Atlantic was wild, romantic, and beautiful. I loved it. In my first novel, *In the Twelfth Year of the War*, there is a brief description of that sailing:

> From the iron grimness of New York winter, the big ships would pull away, decks buried in snow and ice; and for three nights the crew would stand the bridge watches wearing all the clothes they owned, while the North Atlantic smashed at the hull and swept the lower decks. Everything was battened, dogged, and secured, and the wind and sea would rip at the corners and edges of things, making sounds like hungry animals. The men on watch, with frosting on their eyebrows, staring into the stinging ice of the spray and the cut of the wind, would curse as though cursing were prayer. Then on the third night the sea would calm and the wind go warm, and

after that there were three more nights of perfect stillness on the water and ripples from the setting moon and the contented chug of the engines in the ventilators, and three days of rope-horseshoes on deck, men lying around shirtless and braised in the tropical sun until they cooked deep down in the muscles. Finally Cortés or Barrios would slide up over the horizon and the white ship would ease past yellow beaches and slender palms and green mountains to the wharf, where brown boys splashed in the clear water and the voices of jukebox sirens called, called, called from the waterfront bars.

Honduras and Guatemala were lush and picturesque, but very poor. It was my first glimpse of the poverty of the underdeveloped countries, and it put a chastening perspective on my own depression childhood. Cuba was much the same, but it was a longer stay and therefore more interesting: carrying general cargo (not oil or that later quick-loading device, containers) meant that you had a few days of loading time in every port, enough to scout around, talk to people, and get a feel for the country. So Cuba, the "old" Cuba of dictator Batista, became the incubating locale for my first novel.

By the time that trip was over, it was too late to risk missing the beginning of fall semester again on a long ocean voyage, I stayed with my grandmother and aunt in Kendallville (my parents having just moved to Chicago) and worked all summer on a farm owned by my former high-school track and basketball coach, Charles Ivey. (I had lettered in basketball, and in track had set a school record in the hundred-yard dash that stood for some years.) He and his two sons and I worked those fields eight hours a day and came home at night genuinely worn out. Farming, in that time and place, was exclusively a matter of muscle—no air-conditioned stereo tractors, just a lot of tug and haul, lugging steel irrigation pipe, stooping for hours to dig potatoes, chopping out milkweed and thistles, hoeing. Weeding with a hoe requires a precise, almost surgical concentration—hit that weed, miss the corn sprout right beside it—which, after a few hours, becomes downright painful. (The principle of hell is that anything done long enough and without letup becomes intolerable.) And making hay the old-fashioned way, as Robert Frost accurately describes it in "The Death of the Hired Man," is one of the hardest, dirtiest, itchiest jobs in the world. I worked two summers on that farm while in college, and a third summer on a farm run by another high-school teacher, Laurence Baker. Both men specialized in flowers (iris, glads, peonies, delphinium), but there was enough livestock, orchard, cornfield, and hayfield work to keep things varied and interesting. And I made enough money, at sixty cents an hour, to keep from going hungry back at college, when the meager GI Bill money ran low.

A perpetually needy student, I was grateful for any odd jobs I could get. In high school, I delivered magazines and circulars, and clerked part-time at J. C. Penney. During college and graduate-school holidays, I often delivered mail for the post office, and on special occasions worked as a traffic director. I was a janitor at the Lincoln Life Insurance Company in Fort Wayne and at the Desert School in Tucson. My wife and I both worked, our first married summer, at the General Electric plant in Fort Wayne: I was on a multiple-head drill press; she wound armatures. Another summer we both worked nights at the A. C. Nielson Company in Chicago. Once I had the mixed fortune to serve as the judge of a jingle contest for a mattress company ("When you sleep on a Sealy, you'll say / This mattress is strictly OK . . ."). Holding out for a ship in Houston, I worked for a while as a typist for the Burroughs Adding Machine Company (the only man in the office, surrounded by women typing what seemed like two hundred words a minute), and in New Orleans, hard up as usual, I did day labor, cleaning out old Liberty ships for mothballing (the filthiest work I ever did, I think), and once, in extremity, sold a pint of blood (for seven dollars, the going rate) to buy enough bread, peanut butter, and oranges to hold out for the next ship. Things were touch and go back then.

We read sometimes that the "modern" world came into focus not at the turn of the century and the death of Queen Victoria but after the sea change of World War I. As I now see it, the change of spirit after World War II was equally momentous: from an endless depression into comparative prosperity; from a self-imposed national isolation into world leadership; from a lingering conservatism into more progressive thinking about social matters. From two of those fresh new social ideas I was the direct beneficiary: the GI Bill of Rights and the Fulbright Scholarships to Europe. When I was in high school, it was hard to imagine how I could ever manage to go to college. Inexpensive as the costs now seem, they were still prohibitive to a family that had trouble meeting even daily expenses and with a college system that offered far

fewer scholarships than it later did. The GI Bill solved that problem. I was only eligible for three years of college, but by taking extra courses every semester, I managed to finish the bachelor's degree in three years.

Having been a college professor for a long time, I'm aware that not everyone is thrilled by an undergraduate education; but I can't help wishing that all students could feel the same sense of challenge and adventure that I did in those years at Northwestern University. Much of the excitement was due to the special new B.A. Program that Northwestern had just inaugurated and which I had waited almost a year for: it was an interdisciplinary learning experience that focused on anthropology, sociology, and history, but included the full complement of the arts and sciences. For the first time, I began to see how all of those ordinarily compartmentalized "fields" of learning connected to and fed upon each other; how ideas and events developed and cross-fertilized and gave each other perspective. It made me understand, for the first

"Leaving my mother's house in Tucson to go back to the sea," 1948

time, what "education" means; as I said earlier, our understanding depends heavily on contexts. It was, in short, an introduction to that widely neglected and widely undervalued experience: intellectual excitement.

I soon realized that I had found my occupation. What could be better than a lifetime spent trying to foster that excitement in others? I decided to be a teacher, a professor of literature, and, with any luck, a writer, too. So I majored in English, concentrated on creative writing, and managed to write poems and stories despite the incessant demands of other college classes and, later, the pressures of graduate-school courses.

Besides the invaluable B.A. Program, another important thing happened to me at Northwestern. In French class, I met Margie—Marjorie Haberkorn, my future wife—and we struck up a friendship that soon became a romance. After our sophomore year, we both took leave of Northwestern, she to spend her junior year at the Sorbonne in Paris and I to go back into the merchant marine—partly because I needed money, partly to see more of the world, partly because I wanted to do some independent reading in philosophy and science, and partly to try to work out my own philosophy of life. I know that sounds quixotic and a bit sophomoric (I *was* a sophomore); but it was also a matter of being twenty-two and full of enthusiasm for just about everything. I don't feel apologetic about it; it was in fact one of the best years of my life.

Not that everything was rosy. During my first year at Northwestern, my parents began to live separate lives. At first I wasn't aware that it was a permanent situation, because it happened so gradually. In 1946, my mother's arthritis had become severe, so a few months after my parents moved to Chicago, my father drove my mother and my sister Ann to Arizona—reputedly a good climate for arthritis sufferers—where they were to stay in a hotel temporarily, while my father went back to Chicago to finish up some business there, presumably to return to Tucson later.

But my father didn't return then, and as time passed, it became more and more obvious that he was not going to; we found out that he was living with another woman. So our family was never reunited again, except briefly at Margie's and my wedding in 1950. My mother didn't believe in divorce, so my parents remained officially married until her death in 1976. My father, always financially precarious, sent very little support money to

her and my sisters, even at first, and after a few years, nothing at all.

We were all distressed, of course, but since my sisters were younger, they were more affected than I was by both the separation and the privation. Barbara, a freshman at Rockford College, dropped out of school to go to Tucson, to support herself and our mother. On the scanty GI Bill, in college, I couldn't help out much. I did send my mother half of my merchant marine income in 1948 and 1949, but it wasn't until I got my first full-time teaching job in 1955 that Margie and I could contribute significantly.

My mother was wonderfully resilient through her long ordeal. She may not have had many hours of undiluted joy in her difficult life, but by her positive attitude, she was an inspiration to her children, grandchildren, and others. She lived with, or near, Barbara for a long time, and then spent her final years in the homes of my sister Sara and her husband, Jerry Elliot, and their family, and then with my sister Ann and her husband, Hank Belcher, and their family.

My father continued to live in Chicago for the next forty years, as a designer and builder of large machinery—conveyors, incinerators, pulverizers—but barely made ends meet, and certainly never made the fortune he always envisioned "just around the corner." However, he managed to remain healthy, more or less self-sufficient, and always working, until his recent death at age ninety-two.

It was partly a family money problem, then, that sent me back to the merchant marine in 1948. A large percentage of the U.S. merchant tonnage at that time was still made up of Liberty ships. Built hastily during World War II (thirty days from keel to launching), to carry arms and soldiers to Europe and the Pacific, they were slow (ten or eleven knots maximum) and ungraceful; and by 1948, they were expendable. Shipping companies were ordering newer, faster ships; the Liberties were being mothballed in New Orleans, Norfolk, and elsewhere; and those that were still operating weren't being maintained with any diligence. "Rust bucket" was the right term for them. But there were so many of them still afloat that they were the only vessels I shipped out on in 1948 and 1949, and I actually grew fond of them, chipping away at their accumulating rust by day, and steering their ungainly ten-thousand-ton hulls through heavy Atlantic swells by night.

I shipped out of New York, New Orleans, and Houston; we carried general cargo to the North

Sea and around the Mediterranean and to the Caribbean, and midwestern wheat to a hungry postwar Italy; we made Salonika, Piraeus, Trieste, Naples, Leghorn, Genoa, Cádiz, Seville, Bremen, and Havana. In almost every European port, Margie was there to greet me. After receiving my radiogram as to where and when, she'd leave her studies at the Sorbonne, travel by TWA or the Orient Express, and meet me on the pier. My shipmates had never seen anything like it: a girl in every port, and always the same one. We were officially engaged on November 3, 1948, at our first rendezvous, in Trieste, which, at the time, was still an international free city, a sort of political no man's land: exotic, ancient, romantic. To the two of us, it seemed perfect—except for the painful separation afterward.

My self-directed reading program went well, too. Every time we hit port in the United States, I'd find a bookstore that carried the inexpensive Modern Library series (later defunct for years, but now being revived) of the classics of literature, philosophy, and science, and buy enough books to ballast my sea bag. I also read in port, while waiting for ships. I read Pascal in my slightly mildewed rooming house in New Orleans, and the Vedas and Upanishads at the New Orleans public library, where I got stack privileges. In Houston, in the park outside my shabby hotel room, I read Schopenhauer. In New York, I read Hobbes and Locke in the hiring hall and on the subway (consequently sometimes looking up to find myself past my stop, deep in Brooklyn). By the time the year was over, I had read and pondered scores of difficult books; but the most significant of all for me was Charles Darwin's *The Origin of Species.*

In the preface to my volume of poetry, *Darwin's Ark,* I described my first encounter with that book:

> I read [it] in noisy mess rooms, surrounded by cribbage-playing seamen. I read it in my bunk at night, the persistent bedlamp sometimes infuriating my watchmates. I read it on deck in the sunny waters of the Mediterranean, meanwhile collecting extra hazard pay because stray floating mines from World War II were still sinking ships there. The 1948 marginalia reinforce my memory of being interested in the mechanisms of natural selection, but the more detailed marginalia indicate that what most held my attention, in both *The Origin of Species* and *The Descent of Man,* was the information bearing upon the relation of human beings to the rest of nature, and the philosophical implications of evolution.
>
> I am sure it is difficult for anyone reared in a more enlightened time and place to imagine the sense of exhilaration in a young person schooled in midwestern fundamentalism, reading Darwin and understanding evolution for the very first time. But I recall that experience vividly: the overwhelming sanity that emerged from Darwin's clearly thought out and clearly written propositions; the relief at being finally released from a constrained allegiance to the incredible creation myths of Genesis; the profound satisfaction in knowing that one is truly and altogether a part of nature.

With Marjorie Haberkorn, Rome, 1948

So the year was a success in a lot of ways, and by the time Margie took her *Degré supérieur* with *mention bien* in 1949, and we got back to Northwestern for what was suddenly our senior year, we were a couple, a team, together in class and otherwise, and separable only by those quaint rules that put the girls into their sorority-house bedrooms on schedule, and sent the boys home to their separate quarters—where, nevertheless, the two of us continued to commune on the telephone. We did work hard, though: Margie got straight *A*'s that year, and I made Phi Beta Kappa, and we both decided to be teachers.

For many women at that time, it was the age of the P.H.T. degree ("Putting Hubby Through"), and both of us accepted that male-oriented notion without much question. We had no money at all, and scholarships were both rare and scanty, so our plan was for Margie to support us both by teaching high-school French while I sweat out the Ph.D. and got a university teaching job, whereupon she would go to graduate school herself.

That's almost how it worked out. We graduated in 1950, were married on August 19, borrowed the family car from Margie's always helpful parents, Ted and Martha Haberkorn, spent an energetic hiking and climbing honeymoon in the Smoky Mountains, and moved to Ann Arbor, where Margie had a nearby job offer.

Not in high-school French, however. By 1950, the baby-boom generation had only reached the grade schools, which meant that that's where all the jobs were, so that's where Margie had to teach for three years while I was in graduate school. An overcrowded fifth-grade classroom in a tough school and the lack of support from the school administration made her first job disappointing, so we were both overjoyed when, at the end of my A.M. year at the University of Michigan (and our first year of marriage), I won a Fulbright Scholarship to France. It rescued Margie (temporarily) from the ten-year-olds, gave her a second year to study in her adopted country, and gave me the exciting opportunity not only to continue my studies but, after five years of French classes, to see France at last.

Everyone warned us that Lyon was a "closed" city, but we found it friendly and welcoming, and enjoyed our work at the university, where Margie continued to refine her French and I studied comparative literature (heavy in English, with the Ph.D. examinations always in mind). Two of us living on a single scholarship was a bit tight, but, having been depression children, we were such disciplined economizers—making do on student restaurant meals (twenty cents apiece) or vegetarian dinners at home (even cheaper), cheered by an occasional sparkling *vin mousseux,* which in France cost less than soft drinks—that we not only lived within our income but stretched it to include quite a bit of low-budget travel: throughout France, and to Germany, Switzerland, Austria, Spain, Italy,

"Margie, in our senior year at Northwestern," 1950

England, Scotland, Ireland, and into the Algerian Sahara: Bou Saâda, Biskra, El Oued.

By now a well-schooled Darwinian, I was especially thrilled by a visit to the caves of Lascaux, where, on the day before Christmas, in 1951, we and two friends were taken through that vast museum of Paleolithic art. Our guide was the young man who had discovered those important caves only ten years before, when his dog had disappeared through a hole in the ground, and he had followed to rescue the dog. The five of us spent a long time down there, marveling. When we left, we took the train to Santander, in Spain, where, three days later, we were repeating the experience at the magnificent Cro-Magnon caves of Altamira. Many years later, Margie and I got to La Pileta, too, in southern Spain, and later still to Kakadu, in Australia. Each time we were astonished at the remarkable beauty and achievement of the ancient art.

That year we learned both from books and from traveling, and at the end of our stay, I received a graduate fellowship at Northwestern. We were happy to return there, and Margie went back to work, teaching fifth grade in a private school in Chicago, and then in the renowned Winnetka school system, before getting her first high-school teaching appointment in Arlington Heights, where she could finally teach what she wanted to teach: French, as well as English literature. She worked very hard at all of those teaching jobs, while I kept my nose firmly to the grad-school grindstone and, in the final two years, also taught freshman composition on an assistantship. By 1955 I had passed my twelve-hour Ph.D. written examinations, finished my dissertation on "Darwin and the Literary Critics," and begun looking for a university teaching position.

One of the best openings that year happened to be in our home state, as Instructor in English at Indiana University, at the impressive salary of $4,500 a year. (Harvard and Yale were paying new Ph.D.'s only $3,600.) Led by its already legendary president, Herman B Wells, the university in 1955 had a vigorous and engaging faculty, and we soon made good friends across the spectrum of departments, all of whom are still our valued friends. Margie taught French and English as an Associate Instructor, completing a Master's in 1958 and later becoming a member of the regular French department faculty at Indiana University in Indianapolis. I went through the academic ranks on schedule, from Instructor to Professor, and was pleased when in 1982 I was promoted to Distinguished Professor, a title awarded to only about one percent of the faculty.

I always felt privileged to be a teacher. Part of the pleasure of the work is, of course, love of one's chosen subject. Another part is the continuing contact with students, especially the good ones, whose quick minds and considerable talent are always a delight. In my later years at Indiana University, I taught, for the most part, graduate courses in creative writing; quite a few of my M.A. students became good friends, and we still stay in touch.

Margie and I were happy with our busy and varied lives in Bloomington, and also glad to be able to travel and explore the larger world, during summer vacations and occasional leaves of absence when we were invited to teach in other institutions, including Columbia University and the State University of New York at Purchase. By far the most interesting of our outside teaching jobs was with the International Honors Program, for which

Margie and I were both instructors and administrators in 1960–61 and 1962–63. That school, still operating, is a highly structured and demanding program in which three or four professors take twenty-five American college juniors around the world by air, spending the academic year in stays of two to four weeks in various countries of Asia and Europe, the students living with local families in each country. During those two years, we lived in and studied, both by textbook and by close observation, the cultures of Japan, Taiwan, Thailand, India, Iran, Israel, Egypt, Turkey, Greece, Italy, Germany, Poland, Russia, France, and England. It was an intense, difficult, and rewarding experience, from which the professors learned at least as much as the students.

A somber dividend from those years of travel and study was our being able to see the effects of overpopulation at first hand. Margie and I had both been interested in that subject for a long

"My family gathered for our wedding, August 1950": (clockwise) father, William Russell Appleman; mother, Gertrude Collins Keller; the author; and sisters Barbara, Sara, and Ann

"Talking about overpopulation with Prime Minister Nehru in New Delhi," 1962

wretched peasants of Iran, of Brazil, of Turkey—must look to a future of little hope, unless we help them. Those people I saw in Calcutta two years ago—people with arms and legs like brittle sticks, living out their brief lives in the streets, homeless and hungry—*those people are still there.* And there are a lot more of them now than there were then.

Referring to the Catholics, Communists, and simplistic economists, a review in the *New Yorker* concluded: "Appleman discusses with great power the absolute need to change these attitudes if we are to survive on our meager planet."

That book was classified as "sociology," which says something about my rather unconventional interests as a professor of English. The book preceding it, *1859: Entering an Age of Crisis* (Indiana University Press, 1959), which I coedited with two of my colleagues, was classified as "history." And my first major publishing experience, in 1957, with the same two friends, William Madden and Michael Wolff, was to found and coedit a highly successful interdisciplinary journal called *Victorian Studies* (now in its thirty-seventh volume), which encourages and publishes articles on science, history, and philosophy, as well as literature.

My extracurricular activities were also often nonliterary. Always deeply concerned with civil liberties issues, I cofounded (with the distinguished professor of law, Ralph Fuchs) the Bloomington Civil Liberties Union; served as faculty adviser to the Indiana University Civil Liberties Union; and helped organize civil rights freedom marches in Bloomington, in the 1960s. I was also president of the IU chapter of the American Association of University Professors, and served on the national AAUP Committee on Students' Rights and Responsibilities and on the national council of that organization. And I worked on committees of the National Endowment for the Humanities, including an NEH supervisory committee for a pioneering course in medical ethics at the Columbia University College of Physicians and Surgeons.

Lest all that sound excessively nonliterary, I should perhaps add that for years at Indiana University I chaired the Creative Writing Program. I was also a poetry consultant to the Indiana and Kentucky Arts Commissions, and have been associated for a long time with four New York–based literary organizations: as a member of the governing board of the Poetry Society of America and the Poets Advisory Committee of Poets House, as a guest editor for the Academy of

time, and during our two years with the IHP, had discussed it with Planned Parenthood leaders in Thailand, with Prime Minister Nehru, and with other officials in Asia. I had some urgent personal thoughts about the ethical, political, and economic aspects of overpopulation, and eventually put them into my early warning book, *The Silent Explosion* (Beacon Press, 1965). In his foreword, Julian Huxley wrote, "The special value of Professor Appleman's book is that it reveals the moral nature of the population problem." After seven chapters analyzing the motivations and tactics of the various parties who were obstructing sensible progress on population limitation (the Communists, the Catholics, and those I called the "cornucopian" economists), I summed up the urgency of the crisis in this last paragraph:

> What all the statistics mean, finally, is that the dusty children in the streets around Sealdah Station [in Calcutta], the skinny people in the shacks and sampans of Hong Kong, the frowning refugees in mud huts in Jordan, the

American Poets, and as a consultant to Poets and Writers, Inc.

In fact, despite many other interests, I've always thought of myself primarily as a writer. I began writing poetry as a child, and continued in high school, in college, and in graduate school. After we moved to Bloomington, I started to publish regularly in the literary magazines. As every poet knows, finding a publisher for your first book is hard. Like Robert Frost, I was forty when I finally did, and like him I had to turn to England—in my case, to the Byron Press at the University of Nottingham—which in 1967 published a handsome volume of my poems, called *Kites on a Windy Day.* That was followed the next year by my first American book of poetry, *Summer Love and Surf* (Vanderbilt University Press), a book so beautifully produced that it won that year's design award from the American Association of University Presses.

In our early years at Indiana University, Margie and I also collaborated on a number of plays, but I was never satisfied with my own work on them, and when I finally decided to devote all of my writing time to poetry and novels, Margie continued to write plays on her own, which have been produced in New York, Los Angeles, elsewhere in the United States and Canada, and as far away as Finland, where one of her plays ran for two and a half years in repertory. We flew to Helsinki to see it, and didn't understand a word, of course; but the Finnish audience and the local critics responded with enthusiasm. As a side benefit, we traveled north to cross the Arctic Circle, and received the traditional mock "initiation."

After the mid-sixties, I began to publish books at fairly regular intervals. In 1970 there were two. One was a novel based on my merchant-marine experiences, *In the Twelfth Year of the War* (Putnam). I had worked for five years on that book, so I was pleased when the *New York Times* reviewer declared it "a beautifully written novel . . . as auspicious as the fictional signs can be."

The other 1970 book was a Norton Critical Edition, *Darwin,* which became a popular college textbook and is now in its second edition and its thirty-third printing. In that book I brought together Darwin's central texts, along with a great deal of subsequent commentary on the importance of Darwin's thought to the modern world, and concluded with an epilogue in which I tried to evaluate Darwin's intellectual legacy. Stephen Jay Gould later called it "the best Darwin anthology

With Ronald Gottesman at an Indiana University civil rights march, 1963

on the market." In 1975, I also edited for the W. W. Norton Company an abridged edition of *The Origin of Species,* which is also still used as a textbook in many college courses.

I mentioned earlier that Darwin taught us, among other things, the value of context; and that, since Darwin, we have come to understand that we cannot really know ourselves without reference to our prehistoric ancestors: hunter-gatherers, Neolithic, Paleolithic, protohuman. It makes a difference to us that we are not some special creation from the forehead of Zeus or from the snap of godly fingers, but rather the product of an endless and universal evolutionary process. That knowledge requires us to be truly moral agents, responsible for our own decisions, for our own lives. Ideologies that deny or ignore that long development cut us off from our true origins and therefore from any hope of genuine human understanding, responsible ethics, or a sound philosophy of life.

In my epilogue to *Darwin,* I pursued some of these implications of evolution:

The activities of science, relentlessly pushing back the margins of the unknown, have in effect been forcing the concept of "God" into a perpetual retreat into the still-unknown, and it is in this condition that "God" has frequently come to have meaning for people. The final retreat is of course into the strongholds of the Infinite and the Eternal, and with the scientists' continuing success in exploring the littleness and vastness of the finite, one may assume that, for any practical purpose, that final retreat has long since occurred. The implications of all this have led some people to a renewed humanism: to the proposition that humans, cut off from theological presumption, might still have sufficient reason to exist—even to respect themselves—simply as human beings. . . . People now seem able to view the human condition not in terms of a fall from grace to degradation but rather as the reverse—as a long struggle to escape from mere animalism, red in tooth and claw, and to establish upon ourselves—upon our own best knowledge of ourselves—a tenable ethical ground.

Evolution, for billions of years an impersonal biological function, became, with the arrival of *Homo sapiens*, a conscious and potentially moral process.

So it is not after all strange, or even unusual, to hear the very scientists who remind us of our cosmic littleness at the same time assuring us of our individual dignity in terms which, if not so dogmatic as those of the theologians, are nevertheless heartening. . . . Some scientists have gone further than this and argued that a scientifically accurate view of the world is the best basis for ethics. "Duty arises from our potential control over the course of events," Whitehead proposed; "where attainable knowledge could have changed the issue, ignorance has the guilt of vice."

Thus, I continued:

I would propose not that Darwinism has killed human values . . . but something nearer the reverse: that since Darwin, we have been forced . . . to mature to finiteness. I mean maturing as human beings not simply by realizing that there are no usable absolutes for us—for that mere realization is still a kind of adolescence—but by accepting our finiteness and learning to live with it with some degree of sanity and integrity.

And I concluded:

There is grandeur, Darwin insisted, in his scientific view of the world, for, he said, it ennobled humanity. Man has risen, he added later, "to the very summit of the organic scale; and the fact of his having thus risen, instead of having been aboriginally placed there, may give him hope for a still higher destiny in the distant future."

1976 was another two-book year: I edited the Norton Critical Edition of Malthus' *Essay on the Principle of Population*, which was a natural follow-up to my previous work, both because Darwin got his central idea from reading Malthus, and because I had published *The Silent Explosion* a decade before. Like *Darwin*, the Malthus *Essay* has been more and more widely used in American colleges, as the population explosion becomes more and more obviously the critical social problem of our own (and, alas, the next) century. In my introduction to that book, I wrote:

At the end of each day, the world now has over two hundred thousand more mouths to feed than it had the day before; at the end of every week, one and one-half million more; at the close of each year, an additional eighty million. Aware of these alarming statistics, many national governments, influential institutions, and private enterprises are trying to encourage increased production of all the necessities of life, particularly food, in the hope of preventing mass starvation, privation, and social disorder. Fortunately there has been enough success in recent years to forestall, at least temporarily, a major disaster; but some serious regional famines have already occurred, and in the world's poorest countries, where population growth is most rapid, the lives of hundreds of millions of people are constantly plagued by hunger and by diseases aggravated by malnutrition. Humankind, now doubling its numbers every thirty-five years, has fallen into an ambush of its own making; economists call it the "Malthusian trap," after the man who most forcefully stated our biological predicament: population growth tends to outstrip the supply of food.

It is a sad reflection on human intelligence that even as I write this, in 1993, the world-wide population crisis is still not being addressed with any clarity or vigor. And after twelve years of Presidents Reagan and Bush denying American

In Antibes, during the summer of 1968

assistance to U.N. family-planning programs, the world has sunk deeper and deeper into the Malthusian trap. The Population Reference Bureau has just reported that world population is now increasing at the fastest pace ever.

Throughout all those years, I continued to write poems, and my other 1976 book was a third volume of poetry, *Open Doorways* (Norton), which some poets and critics considered a major development in my work; James Wright called it a "beautiful fruition." Although much of the book consists of lyrics and love poetry, there are also a number of poems that address social problems. "Memo to the 21st Century" (quoted above), for instance, reflected the population problem; and "Revolution" was an expression of the civil rights movement. But another social debacle had occurred during and after the publication of *Summer Love and Surf*—the Vietnam War. Although I was in uniform during World War II, I was, for many reasons, affected more profoundly by the Vietnam conflict. The deep sense of shame at the illegal, illogical, and immoral U.S. involvement in Vietnam and Cambodia was anguishing to any reasonable person in the sixties and early seventies, and many American poets responded vigorously against it. During that time, our protest poetry appeared mostly in the literary magazines, and now it can be found in the Vietnam anthologies, such as W. D. Ehrhart's *Carrying the Darkness,* and

in more general volumes like Daniela Gioseffi's *Women on War.* It was one of the rare occasions in recent years when large numbers of poets responded to a social crisis.

After the war was finally over, I thought back to the touching experiences Margie and I had had in Cambodia in 1962, when we were there with the International Honors Program, and what had happened to that unfortunate country in the years of American (and consequent Khmer Rouge) destruction there, and asked, in poetry, if we, as a nation, had learned anything at all from our self-inflicted catastrophe. The poem was published on the Op Ed page of the *New York Times* on December 31, 1975, and was included in *Open Doorways.*

Waiting for the Fire

Not just the temples, lifting
lotuses out of the tangled trees,
not the moon on cool canals,
the profound smell of the paddies,
evening fires in open doorways,
fish and rice the perfect end of wisdom;
but the small bones, the grace, the voices like
clay bells in the wind, all wasted.
If we ever thought of the wreckage
of our unnatural acts,
we would never sleep again
without dreaming a rain of fire:
somewhere God is bargaining for Sodom,
a few good men could save the city; but
in that dirty corner of the mind
we call the soul
the only wash that purifies is tears,
and after all our body counts,
our rape, our mutilations,
nobody here is crying; people who would weep
at the death of a dog
stroll these unburned streets dry-eyed.
But forgetfulness will never walk
with innocence; we save our faces
at the risk of our lives, needing
the wisdom of losses, the gift of despair,
or we could kill again.
Somewhere God is haggling over Sodom:
for the sake of ten good people
I will spare the land.
Where are those volunteers
to hold back the fire? Look:
when the moon rises over the sea,
no matter where you stand
the path of the light comes to you.

With the proofs of Apes and Angels, *1988*

In 1981 my second novel, *Shame the Devil,* was published by Crown. Partly inspired by seeing a church in Rome that was built out of the scavenged stones of an earlier pagan temple on the same site, which itself was built over an even older Mithreum, the novel is a cross-cultural fantasy, exploring what might have transpired if the Vikings, in their sundry travels, had picked up the mysteries of Mithra and transported them, via the St. Lawrence and the Great Lakes, into the limestone caves of the American Midwest. The book is a satire and a social parable—George Garrett called it "at once a satire and an elegy, altogether wacky and wonderful." Despite its playful surface, it is intended to make a serious comment on belief and hypocrisy, on tradition and reason, on social good sense and social extravagance.

In my next book, *Darwin's Ark* (1984), two of my main interests in life, poetry and evolution, came together, and the fine artist, my good friend Rudy Pozzatti, illustrated it handsomely. The lead poem, about the implications of Darwin's work, shows that book's intentions and style:

The Skeletons of Dreams

He found giants
in the earth: Mastodon,
Mylodon, thigh bones
like tree trunks, Megatherium, skulls
big as boulders—once,
in this savage country, treetops
trembled at their passing.
But their passing was silent as snails,
silent as rabbits: nothing at all recorded
the day when the last of them came
crashing through creepers and ferns,
shaking the earth a final time,
leaving behind them crickets,
monkeys, and mice.
For think: at last it is nothing
to be a giant—the dream
of an ending haunts tortoise and Toxodon,
troubles the sleep of the woodchuck
and the bear.

Back home in his English garden,
Darwin paused in his pacing,
writing it down in italics
in the book at the back of his mind:

When a species has vanished
from the face of the earth,
   the same form never reappears . . .
So after our millions of years
of inventing a thumb and a cortex,
and after the long pain
of writing our clumsy epic,
we know we are mortal as mammoths,
we know the last lines of our poem.
And somewhere in curving space,
beyond our constellations,
nebulae burn in their universal law:
nothing out there ever knew
that on one sky-blue planet
we dreamed that terrible dream.
Blazing along through black nothing
to nowhere at all, Mastodons of heaven,
the stars do not need our small ruin.

In 1986 the Echo Press produced a series of new Pozzatti lithographs illustrating eleven of my poems, which were hand-set by Frederic Brewer. The lithos were done on Japanese mulberry paper, in a limited-edition boxed folio called *Darwin's Bestiary*. Signed by Rudy and me, it sells for a thousand dollars a copy, and since it's more Rudy's creation than mine, I feel free to say that it's a very special work of art.

Throughout the eighties, I had been writing another novel, of a kind that many authors produce as their first book: a bildungsroman called *Apes and Angels*. It was published by Putnam in 1989, and recalls the autumn of the year 1941, from Labor Day to December 7, in a small town in Indiana named Kenton, modeled after my hometown, Kendallville. In the background of the book, World War II is raging in Europe, Asia, and Africa, and Americans are furiously debating whether or not we should enter it. The isolationist America First movement had strong roots in the Midwest in 1941, and on one occasion, my father (a right-wing Republican and an unyielding isolationist) took me to Fort Wayne to hear Charles Lindbergh warn the country against getting involved in the war. I was fifteen, and hadn't yet evolved my own political views, which in time would become the opposite of my father's.

In the foreground of the book, adults are trying to earn their living in the endless Great Depression, while kids are going to school and desperately trying to find out for themselves what makes them tick. The book is partly a remembrance of times past, partly character study, and partly social scrutiny. *Publisher's Weekly* said of it:

"Appleman evokes small town America on the eve of Pearl Harbor without nostalgia or condescension—an impressive feat." When Margie and I returned to Kendallville for my forty-fifth high-school class reunion, which fortuitously occurred just after publication of the book in 1989, I was delighted that the local press and townspeople responded to it so favorably.

Even though much of my work is iconoclastic, and Kendallville can hardly be called unconventional, the town's hospitable response reassured me about the often maligned midwestern qualities of friendliness and generosity; there are worse things in the world. Two years later, my latest book of poetry, *Let There Be Light* (HarperCollins, 1991)—clearly atheistic and antitheological—again received good reviews in the local papers and drew positive comments from my hometown friends, including some of the churchgoers. When *Poets and Writers Magazine* published my article "Controversy, Censorship, and Poetry" in 1992, the editor chose to accompany it with a poem from *Let There Be Light* which draws upon one of my Kendallville memories.

And Then the Perfect Truth of Hatred

There was a preacher in our town
whose Sunday text was the Prince of Peace,
but
when he looked out at the Monday world—
at the uppity blacks and pushy Jews
and sassy wives and sneaky heathen—blood
scalded his face as purple as if
he'd hung by his heels. Then
his back-yard, barber-shop, street-corning sermons
scorched us with all the omens of siege:
our roofs aflame, tigers at the gates,
hoodlums pillaging homes, ravaging
wives and daughters, the sky
come crashing down,
and we gazed into his blazing truth
of Onward Christian Soldiers,
A Mighty Fortress Is Our God,
Soldiers of the Cross. No question now
of sissy charity, this
was the Church Militant, burning
its lightning bolts across
our low horizons.

It's been a while since that preacher went off
to the big apartheid in the sky,
and the only hint of eternal life
is the way he resurrects each week
to sell salvation on the screen.
He's younger after all these years,
in designer suits and toothy smiles,

but we know him by the cunning eyes
where he harbors his old stooges,
Satan, Jehovah. He calls them up,
and across the country, glands begin
pumping bile into our lives:
sleet storms in the voice,
cords in the neck like bullwhips,
broken promises, broken bones—
the wreckage of his deep
sincerity.

As I write this in 1993, the images from those early years come back with a freshness that makes them seem almost contemporary, despite what I earlier called their nineteenth-century feeling.

In 1976 we moved to Manhattan—a far cry from Kendallville or Bloomington—partly so that Margie could better pursue her career as a playwright. She applied for a position at New York University, to teach playwriting, and was soon promoted to Assistant Professor of English there. For several years, she taught playwriting at Columbia University, as well. I stayed on as a professor in the Indiana University English department, so for eight academic years, until 1984, I commuted weekly between New York and Bloomington.

Our marriage has been a genuine partnership, and we both feel privileged to have had the opportunity to learn and grow together, as well as to help each other with comments and criticisms on our respective writing projects. Of course, it's inevitable that I would have written poems about us, as has Margie. One way to trace the distance we've come together is to compare one of my early love poems with a later one. In 1964, when we were visiting my sister Barbara and her husband at their apartment in Malibu, I wrote this poem, which would become the title poem of my second book of poetry.

Summer Love and Surf

Morning was hesitating when
you swam at me through wave on wave
of sheet and blanket, glowing like
some dimly sighted
flora at the bottom of the sea.
Around your filmy hair, light
was seeping in with water-sounds,
low growling in the distance, like
dragons chained.

After our small storm dwindled,
we faced the rage outside, swells
humping up far out and charging in
to curl and pause
and dash themselves to soapsuds on

the stork-legged pilings of our house.
The roar was hoarser now, the wrecks of kelp
were heaping food for flies,
our long-nosed sand birds staying
close to dry land; farther out,
pelicans arched their wings in quick surprise
and gulls screamed urgently.
The call was there:
we fought the breakers out
and rode their fury back, triumphant
and again triumphant, till
at last, ears stuffed with brine and heads a-spin
like aging boxers battered,
we flopped face down on hot sand, smelling sun
and salt and steaming skin. Your eyes were
    suddenly
all sleep and love, there in the sun
with sea birds calling.

The sky goes metal at the end,
water, gray and hostile, lashing out
between the day and night. Plastic swans
are threatened; deck chairs, yellow towels,
    barbecues
stand naked to the peril, as if it were
winter come by stealth.
Still later, in the lee of dark and warmth,
we probe the ancient fear: at night
the sea is safer under glass, the crude,
wild thing half tamed to shed its past—
galleons sent to fifty fathoms, mountains
hacked to rubble, cities stripped.
At night the sea, barbaric bellows stifled,
sprawls outside the window, framed
like a dark, unruly landscape.
Behind us is a darker kind of dark:
I watch your eyes
for signals.

The music makes a pause for prophecy:
"Tomorrow, off-shore breezes and . . ."
Warmth to each other's warmth, we do not listen.

Twenty-five years later, I published the following poem in *Poetry* magazine, and it was included in my latest book, *Let There Be Light:*

Anniversary

Maybe it wasn't strange to find
drums and cymbals where
there might have been violins, maybe
we couldn't have known; besides,
would it have mattered?
See what the years have left behind:
a thick scar in the palm of my hand,
a ragged one running along the arm.
And you:
I know your scars at midnight
by touch.

Everything we've learned, we've picked up
by ear, a pidgin language
of the heart, just
enough to get by on:
we know the value of cacophony, how to measure
with a broken yardstick,
what to do with bruised fruit.
Reading torn maps, we always
make it home, riding
on empty.

And whatever this is we've built together,
we remember sighting it skew, making it plumb
eventually, and here it stands,
stone over rock. In the walls
there are secret passages
leading to music nobody else can hear,
earthlight nobody else can see. And somewhere
in a room that's not yet finished
there are volumes in our own hand, telling
troubled tales, promises kept, and
promises
still to keep.

Now that Margie and I have both stopped
teaching in order to concentrate on our writing,

we live much of the year in the village of Sagaponack, in the township of Southampton, at the east end of Long Island. After so many years of academic genteel poverty, we feel fortunate to be able to live in such a beautiful area. The Hamptons abound with writers and artists, many of whom are our close friends. We've also kept our little apartment in the East Village in New York, and spend time there when Margie is busy with various theater projects, often at the Circle Repertory Company, where she has been for many years a member of the Playwrights Lab, and where several of her plays have been produced. In the last few years, she has also had half a dozen productions in the Los Angeles area, so we have also spent a good deal of time there—which is particularly welcome, since two of my sisters live nearby.

It's probably already clear that travel has been important to us all our lives. That would have seemed improbable when I was a boy, because back then, people traveled less. A trip from Kendallville to Chicago, 150 miles away, was a rare

"Margie at the wheel of Barbara and David Vest's boat 'La Dolce Vita,'"
Malibu, 1964

*On a reading tour with Margie,
Seattle, 1991*

venture. There was no plane travel to speak of, and jets, of course, hadn't been invented. Everyone went by car, bus, or train, and a long trip was a major, time-consuming enterprise, which few people (and certainly not my family) could afford very often.

All of that changed for me after I joined the army during World War II and found myself in Texas for the summer, South Dakota for the winter, Alabama and Florida for the summer, and Ohio for the winter. Climatically it was backwards, but still it was travel, and beyond my previous experience or expectations. Then came the merchant marine, and at the age of twenty, with the world so fresh and unexplored, every new locale was an exciting learning experience. After our marriage, Margie and I traveled whenever we could, and were adept at doing it "on a shoestring." Besides the countries of Asia, Africa, and Europe mentioned earlier, which we explored during our two years traveling around the world with the International Honors Program, we've taken trips to or through all but one of the fifty

states and have been back to Europe frequently—most often to France, our "second country," but also to many other countries in Eastern and Western Europe. We've visited parts of the Caribbean and have been a number of times to Mexico, where our interest in prehistoric monuments and artifacts led us to the Aztec pyramids at Teotihuacán and the Mayan ruins at Chichén Itzá and Tulum. That same interest took us to the ancient ruins of Baalbek in Lebanon and, by way of Damascus, to Jerash and Petra in Jordan. Recently, a former student whose family lives in Guatemala gave us an intimate look at the hinterlands of that beautiful and troubled country, and while there we had the opportunity to study the Mayan monuments at Tikal. In our Darwin-inspired search for ancient human connections, we have recently gone to see the spectacular rock art at Kakadu in Australia and the richly carved petroglyph sites in Arizona, Hawaii, the Dominican Republic, Puerto Rico, and the Virgin Islands.

Looking back now on some forty years of writing and publishing, I am also looking forward to more of the same, partly because writing is a way of constantly taking stock, of reminding oneself what is really important. What's important to artists is their art; what's important to humanitarians is betterment of the human condition. I have never seen any good reason why these goals should be mutually exclusive. Indeed, they were usually considered symbiotic until our own anomalous century.

In my latest book, *Let There Be Light,* I tried to achieve that kind of symbiosis in poems that weigh the abuses of organized religion. As I wrote recently in an article for *Poets and Writers Magazine:*

> Religions all around the world are openly and regularly betraying their professed ideals of love and charity by provoking mass murder: Catholics killing Protestants (and vice versa) in Lebanon; Muslims killing Hindus (and vice versa) in India; Hindus killing Buddhists (and vice versa) in Ceylon; Jews killing Muslims (and vice versa) in Israel; Muslims killing Christians (and vice versa) in Egypt and Azerbaijan and Nigeria; Roman Catholics killing Orthodox Christians (and vice versa) in Yugoslavia; Sunni Muslims killing Shiites in Iraq; and Shiites killing Baha'is in Iran. During the Persian Gulf war, when Saudi Muslims and Iraqi Muslims did their best to kill each other, both sides called it a "holy" war. Saddam Hussein told his troops, "The angels are at

your shoulders," and exhorted them to make the "infidels" swim in their own blood. Meanwhile, George Bush called for a "national day of prayer" for the "holy gift" of freedom— and then sent hundreds of Americans and hundreds of thousands of Iraqis to their death, in order to reinstate a brutally repressive Islamic dictatorship in Kuwait.

World history is full of accounts of fanatical ideologies careening toward human tragedy; but rarely has there been a more forceful demonstration of the disastrous effects of religious ideologies than at this moment . . .

Brought up in midwestern fundamentalism, I understand the depth of self-righteousness that motivates religious fanaticism, and I understand how difficult it will be to convert it to anything socially beneficent—so difficult, in fact, that I am on that score very pessimistic. But we cannot live useful or even contented lives as pessimists, so we have to persuade ourselves, somehow, to think that we can change things for the better. As long as the ominous threats of overpopulation and militant religious fundamentalism continue to obstruct social improvement, there will be much to do.

That thought leads me to one more reflection on my years in the merchant marine, half a century ago. One of the Liberty ships I worked on back then was the SS *William Phips*. Hardly a household name now, William Phips was the judicious governor of Massachusetts who, on October 12, 1692, ruled that "spectral evidence" would no longer be admissible in courtrooms. As Bette Chambers recently wrote in *Free Mind*:

> Before Governor Phips made his ruling, nineteen people had been put to death for witchcraft. All told, fifty-two people had been charged, many on the basis of hysterical utterings from a gaggle of schoolgirls. Since it was a "given" that malevolent spirits existed, those condemning their fellow citizens felt they were carrying out the intent of the deity.

Three hundred years later, we are still in sore need of the levelheadedness of a William Phips; and fortunately, his spirit is still with us, even in these beleaguered times when we are threatened on all sides by religious excess. As I concluded in my *Darwin* epilogue:

> Looking back at a million years of our struggle to be human, at our errant and painful attempts to be a special kind of animal—the animal who thinks, the animal who creates—it seems to me that despite our shortcomings, we have some cause for satisfaction. "Thought makes the whole dignity of humankind." Yes. Despite its simplicity, despite our sad reflections on the inadequacy of our thinking, on its stunted and twisted travesties in history and our daily lives, we must end by agreeing with Pascal. *Homo* is unique and valuable precisely because he is *sapiens*. We are worth keeping because, given our remarkable past, we may continue to hope that we have, as Darwin surmised, "a still higher destiny in the future."

Meanwhile, we do the best we can with what we have. Star-stuff though we are, we can take satisfaction and pleasure from the fact that we are also earth-stuff, intimately a part of our own past, as

> challenges sing
> in the sway of treetops,
> in the flutter of sparrows,
> in chirring and stalking,
> in waking and ripening—let
> there be light enough, and
> everywhere backbone stiffens
> in saplings and clover. Praises, then,
> to sunfish and squirrels,
> blessings to bugs. Turning our backs
> on the bloody altars,
> we cherish each other, living here
> in this brave world
> with our neighbors, the earthworms,
> and our old friends, the ferns
> and the daisies.

> (From "The Daisies Will Not Be Deceived by the Gods," in *Let There Be Light*)

BIBLIOGRAPHY

Poetry:

Kites on a Windy Day, Byron Press, 1967.

Summer Love and Surf, Vanderbilt University Press, 1968.

Open Doorways, W. W. Norton, 1976.

Darwin's Ark (illustrated by Rudy Pozzatti), Indiana University Press, 1984.

Darwin's Bestiary (illustrated by Pozzatti), Echo Press, 1986.

Let There Be Light, HarperCollins, 1991.

Fiction:

In the Twelfth Year of the War, Putnam's, 1970.

Shame the Devil, Crown, 1981.

Apes and Angels, Putnam's, 1989.

Nonfiction:

The Silent Explosion, Beacon Press, 1965.

Editor:

(With others) *Victorian Studies*, 1956–64.

(With others) *1859: Entering an Age of Crisis*, Indiana University Press, 1959.

Darwin, W. W. Norton, 1970.

Charles Darwin, *The Origin of Species*, W. W. Norton, 1975.

Thomas Malthus, *An Essay on the Principle of Population*, W. W. Norton, 1976.

Contributor to periodicals: *American Review, Amicus Journal, Antioch Review, Approach, Arizona Quarterly, Author's League Bulletin, Back Door, Ball State University Forum, Beloit Poetry Journal, Bluefish, Chicago Tribune Magazine, Coastlines, College English, Columbia Forum, Confrontation, Creel, Denver Post, Dryad, Fair, Falmouth Review, Fire Island Tide, Folio, Free Inquiry, French Review, Harper's Magazine, Hawaii Review, Indiana Review, Intervention, Kentucky Poetry Review, Ladies' Home Journal, Light Year, Literary Review, Long Island Quarterly, Malahat Review, Massachusetts Review, Midwest Quarterly, Modern Fiction Studies, The Nation, New England Review, New Republic, New York Herald-Tribune, New York Quarterly, New York Times, New York Tribune, North American Review, North Atlantic Review, Out of Sight, Partisan Review, Poetry, Poetry Northwest, Poets & Writers Magazine, Prairie Schooner, Poetry Society of America Bulletin, Publishers Weekly, Pulp, Quartet, Sewanee Review, Sierra Club Bulletin, Southern Humanities Review, Southern Poetry Review, Sumac, Spectator, Tendril, Tri-Quarterly, West Coast Review, Wind, Yale Review,* and others.

Ben Bova

1932-

I was born the day Franklin D. Roosevelt was first elected president: 8 November 1932. It was the nadir of the Great Depression. I am told that on my first Christmas the family fortune consisted of an unheated one-room apartment on which the rent was owed, a seven-week-old baby (me), one dime, and a can of Campbell's pork and beans.

Oh yes, and my father had lost his job.

During that cold, hard winter I contracted rickets. I have been an asthmatic all my life. So much for the sad part of my story.

We lived in South Philadelphia, on those narrow streets with the row houses that many people saw in the 1976 motion picture *Rocky*. It was a working-class neighborhood, pretty tough, but relatively safe because everybody in the neighborhood looked out for one another. And all children obeyed all adults. Or else. Physical punishment was not considered child abuse in those days.

Four years minus two days after my birth, my brother, Robert, came into the world. A little more than three years later, my sister, Barbara, was born. Aside from occasional dogs and cats, our family was now complete.

My father worked all his life as a presser in men's clothing factories. My earliest memories of Dad are of him warning me, "If I ever catch you near a pressing machine I'll break both your arms." We children were expected to do better than our parents. Education was the key to climbing the ladder of success.

Without realizing it, my father taught me something that became crucially important to me. He is a great storyteller. He would keep us three kids in stitches telling tales about his own youthful escapades, tales that always ended with a stern "Don't ever let me catch you doing something like that!" I learned to tell stories from my father, a knack that is the foundation of my writing career.

I started school in 1937 with kindergarten. The Philadelphia public school system was no great shakes, but at least we were taught the basics. Discipline was strict, and unruly kids were sent to a

Ben Bova

special class called O.B. I do not remember what those letters stood for, except that we jokingly referred to them as "Obedient Boys." Thirty boys and girls in a class was typical. Some of my grammar school classes went as high as forty. But we behaved ourselves and learned. Or else. Parents expected to see good marks on their children's report cards. Otherwise, they might put good marks on their children's anatomies.

Philadelphia offered something else that was vitally important to me: the Philadelphia Free Public Library. My mother was a reader, and she brought me to the South Philadelphia branch of the library as soon as I entered first grade. The children's library was arranged by school grade level, and the great trick was always to take books from a level or two higher than your own grade. I thought I was sneaking a hard-earned victory past the librarians when I checked out books beyond my grade level. Now that I look back on it, I think they knew about it all the time. But those "illicit" books were a challenge that I could not ignore.

My constant battle with asthma kept me frail, weak, and often the butt of the stronger kids' hazings. I found refuge from the rough world of South Philadelphia in books. I did not know it then, but the path of my life was being shaped.

One day, while in junior high school, we went out on a class trip. When the teacher announced that we were going to a museum, loud groans issued from most of us. Museums were dull! All you could do in them was look at some dusty exhibits that did not mean a thing to you. And you had to be quiet.

The museum turned out to be the Franklin Institute, Philadelphia's science museum. In Philadelphia, almost everything is named after Benjamin Franklin or William Penn. Come to remember it, our history classes were rife with the names of Benjamin Franklin, Benjamin Rush, and Benjamin West: three prominent Philadelphians. Since my name was Benjamin, I was teased mercilessly about those deceased notables.

Off we went in a school bus to the Franklin Institute, happy to be out of the classroom but less than enthusiastic about visiting a museum. However, the Franklin Institute was different. There were "hands on" displays where you could push buttons, turn cranks, and watch things happen. There was a real locomotive you could climb into! It was fun. And interesting. And you could talk out loud.

Then they trooped us into the Fels Planetarium, named after the man who had made his fortune on Fels Naptha soap, a powerful brown hand soap that took off a couple of layers of skin along with the dirt attached to same.

It was a weird place: a big circular room with a domed roof and this strange black machine sitting in its center like a giant ant. (This was about 1945, long before "sci-fi" movies made giant ants popular.) A man entered the control booth and began speaking to us in a soft, almost hypnotic voice. He told us that the city is not a very good place to look at the stars, because of the dust and glare from streetlights. He said that the best place to see the stars is out in the middle of the ocean, where it gets very dark at night and the air is clear. As he spoke,

he gradually turned down the lights until we were sitting in total darkness. I mean, *total* darkness. Not a gleam of light. It was scary.

But before we had a chance to panic he turned on the stars. The whole dome lit up with heaven's glory. We all gasped at the sudden beauty. It turned me on. That moment changed my life utterly. In that one instant I became hooked on astronomy. Soon I discovered there were people who were dreaming of flying out into space; I became interested in astronautics. And eventually I learned that there were stories about the future, where people went to the Moon and Mars and beyond. I had found science fiction.

But I am getting ahead of my own story. The lecturer at the planetarium turned out to be the same man who had devised many of the "hands on" exhibits in the rest of the museum: Dr. I. M. Levitt. He was a slight, soft-spoken man. In my young eyes he seemed very old and wise, although he could not have been much more than thirty at that time. He was very wise, though, and he turned into a good and treasured friend. I became a regular visitor at the Franklin Institute and Fels Planetarium. Dr. Levitt became virtually my private tutor on astronomy and science in general.

Many years later I was asked to write a book for youngsters about lasers, part of a series of science books sponsored by the institute. I had the exquisite pleasure of dedicating the book to Dr. Levitt.

"Lev" influenced me enormously and our friendship has lasted over four decades. Next to my parents he had the biggest impact on me, although there were many others whose influence was almost just as great.

The next one was Mrs. Jaffe, an English teacher at Thomas Junior High School. She did not take that much special notice of me, in particular, but Mrs. Jaffe insisted that all her students learn to speak English correctly and pronounce it reasonably well. Our South Philadelphia slang was all right for street corners, she told us, but if we expected to get anywhere in the world we should learn to speak like civilized men and women. She was strict about it. And she was right.

It was in the tenth grade that I met the next truly powerful influence on my life: George Paravicini. He too was an English teacher, at South Philadelphia High School for Boys. It was now 1946, but Southern High was still sexually segregated. The two sections of the school were separated by a barrier that must have been the model upon which the Berlin Wall was based.

Mr. Paravicini was the faculty sponsor for our school newspaper, *The Southron*. He recruited the paper's staff from his English classes. After the first classroom writing assignment of the semester, he asked me to join the newspaper staff. He added that if I did so, I could skip the regular English class next semester in favor of the class he taught on journalism. He was a kind, witty, patient man—a wonderful teacher, with a marvelously dry sense of humor. He died in 1978, but not before I dedicated a book to him; a book about writing, of course.

For the next two-and-a-half years I worked on *The Southron* with a great team of guys. In our senior year we put out our class yearbook, as well as the newspaper. Journalism was fun.

But even then I did not dream that I would become a writer. My generation of South Philly young men was encouraged to aim for steady work, a career with security. I was looking forward to becoming a chemical engineer. I enjoyed my high school chemistry classes, and even helped to cause a mass evacuation of the school the afternoon we brewed up a batch of poisonous chlorine gas.

So I applied to several colleges that offered curricula in chemistry or chemical engineering.

Meanwhile, the group of us who had put out the school newspaper and class yearbook decided that we would go into the magazine business. Immediately after graduation from Southern High (the summer of 1949) we published what I believe to be the nation's first magazine for teenagers: *Campus Town*. It was aimed specifically at the high school population of Philadelphia and it was an enormous success. We sold every copy of our first three issues. Yet, somehow, we went broke. That experience showed each of us that there was more to the publishing business than putting out a popular magazine. Our team broke up; we went our separate ways to college.

I received a rude shock when my college entrance tests showed I did not know enough about chemistry to be accepted by any school. I had received straight *A* grades in all my high school science courses. This was my first realization that my public school education was not first-rate. An *A* meant nothing; I simply did not know very much about chemistry.

I had another iron in the fire, though. I applied to Temple University's department of journalism—at that time part of the university's business school. And was accepted. Temple was (and still is) the working man's university in

Philadelphia, a concrete campus set in the middle of the worst ghetto neighborhood of the city.

My family could not afford my college expenses, although I still lived at home. I worked nights, first as an usher in movie theaters and then got a job as a copyboy at the *Philadelphia Inquirer*. It was perfect for me. It was real journalism. And since the *Inquirer* was a morning newspaper, the hours were from 6 P.M. to 3 A.M., I could go to classes during the day and work at night. I slept on the city busses that took me back and forth. The drivers came to recognize me and would faithfully wake me when the bus reached my stop.

I received an important lesson about newspaper writing from one of the elderly senior editors of the *Inquirer*. One summer evening he took me for a walk through the streets of row houses behind the newspaper's building. Working men were coming home, sitting on their front steps, reading the evening newspaper (our competition). It was obvious that for many of these men, reading took great effort.

"That's your audience," said the old-timer, who claimed to have been a copyboy when the Johnstown Flood struck. "If you want to write for newspapers, sonny, you've got to be able to take the most complicated things happening in the world today and write about them so that *they* can understand it."

Clarity is what he was talking about. I never forgot that lesson and have always tried to write as clearly as I could.

In my senior year (1954) I took a reporter's job on a suburban weekly, the *Upper Darby News*, and got married. Working for the weekly was a great experience; the marriage was not. But in those days of the Silent Generation you stayed married and made the best of it. I'm afraid the best was not very good at all. We remained married for seventeen years, adopted two children, but were never really happy with one another. It was not until 1970 that we finally separated and ultimately divorced.

In 1956, while still working in Upper Darby, I saw a newspaper advertisement that startled me. The Glenn L. Martin Company (it had not yet merged itself into the Martin Marietta Corporation) was looking for engineers for Project Vanguard—"Man's first step into space." The United States was planning to put one or more artificial satellites into orbit during the International Geo-

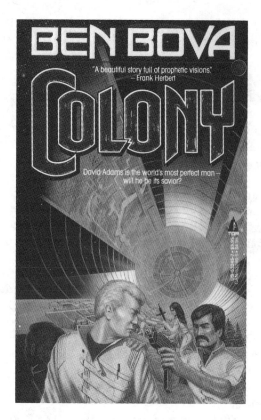

From Colony, *written by Ben Bova*

physical Year, an eighteen-month-long period of scientific studies that would begin in 1957.

Man's[1] first step into space! I had to be part of that! I made an appointment to meet the recruiters who were interviewing engineers at a downtown Philadelphia hotel suite. When they asked me what kind of an engineer I was I replied that I was not an engineer at all, but a writer who could translate what the engineers were doing into language that the general public could understand. I pointed out that since Vanguard was bound to be very much in the public's eye, they were going to need someone like me.

They agreed and hired me! I did not have to tell them that I would scrub the floors and wash the windows, just for the chance to be part of "Man's first step into space."

We moved to the suburbs of Baltimore, which must be the ear-nose-and-throat capital of the world. My asthma was terrible for most of the two

_____

[1]In those primitive days before the Women's Movement, "man" was assumed to mean the entire human race.

years we lived there. But my work on Vanguard was tremendously exciting.

Vanguard, of course, was destined *not* to be the first satellite put into space. On 4 October 1957 the Soviet Union launched *Sputnik,* and the Western world reacted as though a space-age Pearl Harbor had hit us. With some reason. By orbiting a satellite, Moscow proved to everyone that it had rockets capable of depositing hydrogen bombs on any city in the world.

The Vanguard program was run by the U.S. Navy, which was not terribly disturbed by the Soviet triumph in space. Then Wernher von Braun offered to put up an American satellite in ninety days. At that time von Braun worked for the U.S. Army. The Navy went berserk. Interservice rivalry was apparently more important in Washington than the Cold War. The Navy ordered our Martin team to launch a satellite right away, even though we were still in the testing phase of our Vanguard rocket. The result: Vanguard Test Vehicle No. 3, with a two-pound test satellite in its nose, blew up ignominiously a few moments after being launched on 6 December 1957. By that time the Russians had put a half-ton satellite into orbit, with a dog inside it named Laika.

All during this period I was writing fiction in my spare time. Actually, my first published fiction was in *Campus Town* magazine, where I was the fiction editor as well as the sports and features editor. To keep myself honest, I had all the other editors read my stories before I put them into the magazine. My first sale outside *Campus Town* also came when I was seventeen. It was a short science-fiction story that a local Philadelphia magazine bought. Alas, the magazine went into bankruptcy right after I cashed the five-dollar check they sent me. That taught me an important lesson about the business of writing: cash all checks immediately.

I had written my first novel back in 1949–50 when I was still living in my parents' house in South Philadelphia. I laboriously typed it on a Smith-Corona portable, literally placed atop an orange crate, in the basement of that narrow row house. The novel was about the first man to land on the Moon: his name was Chester Arthur Kinsman. The plot of the novel was that the Russians went into space before we Americans did, so the U.S. launches a crash program to put Americans on the Moon before the Russians can get there.

That novel was rejected by every publishing house in New York. Now it was 1957 and the Russians really were in space ahead of us!

Shortly before *Sputnik* went into orbit, our Martin plant was visited by Arthur C. Clarke, who was working on a book about the first artificial satellite—at that time, we all thought it would be Vanguard. Clarke was already well-known for his prophetic nonfiction writings about the future as well as his visionary science-fiction stories. I was given the job of escorting Arthur through every aspect of the Vanguard project, and we became good friends during the few days of his visit.

Then I did something that still makes me blush whenever I think of it. As Arthur was leaving for his home in Ceylon (now called Sri Lanka), I handed him the shoebox full of my novel manuscript and asked him to read it and tell me what was wrong with it.

Generous and kind man that he is, Arthur took the tattered manuscript all the way home with him, read it with great care, and sent me a detailed letter of enormously helpful criticism, together with the manuscript, at his own expense. Twenty-five years later, when my novel *Millennium* was published (in which Kinsman is the central character) I made certain to personally hand Arthur the first copy off the press.

On St. Patrick's Day 1958 we finally got a Vanguard satellite into orbit—with a St. Christopher's medal welded to its guidance system. (St. Christopher is the patron saint of travelers.) I had already grown disenchanted with the Martin Company and was looking for a better job.

Meanwhile, I was still trying to sell my fiction. Years earlier an editor at the Winston Company, a publishing house in Philadelphia, had given me some encouragement about my novel. He did not like the plot—with the Russians getting into space before we Americans—not because he thought it was silly, but because he feared that Senator Joseph McCarthy and his witch-hunting allies would "make life miserable for us" because my novel suggested the godless Russian Communists might be smarter than we are. He suggested I try writing a novel that had absolutely no connection with current politics.

Between his suggestion and Arthur Clarke's encouragement, I reluctantly began to write a thinly disguised novel about Alexander the Great, set far in the future and cast against an interstellar background. It was pure blood-and-thunder, with the good little Terrans (that's science-fiction jar-gon for Earth people) set against the implacable reptilian invaders who had conquered all of the Milky Way galaxy except for our tiny sector. Of course, we good guys win and conquer the whole galaxy.

Winston bought it. *The Star Conquerors* became my first published novel. What's more, the editor was fascinated by the astronomical background of the novel, which I assured him was accurate. He suggested I write a book about stellar astronomy. *The Milky Way Galaxy* was the result, a few years later, the first of many nonfiction books I would write on subjects as diverse as astronomy and dinosaurs, particle physics and divorce.

By that time my wife and I had moved to the Boston area. I had been recruited by a strange organization that called itself the Physical Sciences Study Committee. PSSC had been started in the mid-1950s by a handful of professors from the MIT physics faculty. They were dreadfully disappointed with the quality of freshmen coming into MIT. The kids did not know any high school physics, despite getting excellent grades. It sounded terribly familiar to me. But instead of rejecting these bright, though ignorant, students, the MIT professors decided to do something useful. They wanted to create a course in physics for high schools.

Sputnik and the furor it caused helped PSSC to raise both money and interest. Science education was a hot topic in the wake of the Soviet successes in space. Physicists from many universities around the country, and even overseas, came to help PSSC.

I was recruited to write motion pictures. My on-camera "stars" were Nobel-level physicists doing high school experiments with homemade equipment consisting of toothpicks, soda straws, toy trains, and the like. It was enormous fun. Among the people I worked with was Albert V. Baez, a marvelous physicist and teacher who will be forever known to history as the father of the folksinger Joan Baez. I sometimes drove teenaged Joannie and her sister Mimi to their guitar lessons. The first time Joan sang in public, I believe, was at one of our PSSC picnics. Even the breeze stopped blowing to listen to her incredibly beautiful voice.

PSSC was a temporary thing. It took several years to do the job, but once the task of creating the high school physics course was finished, I began to look for a more permanent position. I found one that would last a dozen years when I joined the Avco Everett Research Laboratory as a science writer.

The lab was an independent branch of Avco Corporation, which at that time (it was now 1959) was a billion-dollar, highly diversified company. Avco was into everything from airplanes and missiles to radio broadcasting and motion pictures. The Avco Everett Research Laboratory, located in Everett, Massachusetts, was the brainchild of Dr. Arthur R. Kantrowitz, another of the major influences on my life. The lab specialized in the physics of high-temperature gasses. We were internationally known as hot-air specialists.

Seriously, AERL was a high-voltage place where we worked on ballistic missile re-entry problems, missile defenses, high-power lasers, magnetohydrodynamics (MHD, mercifully), superconducting magnets, and even artificial hearts. Thanks to the lab's pioneering work on re-entry physics, Avco built all the heat shields for the Apollo command modules that carried our astronauts safely home from the moon.

For me the lab was better than a university, for I worked daily with some of the brightest scientists in the world without the confining strictures of academia. I rose from science writer to head of the lab's marketing department—a department I created. Under Kantrowitz's tutelage, a person could move as far and as fast as he or she chose to. He was a driving force, and remains a steadfast friend.

I was often twitted by the scientists once they learned that I wrote science fiction. It became something of a badge of honor. I was known as the lab's resident science-fiction writer, and I helped to write reports and proposals that sounded like science fiction to the uninitiated. But these "fictions" came true.

For example, in the mid-1960s lasers were little more than scientific curiosities, often described as "a solution looking for a problem." Their major drawback was that they produced too little power output to be useful outside the laboratory. Kantrowitz was convinced that, with our knowledge of high-temperature gas physics, we should be able to invent truly high-power lasers. Which the scientists of the lab did. I helped to arrange a top-secret briefing in the Pentagon in February 1966 to inform the Department of Defense that we had invented the gasdynamic laser, which would eventually lead to the Strategic Defense Initiative, often called Star Wars. According to no less an authority than Prime Minister Margaret Thatcher, it was the advent of SDI that convinced the Soviet military that they could never overpower the West. As a result they did not oppose Mikhail Gorbachev's reforms—which eventually led to the collapse of the Soviet Union.

Our move to the Boston area brought two blessings: one, my asthma was much less severe; and two, I met Isaac Asimov. Isaac soon became like a big brother to me; we loved each other like brothers right up to the day he died, in 1992. He helped me to establish my name in the science-fiction magazine field, in a semi-strange way.

Not long after we had first met, Isaac phoned me to say that I would soon receive a call from a magazine editor in New York, asking me to write a series of nonfiction articles about the possibilities of extraterrestrial life.

"She asked me to write the series," Isaac told me cheerfully, "but I'm too busy with other things. So I told her that you should do it because you know more about the subject than I do."

I almost fainted. Isaac was a Ph.D. chemist, a professor of biochemistry, one of the most famous science-fiction writers in the world, and a prodigious writer of nonfiction about science, as well. I was a neophyte with one blood-and-thunder novel and a book about astronomy to my name.

Isaac sensed my unease. "Listen! I'll tell you everything I know about the subject, and you must know something that I don't—so you'll know more than I do!"

He was as good as his word, and that series of articles established my name among the science-fiction faithful as a serious writer who knew about science. In fact, while writing that series I made an original contribution to astrochemistry, although it went unnoticed by the scientific community. I suggested that organic chemicals, the building blocks of life, might exist in interstellar space. The common astronomical wisdom at that time was that complex chemicals could not form in deep space because the harsh radiation of the stars would tear such molecules apart as soon as they formed. I made my suggestion in an article printed in 1962. The following year radio astronomers made the first discovery of hydroxyl molecules in interstellar space. Within a decade they had found dozens of different organic molecules out among the stars.

One reason why my speculation was ignored by professional scientists was that my articles were being published in a science-fiction magazine rather than a scientific journal. The magazine was *Amazing,* the first science-fiction magazine to be published (started in 1926 and still going strong). The editor was Cele Goldsmith, who has remained a good friend ever since. Now she is Cele Goldsmith Lalli, and the editor of *Modern Bride* magazine.

The top magazine in the science-fiction field was *Analog,* edited by the renowned John W. Campbell, Jr., the most influential editor the field has ever produced. He was yet another powerful influence on my life. I wanted to sell fiction to John Campbell—every science-fiction writer of that era wanted to "sell" Campbell. John was demanding, but extraordinarily helpful to new writers. When he did not like a story submitted to *Analog* he did not merely reject it, he sent back a letter that was sometimes longer than the story itself, a letter filled with helpful criticism and bursting with ideas for the kinds of stories he was looking for.

When I sold my first short story to *Analog* I figured that I had "arrived" as a science-fiction writer. But I did not dare give up my job at Avco Everett. For one thing, I enjoyed it too much. I liked the people and found the work fascinating. They—and it—gave me a lifetime of material to write about. For another, by this time we had adopted a boy, Michael, and a girl, Regina. And bought a house. The security of a steady job was very comforting. A writer's income is never secure.

So I settled into a routine. Every day I would rise before the sun did and spend an hour or two writing. Then I would go to the lab. As I became more deeply involved with marketing the lab's research, I spent more and more time on the road: I was in Washington or at Wright-Patterson Air Force Base in Dayton almost weekly. Once we began working on high-power lasers I travelled frequently to the Air Force Special Weapons Laboratory at Kirtland AFB, just outside Albuquerque. It was on those Avco trips that I first fell in love with the southwestern desert.

I was selling both fiction and nonfiction; books and magazine pieces. My marriage was miserable, and I now realize that my constant travelling did not improve things at home.

It was during this period in the 1960s that I was first invited to the Milford Science Fiction Writers' Workshop. The workshop was the brainchild of Damon Knight, James Blish, and Judith Merrill—all very successful science-fiction writers. For one solid week each June some two dozen writers convened in Milford, Pennsylvania, to talk, eat, breathe, dream nothing but writing. It did not have to be science fiction; any kind of fiction writing. Attendance was by invitation only, you had to be a published author and you had to bring

an unpublished manuscript for all the other writers to read and criticize. Each morning we read one another's manuscripts. In the afternoons we critiqued two or three of them. Evenings were spent in more general discussions about publishers, agents, writing habits, and other aspects of the business and art of writing fiction professionally.

I cannot point to any specific piece of knowledge that I picked up at the Milford conferences, but I know that they were immensely helpful to me as a writer. Not only did I learn a great deal, but I met fellow writers who soon turned into lifelong friends: people such as Gordon Dickson, Harlan Ellison, Anne McCaffrey, Keith Laumer, Kate Wilhelm, Joe Haldeman, Gardner Dozois—it is a long list of cherished friends and colleagues.

Harlan became a good friend despite his reputation as the *enfant terrible* of science fiction. The actor Robert Culp once said that being a friend of Harlan's was a test of one's maturity. Despite the fact that we lived on opposite coasts (he lives in Sherman Oaks, in the Los Angeles area)

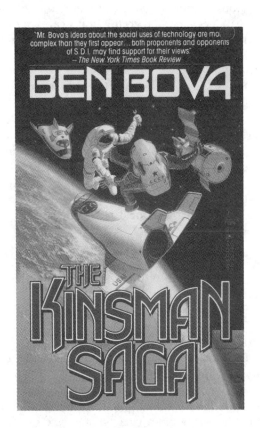

Cover from The Kinsman Saga,
written by Ben Bova

Harlan and I wrote a short story together, titled "Brillo." It was about a pair of policemen, one very human, one a robot. Campbell published the story in *Analog*, the first time Harlan had ever appeared in the magazine. That delighted him.

Then he was approached by certain people from Paramount Studios and ABC-TV who wanted us to turn "Brillo" into a television series. That delighted both of us. We worked hard on the script for a ninety-minute pilot and on plot outlines for thirteen full-hour segments. But the Paramount and ABC people abruptly told us that they were dropping "Brillo." We were stunned—even more stunned when, about a year later, they brought out "Future Cop." It was our script but we received no credit, no payment. We sued. It took four years, but we won the case. It was the first time any writer had won a plagiarism suit against a major studio. But, as we knew all along, the defendants were incredibly guilty.

When I first started going to the annual Milford conferences, I brought my wife and children. Milford is a pleasant place in the foothills of the scenic Pocono Mountains. There was plenty for the kids to do, lots of babysitters available, and the spouses joined the writers for the evening sessions. Yet after a couple of years my wife decided to remain at home and let me go alone. It was just another sign of how far apart we were drifting.

In 1970 my wife and I finally separated. I vowed that my salary from the lab would go entirely to her and the children. I would live on what I earned from writing. So I rented a studio apartment just north of Boston and became a bachelor—really for the first time in my life. I had gone directly from my parents' home to married life, back when I was twenty-one. Now, at thirty-eight, I was living alone for the first time. And loving it.

Within a few months two things happened that changed my life utterly.

First, and most important, I met Barbara, on 12 March 1971, at a science-fiction convention in North Andover, Massachusetts, of all places.

Like parallel lines that run alongside each other without meeting, Barbara and I had led very similar lives. She too had married young and unhappily. She too had split from her husband in 1970. She was not particularly interested in science fiction, however. In fact, she did not even know that science fiction existed. She had brought her three children to North Andover for the weekend because a friend—who was a science-fiction fan—had told her that there would be a conference of interesting people there, the hotel did not charge for children, and it had an indoor swimming pool. I had come to the convention with Michael and Gina because I was now an important-enough writer to be invited to science-fiction conventions. I saw my children only on weekends, and not always then; my ex-wife sometimes refused to let me see them.

I met Barbara that snowy Friday afternoon and with one flash of her beautiful brown eyes I fell in love. Our five kids quickly learned to look for us in the hotel's bar; we spent hours there, telling each other our life stories. We have not been apart from each other for longer than a few days ever since. In 1974, after both our divorces became final, Barbara and I married. Happily. We share our lives completely. Her children—Kenneth, Seth, and Elizabeth—have become as close to me as my own Michael and Regina.

Barbara wrote two books and got them both published. Then she decided to become a literary agent. She quickly became quite successful at it. After watching her at work for a couple of years I asked her if she would represent me. This was not a simple request. It is not easy for an agent to represent his or her spouse. The problems are deep and complex; marriages have been shattered that way. But ours merely grew stronger. As I said, we share our lives completely and very happily so.

When we first met, however, Barbara lived in West Hartford, Connecticut, while I still lived in the Boston area. We spent a lot of time on the highways between the two locations: me visiting her, she visiting me, or sometimes we met halfway between.

Shortly after we met, John Campbell died, very suddenly and unexpectedly. I was asked to take over his position as the editor of *Analog* magazine. In the world of science fiction, this was akin to being tapped to be Pope, or drafted to run for President. You are terribly afraid that the job is beyond your capabilities, but you dare not refuse it.

Campbell had edited the magazine since 1937, when it had been titled *Astounding Stories*. He had almost single-handedly moved science fiction away from juvenile pulp adventures to thoughtful, realistic fiction. He was such an imposing, commanding figure in the field that we all just assumed he would go on forever. And, in truth, he was only sixty-one when he had a fatal heart attack. He was

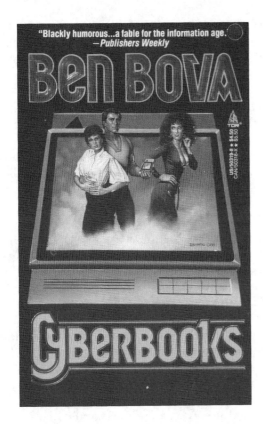

From Cyberbooks, *written by Ben Bova*

a man of strong opinions, and a chain-smoker. He never believed the Surgeon General's report on the health hazards of smoking cigarettes.

At that time, being the editor of *Analog* was the most powerful and prestigious position in the science-fiction world. Why did the magazine's publisher offer the job to a part-time writer? After I had held the job for a year or so, I asked the executive who had made the decision.

Analog was published then by The Condé Nast Publications Inc., one of the biggest magazine houses in the nation. They published *Vogue, House and Garden, Mademoiselle, Glamour,* and many other big, slick magazines. They had acquired this little digest-sized science-fiction magazine back in 1960, when they had bought out Street and Smith Company.

The executive who had to find a replacement for Campbell (and who later became president of the company) knew nothing about *Analog.* None of the executives knew a thing about the magazine except that it made a small profit every month, it was run smoothly by Campbell and his assistant

Katherine Tarrant, and it published both science-fiction stories and science-fact articles. So the executive asked Miss Tarrant to draw up a list of potential editors, drawn from writers who had contributed both fiction and fact pieces to the magazine. Katherine, in turn, asked half a dozen of the magazine's steady contributors to draw up such lists.

As a part-time writer, I was not one of the magazine's steady contributors. Yet my name appeared on every list. So did the names of several others, most of whom were better known in the field than I. But the executive picked me. Why? When I asked him, he replied that he had tried to read a science-fiction story and a science-fact article by each person on the lists. "Ben," he said, "you were the only guy I could understand!"

Score one for newspaper training. Clarity counts.

I felt a bit apprehensive about leaving Avco Everett for the totally different job of editing *Analog.* After all, I wondered, what if I'm a bust as an editor? What then? Kantrowitz was more than helpful. He made a consulting agreement with me that essentially would allow me to come back to the lab whenever I chose to.

Barbara and I took an apartment in the Gramercy Park section of Manhattan. I spent most of each week in New York, then repaired to West Hartford for the weekends. The biggest part of the *Analog* job was reading the hundred or so manuscripts that came into the office each week, which I could do in Connecticut as easily as in New York. I did well enough to win six Hugo Awards[2] as best editor. And I discovered a hatful of new writers. It was a thrill to be able to help youngsters start their careers, just as Arthur Clarke and Isaac Asimov had helped me.

While we were living part-time in Manhattan I was asked to teach a science-fiction film course at the Hayden Planetarium. I have a warm place in my heart for planetariums, and I easily agreed. We showed old sci-fi flicks on the dome of the planetarium chamber and discussed the films afterward. The planetarium's director commented that I was the only man he had ever seen who could

---

[2]The Hugo is named after Hugo Gernsback, who published the first science-fiction magazine in 1926. It is awarded by the fans who attend the annual World Science-Fiction Convention and is considered one of the two most prestigious awards in the field. The other is the Nebula Award, given by the Science Fiction and Fantasy Writers of America (SFWA).

hold an intimate conversation with two hundred people. The following year I taught a course in science-fiction history in one of the museum's classrooms. Many years later I taught a summer semester course in science-fiction writing at Harvard University.

I kept on writing, of course. It was during those years of the early 1970s that I found my metier as a novelist. I began to write novels set in the very near future, novels that looked at the dramatic consequences when big science and big government impact on one another.

In 1976 *Millennium* was published and soon became my most successful novel (until *Mars,* published in 1992). *Millennium* was Chet Kinsman's story, the story that began with my first attempt at writing a novel back in 1949. I would like to think that *Millennium* would have been a contender for science fiction's major awards. But since, as the editor of *Analog,* I held such a powerful position in the field, I withdrew my work from consideration for all awards. In retrospect I think I made a tactical blunder, but I feel that if I had to do it all over again I would do exactly the same thing.

I feared, of course, that people would vote for my work because they wanted to flatter me—or flatter the editor of *Analog,* rather. I realized that my popularity among writers and fans had jumped several quantum leaps once I was named *Analog*'s editor. When I eventually stepped down from that position, many of those "friends" disappeared.

It took me a quarter-century to finally get Kinsman's story in print. My next novel took about three months to write.

It came about largely because of Harlan Ellison. Harlan created a science-fiction television series titled *The Starlost.* It starred Kier Dullea, the star of Stanley Kubrick and Arthur Clarke's *2001: A Space Odyssey.* It turned out to be, through no fault of Harlan's, the worst TV series ever put on the air. But we did not know that at the outset of the project. Harlan asked me to be the science advisor for the series. I agreed, and soon was shuttling from New York to Toronto, where the show was being videotaped.

My job was to spot scientific inaccuracies in the scripts and devise ways to correct them without destroying the entire script. Which I did. I was thanked graciously and paid handsomely. And my advice was ignored. The shows went on the air with all the scientific gaffs in their original splendor, and a full-screen credit at the end for BEN

BOVA—SCIENCE ADVISOR. Harlan had long since quit the series, disgusted with the low caliber of the scripts and production values. After a few episodes the show was cancelled: a mercy killing. It still pops up in reruns here and there, however, and I still cringe to think that my name is attached to it.

The entire affair was so ludicrous that I dashed off a comic novel titled *The Starcrossed.* Many readers have told me they laughed themselves sick over it. Those who know Harlan spot him as the harassed genius in the novel.

Colony was a far more serious novel, and one that exemplifies one of the hidden pitfalls of the publishing industry. In 1977 the head of Pocket Books asked me to write a novel about an O'Neil colony. He wanted it fast because he wanted to publish the very first novel about this hot new topic. Gerard O'Neil, a physics professor at Princeton, had recently come up with the idea of building huge habitats in space and making them completely earthlike. Thousands of people could live in such a habitat in complete comfort. If I could turn in the novel quickly, the publisher promised me, he would use every ounce of Pocket Books' clout to turn it into a national best-seller.

I worked furiously. The novel contrasted the luxury of the space colony against the growing poverty of the poor people who remain on Earth; a metaphor of the growing gap between rich and poor in our global society. I delivered the completed novel slightly ahead of my deadline. Fast as I was, though, I was not fast enough. The head of Pocket Books quit the company just weeks before I turned in the manuscript. The publicist who was going to make *Colony* the hottest book of the season quit with him, and the editor I had been working with was fired. The novel became an orphan. Though *Colony* has sold hundreds of thousands of copies, in several printings, it never broke into the industry's best-seller lists, as we had originally hoped it would.

A curious thing was happening to me. Or, rather, to my novels. Although they were being marketed by their publishers as science fiction, a sizeable segment of science fiction's diehard fans disdained them. They were too realistic; not futuristic or fantastic enough for many of the fans. On the other hand, a large number of people who ordinarily did not read science fiction read my novels and enjoyed them. My audience was partly within the science-fiction fandom, and partly outside of it.

Many of my non-science-fiction audience came from the fields of scientific research and aerospace engineering. I was still very interested in the space program, and was an active member of several pro-space activist organizations. I became president of the National Space Society for several years. I am still a member of NSS and several other space activist groups.

In 1978 I realized that I had been editing *Analog* for nearly seven years. A large part of my original motivation for accepting the position had been to make certain that the magazine did not die without Campbell at its helm. It now was clear that *Analog* was doing fine and would survive another change in editors. The truth is that although I enjoyed running *Analog* I really wanted to write full-time. That had been my ambition since I had been working on newspapers. And by this time my income from writing exceeded my salary as an editor. If I could write full-time, I reasoned, I

would be completely happy and financially better off.

So I selected my successor, Dr. Stanley Schmidt, a physicist and writer who was a steady contributor to the magazine. He is still *Analog*'s editor. I retired from my accidental career as a magazine editor.

For about a week.

While I had been winding up my work at *Analog*, Bob Guccione had been preparing to launch *Omni* magazine. This was really a case of great minds running in the same channels, because I had suggested to Condé Nast's management that the company start a new magazine, to be titled *Tomorrow!* I envisioned a big, slick, national magazine that would attract wide readership and heavy advertising revenues. Most of the magazine would be nonfiction about the future: not just science, but the future of the stock market, vacation resorts, women's fashions—everything in the world has a future angle to it. Of course, *Tomorrow!* would also carry futuristic fiction by the best science-fiction writers in the world.

Condé Nast's management considered my idea carefully, then decided against it. "We know how to produce magazines for the women's market," the company's president told me. "We don't feel comfortable with a magazine about the future." So they brought out *Self* instead, and have done extremely well with it.

Meanwhile, unknown to us, Bob Guccione was planning a magazine to be titled *Nova*. As I was getting ready to leave *Analog*, Bob and his wife, Kathy Keeton, invited me to their brownstone mansion and showed me their plans for this new magazine. It was so close to my idea for *Tomorrow!* that I was staggered. Then they asked me to be the new magazine's editor. I was flattered, but I declined. "I'm going to write full-time," I told them. "I'd be happy to contribute to *Nova*, but I don't want to be its editor."[3]

They picked another editor, who then asked me to be the magazine's fiction editor. Again I declined, but suggested they hire a young woman who had worked as my assistant at *Analog*. They did.

Then the *Nova* television show went to court to prevent Guccione from using "their" name for his new magazine, claiming that the publisher of *Penthouse* would associate "their" name with smut.

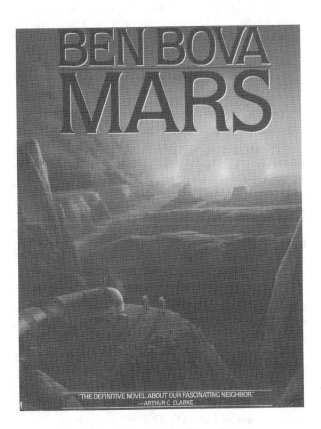

*Book jacket illustration from
Bova's novel* Mars

---

[3]And, truth to tell, I thought it might be just the tiniest bit silly to be Bova from *Nova*.

The court took the matter under advisement at just the time the first issue of the magazine had to go to press. Guccione and his staff spent a harried weekend running off every combination of four letters that a computer could spew at them and finally settled on the name *Omni*. I think *Omni* is a perfect name for the magazine.

As if that was not enough trouble, the fiction editor I had recommended ran off to get married just as the first issue of the newly renamed *Omni* was going to press. She did not intend to return, either. I received a phone call: "I don't have a fiction editor and it's all your fault."

Reluctantly, I agreed to sit in as fiction editor until they could find someone else. I found myself enjoying the job immensely. I was able to publish a broader variety of fiction than I could at *Analog*. Indeed, stories that I had reluctantly rejected years earlier because they did not fit *Analog*'s audience now came back to me, still unpublished. I was happy to give them their chance in the sun.

Two years later I was promoted to top editor when the original top dog suddenly quit. It was an emergency move; they needed someone immediately to fill the position and felt that if an editor were brought in from outside he or she would inevitably want to get rid of the existing editorial staff in favor of his or her own choices. So I took the top job and the rest of the staff kept their positions.

By the middle of 1982 Barbara and I realized that I had been with *Omni* for four years. Whatever happened to my cherished goal of writing full-time?

It was tough to leave *Omni*. Bob and Kathy treated us royally. We travelled all over the world first-class, helping the advertising and circulation departments to establish *Omni*'s credentials as a high-class magazine about the future, not merely *Penthouse* in space. We were highly successful; *Omni*'s readership grew to some five million per month, five thousand times more than *Analog* or any previous science-fiction magazine had ever attained.

But I longed for a quieter life where I could concentrate on writing. And my reputation as editor of *Analog* and *Omni* was overshadowing my reputation as a writer. I became an editor by the accident of John Campbell's sudden demise. I went to *Omni* because a young woman eloped. What I wanted most in the world was to write, and to be recognized as a writer, not an editor.

So I retired from editing. This time for good.

In the decade since 1982 I have concentrated on writing novels set in the near future, thematic novels that explore the interactions where big science meets big government or big corporate power. I have long believed that the true strength of science fiction is to examine the world around us by showing how science and technology are changing our lives. No other branch of contemporary literature has accepted this challenge; indeed, most of science fiction ignores it, too, favoring instead dystopian hand-wringing or juvenile adventure tales.

To me, science and its offspring technologies are the driving forces of human societies. Since the first proto-human used a twig as a digging tool, human beings have been developing tools to deal with the world around them. Our tools have worked so well that today we face the problems of our huge success: overpopulation is the root cause of the pollution, famines, crime, and wars that threaten our survival.

That is what I write about, for the most part. (There is a notable exception, which I will talk about in a few moments.) Science and technology are the driving forces that move us forward into the future. All other human institutions are essentially backward-looking, intended to maintain the status quo. Religion, law, social custom, they are all attempts to make tomorrow exactly the way yesterday was. Science and technology are always discovering new things, new capabilities. That is why they are so often feared or even hated.

What a canvas to work upon! The three-volume *Voyagers* novel, for example, ostensibly deals with the impact of our discovery that we are not alone in the universe; there are intelligent extraterrestrials who have sent a spacecraft into our solar system. The first novel is set in the 1990s, the second and third volumes move the story forward approximately a quarter-century. Extraterrestrial intelligence may seem purely the stuff of science fiction, yet the *Voyagers* tale is actually an examination of how the human race reacts to new technological breakthroughs. I use the aliens as a metaphor for a powerful new concept—nanotechnology, devices as small as viruses that are used to repair the human body from within. Nanotechnology will one day alter human societies much more profoundly than the invention of nuclear power.

While most of my novels deal with such themes, I have also written a series of novels about a time traveller named Orion. The *Orion* novels smack of fantasy more than science fiction: Orion is nearly superhuman in his capabilities. He was created by highly advanced humans some fifty thousand years in our future and sent back into time to do their bidding at various key points in human history and prehistory. He has fallen in love with one of those highly advanced humans, who are so far beyond us that they are virtually gods and goddesses in their powers. And this "goddess" loves Orion, too, but they are constantly being pulled apart by the other gods and/or the exigencies of Orion's tasks in time.

Orion started as something of a lark. I have always been curious about the fate of the Neanderthals, a species of humans who were just as intelligent as we are, but who disappeared with disturbing suddenness at the end of the latest Ice Age. What killed off the Neanderthals? To find out, I wrote a novel in which a time traveller—Orion—shows me what happened.

That is what my novels do for me. I begin with a few characters with a basic conflict, and then I turn them loose. The characters create the story. They show me what is happening. They resolve the original conflict. When I first started writing I used to make fairly detailed outlines. Soon I found that the outlines were too restrictive, too confining. Now I let the characters create the story. First drafts can be hell, because I do not yet know the characters well enough to be comfortable with them and to have them behave the way *they* want to. But later drafts are much easier, and the end result is a far more realistic, credible novel. At least, I think so.

The novel *Orion* turned into a moral struggle between Orion and his "gods." In subsequent novels I have set Orion before the walls of Troy (and Jericho, which fell at approximately the same time Troy did); sent him back to the Mesozoic Era; and had him serve Philip II of Macedon, father of Alexander the Great. *Orion* is a welcome change of pace from my thematic novels.

Thematic novels try to make a point. If the writer is not careful they can become propaganda rather than good fiction. They also carry certain other inherent risks. For one, by writing novels set in the very near future, the author runs the risk of having history catch up with him. *Millennium*, for example, is set in the month of December 1999, for the most part at a base on the Moon that houses hundreds of people. There will be no such lunar base by 1999, and many of the other details of *Millennium* are wrong. But the basic theme of the book—the idea that the coming of ballistic missile defenses in orbit, Star Wars, will fundamen-

The author

tally change global politics—that theme has turned out to be absolutely valid.

Several years before the 1991 Persian Gulf War and President George Bush's call for a "new world order," I wrote a novel titled *Peacekeepers*. Based on the research I had done for nonfiction books about the Strategic Defense Initiative (*Assured Survival* and *Star Peace*), the novel foretold the advent of an armed, permanent International Peacekeeping Force that has the power and responsibility of stopping aggression wherever in the world it might appear. Such a peacekeeping force does not yet exist, but it may well be brought into being within a decade; otherwise the world will continue to be racked by genocidal wars.

There is another risk in writing thematic novels. It is that critics base their evaluation of the novel not on the fiction itself, but on their own perceptions of the author's politics. Again, *Millennium* affords a good example. The novel was first published in 1976 and was received very kindly by the critics. The popular response to it was so positive that I wrote a "prequel" novel, *Kinsman*, in which I weaved together the stories of Kinsman's earlier life. In 1987 I put the two novels together in *The Kinsman Saga.* By that time, a good deal of my fiction had come true. Both the United States and Soviet Russia were working on orbital defenses against ballistic missiles. The Soviet version of Star Wars was called Red Shield by Moscow.

The *Saga* was attacked by critics who were politically aligned against Star Wars. The same novel that they had praised ten years earlier they now condemned as "hawkish." Meanwhile, real hawks scorned the novel for its internationalist sentiments and the idea that Americans and Russians could work together toward global peace. For several years afterward, no matter what I wrote, certain reviewers commented on their views about my politics instead of the novel they were supposed to be reviewing. I felt as if the ghost of Joe McCarthy were laughing at me.

Then came *Mars.*

Ever since I was a child at the Fels Planetarium I had wanted to write the definitive novel about Mars. Not a science-fiction adventure, but a realistic novel about the first men and women to explore the red planet, and the politics and families and loves and hates behind their historic mission.

When I first started working on *Mars,* the novel's protagonist was an American geologist. But something in the back of my mind nagged at me. Among the research materials I had amassed for the novel were hundreds of NASA photographs of Mars. Some of the terrain reminded me powerfully of the rugged desert landscapes of New Mexico and Arizona. Then it struck me. My protagonist, Jamie Waterman, was part Navaho. His father was an anglicized Navaho and his mother was descended from the Mayflower. Jamie spent his boyhood summers with his grandfather, who always tried to remind the boy of his Native American heritage. Jamie is a man torn between two worlds: the Anglo and the Navaho. The differences between Earth and Mars become symbolic of the two worlds within Jamie's soul.

Mars has become the most successful of my novels to date, in terms of sales and critical reception. It has been cited as an example of how a novelist can combine strong characterizations with an accurate cutting-edge scientific background into a powerful story.

That is what I try to write about. People at the edge of human capabilities. The human condition, whether it is in the perpetual winter of the Ice Ages or on the cratered plains of Mars. By going beyond the here and now, by stretching my sights past the limits of Earth and reaching out into the vast stretches of space-time, I can test the human spirit in ways that contemporary literature does not even imagine. My work is usually marketed as science fiction, but I regard my novels as explorations of the near future, stories that show how science and government are shaping our lives, tales of real human beings at the frontiers of knowledge.

Some of my "science fiction" is now history. The Space Race of the 1960s, the Strategic Defense Initiative (Star Wars), videogames and virtual reality and international peacekeeping forces: I explored each of these concepts a decade or two before they became part of our real world. Now I look forward to the human exploration of Mars and the development of genetic engineering and nanotechnology and a host of new possibilities. They are all grist for my mill. They are the raw material for exciting fiction, and the foundation of the world that we will live in tomorrow.

I want to show that world to my readers.

BIBLIOGRAPHY

FOR ADULTS

Fiction:

THX 1138 (adapted from the screenplay of the same title by George Lucas and Walter Murch), Paperback Library, 1971.

As on a Darkling Plain, Walker, 1972.

When the Sky Burned, Walker, 1973.

The Starcrossed, Chilton, 1975.

Millennium, Random House, 1976.

The Multiple Man, Bobbs-Merrill, 1976.

Colony, Pocket Books, 1978.

Kinsman, Dial, 1979.

Test of Fire, Tor Books, 1982.

Privateers, Tor Books, 1985.

Prometheans, Tor Books, 1986.

The Kinsman Saga (includes *Kinsman* and *Millennium*), Tor Books, 1987.

Peacekeepers, Tor Books, 1988.

Cyberbooks, Tor Books, 1989.

Mars, Bantam Books, 1992.

(With A. J. Austin) *To Save the Sun,* Tor Books, 1992.

(With Bill Pogue) *The Trikon Deception,* Tor Books, 1992.

Empire Builders, Tor Books, 1993.

Triumph, Tor Books, 1993.

"Voyagers" series:

Voyagers, Doubleday, 1981.

The Alien Within, Tor Books, 1986.

Star Brothers, Tor Books, 1990.

"Orion" series:

Orion, Simon & Schuster, 1984.

Vengeance of Orion, Tor Books, 1988.

Orion in the Dying Time, Tor Books, 1990.

Short-story collections:

Forward in Time, Walker, 1973.

Maxwell's Demons, Baronet, 1979.

Escape Plus, Tor Books, 1984.

The Astral Mirror, Tor Books, 1985.

Battle Station, Tor Books, 1987.

Future Crime, Tor Books, 1990.

Challenges, Tor Books, 1993.

Nonfiction:

The Milky Way Galaxy: Man's Exploration of the Stars, Holt, 1961.

The Fourth State of Matter: Plasma Dynamics and Tomorrow's Technology, St. Martin's, 1971.

The New Astronomies, St. Martin's, 1972.

(With Barbara Berson) *Survival Guide for the Suddenly Single,* St. Martin's, 1974.

(With Trudy E. Bell) *Closeup: New Worlds,* St. Martin's, 1977.

Viewpoint, NESFA Press, 1977.

The High Road, Houghton, 1981.

Vision of the Future: The Art of Robert McCall, Abrams, 1982.

Assured Survival: Putting the Star Wars Defense in Perspective, Houghton, 1984, revised paperback edition published as *Star Peace: Assured Survival,* Tor Books, 1986.

Welcome to Moonbase!, Ballantine, 1987.

The Beauty of Light, Wiley, 1988.

(With Sheldon L. Glashow) *Interactions: A Journey through the Mind of a Particle Physicist and the Matter of This World,* Warner, 1988.

Editor:

The Many Worlds of SF, Dutton, 1971.

Analog 9, Doubleday, 1973.

SFWA Hall of Fame, Volume II, Doubleday, 1973.

The Analog Science Fact Reader, St. Martin's, 1974.

Analog Annual, Pyramid, 1976.

Aliens, Futura, 1977.

The Best of Astounding, Baronet, 1977.

Exiles, Futura, 1977.

Analog Yearbook, Baronet, 1978.

The Best of Analog, Baronet, 1978.

(With Don Myrus) *The Best of Omni Science Fiction,* four volumes, Omni Publications International, 1980–82.

The Best of the Nebulas, St. Martin's, 1989.

(With Byron Preiss) *First Contact: The Search for Extraterrestrial Intelligence,* New American Library, 1990.

FOR YOUNG ADULTS

Fiction:

The Star Conquerors, Winston, 1959.

Star Watchman, Holt, 1964.

The Weathermakers, Holt, 1967.

Out of the Sun, Holt, 1968.

The Dueling Machine, Holt, 1969.

Escape!, Holt, 1970.

The Winds of Altair, Dutton, 1973, expanded edition, Tor Books, 1983.

(With Gordon R. Dickson) *Gremlins, Go Home!,* St. Martin's, 1974.

City of Darkness, Scribner, 1976.

"Exiles" trilogy:

Exiled from Earth, Dutton, 1971.

Flight of Exiles, Dutton, 1972.

End of Exile, Dutton, 1975.

The Exiles Trilogy (contains all three books), Berkley, 1980.

Nonfiction:

Giants of the Animal World, Whitman, 1962.

Reptiles Since the World Began, Whitman, 1964.

The Uses of Space, Holt, 1965.

In Quest of Quasars: An Introduction to Stars and Starlike Objects, Collier, 1970.

Planets, Life, and LGM, Addison-Wesley, 1970.

The Amazing Laser, Westminster Press, 1972.

Man Changes the Weather, Addison-Wesley, 1973.

Starflight and Other Improbabilities, Westminster Press, 1973.

The Weather Changes Man, Addison-Wesley, 1974.

Workshops in Space, Dutton, 1974.

Notes to a Science Fiction Writer, Scribner, 1975.

Science: Who Needs It?, Westminster Press, 1975.

Through Eyes of Wonder, Addison-Wesley, 1975.

The Seeds of Tomorrow, McKay, 1977.

Contributor of articles and short stories to periodicals, including *American Film, Astronomy, Science Digest, Smithsonian,* and *Writer.* Member of editorial board of World Future Society and Tor Books, 1982—. Editor, *Analog,* 1971–78, and *Omni,* 1978–82. Bova's manuscripts are collected at Temple University, Philadelphia, Pennsylvania.

Bruce-Novoa

1944-

When my father—the descendant of Scottish Protestants who since arriving with William Penn to found Pennsylvania had spent three centuries tracing an east-to-west migratory trajectory across space and time from the English colonies cum United States to whatever territory temporarily occupied the westerly edge of the expanding republic—turned south to travel from Colorado to Mexico, then converted to Catholicism to marry a woman of French-Spanish descent, it marked a monumental deviation from the family norm. It was previously risked only by young Lawrence in the 1860s who foolishly enlisted in time to be wounded defending the Hornets' Nest at Shiloh where the Confederates took him prisoner; during his incarceration, with one foot literally in the grave, he too wrote an autobiographical account to fathom why seventh-eighths of his body so missed its amputated lower leg that it would slowly follow the limb into death. The deviation was no less monumental for my mother—youngest offspring of a Mexican lawyer and Supreme Court judge of Gallego ancestry (the clan won nobility for devising a way to make horse tracks point in the opposite direction!) and his French wife, herself the daughter of a civil engineer whose sojourn in America to oversee the construction of Tampico harbor turned into a permanent immigration when yellow fever planted him firmly in New World soil—who moved to the United States after World War II at the age of thirty-seven with her four children. The youngest, I was less than one year old when we arrived.

In volume 4 of this same series, my friend and fellow Scottish-Mexican American John Rechy summarized the pros and cons of autobiography: "I am able to reconstruct my life . . . and so provide structure to what is shapeless, reason to anarchy—and the only meaning possible, a retrospective meaning, imposed— and the only truth, one's own. That is, autobiography as novel." I agree, John, but structure follows a plan and I've never had one; and what I discover as I look back is movement, yes, and inertia, but the absence of a plan. Sometime back we all set off on a trek to

Bruce-Novoa, 1988

somewhere, and reason, meaning, and truth have been invented on the march, improvised at moments when circumstances imposed on our normal precipitous flight a becalming pause that required or permitted retrospective justification, like Cousin Lawrence writing home about his fatal detainment. A contract from Gale Research creates the circumstance, while a sabbatical provides the pause in the pattern of my days, and here I sit trying to reconstruct myself . . . or a self for public consumption. Another intimate, Sheila Ortiz Taylor, says we choose our metaphors; hers, the ever-shifting fault line, would suit me fine. And yet another, Juan García Ponce, insists writers must not take literature to life, but life to literature, that realm of the possible where anything can happen without

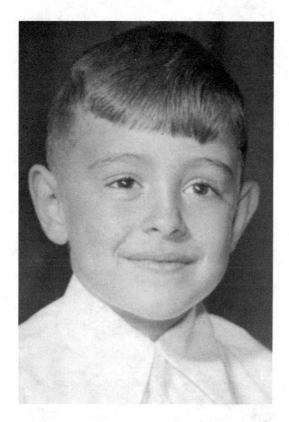

The author in 1953

dependence on outside reality. In literary space the proper noun is a momentary mask on anonymity; autobiography, a fiction of desire perpetually suspended. And yet, and yet . . .

One of the requirements imposed on my father before his marriage proposal was accepted in 1932 was that he promise never to leave Mexico. But when his draft notice arrived in 1944—the risk he ran for maintaining his U.S. citizenship—he had no choice, so he took us to San Antonio, Texas, where my mother's brother had a medical practice, and reported for duty. Luckily, the army discovered he was a CPA and posted him in Boston. Upon his release we were to return to Mexico, but there came a summons from the elegant old woman we all called *Tía* (Aunt), actually my father's aunt, who had helped raise him. She needed his assistance in running the family business in Denver. Caught between two family commitments, he moved the family north

instead of south, a decision that turned his children into Usonians[1] instead of Mexicans.

In 1946 we retraced my father's route of deviation back to where he had broken from the Bruce clan's east-to-west project. Yet, we sons and daughters of this Mexican-Usonian fusion had been born under the sign of a demagnetized compass, *sin norte* (without north), as we say in Spanish. Save for my brother who remains in Denver, the rest of us have wandered from state to state, country to country, without fully taking root: perpetual sojourners, we continue a tradition of travel, but now without a set goal or direction. Once you leave the place you grew up, everything else is migrant labor.

However, it's not that clear cut, because my sense of direction, while not programmatic, is corporeal. With a stability my own son has never enjoyed, I was given a quarter of a century of permanence in the same house of the solid-brick-on-a-full-basement-type construction, about which Texans and Californians can only dream. Set on a corner, it faced both west and north. If I left for school out the back door, I was heading east, where an irrigation ditch traversed the yard carrying summer water to the Italian farmers on the outskirts of town; but mostly I exited north from the kitchen toward Rocky Mountain Park with its football fields for grade-school teams and its lake that froze over for winter skating; and to my left— west—the mountains right where all mountains should be. (Years later, when people asked me why I would give up a tenured position in Santa Barbara, I would mumble something about administrative corruption or the geriatrics-ward feeling of the campus, but much of my discomfort, I'm now sure, came from that range of peaks brazenly mislocated to the northeast.)

An image from 4598 Grove Street: the ceiling light fixture in my room, a circle of opaque glass on which compass readings were painted in blue-and-red nautical motifs; spinning North's curved anchor to meet the rising sun outside my bedroom window, I reoriented reality to my own axis mundi. The books read in that and every other room of the house served the same function—though I never thought of reading in terms of function, just as what gave me the most pleasure . . . until, that is, Mike Ashton's Halloween party in seventh grade: Honky Tonk *laying down the bass riff*

---

[1]Frank Lloyd Wright's term for products of the United States.

of our times and fascinating young females teaching us how to follow the beat. If I search for meaning, John, it's there, but in Sheila-like metaphors: I, as a Mexican bandit, she as a Japanese geisha, dancing to black music in a middle-class Anglo's basement, surrounded by friends of Irish, German, French, and Italian extraction, especially the latter . . . my life seems to perform itself in Mexican costume, playing the outlaw on an Anglo-American field predefined by black strategies of engagement, but mostly among European ethnics tracing out the extemporized choreography of the American Dream, doing the right thing at the right time no matter how ephemeral it might seem. But beneath it all, what drives me still: being in full, rhythmic motion with a woman I'm falling in love with yet not knowing exactly who she is, where we're going, or how it'll turn out—the excitement of physical and mental discovery in and through sensual encounters in which the heightened perception of identity suddenly blurs into the anonymity of pure act . . . and after, the persistent memory of her leaving before I can discover much more than a name, and I've never been good with names; images are my forte: a blonde Italian-American in Japanese garb swaying like Sweet Little Sixteen, which neither of us would reach for a number of years, but nothing would change when we had. Still hasn't, much.

Other images, however, compete as sources. I love books, as I started to say, but reading began as a miserable experience. I never could justify that painful memory with my adult career as an academic and writer until one night in 1980, after lecturing at the University of Mexico, when I overheard my father say somewhere on the fringe of my senses that "when John started school we discovered he was dyslexic," and suddenly doors as massive as the locks on the River Neckar in front of my apartment in Heidelberg opened, flooding me with the repressed frustration of having to learn to rearrange signs that my eyes saw clearly distributed in an order apparently all my own. And back then no one was going to help me but my parents. Nightly we worked. Could that be why reading became such an intense pleasure when I mastered it; why I have spent the rest of my life proving I can read the common code, although still actually seeing everything in an order all my own?

There was football, too. I had no choice. The dog days of August followed by the yellowing of the park's grassy practice field and the cottonwood puffs filling the sky meant football, at which my brother Jimmy was a star. It became a way of life that almost took me to college on a scholarship.

Two things released me from that fate: my father's indecorous announcement in front of my embarrassed girlfriend that he wasn't going to pay the several thousand dollars an Ivy League university estimated would be my cost over and above the scholarship, and being named to an obscure High School All-American team my senior year. After basking in the news of my selection, I felt released. It was finally a level of recognition beyond my brother's, so I no longer had to play in college. For another year, perhaps in an attempt to retain an identity housed in the tissues of my body, I continued working out to build up to the two hundred and twenty pounds at which Dartmouth told me to report, but simultaneously I was coming to accept that it was better to study with the Jesuits at Regis College and be a rock musician. It made sense, my sense, now that I didn't have another standard to live up to. At five feet eight and a half inches I might play football for an Ivy team, but there was no future in it past graduation. Besides, playing football tires you so that you're lucky if you can do anything with a woman before your

Father, James H. Bruce, 1930

curfew has you back in the dorm. A rock musician has the best view of dozens of women every night, dancing just a few feet away, and after work, though you're tired, your body is on a sort of intense high just right for the sensual exploration to which lead singing and playing bass guitar are perfect foreplay, as I have written in my story "Satisfaction." Perhaps some might say that football is similar, but I've never cared for violent sex.

Where are we in this? I warned you. No structure, more like a nomadic wandering across what for others must seem like a well-drawn map. But it's my life . . . at least in the writing, although it belonged to others as well—maybe even more.

I grew up on the edge of my parents' forties, their best days, as my mother would remember later, after bankruptcy sent them back into migration, first to California and then to permanent exile in Texas. But in 1950 they built the house my father had promised her when they came north, and while she had to do housework none of her relatives in Mexico would ever soil their delicate hands with—*para eso son las criadas* (for that there are maids), they would say—she could enjoy the security of financial and social stability.

In contrast to her name, Dolores, which means pain, my mother had a gift for pleasure and fun none of us have inherited, a way of forming with her mere presence a center of lively conversation or song or intense admiration by men and women alike. Nightly, around our kitchen table, their friends came to talk into the late hours, drinking wine and discussing mid-century topics like María Callas's brilliance, Italian New Realism, Malraux's *Metamorphosis of the Gods*, the Communist threat to Catholicism, the death of Frida Kahlo, whom my mother remembered seeing often when they were young, or anything at all. Men I would later know as my university professors or a city councilman or the councils from foreign countries sat around the table. When still very young, after praying the required rosary for Stalin's conversion, I would sneak back out of bed and hide under the dining room table to listen and fall asleep. By the time I was ten I was allowed to sit at the table and even comment once in a while.

Colorado may not seem a cosmopolitan haven, but we lived an incredibly international existence. In the family we were interlingual: my parents spoke mostly Spanish, and we children, English. In classic immigrant fashion, my mother learned English from us, especially while trying to help us do homework. When I was in third grade she couldn't understand my complaint about a silent letter in *knife*. She told me to pronounce it as a German would: "Ka-nife." My teacher saw it differently, but a veteran dyslexic like me had already learned to mediate between contradictory readings of the same sign. Besides, I knew all the while that my teachers just weren't smart enough to understand. After all, none of them were Mexicans, so how could they be as intelligent as Mexicans—yes, it was prejudiced, but it seemed right then. Later it shocked me to discover that people could suffer from exactly the opposite prejudice. If I had to choose, I'd keep mine.

From 1952 to 1956 many of the weekday/night conversations were in Italian, while the weekend gatherings tended towards Spanish. During the day, when I must have often skipped school to accompany my mother, I found myself listening to French as my mother spoke to close friends, or German, when she painted with a group of Austrian expatriates who used English only to talk to us, preferring German among themselves. I thought everyone lived this way, just as I thought coming home after school to snack on escargot, or going to the mountains to hunt mushrooms or make wine, or listening to opera every Saturday while my mother sang along or explained the historical context of anything and everything, or traveling to Mexico City some summers was common experience. If given the choice back then between doing something with my peers and accompanying my parents, the latter carried the day.

Among the adult friends was Howard Shorty Beck, a retired engineer who had worked the Mexican oil fields after the Revolution before being transferred to develop Maracaibo. He was my favorite oral mentor. You see, Shorty wasn't supposed to drink much anymore—some betrayal of the body I have begun only recently to understand firsthand—so his charming wife Chela kept one eye on the bar while making small talk at a cocktail party or playing canasta in the living room. Shorty loved good Scotch whisky, but with his access checked by Chelita's watchful eye, I was recruited at an early age to procure refills, which came to mean one for each of us. Between sips he would narrate his adventures in Sonora, Tamaulipas, or Mexico City, how his military friend executed a dozen or so men one by one with a forty-five bullet between the eyes and then got furious with Shorty for throwing up in his car, or when the same friend responded to Shorty's complaint about pilfered copper wire by decorat-

RECITAL DE CANTO

Carolina Pérez
(del Conservatorio Nal. de Música)

presenta

a

su discípula

Dolores Novoa de Bruce

en su primer recital de canto.

Sala Schifer (Venustiano Carranza No. 21 altos)

Jueves 29 de abril de 1943 a las 20.30 horas (8.30 p. m.)

PROGRAMA:

I

Nina	Pergolesi
Voi che sapete (Nozze de Figaro)	W. A. Mozart
Aleluya	W. A. Mozart
Caro Nome (Rigoletto)	Verdi

II

Si yo te hablara de mi pena	Schumann
Les trois prieres	Paladilhe
Premiere danse	J. Massenet
Les Roses d'Ispan	Fauré
Bonjour Suson	Leo Delibes

III

Berceuse	E. Zubeldía
La Molinera	E. Zubeldía
Jota	M. de Falla

Al piano la profesora
Ana Ma. H. de Burgos

A flyer announcing a recital by Dolores Novoa de Bruce, 1943

ing every telegraph pole between Tampico and the company's field office with the corpses of suspects, strung by the neck and rotting in the same merciless coastal sun under which my great-grand-father Charles Roumagnac had succumbed to fever half a century earlier and under which I would do social work a half-century later. When in

1968 I told Shorty the rumors of a massacre of students in Mexico City, he recounted the machine-gunning of oil workers in Tampico and the army's attack on taxi drivers in Mexico City's central square. Now I mix these stories with my own—walking through tear-gas-filled streets of Mexico City the night Ruiz Cortínez was elected, hours of conversation with Juan Rulfo, setting up a summer school in Lomas del Real where domestic pigs roam the streets gnawing on drunks or babies alike, and harvesting Blue Crab claws as a survival technique—as if I had seen them all myself, and invariably some student will ask, professor, how old are you? Counting Shorty, my mother, a couple of uncles, my *Tía* and her black companion Cornelea, my *nana* Tomasa, all of whom I haven't even gotten around to yet, and so many others I've forgotten, I'd say ancient.

Then there were those trips to *La Capital,* Mexico City. Those words, *La Capital,* symbolize well our interculturalism. For me there has always been one *Capital* in Mexico and another capital, Washington, D.C., but while the latter remained an ideal abstraction until 1976, the former was the fantastic reality of my youth. *México:* dark, luxurious homes in Tlalpan or in Condesa Hipódromo, corner of Aguascalientes and Chilpancingo, where nothing seemed touched by human hands, and silence reigned until after noon, at least everywhere but the kitchen where ruled Tomasa, the smiling *cocinera* and part-time *nana* who managed to understand my English-Spanish brew. She took me to the market to hear the gypsies sing Spanish songs and saved food for me to get me through the long hours between lunch and the snack they called dinner at 9:00 P.M. *México,* where I learned, although never mastered, the trick of not looking out the car window and thus making disappear the reality of insistent but patient hands and eyes begging from the curb. *México,* where my grandmother taught me that even relatives can cheat, and some of them habitually. *México,* that never could be my mother country because as soon as we arrived my mother would drift away to become a different person, one that reappeared at lunch, perhaps, or on television: one night while watching live coverage of an opera premier I saw her pass in front of the camera among a parade of elegant spectators. Only in Colorado did she become again mine, the one who spoke French with her friends or Italian with the choir director, the one whose private melancholy flashed into public joy, whose elegance and beauty made people in Colorado ask where she came from—an exotic Latin, obviously, but they couldn't imagine her origin because she didn't conform to the image of the "Mexican" held by most U.S. Americans. "Oh," the butcher exclaimed when I told him who my mother was, "you mean the one who looks like a duchess?"

Yes.

Torn photo of young Dolores Novoa, taken about 1920

Back home we shared her *México* through what now seem too few anecdotes: hiding under her *nana's* skirt when the Zapatistas invaded the house with orders to execute my grandfather for some personal grudge; having almost nothing to eat during the harsh years of the Revolution; being forced to drop out of the conservatory although she was one of only two students who could sing the full range of Lily Pons because her mother considered singing a useless pursuit for a woman of good family, then being sent out to work as a secretary as if that were somehow a more appropriate career, so that she could help support her male siblings who studied law and medicine; being approached by Sigueiros to model for him, a request rejected by her mother; meeting a young American with the "in" look of an aviator and eventually marrying him because he just kept nagging. . . .

Another image of images: my mother's sense of autobiography. When my parents were about to move from Denver in 1975 I found my mother sitting at the bottom of the basement steps cutting old photographs in half. "No quiero que nadie las vea cuando me muera (I don't want anyone to see them when I die.)" She wanted to leave no images, especially of the life that had been so radically altered when she was forced to leave Mexico, of the girl who had grown up to expect something very different from life. In my passive way I only protested, but let her continue. My sister Lillian caught her repeating the deed a decade later, tearing them this time, but managed to save the one shown here. I feel that rip through everything I do . . . and whenever possible refuse to be in photos: I may not have time to rip them up.

Of my father, I heard almost nothing directly from him. Later I came to know that he told his life to my brother and probably didn't feel the need to repeat it. To explain him would be to invent. What remains in memory is his wanderlust, as if the Bruce blood insisted he travel further, see more, but never prepare for what might happen up ahead. Even at eighty, Eurail Pass in hand, he set off for Budapest with no knowledge of German or Hungarian. My mother had died a year earlier, so he no longer could count on her linguistic skill or charm to negotiate borders. I was teaching at the University of Erlangen-Nürnberg at the time and dedicating every off-hour to finishing my novel *Only the Good Times,* so I could not accompany him. He returned as always, somewhat battered by the crowds, having been fleeced in Vienna and almost trampled in Munich, but happy because in Budapest the Catholic family he was taking something to as a favor had treated him well. To me he seemed guileless, scarcely fit for the modern world; a CPA who loved numbers but had no business sense, who trusted others and got burned every time. It wasn't long after that trip that he began to decline, his body literally curving in on itself without my mother to remind him to stand straight. He began to wait for death, but just couldn't bear to sit still for it, planning to drive across the country or fly to Mexico City, or visit anyone who would receive him. Stubborn as always, a mystery to me.

But in the 1950s and early 1960s he gave us a good life. Not at the level of the wealthy relatives in *La Capital,* but a solid, middle-class life without major worries. A normal life, you might say, with minor differences, like discussions about art, history, classical music, and Mexico. We frequented the movies, but often at the Spanish-language theater on Denver's west side where none of my school friends ever set foot. And my mother had an understanding with the manager of the Vogue, Denver's foreign-film theater, so I was allowed in to films rated even then adult only. Perhaps reading rapid-fire subtitles was the real cure for my dyslexia.

If I learned anything from these films it was that there coexisted different versions of the same reality; that within the same geographic and temporal space so many perspectives are possible that truth must always be relative. For example, the *U.S. Marine Hymn,* without any change in the words, bespeaks national glory and pride or the history of U.S. imperialism, or that Zapata and Pancho Villa weren't everybody's heroes. It's all a matter of perspective.

In fourth grade theater fascinated me. I organized a group to present brief skits to our classmates. I adapted classic novels—Dumas, Stevenson, Cooper—or contemporary films like *The Sands of Iwo Jima.* My taste was and still is radically eclectic. I would give out the roles at morning recess, rehearse during the lunch hour, and premier at the two o'clock break. I don't remember writing any original piece, but I still retain basic discoveries of directness of dialogue and gesture.

That same year when we read a children's version of *The Iliad* it seemed such a disappointment compared to my mother's high praise for the poet that I dedicated a couple of weeks to his dual epic. When the class was supposed to be doing penmanship exercises—Palmer method, floating elegant swirls across the ruled pages with a rhythmic movement delicately balanced on the forearm—I would speedily fill the required space in two seconds or less and whip out my copy of Homer. My penmanship still shows the ravages of neglect, but I also retain a passion for that mixture of history and myth, and in truth I have never been able to distinguish well between the two. They remain in my mind two genres of literary invention. History itself, which I would take up seriously in fifth grade, struck me as a magnificent, multivoiced novel, and I devoured it.

My continual confrontation with authority started in fifth grade on so many issues that I came to expect some punishment at least once a day. First the good nun complained about my lack of attention and refusal to cooperate, especially when she would ask a question about material she had written on the chalkboard. Finally, she relegated me to the last seat in the last row and stopped calling on me. With other recalcitrants I passed my time drawing or reading on my own. Then one evening my mother noticed me squinting at my dinner . . . I can still remember the glow of a neon sign across the street from the optometrist's shop when I realized that those lights all over town could be read by almost everyone. But mostly I remember how brilliant the world glows if only you have the right lens through which to see it.

I finally could see the handwriting on the wall, but confrontation had become my style. I had a reputation my teachers seemed intent on maintaining, but our arguments did shift in character, becoming more intellectual and closely related to writing. I used my outside readings to comment on the limited scope of our classroom discussions. When I wrote a debunking essay on Thanksgiving implying that Pilgrim women were left at home to allow their men to feast on more than turkey, I had to produce my sources. When I pointed out that the Inquisition existed in every European country before it was allowed in Spain and that more heretics were killed in France in one night than in Spain's history, my parents received a call. When I read *Mein Kampf* as my project on World War II, I was sent to report to the pastor—as I was leaving, Sister Hope called me a Communist, so I stopped to explain the difference between communism and Nazism, but she ran down the aisle screaming, "Out, out." So much for reading.

As for writing, I learned to fashion an essay thanks to the extra attention granted me almost daily by my teachers. After school I would write short essays of five hundred or a thousand words on such topics as "Why I Should Respect My Teacher," or "The Virtue of Humility," and my favorite, "Pride as Satan's Tragic Flaw." I couldn't have asked for better training, available exclusively to rule-breakers.

In high school I was continually told that I was a terrible student. Not that I got bad grades, but I never had to apply myself to get good ones. On the other hand, I dedicated myself furiously to extra-curricular diversions: football, music, and girls. Sophomore year I fell into two activities that later would turn into professions. My favorite teacher asked me to take over her world history class when she got sick. She justified it to the principal, my arch-antagonist from day one, by claiming I was, after her, the best-prepared person in the school. The arrangement continued for three years, but somehow I've never stopped pretending I'm a teacher. I also accepted the invitation to sing with a rock band and wrote some teenage angst songs with the lead guitarist, Mike Johnson, who later joined the New Christy Minstrels and now records

for RCA. Senior year we formed another band that would stay together all through college, playing steady jobs for good money in those years. We worked nightly in the best clubs in the Denver area.

Playing music taught me in a concrete manner that the performance is as important as the piece itself, and that quality is not always what moves people, but rather volume, enthusiasm, and the unexpected, although always within the context of the familiar. Most important, I discovered that words transcend distance, that voice and sight can at times assume tactile qualities, and that body and mind can dissolve into each other, but only momentarily. It's like sex, but then so is writing or teaching when everything is flowing just right.

Meanwhile, the Jesuits took charge of my days. At times Joe Elkins, our rhythm guitarist, and I went to our first class straight from an all-night practice. We kept each other awake. Joe had to answer questions for me, because I couldn't talk until noon, when my body would start its gradual up cycle that would peak around eight with the first blast of the amplifiers. But we never missed class, and in return the Jesuits transmitted a solid base of learning, although not yet specifically literary. I was still enamored of history, my major, with psychology as a minor and the equivalent hours in theology and philosophy as another major. In philosophy I experienced the change-over from traditional Thomism to existential phenomenology; history fused with theology in a fortunate reading of Mircea Eliade; in psychology, though Freud was unavoidable, my preference ran toward William James and the even more radical theories of European empiricism with its recognition that subjectivity is merely a necessary fiction. We took two years of required English lit organized by Father Boyle, who insisted that all freshmen memorize Shakespeare's Sonnet CXVI, learn to chart images and do so before coming to class to avoid stupid questions, and read *King Lear, Romeo and Juliet,* and Molly Bloom's monologue from *Ulysses* with an attention to every detail. In short, we were oriented to center our reading on or through the possibility of love as the essential human question. It's stayed with me ever since, although actually it only confirmed and authorized my predilections. I wrote an unbearably existential play that impressed some fellow students and spawned at least one term paper in an ethics course, but my efforts at the time went mainly into songs, ballads mostly, with slightly exotic chord progressions and mournful lyrics . . . sort of Roy Orbison evolving towards Chris Isaak.

At the start of my senior year the band was approached to do some recording and touring, but something else came up (it always has). Spanish literature in the fall of 1965 was performed for us by a Chilean woman who looked and moved like a singer from Brazil 66. I decided to make Spanish a career, though I had no idea what that entailed. I just knew I wanted to spend time with her and it seemed the best way to claim her attention. When I approached her to request a tutorial, she assigned me the novels of Miguel de Unamuno, the great Spanish existentialist who, I discovered, was obscenely prolific in almost all genres. That should have discouraged me, but mine was a passion of mind and body, so I quit the band and dedicated my nights to reading. The rest of my life has flowed from that decision, although less from my teacher's sensual charms than the reading of Unamuno: the importance of cultural history filtered through literary texts whose variety and inherent contradictions are purposefully maintained and even utilized within a phenomenological field in which a deep structure relates all the disperse elements. One book especially impressed me, *En torno al casticismo* with its obsessively phenomenological vision of fragmented reality, tied to a responsibility to structure from chaos, a cosmos through the word, a tool, however, whose notorious unreliability imposes the inevitable conclusion that one cannot write something, or on something, or even about something, but only at best around-and-about something (literally *en torno de*), without the hope of ever capturing completely either the object of literature or literature as an object, because representation is never entirely adequate and language always exceeds the reach of individual expression. Yet within the practice of writing there may be the possibility of coinciding, however ephemerally, with another, the reader—which was my original purpose for the project, although instead of a passionate affair with my professor, who took much too literally the term independent study, I rediscovered my mother.

My reemersion into Spanish led me, logically, to my personal fountain of knowledge, my mother; it also produced the first change in my name: I added my mother's Novoa to my father's Bruce. Sometime during the next two years I would begin introducing myself as Juan to new acquaintances. All part of sentimental ethnicity. My mother and I began, however, a more significant reorientation of both our lives when we started to read every-

thing together, a custom that continued until her death twenty-four years later. At first it arose from expediency—I needed her ability to translate instantaneously the hundreds of words my severely limited exposure to Spanish had never brought me into contact with—but over the years it engendered a closeness few people achieve with a parent. She became a colleague and even a collaborator, my proofreader, editor, commentator, and critic. Years later she would appear at my lectures and invariably question my statements or offer her own insights, sometimes deliberately contradictory to balance my perspective, like the time I was explaining José Vasconcelos's rancorous spirit as a result of his frustrated political campaigns for the Mexican presidency, and my mother raised her hand and quipped, "Pepe wasn't like that, at least not at home. He was fun and full of joy."

As I proofread this I am struck with the same objection I had when I first saw The Graduate: *How can this college student in the mid 1960s ignore Vietnam and act as if he could choose any career*

High school, Denver, Colorado, 1960

With his son, Juan Carlos,
New Haven, 1978

without having to worry about the draft? In the midst of reorienting my life, I was no exception to the panic that gripped the Class of '66 as Lyndon Johnson committed a hundred thousand troops to Vietnam during our senior year. But we, who had been weaned on World War II movies, not only believed we were doomed to serve but assumed it our duty to accept the privilege. Prevailing wisdom had it that you could wait to be drafted as a common soldier in June or join as an officer before graduation. Remember, this was before the police action degenerated into a purposeless war. There was no antiwar movement in the winter of 1966 because there was hardly yet a war. So I admit I tried to volunteer. I even passed the written exam for naval officer's training along with my best friend, Johnnie McNulty, whose portrait appears in Only the Good Times, *but I flunked the physical. I didn't even get to undress. A noncom took one look at my glasses and marched me past a long row of young men clad only in their undershorts. "Officer material," he explained to them, instilling in us all from the start a sense of distance and privilege inherent in the rank I would be*

destined for once beyond this room. He told me to remove my glasses, flipped the switch on a projector, and said to me, "Top line." Under normal conditions perhaps I could have squinted and made out the letters, but I had pulled a near all-nighter reading Unamuno with my contacts on, so my eyes were barely focusing even with glasses. "What line?" I stated more than asked. "You can't see anything?" "A circle of light." "Can I borrow these?" he asked, pointing to my glasses, and then held them to his eyes. "Yeh, they're there. Sorry," he said as he jotted a couple words on my form. Back at the recruiting office the sergeant read them. "Legally blind! Oh, well, I can get you into the marines," he added, without missing a beat. "We help each other." "No thanks," I said as I fled. Not me. If I was going in it was with my best friend to the navy or nothing. Cousin Lawrence had braved it out in hand-to-hand combat and what had it gotten him? Another relative, Aquiles Cerdán, had naively believed the Mexican Revolution would start on time and won the dubious honor of being remembered in the history books as the first casualty when he got himself killed trying to hold off the Federal Army. No, my family knew all too well the dangers of volunteering for any combat on land. Some lessons from tradition are worth remembering. I confess that that's when graduate school became more than a possibility or even a desire—it was my deferment. Over time one shuffles certain events that once seemed so important into brackets, then blocks them off to delete them from the screen . . . but they float stored in a subfile of some memory bank, biding their time.

I was not prepared for graduate study in Hispanic literatures, so right after graduation from Regis I went to Saltillo in northern Mexico for intensive courses to complete yet another major, this one in Spanish. I also went, in true immigrant fashion, back to find my roots. Had I majored in American literature perhaps I would have realized just how trite the effort was, but back then Louis Adamic was not required reading. My reception was mixed. I appeared Mexican enough to be passed over when native-speaking tutors were assigned to the summer students; the director suggested I just hang around with other Mexicans. The *Señora*, in whose house many of the female students lived, zealously guarded her charges against local Mexicans and gringos alike, but she was charmed by my old-fashioned manners and eagerness to hear her childhood memories of the Revolution. In return for listening to her recount Villa's storming of the city and much more, she granted me access to her home, including the young women's rooms. I felt quite at home. Yet, when a pair of LSU students who played for the local basketball club in the regional tournament departed without bothering to return their uniforms, my friend Chon said, "I don't understand your people." My people? A couple of years later Rosario Castellanos, the Mexican writer whom I was lucky enough to have as a visiting professor, told me of hearing the identical words from a Lacandón colleague she considered closer than a brother. One becomes what one is perceived to be and no matter how much effort is expended in pretending, the results are not entirely under our control . . . Castellanos was not an Indian nor I a Mexican, or at least not a Mexican Mexican. But in 1966 I had not come across a viable alternative, since I was not yet ready to be simply Usonian.

My faulty preparedness for graduate studies need not have worried me so much because it was overshadowed by the less than stellar preparation of my professors—with the exception of one of the old school, José de Onís, who informed me shortly after arriving at the University of Colorado in Boulder that my basic problem was that I knew nothing about Spanish literature. He was right, of course, so I proceeded to systematically read through the centuries. Working through the night was nothing new. In the past I had studied for exams and played bass at the same time, so to be free to concentrate on reading alone was a luxury. I caught up quickly, but even so my graduate education was scandalously lacking in orientation, which in turn allowed me to continue my eclectic Jesuit ways. I wrote a master's thesis on Unamuno, studied Octavio Paz and Juan Rulfo in depth, and in 1969 traveled to Mexico with a fellowship to write a dissertation on Carlos Fuentes—a fellowship that was also used to pay for our honeymoon, after marrying my steady of ten years, Mary Ann Giroux Smith, who, despite the many reasons I have given her for being otherwise, is still my wife.

When everything seemed decided and firmly in place, two unexpected events once again changed the course of my life: the discovery of a Mexican literature unknown in the United States and, simultaneously, the Chicano movement. Family connections in Mexico City facilitated meeting the top literary critics, who in turn introduced me to writers I had never heard my professors mention. They shared in common a surprising lack of the rural stereotypes predominant in the Mexican literature taught in the U.S. Their settings were urban and contemporary; their rhythms that of rock music, crowded streets, and cafe society; their concerns were no longer the grand historical myths of the Revolution but personal relationships and loving couples, although often delving into perverse zones of affection. We had much in common and some of those I met that summer have become close friends, like René Avilés Fabila and his wife Rosario Casco Montoya.

Back in Denver, Colorado, after the honeymoon, when I reread the new material with an objectivity distance allows, what impressed me most was the work of a man I had not met, Juan García Ponce, a prolific writer of short stories, novels, and essays on both literature and art. The origin of my fascination, I came to realize, was that my intellectual, artistic, and sexual wanderings coalesced in his work. The same elements reappeared, although modulated through his obsessive erotic voyeurism: phenomenology, now with a strong dose of Merleu-Ponty; the sacred, but filtered through Pavese, Musil, Blanchot, and especially Bataille; and Freud, of course, but reconceived through thinkers more attuned to sexual liberation, like Marcuse and Norma O. Brown. And once again everything focused on the essential question of the possibility of love in a society that foregrounds personal identity, which ironically raises the greatest barrier to the encounter with the other. I decided to change my dissertation topic.

García Ponce was the logical step after Unamuno and Paz, with the distinct advantage of cultivating an open and voyeuristic eroticism. He, too, knew that presence can be distant and that the word or the look can be tactile. García Ponce educated me: I set out to read not just his voluminous writings, but the complete works of anyone he mentioned in his essays. It took me three years to carry out the project, with the aid of several fellowships, including one from U.S. Steel that arrived one day by express mail and was a total surprise because I had not applied for it.

Meanwhile, at the university the great youth coalition of 1960s counterculture was fragmenting into micro-interest groups, and one element crystallized into the Chicano movement. Although I had no sympathy for the obnoxious youth who first mentioned the word to me, I discovered in the term Chicano a name for my perceived state of existence between Mexican and U.S. cultures—it was too early to understand that that state is exactly what makes me Usonian. Since we had no Chicano professors to speak of, or at least none who cared to speak to us, even a graduate student like me could play a significant role. I was drafted to act as a faculty adviser in confrontations with the administration and then to teach the first courses in Mexican-American Studies at the University of Colorado. My new-found ethnic identity was a shock to some, including close friends and family, and a threat to others who could not fit my middle-class, nonbarrio character into the image of a Chicano radical. But from the start I, too, realized an unbridgeable difference between what the militant cultural nationalists wanted to offer as an essential Chicano identity and what I represented for them. So I participated only when invited and meanwhile continued my readings into the world being opened for me by Juan García Ponce.

In 1972 I felt prepared enough to return to Mexico and begin the actual writing of the dissertation, which included plans to interview the author. Everyone counseled me against the project. García Ponce's writing, they advised, was esoteric and extremely difficult, and even harder would be trying to deal with the author. García Ponce was infamous as violently aggressive and intolerant with friends and opponents alike. Although he and José Luis Cuevas were intimate friends, when the latter once served a Mexican wine, Juan threw the bottle through Cuevas's window and stormed out. José Donoso confided to me that when he lived in Mexico García Ponce terrified him so much that he did not speak in his presence—the man had the reputation of an intellectual buzz saw. Such were the horrors I was told about him, but for some reason my reception was more than affable and our eventual relationship could only be described as close, which surprised and even angered some. He may have been flattered by my near memorization of his writing; maybe the interviews on each novel gave him the opportunity to relive them from a different perspective; or perhaps because, despite what he says, it matters to him that his readers understand his work, and even more important, live them. I don't know why we hit it off, but it was marvelous: each week Juan lectured on one of Robert Musil's works to a group of young writers—Alberto Ruy Sánchez was among them—and another two nights a week we conducted the interviews . . . we, I stress, because I met a student working on her thesis as well and we joined forces to collaborate. Eventually the experience sifted itself out into two short stories now included in *Manuscrito de origen* and several of the poems in *Inocencia perversa/Perverse Innocence.*

One more result of the trip: in deference to Juan García Ponce, I decided never to use my first name in print. It has caused confusion at times and provoked some editors to insert a first name, but I still insist there is only one Juan.

I returned to Colorado intent on finishing the dissertation, but once again I was distracted by political events at the university. The Chicano students asked me to assume the directorship of the new program, and with my fellowship expiring I needed to find some means of support, so I accepted. I endured it for over a year until I found myself in a meeting with the university's vice president, writing notes to myself asking what I was doing there. I hate administration. It consumes you. After a year I had written nothing on the dissertation and only managed a couple of short stories, some poems, and a few paintings. I did help the students put together a literary magazine, *Sirocco,* made up of six chapbook-style sections, one of which, *Homenaje a Vlady,* gathered a sampling of my poetry, fiction, song lyrics, and illustrations, but the publication only exacerbated the feeling of being trapped in an eight-to-five job as I had sworn I never would be. Finally, I took a leave of absence and finished both the dissertation and *Inocencia perversa.* The latter was accepted by Baleen Press, whose all-female editorial press had no preestablished norms for Chicano writing— they let me design the cover and bilingual layout of mirroring pages. I also published my first essays and a story with the fledgling *La Luz,* one of the first nationally distributed Latino magazines.

My publications established the outlaw position I still maintain in relationship to Chicano studies. When other Chicanos were attacking the system for excluding us from participation, I chided those same Chicanos for excluding large sectors of our own people who did not fit the militant ethno-political profile. I rejected ethnic essentialism based on characteristics tied to a culture of poverty, or on narrowly selected elements of Mexican culture, or on regionalism. I insisted on broad parameters of acceptance that were able to embrace and promote many different versions of Chicano experience, all equally valid. "Freedom of Expression and the Chicano Movement" called for allowing Chicanos to be whatever they want to be and to develop their arts in any form they desire. And when the favored expression of Chicano writing was social protest, my fiction and poetry obsessively concerned itself with personal and erotic relationships.

I never intended to be anything. I didn't plan a career; I had no such idea. I studied because school was the structure that organized our lives, and because, other than being with women, studying was what I enjoyed most: reading, thinking, and retelling it in the context of everything else you know—and to combine the two, women and studying, whenever possible, is ideal. I never dreamed anyone would pay me to do it for the rest of my life. So when the Spanish department secretary at Colorado asked me what I planned to do after receiving the Ph.D., I sincerely had no idea. I had not thought in terms of utility, but pleasure. It was April 1974, and all I knew was that I'd do anything rather than return to my position in administration. With a look of disbelief or maybe pity, the secretary handed me a publication I had never seen before: the MLA Job Listings. Of course, there was almost nothing left so late in the academic year: two positions at the University of California, Santa Cruz, and another at Yale. I hurriedly sent off my one page vitae.

Santa Cruz told me I was the top candidate for the positions in both colleges, but that was before they saw me. They were shocked by my unswarthiness, as one professor admitted, and put off by my refusal to make excuses for my interest in the "bourgeois literature of García Ponce"—I could tell they had a different definition of bourgeois, because for me they incarnated the concept. When asked at one college what I would teach besides Chicano literature, I said a course on eroticism. Someone asked if there was much eroticism in Chicano literature, to which I responded, "No, but there should be." The interview was over. At the other college they began by asking how I would teach Chicano literature. "As literature," I replied. The only member of the committee who agreed was an Asian-American student. As I was walking out a black sociologist told me, almost in a whisper, that he also agreed, but that neither the white liberals nor the Chicano militants were ready for it. I learned that the academy generally seeks specimens, not experts. Luckily they disliked me, which saved me from having to start out hamstrung by a political correctness that has only grown stronger over the years.

Yale was my only other possibility, but Emir Rodríguez Monegal, the department chair, told me it was too late for them to make an appointment; their search was closed. However, after we talked about my dissertation and mutual acquaintances in Mexico, he invited me for an interview. Ironically, in comparison to supposedly liberal

Bruce-Novoa with wife, Mary Ann, and their son, Juan Carlos, Heidelberg, Germany, 1984

California, Yale is a haven for the nonconformist. I went for a year and stayed nine.

Yale was ideal. The Chicano students, besides being uniformly brilliant and extremely talented, were from such different regional and social backgrounds that no one definition of cultural experience could impose itself as the authentic standard. After some struggle, it became our working principle to accept that anyone of Mexican heritage living permanently in the United States is Chicano and that anything he or she does is Chicano culture. And we flourished. One would have had to have been a vegetable not to notice the Chicano presence at Yale between 1974 and 1983. We had the most active center on the East Coast, with daily lunches, weekly poetry readings, monthly visiting lectures, several national conferences, and our own graphic arts collection and literary magazine, *Cambios/Phideo*. The night before we published the first issue of the magazine, we painted its name in monumental letters across the construction barriers on Old Campus Yard, the sacred heart of Yale tradition. We were a spectacle. I wrote a novel, *Mexican Illusions,* and even had the good sense not to publish it. I was an adviser to the Library of Congress, a lecturer at the Foreign Service Institute, undergraduate director of Latin American Studies, author of three books, dozens of articles, stories, and poetry, and the father of a beautiful boy, Juan Carlos, who was born in New Haven and who, like his father, assumed Yale was his playground . . . but, alas, I was without tenure. It was too good to last.

In 1983 I found myself a Fulbright professorship at the University of Mainz, West Germany, an adventure that saved me from the potentially fatal post-Yale blues. If I had to be back on the migrant circuit it might as well be in Europe. I helped organize the first of what has become the biennial conference on Latino Cultures of North America, and in Paris, working with Genevieve Fabre, founded ADECLAN (Association Pour la Diffusion et L'etude des Cultures Latines D'Amerique Du Nord), an association that tries to coordinate activities of European researchers in the field of Latino cultures in the United States. I have returned to Europe yearly to lecture and work with students, some of whom are now professors themselves.

Over the last decade I have continued to wander Stateside as well, from Santa Barbara to San Antonio and eventually to Irvine, never being fully at home anywhere. In Irvine I preferred a home without a view rather than struggle with mountains again misplaced to the northeast. Nevertheless, I behaved dutifully if somewhat mechanically, and my lecturing activity and scholarly output if anything increased. My anthology *Retrospectiva del cuento chicano* won the Fuentes Mares literary prize, an essay on Cabeza de Vaca was awarded the Plural Prize for best critical essay, my reconstruction of the original version of a landmark Mexican novel *La sombra del caudillo* was the National University of Mexico's showcase publication in 1987, the *Heath Anthology of American Literature* finally appeared after a decade of collective editing efforts, and I was invited as a visiting professor to Harvard . . . but I missed the nurturing environment we had created for ourselves at Yale, especially for creative writing—an environment strictly historical now, since, as students have informed me, it, too, disappeared from Yale in 1983.

It wasn't until I returned to Germany in 1990, on a second Fulbright, that writing began to flow naturally again. Perhaps it was my mother's death at the end of 1989—it voided any project I was working on at the time. Although I lived close by, she died so rapidly I couldn't get there in time; our last conversation was a request to go see her soon because she was afraid, and I promised I would,

but . . . Or perhaps it was the fact that I had a month with nothing to do, no telephone or even a radio, far from family and friends, in the amenable city of Erlangen where everything one needs lies in walking distance. Whatever the reason, I spent up to twenty hours a day writing what is now *Only the Good Times,* my second novel, but the first to be published, presently in press at Arte Público.

For the first time in almost a decade I wrote without thoughts getting in the way, although, ironically, my narrator can't manage to do the same. Much like me, he is a man who has let circumstances guide his life; but at least he stays closer to the subjects that matter most, refusing to compromise as much as I. The first readings from the manuscript, in Germany and Austria, went well, but back in the States mainstream publishers and agents kept telling me that they didn't see enough ethnicity in it. One told me that he had in mind something more like *Good-bye Columbus,* but Chicano. Another advised me that there is no market for middle-class Chicano characters, so I should recast my narrator as an ex-gang member from the inner city and spice it up with local color by including some of the interesting types, that is, if I wanted it to fly. He had invited me to do breakfast as we discussed the manuscript. "I like the way you incorporate film," he said. "It's good to think film, but can your people relate to these characters? [*Your people,* again!] You need characters people recognize, like these guys," and he motioned towards the waiters. "Sure," I answered, "like maybe a boxer with a drug problem, whose family fled the Mexican Revolution."

Ironically, it was Arte Público, the major Latino press, that did not insist on more ethnic content. Julián Olivares, my editor, immediately understood that the story is about sex. He appreciated the metatextual playfulness and even encouraged the use of footnotes for the editorial dialogues and the open discussion of the conflicts among the writer, the agent, and the publishers about what kind of book is being created. Now, if I can get the cover editor to do the layout the way I envision it, the game will be presented graphically—one printed title crossed out, as if by the same hand that has written in another above it—but we control so little of what eventually represents us, which, by the way, is another of the main topics of the novel.

In the end, there may be no structure to be found here, but my ancestors' images persist: tracks that pretend to retrace themselves back

Cousin Lawrence Bruce

against the unyielding monolinearity of time, the constant movement across frontiers to start anew in the name of tradition, but with a willingness to adjust, assimilate, and synthesize . . . but mostly I return to Cousin Lawrence writing against time, knowing that the part of him left behind would eventually win out over the rest, yet through his desperate text managing to survive more patently than all the rest of us who live our normal lives and disappear, imageless in our perpetual migration. When I invent myself yet another name, it will be Lawrence. Just Lawrence.

BIBLIOGRAPHY

Fiction:

Homenaje a Vlady ("Tribute to Vlady"), University of Colorado, 1973.

Manuscrito de origen ("Manuscript of origin"), Gijalbo, 1993.

Only the Good Times, Arte Público Press, 1994.

Nonfiction:

Leonardo Carrillo and others, editors, *Canto al pueblo: An Anthology of Experiences II* ("Songs to the people"), Penca, 1978.

Chicano Author: Inquiry by Interview, University of Texas Press, 1980.

Chicano Poetry: A Response to Chaos, University of Texas Press, 1982.

La literatura chicano a través de sus autores ("Chicano literature through its authors"), Siglo Veintiuno Editores, 1983.

RetroSpace: Collected Essays on Chicano Literature, Arte Público Press, 1990.

Poetry:

Inocencia perversa/Perverse Innocence, Baleen Press, 1977.

Translator:

(With David J. Parent, also author of afterword) Juan García Ponce, *Entry into Matter, Modern Literature and Reality,* Applied Literature Press, 1976.

(With Margarita Vargas) Juan García Ponce, *The House on the Beach,* University of Texas Press, 1994.

Editor:

(With J. Lawhn and R. Saldívar) *Mexico and the United States: International Relations in the Humanities,* San Antonio College, 1984.

(With Renate von Bardeleben) *Mission in Conflict: Essays on U.S.-Mexican Relations and Chicano Culture,* Gunter Narr Verlag, 1986.

Martín Luis Guzmán: "La sombra del caudillo," versión periodística (newspaper edition), Universidad Naçional Autónoma de México, 1987.

Antología retrospectiva del cuento chicano ("Retrospective anthology of Chicano short stories"), El Consejo de Población, 1988.

(With Rolando Romero) *Salvador Elizondo, Material de Lectura* (reading material), Universidad Naçional Autónoma de México, 1989.

(With Paul Lauter) *The Heath Anthology of American Literature,* Heath, 1990.

Contributor:

Felipe Ortego and David Conde, editors, *The Chicano Literary World—1974,* New Mexico Highlands University, 1975.

Teresinha Pereira, editor, *Christmas Anthology,* Backstage Book Stores, 1975.

Carmela Montalvo, editor, *El quetzal emplumece,* Mexican American Cultural Center, 1976.

Elizabeth W. Trahan, editor, *CNL-Quarterly World Report: Proceedings of CNL-MLA Meeting December 1982,* Bagehot Council, 1983.

Contributor of articles, poems, and stories to literature and ethnic studies journals and literary magazines, including *Mango, Puerto del Sol, Riversedge,* and *Xalman.* Also editor of *La Luz* and *South Western Literature.*

Matt Cohen

1942-

Our house was always filled with books. My mother always was—and still is—an avid reader of whatever she considered the latest or most interesting available fiction. My father was a self-declared "old-fashioned" scientist who loved to lecture on the rational attributes of "the scientific mind" while priding himself on his interest in the arts. He also had the insomniac's habit of staying up half the night reading novels—a trait I inherited.

There was never a time my parents' house did not contain books I wanted to read, and from an early age I was addicted to novels. In the mid-fifties there was nothing inconsistent about escaping homework by simultaneously listening to rock and roll and reading the great American and European novels of the day. In fact, the two went well together.

As a teenager I read because reading gave me windows into worlds I wanted to know—worlds I *needed* to know. I read all sorts of books but mostly fiction—including science fiction, science, and a lot of biography.

To me it seemed self-evident that the novel was the king of all book forms. I could never get enough novels. My sources were my parents' house, bookstores, and the Carnegie Library near my school. Sometimes I would baby-sit for my parents' friends' children and part of the excitement, aside from being offered more desserts than I got at home, was examining their selection of titles.

On one such expedition, when I was fourteen, I discovered *Ulysses*. It was New Year's Eve, and since the description on the cover included "unexpurgated," I picked it up expecting a *Peyton Place* type of experience. I managed to finish the book before its owners returned, and often wondered afterwards if this concentrated exposure caused some sort of syntactical short circuit.

I would read novels instead of doing my homework, read novels in class instead of listening, read novels in any spare time that presented itself.

But it never occurred to me to take up the official study of English literature. For one thing, it

"With my parents, Morris Cohen and Beatrice (Sohn) Cohen," Kingston, 1943

seemed queer to me that for a Jew—even a lazy or agnostic one like myself—to study English would be the moral equivalent of taking conversion classes.

Secondly, I think reading so many novels had made me regard fiction as a populist form. Even in high school, English classes seemed to concentrate on what was most dead in books, whereas I was interested in what was most alive.

I read American fiction, a little British fiction, European fiction in translation, and Canadian fiction. As a spectator I was most attracted to the European fiction. The part of me that liked to simultaneously read and listen to rock and roll felt most at ease with the American fiction. But I was Canadian. However, I found the Canadian fiction completely puzzling. The voice of its writers seemed to me congruent with the voices of strict and forbidding teachers. This seemed all wrong to me. The great attraction of fiction was the explosion of possibility. Yet the Canadian writers I read seemed to be saying that the least deviation from the norm would be severely punished. A nascent child of the sixties, I naturally found this moralism unappealing.

In 1969 my first novel, *Korsoniloff,* was published. A character in a later short story would eventually use his spare cash to buy up and destroy all remaining copies of his published poetry. That is approximately how I came to feel about my first novel, though I was spared the expense. At the time, the novel was assessed in two ways which I particularly remember. The first was on CBC radio. Toronto's most eminent literary journalist, William French, had been charged with the task of reviewing five novels on the same program. All were first novels and had been brought out simultaneously by the same publisher. For Canada, this was a noteworthy event. The novels, their authors, and the reviewer had been gathered together so that the occasion could be marked on the national airwaves.

"My brother Andy (on soccer ball) and I in our apartment in Cambridge, England," 1948

As is well known in publishing circles, unkind criticism of first novels is considered impolite. Therefore, after praising as he could the other four novels, Mr. French noticed mine was "of interest" and passed on.

Fate, perhaps posing in the guise of an insane antiliterary arsonist, provided the second assessment: a warehouse fire that destroyed most of the copies of my book—along with those of my fellow first novelists.

Between the date of publication and the warehouse fire, I had enjoyed being a published novelist. It was a feeling of satisfaction that lasted for a few months and was filled with fantasies about movie deals, seaside villas, and fevered all-night workouts with my trusty portable Olivetti. I was twenty-seven years old and, though I had been writing for what seemed to me a long time, I had no intentions of becoming "a writer" in the official sense of the word. Official "writers," as far as I knew—I had never actually met one—wore carefully creased grey flannels and clever little ascots tucked into their neat, white shirts. They spoke with cultivated accents and exchanged refined comments in letters which were eventually collected and published in leather-bound volumes. My own situation was a lot less formal.

When I decided to try writing a novel, my method was the following: I would type at least a page and a half each day. My hope was that when the pile got big enough, I could sort through it and find something good.

With my first published novel (only a hundred pages long) consigned to oblivion, it was time to develop other plans.

I had been living in Toronto for almost a decade. Arriving in 1960 to start university, I'd graduated in 1964 with an honours degree in political economy. I continued into graduate school, supposedly in political theory but in fact I used my scholarships to finance writing short stories—and a complicit professor even permitted me to do my master's thesis on the political thought of Albert Camus. By the time my novel went up in flames, my academic career was over, and I was embarked on a new career, as a journalistic.

Unfortunately, I had no clients. In any case, in those days Toronto was suddenly full of writers. They congregated in bars, taverns, at the race track, in restaurants where publishers or editors might buy them lunch. There were big publishers like McClelland and Stewart, and Macmillan, and there were also numerous literary presses, like Coach House Press and Anansi.

Exciting times. At least they seemed exciting to me. In the mid-sixties, after a night of doing what people did in those times, I would go out and walk the streets as the sun came up. The brick fronts of Toronto houses had been painted a wide variety of colours by the waves of European immigrants then coming into the city. Greens, reds, purples all glowed with the rising sun, and in this weird and riotous morning rainbow I would feel full of promise and good luck.

But by the end of the decade the city had somehow lost its lustre for me. My girlfriend and I spread out a map of Ontario and began thinking about where we might like to live. Weekends we would drive out to the country to look at farms and cottages for rent. One day my birth certificate happened to fall out of my wallet. I had been born in Kingston, Ontario, and, I now noticed for the first time, Kingston is in Frontenac County, a rugged infertile agricultural outback that shoots north from Kingston on Lake Ontario to piney lake country in the pre-Cambrian shield.

A few months later we were sitting in an unfurnished farmhouse whose previous owners had left a new layer of brown wrapping paper on the kitchen floor. The house was in Frontenac County—which I have since renamed Reality. There was a well in the front yard, an outhouse on the far side of the barn, a couple of feet of water in the basement.

I was not yet thirty years old. Aside from my novel I had a few unfinished manuscripts waiting for a stroke of genius, a Ping-Pong table, a chain saw, a car I'd bought during a year of teaching. I also had several cartons of books that were supposed to turn into the Ph.D. thesis I still pretended to believe I would write.

We were in an area that seemed to have little need for journalism. I did go speak to someone at the *Kingston Whig Standard*, but when they offered me fifteen dollars an article, to be submitted on spec, I decided to accept an alternative form of employment: a local carpenter, who thought I must be a hippie because of my long sideburns, offered to hire me as his "assistant." My job would be to do whatever he told me.

I met this carpenter in a strange way.

We moved into the house in May. Because of the season we hadn't thought about heat, but when the sun went down it got chilly. By the time morning came, the house was freezing. In the basement was a wood furnace, handily raised

Matt at seven

above the water, and a pile of wood. Using my Ottawa Valley boy-scout background, I started a fire. But the house was big and the fire seemed small. Not having had previous experience with wood furnaces, I kept throwing on more wood. By noon the house was extremely hot. The exposed stovepipes had turned red. We began to be afraid we were going to burn the house down.

I ran out to the front, pumped a bucket of water from the well, trundled it down the basement stairs, and threw it on the fire. There was a mighty hissing but the fire continued. I then remembered another scouting lesson. I grabbed a shovel, filled a bucket with earth, then threw *it* on the fire.

This worked. The fire went out. Soon instead of having a fire we had huge clouds of smoke coming out the chimney.

My future employer, the carpenter, was driving by and saw smoke rising from the house where the city people had moved in. He waded down to the basement to see how cleverly I'd handled the situation. Probably that was when he decided I would be a good man to hire.

Rituals of Acceptance

One Hallowe'en night the telephone rang at four in the morning. "Fire!" announced a neighbour's voice. By the time I had pulled on my jeans and work boots, a truck was idling in the driveway. I jumped in. A few minutes later we had pulled up in front of a long-vacant house a couple of miles away. A ring of trucks surrounded the house, their headlights shining towards the fire. We stood in front of the trucks and drank rye while the house was consumed. The temperature was just above freezing, but the fire kept us agreeably warm. Some of the men had brought picks and shovels, there were also axes and a chain saw—but there were no trees near the house, it was too late in the year for the grass to burn, and the few nearby bushes were simply thrown into the flames.

The next morning I drove back to see what would be left. Everything wooden had burned, but the stamp-patterned tin from the ceilings was still intact: it was lying in the stone foundation, the paint burned off.

Tin and stone—they were the typical leftovers from fires. The foundation stones were squared chunks of granite. With my hand against them, I could still feel the warmth of the fire. The house and its foundation would have been a little more than a hundred years old, built in the 1850s or 1860s, when the area was settled by Scots or Irish too unlucky to have gotten land grants in more fertile areas of the province. Standing in the midst of that foundation, I couldn't help noticing that there was a lot of stone—and a lot of carrying, splitting, and lifting—for the amount of space it had managed to surround.

*

Another night phone call: it is January, minus thirty. A neighbour's cow is stuck in a field. The cow had been trying, unsuccessfully, to have a calf in a barn far from the house. The neighbour decided that the cow was in so much difficulty, she should be brought to the heated barn beside his own house. But snow had made the road between the barns impassable, and the cow, weakened and in labour, could not be led across the fields, which were hilly and slick with ice. The neighbour had

had the brilliant idea of rolling the cow onto a piece of plywood, which he would use as a toboggan to slide the animal across the ice.

This might seem an impossible feat of strength—in fact it was, though the same neighbour once observing me with a shovel and planks trying to get my car out of a ditch just lifted it onto the road.

Eventually a small group of us ended up pushing and sliding the cow-laden plywood to the home barn. It was a brilliant night, half a moon made the icy hummocks of the field glisten, and you could smell the woodsmoke from the fires of the farmhouses. For a while we could hear the cow heaving, then it was only our own panting.

That summer I went into the beef business with my ex-carpenter employer. The idea was to buy steers or cows in calf at sale barns, pasture them on our farm, then sell them in the fall. As our capital was limited, we ended up spending almost as much on penicillin as cattle. But cattle don't like needles any more than people, so we became quite expert at veterinarian hockey: one of us would body check a cow into the corner of a stall—then, while it was temporarily immobile, the other would plunge the penicillin home.

*

Meanwhile I was observing all these cows. I realized that in their social behaviour they were exactly like people except that, being stupider, they went through everything in slow motion. This was ideal for me since I'd never quite figured things out in fast motion.

With my new insights into human behaviour that I gleaned from watching cows, I was writing fast. In a period of less than a year I finished my second novel, rewrote a book of short stories, wrote another novel. The second novel, the hallucinogenic story of a fictional Ottawa Valley rock star who named himself after a popular breakfast cereal, was well received by both critics and warehouse. But my editor and publisher were split about the new one—the story of a group of painters in downtown Toronto. Instead of revising it, I suggested I start on another. This eventually became *The Disinherited,* a novel I ended up writing while mostly in bed, in a third-floor apartment in Toronto whose eaves were so slanted I had to sit down to cook or go to the bathroom.

When I finished the first draft of *The Disinherited,* I went out to the West Coast for almost a year.

Then I returned to the farm, finished a new novel, *Wooden Hunters,* ran out of money, accepted a one-year post as writer-in-residence at the University of Alberta in Edmonton. Edmonton was supposed, in contrast to rural Canada, to provide an urban experience. However, I spent most of my time behind a desk, typing. There I wrote *The Colours of War* but failed to discover downtown Edmonton.

I did, however, have the essential urban experience: my personal life fell apart. This meant, among other things, that when the year in Edmonton was over, I wouldn't be going back to the farm.

After a brief stint in Toronto, which did have a downtown I could find—featuring, in my case, a lot of opportunities to play pick-up basketball and the odd chance to resume my nonexistent career as a journalist—I went to England for a year. There, for the first time since I'd started writing my first novel, I excused myself from the daily fiction quota. This lasted only a few months, but was, I suppose, the first major recognition on my part that I might have written myself so deeply into a rut that, rather than being able to write myself out the other side, I might have to stop and actually decide what I was going to write.

This idea ran contrary to my thoughts about writing. I had always believed in proceeding according to instinct. While my writing seldom approached stream-of-consciousness, my basic theory, at least for myself, was that the best thing to do was simply to sit down and type—and then worry afterwards about what was good. The alternative—deciding what to write on the basis of theme, subject, symbols, etc.—made fiction seem like an academic exercise best performed by critics. At the time this seemed absurd, but of course since then critics have revised their ideas of criticism and now dominate what used to be their subject matter.

One of the best things that happened to me during my time in England was that I got tired of the food and the cold—this was the last winter before Thatcher's election and everyone was depressed in every way—and decided to spend a month in Paris. Once there—my first time back since I'd spent a month there at the age of twenty-one, supposedly researching my thesis on Albert Camus—I realized this was a necessary location. I tried to understand French, wandered about, generally enjoyed the sensation of sinking into the most congenial of cities for threadbare and footloose writers.

"When I was starting to write," 1968

The Disinherited (1974) was the first of four novels centred around the fictional town of Salem. The others were *The Colours of War* (1977), *The Sweet Second Summer of Kitty Malone* (1979), and *Flowers of Darkness* (1981). By the time I got to *Flowers of Darkness* I was back from England and, thanks to a couple of ghost-writing jobs, living on another farm—or at least an abandoned farm, a marshy tract of land, still in Frontenac County, with a log cabin I was finishing myself and a huge beaver pond. I wrote *Flowers of Darkness* during a summer heat wave—it is a nightmarish gothic book, and during the time I was writing it I would shake off the terror it inspired by going out at midnight and jogging down the deserted dirt roads through clouds of rolling mist.

Others would have found it unpleasantly hot but I didn't. That was because I had spent the previous winter living in my cabin without electricity, telephone or a furnace. All I had for heating was a wood stove so inefficient that the bucket of water in the cabin would have a layer of ice in the morning. For various reasons I found this all quite perfect, but I wasn't necessarily eager to repeat it.

In the summer of 1979, electricity and telephone were installed, and I replaced the old wood heater with an efficient airtight stove. I had a truck, somewhat dilapidated but operational. I had no mortgage and absolutely no savings. My only employment was writing book reviews at eighty-five dollars each for Ken Kilpatrick of the *Hamilton Spectator*. He must have suspected he was supporting me—he certainly allowed me to review a lot of books.

One day I was sitting among my two-by-fours wondering how I would buy the material to make walls when the telephone rang. Thinking it was another book review on the way, I tried to calculate how many times I would have to multiply eighty-five dollars to finish my house. In fact, the call was from the University of Victoria, offering me a one-year job teaching creative writing. Whoever had been intended to fill the position must have changed his or her mind, because it was only two weeks from the start of classes. But I had just finished my novel, I had friends in Victoria, which was only a few thousand miles away, and I would be paid. They even offered to send me gas money. I decided I was very available.

I set out for Victoria in September 1979. The third of the Salem novels—*The Sweet Second Summer of Kitty Malone*—had just been published, and I had just finished a first draft of the fourth. During

"At the farm, trying to learn to wear my hat straight," 1971

the 1970s I had written six novels, two books of short stories, two books for children.

The thoughts I'd had during the intermission from writing in England now returned. Just before starting *Flowers of Darkness,* I'd gone to my publisher—Jack McClelland of McClelland and Stewart—and he'd asked me if I could "go back to the well one more time." With this last book it seemed to me that that's what I'd done. Although on the surface the book was better constructed and written than any of my others, I felt that I had exhausted the source. Not only that, but the actual movement of the novels had reflected a change in the countryside. I had begun the cycle typing blindly, as I believed suitable, but over almost a decade I'd become aware that the novels were not only portrayals of various individuals and families, but also of the changing relationship between people and the land, a portrayal of the way that relationship evolved as more and more technology—from tractors to milking machines—became available to the farmers, and then evolved again as the landscape was transformed from one which was entirely rural and the centre of its own universe, one in which each man had to wrest his living from the physical ground, to one in which all countryside was the hinterland of the ever-encroaching city.

I could have kept on writing this series of novels indefinitely. I would imagine myself, old and hoary, a sort of minor league Tolstoy with my dozens of books all about the same thing—the official guardian of my own museum. This wasn't too appealing. Having grown up in Ottawa, a civil service town, I had no desire to become the civil servant in charge of keeping my own writing in line.

On the other hand, I had no other plans. So, it seemed to me, a year of being paid to teach during which I would see old friends and read a few books while I reflected on all this was probably a good idea. To prevent recidivism, I wrote a preface to *Flowers of Darkness* saying that it would be the last of the Salem novels. I hoped this public promise would be difficult to break.

Victoria is at the southern tip of Vancouver Island. As well as being the Canadian city with the best weather—and therefore, outside of Florida, Canada's most sought-after retirement destination—it has always had a lively literary life. When I arrived, while waiting for the apartment I'd arranged to rent to be ready to occupy, I stayed in the ocean-side guest cabin of a friend. These friends had a dog called Georgie. Since I was quite restless from having just driven across the country, and since I was otherwise dogless because I'd decided my own dog, an incredibly intelligent Border collie called Teddy, would be better off staying in the country with neighbours than trying to adapt to apartment life, Georgie accompanied me on many walks those first couple of weeks.

My friends' establishment was near the Sooke ferry landing. Every night, an hour or two before midnight, Georgie and I would set out. The smell of cedar, the wind off the waves, the occasional sound of a ferry horn, the rustle of deer in the underbrush. One night Georgie and I were out walking in the rain. We passed a break in the trees and through the blackness, shining across the water, came a weak yellow light. I could see Georgie's silhouette against the sky, the jagged outline of trees, hear the sound of waves breaking on the rocky shore. Suddenly I found myself thinking about how strange it would have been to be a Jew, a doctor, fleeing across Europe hundreds of years ago. Someone alone and in flight, however not in a society like our own where moving is as easy as driving your truck or car a few thousand miles and borrowing a friend's dog to take a walk, but in a situation where once outside your own enclave you are irrevocably a stranger and outsider.

This doctor, it seemed to me, would have come from Spain, where Jewish civilization peaked in the early Middle Ages; he would have been educated in one of those Jewish universities in Cordova or Toledo, someone who could neither fit into his own community nor any other, someone whose ideas of science had somehow set him apart from the way others thought and made him, unconsciously, a precursor of the Renaissance: one of those men and women who—because of the particular details of their lives—were put outside the received ideas of the world at that time and found themselves unable to take for granted what everyone else blindly believed.

While I stood on the road, looking at the water, the entire plot of a medieval historical novel came into my mind. The doctor, from Spain, would be going east—against the current of the Renaissance which moved west—therefore in the span of his own lifetime he would cut across the whole change of the Renaissance, two centuries of history. All four of my grandparents were from Russia and, as I imagined the doctor moving east, I saw him going finally into the heart of the old world, Russia, a mythic tangle which existed in my

imagination without my really knowing anything about it.

I kept walking. When I got back to the cabin I wrote down the outline of the novel. The next day I started teaching.

I was still revising and reworking *Flowers of Darkness,* but every now and then I would tinker with the outline. I didn't think of the prospective book as one for me—after all, I was a person who wrote contemporary experimental novels of alienation, etc., but I couldn't help filling in the outline as an exercise. Then one day, a couple of months later, I decided to make a list of everything required to write the novel. Research, first of all. This would mean going to Europe and following the probable course of the doctor. The main European centres of medical knowledge were in Spain, France, and Italy. Were I to follow him to these places, I'd have to learn enough of each of these languages to do research.

My French was very poor. I knew no Italian and, although I'd used some high school Latin to pass a laughable second language exam in Spanish for graduate studies, I could not remember a single Spanish word.

Fortunately, fate had offered, in addition to what otherwise might have been an impossible project, an ideal travelling companion, whose first language just happened to be Spanish. That summer we found ourselves in Toledo, staying in a hotel which was a reconstructed Cardinal's palace. I started having the dreams of the main character, Avram Halevi. I decided that even if the novel was hopeless, the research would provide me with an education.

When I came back from Toledo, I started reading more intensively and also taking French classes. The following spring I went to Bologna, Italy—the site of Italy's oldest and most open medical school. The huge cathedral was still in place, though surrounding it, instead of the brothels which used to serve as student residences during the time of my novel, were hotels and boutiques. After Bologna I went to Montpellier, a city in the south of France renowned for having been a university town since the thirteenth century and having Europe's oldest medical school. I spent my days in the municipal library, which had a huge collection of books about the city in that era.

From being in Victoria wondering how I would get to Europe, I had moved to the point where I spent three days in France reading an account, in Portuguese, of a travelling fair. I was getting, in a permanent way, the kind of spinning

"Typing for the camera while working on Sweet Second Summer of Kitty Malone," Toronto, 1977

sensation I'd first experienced on an afternoon walk in the north Ontario bush when, in the midst of some hilly birch-covered terrain, I looked up at the sky only to discover that, although I could see the sun, I'd forgotten to note in which direction I should be walking in order to return to the car. On that occasion I was saved by a set of hydro wires over the next rise.

From the Montpellier situation, however, I've never returned to my original bearings—whatever they were.

I *did* stop reading—of which I'm not sure I understood a word. I came back to Canada with a suitcase full of notes and books. Gradually over a two-year period these became a novel, *The Spanish Doctor*. Unlike any of my other novels, my publishers believed this would be a great commercial hit and, relatively speaking, it has been. However, this was initially obscured by the fact that my father died on the day it was first published, and on the day of his funeral large and scathing reviews were published in Canada's two biggest newspapers.

All things considered, when my companion reverted to her traveling mentality, suggesting she use a forthcoming maternity leave as an excuse for us to go live in Paris for a year, I found it an excellent idea. The critics of *The Spanish Doctor*—and there were many—had suggested I was deserting my talent by writing about something other than rural Ontario. Since many of the same critics had ten years before accused me of deserting my talent by writing about rural Ontario instead of writing experimental short stories, their advice alone would have been good reason to go to Paris.

But, in fact, I had other motivations. After fifteen years in the hothouse scene of Canadian letters, I was ready for a substantial change. It was true that I had been lucky enough to begin writing and publishing at the very moment when Canadian literature—at least quantitatively—was taking its great leap forward. Until the late sixties, although there were some excellent Canadian publishers, most fiction published in Canada had also to be co-published, for financial reasons, in either New York or London. But coinciding with the surge of Canadian cultural nationalism in the late sixties—a surge not unrelated to anti-American sentiments brought on by the war in Vietnam—were technological advances that made it possible for fiction printed in shorter runs to be economically viable.

By the late sixties numerous literary presses—House of Anansi Press, the Coach House Press, and Talon Books are just some of the most obvious and most enduring—had been established across the country. Each year brought new writers into print. Previously established writers, too—writers like Ernest Buckler, Margaret Laurence, Hugh Garner, Morley Callaghan, Sinclair Ross, Ethel Wilson—found a new generation of readers.

The audience for Canadian books was so avid that public readings in universities, bookstores, libraries, art galleries, venues of all kinds became popular across the country. I gave my first public reading surrounded by totem poles at the Royal Ontario Museum. They still rank among my most attentive listeners though, in the years that followed, I gave hundreds of other readings. These readings were a great way to meet audiences, sell books—but, most of all, to learn about the country.

Along with the new books and new readers came new organizations. The Writers' Union of Canada—of which I was a founding member—held its first national meeting in 1972, after a year of preliminary get-togethers in which awestruck newcomers like myself got to meet and learn from figures who had been hitherto mythic. One of the first goals of the Writers' Union was to obtain Public Lending Right—compensation for books held in libraries. The year I was chairman of the union, following a stint as vice-chairman, was the year we were finally able to get a government commitment—and funding—for that program.

But to me it seemed that unlike the 1970s, the 1980s were not so much a time of cultural blossoming as of business activity. Publishing, in Canada as in other countries, had to bend to the prevailing economic winds. The success of big business and the fact that it was able, for the first time in at least my memory, to install the corporate ethic in the public mind meant that people working in publishing houses and in the cultural sector seemed to find it perfectly normal to judge books by their economic potential. "Every book a profit centre" became the rallying cry of publishing—even though this idea was at best a futile hope and at worst a very destructive demand. After all, poetry books don't make profits. And if the

The cabin under construction in "Reality,"
Frontenac County, Ontario, Canada, 1978

occasional literary or first novel does break out for the best-seller lists, it's still true that most books do well to break even.

But there were profits to be made in publishing. Publishing companies were being bought and sold in London and New York, and this had a tremendous impact on Canada for two reasons. Firstly, because publishing in Canada—though not necessarily the publishing of Canadian books—is dominated by foreign-owned firms. As these companies expanded in the eighties they often expanded their lists of Canadian books—creating new opportunities for many writers but also changing the climate of the publishing of Canadian books and preparing the way for the collapse when they got out of Canadian books at the end of the decade.

Secondly, Canadian companies themselves went through changes of ownership for the same reasons. Often this ended in disaster—as when one highly respected small company, Lester and Orpen Dennys (who happened to be my publisher), was forced into bankruptcy following a series of ownership changes that left it as a small company held by a merchant banking group who had larger losses on their minds. Many other reputable houses also went bankrupt—others were saved by mergers, then "restructured" into hollow shells.

By the time we left for our year in Paris, this process was already under way. Besides, following my research for *The Spanish Doctor,* I had continued going to Europe as frequently as possible. For two months I had been visiting professor at the University of Bologna in Italy. I'd also spent over a month in Paris, fortunately one during which the franc was at a historic low, researching a new novel. It was a period, perhaps one which still continues, when I was comfortable anywhere and nowhere. The Canada for which I'd had such optimistic hopes during the sixties and seventies had evolved into a fractionated country whose government and business class was trying to finance itself by selling the country's birthright—if only it could discover what it was and who might be interested in buying it. (Interestingly, many of the most prominent of this group are now either dragging their giant companies into bankruptcy, or hastily retiring from public office in order to avoid the forthcoming election.)

The new novel, *Nadine,* was the story of a woman's attempt to reconstruct herself—both physically and psychologically—after throwing herself on top of a terrorist's grenade in front of a

Jerusalem hotel. Nadine had been born of Jewish parents during the Nazi occupation of Paris, then left in the care of her aunt while her parents tried to flee.

This was in all respects a difficult novel for me to write. When we arrived in Paris for our year, it seemed to me obvious I should turn away from difficult psychological novels like *Nadine,* or controversial historical novels like *The Spanish Doctor.*

Now, it seemed to me as I strolled the streets of the City of Light, was the ideal moment for me to become someone else and write a truly commercial novel, one which would make my children grateful. All I needed was another name and the right novel.

In those early weeks many names sprung to mind, but the novel itself was slower in arriving. I knew what was necessary: a spy novel featuring the decaying Soviet empire. My only problems were that I knew nothing about Russia, spy novels, or even how to write a novel with plot.

Meanwhile our family life was complex and crowded. It was a situation of two adults, two teenagers, a four-year-old, and a baby crammed into a very small three-bedroom apartment in the seventh arrondissement.

The view out was spectacular: from our balconies we could see the Eiffel Tower and the Invalides. Inside, things were a little more squalid. The baby slept in the windowless closet of the "master" bedroom—a room which would have been big enough to walk around in had it not had to contain our bed, a horsehair monstrosity that must have contained the remains of Napoleon's cavalry. The second bedroom was occupied by our teenage son. Faced with the trauma of attending a bilingual school, he was coping by making American friends and learning how to drink beer and discuss the NFL. The third bedroom was occupied by our teenage daughter and our four year old. The teenage daughter became bilingual in about fifteen minutes while the rest of us struggled. I placed the four-year-old boy, who knew no French, in a local school. In the yard, while the teachers smoked cigarettes, the children practiced karate. Remembering a similar experience inflicted on me when I was a child spending a year in Cambridge, I actually removed my son from this school, much to the astonishment of the teachers who apparently felt this was the way for foreigners to learn, and put him in a Montessori school where he learned to sort blocks, dress impeccably, and speak with a perfect Parisian accent.

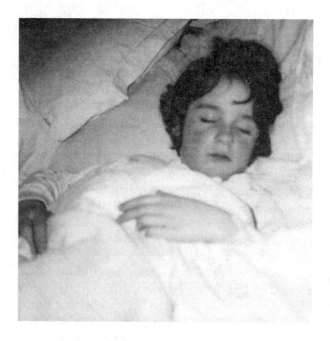

"Daughter, Madeleine, looking angelic . . . ,"
1992

All of this kept the apartment busy. In order to make time for ourselves, my wife and I hired a nanny to take care of our baby. But the baby hated her, which meant that we had to stay home and baby-sit for both of them.

At first I didn't mind all this. I thought it would help inspire my novel, which was going nowhere. Then I got desperate. Finally we decided to get rid of the baby-sitter and split the duties between us. With some of the money saved, I rented what was called a "maid's room." Here, perched in a tiny cell on the seventh floor of an apartment building near the Champ-de-Mars, I would retreat after my child-care stints to write the great commercial success.

I invented an incredibly violent British lady detective who chewed toffee while committing grisly deeds in the name of the Queen. Could I help it if she looked exactly like the hated grade one teacher I'd had in England? I gave her a walk-up in Hampstead and an unsavoury boyfriend. Of course, she was brought on assignment to Paris. I put her in a bad hotel and had her chasing various suspicious characters around the various streets I walked every day.

At Christmas it snowed in Paris. Our fashionably located apartment was not equipped for cold weather. It was necessary for each person to take two baths a day in order to keep their core body temperature high enough to prevent hypothermia. The plumbing burst and the bathtub began to drain into the courtyard. This was embarrassing. By this time I had over a hundred pages. The cold snap seemed to last until Easter. By the time we fled Paris for a month in the south—in March—I had half a blockbuster.

In Provence it was warm. We found a tiny stone house to which we have returned compulsively ever since. In that stone house, sixteen months later, in the midst of an incredible August heat wave, I finished the first draft of the novel that was to have made me millions.

My wife and I had a bottle of wine to celebrate, then I made her read it. Then I read it. Fortunately, during the time I was writing the novel, I had also written other stories and articles. Some of the stories were collected in *Living on Water*. Others became the basis for a satiric novella composed of three linked stories about expatriates in Paris, *Freud: The Paris Notebooks*. Thus, when I threw my blockbuster in the garbage, I didn't have to think I'd entirely wasted the past two years.

Writing the blockbuster—although it was actually only a mere 550 pages long—was probably the closest I have come to achieving wealth and worldwide fame. The good part is that I got to walk around Paris, eat terrific food, drink great wine, and sit in cafés absolutely convinced my novel was going to be an explosive success. "This is it," I would say to myself. For once I was right. That was it.

Returned to the real world of Toronto and my wife's job here, I managed to salvage a few pages from the blockbuster and ended up with *Emotional Arithmetic,* a novel which is linked to *Nadine*. The novel, in its final form, began from a single image: I was looking through some photographs I'd accumulated during the writing of *Nadine* and included amongst them was one of a group of Jews being boarded on a train destined for Auschwitz. It was late in the war, and there was no doubt that the prisoners knew where they were going and the fate that awaited them. One man, as he was climbing onto the train, had turned his head to look at the camera.

At the particular moment I was re-inspecting this photograph, it occurred to me that this man, a man whose name I could never know, was aware both that he was looking at a camera and that, by looking at the camera, he was looking at someone—like myself—who would one day look back at him. There he was, going off to his death while

I, forty years later and comfortably ensconced in my office, was watching.

What, he must have wondered, would someone in what to him would be the unknowable future think of his or her fellow human beings being loaded into cattle cars and sent off to die?

Looking at this picture, it seemed to me I was being subpoenaed as a witness to this event.

I began reading more about the German occupation of France, Drancy—the internment camp where Jews were kept before being sent off—the conditions of life in Paris and Vichy France during the Second World War.

I had no desire to write a history of this period—excellent accounts already existed. What was required of me, by the image I could not shake, was to somehow imaginatively live through and recreate the situation.

Emotional Arithmetic was the result—a book which finally took me four years to write and which still haunts me—even in the literal sense that I am currently writing a screenplay based on it.

"Son, Daniel, looking mischievous . . . ,"
1992

For those of us whose ancestors—or who ourselves—came from places which have been destroyed by catastrophes of war, technology, events too numerous to list, the past is unreclaimable in almost every sense. But, though we can't claim it, it claims us.

My generation has lived most of its life in the shadow of the Second World War. Even though new crises may now dominate the world, that war's shadow—at least for me—has never entirely dissipated. On the other hand, so much time has passed, and the visible focus of history has moved to so many other parts of the world, that I now realize my own growing up is not so much a universal experience as one in many ways typical. We live in a time when increasing numbers of individuals are refugees from gigantic situations they can never fully understand, let alone resolve. Living in the present and looking forward, instead of being dominated by all the terrible things that have happened in the past, has become an almost impossible challenge for hundreds of millions of people.

It is hard not to think we are entering into one of those turbulent historical periods during which so much will be remade that our grandchildren will look back upon our era just as we, as schoolchildren, looked back on the dimly lit nineteenth century.

I once read somewhere that autobiographies should be written either by people who are just commencing their lives as adults, or those who have attained the maturity and wisdom adult life has to offer.

This seems to me an excellent rule, though unfortunately I am not in either of these situations.

The novel I have just finished, *The Bookseller,* is the fictional memoir of a man in just this position. Looking both backwards and forwards at the same time, he is forced to the inconclusive conclusion that while he may now rewrite and interpret his past, he must still devote most of his energies to considering the future. Meanwhile, as he says, "I am willing to believe anything. I am even willing to believe that the night which is coming is only an ordinary night, a night like other nights, a night to be followed by a day like other days. A day during which the entire universe could hinge on a cough, a sigh, a book opened at a random page, the first person who walks through the door."

"Parents, looking exhausted"—Matt Cohen with his wife, Patricia Aldana, 1992

BIBLIOGRAPHY

Fiction:

Korsoniloff, Anansi, 1969.

Johnny Crackle Sings, McClelland & Stewart (Toronto), 1971.

Too Bad Galahad (for children; illustrated by Margaret Hathaway), Coach House Press, 1972.

The Disinherited, McClelland & Stewart, 1974, Penguin Books (London), 1987.

Wooden Hunters, McClelland & Stewart, 1975.

The Colours of War, McClelland & Stewart, 1977, Methuen (New York), 1977, Penguin Books, 1987.

The Leaves of Louise (for children; illustrated by Rikki), McClelland & Stewart, 1978.

The Sweet Second Summer of Kitty Malone, McClelland & Stewart, 1979, Penguin Books, 1987.

Flowers of Darkness, McClelland & Stewart, 1981, Penguin Books, 1987.

The Spanish Doctor, McClelland & Stewart, 1984, Beaufort (New York), 1984, Penguin Books, 1985.

Nadine, Viking (Toronto and London), 1986, Crown (New York), 1987.

Emotional Arithmetic, Lester & Orpen Dennys, 1990.

The Bookseller, Knopf, 1993.

Short-story collections:

Columbus and the Fat Lady and Other Stories, Anansi, 1972.

Night Flights: Stories New and Selected, Doubleday, 1978.

The Expatriate, General (Toronto), 1982, Beaufort, 1983.

Café le dog, McClelland & Stewart, 1983, Penguin Books, 1985, published as *Life on This Planet and Other Stories,* Beaufort, 1985.

Living on Water, Viking (Toronto and New York), 1988, (London), 1989.

Freud: The Paris Notebooks, Quarry, 1991.

Poetry:

Peach Melba, Coach House Press, 1974.

In Search of Leonardo (illustrated by Tony Urquhart), Coach House Press, 1985.

Other:

(Editor) *The Story So Far 2,* Coach House Press, 1973.

(Editor with David Young) *The Dream Class Anthology: Writings from Toronto High Schools,* Coach House Press, 1983.

(Editor with Wayne Grady) *Intimate Strangers: New Stories from Quebec,* Penguin Books (Toronto and London), 1986, (New York), 1987.

(Translator) Gaétan Brulotte, *The Secret Voice,* Porcupine's Quill, 1990.

Cohen's manuscripts are collected in the Mills Memorial Library at McMaster University.

Aaron Elkins

1935-

Aaron Elkins in his workroom, 1992

My father, Irving Abraham Elkins, came to America from Minsk in 1911, when he was twenty-one.

Or maybe it was Pinsk. Possibly he was nineteen, not twenty-one, at the time, and it may well be that his actual year of immigration was 1909, when he was seventeen (or nineteen).

This is by way of saying that I may have a little trouble with this essay. A bent for candid, straightforward autobiography is not part of my heritage. It certainly wasn't that I never asked Dad about his early life. I asked him, all right; I just got different answers, or more often, a flap of the hand, a shrug, and a bemused "What do you want to know that stuff for?" All frequently without looking up from his after-dinner New York *Daily News* or *Daily Forward*.

In the thirties and forties, immigrants were still looking ahead, not back. America was all-important, the Old Country was something to forget as thoroughly as possible. Besides, it wasn't a good idea to talk too much, especially if you were not just an immigrant but a Jewish immigrant. American anti-Semitism, taking life from Hitler's successes, was thriving. The proudly pro-Nazi German-American Bund was holding mass rallies in Madison Square Garden, the Christian Front had "Buy Christian" as its slogan and was mounting a boycott of Jewish businesses, and the vicious Father Charles Coughlin, perhaps the most popu-

Aaron with his mother, Long Island,
New York, about 1937

cossacks, the wretched poverty. A grown-up without an accent was something you noticed. Throughout my young life I envied my friend Lyle, whose father could talk so knowledgeably about the Dodgers and the Giants, and who spoke—and walked, and laughed—like a native-born American. (He wasn't.)

Whatever Dad did before he left Minsk (Pinsk?), I never did learn. He must have gone to school, because he could read and write and do numbers. Here in America, he worked as a machinist at the Brooklyn Navy Yard while I was growing up and, when he could, he puttered away at inventions that were bound to make us rich someday. Some of them he patented. The story was that, years before, he had invented the bicycle coaster brake and sold it for four hundred dollars to Schwinn, who made millions with it. I don't know if it's true or not. The inventions I do remember were less exciting. There was a question-and-answer game called The Wise Old Owl, in which a cutout of a (surprise) wise, old owl was manipulated to point with its beak at answers to hundreds of educational questions about arithmetic, geography, history, and spelling. He really believed kids would go wild for it. He was working the night shift at the Navy Yard at the time, and for months he spent his weary days walking all over New York City with an increasingly beat-up cardboard prototype, carrying it to every Woolworth's and Kresge, trying to get them interested. You can imagine how they queued up for it.

And then there was the Elkins Handy Holdall, another winner. I was eleven or twelve then, and I remember it more clearly than any of the others because on many a grim weekend, while my friends were out in the sunny streets—I could hear their shouts and laughter—I was at a makeshift wooden contraption in our storefront apartment, sulkily working the foot treadle that stapled strong, flat rubber bands to glossy, 8½-by-11-inch photographs of neatly arranged pens, pencils, rulers, and compasses. Protractors too, I think. That's what the Elkins Handy Holdall was: a colored photograph of school implements on cardboard, punched with three holes along one side so that it could be inserted at the front of a loose-leaf notebook. The rubber bands were designed to make pockets into which you were supposed to stick your otherwise hard-to-carry implements. The ruler went right over the picture of the ruler, the pencil went where the pencil photograph was, and so on. Children would no longer have to carry ruler boxes.

lar radio personality in America, was spouting out-and-out anti-Semitism to enthusiastic radio audiences nationwide. No, you never knew what the future held, you never knew what *they* could use against you. Roosevelt was wonderful, but every American wasn't Roosevelt. It happened in Russia, it happened in Germany, it could happen here.

And so they learned to muddy the waters, to obscure their pasts, to cover their tracks, and after a while it became a habit. And then they found they couldn't get the facts straight themselves anymore. At least I think that's the way it worked. In any case, the upshot was prevarication, gaps, holes, and "What do you want to know that stuff for?"

It wasn't any different with my friends' fathers. In the Brooklyn of the 1940s, in the six-story tenements on Blake Avenue and Amboy Street, everybody's parents were immigrants, or so it seemed to me then (and seems to me now). We were all the children of foreigners who had fled from Eastern Europe to escape the pogroms, the

Dad was so sure he was going to make it big with this one that he borrowed a thousand dollars on it from Mr. Goldberg, the tailor across the street, so that he could hire someone to help him peddle it to the stores. He advertised for a salesman in the *New York Times*, as I recall, and those had to have been tough times for salesmen, because we must have gotten fifty responses—confident, bragging letters, lists of references, three-page resumes (and these were the days before Xerox)—all in hopes of what was manifestly a shabby, scrambling, footslogging job. Most were handwritten. Many were from other immigrants.

I can remember Dad sitting at the kitchen table with a dozen letters spread out in front of him, slowly shaking his head. I thought he was having a hard time picking his man, but it wasn't that at all.

"Oy, *kinder*," he said, and he really sounded sad, "I wish I could give you all a job."

I spent a lot of miserable weekends stapling those things, and Dad worked himself to exhaustion with them, and I suppose the salesman—a red-faced man named Jake who smelled of cloves and looked like a salesman—did his best. A few stationery stores accepted some, and Jake actually talked Woolworth into taking a few gross on consignment (what a day that was). But of course the customers wouldn't buy it in the stores, and the thing went bust.

I remember that it took a long time to pay back Mr. Goldberg, and that Mom was bitter over it and Dad was depressed, and I think that was the end of his career as an inventor.

But I remember a success story too. This was a little earlier, during the Second World War, when he developed a mechanism to safely jettison a burning airplane engine. The Navy had no use for it, so he offered it to the Army Air Force and received a gold-rimmed certificate with a big *E* on it—for Excellence?—over which he wept with pride, and laughed, and then put up on the wall, where it was still hanging when I went away to graduate school in 1957. I don't know if the Army ever put his invention to use or not. Dad never got any cash for it, of course.

Mom, Jennie Beatrice Katz, was born in New York of Russian immigrant parents, and she had learned from them to be as tight-lipped about her past as Dad was. I was nine or ten before I found out that my sister Sonia was actually my half sister, the offspring of my mother's previous marriage—which in itself was staggering news to me. Even then, I didn't find out from Mom (or Sonia, for that matter), but only through some remark I wasn't meant to overhear. And I was well into my thirties, maybe my forties, before I finally learned Mom's earlier married name (Pastelnick), also without any help from her. Mom died in 1992, at the age of eighty-nine, and in all her long life, I never wormed out of her what Mr. Pastelnick did for a living, or where they lived, or what his first name was. But then I don't know what her father's name was either, or what relationship the mysterious, seedy old man named Hennoch (Was that his first name? His last name?), who seemed to live on and off in my maternal grandmother's apartment, was to the Katz family.

There were plenty of other mysteries on both sides of the house; things that were never, ever talked about and things that broke the surface occasionally, precipitating wild arguments. My mother would cry, and scream, and break dishes; my father would put his fist through the wall or literally tear out his hair. These were no more than once-a-year occurrences in an otherwise subdued relationship, but they were so terrifying and unsettling that I stopped asking questions. I was starting to see deep, unexplained tensions and undercurrents between my parents, even in the quiet times, and to tell the truth, I stopped wanting to know any more than I already did.

I spent a lot of time outside in those days, playing stickball and punchball with my friends, or making our first fumbling advances to the girls in the neighborhood, or just exploring the run-down streets on our own. I remember it as fun. I remember how sincerely we wished that we could all stay twelve forever, that nothing would ever force us to move out of Brooklyn or, more specifically, out of our beloved Brownsville section of Brooklyn.

It was a childhood made for a writer, I suppose, filled with grist for the mill. Plenty of novelists have since turned similar grist into gold, both literary and commercial. Coming-of-age-in-New York has become a respectable genre all to itself. Perhaps if I had realized a bit earlier than I eventually did that I was going to end up as a writer, I might have tried to join that crowd. But I was long, long out of New York before that ever happened.

This brings up a point that is addressed in every writer's biography or autobiography, and now would seem to be the time to raise it: When did I first know that I was meant to be a writer? One of the things to be learned from authors' accounts of their lives is that the writing impulse tends to come early. Over and over one finds phrases like "The urge burnt in me from earliest times," or "Certainly, by the time I was eleven, I knew that I was meant . . ."

Well, here is mine: The urge to be a writer first entered my mind at the tender age of forty-three. And even then, somebody else had to put it there.

But this is to anticipate a little.

Why I never seriously entertained thoughts of writing as a boy I'm not sure. But wanting to be an author would have been presumptuous and unrealistic, like wanting to be a baseball player, or a film actor, or an opera singer. People like that lived in a different world, and it was a world that tenement kids from Brooklyn could never hope to get into. As a matter of fact, kids from Brooklyn were getting into it all over the place, and had been for years. I just didn't know it.

But I was a great reader as a boy and had from somewhere formed an enormous respect for writers. I can remember once when someone—I'm not sure, but I think it was a now-obscure mystery writer named Bruno Fischer—was pointed out to me in a cafeteria, and I spent the rest of my meal sneaking fascinated, surreptitious glances at him to try and read his expression. What deep thoughts was he thinking as he chewed away on his veal cutlet? What perceptions was he forming and honing from the lively scene around him?

Now I'm a writer myself, and I know better.

My first taste of literary acclaim came when I was ten. I was home from school for a day, sick in bed with something, and for a reason I no longer remember I decided to try writing a poem; possibly it was a class assignment. Anyway, I remember approaching it in earnest. I spent most of the day on it, and I thought the finished product was dandy. I copied it carefully into one of those piebald composition books and read it aloud to my class. It was called "The Boogeyman."

My teacher thought it was a dandy too, and for months to come I did the fifth-grade equivalent to dining out on it. If there was a school recital, there was little Aaron Elkins on the stage reading "The Boogeyman." If there was a PTA night, there was little Aaron Elkins and his damned "Boogeyman." I gobbled up the adulation, of course, and in a way it was surprising that I didn't see that there might be something in a literary career after all, but I didn't.

I always have wanted to see it in print, however, so now, to that end, I am going to take advantage of the nice people of *Contemporary Authors Autobiography Series.*

Here then is my earliest work—published in these pages for the first time:

The Boogeyman

Every night when the lights are turned down low,
I hear and see the boogeyman come in and say hello.
I huddle under the blankets in fear
And wonder—is he there or is he . . . *here?*
Then I run like a mad fool,
And then my mother wakes me up—'cause it's time to go
To school!

Looking at it now, one can certainly see why it was such a hit. It has everything: a sympathetic protagonist, gut-wrenching suspense, a twist at the end, and a clean, punchy resolution. Why wasn't it even more successful? Why did it take so long to get into print? Who can say? Possibly, the meter is not everything it might have been. But whatever

In Brooklyn, New York, about 1944

the reason, this promising beginning was followed by a four-decade hiatus in my literary career.

Those thirty-seven intervening years were, all in all, a pretty uneventful interlude and not likely to be of much interest to anyone out there. Inasmuch as I wasn't writing or thinking about becoming a writer, they do not have even the dubious virtue of being a "writer's life," so if you don't mind, I think I'll merely sketch them in, without going into a lot of detail.

In other words, what do you want to know that stuff for?

In grade school and junior high school I was a pretty good student, but in the last year of high school my grades plummeted, not for want of trying. For reasons I never have understood, the mathematics and science that had always come so easily to me was suddenly impenetrable. I managed to graduate, but barely. "Good luck to a boy who means well," was what my algebra teacher, Miss Sibley, wrote in my autograph book, and it makes a perceptive if double-edged epitaph for my high school phase.

It had been determined years before that I was going to go to college, and the only school that had ever come into consideration was Brooklyn College, about a twenty-minute bus ride from home and more important—overwhelmingly important—free. But now it turned out that my average wasn't good enough to get me in. Nor was it good enough for entrance to City College in Manhattan, about a forty-minute subway ride. It was good enough for Hunter College in the Bronx, a then brand-new campus of what is now called the City University of New York.

Hunter was a full hour-and-a-half subway journey from home; three hours a day on the BMT and IRT, with two transfers each way. Five days a week, ten months a year, from 1952 to 1956. The subways were better then than they are now, but they weren't much fun. If only I'd been a writer at the time, I would have had plenty of time for thinking deep thoughts and polishing and honing my perceptions. Mostly, however, I read other people's novels—Louis Bromfield, Irwin Shaw, John P. Marquand, Jerome Weidman—or stared out the window at the tunnel.

I came close to flunking out in my first year, but then I wandered dubiously into an anthropology course and suddenly remembered how exciting education could be. I had a major, and my grades became respectable again.

When I informed my parents that I planned to be an anthropologist, something they could never

As a graduate student in Arizona, 1956

have heard of before, a kitchen-table conference was called. "Can you," my father solemnly asked, "earn six thousand dollars a year at this?" I said I was sure I could (I had no idea), and the matter was settled.

By the time I finished at Hunter in 1956, my grades had improved enough so that I got a small scholarship in physical anthropology to the University of Arizona. I made ends meet by boxing professionally, of all things, under the name Al Blake, and even managed to put together a winning record, but when I got knocked out for the third time in a row, I decided to hang up the gloves while I still had some brain cells left. By that time I had my master's degree and had won a more substantial graduate assistantship at the University of Wisconsin. But I ran into personal and personality problems (you don't want to know) and left after two years without ever getting a doctorate.

What I did get in Madison, Wisconsin, however, was a wife. I met Toby Siev, an occupational therapy student at the university, in 1957, and we were married in 1959. The marriage produced two children, Laurence and Robin, and lasted ten years, nine of which I remember as wonderful and one as miserable; not a bad record, if you look at it the right way. We separated in 1970 and were divorced in 1972.

Early in that marriage I started on a meandering, aimless sort of dual career—in government and teaching—that lasted almost twenty years. There was nothing shady or irresponsible about it, you understand. Never was there a time when I couldn't support my family or come up with the mortgage payments on the new suburban house we bought in Orange County, California. Never was there a time when I didn't have an eminently respectable job, and most of the time I had more than one. But there was an awful lot of bouncing around from one eminently respectable job to another eminently respectable job, and not in any kind of career progression that I or anybody else could apprehend.

In those twenty years I taught at ten different colleges and universities, mostly evening classes but occasionally full-time, in three different subjects: anthropology, psychology, and management. And I worked full-time, mostly as an administrator, for seven different organizations, most of them governmental. It was even more frenetic than it sounds, because I left several of those organizations only to return again later for a second or even a third stint. And then there was a two-year period when I worked during the day, taught a course or two at night, and completed a second master's degree, this time in psychology.

It was hectic but not unpleasant; I was never fired or asked to leave, and my employment records are stuffed with positive evaluations. But it wasn't satisfying either. The thing was, I could never figure out what I was doing serving as the safety and training director of Orange County, or teaching theories of management at California State University, or, for that matter, spending my weekends in the southern California sunshine applying leaf polish to our variegated *Aucuba japonica* hedge.

It was a very nice life, and I knew it; it just didn't seem like *my* life.

The big turnabout came when I married Charlotte—Charlotte Marie Trangmar—in 1972, just one day after my divorce from Toby became final. (I have been known to say, when attempting to be amusing, that I tried being single for a whole day before I decided I didn't like it. The truth of the matter is that I had been living alone, with Toby and the children in faraway Texas, since 1970. So the truth is that I tried being single for a whole two years before I decided I didn't like it.)

When we married, I was the chief of employee development for Contra Costa County in northern

With Toby Siev, "a year before marriage when we were both University of Wisconsin students," Madison, Wisconsin, 1958

California and an evening lecturer in anthropology and supervision at Golden Gate University. Charlotte was an artist selling her sculptures through several San Francisco galleries. That seemed right for her, but my life didn't seem right for me, and she agreed with me on that. It was time, she made me see, to take my life into my own hands and get it moving again, even if I didn't quite know in what direction.

The encouragement took. By 1976 I had started and finished a doctorate in adult education at Berkeley—seventeen years after quitting the doctorate at Wisconsin—I had resigned from my job at Contra Costa County, and I had accepted a two-year, dream position in Europe as a lecturer with the University of Maryland's Overseas Division, moving every eight weeks to a new country and a new assignment.

It was the first bold thing I'd done in decades, and it felt wonderful. Two years later, however, my contract was about to run out, and it was time to come home again. But there was nothing to come back to. I had burnt my bridges behind me, and I didn't want to be a chief of employee development anymore anyway. And I certainly couldn't live on part-time teaching.

We had mailed applications and resumes from Europe to dozens of American universities, but none of them had come to anything. We were winding up an assignment in Munich at the time, and I had begun to wonder gloomily how hard it would be to unburn some of those bridges. Then, out of nowhere one morning, while I was at the dining room table grading a pile of papers on human evolution, Charlotte uttered the Eight Words That Changed Everything.

"Well," she said, "you could always try writing a book."

The seed, thus cast, did not alight on fertile ground. What kind of book was I supposed to write, I demanded to know, and not very enthusiastically either.

"A thriller," she said decisively. This from a woman who had read perhaps three thrillers in her life. "I think you'd be good at that."

I didn't. My most exciting publication to date had been "An Anthropological Analysis of the Skeletal Remains from CK-44, the Smullins Site," published as the second lead article in the *Oklahoma Journal of Anthropology* in October 1959. I wasn't a writer, I was a—well, I wasn't sure what I was, but I certainly wasn't a novelist. I'd never even written a short story. My last serious literary endeavor had been "The Boogeyman."

But by that afternoon, lacking reasonable alternatives, or any alternatives at all, I was mulling over the idea. It was over a dinner of bratwurst and liver-dumpling soup in Munich's Marienplatz that I mutteringly brought the subject up again.

I didn't know what to write about, I told her.

"Write about what you know," she said sensibly.

"You want me to write a thriller about Pleistocene hominid evolution?"

She saw how that might present a problem and suggested that perhaps I might write about my adventures as an anthropology professor.

"You're kidding," I said.

"All right," Charlotte said, "use your imagination a little. Write about the adventures that *might* have happened to you."

By now you may be wondering about my ability to recall verbatim a conversation of fifteen years ago. But this was a pivotal conversation, the starting point of a transformation, and I was aware of it even then. To be honest, I've told the story a lot of times, and retelling has probably condensed things a little and sharpened them up. But not much.

Before that week was out, I had begun *The Need-to-Know Principle,* about the European adventures of Gideon Oliver, a likable, intelligent, witty, attractively quirky anthropology professor (whose real-life model I have never divulged to anyone). Interestingly, there turned out to be all sorts of adventures I might have had. The writing flowed, the characters developed, the plot thickened. But after a few chapters, I began to lose focus. I felt the book needed something different, something offbeat. So in the midst of what I can now see were rather conventional goings-on, I produced a burned car with a few charred skeletal fragments: a tiny piece of the jaw, a bit of tibia, a little chunk of the occiput. Then I put them into Gideon's hands and wrote a long, detailed description of how a forensic anthropologist would go about analyzing them.

Why not? I was supposed to write about what I knew, and what I knew were bones. If they were so fascinating to me, why shouldn't they be at least passably interesting to others?

In any case, after twenty-one densely packed pages, Gideon was ready to make his report to the police. The minuscule fragments, he announced, had belonged to a muscular, thirty-eight-year-old, Oriental male who was five-feet-five-inches in height and weighed 145 pounds.

The police, of course, are smugly skeptical; can this crack-brained, ivory-towered professor seriously expect them to believe that he has deduced all this from a literal handful of bones, and a small handful at that? Damn right, says an irritated Gideon, and for good measure he tells them that the person was left-handed and smoked a pipe.

Mystery devotees will not be surprised to find out that he turns out to be right in every detail, much to the astonishment of the police but not of the reader, who has been at Gideon's shoulder every step of the way.

I finished writing the book after returning to the United States, bought a copy of *Writer's Market,* and began sending query letters to those publishers listed as having an interest in mysteries. Walker and Company, the first publisher to agree to look at the manuscript—after twelve negative responses from other houses—bought it. Ruth Cavin, the senior editor who telephoned me to express their interest, said they would be happy to publish it and would, in fact, be pleased to consider publishing future novels about Gideon Oliver. (This was in response to my original letter, in which I had recklessly and not altogether truthfully said that I had a second such book well under way.) However, Ruth would prefer that the first one be shortened a bit, and that a few patently Ludlumesque elements be deleted as being out of character with the rest of the story. Would that be all right with me?

What a question. There was nothing that wouldn't have been all right with me, as long as they didn't change their mind about publishing it.

In addition, she was not overly keen on *The Need-to-Know Principle* as a title (neither was I) and decided, with my willing agreement, to change it. As a result, my first novel was published in September 1982 as *Fellowship of Fear*. Perhaps, Ruth suggested hopefully (or was it wistfully?) people might confuse it with *The Ministry of Fear*.

To my knowledge, no one did confuse me with Graham Greene, but the reviews were uniformly good, and the sales were as good as was to be hoped from an unpromoted first mystery novel—which is to say modest, but not embarrassingly so.

There were, as I recall, sixteen newspaper reviews that came to my attention, every one of them positive, which, in my middle-aged naivete, was welcome but hardly surprising. What *was* a surprise, however, was how much most of them— and most of the letters from readers—expressed a liking for the skeletal analysis. I had made Gideon Oliver a physical anthropologist because a protagonist has to be something, and inasmuch as that's what I was, that's what he was. The anthropology had been intended as backdrop, not center-stage material. The business with the muscular, thirty-eight-year-old, left-handed Oriental man who smoked a pipe had been put in simply as a bit of "business," a one-time tour de force.

But the reviews and letters made me think again. I was on to something, I realized. Without trying to, I had created what every new mystery writer dreams of: a niche of my own, all to myself, with an appreciative audience and no likely competitors. Under those conditions, one's ingenuity is stimulated. I began to see all kinds of interesting and unusual plots that might involve bits of bone,

Aaron with his father and mother on a trip around Manhattan, 1958

and from then on, Gideon's skeletal detective work, and the field of anthropology in general, became a continuing and critical part of the series.

I had sold my first novel without an agent, but I knew I would need one if I was going to try to earn a living from writing. Among my strengths, such as they are, business acumen does not figure prominently, and I was going to require help in contract negotiations and the like. But not knowing how one went about acquiring an agent, I asked my editor to recommend one. This is not an approach I would suggest to other writers; agents who are on close terms with editors or publishers are not necessarily the best people to represent authors. In this case, however, I was well served. Ruth recommended her old college friend Victor Chapin, an agent in the small John Schaffner Agency in New York. My association with Victor was a good one, but sadly it lasted only a few months before Victor died without my ever having met him. My account was dumped into the lap of Barney Karpfinger, a young agent on the Schaffner staff.

After a somewhat rocky beginning (Barney was overloaded with his own clients and Victor's as well), we hit it off. When he moved to the Aaron M. Priest Literary Agency I went with him, and when a year or two later he opened his own agency, I was the first client for whom he wrote a book contract. In the decade that has passed since then, I have never once even thought about changing agents, and I don't know how many writers can say that.

For the second Gideon Oliver book, I had in mind a plot involving a small band of ancient people that had managed to survive twelve thousand years, unknown to the modern world, in the Neolithic cave complexes of the Dordogne region of France. I didn't see how I could write it without revisiting the Dordogne, but with our financial situation what it was, I couldn't bring myself to risk spending the money to make the trip, certainly not on the remote possibility that I was actually going to make a career of writing.

At the moment, that possibility was extremely remote. Writing was still a spare-time affair for me, something I did from 5:00 A.M. to 6:30 A.M. most mornings. *Fellowship of Fear* had earned me a two-thousand-dollar advance (about average for a first mystery) and further royalties that were, as they say in the business, in the low three figures. These were not living wages, even in 1982. As a result, I had repaired some old bridges and was back

working for Contra Costa County. That was another reason the trip to France was out. I hadn't yet built up enough vacation to let me take off more than a few days.

Further thought suggested that I might get by with a plot involving a band of presumably extinct Indians that had managed to survive unknown to the modern world not for twelve thousand years, but for sixty or seventy years, as a band of Yahi Indians had in fact done in California at the beginning of the century. The question was: Where could I set it? Where could it credibly happen in 1983? Not California, obviously. Was there anyplace within a two- or three-day drive of the Bay Area?

And so *The Dark Place* takes place eight hundred miles north of the San Francisco Bay Area, in the rain forests of Washington State's Olympic Peninsula, the rugged, uncrowded thumb of land that forms the northwest corner of the United States. It took two or three research trips, all of them made with Charlotte, to get the details right, and by the time we were done the place had gotten to us. In another year, when the books were doing well enough to support us, it was where we moved, and we still live there.

Like *Fellowship of Fear*, *The Dark Place* came out to warm reviews—all except the *New York Times'*, which had been generous to the first book. This time it was merciless. "Panning" doesn't begin to do it justice. "Crucifixion" is nearer the mark.

Smart writers do not let negative reviews affect them adversely. In that regard, I am a smart writer; negative reviews don't bother me. But in 1983 I wasn't smart yet. I was devastated. I had just come from an optometric examination in which drops that blurred my vision had been placed in my eyes. I was driving slowly home (I shouldn't have been driving at all) when I passed the library. It was a Thursday, the day the *New York Times Book Review* arrived, and I had been going to the library for the last several weeks hoping to find a review of *The Dark Place* in it, so I stopped in.

The *Book Review* was in, and squinting at the mystery page, I was able to see that *The Dark Place* was the lead mystery review, and a longish one at that. I borrowed a magnifying glass and sat down in a cubicle practically panting with anticipation. My eyes were tearing and blinking. I could barely focus. I was able to make out phrases, but not complete sentences, and I kept losing my place. I saw some nice words—something about the

Sister Sonia and Mother, 1958

spooky rain forest setting and the action scenes—and then, sitting all by itself, a brief, one-sentence paragraph:

"But, oh, the writing."

If I were the sort of novelist who wrote about people's blood freezing, that's what I'd put in here. I couldn't believe that sentence meant what it seemed to mean. But the following paragraphs made it clear that it did. My first negative review, and not only was it a lulu, but it was from the *Times.* It was the worst moment of my life as a writer. I didn't sleep most of that night. My self-confidence, never overwhelming, evaporated. The new book I had begun, set near Mont-Saint-Michel, lost what steam it had and went into a desk drawer while I pottered uncertainly among other writing projects. It was weeks before I got my confidence back.

Had I foolishly been expecting never to get anything but positive reviews? I don't know. I hadn't thought about it. They'd all been good so far; that was all I knew. Do other writers react as strongly to their first negative review? Yes, many do. But, assuming that one keeps writing, more of the same are certain to follow, and the others tend not to be as painful as the first, and after a while a kind of protective scar tissue forms that makes them easier to take. Besides, by then you have

often had the fun of seeing your friends and colleagues similarly skewered, which helps a lot.

People who are not writers might think that authors would be well-advised to read their negative reviews with particular attention rather than letting a protective skin form. Reviews are, in a sense, free advice. Isn't there something to be learned from the thoughtful analyses of intelligent and knowledgeable critics? Maybe, but I don't know a professional writer who takes them seriously, and I know a lot of writers.

One reason they don't is that reviewers do not prepare their columns for writers. They write them, as they should, with readers in mind, and that is a different thing. More importantly, a successful writer—successful enough to be reviewed in major newspapers—is no longer a student trying to learn how to write. He or she writes, sentence by sentence and paragraph by paragraph, from the personal conviction that this is the way to say what he or she is trying to say. It can very likely be improved, yes, but not by following someone else's advice on the way it should have been done in the first place. Once you start writing what other people think you should be writing, the issue of just whose book it is arises. And a writer who writes any book but his or her own is heading for trouble—is already *in* trouble.

There are a few authors, of course, who simply cannot ignore negative reviews, and they fire letters back to the newspapers pointing out the errors, oversights, ignorances, and biases of their reviewers. No doubt there is a certain amount of catharsis to be gained from this, but I find it simpler and more soothing to leave the reviewers—who are, after all, only earning their living, as I am mine—to their jobs while I get on with my own work, tranquil and unruffled.

How do I manage to maintain this constructive and magnanimous attitude? Easy. I don't read negative reviews of my books. My publishers don't send them to me, and if Charlotte spots one, she keeps it to herself. Every now and then one sneaks through anyway, but it is no longer enough to bother me. Besides, the reviews, knock on wood, continue to be overwhelmingly positive.

On the other hand, how would I know if they weren't?

A book called *Murder in the Queen's Armes,* set in England, followed, after which I had one of my recurring crises of confidence. It seemed to me that the "skeleton detective" series, while enjoyable to write, well received, and doing moderately well, had run its course. How many plots can you construct, after all, that revolve around solving murders from little bits of bone? And how long can you go on doing it without repeating yourself, or seeming to repeat yourself, which amounts to the same thing as far as readers are concerned?

So, casting about for another subject that might provide an interesting and challenging milieu in which to set a mystery, I settled on art, not at all sure that I was doing the right thing. Friends in the publishing field shook their heads: art mysteries were out of fashion (if they were ever in) and unsellable. But I had gotten deeply involved in the research by then and had come up with what seemed to me to be a nifty plot, and I saw it cheerfully if not always confidently through.

A Deceptive Clarity, featuring a curator of Baroque and Renaissance art named Chris Norgren, turned out to be very much an art mystery; that is, the story centered on some technical, fascinating (to me) aspects of Old Master paintings and forgery, much as the Gideon Oliver books had centered on the technical aspects of forensic anthropology.

Alas, my friends were essentially right. The manuscript did sell, but not for very much. On publication the reviews were scant, and for the first time, there was no sale of paperback rights; indeed, *A Deceptive Clarity* was not to appear in paperback until 1993, six years later.

There was a bright spot: a magazine reviewer read a galley of *A Deceptive Clarity* and liked it enough to want to do a major interview piece on me. The interview was duly conducted by telephone, I was at my brightest and wittiest, and the resulting article was published a few months later. But someone at the printer's, never having heard of Aaron J. Elkins, concluded that the interviewer had a better-known author in mind and corrected the title on his own. The piece was published as "An Interview with Stanley Elkin."

I sincerely hope it did Mr. Elkin some good.

A word about "Aaron J. Elkins," who vanished from sight with *A Deceptive Clarity* to be replaced by the simpler "Aaron Elkins." This small transformation continues to create minor confusion for *Books in Print,* the Library of Congress, and numerous lesser libraries, and to them I apologize. Actually, "Aaron J. Elkins" never was my name. I was born "Aaron Elkins" and was content with it until my late twenties, when I published my first paper in anthropology. Everyone else putting out academic papers seemed to

have at least one middle initial, some had two or even three, and I decided I needed one of my own.

Acting on something I read that said one could change one's name simply by changing it, without going to court or filling out papers (if this isn't true, please don't tell me now), I added an initial of my own: *P.* The name I had in mind was Aaron Paul Elkins, which to my ears had a ring both scholarly and friendly. But before it showed up in print, a far-thinking colleague alluded delicately to the potential for unwelcome drollery that lay in wait for a physical anthropologist whose initials were APE.

I promptly changed it to *J* (for Joseph) and used it for the next twenty years for business and academic dealings. I never had it in mind for my novels, but my original letter to Walker had been signed with it (more distinguished, don't you know), and they put it on the books. It took me four publications to get around to having it removed.

Back to the writing. Chastened by *A Deceptive Clarity*'s nonreception, and in a decidedly gloomy frame of mind, I concluded that I might have been a little hasty in retiring Gideon Oliver, so I went back to the desk drawer in which, three years earlier—in another gloomy frame of mind—I had

With Charlotte in the Tucson Mountains, about 1975

stowed the unfinished manuscript of the Mont-Saint-Michel book. Seeing the title, "Legacy of Death," was enough to make my teeth ache, but the work itself, unlooked at all this time, now seemed salvageable. Retitling it *Old Bones,* I got back to work on it, a complex story of death on the tideflats, bones in the cellar, and buried familial hatreds going back to the days of the Nazi occupation.

When it was finished, I was still in a generally negative frame of mind. The lack of critical attention to *A Deceptive Clarity* had scared me. Most mystery novelists get a fair amount of attention from reviewers for their first book, or two, or three. But then interest withers. Mysteries, after all, tend to be somewhat repetitive and predictable simply by virtue of being mysteries. (You know someone is going to get killed, you know someone else—the protagonist—will try to solve the murder, you know the protagonist will follow many false leads and face many obstacles, and you know that in the end he or she will solve it.) And those of any individual writer are bound to be even more alike than mysteries in general. What a reviewer might say about book number seven by a given writer is likely to be similar, on the whole, to what he or she said about book number two. Thus, better to be on the lookout for new and different writers, of whom there are always plenty, about whom something new and different can be said. Only a relatively small group of authors becomes well-regarded enough, or well-known enough, to continue to be reviewed, book after book. And without reviews, writers fade away. The publishers lose interest and the readers, even if interested, can't find the books.

The sum total of three reviews for *A Deceptive Clarity* had me wondering if I had reached that cutoff point and failed to get by it. I thought of *Old Bones* as my last try at establishing a place as a credible mystery writer. I was over fifty; a long apprenticeship was not in the cards. If this book, hauled from the refuse pile, was just one more unnoticed mystery among the four hundred or so published every year in the United States, I was ready to throw in the towel and look for something else to do.

But things went wonderfully from the beginning. First, the book was bought by Otto Penzler's Mysterious Press, arguably the best of the mystery publishers, and I acquired another superb editor, Sara Ann Freed, who continues to edit my novels till this day, knock on wood.

And then, to my intense surprise, *Old Bones* won the 1988 Edgar—the Mystery Writers of America Edgar Allan Poe Award—as the year's best mystery. That did it. I became an instant celebrity, and I can prove it: at the International Congress of Crime Writers held in New York that May there was an event called the celebrity luncheon, where honest-to-goodness writing celebrities such as Donald Westlake, Evan Hunter, aka Ed McBain, Mary Higgins Clark, and Isaac Asimov joined mystery fans and aspiring writers for lunch and then participated in a panel on writing. The fans, of course, paid for the privilege. Had I reserved a place at this affair ahead of time, I would have been charged thirty-five dollars like anybody else. But as it happened, it was held on the day after the Edgar awards ceremony at the Sheraton Centre.

And by then, of course, I was a celebrity. Early that morning I was pressed into service to join the other celebrities on view, which I did with pleasure. Well, to be candid, it was an emergency, one of the advertised attractions having found it impossible to be there, but all the same, there I was at the celebrity luncheon, a certified celebrity.

The point was brought forcefully home in the course of the afternoon, when I gave my jacket to a shivering attendee in a thin dress and I heard a nearby woman whisper to a companion: "Won't *this* be something for her to remember!"

Clearly, I was in for some heady times.

When Gabriel García Márquez won the Nobel Prize for literature in 1982 he was so overwhelmed by the attendant publicity that he had no time for work. For a year, he said, he had to give up writing and simply be the Nobel laureate, like a reigning beauty queen. So it was for me. There were interviews, appearances, book signings, and congratulatory letters to be answered. All of it was welcome, but it kept me from concentrating on my current novel, and it made for a self-puffery that I hadn't known was there and didn't like. Fortunately, it lasted not for a year, but only for about two weeks (thereby empirically establishing that an Edgar carries one twenty-sixth the cachet of a Nobel Prize), after which I was able to settle down to my writing again.

And settled down to my writing I have remained for the past five years. My life at last has become a "writer's life," enormously satisfying to me, but not so easy to write about. Simply put, writers do not make very good biographical subjects. Flannery O'Connor, expressing comparable

*"A celebrity at last." The author (far right) with Evan Hunter, aka Ed McBain,
and Donald Westlake at a celebrity luncheon, May 1988*

thoughts, says somewhere that the story of her own life would consist mainly of walking from the house to the barn and back again. Except for my having a study instead of a barn, that about says it for me too. Readers of biographies who expect anything very novelistic in the lives of novelists are going to be routinely disappointed and certainly will be in my case. Like most other novelists, I spend most of my time sitting quietly in a room in front of a word processor, making up stories.

In other words, here is where, if I don't watch myself, this is going to turn into a series of six more "And then I wrote . . ." Rather than finish on that dreary route, I thought I might make some remarks about what I write and why I write it.

I am a mystery writer. I am not on my way to grander things. My first book was a mystery, all of my books since then have been mysteries, and I will be very surprised if my last book isn't one. Basically, the reason that I write mysteries and nothing else is that you can write them without having anything to say.

When I say that at a writers conference or in an interview, it's usually treated as an attempt at humor or disingenuousness, but I mean it sincerely. I really do love being a writer. I love the fun and anguish of wrestling with plot and character, of trying to make the words say what I mean. But I don't have anything in particular to *say:* no solu-

tions to the problems of society, no comprehensive grasp of the root causes of the world's evils, no insights into personality and character that millions of others (well, thousands) don't have too. The mystery novel is precisely the vehicle I need: a form with structure, with point, and with a ready readership, but with no need for an over-arching message or theme.

As I see it, I am following in the wake of an old and glorious tradition. The mystery, surely more than any other fiction genre, can boast a long, honorable history of works that are primarily entertainments and diversions—but diversions of high literary merit—by authors such as Edgar Allan Poe, Wilkie Collins, Arthur Conan Doyle, G. K. Chesterton, and Dorothy Sayers.

Some of my fellow writers—and too many of the academics now writing about mystery writing—feel otherwise. They view the contemporary mystery novel as a means of putting forward important political, social, and environmental agendas, of raising consciousness. I don't see it that way at all. Here I am in the middle of my twelfth novel, and I've yet to go out of my way to take on an environmental issue, or a social issue, or just about any other kind of issue. They show up in my books from time to time because the books are set in today's world, but having them show up is different from taking them on. If any reader has ever figured out from my books where I stand on Brazilian rain forests, or overpopulation, or the problems of the homeless, or the plight of the spotted owl, he or she has done it without my help.

There is more involved here than personal preference. I think that issues and mysteries make edgy bedfellows. For one thing, they're an awkward combination for the author. Writing mysteries is tricky business. Writing cogently on issues is tricky business too, but of a different kind, requiring different techniques if it's going to be done well. (High school English teachers have good reason to try to drum into their students' heads the critical difference between narrative and exposition.) Besides, there are other forums, easier and more effective ones, for sounding off on issues. Mysteries have more than enough constraints—the placement and ordering of clues and red herrings, the hiding and holding back of information until the novelistically right time—as it is. Of course it's possible, yes, to weave significant messages into mystery fiction; what I don't understand is why anyone tries to do it.

More than that, the reader that I have in mind as I write doesn't turn to a mystery at the end of a workday or on a rainy Sunday afternoon to have his or her consciousness raised about all the terrifying, patently insoluble problems that grow more threatening and further out of control every day. I worry about a lot of things, but one of them is not a shortage of stress-inducers and frustration-makers, of critical needs crying out for urgent action before it's too late, of simmering problems that will surely mean the end of the world as we know it (and probably the end of the world, period). Television programming and daily newspapers do very well at maintaining general agitation levels without the help of mysteries.

On the contrary, I think that the sweetest, best function of the mystery novel or story is as a decompressant, a consciousness-*lowering* interlude for the intelligent reader. This is nothing to be sneezed at.

"Holmes," Christopher Morley once wrote about Conan Doyle's great detective, "is pure anesthesia." He said it lovingly and meant it as praise. Not anesthesia in the sense of unconsciousness or dullness of perception, of course, but in the sense of relief from pain, worry, and uneasiness. It's still why most readers come to mystery fiction, in my opinion. They come for comfort, for security, for a welcome dose of order in a disorderly and changing world.

Moral issues are a different matter. The mystery is, I think, the most moral of all forms of popular fiction. At least in traditional, "classic"

"On the Nile, hard at work researching a setting." The author with Charlotte and Barbara Mertz, aka Elizabeth Peters, December 1991

detective fiction, which is what I try to write, there are certain predictabilities (which is where the comfort and security come from): actions beget consequences. People get what's coming to them. The good guys win, the bad guys lose, and they pay for what they did. Virtue triumphs, if not in every particular, then for the most part.

When I read a mystery myself, I like to do it in a good chair with a long, leisurely evening before me and a glass of wine or a cup of coffee at my side. And I don't do it to confront the implacable issues of world ecology and human society, I do it to get away from the damn things. I think that's why most other readers do it too.

I must admit some trepidation about confessing to all this, that is, to not being a Serious Writer of Meaningful Fiction. Anthony Trollope's reputation suffered famously when he acknowledged something similar in his autobiography. What will happen to mine? Who knows, would I have been invited to write this memoir for the *Autobiography Series* if the people at Gale Research had known so much about me before? (If you are reading this, it would appear to mean that at least they didn't have a change of heart about publishing it.)

Time will tell, I guess. In the meantime I have continued to write Gideon Oliver novels and Chris Norgren novels with literate entertainment as my primary aim. For as far ahead as I can see, that's what I will keep doing. The one departure was to collaborate on a novel—a mystery, of course—with Charlotte, but it's unlikely that there will be any more of those. Our marriage comes before our joint literary career.

I have discovered that autobiography is more difficult to write than biography, at least in one respect: It's hard to know quite when to stop, or even how. One feels almost as if one should have the decency to die immediately on completion. That dangling, expectant hyphen on the first page (Aaron Elkins, 1935–) gives one an edgy and peculiar feeling.

Like waiting for the other shoe to drop.

BIBLIOGRAPHY

Fiction:

(With Charlotte Elkins) *A Wicked Slice*, St. Martin's, 1989.

"Gideon Oliver Mystery" series:

Fellowship of Fear, Walker, 1982.

The Dark Place, Walker, 1983.

Murder in the Queen's Armes, Walker, 1985.

Old Bones, Mysterious Press-Warner Books, 1987.

Curses!, Mysterious Press-Warner Books, 1989.

Icy Clutches, Mysterious Press-Warner Books, 1990.

Make No Bones, Mysterious Press-Warner Books, 1991.

"Chris Norgren Mystery" series:

A Deceptive Clarity, Walker, 1987.

A Glancing Light, Scribner's, 1991.

Old Scores: A Chris Norgren Mystery, Scribner's, 1993.

Also contributor to personnel, education, and anthropology journals.

James A. Emanuel
1921-

A FORCE IN THE FIELD

PART I

"Third time is the charm." We used to say this as children in the little prairie town of Alliance, Nebraska, facing northward the Bad Lands of South Dakota, and southwestward the rodeo-famous Cheyenne, Wyoming.

Starting now, in Paris, France, my third autobiography, I think of the first one, called *From the Bad Lands to the Capital,* begun when I was twenty-one and working in the honestly named War Department in Washington, D.C.

The opening lines of those 124 pages romanticized the flat, drab plains stretching away from the town; blurred with twilight the sawed-off angles of the low frame house where our family of nine lived (in the sparse Hills Addition beyond the railroad tracks); and borrowed the drifting cry of a low-flying "long-billed bird" to signal the birth of the author.

Almost forty years later, the possible effects of mid-twentieth century American life on the psyche of an African American are reflected in the opening lines of my second autobiography, *Snowflakes and Steel,* written in Paris at the request of the Southern scholar for whom the Jay B. Hubbell Center for American Literary Historiography at Duke University was named:

> When I sailed from New York Harbor on the SS *France* in late August 1971, I did not care whether I ever again saw any place or any person that I had ever known, except for my son and six relatives.

This third autobiography indeed needs a charm, a magical power perhaps beyond me, to relate selectively, to picture and suggest, what happened before, during, and after those forty years—besides normal boy-to-man-to-different-man changes—to explain the shift from romanticizing to hard-eyed isolation.

"My mother and father holding my sister Julia, near the sod house in Valentine, Nebraska," about 1913

A magician needs materials, gestures, and a cooperative audience. Readying the stage for this third performance, I can offer only a chronological series of props (lists of dates, places, and names) illuminated by gestures (wand-waving paragraphs, variable in steadiness) proposing to ferret out incidents and impressions that might have shaped me particularly as a person or writer.

109

At the Edge of the Wild West

1921: Born James Andrew Emanuel on 15 June in Alliance, Nebraska.

1921–29: Family lived in Hills Addition: father Alfred; mother Cora; sisters Julia, Janet, Gladys, Christine; brothers Raymond, Alvin.

Thirty-six degrees below zero, my spit freezing in the air: that was wintertime in Alliance (where, according to a midcentury photo in *Life* magazine, enough snow entered keyholes to pile giant drifts into exterior rooms). Deep snow punctured with black-and-red boots remains my earliest memory: my probably three-year-old self struggling through it. Even then my sensitivity to beauty, normal in children, was forming; and by the time I walked through autumn leaves to kindergarten, I was pleasurably moved by the red, gold, and brown fallen leaves, crisp and curled on the sidewalks.

Boyish delights, however, not aesthetic meditations, preoccupied me outdoors. I was soon, with my little companions, striking wild olives from the trees to feel their oddly fur-like exterior and enjoy their bittersweet taste. At Emerson Elementary School, finding myself stronger than other boys (or perhaps simply faster), I always won friendly tussles. One teacher, noticing my gladiator style, cautioned me not to be "so rough." I was not naturally rough—nor was I talkative; yet the art teacher, Miss Atchinson, made me sit in the wastebasket for talking too much, a punishment from which I rose with several multicolored papers glued to my denimed rear end. Nor would I stand up alone and sing, another teacher found, unlike other pupils in her small class.

Speed and dexterity, more so than sheer muscle power, were my main allies. Although very good at leapfrog and kickball, I excelled in footracing. (At picnics and small fairs, older boys who knew me would win bags of gumdrops through bets pitting me against boys of ten or eleven, giving them headstarts or taking odds.)

Being fast and nimble did not help me much in some Wild Western activities. Riding the Irving family's pigs, bronco style, on their nearby property, I was knocked against fences or thrown into thick mud by those grunting, squealing creatures. More formally, entering the boys' calf-riding competition in a rare Alliance rodeo near the auction

*Paternal grandfather,
Dawson Joshua Emanuel*

grounds, I soon lost my seat on the fast-rolling hide of the bucking animal.

If my sister Christine (whom I made walk behind me to her kindergarten, she being two years younger and, unforgivably, a *girl* whom I was forced to protect) had been faster and tougher, she might have avoided being stolen by itinerant gypsies. But because of chance, superstition, or some prophetic wind blowing to their wagons news of my resourceful mother, those westward-bound nomads released her.

Other passersby enlivened and colored my earliest years:

Indians, cowboys
crossed my town with faces brown
like rocks. They were real.

That "breakaway haiku," from my book *Deadly James and Other Poems* (1987), says enough about those true Westerners. I secretly followed Indian groups onto the prairie, from hiding watched their piebald ponies drawing behind them cowhide stretchers loaded with bundles and children older than papooses. Similarly, I watched hoboes in their camps, drinking from battered, blackened tin cans, growling brief phrases to one another. In contrast, the occasional cowboy who gave my brother Raymond and me a coin to let him tether his horse to some pole in our yard seemed open, ready to let us wear his bandana or examine his spurs.

The real Westerner in my life, I was to understand later, was my father, a fairly tall, strong, light brown-skinned, steel-grey-eyed man who (according to my mother's only unstinting praise of him) "could ride horses no other man could ride." This rare tribute she sometimes balanced with both apparent exaggeration and credible truth: "I've seen him ride horses that

Paternal grandmother,
Mary Robinson Emanuel

would jump eight feet high, then he'd spit blood for an hour afterwards." He was a wide-open-spaces man, married to a woman with a pioneer's spirit but a talent for social, metropolitan life.

Her pioneer experience was also sharply physical, implicit in her stories of mountain lions springing upon people riding horseback in the night, or boldly climbing front porch steps to make crying sounds like those of small children. She knew these cunning beasts personally as a country teacher who once sent her pupils home early after seeing panther tracks circling the school cabin.

What I know of my parents' ancestry, extended by a letter, dated 17 November 1992, from my sister in Denver, Julia E. Williams, can be condensed here. My father's grandfather, born in Luxembourg, emigrated and settled in Rochester, New York, where my paternal grandfather, Dawson Joshua Emanuel, was born. He married Mary Robinson, who bore him my father and four other sons and a daughter.

As for my mother, her grandfather was an English scholar who fathered a boy by an English-and-Malagasy girl and sent him, after the mother's death, with his other two sons to Oxford University, where, reputedly, they all graduated. These people, through alliances unknown to me, became the respected Fisher family, one of whom, Georgianna Fisher, married the Reverend Wade H. Mance, the two becoming the only grandparents I knew, the parents of my mother.

Although I remember my grandfather only slightly (his mother, Eva Mance, was also English), my grandmother, born a slave, seemed a wise, gentle woman—a conclusion I came to after she chastised me in her room, ever so charitably, for having taken a small stick of her peppermint candy. "You shouldn't ever take something that doesn't belong to you," she said, hand on my shoulder, "without permission." A whipping, which I almost never received, would have impressed me less.

Regarding the putative Oxonian men, I was acquainted with but one of their line, Willie W. Fisher of Evanston, whom I found to be a distinguished, amiable, cosmopolite gentleman, apparently a former associate of Vice President Charles Gates Dawes, who served under Calvin Coolidge.

I still do not give much importance to ancestry, and have made no attempt to trace mine. In response to a high school assignment, however, my mother told me that my forebears were African, French, German, and Mohawk Indian.

Maternal grandfather, Wade H. Mance

Certain literary and quite nonliterary references can round out those earliest years made possible by the Emanuel-Robinson and Mance-Fisher romances. My meditative bent, visible at three or four when I would climb the clothesline post or chicken house or grassy cellar top to contemplate the prairie, was obvious to me on my seventh birthday when I sat in our rocking chair to rock and ponder my age. A sense of reserve, also at seven, probably explained my resentment at having to wear a brown bunny costume at school and turn somersaults with other pupils around a maypole.

The meditative and the literary melded that same year in my fascination with imagery in the first lines of poetry I remember hearing in school: Robert Louis Stevenson's "I saw you toss the kites on high / and blow the birds across the sky." And remarkably unique were the family literary sessions held by my mother, all children gathered around her as she read from the Bible, Booker T. Washington's *Up from Slavery,* the *Saturday Evening*

Post, etc. Certainly my love for beautifully cadenced language and gripping sensory effects started in this family circle.

For balance, Hills Addition can fade on a rowdier note: fisticuffs. Fortunately because of my Jekyll-and-Hyde teetering when angered, I was not prone to violence, except in the heat of gang fights led by Retilo Remos on the Mexican side (my side) and Dennis Hashman on the white side. Besides bare knuckles and sticks, we fought with prickly pears. Once, catching me unawares from behind on the way home from school, big Dennis, the not-too-bright teenage strongman of his hard-working family, dealt an ear-ringing blow to my head and dashed away, fearing that some of my gang members might run up. Although I could do nothing but stalk home, crying bitterly, and sit on our rooftop nursing my ear and looking at the prairie, every future group encounter found me giving Dennis a fast series of hop-about stinging blows before some comrade took over, also evading those slower but longer arms.

Other than such gang battles, my only fistfights were with my friend Arthur Meehan, whose sister cut up burlap bags to fashion cowboy chaps to match the scrap-wood pistols and rubber-inner-tube bullets with which we rode marvelously crayoned stick-horses. Once, on a road near the railroad tracks, when he failed to keep his younger twin brothers, Cecil and Sylvan, from flailing their way to his aid, Western honor ended the strife. Much more ominous was my anger against some bully whom I do not remember, mollified only when my father spotted and took from me the brass knuckles with which I was headed for vengeance. "You'd break his jaw with those, James," he cautioned—with a concern somewhat like that of my grandmother reclaiming her peppermint stick.

"The Queen City of the West": An Interlude

1930–31: Family moved to Denver, Colorado (Franklin Street); lived mostly at 2229 Clarkson Street.

Snow, ashes, Mrs. Treadwell, and the Pratt family: these come to mind when I think of our year or so in clean, cold Denver. My father hauled ashes in the snow, Raymond and I searched for saleable empty bottles in the snow, we walked partway to meet our mother coming home from work in the snow, and I wired together a too-small, broken-up sled to race in the snow—all within sight of the snow-covered Rocky Mountains.

It probably snowed during my first week at Whittier Elementary School (my first proximity to large numbers of Black pupils); but the weather did not dim my appreciation of my tiny-town education, about 250 miles away, versus that of big-city Denver when officials advanced me one half year. Whittier served me best through the classes of Mrs. Treadwell, a bespectacled, red-haired woman who seemed to sputter and sizzle as she talked enthusiastically, initiating us into the adroitly spun marvels of La Fontaine's *Fables*, making Renard the fox our getaway man, shifting her glasses and wrinkling her nose as she joyfully read us the drolleries and escapades of crows, wolves, storks, tortoises, ants, and other unforgettable creatures. Another teacher, a younger brunette (who, later reflection told me, was a seductive woman), sat on a corner of her desk, one palm massaging her thigh, and read us a different series of enthralling stories.

Educational on another level, the Pratt family of five, living nearby on Washington Street, made me know what community life in a big city could mean. Unbelievably generous and energetic, Mrs. Pratt was a rather small, brownskinned woman omnipresent throughout their few large rooms, while Mr. Pratt, a master chef, thin and slower but tireless, endlessly baked large pies and cakes—especially pineapple-upside-down cakes—made unstintingly available to the many Depression-weary people, friends or strangers, who passed through their doors.

The Pratts "played the Chinaman" almost daily, sometimes hitting for eye-rolling sums of money; and their middle room was a magnet for hard whist players and riveted observers. Would-be kibitzers were reformed at once by the sight of the revolver that Mr. Pratt sometimes placed on the table when the players' eyes narrowed and the smoke thickened.

When Mrs. Pratt died many years later, her funeral attracted, I heard, more sympathizers than that of any other private citizen in the history of Denver.

Feminists and fishermen might appreciate two more recollections. My eleven-year-old sister Gladys, appearing one day on our back porch munching a sandwich, called out to us boys in the yard, "Whatcha doin'?" Sweating and mumbling a few unallowed "damns" and glowering at a rope tied between a tree and a pole stuck into the ground, we ignored her, it being obvious that we were failing to clear the rope as a high-jumping challenge. After watching two more near-misses, more embarrassing to us now, Gladys put down her sandwich, ran down the steps into the yard, and jumped over the rope: she then disappeared, sandwich in mouth, through the screen door of the porch. Too disgusted to look at one another, we jerked the rope loose and disappeared elsewhere. Our aging spitz, Rover, had calmly watched it all.

As for fishing, my first experiences occurred at Rocky Mountain Lake, Mud Lake, and the Sand Pit with Raymond and Uncle Turner (Mance). I must have annoyed them in the early-morning dark with my repeated "Is it time to wake up yet?" and surely inconvenienced them by ruining the dough bait with too much water. I was thrilled, however, to see my first large lakes, to smell crayfish, to stare at gleaming bass at the Sand Pit, and to hear the eager whir of reels jetting lines out

*Maternal grandmother,
Georgianna Fisher Mance*

and across an expanse of water so dangerous (to one who could not swim).

It could indeed be dangerous I confirmed at the Sand Pit, where my enthusiasm one day, as I hooked a small fish, brought me too close to the Pit's edge. I slipped on the mossy, rocky bank and fell into those waters known to be full of sudden, craggy drops. Feeling water quickly up to my hips and nothing under my feet, I had no time to cry out while I grasped at the nearest rock. Probably I did not hear my own shout, but I felt Uncle Turner's hands pulling me upwards. I never went to the Sand Pit again.

Besides being dangerous sometimes, thrills can be aesthetic and can have moral and comic dimensions. In Whittier's manual training class, I glowed over a viola and a model ship that I constructed; but neither could possess the retrospective beauty of a Colfax Avenue billboard that Raymond and I passed when we sometimes walked to meet our mother. Writing autobiographically at twenty-one, I recalled

"Mother's 'Uncle Will' Fisher of Evanston, Illinois"

the soft, large snowflakes gently spraying my vision of the beautifully lighted billboard. There was a strange, slow, heavy beauty, the beauty of *stillness,* about that sign.[1]

One ethical "thrill"—if a dilemma can be a thrill—seems important for its prefiguring my lifelong tendency to take moral issues seriously. A next-door white neighbor, Mrs. Williams, sometimes left in my nine-year-old care her small daughter, Betty, a lively child who once outsmarted me by smearing detergent over her mouth, nose, eyes, ears, and brow. The tolerant mother later gave me a dime to get a vanilla ice cream cone for Betty and another cone for myself. Returning with the cones, I stumbled into the classic joke: Betty's vanilla cone dropped and spoiled beyond recovery, my own strawberry delight intact. The same autobiography details at length my chagrin, excerpted here:

> Should I go tell Mrs. Williams the truth, that I had dropped *Betty's* cone, thank her for the nickel, and then stride away eating my own cone? . . . [she] could think that I still had the second nickel, and had not really dropped the cone. . . . If I gave the strawberry cone to Betty, I would be asked why I didn't get vanilla for the child; . . .[2]

The comic "thrill"—if a searing disappointment can be a thrill—became a half-a-century-long joke to Raymond, Gladys, and me, participants in the Cheeseman Park Caper, actually a mammoth Easter egg hunt for Denver children. The just-mentioned manuscript pictures us three, equipped with Number 16 paper bags, as pistol shots signalled the end of the one-hour hysteria:

> . . . every bug, cricket, grasshopper, or insect of any kind, hiding under every leaf or blade of grass . . . in every tree or bush or hedge—each had his private home invaded a thousand times by . . . egg-crazy juveniles. I had found . . . not even a *shell*. . . . At last we encountered [Gladys] near a tree, clutching with defiant and triumphant desperation the squashed, unrecognizable remnants of one candy egg. . . .[3]

---

[1]From Emanuel's first manuscript autobiography, *From the Bad Lands to the Capital,* 1943–44, p. 18.
[2]From *From the Bad Lands to the Capital,* p. 17.
[3]From *From the Bad Lands to the Capital,* p. 15.

Books, Harnesses, and Jockstraps

1931: Family returned to Alliance, to 412 Missouri Street.

1933: Entered Alliance Junior High School, where I first read one of my poems to an audience.

1935: Entered Alliance High School.

1936: Worked on Batt's and others' farms in summer.

1937: Worked on Batt's farm and on Worley's ranch in summer.

1938: Worked on Batt's and Krejci's farms in summer. Won ribbons in Chadron College track meet, medal in statewide shorthand contest. Was center on African American professional basketball team, the Five Aces.

1939: Left in January for CCC Camp 786 in Wellington, Kansas, never to return "home" to the family.

The fact that the Denver period had hardly turned the calendar was brought home to me when Alliance school officials wanted to detain me in grade because Denverites had not taught me arithmetical fractions and related mysteries. But when I quickly cracked these codes, I was reinstated—and was even privileged to teach some classmates at the blackboard, supervising and correcting their work on math problems given them. I attended all five schools in the town: Emerson, Grandview, Central (where I scored all five points in the end-of-the-year hockey game), and now Alliance Junior High, continuing the straight-*A* grade groove that was to persist until my doctoral studies at Columbia University in New York, when course grades were not given.

A literary calamity overtook me at the junior high school when I was thirteen. The principal, Miss Wilson, a broad-hipped woman whose skirt swished authoritatively when she walked, decided that I should mount the auditorium stage to read a Thanksgiving Day poem that I had written. Profoundly embarrassed while obeying, feeling hundreds of eyes upon me, I swore that I would never again write a poem. (The writing bug had already bitten me, however, for the *Omaha Bee* newspaper had sent me five dollars the previous year for my brief article "Going Up," in praise of construction at my favorite building, the local library, where I was beginning to spend countless evenings.)

Miss Wilson clings in my memory for another reason: I can still see her standing on "my" stage, explaining to us students why we need not use more than four squares of toilet tissue. A more scholarly connection: under her eyes I won the American Legion School Award by a vote of 119 to 4 over my friend Neil Winegar, to be mentioned later.

During the Miss Wilson years, considering becoming a farmer, I wrote to a distant farm equipment firm for detailed information about the butterfat yield of Holstein cows, possible evolutions in milking machinery, and other technical matters. After getting a reply that a regional sales representative would visit me on a specific date, I made sure that I was not at home all afternoon. Upon returning home from the library that evening, I faced my mother's questions (she was separated from my father, who was working on somebody's ranch or farm while planning his own).

"Yes, ma'am, I wrote the letter," I confessed, begrudging but negotiating her sense of victory in this one of our continual contests in which I outmaneuvered her attempts to force me to reply with a word I detested: "ma'am." She recounted what had happened, from the confused salesman's "Is Mr. Emanuel here?" to her final bottom line, "But he's only a boy."

"Only a boy" or not, I had hard jobs during the school year. Pumping water from the outside well before dawn (the toilet was much farther outside), I did not always manage to keep the flesh of my hand from sticking to the icy handle. Out of Depression-born necessity, Raymond and I, for fuel, gradually tore down the inner wall of the shed-room of the frame house next door, ripping away wooden laths to burn. Oddly, the smallest room of the house was occupied: a genial old Black man from the Deep South, Mr. Riley, was a squatter there, living off greasy cornbread and fatback, often reclining barefoot on two chairs, his yellow teeth clamping a curved pipe full of miasmic Granger Twist. (Our family had lived in that abode before moving to the corner house.)

One haiku in my book *Deadly James* treats that wood-getting; another addresses a similar need:

> Hot bricks in the bed,
> wrapped in rags too torn to wear,
> kept my sisters warm.

Others could have pictured me distressfully wearing secondhand shirts with cut-down sleeves, or corduroy knickerbockers whistle-squeaking at their bunched-up knees at my every embarrassed step.

Our mother hid from Raymond and me what must have been her agony in asking us, for about four years, to perform another task that "kept my sisters warm": to take gunny sacks and get coal (she never said "steal" coal) from the railroad tracks half a mile away. True, we took only coal that had fallen off the cars; but my soul ached during those possibly one hundred trips, Raymond trying to soothe me at first with "Don't cry." Once when a "railroad dick" shouted at us from a distant engine, I dropped my sack and—as Raymond pensively told the story years later—I "really flew." My racing away, I suppose, would have looked funny in a movie. But my grandmother, the lady with the peppermint candy, would not even have been able to smile.

My reaction to the coal-gathering trips, among other forces, moved me to an extreme recourse. Three rooms in the house were restricted as storage space for our landlord, a mild-mannered Black farmer who called his hogs "hahgs" and whose homely wife wore seven dresses at once. One wintry day I cut a neat, two-feet-square hole in one wall (where it was made of building board like Celotex) and began to go through it nightly—carefully replacing the square "door"—to study and sleep in the smallest forbidden room, taking with me a kerosene lamp.

My mother's main criticism of me during those cruel, "most regretful, sometimes even unreal" years, as I wrote of them a few years later,[4] was that I did not accept my role with enough cheerfulness and grace. Before the one-by-one escapes of Raymond and my older sisters to Denver (where my mother had not let the girls go, invited as a popular local trio, to sing on the radio), they added their censure, usually circuitous, to hers. (Over twenty years later, during my few visits to the family, my mother began to reminisce, "All my children were different. I had to treat each one of them differently.")

Recognizing, somewhat inaccurately, my difference, she entered my hermitage one night, sat on the bed and asked, "James, why do you hate me?" I remember well my reply: "I don't hate you, Mama; I just don't think we should have to live the way we do." My determination to "do it my way" made me hold on to my retreat after I was awakened one night by a weight and move-

"They benefited from the task that 'kept my sisters warm': (from left) Janet, Gladys, Christine, and Julia," in the 1940s

ment on my chest, followed by the thump of something hitting the floor and the scratchy sound of skittering feet. My loathing was doubled by my almost vomitory memory of beating a rat to death with a bed-frame rail in our cold shed-room, my mother close by, apprehensively watching. Still I held on to my hermitage. Today I would not be, I think, that resolute.

Summer adventures became either bits of underground ore in my character or poetic staple-to-come. They occurred on the farms of my first employers (Harris, Brown, and Hayes); on the farm of William Batt, a tall, powerful, grey-haired African American who spoke only to grunt commands or laconic questions requiring self-belittling answers; on the ranch of Charlotte Worley, a sun-wrinkled, choppy-voiced, bowlegged woman who gave the impression that she carried a weapon; or on the farm of Adolph Krejci, a red-bearded Bohemian whose overalls always had one suspend-

---

[4]From *From the Bad Lands to the Capital*, p. 24.

er off-shoulder and whose wife served burnt food and sugarless lemonade.

On the Harris farm, where I had to kill thirteen snakes in one day and was first thrown, one sunrise, from a horse, I had the breathtaking task of chasing an escaped bull back home:

> . . . my horse leaped forward. . . . After a long, hard chase, which took me over hills and across gullies, puddles, etc. at a goodly clip, . . . we reached the corral; and there the creature agilely leaped the fence and stood glaring balefully at the horse and me with his chest heaving and red-rimmed eyes full of fire.[5]

Moonlight rides on the same horse were aesthetic pleasures:

> Upon reaching the peak of the hill, I would pull my mount to a halt, crook my leg over the saddle horn, and survey the depth and feel the silence . . . usurped only by the occasional chirp of an insect or the yap of a coyote.[6]

On the Batt farm, where I spent three summers (and where a large bull snake once crawled with me from under a shock of wheat after a rainstorm), I took similar but faster rides over better-known ground on a bay horse that became a subject in my poem "Three Chores One Country Day," which refers to my sad task of burying him after he died, shriveled up from sleeping sickness. Distasteful, more so than sad, was the aftermath of the death of Queen, a partly lame, nervous white mare, for my taciturn boss and I had to skin her before the burial. She had been lively, despite her bad foot, and recently, after my entering the darkening barn without whistling or speaking as usual, I had made the mistake of unhaltering her before freeing her mate. Snorting fiercely, she had reared up wildly, snapped the halter of the other horse like a string, and bowled him head over heels, kicking, before lunging past me—backed flat against the stall—out into the corral.

With one of my haiku, terse as Mr. Batt, I take leave of him:

> He took turpentine,
> Knife and pail—"to nut the pigs,"
> he called it. I learned.

[5]From *From the Bad Lands to the Capital,* p. 28.
[6]From *From the Bad Lands to the Capital,* p. 29.

Adolph Krejci, he of the red beard and slack suspenders, had two giant roan stud horses that were far from droopy. Working on his farm "on loan" from Mr. Batt, I used the team to pull a hay rake, the two-and-a-half-feet-high, curved teeth of which spread through a width of about eleven feet. Riding over long windrows of green Russian thistles one afternoon, I suddenly heard a metallic jostling sound and felt my seat shake and lurch sideways. The long tongue of the rake, jutting forward between the two horses, had become unbolted from its crossbar and dropped to the ground. The giant roans, as if anticipating a fouled arrangement, pranced and snorted, eyes rolling. Almost without thinking, I dived backwards off the rake, saw the vibrating row of teeth dig into stubble near my face before they were jerked upward.

Within seconds the leaping horses snatched away the big rake like a toy dangled behind them, swept it twenty yards before I could stand up. Imagining with panic the violent destruction of equipment and animals that could be blamed on me, I found myself running, not after the horses, but toward the area where their curving, mad path was rushing them. Thinking of nothing but stopping them and the crazily bouncing rake that seemed to be flailing their rumps, I stood squarely in their path, trembling arms upraised. Strangely deliberate as they finally loomed above me, I jumped up, each hand reaching for a foam-sloshed bridle or bit. Miraculously, half a minute later, their heads tossing sweaty foam into my face as I stood, still gripping their bridles, they had quieted enough for me to notice that they had dragged me for about thirty yards and that both of my shoe heels had been torn off.

On the same Krejci farm, or another—the immigrant Krejcis were dispersed in the area—I met my father among a threshing crew of lean, suntanned men arriving near dawn, like me and my rack and team, from neighboring farms. "Hi there, son!" he called. "What the devil are you doing over here?" He chuckled at me climbing down from my rig, remembering me, apparently, as a child. Other men kidded me a little, asking me if I could make it through the rest of the day. They did not know that the previous two weeks had been harder, with me alone daily in a town-sized field, surrounded as far as my eyes could see by windrows of grain that I had to shock by myself.

Although a Krejci threshing-crew mealtime is worth depicting, as well as my sometimes exciting tasks on Charlotte Worley's big ranch (driving a header barge with frightened horses; hauling corn cobs in a standard wagon that caught fire; harrowing a neighbor's crop under, due to vague instructions; and contending on a hayrack with two smartass drifters), I swing shut the farm-and-ranch gate of my youth by condensing one Western-movielike adventure on the Worley ranch.

In late summer, after taking my herd, which included a few horses, from the ranch to pastureland a few miles north, I relaxed in some cowboy's empty shack until time to gather the herd for the return drive. I saddled up in heavy rain and rode toward the cattle, noticing the horses clustered in the far corner. The impossible happened after I dismounted and ground-reined my horse, a dark sorrel, to tighten his bellyband: when I slipped on a mound of fresh cow dung and fell, he bolted and ran away.

Caught in the ridiculous plight of a so-called cowboy who has lost his horse, I cursed my luck but slowly thought of a way to regain him, now tossing his head—mockingly, I thought grimly—among the other horses standing, tails to the rain, in the corner. Removing my wet straw sombrero and quietly crawling back and forth in grass and mud (and cow chips), I nudged the cattle toward the corner. When the horses were hemmed in but still unsuspicious, I moved toward them at a half-crouch, among the cattle. When one of the horses spotted me and whinnied nervously, I dashed forward, grabbed the reins of the retreating sorrel, and leaped into the saddle. Only lightning could have removed me—my mind flashing through the memory of how I had been thrown in a bull pasture from the back of a suddenly buck-jumping horse Raymond and I were riding double to visit our father, how a few snorting bulls had started toward me, how Raymond had whirled the horse around to return and snatch me up, and how only lightning could have removed me from the unwilling horse.

In the case of the sorrel, I behaved badly, whipping him on the way back to the ranch so unnecessarily that he was later somewhat afraid of me. In literature, however, I have respectfully pictured horses and bulls, not only in "El Toro," but also in "A Fable for Animals" and "Challenge, Taken Hard."

Smaller but wilder animals, with excitements and dangers related to them, helped me grow up. I hunted rabbits with the .410-gauge shotgun of "Creepy" Crittendon, whose washerwoman-wife made super-delicious fried corn, and who himself whittled airplane propellers for me and owned a

small place three miles out on the prairie that we called "Mosquito Ranch." Following, for the first time, a jack rabbit along the snowy trail to that ranch, I shot at and missed him, ejected the smoking shell, reloaded, and stalked another one until he paused about 125 feet away. I aimed low, having just learned that the barrel would jump up when fired, and squeezed the trigger. Pow! He did not move. I was disappointed until, crawling close, I decided that I had "drilled him dead center," although my pulp Western magazines would have differently credited the well-aimed pellets. After returning proudly through the town, the jack rabbit slung over my shoulder Davy Crockettwise, I strung my game to our backyard maple tree and did a frontiersmanlike job of readying it for the kitchen.

"Creepy's" friend, Mr. Chandler, father of a Hills Addition family, with a wife still locally famous in 1989 as "Grandma Chandler," sticks in my memory—and is indirectly linked to my longest poem, "El Toro"—because of an ordeal he suffered similar to that in the poetic epic "The Song of Hugh Glass," read to us by a teacher. Gored by a bull in an open field and left for dead, Mr. Chandler crawled all afternoon and evening to eventual safety. (One of his horses, just as plucky, a pork-and-beans-colored four-year-old who would not stand still in harness, was nicknamed "Dancing Dan" by Raymond and me.)

The trail to Mosquito Ranch figures more dangerously in another memory with sequels, as years went by, hard to estimate. One fall day after Raymond and I had been duck hunting, wading in Bronco Lake and lying in the cold marshes north of the cornfields (where most of the ducks were, it turned out), we headed for home. Walking at Raymond's side, carrying a duck or two while he carried others plus the shotgun, I stubbed my toe and dragged momentarily behind. In that instant the "unloaded" shotgun went off, blasting the middle of my old jacket and leaving small burns at stomach level. We agreed not to mention that I probably missed death that day, but I had cause to remember it later in the army and on highways in New York and France.

Unlike my adventures with horses and guns, hardly a shadow fell across the luminous current of my school life. I was the only student who did not cheat on an orientation class exam, according to the teacher (who, by encouraging me to do two semesters' work for her in one term, inadvertently readied me for my departure from

"My single beloved building, the old public library in Alliance"

Alliance before graduation day). However, I was not a teacher-toady, for I made pictorial fun of four of my teachers in the school newspaper (Burns, Salsow, Binfield, and Borgaard), in a prize-winning cartoon series on the front page. More serious drawings had already accumulated in my hermitage at home, where, since my final months at Central School, I had made freehand drawings of Indians, cowboys, and coyotes.

The town library was in Biblical terms "my truth and my refuge," my single beloved building then and thereafter. I can still smell the books, finger the shelves, and see silver-haired Mrs. Prettyman patrolling the aisles with a slight waddle and twinkling blue eyes. She pretended once not to see me in a corner studying sexually informative drawings in a large book with a scientific bias. I read all the fiction and magazines there, probably, except those meant for females. I knew Jules Verne, *Baron Münchhausen*, the "Easy Chair" pages in *Harper's*, and *The Riders of the Purple Sage* by the age of fourteen (as well as the Whistling Kid, the Phantom with all his disguises, and other pulp heroes).

Regarding Zane Grey's daring riders, my sister Julia's letter, already noted, says that the famous novelist chose my father as the best horseman and guide to familiarize him with the Bad Lands and Sand Hills. I remember my father's mentioning his own acquaintance with Harold Bell Wright, a lesser star in Zane Grey's firmament. *Wild West Weekly* and *Ranch Romances* were delicacies that Raymond and I devoured at home in secret, for my mother thought them trash, a view I occasionally shared regarding *Ranch Romances* when I pooh-poohed as "girl stuff" its hugging and kissing.

Perhaps if I had spent high school time thinking about girls—I was the only boy in my Latin class—I would not have received, as class valedictorian, the congratulatory scroll and the scholarship offer from Grand Island Business School, still packed away with the silver and bronze medals won for shorthand, history, etc. Girls also played second fiddle in the concerns of my friend Neil Winegar, a classmate of superior intelligence; he preferred the model airplanes that he built and that I tinkered with. But Neil was rather sour-natured; whereas the prom-queen-to-be, Shirley Grassman, according to her statement in the *Alliance Times-Herald* in 1989, considered me "really a smart guy and a fine fellow."

I was either too smart or not smart enough (if a family anecdote is true) to appreciate a visit to our house made by Fern King, one of the seven other African Americans in the whole school. When Fern left, so goes the story, my mother said, "James, why don't you walk Fern home?" My reply, I am ashamed to say, was "She came over here alone, didn't she?"

On "the oval" or on the basketball court, however, I began to develop an eye for the sweaters of the pep squad. Those female squeals and yells from the stands gave me the glandular push for my ribbon- and medal-winning efforts in broad-jumping and high-jumping at a Chadron College competition to which our first-class high school team was invited. The roar of the crowd, I found when barely tipping the bar during a crucial local meet, was no more moving than its vast groan of sympathy. The relevant newspaper coverage mixed sympathy with praise: "Emanuel, fighting a pulled muscle, jumped Kenworthy to a new meet record." I proudly sewed my large white "A" on a green mail-order sweater I already had (being unable to afford the school's official blue-and-white garment) and wore it sometimes after leaving Alliance.

A sports note worth adding is that when three young men who had recently graduated (Robert and Joe Lewis plus Ernest Green) joined Ralph Jones and me to form "The Five Aces," we performed, even if eliminated in the second round of the Four-State Tournament, as apparently the first professional African American basketball team in the USA. (In the intramurals we had been unbeatable.)

I left Alliance on 9 January 1939. Leaning back on the green seat cover of the railroad coach bound for Mayfield, Kansas, the station nearest to my destination, the Civilian Conservation Corps camp at Wellington, I pondered two of what have remained vital memories, one ideological, one familial. As for ideas, I had already become what I would always be: a person whose civil rights were inviolable. Unforgettable were the several days in Mr. Osborne's civics class when the boy Zack and his dog, alive on the pages, went from municipal office to municipal office, learning Zack's rights. The moral that burned itself into my mind was this: Never, never give up your rights as a citizen; learn them, and treasure them as life itself.

"My mother, 'whose courage never failed,' as reads the dedicatory page of my A Chisel in the Dark*"*

The iron will and ethical stamina enjoined by that memory had become flesh and bone in the person of my mother, whose accomplishment I partially understood at twenty-one when writing of her in my first autobiography:

> Practically alone . . . she managed us [seven children] through school to graduation, during the worst years of our century. She had the rare ability to do so much with so little. Her faith in what she was doing was so great, the odds against her were so many, that the miracle of her achievement, I suppose, had to happen, in order that we who were a part of it might not forget. That she should escape with us without the telling marks of indigence stamped upon our bearing and outlook is the best tribute I believe can be accorded to a mother.[7]

[7]From *From the Bad Lands to the Capital*, p. 25.

But the expression of this truth, for the moment, had been her final advice on the station platform: "Always put your best foot forward."

Bugles, Bales, and Mortarboards

1939–40: Was member of CCC Camp 786, Wellington, Kansas.

1940: Worked in Des Moines, Iowa, as elevator operator.

1941–42: Worked in Rock Island, Illinois, for Brady Iron and Metal Company.

1942–44: Worked in Washington, D.C., War Department, as Confidential Secretary to Brigadier General Benjamin O. Davis, Assistant Inspector General of the U.S. Army and Air Force.

1944–46: Did military service in Philippine Islands and Netherlands East Indies.

1946–50: Earned B.A., summa cum laude, at Howard University, Washington, D.C.

1950: Married Mattie Etha Johnson in Chicago.

1950–53: Earned M.A. with straight-A record at Northwestern University, Chicago and Evanston, Illinois.

Just as school colors and graduations were consistent in my academic life (colors veritably always blue and white, caps and gowns never worn—until the Ph.D.), bugles sounded often in my nonscholastic times, beginning with my Kansas days.

Civilian Conservation Corps Camp 786, as President Roosevelt envisioned it, environmentalist but military-without-weapons in practice. Like other regional companies, for its tree-planting and other conservationist activities, it had, on the paramilitary level, a commander, a subaltern, and a medical officer; and, on the civilian uniformed level, a top kick (first sergeant), supply sergeant, mess sergeant, company clerk, canteen steward, and lower enlisted staff and work supervisors above the mass of enlisted men. (I should think, in the Green Party mid-1990s, such a nationwide anti-unemployment crusade would reemerge.)

The lowest-level "enlistees," except the weakest ones, seemed like men, not boys; and I had never imagined so many Black men in one place. They were rougher, in a different way, than the hardpan crew on the Worley ranch, among them pool sharks, knife-wielders, boxers, would-be thugs, and a bayou-born snake charmer. Some, like my friend Bill Frye, had strict, native intelligence. Having a tough body, quick mind, and social manners more flexible than I had thought, I survived rather easily among them—partly because, being canteen steward and thus in charge of the recreation hall, company store, and mail, I could dish out small favors.

In short, my knowledge of life expanded rapidly. I learned, at table, that "Please pass the potatoes" meant nothing, but that a curt "Gimme shorts on them spuds, man!" got results. With the help of Frye, I chose high-drape trousers, uncommon suspenders, and big-shoulder jackets from swatches in the camp for the regular trips to Wichita. And I made camp friends with Wichita hepcats (Howard Smith, Artie Richards, and the two big cheerful but rowdy Thurman brothers) who knew where to buy illegal "chalk" alcohol and find transient rooms. Although $22 of my $30-per-month salary was an allotment to my mother, $8 was enough for game and riot.

Girls, girls, girls. I met my share, Lorraine, Valentina, and Ruby still being unforgettable names, in rising order of impact. In Valentina's lavender gift stationery box of 1939, I have always stored my high school medals. Ruby is sensually preserved in my poem "Between Loves: A Train from London," as well as in my recollection of a joint descent down the fire escape of a Wichita hotel, foot locker between us, for Lord knows what reason.

After half a century, close-shaven topkick William Wilson ("The Wolf" to us) strides flat-footedly through my memory, barking orders; Willard P. Cropp, the pudgy, serious educational adviser, ponderously sips Coca-Cola at my canteen counter, the bottom button of his shirt having popped out; Leonard Conger, the balding, stuttering master of the dirty dozens, grins and capers at the anger of his victim; tall, long-lipped Solon "Soak" Shepherd twitches one earmuff at his long-awaited letter and does a floppy, double-jointed dance through the door; and "Shithouse Shorty," the gap-toothed, muscular latrine orderly, smilingly pushes a stone-laden wheelbarrow along a plank. "Alley-Oop"; "Dickhead" Price; "Little Depot"; "Frankenstein"; and dark, thin Wendell Johnson, whose reason finally succumbed to his own imitations of Napoleon: the images of these and other camp members seem indelible.

Although intellectually I marked time in the CCC camp, where Mr. Cropp urged me to plan for college despite my poverty, I did write short stories (commended by a soil conservation service man there who had been a Hollywood technician) and published them in the *Chatterbox*. That mimeographed paper contained so much romantic gossip that "The Drape Kid" once tried to grab up all the copies in Wichita to salvage one or two of his love affairs. Regarding one of my stories, Frye asked me with disappointment, "Why did you kill off the lovers at the end?" I shrugged, but I perhaps thought of our friendly camp mate "The Weasel," who had recently died in a car crash, and at whose funeral our bugler had sounded taps.

The comparative cultural lull was accompanied by a temporary ease, even privilege, mixed however with crosscurrents. The only camp member who never had to wear his GI overalls, I lounged after midnight, learning to shoot pool with the night watchman or musing behind my drawn canteen shutters over the various graduation souvenirs kindly sent me by my typing teacher, redheaded Miss Worley. True, I experienced real affection from shapely, tender Valentina, to whom I paid insufficient attention, according to Frye; and, except for the bone-numbing travel (1500 miles by bus and 250 by train), I enjoyed my Christmas vacation in Denver, where I saw Raymond, Julia, Janet, and Gladys; and in Alliance, where I saw my mother, Christine, and Alvin (as well as, by chance, my father). In Alliance I sparkled with dance steps yet unseen by "the locals."

Yet, my "tendency to sobriety and seclusiveness" (part of my self-portrait recorded at twenty-one) was revived in camp by my gang's trips to Wichita's Hollow Inn, Paradise Inn, Commodore Inn, and the bareknuckle Hancock Inn, where we were always frisked at the door: that is, I recognized the cold bedrock beneath the loose, sandy gaiety of such places. The icy part of my consciousness was also firmed by the unfounded suspicions of the latest subaltern, young Lieutenant Jack T. Shannon, who, during my vacation, charged me with mismanagement of canteen funds until he was told that his inventory had overlooked an expensive stock of army footlockers on hand. Lantern-jawed Shannon was the only man in camp that I disliked, and his narrow-eyed, sidelong glances told me that he knew it. I never set foot outside the camp for three months, to make sure that he could not again wedge his juvenility into my business. Although I wanted to reenlist to save money for college, a delicate balance in my mind had shifted. The countdown of morning bugles had begun.

Both Frye and I, like most of my buddies, "jumped down" (camp slang for pulling up stakes) on 26 June 1940. In Frye's hometown, Des Moines, Iowa, I took a room on Sampson Street in the eastside home of his brother Tom, whose wife was named Etta. Quickly I found that the dance halls and taverns were not as exciting as those in Wichita, where our gang had slid gin bottles across the length of the floor to one another, and where, at Hancock Inn, we had seen loud-mouthed women like "Black Sal" attack one another in fistfights.

I found the worst-paying part-time job of my life in Des Moines, where hard times and racism relegated me to operating an elevator, earning $5.82 for a seven-day week, in a building housing the state employment office and the Rainbow Club. Once, after misjudging the threshold on the highest floor, I found my elevator stuck to the ceiling shaft. Crestfallen, I left the building, bought a beer in a café whose red neon lights seemed to flash "All is lost," and returned to the scene of the crime. Behold! Supervisor Ollie, congenially running the elevator, assured me that the catastrophe was normal.

My literary career, running, I thought, almost parallel with catastrophe in terms of rejection slips, was encouraged by Stanley McLaughlin, a fiction-oriented African American journalist whom I had met. Partly because of his enthusiasm for his own projects, and partly because I began to mix my *Wild West Weekly* heritage with my off-elevator reading of Dashiell Hammett and other pulp masters, I wrote an estimated three quarters of a million words in numerous detective and murder mysteries—aided technically by a little red-covered book called *Murder Manual*. (I faintly remember words of encouragement from a writer in the second-floor employment office named Hagedorn.) Dissatisfied with my stories after six months, I burned all of them up.

My dissatisfaction spreading from the root through the tree, I decided to leave Des Moines. Studying maps and newspapers, I planned to go northward through Iowa, try fruit-harvesting work in Wisconsin, then go eastward as far as Cleveland, Ohio, where I thought I might like to live for a while. Failing to get a loan of ten dollars from Julia in Denver, I resolved to initiate my plan with the $1.54 left from a five-dollar loan from Frye. I said to him, on the steps of the departing bus: "I've got to take big and bold steps, or I'll never get anywhere."

I got off the bus in Davenport, Iowa, where a very recent letter from Stanley McLaughlin had asked me to spend my birthday, which was the following day, with him and his friend Leona. Their landlady, a hefty woman named Mary had, it developed after my arrival at his lodgings on West Fifth Street, a viewpoint resembling that of Ellison's Mary in *Invisible Man* (a novel in which I was to jot down over two thousand notations years later). Divining in nature, she surveyed my thin suitcase, gave me a cot and curtained it under the staircase near her spare-time front-room barbershop.

Two days later, deciding to test the job-hunting mysteries of Illinois, just across the nearby Mississippi River, rather than the sidewalks of Iowa, which had probably already yielded me their maximum of luck, I headed for the Centennial Bridge. Halfway across it, I was halted by my first-ever tollkeeper, who apparently found me the first traveler without the nickel needed to continue. I retraced my many steps, holding onto my nickel, and followed his directions to a distant free bridge that crossed the muddy Mississippi into Rock Island, Illinois.

After fruitlessly walking miles in Moline and Rock Island and returning to my starting point, I noticed a large building nearly under the bridge. Not even caring what kind of place it was, having decided it was time to proceed to Wisconsin, I sauntered in and asked the keen-featured busy man behind the counter if he could use a good man.

Surprisingly, I thus secured the last back-breaking job in my life, at Brady's Iron and Metal Company—in short, a junkyard. But there was also a raghouse, where I was put to work hauling on a two-wheel, front-boarded hand truck all sorts of rags, magazines, and papers from the receiving floor (where pedlars and truckers came), upstairs by elevator to the "ragwomen." These usually dusty, tough but friendly foreign women sorted my loads into proper categories to dump into the baling machine, operated (when sober) by "Little Jimmy Ray," a broad-shouldered, short Black man whose talk was unintelligible when moistened with liquor. This crew was sometimes supplemented by "Moon," a cockeyed, snuff-dipping, usually unshaven Black man who normally worked in the yard.

Our job was back-breaking and rather dangerous when we hauled, using a hand truck without front boards for large magazine bales (five-by-six-by-two feet) often weighing a ton. Due to necessary quick maneuvering in limited space, one man had to handle the mammoth bale, even at the most dangerous moments when trucking it across a huge iron plate between the doors of the raghouse and the receiving railroad boxcar. A wrong movement or a subtle failure in strength at that point was cause for bones to be broken by an uncontrolled bale sliding toward iron doorjambs or crashing downward toward junkyard rubble.

The second night after I had handled a few such bales, I almost fell asleep in a Davenport restaurant on Fifth Street. Starting to eat, I was amazed to find my hand too weak to raise my glass of water. When the waitress, a timid-looking woman with shredded-wheat hair, left with my order, I clasped my wrists together and used them to lift my glass. Clamped fists, I found, could manage a knife, fork, and spoon.

Regaining my farmhand toughness in the raghouse, I learned to "double-deck" bales in boxcars (the biggest man in the junkyard being sometimes unable to help when called upon); to drive and back up trucks in the alley without being exposed as a nondriver; to outwit dishonest pedlars who slyly put their feet on my weighmaster scale; and to walk under a sun-baked ceiling across a ten-feet-high pile of magazines carrying a seventy-five-pound box without slipping into holes. And, of course, I said "Sure" when Brady Senior asked me whether I could run the baling machine in a whiskey pinch. Thus continuing my education, I energized myself each noon at a curb by downing a quart of milk and wolfing a dozen cinnamon rolls plus a half pound of baloney. This diet, with extra trousers and shirts worn daily, helped me to survive the cold: I froze my nose a few weeks after Pearl Harbor Day, from continual bridge crossings; and my feet, in icy sympathy, did not warm up until springtime.

My feet, and the rest of me, did catch the Rock Island Rocket for a warming pre-Christmas trip to Denver and Alliance. In the Queen City I saw my three older sisters, all married, and their visitor, Christine, from Alliance, where I afterwards saw my mother and Alvin. Then, with my aunt Grace (Harris) and two friends of hers, I went by auto to visit my father at his own farm. Although his horse had fallen with him minutes before he arrived to find us unclogging our gas line, he let me take the animal for a brief moonlight ride. Putting the horse in the barn later, I chatted with my father, who lent me some money, and said, "Someday I'll try to help you along, James, if I can." After we ate his good cooking and said our goodbyes, he mounted the running board of our car, shotgun cradled in one arm, "to see if I can spot you something to take into town," he said. Nothing popped up or flew away, however, as we drove slowly along, so I shook his hand before he lithely jumped off and watched his free arm waving a faded farewell. I repaid the loan, but I never saw him again.

Raymond, the reason for the loan, who had come to stay with me and for whom I had secured a job at Brady's, had failed to telegraph me my return fare as promised. Back in Davenport (where I now roomed with Booker T. Cribbs and his family at 1128 Ripley Street), I found out that Raymond was in jail. He had been arrested in the Morocco Club in Rock Island in an altercation over the loss of an overcoat—my overcoat, which he had been wearing. The lawyer whom I obtained apparently made a fool out of the arresting officer, who had plainly abused his powers. I later shared Raymond's admiration of the lawyer's reply when asked his name by a court clerk: "Weinstein, thank you, past master of law; and I believe in my freedom!" But I did not share his belief that it was acceptable to wear my clothing without my permission; and, less acceptably, he had earlier worn my favorite, Wichita-haloed, blue-and-grey trousers without the magic password.

Raymond and I were on the fringes of an enterprise that would have again involved legal counsel had it gained full support. We were to be on the staff of Stanley McLaughlin's proposed first African American newspaper in the Quad-Cities area (Davenport, Rock Island, Moline, and East Moline). Unable to garner enthusiasm equalling his own, Stanley was upstaged by a man from Kewanee, Illinois, who came to town and founded the *Bronze Dispatch*.

As for Raymond, whose smile in those days was larger than his purse, and who was rejected as a volunteer for the air force because of his race, he successfully volunteered for the army. At 5:50 A.M. on 11 April 1942, we prepared to part, I donning my two pairs of trousers and two shirts, he sitting on the edge of the bed, smoking. He was undoubtedly, like me, thinking of our boyhood, when we had been asked to act like men before our time, when we had been given too little, denied too much, and asked to shoulder burdens meant for those wiser and stronger than we were. But now we merely exchanged some light banter and shook hands. I stepped out abruptly, onto the frosty sidewalk and, as was my custom after saying goodbye, did not look back.

"My brother Raymond, at 412 Missouri Street, Alliance," 1938

In Davenport, alone more than ever, I survived; but, more so than in the CCC camp and Des Moines, intellectually I stood still. My Corona portable typewriter, bought near the Des Moines River and finally paid for near the Mississippi, gathered some dust. I was not closer to college, although I had saved about a hundred dollars' worth of perspiration in a post office account. "Uncolleged" people had schooled me a little: a magician and ventriloquist named Louis McBride, rooming for two months at the Cribbs' with his charming wife, had used his deck of cards to demonstrate to me that gambling paid off only for professionals; and "Moon" himself had taught me some humility by shouting at me almost angrily in the raghouse one day. "Sesame! Sesame!" he cried, veritably jumping up and down, cockeye glaring, sweat and mattress straw and loose snuff sticking to his beard. Disappointment, curiously, seemed mixed with his exasperation after hearing me mispronounce the word as *sea same*.

Girls had been the agents of instruction as well as pleasure. One named Geraldine led me to the knowledge of curative blue ointment, the druggist probably guessing that it was not "for a friend of mine," as I had pretended with a straight face. Another one, popular Nettie, a Freemana Davenport native, wild and pretty and essentially good-hearted, zinged along at what was my speed, but jockeyed a length ahead of me on Saturday nights to keep "China Boy," "Railhead," and other Monte Carlo Club regulars in their proper lanes. She was just as quick-witted one night when her mother returned home unexpectedly and sat talking with us. I can still see Nettie's carelessly flung panties clarifying in my focus, still draped over the radio after the knock on the door, and hear her changing the conversation geometrically, diverting attention from her subtle movement toward the delightful article.

Averaging $22 weekly at Brady's, I remembered that my grade on a Federal intelligence test taken on 19 July for a job as messenger at the Rock Island Arsenal had yielded nothing. Yet, often that fall I saw, crossing the bridge with me but headed for the arsenal, white boys who had taken the exam on the same day. I had had to write "Negro" in one space on the test sheet, which had not diminished my score of 98.87. I still keep the official notification of that score, as well as the sheet indicating my marks on tests in shorthand and typing given the following March for a stenographic job in Washington, D.C. Although the carriage return lever of my ancient Corona failed me in the test room, I scored 89.79, with a mark of 98.75 in shorthand. Then I waited, wearing two of everything but shoes when crossing the Mississippi to Brady's.

When the notice of my appointment to a civil service job in Washington, D.C., arrived on 12 April 1942, the day after Raymond's departure, the weariness that sometimes bent my shoulders lifted magically, the grime left my face in the mirror on Ripley Street. I quit my job two days later and spent eight days relaxing and packing a save-all-this trunk to be sent to Denver. To carry my Washington suitcase, I used the title "Mister James" given me respectfully by the Cribbs children; and, to make that bag lighter, after I caught the 10:10 A.M. train on the 21st, I daydreamed of a life where Stella and Maggie, the most picturesque of the dogged Polish ragwomen, as well as "Babe" and Roy, the foreman and the youngest of the junkyard crew, would rest in my memory as witnesses to the likelihood of survival, rather than as carriers of the virus of desperation.

Two weeks earlier, grimy and aching amidst a pile of especially filthy rags and papers at work, I had kicked aside a frayed silk-stocking nest of newborn mice and stared down at a startlingly clear page from *Liberty* magazine. "The lights of civilization," I had read, I think, in the boldfaced bottom lines, "are going out all over the world. We shall not see them lit again in our lifetime.—Sir Edward Grey, 1914." To me, the lights were coming on, even though a terrible world war had just begun.

In Washington, rooming with the Perry family at 27 R Street, N.W., I became the confidential secretary of Brigadier General Benjamin O. Davis, Sr., in the War Department's Office of the Inspector General, housed in the Riverside Apartments Building, not far from the Lincoln Memorial. I replaced Hollis A. Woods, a very able, industrious, intelligent African American, who, after the war, became my friend, introducing me to his own friend—and opposite—postal clerk George Webb, who could philander, talk politics, and perceive literary beauty with equal ease.

General Davis, the first Black general in the USA (who "came up through the ranks, taking an exam every step of the way" and without influence, he said) was an irreproachable gentleman and an agreeable boss. He was a member of President Roosevelt's "Black Cabinet"; and, as assistant inspector general, made many inspection tours throughout the USA and abroad, writing detailed reports on matters ranging from mess hall sanitation, through delicate staff problems of commanding officers, to death-dealing racial clashes from Georgia to Texas. From him I learned how General Eisenhower's fingers and legs moved as he discussed vital strategies in England. In General Davis's office, taking shorthand notes as lieutenant generals examined with him the pitfalls in devising Puerto Rican soldier policies, I learned the governmental biases and prejudices that nerved executive orders and crucial memoranda. Taking my oaths seriously, I kept to myself all the classified information that came my way.

General Davis and his family, a social set of people new to me, invited me to their holiday dinners in 1942, when I met their charming daughter Elnora, and in 1943, when I received as a present an engraved leather toilet kit of such quality that I still carry on trips its last, taped-up remnant. I met "B.O.D., Jr.," then a straight-backed West Pointer, who soon commanded the 99th Fighter Squadron in Europe and later became a general. My job also brought me into contact with other eminent Black men: the fabled Walter White; Judge William Hastie and his successor, Truman K. Gibson, each a special assistant to the Secretary of War.

A friendly, complimentary letter from the White House was to be my final bond with Lieutenant General Howard McCrum Snyder, the Surgeon General of the army, when I walked his floor in the Inspector General's office. He was the personal physician of President Eisenhower when he wrote me the letter.

My family bonds were firmed in a new way when my sister Christine, whom I had made walk behind me to kindergarten, followed me to Washington two months after my arrival. Alliance being only one-hundredth the size of the capital, she adjusted well, with intermittent help from me, to her civil service job. As months went by, she and her leopard-skin coat and dance-loving slippers became almost Washingtonian. She and James Wesley, a brilliant young man from Charleston, West Virginia, both rooming at the Perrys', became dancing-party friends; but, finding him sitting more than once with his bags packed, I had to persuade him each time to give Washington another chance. (When he visited me years later in Mount Vernon, New York, he was chief of cardiology at Harlem Hospital.)

Raymond came to the capital too, but only briefly (exactly one year after he had come to Davenport), as a corporal temporarily based at Fort McClellan, Alabama. I saw the other family members during a trip to Denver, where my mother and Alvin had moved in August 1942, and where I heard Alliance news of Lewis-Jones-King marriages. I took in gin and philosophy from Uncle Turner and talked on the street with pretty Dolly Batt, daughter of the laconic farmer who had once said of me—my mother confessed—"That boy'll never amount to anything: he don't respect his elders."

Four girls remain names in my Washington life, two of them set in boldface. Frances Kimbrough, a New Yorker with a melodious voice, introduced me to her city and charmed me by singing the lovely song "Skylark" while we danced in a nightclub. Nona Ashby, another New York girl with dash and a fresh take-charge manner, swished into my ken at a northeast Washington party (where I also met an appealingly soft-natured girl named Marjorie Robinson, whom I remember for inviting me to enjoy a bubble bath in her apartment just after the war). Nona and I went to New York, where I had a jolly time with her

family, but afterwards the days of our association were numbered. On Valentine's Day, two cards in my mail were unsigned, one with a postmark that lost the game, the other with handwriting that former-mystery-story-writer-me compared with old Christmas cards. Nona had asked a girl that I knew to send the nameless card.

Yet how do these stack up against "Zany," my nickname for a slim, dark Washington girl who told me, enfolding her drink in her arms, that she would chain her ideal lover to her bed and feed him raw eggs until inventory time?

"Chili" (Georgietta Childress by name), an attractive girl from Chicago, cut a wider swath through the field of my social life. I met her in the assignment pool for newcomers, on Eighteenth and Pennsylvania, where, instead of joining complaints about idle days, I read Benjamin Franklin's engrossing *Autobiography,* which I had rescued from Brady junk. With Chili, I satiated myself in the glitter of nightclubs and parties. Having become an amateur chiromancer, I entertained a few people at these parties, especially girls, by reading their palms. Chili's engagement to be married, unknown to me, loosened the tie between us in preparation for the legal knot she was to celebrate in July 1943. I turned at once to glamour girls whom I had met through Webb (Adella Shields, Dorothy Herriot, and Marguerite Thomas in particular), soaking in their instruction along with their pleasant company. And I even reread a gratifying letter that had come at Christmastime from Nettie in Davenport.

Less glamorous, yet more so, was "Kat" (Katherine Smith), an Atlanta peach mixed with a Philippine mango, tinted with strains as remote as Hawaii, Guatemala, Peru. I never asked her about lineage, but she was from Atlanta, first seen by me at the wedding (25 May 1943) of Mary Threet, a friend of Christine's whom I nicknamed "The Chile." Surveying a group of girls waiting at the foot of a staircase to catch the bride's bouquet as a forecast of good luck in courtship, I singled her out as the good-luck girl, saying "It'll be you." Later, the two of us conversing and swaying on streetcar straps, bound for U Street, she reminded me, "You don't even know my name." My pencil was already in my hand.

Kat, socially formal because of her Atlanta background, must have thought me curiously unpolished, worthy of study. I, on the other hand, found her both childlike and voluptuous, unconsciously sensual in her smile, in slight movements of her body and head. She did the impossible in luring me to church on New Year's Eve, when I should have been drinking toasts with good-timers, and in dragging me several times to the same church, where she prepared current-events summaries, gave monthly Bible readings, and did other services that made me pinch myself for orientation. More normally, I played whist, even bridge, with her and spent time with her kindly mother when she visited Washington.

Not only did she try to churchify me, but Kat also stirred my initiative in more interesting ways. After studying the *Congressional Directory* at the IGO, I suggested to her a visit to a session of Congress. First visiting Congressman Miller of Nebraska and Ramspeck of Georgia for passes (the former adding a pass to the National Art Gallery), we observed the post-Easter session, not an efficient one, where Congressman Hébert of Louisiana took thirty-five minutes to defend himself gratuitously against aspersions in some newspaper. On a tour of the Capitol, I whispered to Kat some facts I had dug up, among them that a West Indian physician, Dr. Thorton (from Tortola), had advanced a plan for the Capitol that had been chosen from a group of about fifteen. At the art gallery, I looked closely at paintings by Rembrandt, Monet, Manet, Whistler, and others for the first time. Kat, I decided, was a good influence.

Even if I had wanted to, it would have been hard to ignore Washington culture. The "wedding girl," as I first thought of Kat, went with me in late February 1944 to a command performance at Constitution Hall, where Hans Kindler conducted. (I sat there remembering all the beautiful 78-rpm records of Caruso that my mother had played on our Victrola in Alliance.) The previous year, I had seen *La Traviata* with her, performed by the National Negro Opera Company of New York at the Watergate on the Potomac.

On the lowest rungs of the cultural ladder, I had two other entirely new experiences. First, I set foot inside a YWCA (with Kat). I felt out of place—just as I might have felt in a YMCA—however, a girl who danced with me and felt my tension said two words that were magic to me, then and in later years: "Just relax." I never saw her again, but her name is still like a bit of money in the bank: Sylvia Scott.

Second, I went to a place described thus at twenty-one:

> . . . in my childhood I had thought of [teas] with abhorrence, always having pictured sickly looking, large-eyed children playing mammoth

instruments to produce music which the listeners applauded with stiff, pretentious, and often hypocritical daintiness while they munched tiny, sugar-coated cookies and sipped tasteless tea from miniature cups.[8]

On this St. Patrick's Day, with the "wedding girl," I found those very cookies, cups, and tea. But the musicians were not children, and they were good. I could hardly believe it.

Although new experiences were feeding into my life, I did not recreate them in literary forms I had used before. My D.C. acquaintances had no reason to encourage me, although Adella Shields of the Bureau of Engraving (met through Webb) conversed with me about books, plays, and music and wanted to write a satire on her place of employment. One other casual acquaintance, Mamie Burns, said that she wanted to write humorous material. To me she *was* humorous material, in that she could produce it at will from her mouth, moving about her house in company. Perhaps if she had chewed on a pencil long enough, her literary career would have zoomed.

New experiences were in store for Wesley. He who had so often packed his bags to give up on Washington, finally had to pack one at the behest of the Army Induction Center. As I said goodbye to my genial next-room neighbor and thought of Raymond's rejection by the air force (which later changed its racial policy), I remembered that, during an air-raid drill, when citizens on the street had to take immediate shelter, Wesley and I had been refused entry into the vestibule of a "white" church by its minister. That was preparation, perhaps, for years to come.

Although I knew how to avoid military service, through my study of *Army Regulations* sections on malingering, I also knew that army service, because of veterans' educational benefits, was my only route to college. The processes by which I reached my decision to join the army—long, rigorous, and exact (requiring about five hundred words of close explication in my first autobiography)—can be reduced to two steps. First, I used a worn little card in my wallet, dated "11/20/43," labeled on one side "CRITERION OF VALUES" (ranging from "strength of character . . ." down to "service to mankind"), and on the other "LAW" (specifying my steps in making

---

[8]From *From the Bad Lands to the Capital*, pp. 118–19.

decisions, starting with isolation of "the truth of the issue" and ending with immediate pursuit of the resolution).

Second, as an aid I used an irrefutable system learned in my orientation course under Miss Hart in high school: listing pros and cons of the issue, striking out opposing arguments of equal weight, and emerging with a yes-or-no logical conclusion.

After six hours of uninterrupted concentration on my calculations, I found my decision, then on the next day, 15 March 1944, reviewed my efforts, almost hoping for an error. I had overlooked nothing. I must join the army. The draft board gladly acted on my come-and-get-me letter written the same day. On 17 May I passed the physical—with no regrets during the two-month interval.

General Davis, on the following morning, asked me about my plans, War Department memos having made possible my retention in uniform in the IGO as his assistant. Believing that my acceptance of the privilege would reduce my recent torturous moral journey to a butterfly's pause, I returned his straight glance with "I'll take my chances with the men in the field."

His hand fell decisively upon his desk; and he said, among other things, "The way you have expressed yourself, I feel good about you," adding that he had become attached to me and had always felt very free in talking to me, for some reason. (Years later, after his retirement, a holiday letter from his daughter Elnora reported to me that "the General" always described me as "the best secretary I ever had.")

On Sunday, 28 May 1944, as I walked around the Natural History Building of the Smithsonian Institution, I knew that I would soon be hearing bugles again, this time as a soldier in the war "to make the world safe for democracy."

At the end of basic training at Fort Devens, Massachusetts, I felt sure that I was bound for officer candidate school, for Captain Richard F. Kane, my New York-born commanding officer, told me that I had made the highest score in the regiment on a screening test. "You'll make a fine officer," he predicted. Although he might have been correct, the USS *General A. E. Anderson* soon carried me not to OCS but on a thirty-six-day, enemy-submarine-dodging voyage to Manila Bay. During the crossing, I was once given radio headphones to record messages in shorthand; perhaps the staff anticipated the message that I was the first to hear: the death of President Roosevelt.

As a private in the 642nd Ordnance Ammunition Company, I led Filipino dunnage crews into jungle-edge areas to fell the tall trees needed to secure and protect large "ammo" shells. Thus I met seven-year-old, smiling Leonardo Eusebio, who stealthily drove the crew's tractor into a tree; later he taught me to make poultices from leaves and to fashion bamboo fish traps; also he offered to get and sell me miscellaneous items, his pockets regularly stuffed with coins and bills. But earlier he had hidden in a hole in the ground for two years, living off sweet-potato roots. "Look, Mahnwail!"— for so he pronounced my name—"I lived over there," he pointed one day, then wanted to buy my boots. (Later I gave a pair of boots to a Filipino artist in need, Benjamin Hechanova, who in exchange painted two strikingly natural scenes for me on the reverse sides of discarded military signs.)

Danger threatened me visibly only twice in the Philippines, in quite different ways. On night guard duty at a water point in the low hills above the company position on Mindanao, three companions and I exchanged rifle fire with Japanese stragglers known to be north of us. I never learned whether my rating as an expert had any effect on the Japanese, but the sound of bullets ripping the canvas above us was useful information for our four replacements.

The second danger surprised me off the seashore near Cagayan when I was wading in deep water (I could not swim) with Keyes, a New York tent mate. Revolving my body horizontally in the water for fun, I stopped to stand up, only to feel my feet kicking into nothingness, then into water. Choking and sinking fast, I managed to realize that I was upside down, stomach up, and I whirled over into a posture enabling me to stand and raise my spouting mouth above the water.

Moments after having saved myself from possible drowning, and sensing Keyes at a hazy distance, I saw an upraised, triangular fin piercing the water toward him. "Watch out, Keyes!" I shouted. "There's a shark!" Both of us, straining mightily to *run* in water, splashed and heaved fearfully toward the shore, the deadly fin turning as we turned. Blinded by alarm, we could not see the shark turn away unexplainably. Keyes, not as hardy as I, lay slobbering and panting on the pebble-spotted shore as I watched him thankfully. (Less dangerously, perhaps, an adventurous soldier nicknamed "Shag" and I, leaving the same shore for a nearby town rumored to be overpopulated with girls, overturned in the tiny boat and gave up

*"Staff Sergeant Emanuel, on furlough in Denver,"
spring 1946*

in time for me to wade ashore, drenched and chastened.)

My buddies called me a "good soldier"; and more than one of them, the Philadelphian Leon Constant in particular, considered me a "cool cat." I earned the former praise by disappearing into the jungle to avoid the unwanted assignments that we plainly called "shit details." The latter name was applied to me after a few soldiers in the night queue awaiting service before a darkened Filipino hut saw me getting my five pesos back from the wizened little man in charge. A third appellation, given me by some laundry girls from Bugo and a few people in Cagayan, had some link with whatever cool I could muster: "the soldier who speaks Visayan."

Along Cagayan Bay and in the town, which bordered the Sulu Sea and faced Visayan islands to the north, I tested the phrases taught me by Leonardo, Dulzura, Feling, Marciana, and, of course, the laundry girls. Thus I earned slow nods and crinkled smiles from the cigar-brown, low-squatting vendors of stubby bananas and stinging rice wine. One Filipino family there honored my birthday in its bamboo house-on-stilts, politely dishing unfamiliar meat and thick sauces that did not go down easily, even with the sharp wine.

My good soldiering, jungle style, was followed by some literary effort, as well as some unexpected community action. I wrote a seven-stanza poem called "Dark Soldier," which included the lines "You were maligned, dark soldier, / While you were in the fray. / The onslaughts of your countrymen / Beshamed the American way." The enemy propaganda queen "Tokyo Rose" would have clasped those lines to her kimono had she seen them and found their source: the harassment of African American soldiers by military police from the "Dixie division" (31st Infantry), along with the spread of racist slander to infect Filipinos.

Community leaders, however, in cooperation with members of the Black 93rd Infantry Division (to which I was transferred two weeks after the atomic bombing of Hiroshima), arranged what they described as a "mountain forum" of eighty participants to combat the "whispering campaign." I made a detailed account of the proceedings, entitled it "Report from Mindanao," and sent it on 15 November for possible publication by *Reader's Digest,* to which I had a gift subscription given me by a New Jersey girl. The forum positively shaped Filipino opinion, but I received a negative reply from the USA.

Two goodbyes, in August and September of 1945, add feeling to my meager recollections of my first two months with Headquarters, 93rd Infantry Division. Huddled tents, warm beer, and outdoor movies watched in mud and rain are my final images of the island of Morotai in the Netherlands East Indies, where we awaited the move to the Philippines and return to the USA for demobilization. Much more vivid is my memory of Leonardo Eusebio and his smaller friends, just before my departure in August, splashing forward among water buffalos in the Tagoluan River, waving and shouting "Goodbye, Mahnwail! We will never forget you, Mahnwail!"

The other goodbye was the word itself, closing as an omen a V-Mail letter written on 17 June by my father. In late September, I learned that he had died.

The angel of death whispered to me once during that August plane-and-boat trip from Del Monte to Leyte to Morotai. Having missed one plane, I was the only passenger on a small landing boat near Leyte carrying four unshackled but rather emaciated Japanese prisoners. Seated on the gunwale, my feet dangling above my gear and rifle on the flat bottom, I saw the soldier in charge of the prisoners at the other end lean over the side of the boat to vomit—having momentarily laid his rifle aside. Instantly the most fit and alert of the Japanese sat upright, looking first at the rifle, then at me, the question being whether he could cross the distance to the guard's rifle before I could jump down from the gunwale and grab mine. I was about to leap down when he relaxed. And the angel turned away.

In the springtime, back in the USA at the demobilization center at Ogden, Utah, I found myself standing before a captain's desk as the only man in the regiment ineligible for discharge (lacking seventeen days of required service). "We're going to send you to Alabama," he said. As if holding back from a death chamber, I replied quietly, "By God, I won't go." He paused, seemed to study the double row of ribbons and stars on my chest, while I was seeing again my poem "Dark Soldier" pinned to the bulletin board of our USA-bound ship. He explained that he could send me to Fort Benning, Georgia, and could add a fifteen-day furlough to the orders.

After a cross-country, riotous furlough, I found myself being studied again, this time by an old Black man sitting across from me in a smoky, cinder-whipped Southern Railway coach bound for Columbus, Georgia. "Son, things are different down here," he said kindly, seeing me watch the almost snarling food vendor passing rudely through the all-Black coach.

Things were indeed different. Stationed for my final two months with the 25th Infantry Regiment at Fort Benning, I went into town only once, taken there by an officer investigating the shooting of an African American soldier by a Columbus policeman. In the hospital, I recorded in shorthand the halting words of the dying soldier, my ear close to his moist, whispering lips. Newly arrived in Columbus for a change of assignment, he had been accosted by the policeman. "He told me to take my hands out of my pockets," I barely heard. "I guess I didn't do it fast enough, because he started shooting. He shot me seventeen times." Maybe the soldier got the number wrong. But he died.

Discharged on 6 July 1946, I went to Washington, D.C., where the GI Bill allowed me to attend Howard University. But first I had to be reminded of racial policy in the nation's capital. Seated in uniform at a lunch counter, I ordered a Coke. The Black waitress said she could not serve me. Because of quick, consuming anger, I imagined the long mirror behind the counter shattering from my automatic rifle fire. For two hours, I sat waiting for the manager; and when he approached, a hot-biscuit-faced, blinking, white man, I gave him a short, fiery lecture damning racism in Washington as "worse than Hitler" and strode away, deeply unappeased.

Although three years earlier I had laughed at James Wesley for suggesting that I enroll at Howard, I was now ready for serious study there. No girls, as autumn approached, really distracted me: Kat had disappeared; and one of the letters received on Morotai from "Little D," my nickname for a Washington girl named Evelyn, lovely in all ways, had said, "Before I got married [a week ago] I tried to think of any possible person that could be hurt . . . , but somehow I could not imagine that you would honestly care."

What I cared about was making the most of the opportunity for which I had gone to war: the chance to go to college. Professors already famous, like Alain Locke, invited me into their offices to offer whatever help I might need. John Hope Franklin showed me, from his desk drawer, the opening paragraph of his manuscript of *From Slavery to Freedom*. Sterling Brown, inviting a few of us students to a restaurant dinner, regaled us with his easy magic as a raconteur.

Unaware that I would never again have such remarkable classroom teachers in a single university, I enjoyed the tutelage of John Lovell, Frank Snowden, and Margaret Just Butcher. I was in a class taught by the charming Mrs. Butcher, a group as capable as any I was to join or teach later (Jett, Washington, Lyons, Coffee, and others), some of whom she invited to her home for lunch. All I could think of to write in her guestbook was "Pass the eggs, please."

I profited for four years from these extraordinary professors, ironically because of racism. Since, at that time, white universities in the USA would not hire them, they tended to congregate at Howard, which was then styled "the capstone of Negro education."

For feminine company during those years, I did not scout the campus, although Gloria Edmunds and Loretta Wilson were my favorite occasional classmates. (I once astonished Gloria by straightening up from a hallway water fountain with masses of white foam bubbling from my lips—having just mistakenly brushed my teeth at home with shaving cream instead of toothpaste.) Neither did I depend upon Nona, who knew the Wilson family with whom I roomed on Thirteenth Street, N.W., and who flashed pleasantly across my student life without disarranging my desk.

I met Jessie Poole (through Webb), another Bureau of Engraving employee: poised, good-looking, intelligent, and slightly motherly. Instantly likeable, she shared most of the cultural events and entertainment that I could afford. When mentioning her father, she would laugh, "Oh, that man Elijah! The things he used to say!" (It occurred to me only a few years ago that she was the daughter of the Elijah Muhammad who founded the "Black Muslim" movement that involved Malcolm X, but I never researched my conjecture.)

I remember Jessie, not only for her durable tenderness, but also for her chance connection with a misfortune that overtook me in her presence. Preparing to leave her apartment one night, I discovered that I could hardly raise my left arm. Afterwards I never told her (nor anyone else to this day, except for three women) that I remained afflicted with polio.

The polio attack and its lasting effects did not hamper my literary advancement. Majoring in English literature (I was the founding president of the English Club) and minoring in psychology, I published a few poems and a short story in Howard's *Hilltop.* As for national publications, several of my poems appeared in *America Sings,* a college anthology series; and in *Ebony Rhythm,* a collection of African American poems edited by Beatrice Murphy. (When red-baiters troubled the editor and most of her friends were afraid to speak up, I wrote a letter in her defense—remembering Zack and his dog, as well as the words of my brother's lawyer, "I believe in my freedom!")

During those Howard years, I intensified my creative writing in New York during the summer of 1948 in a twelve-by-six-foot windowless room in the Bronx, on 155th Street near the "Home of the Yankees," the Polo Grounds. I completed a partly autobiographical novel called "Vengeance Is Mine" and worked hard on a volume of eighty-four poems called "Dreamspots"—all by writing constantly, seeing no friends, climbing through the skylight to get air or to sit on the roof at night.

Professors Butcher and Lovell read the novel; and Pearl Buck, who kindly visited Mrs. Butcher's class in 1949, giving us advice and taking away samples of our writing to examine, read my first two chapters. Because I left Howard before graduation in 1950, having enough credits for the B.A.,

I had no more contact with the Nobel Prize-winning novelist, but classmates reported that she said of my work, "If the rest of the novel is as good as these first two chapters, it is a good novel."

That "if" clause was decisive for two publishers. Farrar, Straus, and Cudahy returned the manuscript, wanting to see my "next novel"; when Little, Brown, and Company sent it back, I never opened the big envelope, assuming it contained a flat rejection. Since Twayne Publishers did not name my "Dreamspots" volume the winner of its contest, I hid it in a trunk (and did not examine it closely again until early February 1993, when I judged about five of its poems worthy of publication today).

My creative writing lapsed when I shifted to Northwestern University's Chicago campus, partly because I got married (to Mattie Etha Johnson of Chicago) and put on the grueling harness of graduate studies plus full-time or part-time jobs that I was to bear for twelve consecutive years. On Northwestern's Evanston campus, however, I published the poems "Illegitimate Child" and "War" in the magazine *Profile,* and I received encouragement from Professors Joel Hunt and Zera Fink. The former read "Vengeance Is Mine" and found the portrait of the mother "unforgettable"; the latter read my "Sonnet for a Writer" to the Wordsworth seminar after announcing, "Mr. Emanuel is a poet."

Being the only Black student pursuing an M.A. in literature on the Evanston campus, I had to pass muster with each professor (Arthur Nethercot, the vampire-lamia specialist, asked me in his office, rather kindly, "I presume you know how to write a research paper?"); but all of them graded me fairly. I decided not to apply the second half of my two-year John Hay Whitney Foundation grant to doctoral studies there. Although husky-voiced departmental chairman Frederic Faverty told me, "You would have done well, staying with us," I remembered Northwestern's flimsy reason for rejecting my appeal for scholarship aid ("We have numerous qualified candidates"), and I recalled that a test grade of 98.87, linked with the word "Negro," had not qualified me for a job as messenger.

In Sandburg's "City of the Big Shoulders," I cast my first municipal vote, disappointed to be offered two dollars, Chicago style, to favor Mayor Daley's man. I learned to say, familiarly and without rancor, "There's our mail thief, Harry!" whenever I spotted the loose-walking young man who would continue free unless caught in the act, as two detectives told me at 4547 Calumet Avenue without glancing at my mailbox. I learned to fish, leaving the Hog-Butcher city to join in-laws in Niles, Michigan, for fast, beer-sipping drives to Pawpaw, whose weeping willow-fringed lake held big carp smart enough to break nylon line without resisting it.

Meanwhile I worked in downtown Chicago as civilian chief of the preinduction section (which for a while contained sixty people) of the Army and Air Force Induction Station. After the promise of an admittedly deserved promotion was not honored for the second time, I resigned, recording as my official reason "Deterioration of the integrity of the Station Command." The personnel officer, studying the phrase, asked me, "What does this mean?" My reply: "Exactly what it says." My section members gave me a splendid briefcase at the farewell party; and among separate gifts from them was a copy of the *Reader's Encyclopedia* from Voyle Stewart, a theosophist, who urged me on the flyleaf to "make known [my] thoughts to the world." Several years later, he wrote on a greeting card, "You have become a legend here."

"The Windy City," before that instance of a promise deferred, had sharpened my notions about race. In early 1950, traversing Polish, Italian, Black, and Jewish enclaves while job-hunting, I had unconsciously taken a crash course in economic discrimination. One sympathetic young man in a factory employment office on Pulaski Avenue had told me frankly that he could not hire me because of my race. A Jewish businessman named Abrams, before telling me to try the *Chicago Defender,* had said, "I don't see why your people don't help you. If nothing else works, come back to me and I'll see to it that you get a job." The *Defender* had hired me for catchall duties, from going out for cigars to writing "Bud Billiken Day" news coverage; and once I had been asked to mark each line of a speech by the publisher to indicate pauses needed for a rhythmical delivery.

Working at that "race newspaper," I had learned how Chicago, the Nation's Freight Handler, handled dead bodies, both human and canine: those white in pedigree merited interment in white cemeteries; others received their rituals on segregated grounds. Working at the induction station, I had learned from personal experience that Chicago treated living bodies the same: it had been a Black nurse, part of a Black staff, who had sewed up my cut finger without any anesthetic but my sudden profanity (to which she had objected); and it had been a Black institution to which my

wife, seriously ill with a miscarriage, had been transferred from the emergency room of a white hospital.

After leaving Chicago for New York City, I spent almost a decade of part-time work and study to earn a Ph.D. at Columbia University. My doctoral studies began uncongenially in the office of the head of the English department, Marjorie Nicholson, who was dissatisfied to find that the only foreign language that I could read was Spanish. I stiffened and grew cold, reminding her that my background fulfilled requirements specified in the bulletin. "I have never asked a candidate to get up more than one language in a year," she stated, "but I am asking you to get up two." I nodded like a soldier receiving orders, and I departed like one.

A year later, in the same office, she was relatively friendly, insofar as her austere nature permitted her to be. "You have done well, Mr. Emanuel," she admitted, for I had taught myself *three* languages (French, German, and Latin) sufficiently to pass the requisite exams.

As a souvenir of that maximum effort, I kept for thirty years my shorthand notebook filled with German vocabulary and splotched with what were once hot soapsuds leaping from a bathtub of diapers up to pages suspended on a string before my eyes. For several weeks after New Year's Day, 1954, I had to mix and heat formula, wash diapers, and provide rock-a-bye services for James, Jr., who was to be my only child.

When my Bronx landlord on 169th Street, an African American lawyer named George Hicks, found me painting a secondhand crib, he said approvingly to his wife Kate, "See the kind of people I have." He found out what he had: trouble. Upon inquiry, I learned officially that my rent was almost double its legal maximum. Studying the New York State Housing Laws in the public library, and copying those applicable to my case, I secured a lawyer, David Minckoff, through the Bronx Tenants League and took Hicks to court. I learned something about lawyers and judges when the judge made Hicks repay me some illegal rent received but also ruled, for unspecified reasons, that I must vacate the lodgings. Zack and his dog and I had won, and my respect for Plato's ideas about justice increased.

New York landlords were not finished with me. One asked me on the phone, speaking of his newspaper ad, "Are you Spanish?" Necessarily telling him my race, I heard him say, "That won't help you out here." I replied, "It will help me to act like a man wherever I am." Slamming the receiver down did no good. Other landlords and other slammings only reinforced the lesson. I had to accept a Brooklyn landlord's offer. But he was Black, his Monroe Street house was in the ghetto, and its rodent population had proprietary habits, using the top of the stove as an evening observation post, rummaging through the chest of drawers before the nightly ritual that I called "clearing the room," and leaving their droppings in the baby's crib to be gasped at each morning.

The telltale crib forced me to write a letter of complaint about my housing problems to the *New York Times*. After the sympathetic reporter said that a "fingers-in-the-till" story was the kind of news usually sought, I somehow thought of Virgil Motley, the Alliance Black man made so desperate by the Depression that he wrote to President Roosevelt for a job. (He got the job.) I wrote to the Chief Landlord himself, Mayor Wagner, pithily stating why I considered my plight a disgrace to the city. The mayor gave me three choices among low-income city housing projects; thus I lived at 195 Hoyt Street in Brooklyn from 1956 until I earned my doctorate in 1962.

"Low-income" fit my case. My face swollen from some infection (rodent related, apparently), I delayed medical treatment until a pharmacist warned me to hurry to a doctor lest the trouble reach my brain. Ignoring the scheduled second visit was a risk I took to save the $2.50 involved, the result being a lifelong scar on my cheek. The fee saved was worth fifty bus trips to the nursery where I took Jimmy starting in late 1957. To save the nickel, I always walked back. (The bus driver was so accustomed to seeing me board his bus with the child clasped in one arm that when I got on alone one day, he asked me almost suspiciously, "Where's the little boy?")

The nursery trips were necessary because my university teaching career started in 1957. In 1956, having spent two years teaching at the Harlem YWCA, I mentioned the prospect of my getting a post in Columbia's evening division to its director, Vernon Loggins, who had spent ten years writing his important book *The Negro Author*. His response was "Why don't you try Howard University?" He and others indicated that I had no chance of being hired by the City College of New York, which had no Black staff in its English department. Of course, I wrote directly to that office. The chairman of the downtown branch, Robert Dickson, hired me; and I remained with

the City University of New York from 1957 until my retirement in 1984.

My curiosity about the causes of racism and my related decision to study American literature cost me an extra two years at Columbia, for English literature had been my field. What I learned about African American literature I had to dig up alone. From this new world I chose three men in 1958, each eminently suitable for my dissertation: W. E. B. DuBois, Richard Wright, and Langston Hughes. On 27 October, I wrote DuBois at his Brooklyn address, explaining why he was my first choice. I still have the unopened envelope returned to me stamped "Unclaimed." I then wrote Richard Wright in Paris. Although no reply came, I read after his death two years later that he had been assembling notes about his short stories, the intended subject of my dissertation.

It was Langston Hughes who answered me promptly, from his apartment on 127th Street in Harlem, offering his cooperation. For two years or more, my life as a doctoral researcher was a dream fulfilled: my finding in his basement forgotten literary treasures; recording his answers to first-time questions; and, during his absence, in Europe or elsewhere, whirling in his swivel chair at his desk, tapping my toes against his file cabinets. Facing my Columbia interrogators (twice the normal number) at the defense of my *The Short Stories of Langston Hughes*, I naïvely had no note cards to preserve their questions, knowing the truth of the author's statement to me: "You know more about my stories than I do."

My final four years at Columbia brought various innovations, personal and literary. My son was discovered to be a near-genius and was transferred from kindergarten to an "IGC" school (one for intellectually gifted children); and my fourth and last graduation trapped me into my first appearance in cap and gown. As a writer, I appeared for the first time, in 1958 in a scholarly journal, *Phylon*, in the form of my "Sonnet for a Writer," which won *Flame Magazine*'s Certificate of Merit that year. In 1959 I broke a subtle racial barrier, apparently, among Black poets by writing a poem that emphatically and positively presented the word *Black:* my "Negritude," which appeared in the *New York Times* in 1964 with each of its twenty-four lines beginning with that then-unpopular adjective.

Leaving Columbia's campus the day that I saw official proof of my having earned the Ph.D., and passing shouting children in a playground on Morningside Avenue, I felt tears in my eyes. If they only knew. Yet, with a doctorate under my belt and a foothold in a major university, I remembered some immortal words from a Greek tragedy studied in Frank Snowden's class at Howard: "A day can uplift and a day can prostrate all that is mortal."

PART II

Blackness Can: A Dream Like Steel

1961: Lived at 195 Hoyt Street, Brooklyn, New York. Published my first scholarly article, "Emersonian Virtue: A Definition," *American Speech*.

1961, 1963: Published pioneer articles urging interest in African American literature: "A Glance at Negro Authors," *The Ticker*, followed by "The Invisible Men of American Literature," *Books Abroad*.

1961–68: Continued my career launched by the *New York Times*'s publication of 19 poems from 1959 onward.

1961–69: Published series of poems in *Phylon*.

1961–77: Published articles on Black literature in journals (*Phylon, Negro Digest/Black World, Negro American Literature Forum, Readers and Writers, Freedomways, CLA Journal*) and books (*Langston Hughes, Black Genius: A Critical Evaluation; Native Son: A Critical Handbook; Black Expression; The Black Aesthetic*).

1962: Moved to 405 Nuber Avenue, Mount Vernon, New York. Gave first solo poetry reading, Baruch College of the City College of New York.

1962–70: Published series of 13 poems in *Negro Digest/Black World*.

1963: Published first book reviews (*New York Times Book Review* and *Books Abroad*).

1965: Won Eugene F. Saxton Memorial Fellowship.

1966: Entered politics, campaigning for a seat on the Mount Vernon board of education. Taught the first course in Black poetry accepted by the City College of New York.

1967: *Langston Hughes*.

1968: *Dark Symphony: Negro Literature in America* (with Theodore L. Gross). Received invitational Senior Fulbright Grant for professorship at University of Grenoble, France.

1970: *Panther Man*. Made tape-recorded interviews of Gwendolyn Brooks, Nikki Giovanni, Don L. Lee, Dudley Randall, and Sonia Sanchez. Was member of five-person Black group that, in person at Albany, persuaded state education department to make statewide instruction in African American literature mandatory.

1971: Was included for first time in a literary reference book, *Broadside Authors and Artists: A Biographical Directory*.

The 1960s, more so than any decade, gave muscle and fervor to the African American cause with simple phrases and simple ideas. W. E. B. DuBois's poem "The Song of the Smoke" (1899) rallied Black men of the oncoming century with its lines "I will be as black as blackness can, / The blacker the mantle the mightier the man." A generation later, Langston Hughes, who told me that DuBois was his "intellectual godfather," won a tearful embrace from Mary McLeod Bethune (one of President Roosevelt's "Black Cabinet" and founder of Bethune-Cookman College) after reading his "The Negro Mother" (1931). The poem's speaker (perhaps half my slave-born grandmother and half my unconquerable mother) recalls:

Three hundred years in the deepest South,
But God put a song and a prayer in my mouth.
God put a dream like steel in my soul.

Inspired by all three of these giants—the austere, many-faceted DuBois; the imperishable, warm-hearted Bethune (who, in the early 1950s had invited me to teach at her Florida college); and the mellow, indefatigable Hughes—I began the decade with an attempt to rouse the USA from its twenty years of slumber (since the excellent anthology *The Negro Caravan* in 1941) on the unfelt body of African American literature. But I had no way of knowing the effects of my cattle-prod essays, "A Glance at Negro Authors" and "The Invisible Men of American Literature."

In 1962, as my publishing career began to accelerate, my City College career as faculty advisor of the downtown campus literary society and its publication *Phoenix* hit a bump. A column in one issue, suggesting some past connection of CCNY with Communism, resulted in my being called on the carpet in the office of Dean Emmanuel Saxe, a sturdy, keen, authoritative man. I can see the scene now:

"I think that you have done City College a disservice," Dean Saxe stated flatly from his desk, index finger on the offending column.

"I don't think so," I replied evenly.

Our discussion was brief. No wasted words. No charges. No excuses. The Dean's last words were "I think we understand each other better"; mine "Yes, I think we do."

The *Phoenix* staff and the literary society presented me with a plaque (the first ever given to a teacher there, I was told) engraved with ". . . for his advice, assistance, and always genial disposition." Dean Saxe also gave me a gift: his observant interest in my poetry during the following years.

My first four suburban years were no preparation for the storm to come. James, Jr., now eight (whose teachers in Brooklyn had transferred him to an "IGC" school), was comfortably installed in a largely Black neighborhood school that left him happily unchallenged by his homework. The fish in Michigan's Lake Pawpaw were voracious and uncunning, although their wilder cousins in Canada, I found, proved reclusive, xenophobic.

From Westchester County, during those four years, I mailed poetry and prose works that were published in the midst of historic events, sometimes reflecting them. In 1962, when James Meredith, guarded by U.S. marshals, enrolled at the University of Mississippi as the first Black student there, I published poems against American and German racism in the *Negro Digest* ("Bill Collector in Harlem" and "When I Read of the Rose of Dachau . . ."). In 1963, two weeks after the momentous March on Washington by more than 200,000 people, my poem "Emmett Till" appeared in the *New York Times,* soon followed in *Books Abroad* by my aforementioned wake-up-America essay. In that same year, when Kenya's independence continued a trend, one of my first book reviews examined Langston Hughes's *Poems from Black Africa* for the *New York Times Book Review.*

In 1964, when the Civil Rights Act was passed and "white backlash" parents in New York crowded huge demonstrations against integrated schools (protests called surprisingly "hostile" and "hateful" by Martin Luther King, Jr.), I published relevant poems: "Negritude" in the *New York Times,* "Effigy" in *Negro Digest,* "Freedom Rider: Washout" in *Freedomways,* "Black Muslim Boy in a Hospital" in the *Midwest Quarterly,* and "Eichmann, Slide No. 6" in *Renaissance.* I kept my literary distance, however, in 1964 with the publi-

cation of eight other poems that concerned, not racial strife, but athletes, farmers, women, children, weddings, humor, and condolence.

In 1965, "our shining Black prince," as Ossie Davis eulogized Malcolm X, was assassinated on 21 February. The following month *Negro Digest* printed my poem on the firebrand's favorite subject, "The Negro." A few weeks later the same journal published my contribution to its symposium, "The Task of the Negro Writer as Artist"—a task not unrelated to the voting rights for which Martin Luther King and his associates of the Southern Christian Leadership Council were then demonstrating in Selma, Alabama.

In the spring and early summer of 1966, the thirteen riots and lesser disorders that signalled African American discontent were only a part of the environment that radically changed my life. "Black Power!"—the resounding afterclap of the Meredith March from Memphis, Tennessee, to Jackson, Mississippi, in June—was mere rhetoric to me in comparison with the sincere entreaties of a group of Mount Vernon's Black leaders that persuaded me to fight the segregated school system by competing for a seat on the city's board of education. The NAACP (National Association for the Advancement of Colored People) had concluded that the city's largely Black schools, like the nearby one attended by my son, lagged, grade by grade, two years behind nearly all-white schools in more restricted neighborhoods.

Thus, with the incunabular naïveté of one fresh from sixteen years of note-taking in graduate seminars and in the stacks, I unknowingly entered the often grubby domain of politics.

I learned fast. When middle-class Negroes, at a swank fund-raising private meeting, said, "We have to find an image for you," I replied without thinking, "I don't need an image" and fell back on a burlap-textured comparison to Popeye: "I yam what I yam." Result: they kept their money, as well as their insulation from political upstarts who did not know who was who. When I held a similar meeting with influential Jews, explaining to them that Black leaders had vowed mutual fidelity to a Blacks-only campaign, to raise the political consciousness of the city's African Americans, my hosts thoughtfully agreed to keep their money, saying "We understand." (Others understood also, for upon leaving the elegant suburban home, I found my automobile sabotaged.)

The fast learning continued. When "Augie" Petrillo, a powerful contractor with reputed Mafia contacts, offered me a substantial contribution, I politely refused. Result: my Black backers, totaling the sums rarely offered and now "lost," began to scratch their heads to a new rhythm. When I told the Italian Civic Association, in a building described to me by my campaign manager as "Mafia Headquarters," that housing patterns in the city were "cowardly" and sufficient to drive away "a Black family with any self-respect," the chips were down. When Mayor Vaccarella sent a Black underling to my house to bring me in for "a talk," I replied, "Tell the Mayor that I don't need to talk with him."

Then the shit hit the fan. Black Mount Vernon leaders exiled me from their company and their aid, fearing that I coveted their political clout. They forced the NAACP youth workers to abandon me also, leaving me utterly alone to walk the streets in wintry weather to carry out the plan that I never forsook: arousing ordinary African Americans to a sense of their political power and duty. (Betty Shabazz, the widow of Malcolm X, had counseled me with tips on approaching whites—wise advice that I no longer needed.)

Common Black people responded immediately to me (and to my twelve-year-old son, who walked with me sometimes), opening their doors, showing family photo albums, offering refreshments, saying, "Nobody ever came asking for our votes before." They took action also, registering to vote, I was later told, in unprecedented numbers, some hobbling with canes. My recollection of them, and of their children who helped in the campaign office (and who wrote me thank-you letters, inspiring my poem "To the Negro Children of Mount Vernon"), remains a cordial souvenir of a decade that, in particular ways, severely tested my endurance.

Even with the slack integrity and ultimate collapse of my backers, I lost the election "only by a nose," as the gesture of one repenter indicated. Langston Hughes, on whom I was then writing a book for the Twayne's United States Authors Series, said, "You're lucky you didn't win. All those board meetings," he added, shaking his head. Politicians, I had learned, were not my kind, regardless of color.

Two other poems—the one just mentioned having compared my sidewalk companion and me to Batman and Robin—were the literary fruit of the campaign. The *New York Times* printed "A Poet Does Not Choose to Run," the editor aware, perhaps, that television publicity had implied my connection with aggressive civil rights activity rather than educational policy. The end of the poem states what I still believe: a poet, unlike a politician on the platform, "sits in silence, / His pledge to rearrange / The clues of some wild track, / Trail it lonely out, / And lone come back." In 1966 also, *Negro Digest* published "In Black Suburbia," in which a civil rights worker requesting signatures on a petition for equal education for African American children does not quite perceive the depth of Blackness in the home where he stands.

A nonliterary fruit of the campaign, not as strange as it should be, was my firsthand knowledge of two facts: that Blackness will not guarantee brotherhood in a political team, and that there is no civil purpose or action so essential, humane, or elevated as to protect the citizen pursuing it from invasion of his privacy by official agencies. The sabotage of my car was the hooliganism typical of racists, and the refusal of local tradesmen to provide services requested (such as repairs to my house) was perhaps retaliation for my having planned and executed a Black boycott of Mount Vernon merchants as a pressure tactic. But the openings of my mail (like the intrusions into "at least 215,000 pieces of mail" by the CIA in its campaign against "thousands of Americans from 1953 to 1973," according to the *New York Times* of 8 January 1978) and the photographic surveillance that seemed to occur were interference of a different magnitude.

I recorded my concern in a letter to Senator Robert Kennedy, including other details resembling accounts by civil rights activists elsewhere. His thoughtful response confirmed what many African Americans were still risking because of Zack and his dog.

Official abuse of my privacy poisoned the year in ways especially abhorrent to Black people because of the intraracial betrayal involved. A Black spy whose construction-business card read "Mr. Dudley," and whose grey Volkswagen Beetle carried a New Jersey license plate, smooth-talked his way into my house during my absence and sized up the ground-floor rooms. (My poem "For 'Mr. Dudley,' a Black Spy" catches him in the act: "I saw you / know you mixing Judas paint / with Judas praise when you pushed in / that startled woman's door, / . . . / and in your peeling mind already Judas pipes / installed to plumb, to bug the private hearts, / to taptape fireside bedside table talk.")

"Mr. Dudley's" real license sent him elsewhere, bebop-striding among Black students demonstrating on Columbia University's campus, mingling jocularly with protesters at the United Nations Building, dropping in on various student groups. When I described him to two different acquaintances as tall, light-skinned, freckled, and ambling in his walk (a pretense, apparently), each replied with the same "Oh! I know that man!" Margaret Ketley, a teacher, had seen him with students, while Mary Jones, a New York City board of education official who had served with me on the Black team at Albany, had seen him at the United Nations. His mission was clear after I heard one evening, "Dad! Quick! Come here!" Running upstairs, I saw "Mr. Dudley" on television, declaiming what "Harlem would not stand for" in the case against popular Congressman Adam Clayton Powell. My poem took his snapshot in his new guise: "you lisping cute / for Adam, tricking Clayton / fooling Powell, fronting cameras / that choked that big white collar round your neck, / you strangling, / spit missing Bimini."

The infiltration by "Mr. Dudley" and related events were sinister enough to help feed an almost gothic horror into my life. I cannot say, without scientific authority, that my wife, Etha, went mad. I am wholly authoritative only in recounting here, as personal history, some of the bare facts, the mere outline of all the drama that came to pass.

Often, during the two years 1966–68, about 4 A.M, I was stirred from sleep by fingernails digging into my shoulders and moist lips pressing my ears with fragmentary accounts of the machinations of miscellaneous people, in Mount Vernon and at Columbia University, to drive her insane. "Watch out," the labored breath would always conclude, an arm squeezing me with "they're after you, too." Groggy with mixed, before-dawn memories, I habitually rose from bed, surprised to see a relaxed, half-smiling face on the pillow behind me—too easily awakened, however, by any uncalm gesture that I might make.

Whenever, during daylight hours, she wished to speak of uncommon things, she would ask me to drive her upstate into a wooded area or to a similar spot near the Major Deegan Highway, where she would whisper her fears and warnings. That was on weekends. During the week, she crimped herself with Cassandra-like rigidities—when James, Jr., freed himself too soon from his homework—or flashed homemade signals or, worst of all, came to my attic study to drum into my overburdened consciousness the hidden meanings of the day.

I had learned about Mississippi, where she had been born in Yazoo County, and heard from her about her youth there, before she was given by her mother to her childless aunt in Chicago to raise further. Her six brothers, most of them my fishing buddies, and her sister had indirectly taught me what separation from them had meant to her. I had often observed her resentment of some of their habits, her scolding of them after a single day of renewed association.

"Mattie," as they called her, although I called her Etha, was indeed a scold, a nag—although *nag* is too dishrag-limp a term to salute her capacity to rival Dame Van Winkle. She was absolutely first-class, world-grade, in that art. When she canted one leg, fitfully rested one hand on her hip, darkened in her eyes, and lashed out with blood-honed, thin-slicing vituperations, somebody's heart had to bleed.

I ran out of blood, in a sense, but held on for a few years. Racism in the Deep South, I felt, had damaged her psyche as a Mississippi girl in such a way as to make it support her drawing blood from others as a means of healing herself. Looking through Richard Wright's Mississippian "knothole in the fence," she had probably seen my campaign and its cruel aftermath as a Southern-style, almost demonic hoax. "Will you lead me back?" she implored in one predawn holding pattern. "I'll try," I whispered foggily, in that fingernail grip; but I knew, even half-asleep, that the landing field of her reclaimed sanity would be narrow and short. And the weakening effects of continually broken sleep and injections of delusive fears clouded my vision as a pilot.

My personal ills during what the *Dictionary of American Negro Biography* calls the "great black upheaval" of the decade did not debilitate me as a writer. In 1967 not only did I publish *Langston Hughes* (in the preface of which I urged the American literary establishment to face the challenge of Black works), but, in addition to two essays, eight of my poems appeared. Three directly or indirectly concerned the revolutionary mood of DuBois's "Blackness Can" and its national effects: "White Power Structure" and "Son" in the *New York Times,* and "To Harlem: Note on Langston Hughes" in *Free Lance.* Albert Camus would have thought "A Cabinet of Few Affections" (in *Imprints Quarterly*) existential. Others explored the meaning of youth or satirized advertising techniques. Meanwhile, in Detroit and Newark, the racial upheaval underwent such violent throes as to give birth to the Kerner Commission on Civil Disorders.

In 1968, after a springtime chilled and numbed by the assassinations of Martin Luther King in Memphis and Robert Kennedy in Los Angeles, a poem was born of a question asked by a nine-year-old boy at a reading for pupils that I gave on Long Island. "How did you become a poet?" he wanted to know. Hence "For the 4th Grade, Prospect School: How I Became a Poet." A free-roaming question could pull up here: What is the connection between becoming a poet and becoming a martyr? The answer, in childlike terms, opens the poem: "My kite broke loose, / took all my string / and backed into the sun. / I followed far as I could go / and high as I could run." Perhaps not much more can be as briefly said, I concluded, about idealism and the pursuit of it within the limits of human endurance.

That same year, cemented in the desperations of countless ghettoes, African Americans peaked their end-of-an-era recognition that nonviolence was a limited tactic by rebelling throughout the "long hot summer" predicted. The Deep South headlined its historical passion for racial brutalities, bragging, as reported by *Jet,* about the nearly two hundred Black bodies thrown into its rivers. My poem "Where Will Their Names Go Down?" imagined the corpses "Sunk link by link— / Socket, bone, and upright knee— / Muscled down dead / In the Tallahatchie, the Mississippi, and the Pearl." (I had previously written the New York headquarters of the NAACP suggesting that the names of all Black people martyred for demanding their constitutional rights be regularly inscribed in the Congressional Record, but had received no response.)

Literary Black journals, not obsessed by revolutionary moods, sought balance. In 1968, *Negro Digest*'s Hoyt W. Fuller printed not only "Where Will Their Names Go Down?" and my essay "Fever and Feeling: Notes on the Imagery in *Native Son,*" but also my nonracial poems "The Burlesque Queen" and "Lovers, Do Not Think of This." *Freedomways* and *CLA Journal* published my substantial essays on Langston Hughes's short fiction and his literary experiments, respectively. Broadside Press brought out my first volume of poetry, *The Treehouse and Other Poems* (a title suggested by Langston Hughes, who had died in 1967). Among its twenty-seven poems, five were to be ranked, in terms of reprintings and popularity with audiences, among my best-known works:

"Emmett Till," "A Negro Author," "Get Up, Blues," "The Treehouse," and "The Young Ones, Flip Side." Dudley Randall, the founder of Broadside Press, also had me read the volume onto a tape to initiate the "Broadside Voices Series."

In 1968, too, a major effort of mine, shared with Theodore L. Gross, bore fruit when Free Press in New York published *Dark Symphony: Negro Literature in America,* an anthology with thorough introductions to periods and individual writers. The book was meant to break the barrier held firm by the almost thirty-year-long neglect of Black literature by American publishers. Measured by various criteria over the years, *Dark Symphony* achieved its goal.

My records of this crucial year, 1968, show the flourishing of my literary correspondence (if not the expenditure of time and energy demanded to maintain it); and they reflect, in part, the rapid expanse of my personal contacts with predominantly Black writers and editors. Among those records is a chart of such contacts, extended from 1968 to cover correspondence with individuals for periods ranging from two to ten years. Most of the letters involved Dudley Randall of Broadside Press (100), Hoyt W. Fuller of *Negro Digest* (58), and Arna Bontemps (24). Other Black correspondents included Addison Gayle, John A. Williams, Ralph Ellison, Samuél Allen, John Henrik Clarke, and Ishmael Reed among writers; Ossie Davis and Vinie Burrows from the stage and screen; Tilman C. Cothran and Therman B. O'Daniel among editors. Robert A. Bone became my principal non-Black correspondent; and outside the USA, letters involved Paul Breman in England (24), Gianni Menarini in Italy (14), and Michel Fabre in France (9).

This literary harvest of about four hundred letters, involving at least forty other writers and editors, probably belongs in a major cultural collection, since it presents firsthand perceptions of years crucial to the maturing of the nation.

Three gleanings from this field—personal, literary, and sociological—might provide a departure from 1968. Personal encouragement came with Dudley Randall's mid-October correspondence in the form of his remark that a Mrs. Jane Yawn of Wilberforce University had called me "a black Robert Frost." Literary enlightenment wider in significance came to me on 27 January 1967, actually at a dinner party given by Robert Bone in New York, where I observed Ralph Ellison personally for the first time. Closely pursued by a few Black guests at odds with a point in his literary philosophy, Ellison leaned back in his chair, rolled his smoking cigar between his fingers; and like Captain Ahab teasing Starbuck into "lower" yet "deeper" levels of thought, the author of *Invisible Man* receded, calmly voicing his heavier and heavier defenses, until he seemed to disappear into a filmy cavern suggestive of pure logic.

Perhaps more psychological than sociological was the phenomenon glimpsed through a letter to me from a white teacher in the USA. Commenting on his admiration for *Dark Symphony,* he wrote that a number of his students were crying during their discussion of certain works in the book. That they should willingly undergo the pain of facing the meaning of so-called "Black experience" seemed to me a hopeful sign.

The difference between 1968 and 1969 was the difference between the USA and France, sharpened and yet mellowed by the potluck of my meager French vocabulary, with no backup from Etha and Jimmy. The latter, becoming "James" as he quickly absorbed the language and habits of his friends at Grenoble's Lycée Champollion, became also the unconscious fulcrum of the family plank, weighted at its ends by parents facing strikingly divergent challenges. While his mother wrestled with dark phantoms born of her recent fears, and while I walked the tightrope between preparations of lectures for new-style French students and my pretense of composure in our mountain chalet, the new James, family translator and shaker of bannisters, inspired my poem "Fourteen," in which

> unbroken doors agape behind him
> gasp, and bannisters are lurching
> bending up the stairsteps three-in-one
> he skims, punching a grab of cake
> through jacket sleeve and out again
> caught in his snatched-up cap
> and bounding down again, doors
> standing back.

The final lines of "Fourteen" ("where do you think—oh, think— / you are going?") came from the abyss that gaped beneath almost all of my experiences of that Fulbright year, ranging from those imbued with bone-chilling horror to those perfected by instant delight. The mild exhortation "oh, think" reflected my hope that James knew, and yet did not know, the mortal danger in which he lived. His mother, resuming her practice of predawn, in-bed confidences, had whispered to me

that a voice had been telling her to kill both him and me.

One night soon thereafter, having taken the precaution of beginning to sleep in my attic study, I was startled awake by hearing James cry out twice downstairs, "What are you doing in my room?" My heart beating with quick pains, I ran down to his lighted bedroom. His mother stood in her eternal blue dressing robe, a slightly puzzled frown on her face, dangling one of his green socks in her hand. He had leaped out of bed and stood like a basketball player from whom the ball had just been adroitly stolen, a half-angry, half-amazed glare in his sleepy eyes. She turned aimlessly, seemingly unaware of our presence, explaining, not to us, but to some vacancy enveloping her, that "they" had told her to get rid of all of his clothes that were green, and that then he would be safe.

It cannot be overestimated that American racism lay behind the tragic plight of his mother. The "wide, wide wonder of it all," to borrow a phrase and support a theme in James Weldon Johnson's "O Black and Unknown Bards," is that somehow my poetry (like that of most African American poets), grooved in the cosmic trail of cause and effect, has not been continually laced with racially informed bitterness.

From that Seyssins attic of our seven-room chalet in the Belledone range of the Alps, whose "Three Sisters" peaks towered above us, six more poems issued forth. "For 'Mr. Dudley,' A Black Spy" came next, charged with personal history widely racial in significance. Oddly, working on that poem, firing my memories of 1966 into free-verse patterns, I reached a turning point in craftsmanship. Automatic first-word capitalization, line by line, disappeared. Rime was out, free verse was in, except for what I grew to call "ten-minute poems," light occasional verses for friends.

Among the five other poems, only "Flirtation" was completely nonracial, but it resembled its wintertime companions in its somber conclusion. "Christ, One Morning" developed from the tactfully impatient table blessing "Jesus saves" and from my bothersome speculation that Jesus was never pictured as laughing. My finger-drumming notion was shared by a CCNY colleague with a ministerial background, William Turner Levy (who knew Eleanor Roosevelt, and who had in 1962 told me of the former First Lady's admiration for my poem "A View from the White Helmet," written to salute the new strength of Africans battling for independence).

One poem saluted a different strength: that of the psyche in resisting destructive attacks—one of the functions of humor. Thus "Black Humor in France: for Etha" sprang from a prank imagined by the weakest family member. She leaped from the bathroom one afternoon and shouted at my back "Boo!" Turning, ready for quick footwork, I saw her lips smiling in a white mask of soapsuds, her head bobbing clownishly as she mocked me in a downhome accent with "White folks scareya, hunh?" Hopping about, she chanted "Think white! Think snow!" (white-backlash phrases recently devised to counter the Black Power and think-Black slogans so upsetting to conservative Americans). The comic thrust of the poem pulls back for its final image: "all those faces, / clean and white, / that came up from behind." The residual idea, an enormity beyond reason, beyond forgiveness, is that skin-color can be so irremovably the signal for a person's lifelong abuse by his own countrymen. The image suggests, of course, that racists are cowards.

The mood that usurped the humor in that poem was fully exercised, in February too, when I read remarks and news about the deaths of two famous men who had figured briefly in my recent life, Richard Wright and Robert Kennedy. The lines ". . . the CIA poisoned Richard Wright," on page fifty-two of the latest number of *Negro Digest,* stunned me into a rush of memories: the sabotage of my car, the furtive photographers, my opened mail, the clean-shaven faces of government agents and "community service" men, and the Boy Scout master who had reputedly spit at young Black girls demonstrating in Mount Vernon for school integration (and from whose Cub Scout unit I had consequently withdrawn my son). "Item: Black Men Thinking" was the resultant poem, which closed with an accurate reflection of my feelings: "no antidotes (page fifty-two) / for any Native Son, and none for me, / . . . / the scar becoming slowly man, / nerved to clash with monsters."

Truth and poetry not always wearing the same clothing, I must add that only mistrust of governmental ethics condones a full suspicion of foul play. But biographical records credit Wright with potentially fatal behavior: his speech at the American Church in Paris shortly before his death in which he revealed individuals, dates, and places connected with espionage directed against Black men abroad. Two Black men who knew Wright told me their opinions: Langston Hughes, saying in 1960, shortly after the death of the author of *Native Son,*

that he "seemed all right" practically on the eve of his demise; and Leroy Haynes (then proprietor of Haynes' Soul Food Restaurant in Paris), saying two months before I started work on the poem, "Yeah, Dick's death was strange, mighty strange." (A year or so earlier, the African American poet Julia Fields, telephoning me from Alabama or Tennessee, had shared her worry and wonder about the apparently too-fast disappearance of treasured Black men.) But the French authority on Wright, Michel Fabre, told me that he had found nothing suspicious in his death.

Not suspicion of foul play in death, but wonder over the power of simple charity and the continuity of brotherhood, as roused by death, controlled the other poem born in the chalet of Madame Disdier (our Grenoble-based landlady). The momentary situations, on 5 June 1968, of the fatally wounded Senator Kennedy and the Ambassador Hotel busboy Juan Romero, who cradled RFK's head in his arms, were suggested by an article in the *International Herald Tribune.* I wanted to praise Kennedy's vision as I had seen it while watching him, on television, in shirt sleeves in Harlem, walking with African American and Hispanic people, listening to their talk about their needs. Remembering Ralph Ellison's splendid passage in *Invisible Man* describing three average Harlem boys (like Juan Romero) as history's possible "ace in the hole," I wanted to deepen RFK's vision into a prophecy of the American nonwhite as the "new man" of the future. New Jersey road crossovers that I had driven on became the metaphorical equivalent of the assassinated man's insight. His memorable near-death query, "Is everybody all right?" put him squarely in the busboy's human class, bonding the generations. Kennedy saw the bond, and Romero felt it. Kennedy had the vision; but Romero had the chance to become its emblem, the future's "ace in the hole."

With this poem, "Crossover: For RFK," spring came early, along with talk of travel; and my creativity stopped when the vagaries of "the lady of the house" took such a turn as to make me pile furniture against my attic door before trying to go to sleep. A needle discovered under a chair cushion was recognized as malevolent and was thrown into the road. Three stars in the sky stood for three people in the chalet, and two were flickering weakly, a bad sign. While we were driving later in Spain (my attic-orientation kept me, never Etha, at the wheel), stand-up electrical equipment in the hills became giant assassins closing in on us for the kill, while an oversized Jesus Christ loomed higher up against the grey-brown mountainside—or so James and I were told. As the television star Jack Paar used to say, I kid you not.

The Volkswagen took us farthest southward to Toledo in Spain, Naples and Capri in Italy; farthest northward to Copenhagen and Skanderborg in Denmark. In between, we visited Switzerland, Germany, and Holland. Chaucer attracted us to Canterbury, where I unwittingly contributed my umbrella to the Cathedral; and many other great spirits lured us to London. Since we had never been in Europe before, our teeth nearly dropped out at many sights. James, who seemed to project a nonchalance at key moments, gave himself away in Spain when his mother chided him for pocketing "common old rocks" at the cathedral in Burgos. He frowned at her in amazement and retorted, "How can any rock here be *common?*"

Two examples of the physical and emotional trials endured during our trips can convey the bad patches. At Puttgarden, as we waited in the car to cross the Baltic Sea into Denmark, James enthusiastically admired the scene at the ferry landing. At once, his mother began to drum her feet frantically against the floorboard, crying, "It's a trap! A trap! We're going into a trap!" My embarrassment under the stares of other drivers and their open-mouthed passengers made me want to sink beneath that same floorboard; but I could only grip the steering wheel harder and wonder what the next seizure would be like.

The other example, more common and more dangerous, was an auto accident that occurred near Schleswig-Holstein just after we had crossed the Danish border into Germany. A car speeding toward us on the highway had a blowout and whirled forward directly in my lane. I could do nothing but steer straight onward and take the smash head-on. Neither James, riding in the back, nor I was hurt, but Etha suffered a fractured foot bone that required a cast. During our week-long entrapment in a hotel, only James, now fifteen, seemed lively, apparently stimulated by the close attentions of a German young woman in the hotel bar.

A pleasant literary souvenir of Denmark lingered—to offset another ferry-landing-type scene in the main restaurant serving my conference colleagues in Skanderborg. A number of women, teachers from different countries, persuaded me to hold an after-hours discussion with their group

concerning Black America and its literature. They were intrigued, during the give-and-take that lasted until 2 A.M., by a favorite notion of mine related to their wonderment that Black Americans held on to their humanity: that if we Earthpeople are ever subjected to psychological warfare by intelligences now beyond our ken, African Americans will survive longest because of their already enforced adaptability to irrationality.

Preparing for a return to the USA, I surveyed the meaning of my year abroad. Due to the dire restrictions of my family life, I knew almost none of the faculty except my congenial departmental chairman (Jean Wagner) and his wife, plus the also likeable head of the American Library, Madame de Bertrand. I had never donned a pair of skis. I had learned little of France's history or politics. As the date for boarding the SS *France* drew near, I felt that I would remember only an odd selection of experiences: the pleasant, leathery aroma of our living room; the long walk up and back down the mountainside after locking myself out of my car in Grenoble; my standing alone many mornings at the darkened kitchen window watching James trot down our slope toward the school bus; his brilliant performance in the Volkswagen in the heart of Madrid, using only the little map in the *Michelin Guide* under his flashlight's beam to guide me out of the city; and, finally, the attic furniture piled against my door to prevent my being taken by surprise in the night.

But, to use the title of a poem by Langston Hughes, I was "still here." So was James, the only one who had learned French (and whose headmaster had written a commendation for his scholarship and *joie de vivre*). So was his mother, who seemed, like him, to be unaware, as we packed, that anything insidious had happened in Madame Disdier's chalet or during our travels.

New York and City College in the autumn of 1969, I found after my return, were of course still there too, but were suffering from the new malaise: a foretaste of smoke, perhaps, from burning classroom buildings, or, as Cornell University officials would have diagnosed it from experience, an apprehension of armed Black students demanding changes in curricula or in dormitory patterns. Even as Columbia University had delivered a warning in the form of its underground passageways erupting with riot police—its own professors assaulted—nearly 10 percent of young African Americans now saw themselves as revolutionary in outlook, and four times as many

"My son, James, Jr., who would risk his life for a button," 1970

were ready to commit or condone violence to secure their rights. They read Eldridge Cleaver's *Soul on Ice* with the addictive fervor with which some people read horoscopes.

I joined other Black writers in shaping a racial literary voice that might both support and moderate the justifiable clamor from the thinking ghettos. *Negro Digest*, between July and September of 1969, published, along with my "Black Writers' Views," essays on the Black aesthetic by Addison Gayle, Melvin Dixon, and Amiri Baraka, that aesthetic powering a new thrust into the history of American literary criticism. Offering a vehicle to the mounting controversy, *The Black Scholar* was founded; Black writers not uniformly in the same camp appeared in Clarence Major's *The New Black Poetry*, and their brother-critics fed their ideas into Gayle's *Black Expression*.

The year 1969 was unusual historically. Books of poetry and novels by African Americans, with proud, assertive, admonitory titles, burst upon the scene: Nikki Giovanni's *Black Judgement*, Don L.

Lee's *Don't Cry, Scream!*, Larry Neal's *Black Boogaloo*, John A. Williams's *Sons of Darkness, Sons of Light*, Sarah Wright's *This Child's Gonna Live* (I had known Sarah at Howard University), and Ishmael Reed's oddish *Yellow Back Radio Broke-Down*.

The year ended with a murder and a poem worthy of discussion as a single phenomenon. In early December, the Chicago police shot to death Fred Hampton and Mark Clark as they lay sleeping before dawn. The two young men were Black Panthers. Although they were not members of my party—nobody ever was or will be—I worked in anger, a few weeks later, on the draft (in shaky handwriting) of "Panther Man." I remain unapologetic about what has been called the "strident" tone of the poem, which begins with "Wouldnt think / t look at m / he was so damn bad / they had t sneak up on m, / shoot m in his head / in his bed / sleepin" and ends with "Tell m, Panther! / Get up out yr dead bed / if THATS the way he is / even yr GHOST / can take m."

Someone wrote that he was sorry that I had included "Panther Man" with other poems in book form. At my reading at C. W. Post College (its name as I now remember it) on Long Island, a woman in the audience of teachers complained that the poem would foster racial animosity. But when I read it to a group of Black students at Bronx Community College, they stood up in unison and roared their approval. And when I questioned new James about a Black Panther button he wore, saying "Would you risk your life for a button?", he replied calmly, "Yes, if I can't wear it."

Later in January in Albany, New York, the Black scholar Blyden Jackson examined "Panther Man" and asked me to read it to our five-member African American team of educators that had come to the capital to persuade the state education department to make obligatory the teaching of Black literature in all New York schools. Their compliments were mixed with our consensus about our mission: as Joe Louis would have said, "We fought hard, and we won." (The official brochure proclaiming and defending that new policy carried my poem "For the 4th Grade, Prospect School: How I Became a Poet" on the reverse of its cover.)

The rest of 1970, with President Nixon's program of "benign neglect" of African Americans as background, brought expanding literary activities. Thank-you letters, with laudatory phrases about my poems and lectures presented as an invited writer, began to accumulate in my files, among them a 16 January letter from "Sister Georgia" of the Academy of the Resurrection in Rye, New York, consisting largely of separate paragraphs by seven students. One girl's comment was typical:

> What I liked best about your discussion of black power was the way you attached the two words—yet showed the depth of meaning for each word. You're a really smart man!

Moving from students to graduate students, I quote from a 12 May letter from Terence Q. O'Neil of the University of Notre Dame, who had telephoned me for information for use in a seminar:

> Armed with the absolute inside dope on your poetry, I led a class discussion on April 23 which was—well, let's just say it had style.
> I began the class with a short biography of you, then dropped something like, "While talking with Mr. Emanuel the other night. . . ." One by one, these mouths started to hang open, until the prof finally said, "Mr. O'Neil, did you say you *talked* to this man?" It was classic.

These two letters are more important than they seem. In the career of any writer, strewn with the wreckage left by critical neglect, hackwork, or tomahawk sanctions, genuine praise from any quarter is welcome nourishment. Sustenance came also from Professor Myron Simon's 29 January letter from the University of California at Irvine, saying that "both [my] public lectures . . . and the question periods following were absolutely first-rate." An academic tribute to us three professors who had argued at the capital the case for African American literature was dated 10 April, Jerome Flax telling my departmental chairman at CCNY:

> Young black people working in public school education have been filled to bursting pride by the triumphant performance of three black scholars. . . . these young black people will never again doubt . . . their own ability to compete on any level in any context.

Academics worth their salt hold the line when literary values they firmly believe in are challenged. I bounced against such a line in Ripon, Wisconsin, in April, presenting to a university group various Black American poems. After hear-ing me read a poem by Nikki Giovanni, one reiterating conditions despite which "the revolution will go on," a professor suggested, in essence, that Nikki's lines "were not poetry." What followed was argument, not dispute or contention, in which I, having had my perceptions honed on masterpieces, was not forward in championing the "poem."

Nikki Giovanni and Sonia Sanchez became more than names to me in 1970, when I interviewed them (Nikki on 11 September, Sonia on 1 September) in New York, after having driven to Chicago in July with James to talk with Don L. Lee and Gwendolyn Brooks. Even today those interesting interviews (taped except in the case of Gwendolyn Brooks) are relatively unknown. But images and facts learned face-to-face live on: Nikki "escaping" Delaware by an edge gained through leaving her telephone off the hook; Sonia explaining how the haunting testimony of a young patient at Phoenix House had made her begin, the same night, her moving poem "summer words of a sistuh addict"; Don (now Haki Madhubuti) limbering his knee alongside my tape recorder, declaring "There is no such thing as a negro" (one of his informing reasons for not capitalizing the word) and informing me with a slight smile that a "hog" in one of his poems was a Cadillac; and Gwen (as I grew to call her) demolishing my theory that the ritualized killings of British people in India by thugs explained precisely her pattern of images in her fine sonnet "First fight. Then fiddle." A fig for literary detectives! I thought, hearing her little bombshell, "No, I didn't know about thuggee."

Two poems typical of the diversity in my themes (one having nothing to do with race, the other having everything to do with race) began and ended my bibliography for the year. "Fourteen," with its completely nonracial dragging shoelaces and shaking bannisters, was published in January by *Black World* (the rebaptized *Negro Digest*), whereas "Church Burning: Mississippi," in which "Christ came down in flames, / A smoke-smile on His lips / And black of face," appeared in the anthology that closed the year, *The Poetry of the Negro, 1746–1970*.

That same inclusiveness was evident in my most aggressive book, *Panther Man* (1970), among whose twenty-three poems eight were devoid of racial implications. "Black Poet on the Firing Range" asked reticent African Americans the chiding question "dont wanta join th game they played / on yr mamas stomach an yr daddys back?" But in "Furnace in May" it was Everyman who burned up the love letters, "every miss-you miss-you / crisping up to Dearest / scorching down to All My Love." / Two dissimilar poems in *Panther Man* that have been consistently popular with audiences in the USA and in Europe for twenty-five years follow convergent lines in a single pattern of human experience: both "For the 4th Grade, Prospect School: How I Became a Poet" and "Old Black Men Say" suggest the subtle function of the affections in the movement of innocence toward wisdom.

In 1971, the year that revolutionized my life, my literary publications combined with my performance of duties at the City College to evidence an order and stability made possible by discipline rather than normal routine. My idea of publishing Black scholars' appraisals of the works of Black poets, wholeheartedly accepted by Dudley Randall in his letter of 16 November 1968 to me in Seyssins, bore its first fruit in *Dynamite Voices 1: Black Poets of the 1960s.* Written by Don L. Lee, it was the beginning of the "Broadside Critics Series," the first of its kind in American literature. As general (and only) editor working mostly in Toulouse, I was to complete the series for Broadside Press within four years, closely editing essays by Addison Gayle, Bernard W. Bell, Houston A. Baker, and William H. Robinson.

In 1971 also, my long essay "Blackness Can: A Quest for Aesthetics" appeared in Addison Gayle's controversial anthology *The Black Aesthetic.* A literary genre hardly argumentative, but necessary, was still engaging my efforts: the book review. The *New York Times Book Review* had printed my comments on June Jordan's *Who Look at Me* in November 1969; but I chose to become a regular contributor to *Books Abroad,* which had published my reviews of fiction and poetry by Peter Ustinov, Robert Hayden, Charles W. Chesnutt, and Sylvia Townsend Warner. I continued, in the next few years, by reviewing works by John Berryman, Gay Wilson Allen, Maxwell Geismar, Hortense Calisher, John Figueroa, and others.

The summer of 1971, although its spiritual and psychic heat generated a revolution in my career, was perhaps one of those bitter seasons in human life that need not be recorded. The mental aberrations already pictured in my chronicle, with images of madly stomping feet, Ophelia-like wandering with a green sock, and fingers pointing out grey giants striding through the mountains, need not be replaced by my attempts to present key scenes in which my life force was steadily drained by the deadly swordplay of a tongue thrusting at

"My publisher Dudley Randall, in New York in 1970 with me, our 'Broadside Critics Series' about to become a first-of-its-kind in the USA"

my heart. Histrionic but true, those episodes might be curiously unproductive in the memories of the many readers who have either gripped the hilt or bled at the tip of that blade.

"Run for your life!" as a phrase in fiction became "Sail for your life!" in my desperate reality. Thus I go back to page one, to its quotation of the opening of *Snowflakes and Steel:*

> When I sailed from New York Harbor on the SS *France* in late August 1971, I did not care whether I ever again saw any place or any person that I had ever known, except for my son and six relatives.

Shifting Gears and Driving On

1971–73: Lived two years at 10, rue Marie, Toulouse, France, as a professor at the University of Toulouse. *How I Write/2,* with MacKinlay Kantor and Lawrence Osgood. Five essays in the reference book *Contemporary Novelists.*

1973–75: Lived at 84 Park Avenue, White Plains, New York, then at 240 Garth Road, Scarsdale, New York. Divorced. Essays in books (*Modern Black Poets* and *The Black Writer in Africa and the Americas*).

1975–76: Lived at Górskiego I/7 and at Wieluńska I,74 in Warsaw, Poland, as Senior Fulbright Professor at the University of Warsaw. Essays in books (*A Singer in the Dawn* and *Interculture)* and in a journal (*Black World*).

1976–78: Lived at 240 Garth Road, Scarsdale. *Black Man Abroad: The Toulouse Poems.* Essay in a Toulouse journal (*Caliban*, XIII). Moved in July 1978 to 55 Sinclair Road, London, England.

1979: Lived at 14, avenue du Maine, Paris, then at 3, rue du Midi, Toulouse. First scholarly essay on me in the USA, Marvin Holdt's "James A. Emanuel: Black Man Abroad," in *Black American Literature Forum.*

1980: Lived (from September) at 201, rue de Vaugirard, Paris. *A Chisel in the Dark: Poems, Selected and New.*

My commitment to literature helped me cross the Atlantic without immersion in bitter memories. I began work on six essays promised to editors: critical pieces on James Baldwin, Leroi Jones (not yet Baraka), Margaret Walker, Ann Petry, Julian Mayfield, and George Moses Horton.

My commitment to my new self helped me sit and half-lie all night in my Volkswagen alongside the Canal du Midi in Toulouse after having driven all the way from Le Havre only to find my villa at 10, rue Marie not available until the next day. Compared with the cold, cramped discomfort of that first tiny living space that I could call *mine*, the eleven-room house and large 1970 Chevrolet that I had left behind were rude and alien.

New James, Sr., to be defined, required policies. My first rule of new life formed while I was waiting in line for my *carte de séjour,* or residence permit, at police headquarters. Uncertain that I was in the right queue, I changed lines. I felt good about the suddenly alive Rule No. 1: Resolve doubts by action, even mistaken action. The action in this instance happened to be correct. (My old infantry injunction "Don't just stand there; *do* something!" was still valid.)

There were new things to do in my new life: the *Section d'anglais'* regular "Amicale" outing in the scenic countryside, dinner invitations, intimacies sifted from multiplying friendships—a different planet, seemingly three lifetimes rather than

three years removed from the weirdly changeable atmosphere in the Seyssins chalet.

Learning to ski and skiing dangerously without having mastered all fundamentals were two activities excitingly new to me. When December snows fell in the Pyrenees, I joined a bus load of colleagues and students headed for Monts d'Olmes. Although I was later to ski at other stations (Peyresourde [with its unthinkable toilets], Les Agudes, Ax-les-Thermes, Pas de la Case, St. Lary, etc.), I never again, fortunately, had a day on the slopes quite like this first one.

No skier would have worn any visible garment that I displayed: long overcoat, old brown trousers, unlined gloves, outdated sunglasses. My Grenoble fur-lined boots were okay, as was my bare head (from which a cap would have exploded, even later, since my efforts on snow were always arduous enough to generate excessive steam-heat at scalp level).

In my beginner's group (*niveau* 7), I discovered that every move a novice makes is impossible, once his boots are clamped into the *fixations:* standing up, remaining in place, turning or moving an inch, and slowing down—not to mention stopping. I seemed to do nothing but rise and fall, whether trying to stand or move, the seat of my trousers wet, my hands stinging and cold, my eyes wet with snow-tears. The instructor, a pretty girl, always marveled, I was later told, that I stood up after each fall as the afternoon sun waned. She predicted, the account went, that I would become an excellent skier.

Although the prophecy did not come true, I had the satisfaction of being told that evening by Albert Poyet, a *Section d'anglais* friend and veteran skier, "I hear that you have much courage." I did not reply with the truth: that because a pretty girl had been watching me closely, I simply had to keep trying.

Snowflakes and Steel, my archival second autobiography at Duke University, details my ski adventures, two of which bear upon my two relevant poems, "Ski Boots in Storage" and "My Animal: Accident at Pas de la Case," and concern friendships made in Toulouse. At Pas de la Case, a ski station bordering Spain, after riding a T-bar past my personal danger point on a new slope, I edged downward at too sharp an angle and ploughed with twisted skis into the snow. Later in my hotel room, my skiing companions Jean Loze, Monique Malterre (later his wife), and Françoise Rives (deceased since then, 1972) examined the

"My skis and I in the Pyrenees," 1973

wound along the frontal bone below my knee, Françoise applying what looked like iodine.

The other accident involved companions important in different or more lasting ways. At St. Lary, where I went the same winter with two couples, Marie-France and Alain Bertrand, as well as Lee and Patrick Audhuy, a skier slanting down the mountainside collided with me at right angles as I, too, was descending. After I had leaped into the air, knowing that his skis might cut my legs, his swift contact knocked me whirling into the snow. Soon, Marie-France's changing facial expression above me let me know that, lying there, I had muttered a negative reply to her "Are you hurt?" She became my constant friend, as Lee became one of the first critics of my poetry.

I remember Alain for giving me my proudest moments in the Pyrenees. Finding me one afternoon too high in the mountains for my skills, lying in my usual position, flat on my back in the snow, he said in French, "What are you doing up here?" and added, "Suivez-moi (Follow me)." Patiently crisscrossing down the mountain, waiting for me to get up every time I fell, he refused silently to go on without me when I motioned him onward. Nearing the bottom, I fell hard, felt sharp pains, and scarcely had the willpower to lock on my skis again and finish the run. Even though my foot was to swell to half again its normal size the next day, I enjoyed my best moments "in the snowflakes" when he and Marie-France, standing at the finish, gave me a round of applause as I "snow-ploughed" to a halt.

All of my colleagues and acquaintances were not skiers, of course, among them Marvin Holdt, an American from Tennessee committed to life in France. He had introduced me to his friend, the just-mentioned Marie-France Bertrand, head of the American Library in Toulouse, frequented by all students and faculty involved in American Studies. A brunette with dash in her musical voice and a hint of diffidence (except when she talked) in her quick, dark eyes, Marie-France was to resume the name Plassard after her divorce from Alain. She and Marvin and I, often seen together—once at lunchtime doing linear dance steps beside the fountain on Place de la Trinité—have formed a lasting trio for good times, travel, and pleasantries.

Travel and cultural expansion with Marie-France began in April in London, where I first saw the ballet *Swan Lake,* at the Prince of Wales Theatre, and *Under Milk Wood* the next day at the Odeon, then something at the London Coliseum. My new education continued, again with Marie-France, in July at the popular festival in Orange in southeast France, where I heard Monserrat Caballé (another first-time experience) sing *Il Trovatore,* followed the next day in Avignon by La Comédie Française's presentation of *Richard III.* In early August, nearer "home," I saw in Albi an exhibition of works by Bonnard. But during that summer travel, typical of years to come in its diversity of place and enlightenment, nothing matched *Swan Lake* for its initiatory thrill, nothing equaled the lady from Barcelona for the heart-catching drift of pain in her rendition of *Il Trovatore.*

Among the twenty or more names that I could add to those already mentioned, concerning colleagues with whom I more than once skied, dined, or had serious conversations, six denote people whose contact with me is still active after twenty years: Gérard Cordesse, whose daughter Alix revived my will to write; Ellen Epstein, who has admitted an admiration of my poetry; Maurice Lévy, largely responsible, with Cordesse, for introducing American literature into the university curricula in Toulouse; Françoise Poyet (and her husband, Albert), whose energy animated all cordial projects in the *Section d'anglais;* Marcienne Rocard, who is related through her husband Jean-Michel to the recent prime minister of France and whose letters are as buoyant as her person; and Anthony Suter, scholar and poet, the only person who has kept track of, and continued to write about, my poetry.

"And a Little Child Shall Lead Him," the title of Chapter IV of *Snowflakes and Steel,* tells how three-year-old Alix Cordesse waved her wand and made me a poet again. At aperitif time at her parents' dinner party in Rabastens, near Toulouse, she was surprised to find that I did not know the names of animals in her colored picture book. Repeating the French words for *cow, pig, goat,* etc., she twisted her head up with increasing, smiling curiosity, turned the page, and pointed to the picture of a key. Leaning harder with her elbow on my knee, she looked at me with an insistent, unspoken question. I did not know the answer.

With a half-victorious, chocolate-stained smile and a quick glance at her parents, she put her finger on the key. She said twice, with a small emphasis: *"Clé, clé."*

"The room swam before my eyes" is true beyond the pages of a cheap novel. Alix was giving me the key, was opening the door on a problem that I had discovered in April in London while trying to begin a poem about my ski accident at Pas de la Case: I could not write; I had not yet recovered from the previous year in Mount Vernon.

In the late afternoon of 4 June 1972, it took fifty-five minutes to write "For Alix, Who Is Three," a poem born of such magic that I have never been able to read aloud this poem about the French child

> who in foreign country
> of her eyes and chocolate smile
> gave me the key
> the *clé*
> I will throw away
> if ever I want
> to lock my doors again.

I knew that this would be only the beginning of a series that I would call *The Toulouse Poems.* I was ready. I was fit again.

Several poems that followed can be mentioned briefly, while two or three others merit particular comment. "It Was Me Did These Things," written in mid-June, shortly after my revival through Alix, and inspired by her younger brother Sylvain, adopted a tone not found, perhaps, in any other poem of mine: the wayward cool of a free spirit shrugging off incredible happenings. Its unfettered, off-the-shoulder style probably expressed my reason for being in France: starting with a piece of cheese falling through the air, it ended with a half-mocking, half-serious reference to idealism, the "Most Beautiful Horse" the innocent ride.

The following week, the ski poem gained the title "My Animal: Accident at Pas de la Case" and was finished without unusual difficulty. (Lee Audhuy—one of my trio of Toulouse critics, with Anthony Suter and Marvin Holdt—had suggested in a letter dated 13 March 1973 that Pas de la Case be in the title, "so people would know it's a place.")

For the poem written the next month, July (during which interval my younger brother, Alvin, died in Denver), I seriously considered only one title, "The Ones Who Did It," *It* referring to the poison of racism. The poem showed the guilty ones

> feeding hatred deep to Douglass, Wright, and
>   Hughes,
> feeding it sharp to Malcolm, feeding it hard:
> whiphand beat Frederick once and raised a manly
>   scar,
> cursemouth lashed Richard up his own great hill,
> pushed Langston's Blackness in his face
> until he hugged it there,
> spiked Malcolm's path with devildeeds
> until his armor bristled with all brave reply.

The harsh poem revealed what they aimed at their Black victims:

> deadly arrow, hate-stare,
> back-of-the-hand slap into bushes of life,
> curse for breakfast, threat for lunch,
> and for evening meal
> lash and chain and pistol ball
> leerlaughing.

Unconscious indifference, rather than active racism, was the subject of a poem written near Thanksgiving. Maya Biasio, a girl who sang with her guitar at Le Petit Bedon in Toulouse as eleven of us (Albert Poyet being the host) dined pleasurably, scored zero in competition with our conversation. My poem caught her seated in the door

> she filled with lean and tinsel gestures,
> a float of rising hair and wing of elbow, hips
> that rested on some hidden thing that rocked
> as if to soothe her body's moan.

My own inner music and my body's gratefulness for it were the subject of an earlier (January) poem, "For Madame Plassard, a Thanks," important for its setting, Le Barry, the country home of Marie-France's mother, Christiane Plassard-Naples, in the Gers region of southwest France. Always given the largest room in that lovely mansion during countless visits there for twenty years, I have written much poetry in "my room."

The poem reflected my occasional tendency to borrow words or short phrases from authors whom I admire, such as Thoreau, Melville, and Hawthorne. It showed me comfortably in bed before dawn in relatively new surroundings (on an early invitation to Le Barry), contemplating "A bed of rest and quiet, simple thing / and high enough for me to reach and pull aside / far-other drapes." Those "far-other drapes" took their adjective

directly from the end of Hawthorne's jewel-like story, "The Artist of the Beautiful."

By contrast, a potential touch-me-not companion-poem to "It Was Me Did These Things," or a toughening of the sarcastic tone of "Whitey, Baby" (a poem in *Panther Man*), an April-born fragment remained a fragment. "You Wanta Help Us Black Folks?" battered a sincere poetic effort of Pierre Senouillet, who had been a student in my advanced class at the University of Toulouse. My fragment thrust questions like "wanta eat some of this dirt?" and "wanta put out yr eyes n see it all clear / (like that angry cat way back in Greece / who came to crossroads / and found his mama cryin there)?" A fragment, a flexing of muscle in the reanimation room, stirred by Pierre's "Black Man Listen."

Other fragments were the fits and starts of the summer, written on scraps of paper in dim light in the once-sinister Conciergerie (on ironical uses of the word *crucifixion*), in the Hotel Lido near Valencia, Spain (on dead birds on the roads in Scotland), in the Hotel Duminy in Paris (on a swank French girl versus her flabby American opposite). One ten-minute poem, conceived as a fragment or bit of verse to be offered to Marie-France with a flower, turned out to have that drift of sense and feeling that belongs exclusively to poetry; so I gave it a title, "May Rose for 'Mees'":

> A rose away from where you are
> is distance that I know.
> A rose that bends across your path
> is with me when I go
> and come and go and come again
> and rest at last to know
> that going there without you
> makes distance ever grow.

A similar piece, the only published one among numerous three-minute and ten-minute verses dashed off to accompany flowers for Marie-France, is the following (obviously ten-minute) poem, entitled "A Birthday Rose for 'Mees'":

> This rose that sheds some mist for you
> does nothing more than I must do.
> This rose that stands you in its sun
> does little more than I have done,
> does nothing more than start the race
> that I have run in this still place.
> It cannot drop one petal more
> than those I've added to my store
> of memories affection knows
> more intimately than any rose.

Madame Plassard with Marvin Holdt and Marie-France, at Le Barry, 1976

The romantic bent evident in these "rose" pieces was new in my poetry, having gleamed previously only in "Lovers, Do Not Think of This" and "Wedding Procession, from a Window," both written in the mid-1960s and both marked by grim conclusions. One year after my night in Hotel Volkswagen by the Canal du Midi, however, I found myself composing lines that would become my very first love poem. My Toulouse critics liked the final version immediately, Lee Audhuy, who was then making a study of Robert Lowell's poetry, writing me that the final stanza was "perfect." Marvin Holdt, in a later published essay concerning my "Toulouse Poems," called it "one of the most moving love poems I know." And Houston A. Baker (now a leading African American critic) sent me a letter, after seeing the poem in April 1973, saying that I was now obviously sure of myself as a poet.

"Lovelook Back," patterning leaf images to fit its theme ("trees," "windy stems," "meadow," "grass," "cover," "buds," and "bloom") and moving from boyhood to adulthood, ended thus:

Leave-taking now is tender part of you
I dare not
touch
but with this hand that once waved
to the hills.

Something less and yet more than a love poem was "For 'Mees,'" Mees being a nickname for Marie-France, originally an acronymic by-product of an outlandish narrative tale interspersed with tuneless ditties that I made up to amuse her. On 16 June 1972, I interrupted my lunch in my villa to compose twenty-one lines of the poem (writing "on top of warm stove," the draft recorded) in ten minutes. By July, my intention to work into the poem references to my travels with Marie-France resulted in such lines and phrases as "the Barcelona blacksmith's dizzy spires" (those above Gaudi's almost frightening stairway from the top of the surrealistic temple, Sagrada Familia); "the Tarn's deep deepest gorge" (the river into which I was almost swept by a rockslide while fishing); and "all the Isle of Skye could say / in voice of mountain-rock and mist" (the Inner Hebrides isle where

"Marie-France (nicknamed 'Mees' by me) in 1973, when 'For Mees' was written"

Marie-France contributed her camera to the sunken treasures of the misty waters).

"For 'Mees'" also recalled my picture-taking along the amazing Giant's Causeway on the northeast coast of Northern Ireland, as well as historic Dublin and barbed-wire barricades on the streets of Belfast, where soldiers forbade me to stop my Volkswagen—and where the hotel we stayed in, the Skylon, was bombed a week or so later:

Saw you pose among a thousand perfect stones
where legendary giants fought upon the Causeway
in battleboom we drove against in Belfast
(then shaking soldiers from her sleeves,
rolling from her barricaded skirts those drums of
     steel
and, suckling daily, in her years of death, some
     killer-child)—
all agonies dissolved in Mulligan's Bar
in gin and Joyce and a Dublin cat
who yawned upon the history of his chair.

The "killer-child" reference, coming from an *International Herald Tribune* article, "Northern Ireland's Children of Hate" (9 August 1972), concerned children who cheered after killing a soldier, but burst into tears upon hearing thunder, thinking it a bomb. The pitiable reference became a poem on its own, the tables turned, when, in a Dublin tavern, Marie-France and I saw a small, handsome boy, slightly smiling, enter the swinging doors selling newspapers. The white-jacketed waiter promptly jerked the boy doorward and kicked him out. Without a word, the boy gathered his scattered papers from the gutter, reentered the tavern, adjusted his cap, and walked about, offering his wares with the same smile. I bought a paper, as did a few other beer drinkers.

The poem was there: in all human and societal relationships that can fall apart, we threaten to wind up trying to give one another the Dublin-tavern kiss-off, a kick in the ass. The title was there: "Kickass." Making Kickass "an ugly prince / whose ugly father, / the King of Kickass, / gave him magic powers / of travel and disguise," I set him on the road to do his mischief—in the guise of both man and woman—from Dublin to Africa to Kansas City (the middle of the USA). His deviltry in Africa and Black America sufficiently indexed his career:

Saw him jungletoothed in Africa
fevered with the beat of longlimbs
Black and gliding on the grass
until his gunwhip plan to snatch and chain them
sprang itself to trap, to coffle gang, to barracoon,
to ship that bled and coughed across the seas
and came to nightmare rest
on shore where Kickass was the king
who hated Black that jeweled his crown
and fanned his path
and washed his feet
and robed his bones
and poured his wine
and pitypillowed his white hairs
till night he loudly died
with "Kickass! Kickass!" burning in his eyes
and wiring down his lips
to teach another bedside prince
his golden rule.

Whereas the poem-born Prince Kickass shifted identities to spread his footwork to new lands, I had shifted gears in August 1972 to push my Volkswagen through new countryside, including Shakespeare country. I thought of Wordsworth in the Lake District while staying overnight at the Sawrey Hotel in Hawkshead, and of Burns while at Ardrossan's Hotel Kilmeny in Ayrshire. I actually shouted to Marie-France and jammed my brakes on, "That's where Carlyle was born!" when the road sign near one fender read "Craigenputtock." In Ullapool, far north in Scotland, I decided that Edgar Allan Poe could have named the town—and written poetry there. Surely he would have joined our brief search for the bruited Loch Ness monster.

We were tourists in 1972 in our admiration of the Royal Mile and Princes Street in Edinburgh, but were adventurers in braving the single-track roads of Ross and Cromarty counties in the north during evening hours. August of the following year found us traversing veritably alone the stretch along the northern edge of Scotland bordering the North Sea between Scourie and Thurso. Driving through Perth earlier that month, I had tried in vain to remember the character in *Moby Dick* who was born there (the carpenter, maybe). My resumed attempts between the coastal towns of Tongue and Bettyhill were interrupted by a simple, unforgettable sight.

Having stopped the car near Coldbackie Bay upon the request of Marie-France, who wanted to cool off near the sea, I watched her dash down the hillside, leaping from grassy mound to grassy mound—to avoid the plentiful droppings of over-fed sheep—her arms outstretched like bird wings exuberant in their choice of liftoff, feathering her fingers to balance her descent, the hem of her red duffel coat flying. I inserted this beautiful image (beautiful in reality, at least) into my poem "Between Loves: A Train from London" several years later, when my life was emerging from what "Craigenputtock Carlyle" would call its "Everlasting No."

Geographically going for broke, we reached the northeast tip of Scotland, John o'Groats, and with a group of tourists (having stored the VW at Noss Head near the town of Wick) crossed Pentland Firth to the Orkney Islands. Pedaling on bicycles the barren stretches between monuments, we examined hieroglyphics on stone below ground and megalithic stone slabs in awesome circles above ground. In Kirkwall, the main town of the Orkneys, I jotted down on 24 August notes for a poem based on the fact that farmers often ploughed up, as annoying obstacles to planting crops, ancient monuments and historically valuable stones.

Returning to John o'Groats, our group faced a difficulty in a way that partially explains why the King of Kickass has not been dethroned. Finding that British Airways did not have a bus waiting to take us to Wick, people took refreshments nearby, turned up the volume of their complaints, strode testily back and forth to the guilty road, devised and revised threats to the airline, but otherwise did nothing.

Since all of these apparently seasoned travelers were blocked below lip-level, I took the initiative, conversed with a local standing beside a small truck, and ended up telephoning a man who agreed to bring a bus to John o'Groats if I would guarantee him payment for the trip to Wick. "Yes," I replied (thinking "by any means necessary"), "I'll get the bus fare."

Although it is not easy to get money from tired people who owe nothing, wallets can be nudged open by patience, reason, and an innocent smile. The lucky group got a late dinner at the hotel in Wick, the bus driver meanwhile kindly dropping me off at the airport. The yawning hangars were so eerily transformed by darkness, utter silence, and my fatigue that my gravel-churning U-turn seemed an escape rather than the prescribed exit from my parking spot. The welcome surprise, back at the hotel, was a meal that Marie-France had persuaded the staff to save for me.

After recrossing Scotland and part of England, somewhere near Manchester one of us mentioned Holyhead, our ferry-landing in North Wales after having left Dublin. In that city of the Easter Rising, we had seen dust-raising folk dances to balance our memory of the more literary Mulligan's Bar mentioned in "For 'Mees'"; and a movie version of *The Doll's House,* also seen there, had inspired in me a few lines of verse while visiting Fitzpatrick Castle in Kilkenny (an Ibsenite flash on the face of an envelope). "Give me a shawl from Galway" had become more than a line to hum, for after ferrying to Ireland at Rosslare, we had taken roads in the south and west as far up as that port city.

Other travel, involving invitations to read my poetry or give lectures, took me back to the USA, as well as to England, the south of France, and Austria. Jay Martin of the University of California at Irvine invited me to lecture there in November 1972 at the Dunbar Centennial, for he thought that my essay "Racial Fire in the Poetry of Paul Laurence Dunbar" would help change current opinion of our first professional African American writer.

At UCI, I renewed my acquaintance with old and new Black stars in the literary sky: Saunders

Redding, Arna Bontemps, Addison Gayle, and others. I met Houston A. Baker, who taped an interview of me on 19 November for Fisk University's Black Oral History Collection. On the distaff side, I made acquaintance with Kenny Williams, then working on her book on Chicago; Sarah Webster Fabio, who offered to write a book on Margaret Walker for my "Broadside Critics Series"; and Willie H. Coleman, a doctoral candidate chosen to be my guide.

One of these scholars spoke to me of Abraham Chapman, whose anthology *New Black Voices* (reprinting four of my *Panther Man* poems) had recently appeared. At the University of Southern California conference the previous spring, Chapman had related to me, between our sips of whiskey in his hotel room, an interesting story about Richard Wright. Wright, briefly staying with Chapman's family in the late 1930s, had slept with the manuscript that would become famous as *Native Son* under his pillow. Composing my poem "Lines for Richard Wright" in 1970, published the same year in *Panther Man*, I repeated that fact:

> Wright slept on it beneath his pillow
> (manuscript to cling and bleed on
>
> . . . .
>
> to press his knothole in the fence
> against a worldbrow waiting
> a blackeye knockout
> too swift for tears).

One other poem resulted from the trip to UCI: stopping in Denver on my return to France, I listened closely to my niece Gwendolyn's remarks about her interviewing unwed mothers-to-be on her job. Staying overnight at my mother's home on Clayton Street, I awoke at 2:45 A.M. to write—on some cardboard from a packaged new shirt—imagined portraits of two interviewees: "Woman, / grimface girl, / the slouch on your chair heavy / with beat of life you want / to kill, / your name your name?" and

> You behind her, you
> with savage freckles,
> with tender curl wethanging
> on your cheek just from the rain,
> downstaring as if floor were all you knew
>
> . . . .
>
> give me some corner of the truth
> you spoon into the floor
> with all your toe, and wipe so solemn.

Gwen was amazed to discover that my piece of cardboard precisely described girls who had unwillingly come to her agency for help.

Poetry reading trips that winter, in February 1973, found me drinking beer with students in an English pub, donning skis in the Pyrenees, and sharing the platform with a truly famous poet in the home city of Great Britain's champion antislavery crusader. At the University of Essex, the lively pub scene was the main event that followed the reading. At the University of Pau, where I found the host, Robert Mane, as animated as a pub, the ski trip was a natural part of the invitation. And in William Wilberforce's what might be called Hull-on-the-Humber, it developed that Robert Lowell found it convenient to read at the same time on 1 February (our reading being afterwards the subject of delightful correspondence from professors Ralph Willett and John Mowat of the Department of American Studies at Hull). Lowell's platform reading—the first I had heard—seemed a bit disengaged, sometimes barely audible (probably due to fatigue); but his later seminarlike performance in a small room, as he answered questions, revealed him to be as masterful as I had anticipated.

The following month brought me my first ride on a German train, listening with some amusement to the sturdy conductor sing out "Gnädigen Frauen und Herren!" politely before announcing each stop between Munich and Innsbruck, where my first lecture and reading were scheduled. Austrian trains, the next few days, taking me to similar appointments in Graz and Vienna, left me with images of peaked Tyrolean hats; thick, long, deep-dyed socks; and teasingly marvelous ski slopes beyond windows. My nonliterary activities were indoor: a *weinhaus* dinner in Innsbruck; a restaurant meal with a young couple in Graz (he with a bandaged foot that I hoped was his recollection of skiing); and my first attendance at the beautiful Vienna State Opera, where, from a seat in the American Ambassador's box with Martha Raetz, I watched a three-part ballet (one title, "Petruschka," staying in my memory).

"Frau Dr. Raetz," head of the Department of English and American Studies at the Institute of Translation—soon simply Martha—arranged for four pretty girls to escort me around the city. I remembered their names for years: Suzy, Gabrielle, Marianne, and Isabel. Two other names lingered with time: those of Norris Garnett, the personable African American cultural attaché who arranged my trip; and Arno Heller, an obviously promising young man at Innsbruck, who gave me a chapter on Ralph Ellison from his "second dissertation" and later became chairman of the Austrian Association for American Studies. (A university student in Vienna, Christa Hofmann, later wrote a thesis on my poetry, as did another at the University of Pau—two agreeable additions to those winter memories of Pyrenees snow, Robert Lowell, and Vienna State Opera chandeliers.)

On 31 August 1973 in Southampton, about to board the SS *France*, I said goodbye to Marie-France (who later wrote me saying, "You didn't even look back"). Looking back was not my custom, and I did not want to look forward. An unwilling voyage, even on a luxury liner, could never promise what my recent travels had stored in the poem "For 'Mees'": "heather on the browning hills," "sentinel moments large and breathless," and "champagne cork at a table in the sun."

Since 1973–78 outdaggered 1966–71 in its thrusts at my vitals, that period is best presented in its essence, life-giving whenever possible. To references to the calendar that opened this chapter, I shall add only some events that illuminated for me the effect of the period on my life or outlook.

My filing for divorce in September 1973 and the events that led to my getting it the following July, excruciating and revelatory as they were, need not discolor these pages. My poems "White-Belly Justice: A New York Souvenir" and "A Bench to Bear" sufficiently document how I was affected, intestinally and ideologically. Treachery, greed, vengeance, and justice seemed, in my damaged sight, to nose about in the same trough; but loss and gain walked hand in hand: even though, through contrived theft, I lost most of my literary treasures (letters, holographs, and assorted documents from Langston Hughes, Mary McLeod Bethune, and other famous people) and, through betrayal, lost all of my property except my old Volkswagen. I learned rather quickly that I needed nothing of what had been taken from me.

Roughly one year after my divorce, a phone call from the State Department in Washington—in

"Le Barry, terrace side and front (two windows of my customary room at extreme left)"

the person of Georgene Lovecky, program officer for Eastern Europe—let me know that "We'd love to have you go to Warsaw." The magic wand wafted me into a Fulbright year of experiences too amazing to convey except through a novel: floating on a river raft near Czechoslovakia, staring at the Seven Dwarfs formed entirely of salt in a deep mine in Katowice, kneeling (by official necessity) to glimpse briefly the sword-gashed cheek of the closely guarded Black Madonna in Czenstochowa—and, in a store in which I had been overcharged for three bottles of wine, fiercely saying "Nie!" to an uncooperative clerk, barring the counter behind me with my arm and shifting to English with "Nobody moves a goddamned inch until I get my money back!"

I met many Poles, from the friendly children at my second lodgings at Wieluńska No. 1 (running up to ask for the time, pointing to my watch, just to hear me speak Polish) to "Pani Rut" (my first landlady, whose eyes glittered like glass agates and fluttered with nervous irregularity, and whom I had to order, finally, never to return to Górskiego No. 1 without telephoning in advance). Among them, resting in the middle of any pain-pleasure graph, Irena Dobrzycka, who headed the English Institute of the University of Warsaw, was central in what furnished the title of my poem "The Warsaw Experiment."

Chapter IX of *Snowflakes and Steel*, "The Devil of the Vistula," details what happened after I wrote a memorandum to the pertinent university official listing the corrective actions that had to be taken regarding my circumstances as Senior Fulbright Professor that lay within the university's accepted responsibilities. After my deadline for reply, 12 January 1976, passed, I warned Marie-France—who had arrived in mid-October to share my adventures and shop for nonexistent necessities—to return to France before the *milicja*, sure to link her with my revolutionary intentions, refused her the exit-visa without which no person could leave Poland. (She would not leave.)

Using as my example Martin Luther nailing his ninety-five protestations to the church door in Wittenberg in 1517, I tacked onto the main bulletin board of the university a four-by-six-inch note card headed "I charge the University of Warsaw." After terse references to the institution's responsibilities, it concisely listed my four unredressed complaints. Result: Dobrzycka, stern-faced and agitated in her office, the nervous tic of her eyes accentuated—much unlike the smiling woman who had recently congratulated me on my

having guided thirteen of her students through their master's theses—informed me that she was convoking a punitive meeting at which the American Embassy and the university would be represented. "Fine!" I said curtly, then departed.

During the tense two-hour meeting in Dobrzycka's office, her main point was that my posted complaint seriously harmed relations between the USA and Poland with regard to the Fulbright program, to which I replied that no self-respecting American would tolerate the circumstances basing my complaint and that enforced submission, as a practice, would be sufficient cause for the USA to abandon the Fulbright relationship. "But you wanted to harm the university, didn't you?" Dobrzycka persisted, firing her biggest shell, which left her vulnerable to my next shot from the hip: "You must have a low opinion of Americans. You assigned me an overload of work, illegal according to your own regulations. Other Americans might have taken it, but not me." Her facial muscles sagged; and when Wiesław Furmanczyk, my amiable but not especially valiant office companion, said that the overload was his fault I knew that I had won.

A few days later at the embassy, Jim Bradshaw, the press officer (he of the Tennessee swimming-hole stories), took me into his office and closed the door on his Polish secretary. "I hear you had a little trouble," he said. "A little," I replied. "Why didn't you come to us before?" I told him that I always tried to take care of my own troubles. Inching his chair forward, he gave me the embassy's position, saying, in brief, that it was time that somebody did something about the university. He concluded with "We're glad that it was a Black man that did it, and we just want to thank you for it." Tennessee Jim talking to Zack and his dog.

Six weeks after my unbelievable return to Western Europe, I said another goodbye to Marie-France:

> We were, perhaps, like two discharged war veterans who had somehow been thrown together continually for a long time, in the same foxholes: each needing freedom from the memories of combat, each unable to forget having been saved by the other.[9]

---

[9]From Emanuel's second manuscript autobiography, *Snowflakes and Steel: My Life as a Poet, 1971–1980*, p. 189.

My most unusual activity in 1977 occurred in January: my participation in FESTAC, the second World Black and African Festival of Arts and Culture, in Lagos, Nigeria, where I read from my poetry in the National Theatre on 20 January. No part of the festival could have equaled the flight from Kennedy Airport, bearing a substantial percentage of the creative genius of the race, offering a spectacle probably unmatched, in the air, in history. I tried to preserve it:

> Traditions of Black music and poetry and art came alive, fleshed out by the spontaneous performances of "stars in the sky"—a romantic phrase unexpectedly realized in undulating arms, rhythmical hips, and velvet voices as shapely women and lithe men rose gracefully from their seats or slipped into the aisle to "do their thing." Snatches of famous songs rose and fell, making way for partial recitations of revered passages of poetry fading out, in turn, to enhance the slow acceleration of drumbeats, the strangely mellow clacking of African instruments on their way "back home."[10]

My running to join the American paraders among the fifty-odd national groups in the gigantic National Stadium on opening day

James Emanuel with Madame Plassard and Marvin Holdt, 1988

was like gliding slow-motion across multicolored grass, itself crested everywhere with revolving, gleaming bushes of various hues and textures. Black arms and chests gesticulated high in the air as men from Guinea on stilts about fifteen feet in height vibrated slowly amidst their sweeping plumes and seemed to float further into the sky. The flowing green garments of pretty girls in the contingent from Zaïre, next to ours, merged, coalescing into both darker and lighter shades as that group reversed its position in rhythm with its momentarily invisible instruments. Elsewhere around us bare feet mixed with sandals; gnarled, ropy hair tossed along with glistening, tight braids; flared white robes caught the same breezes as black coils and crimson swathes and deep-dyed royal-looking trains. Strange musical waves, percussion beats like spurts of conversation, rattlings, clacks, whirrings, and thin mechanical cries—all wove a shifting blanket of sound that kept us in various stances of intense attention even as we loosened up to the diverse richness blossoming in the stadium.[11]

True, I conversed with Wole Soyinka; held in my hands Clarence L. Holte's half-million-dollar contract for the sale of his book collection; sat for a penciled portrait by my roommate, Joe Delaney, brother of "the amazing and invariable Beauford Delaney" (Henry Miller's title) in Paris; and cooled off in the strangely calm waters of the Gulf of Guinea, my privacy—except for my companion doing her best with my camera—unaccountable until I learned that Whitney Young, head of the National Urban League, had been drowned in undercurrents nearby. But among the dozens of thrills not mentioned here, none had the physical grip and mental flush of the come-fly-with-us crossing and the exuberant first-day parade, capped by the omnipresent flaming torch of a decathlon-style Yoruban Shango dancer.

There were no torchbearers in my travels the following summer (to Tunisia with Marie-France in July and to The Hague, where I lived one month with her, at 40 Hilversumsestraat, in August); but there were challenges and resolutions in my poetry writing. At Le Barry, I wrote "A

---

[10]From *Snowflakes and Steel*, p. 197.

[11]From *Snowflakes and Steel*, pp. 199–200.

Harlem Romance," in which the protagonist awoke to reality when "a short black dog pissed on [his] leg." Sexual psychology, one of my contemplations on rue du Midi in Toulouse, wrung itself dry in "The Squeezing of the Bra"; hid its secrets in the "lively bottoms," "flavored arms," and "tittywhirlings" of "Topless, Bottomless Bar, Manhattan"; rose naked from the sea waves in "Ass on the Beach, in Spain"; then both "gigglebraided" and "mudhaired," probably overtaxed potential adherents in "'Even Steven,' Flag for a Lovers' Feud."

Two encouraging publications, wholly and partly on my work, appeared in 1976–77: Marvin Holdt's "James A. Emanuel: The Perilous Stairs," in *Caliban* (Université de Toulouse-Le Mirail), XIII (1976), the first essay to examine closely some of my work, and *Black American Poetry: A Critical Commentary,* by Ann Semel and Kathleen Mullen, a Monarch Notes book (1977) containing the prediction, within a biographical and analytical essay, that "Emanuel seems destined to become one of the major Black poets."

During the following spring, the long-lingering breath of the Dragon (my appellation in *Snowflakes and Steel* for the opposing lawyer in my divorce case) fouled my life with her sulfurous threats to extort from me payments allegedly due from her client. Expecting daily and hourly to find my car seized and towed from its parking space in Scarsdale or in the prescribed lot at City College—a possibility, said my own lawyer—I finally paid for a garage in Connecticut and took an almost daily train to pick it up or return to Scarsdale. Known to keep "dirt files" on judges, the Dragon almost hated me, perhaps because I had called her a thief to her face in a White Plains court building or perhaps, in the throes of redirected vengeance, because her client had made three attempts—my lawyer told me—to have her (the Dragon) reprimanded by the Association of the Bar of New York.

The puzzle of hatred of the victim, made vivid in literature by Claggart's hatred of "the handsome sailor" in Melville's *Billy Budd,* and made horrifying in life by the Nazis' demonic crimes, is too serious for anything less than a series of books, just as the record of other springtime exhalations on the Dragon's tongue is best buried in Chapter XII of *Snowflakes and Steel,* "Dunbar, the Dragon, and Deliverance." (Best buried too, or half buried, is the that's-the-way-it-is advice of my friends, concerning dragonfire: Forget it; Don't let it get you down; You can't change the system; Consider

what happened to me—all giving comfort to the master criminal, the timeserving politician, the seediest bilker on the grimiest street.)

"Dunbar" in that title refers to a February 1978 symposium at Morgan State College in Baltimore, where I gave a lecture revealing surprising similarities between my life and that of Paul Laurence Dunbar. My stay ended with a three-way, fascinating literary conversation lasting until 2 A.M. in the living room of Elaine S. Diaz, who added feminine charm to the memorable remarks of Saunders Redding, whose scholarly eloquence, human complexity, and unwavering decency were reflected in Henry Louis Gates's eulogy of 1988.

A professor at Morgan State, the quiet, gentlemanly Benjamin Quarles, complimented me on my poem "Emmett Till," which, because of hoarseness from a cold, I had to read by placing the microphone almost in my mouth. It is "one of the most beautiful poems in the English language," Quarles said. I recalled a different kind of praise from Yves Le Pellec, a Toulouse colleague, concerning "The Ones Who Did It": the poem, Yves had said, following a reading at Le Mirail, "hit me right in the stomach." I recalled, too, that in Toulouse, where I had taught students about both Emmett Till and the Black men in the other poem, my seminar on African American poetry had bolstered the American studies program. After the turmoil of 1968, the program director Maurice Lévy had told me for the record two weeks before the Dunbar symposium (during CCNY's winter intersession), "the Centre de Recherches sur l'Amérique Contemporaine . . . actually functioned as such for the first time when you taught the seminar."

"Deliverance" in that title from *Snowflakes and Steel* refers to my sabbatical leave for 1978–79 and my half-in-London, half-in-Paris plan to recuperate. My CCNY friends Nathaniel Norment and Raymond Patterson (a poet) promised to truck my belongings from Scarsdale to Long Island for storage in "Nate's" basement. Dave Buckley was to safeguard my most valued books. Thus, just as I had managed to "fly Pan American" from behind the Iron Curtain, my new silver Volkswagen and I were ready to meet in England, expecting no dragons but those selling gasoline on European roads.

Perpetually tanked up on super, I thought of myself as "the tall Black man in the silver Beetle." In West London's Shepherd's Bush area, bounding up the four flights of stairs to my attic apartment at 55 Sinclair Road was like letting out the string of a rising kite. (Stella Smethurst, a friend met in 1972 in Toulouse, had kindly offered me the free use of her flat through September.) Gone was my wrath over my discovery at the port in Southampton that my new VW had been stripped of all accessories not thief-proof, including windshield wiper blades. I was writing again. Shopping and cooking took less time. I knew nobody. Flat No. 9, I felt, would offer me my longest period of sustained creativity.

"Between Loves: A Train from London," taking aboard at least ten years of memories for my first excursion into what Ibsen's Hjalmar would call "splendid isolation," merged the theme of revery-clouded loneliness with the question of how to behave with women. One revery transformed Marie-France at Coldbackie into "oh barefoot Rachel, leaping mounds of sheep-soiled grass / to reach the Scottish sea, / her red coat flying." The advice concerning women was understandably limited: "Be usual." At the end, the poem described man's best experience, as I had known it:

> a prickly train to ride—
> but always stations:
> 　　a few friends far away,
> 　　a life that hugs the ground,
> 　　and, in a lovely while,
> 　　some woman's arms.

In mid-August, an article in *Newsweek* rankled me with its message to jobless Black teenagers: America does not need you; you are obsolete. Combining a 61-line draft called "Black Lookin' Back" in 1972, curiously prophetic of my later reactions to Alex Haley's *Roots,* with alterations of the substance and dramatic framework found in the *Newsweek* piece, I composed "For Young Blacks, the Lost Generation (*Newsweek,* 8/14/78)." The end of the poem drew a tight line between disheartened Black youngsters erased from the economic picture in *Newsweek* and slaves in chains during the Middle Passage resisting the need to puke, the former now soaking-in the constant message:

> they spell it slow,
> especially for you:
> 　　you
> 　　are
> 　　ob-
> 　　so-
> 　　lete

as were your fathers
and theirs before them
back to the one
who held the vomit tight
against his teeth.

Half of the ten poems composed during my five months in London were long, according to my standards, including my four-page "El Toro," in which the sharp-horned star of the corrida charged against the fate that society plans for its bravest men. Another long one, "Officer Liz and the Poem," showed the exemplary poet at work, poised for the dawn of the right structure, who must "be quick with architecture" when the parts of his creation begin to "move as one." London's Cockpit Theatre Poetry Group, which I visited three times, admired my final poem of the season, "Eric, at the Blythe Road Post Office." They praised its picture of dead Eric's mother, shuffling and smelling scraps of paper, "her face a shrunken straw basket / balanced on a huge black knot of scarf," and the line that depicted post office customers as "queues of eyes that widened to and fro" in their recognition and tolerance of her madness.

"For Young Blacks, the Lost Generation," incidentally, was deemed very strong, especially at the end, by Anthony Suter during our pub-hopping along the Strand in September. Moving on up to the shorts—British slang for our switching to whiskey—he read "Between Loves" and commented, "I wouldn't change a word of it."

Later in September, I joined Marie-France in Toulouse for a trip through Spain as far as its busy southern port, Algeciras, where I threw a rock at the Rock of Gibraltar across the bay. There, our Dyane 6 having been struck from behind while stopped at a red light, I was incensed by high-handed police treatment and insensitive court procedures—reminding me of our being surrounded in 1975 by a ring of soldiers with rifles pointed at us in the Guerrero province of Mexico because of my objections to being forced to put all my Volkswagen baggage on the ground, for the ninth time in one day, to facilitate their search.

Not only my vexations in Spain, but also the marvels of Granada (the Alhambra gardens), Córdoba (the awesome La Mezquita mosque-be-come-cathedral), and Seville (the strangely compelling beggars haunting the Giralda area), worked their way into the 127-line "El Toro," together with striking images from the Dyane 6 trail through the Andalusian hills and Sierra Nevada mountains and along the Guadalquivir.

The Volkswagen, not to be outdone, carried me on 5 October through fifteen hours of almost uninterrupted driving from Toulouse to Calais, where I arrived in the dark, red-eyed and stiff from my self-imposed, wonder-if-I-can-do-it trial.

The Beetle, having left Sinclair Road for the last time almost two months later, passed through Boulogne rather than Calais on the way back to Toulouse, and on the way to double trouble. Near Authon-la-Plaine, the accelerator pedal, supersubmissive to my foot, sunk limply all the way to the floorboard. Replaced after towage to Rambouillet, it did its job on the resumed route to "La Ville Rose," even near Moissac, where the previous disaster of Schleswig-Holstein faced me again suddenly: an out-of-control car, this time sliding straight toward me on ice, rather than spinning from a blowout. Reenacting the German nightmare, I steeled myself for the shock. The shock was that the accelerator pedal moved me forward smoothly. I speeded up, the faint sounds behind me in the trail of autos as indistinct as my comprehension of my escape.

Thanks to the monster in my poem "Frankudrackenstein," "Uncle Romy" (then in real life Romi Szramkiewicz, a professor of law at the University of Poitiers and later a special envoy to Pope Jean Paul II), I could occupy his mother's apartment on Avenue Jean Rieux in Toulouse for a few weeks. There I composed one of my rare political poems, "The People Is a Whore," in which the hoodwinked public was a "dandelion girl / asleep on the arm of the enemy, / eased by his clean cheeks and innocent tie." In the small quarters of "Madame Szram" (then in a home for the elderly), I wrote one more poem, not about political smartasses, but about their international betters, diplomats in session, televised while honoring one of their own. "Two Minutes for the Dead" shows them as "The Conscience of the World . . . on camera smothering their cough, / their fist relaxed," musing upon unsavory personal secrets of their past until "the gavelish echo from the cufflink hand" signaled them back to the management of their corner of world affairs.

In Le Barry again for Christmas, anticipating the champagne, fresh oysters, country-made foie gras, pink and green candies, truffles and other chocolates that always made Yuletides pleasant, I spent part of the noon hour on Christmas Day beginning a poem to be called, I thought, "Robin Redbreast in the House." The little bird had indeed been in the house, trapped, after an accidental burst through a window, behind a bookcase shelf of French classics and ponderous legal tomes. He stayed there, in my mind, until I found private rooms a week or so later, with the help of Marie-France and Robert Tricoire, in the large apartment of the painter Françoise Estachy at 14 avenue du Maine, in Paris.

There I completed the poem, rechristened "The Birdpeople," my first Paris creation, which pitted the protective anxieties of birds against the destructive apprehensions of people. Three age groups deployed the human forces: a thoughtlessly hurtful boy, his job-and-family-oriented parents, and his intuitively life-preserving grandmother.

In the same third-floor apartment (of the building where Kahlil Gibran had lived, according to a plaque), I wrote "The Boat Basin, Years Later." Conjecturing a child's reaction to the sight of chairs frozen upside down in a pool in the Tuileries in order to clarify my sensory perceptions, I used subconscious forces probably at work in me near the octagonal basin. I employed techniques remembered from Wordsworth's "Lucy" poems and Coleridge's *Rime of the Ancient Mariner* to mount a scene that merged chaos, dreamlike calm, and tones implicit in "rigid dog," "shudder in the ground," and "I let go of the pool."

In "Worksheets, Flat No. 9," the grotesqueries in my poetry continued to flower in my Paris hideaway. My second autobiography preserved the queer inception of the idea behind the poem:

> Several early mornings in a row, after completing some habitual gymnastic exercises in the living-room [in London], I had staggered to the hallway. . . . My unsteady locomotion had puzzled me, since no riotous night life, or even overly generous nightcaps, could explain it. Then, one morning, the answer had leaped into my mind: the floor was crooked! That sunny-morning illumination had propelled . . . a vein of associations . . . until its richness signaled me through the cover of ordinary events.[12]

In the poem, the poet, learning to walk for the third time, stumbles to his new window and has "doubly strange" perceptions:

---

[12] From *Snowflakes and Steel*, p. 330.

inside, the blackness of the room shrank down my
   leg
to floorboards straight, as smoothly innocent of
   guile
as painless, dry Madonna cheeks upon the wall;
outside, snowflakes untraceably chaotic
dived into caves, laid hills on hills,
rode lavishly with every motion in the street,
slow-draping every meaning, till whiteness had its
   way
by bringing darkness to the world.

Moving between countries to learn to walk alone,
the poet, who started out in an apartment where a
nearby "railroad rhythm" vibrated his stairs, ends
up in one in which he can recall:

> I didn't even move.
> Just walked around and wrote,
> in rhythm with snowflakes and steel.

In the winter and spring of that year, 1979, I
completed three more poems, the first one deemed
venomous by a CCNY colleague, Arthur Wald-
horn. "White-Belly Justice: A New York Souvenir," conceived in stomach cramps and disciplined
calm and branding-iron images, could have but
one subject, the Dragon, "her demon / perceived
as human, as if / it could smell like coffee, wear
smoke in its hair." Concerning the personified
subject, Ugliness, and its extremity, evil, the extent
of man's responsibility was the unknown factor in
what emerged as the necessary ending. Studying
twelve hundred pages of Emerson, the Boston
Sage, for my first published essay had taught me
his definition: evil is "privative." Attending with
Marie-France the movie *Nosferatu* and observing,
at the end, the household servant sweeping away
the restrictive charms holding evil at bay, I added
Emerson to Count Dracula and got the answer for
my poem: evil follows us, needing us, asking, for its
survival, the surrender of our strength against it.
The ugly poem outgrew its black cloak tailored in
Transylvania.

Of the two other poems, both long, "Three
Chores One Country Day" evoked teenage memories of my first, fearful slopping of vicious-looking
hogs on the Batt farm, my legs hemmed in by their
ravenous snouts; my exhaustingly sickening days of
pitch-forking vapory piles of manure; and other
rural experiences, testing the powers of poetry "to
upturn barnyard possibilities / of cleanline form
and lovely motion." I ended the poem with a truth
about my past, present, and probable future:

> It takes me all my life and all my strength
> to do three chores:
> to slop these hogs despite the boar,
> find beauty down in barnyard lore,
> and claim for love some patches on the grass.

The other poem first sprouted when, at a
dinner party in Paris given by Maurice and
Madeleine Goldring, I asked a table companion,
"Who is that man?"—meaning a somehow unusu-
al-looking man whose mild composure perfectly
complemented the relaxed wave in his brownish
hair, palm-sized as if molded there by sympathy
with his continually propping hand that kept his
head in an attitude of reflection. The reply came,
not a name, but "He was at Auschwitz." Conversation dimmed as I tried to connect the drab bunks
and iron rings that I had seen at "Oświęcim" in
Poland with that half-smiling face wavering behind
candlelight and wisps of smoke.

"He Shall Be Nameless," therefore, made his
face emblematic of what the Holocaust had done
and failed to do:

> Weeks afterward, his portrait hung for me
> on any wall it chose;
> one day the eyes greened back, full gingering the
>   hair,
> and generosity of lips poked through a
>   honeysuckle veil
> tried on within a privacy of hedge beyond a
>   country road;
> next moment, angled shelterless between two
>   ancient wagon
>   wheels,
> the smoke-ringed face was dangling near a barn.

His parents were part of the background:
"(they must have kissed his cheeks, / rubbed brief
advice into his hair, / and called him Little So-and-
So in parting)."

Working on the poem, I had thought of the
international lawyer Samuel Pisar, once in Auschwitz, who (according to his reminiscence in the
International Herald Tribune, 3–4 March 1979)
had lived in a "sort of purity" there, had found
"something honorable," finally, "amid all that
degradation and madness." So I returned the
dinner guest to his origins, ending the poem,
"staying where he was, keeping his face, / a
fragrance," and finding in his "honey of remembrance" (the poem's metaphor for the Jewish
sacrifice) some human splendor.

Sweet remembrances for any poet are those appreciative remarks and events that obliterate some thorns along the path. Gwendolyn Brooks, writing me a note about some poems that would appear in my *A Chisel in the Dark* in 1980, heartened me by saying that my poetry had taken "great gallops forward." *Black American Literature Forum* gave me a "special distinction" honorarium for my two poems in its fall 1979 number: "For Young Blacks, the Lost Generation" and "Stiff Roses Bring Their Simple Wish." Arthur Zeiger, visiting me with Ed Quinn (both CCNY colleagues) in February, remarked after reading "Worksheets, Flat No. 9," "Why, this is REAL poetry!" Harry Goldberg, head of the American Library in Paris, wrote me of the "blend of tenderness and strength" in *Black Man Abroad: The Toulouse Poems,* as well as the "earthy language and vivid images."

Two other experiences, one not intended for my ears, the other not intended to be as difficult as it was, were gratifying. Reading before a poetry workshop at Shakespeare and Company Bookstore on 6 March, I overheard a nearby man remark to his companion, "Whew! I need to rest a minute. The richness of it is almost too much for me." (It did not occur to me that he might have been thinking of a *baba au rhum* or an overstuffed nougat consumed just before climbing the stairs.) The two-semester gratification, surprisingly difficult to sustain, came when the University of Toulouse asked me to teach a course on my own poetry.

Asking myself questions about my poems and getting students to ask questions were exercises in honesty, wisdom, and tact. I could only hint at the complexity:

> I kept discovering what they would not ask, and they kept conjecturing what I would not tell; but there remained, between these two negative poles, a common field sparked with their intuitions and with their sidelong glances of comprehension alive in those silences that made us somewhat more than teacher and students.[13]

Poetry readings in other countries, under the auspices of American cultural agencies, led to question-and-answer sessions with a variety of students and teachers. In Spain, for example, just before Christmas of 1979 at a large conference in Santiago de Compostela in Galicia, I not only read my poems but also learned the legend of beheaded Saint James reappearing on his white horse (reminding me of Emiliano Zapata). And, sitting in the medieval cathedral there on the Plaza del Obradoiro, I was amazed, like the breathless watchers around me, to see six men maneuvering with strong ropes and pulleys a huge, burning censer, swinging the flaming and smoking *botafumeiro* in fifty-feet-wide oscillations from the high arch of the transept down back and forth through the aisle where we leaned backwards on our seats, the comet-like censer, veritably a fire-belching stove, grazing their ankles, slowing down, until one of them dived upon it like a cowboy bending from his saddle to bulldog a plunging steer and swung it to a smoking halt.

Five students took me in hand, leading me to restaurants and bars, showing me narrow streets where they had escaped club-wielding mounted police: Luis, their able leader; Beatriz, who had dark hair and smoked cigarettes; Hilda, who had dark hair and smiled pleasantly; Carlos, who did front-line, attentive duty when I read poetry; and Victor, who hid his shivering from the cold when we left our last bar. They termed their town "the rainiest place in Spain." And later on, they wrote me letters.

Two months later, I read in the Samuel Beckett Room of Trinity College, Dublin. I met two well-known poets: Seamus Heaney, who shepherded me to a lunch served by two witty nuns, and John F. Deane, who told me of acceptable poltergeists in his new house and kindly bought me candy and nuts, sensing my hunger, on the way to my reading. A younger, lesser-known poet wedged into my memory too: Frank Gallagher, who, second or third glass of wine in hand, sat on the arm of my luxurious chair in the home of Robin Berrington, an embassy official.

> My eyes, covertly watching the surface of the wine in his glass, saw it undulate like the sea viewed through a porthole of a rocking ship. He raised his finger to accentuate a point he was making to me, his eyes frowning ever so slightly, in the manner of a man who has lost the thread of his thought. His finger sank curiously as his frown deepened, and for an instant I felt a disorientation. . . . Quickly, I realized that I had involuntarily risen a little from my chair—while Frank was falling. He settled calmly into a large pot of poinsettias, his arms upraised, while the fire spurted

---

[13]From *Snowflakes and Steel,* pp. 387–88.

fitfully just beyond one of his feet. He recovered tranquilly among smiles of concern.[14]

Although, during a similar cold season, I read at the University of Toulouse (where "Ass on the Beach, in Spain" drew appreciative gymnastics from some students and a chuckle from the head of the *Section d'anglais*), at the University of Paris III with Melvin Dixon, and at Shakespeare and Company Bookstore (where I had none of my books, after the reading, to sell to people with money in hand), nothing exceeded the flame-and-smoke dip of the awesome *botafumeiro* or the beautiful, slow-motion fall of Frank Gallagher.

Other trips, each remarkable in far too many ways to be mentioned here, merit at least tiny indications of their impact. Driving unintentionally from Paris to Rothenburg ob der Tauber instead of to Toulouse, because of a last-minute phone conversation with Marie-France in Germany, I crossed what seemed a delightful but unreal fairyland of Mother Goose colors and shapes along the river approaching the town.

During an auto trip through Spain and Portugal with Marie-France in August 1979, two small boys in Valladolid, unconcerned over their failure to beg money from us, lay down on their backs on two different low stone walls. The following passage recaptures their unrehearsed, nontouristic gem of a performance:

> Ignoring us completely and never glancing at each other, they began to sing a partly chant-like, partly melodious antiphonal conversation, one scratching the ground absently with a stick as he sang, the other changing his recumbent position with each pause in the exchange. Their sounds, tumbling and climbing, sometimes joyously, sometimes almost querulously, had nearly the purity of the Vienna Boys Choir.[15]

A much different trip, with a group of tourists, to Leningrad (now St. Petersburg) and Moscow in February 1980, afforded me my first view of the beautiful Hermitage museum in "the city of the Neva." Daring to break away from guides and our group, we found special pleasure in travelling the fourteen miles to ice-and-snow-decked Pushkin Village, named after the great womanizing writer of African descent to whom Marie-France was

partially indebted, as a music-lover, for her knowledge of *Eugene Onegin* and *Boris Godunov* (the latter of which I had seen with her). Emboldened by our breakaway success in St. Petersburg, we went alone by tramway in Moscow to Tchaikovsky Concert Hall and, more adventurously, in the dark of night, to a restaurant where we were treated as privileged guests—but where I failed to convince Marie-France, between sips of complimentary champagne, that the bears we had seen in the Moscow Circus had been real.

One thing was distressingly real in Moscow, in the Metropole Hotel: shifting heavy luggage quickly during a change of rooms, I felt a presentiment that became later, back in Toulouse, that dull flutter and almost imperceptible abatement in my left groin that I recognized as a hernia.

A mid-July 1980 vacation flight to Bulgaria—after an *intervention chirurgicale* (so tactfully oblique a term for knifework) at the Clinique de l'Union in Toulouse—took us to Varna on the Black Sea; to Plovdiv, Bulgaria's second largest city, among the hills along the Marica River (pronounced, we discovered, the Polish way); and to the Batchkovo monastery fifteen miles farther, inside of which we saw a girl perched high on a beam, painting or cleaning, as well as shy monks gliding to and fro, unaware of the secret movements of my camera.

From Toulouse to Bulgaria, I had carried the fragment of a poem begun in "La Ville Rose" at 3, rue du Midi, Apartment 129, where I had lived since August 1979. While Marie-France stayed under our beach umbrella at Zlatni Pjasâci, I returned to our balcony at the Preslav Hotel to work on "Scarecrow: The Road to Toulouse," a poem finished the next week where it had begun, in Toulouse.

In this composition, the protagonist saw—as I had seen drowsily in the Dyane 6, with Marie-France driving—the figure of a man "hanging stiffly" from a tree. Startled fully awake, I had felt memories of American lynchings rush to my head: "the rolling scream / our tires must have sucked into the road" in the poem. "What's the French word for *scarecrow?*" had been my question, retained as such in the poem, a thing that "looped out of me like rope to cling to." Marie-France had replied so colorfully with the French version of the birds and the trees and the scarecrows that her words, like mine, wound up in the poem: "'They get in cherry trees'— / the birds, she meant—'and *chuk-chuk-chuk:* / all you get is holes.'" The next lines of the poem were faithful to my reaction: "I

---

[14]From *Snowflakes and Steel*, p. 395.
[15]From *Snowflakes and Steel*, p. 373.

felt the cutting of the beak. The man's head / was gone, back there in the leaves, the limbs" that the car had left behind.

The poem continued, with an intended cause-and-effect interplay taken from our real journey toward Toulouse, the relationships between birds and mankind, and the brutal history of racism. It ended with a representation of the robot-mentality and monsterlike behavior of those who spread misery and terror:

> *DEATH!* sensed and seized,
> the only word the scarecrow-men obey:
>
> they move grotesquely,
> and from their slightest flap of tinsel,
> drift of odor,
> the air is filled
> with chaos.

There were shades of chaos in my life as 1980 neared its end. My "renewable" professorial post in Toulouse had been given by officials in Paris to a political refugee from Chile. Also, following my letters to them, Senator Javitz of New York and Congressman Ottinger, who served the Scarsdale area, had been unable to blot out the dragonstains still on my trail. Thus my tenure at my new abode in Paris, at 201, rue de Vaugirard in a seventh-floor studio (since 1 September 1980), was uncertain in terms of French francs available.

But as measured by hope available, I felt afloat while spending the last few hours of the year watching, with Marie-France, Béjart's ballet *Notre Faust* at the Théâtre des Champs-Elysées. Thinking as a poet and reaching back for sustenance, I remembered that Robert Bone, in the *Teachers College Record*, had believed in my future prospects long ago, comparing my work (in 1967) to that of Robert Hayden and Melvin Tolson. Michel Fabre, in the *AFRAM Newsletter* in Paris in 1978, had described lines in my *Black Man Abroad: The Toulouse Poems* as "*lisses comme un caillou poli* (smooth as a polished pebble)." Naomi Long Madgett of Lotus Press in Detroit had placed a *caillou poli* in the jewel box of my memory by steadfastly working on the proofsheets of *Black Man Abroad* with her neck in a cast after a bad automobile accident. And she had recently published an attractive edition of my *A Chisel in the Dark* (1980).

Ready or not, I gave a champagne salute to the new decade already in motion and felt that I could keep in step—with my own drummer.

"Deadly James" and Afterwards

1981: Moved to 340 East 90th Street, New York City. Resumed post at the City College of the City University of New York.

1982: Attended the "Days of Poetry" Festival in Sarajevo and elsewhere in Yugoslavia in May. "American Poet James Emanuel in Yugoslavia," *Pregled 219* (Belgrade), by Leslie McBee. Essay "George Moses Horton" in *The Dictionary of American Negro Biography*.

1983: Suicide of James, Jr., 16 January. *A Poet's Mind. The Broken Bowl (New and Uncollected Poems).* Visited Barbados and Peru. Lecture, "James Emanuel: Negro Poet to Earth-Citizen," by Douglas Watson, at annual conference of the Popular Culture Association at Wichita, Kansas.

1984: Videotaped poetry reading (1½ hours) at Pace University, New York. Visited the Virgin Islands. Retired. Moved to 28 bis, rue du Cardinal Lemoine, Paris.

1985: USIS-sponsored readings and lectures in Romania and Austria. Read poems to jazz background for the first time, in Paris. Was guest poet at the eighth *Festival franco-anglais de poésie* at the Pompidou Center in Paris. Visited Athens.

1986: Moved to 55 bis, boulevard du Montparnasse. Mother died. USIS-sponsored trips to Reykjavík, Iceland; to the Twenty-third International October Meeting of Writers in Belgrade; and to other cities in Yugoslavia. Read with Edouard Roditi, Gordon Heath, and Ted Joans (videotaped) at the Village Voice in Paris, in homage to Langston Hughes. Began cooperation with Jean Migrenne in his translations of my poetry.

1987: Nicole Lamotte began to illustrate my poetry. *Deadly James and Other Poems.* Joined activities of Art Musique Échange group in Paris. Started visits to Swiss Alps (to Brambrüesch, where Marie-France was co-owner of apartment). Visited Liechtenstein (smallest nation in world).

1988: *The Quagmire Effect.* Gave first-time readings at Oxford University Poetry Society in England and at University of New South Wales in Sydney, Australia (from where I went to the Great Barrier Reef at Cairns). Visited Hong Kong, Singapore, and Malaysia with Marie-France. In Paris, as special guest at the

"Nicole Lamotte, Jean Migrenne, Françoise Labrusse, and Nicole's husband, Jean, as guests of Michèle and Jean Migrenne in Ifs, Normandy, February 1989. I took the picture."

Women's Institute for Continuing Education's benefit, 26 April, met President Valéry Giscard d'Estaing. Brother Raymond died.

1989: At "Days of Poetry" festival in Fougères in Brittany, read in French for first time ("Les jeunes, face 2," Marvin Holdt's translation of my "The Young Ones, Flip Side"). *La Vague à l'Âme* No. 43, bilingual *Poètes Noirs Américains,* consisted of poems by Raymond Patterson and me. Greenwood Press, after a twelve-week contractual relationship to publish my collected poems, ceased its helpful correspondence and replied to none of my August-December letters, nor to my final registered letter of 17 January 1990 sending a twenty-one-dollar check for return of completed MS mailed 28 November. Keith O. Anderson began to illustrate my poetry.

1990: Essay "Black Poetry for a New Century," translated into French by Laurence Lenglet and Diana Schroeter, in *La Traductière,* Paris.

At 17th International Poetry Biennial in Liège, Belgium (theme: Poetry and the Sacred), read my essay "Writing and the Absolute"—calming religious controversies heating up among discussants and audience. Read poetry at the American Church in Paris, with innovation: Gerald Mangan, a Scottish writer, sang with his guitar his arrangement of my song "That's Character, Baby." Joined once the 72-hour "fire readings" benefit to repair damaged Shakespeare and Company Bookstore in Paris. Attended Frankfurt Book Fair. Visited Florence, Italy, with Marie-France.

1991: *Whole Grain: Collected Poems, 1958–1989.* "Interview with James A. Emanuel" (written replies to questions by Jean McIver) in *Negative Capability.* "James Emanuel: A Poet in Exile" was final chapter of *From Harlem to Paris: Black American Writers in France, 1840–1980,* by Michel Fabre. *Kenyon Review* published haiku and my first blues poem,

"Sittin'-Log Blues." Mohamed Al Nama sent me a cassette recording of his voice-and-guitar arrangement of one of my seven song lyrics in *Whole Grain,* "Everybody's Songbird." Read poems at Harambe organization's Black History Festival at St. Louis Blues jazz club on rue Blomet (at No. 33, site of the Bal Colonial, famous nightclub of the 1920s). Read for first time my translations of French-language poems into English, at the *Festival franco-anglais de poésie.* Godelieve Simons exhibited her engravings based on my poetry at Vaison-la-Romaine and twice at Brussels galleries. The new Carnegie Arts Center in my hometown, Alliance, Nebraska, started its poetry collection with *Whole Grain.* Sister Gladys (who had coauthored three books) died.

1992: *De la rage au coeur* (fifty poems in English, same in French as translated by Jean Migrenne). Poems in *African American Review* (more blues and haiku) and in *Prémices* (Belgian journal, adding biographical sketch and photo). Preface to Joans and Bibbs's *Double Trouble,* plus review of Naomi Long Madgett's *Adam of Ifé: Black Women in Praise of Black Men* in *The Black Scholar. Langston Hughes* (1967) appeared on *DiscLit: American Authors—Twayne's United States Authors Series . . . on CD Rom* ("the first full-text CD Rom in the humanities," said G. K. Hall and Company).

Material on my life appeared on fifteen different pages of *Way B(l)ack Then and Now,* by Michel Fabre and John A. Williams; and a curiously adverse, ambivalent review of *Whole Grain,* contradicting a principal fact in my preface, came out in *African American Review.*

Hung my fifteen-panel display of artists' illustrations of my poetry to accompany readings at the Sorbonne conference "African Americans and Europe," at the Cannibal Pierce Australian Gallery and Bookstore in Saint-Denis, and at Oxford University's Maison Française in England. Read twice with Ted Joans and Hart Leroy Bibbs, at the bookstores Shakespeare and Company and Tea and Tattered Pages; twice with Ted, at Galerie 1900Δ2000 (to end his surrealistic art exhibit) and at FNAC Librairie Internationale (where Michel Fabre, introducing us to the audience, compared my poetry to that of Robert Lowell and Robert Frost). Made six appearances in one day at Lycée Saint-Ex-upéry's international festival at Mantes-la-Jolie, after which came forty-eight written

thank-you comments from students. Read from *De la rage au coeur* at Association Grenier Jane Tony in Brussels (selling all twelve books brought with me), with Godelieve Simons reading French versions.

Media treated my work and life: Radio France Culture's "Panorama" program briefly discussing *De la rage au coeur,* and the *Dallas Morning News* (15 March) employing photos and eight columns of coverage.

With Marie-France, saw superb concert by Montserrat Caballé and Marilyn Horne at Frankfurt's *Alte Oper,* vacationed in the spring in Rome, in the fall in India. Explored Normandy and Brittany with Godelieve Simons. Received International Man of the Year 1991–92 award from International Biographical Centre in Cambridge, England.

1993: Read at a literary evening at Université de Paris VII, Institut d'Anglais Charles V (dedicated to Melvin Dixon), and included a page of my "jazz haiku," offering them as a new literary genre. "A Fresh Perspective" review of *Whole Grain* (with bio-bibliographical enhancements) by James de Jongh, in *American Book Review.* Awards, as of 1 May, from major British and American biographical centers: International Order of Merit Award, World Lifetime Achievement Award, the Twentieth Century Award for Achievement, Men's Inner Circle of Achievement Award, World Intellectual of 1993 Award, and Man of the Year 1993 Award.

Perhaps the title of this final chapter—or the fact that what was formerly unrushed, pictorial narrative is suddenly a journalistic series of lean phrases—signals that the curtain is falling on the "wand-waving" planned in the beginning. The present thirteen-year chronology records that I taught, traveled, met people, wrote, and was written about. I trust that readers who responded to my take-my-hand-and-use-your-imagination appeal at the start, musing now beyond the reaches of mere fact, will illuminate in these calendared events whatever shaping graces they left upon my will to write poetry that might live. Those touches of generative magic, whenever I could feel them as nourishment, were the staple of my life as a poet, before—and especially after—my Deadly James, in the unremitting solitudes of his last travail, took on his new name.

The news of his suicide-by-rifle in Michigan, received over the telephone in New York, pinned me against the kitchen wall, I remember, my arms stretched high, clutching at it as if I were trying to climb over it—Marie-France standing there, wide-eyed, one hand raised.

At this moment now, in truth, 27 April 1993, seated at my Olympia machine, I relive lines from my "Officer Liz and the Poem":

And now typewriter roller in my grasp
turns idly back and forth, lifting and lowering
the emptiness in need of words.

Emptiness. His death, the wound from which I never recovered, raised a wall, in the words of a title by Richard Wright, "between the world and me." Its causes, important in firming my view of the world, were twofold: racism-motivated police brutality in California, where he suffered a two-inch skull fracture from beatings in jail; and subsequent, court-based harassment, pursuing him to Michigan, dependent on the police-report charge of assault with a "deadly" weapon, identified as a book satchel.

My life, turning a corner in January 1983, has not followed old paths since then. A veil, lifting and lowering itself as if moved by a moral force obeying its own kinetic laws, still shadows my memory of the past thirteen years. In conformity, then, with the legacy of Deadly James, who gave up his life rather than submit to injustice, I end this chronicle with a kind of eulogistic silence, as a salute to good men that died before their time, and to good probabilities that never came to fruition.

Silence. But always before it, sounds and echoes and images: of how, in Peru near Saqsaywaman ("Sexy Woman," to our guide), I almost fell off a towering mountain ledge, dared by a few of us, into a craggy abyss below because of the *thought* of vertigo, and later marveled at the absolute silence of our small group during a midnight jungle-venture-by-boat on the Amazon River, and back in camp watched the darting antics of a tiny monkey the size and shape of a telephone receiver; how, in India, I plodded far in ten-inch-deep water in a sudden monsoon downpour in New Delhi, walked softly around a cobra in Udaipur, rode an elephant in Jaipur, gasped at the beauty of the Taj Mahal in Agra, and kept in rhythm with a pretty young woman as we danced in a chilly Bombay disco; how I made hundreds of phone calls to Marie-France working in Hamburg, Yorkshire, and Frankfurt to cheer her up; how, at Nicole Lamotte's Normandy studio, "Le Buisson," my emotional reaction to being shown her four illustrations of my poem "Deadly James" made me turn and walk away into her flower garden for a few moments; and how, in Reykjavík, Ambassador Ruwe acknowledged my courtesy call in his office (minus my necktie, as usual) by reminiscing, fingers laced on one knee, about fishing before saying, "One thing you writers can do that we diplomats can't: you can talk with people."

An autobiography is the only literary creation that cannot end—unless its author dies, like the legendary engineer Casey Jones, with his hand on the throttle, headed for the promised land. For me, the promised land, always seeming just beyond my reach, is the poetic masterpiece, that perfect union of words in cadence, each beckoned and shined and breathed into its place, each moving in well-tried harmony of tone and texture and meaning with its neighbors, molding an almost living being so faithful to observable truth, so expressive of the mass of humanity, and so aglow with the beauty of just proportions that the reader feels a chill in his legs or a catch in his throat.

I wish that my autobiography could have pictured a life worthy of producing a few masterpieces. But there is hope: the narrative does not end on this page. . . .

BIBLIOGRAPHY

Poetry:

The Treehouse and Other Poems, Broadside Press, 1968.

At Bay, Broadside Press, 1969.

Panther Man, Broadside Press, 1970.

Black Man Abroad: The Toulouse Poems, Lotus Press, 1978.

A Chisel in the Dark: Poems, Selected and New, Lotus Press, 1980.

A Poet's Mind, Regents, 1983.

The Broken Bowl: New and Uncollected Poems, Lotus Press, 1983.

Deadly James and Other Poems (illustrated by Nicole Lamotte), Lotus Press, 1987.

The Quagmire Effect, American College in Paris, 1988.

Whole Grain: Collected Poems, 1958–1989 (illustrated by Keith O. Anderson), Lotus Press, 1991.

De la rage au coeur (bilingual edition with French translations by Jean Migrenne), Amiot.Lenganey, 1992.

(With Godelieve Simons) *Blues in Black and White*, privately printed, 1992.

Contributor:

Addison Gayle, editor, *Black Expression*, Weybright & Talley, 1969.

Richard Abcarian, editor, *Native Son: A Critical Handbook*, Wadsworth, 1970.

Addison Gayle, editor, *The Black Aesthetic*, Doubleday, 1971.

Therman B. O'Daniel, editor, *Langston Hughes, Black Genius*, Morrow, 1971.

James Vinson, editor, *Contemporary Novelists*, St. James Press, 1972.

Lloyd W. Brown, editor, *The Black Writer in Africa and the Americas*, Hennessey & Ingalls, 1973.

Donald B. Gibson, editor, *Modern Black Poets*, Prentice-Hall, 1973.

Jay Martin, editor, *A Singer in the Dawn: Reinterpretations of Paul Laurence Dunbar*, Dodd, 1975.

Sy M. Kahn and Martha Raetz, editors, *Interculture: A Collection of Essays and Creative Writing* [commemorating the twentieth anniversary of the Fulbright Program at the Institute of Translation and Interpretation, University of Vienna, (1955–74)], Wilhelm Braumueller, 1975.

Rayford Logan and Michael Winston, editors, *Dictionary of American Negro Biography*, Norton, 1982.

Other:

Langston Hughes, Twayne, 1967.

(Editor with Theodore L. Gross) *Dark Symphony: Negro Literature in America*, Free Press, 1968.

(Editor) "Broadside Critics Series" (including Don L. Lee, *Dynamite Voices 1: Black Poets of the 1960s;* Addison Gayle, *Claude McKay: The Black Poet at War;* Bernard W. Bell, *The Folk Roots of Contemporary Afro-American Poetry;* Houston A. Baker, *A Many-Colored Coat of Dreams: The Poetry of Countee Cullen;* William H. Robinson, *Phillis Wheatley in the Black American Beginnings*), Broadside, 1971–75.

(With MacKinlay Kantor and Lawrence Osgood) *How I Write/2* (nonfiction), Harcourt Brace, 1972.

Poems anthologized in *Sixes and Sevens* (London), 1962; *American Negro Poetry*, 1963; *New Negro Poets: U.S.A.*, 1964; *Anthologie de la Poésie Négro-Américaine: 1770–1965* (Paris), 1966; *Kaleidoscope: Poems by American Negro Poets*, 1967; and about one hundred fifteen other volumes. About ninety poems have been published in periodicals, including *African American Review, Black American Literature Forum, Les Elytres du Hanneton, Imprints Quarterly, Inédit, Le Journal des Poètes, Kenyon Review, Negro Digest, Prémices,* and *Renaissance. The Treehouse and Other Poems* and *Panther Man* were recorded by Broadside Voices in 1968 and 1970 respectively.

Author of two previous manuscript autobiographies, the first called *From the Bad Lands to the Capital* (1943–44); the second, *Snowflakes and Steel: My Life as a Poet, 1971–1980*, written at the request of the Jay B. Hubbell Center for American Literary Historiography at Duke University and deposited there in 1981.

Contributor of book reviews to *Books Abroad* and *New York Times Book Review*, and of articles to scholarly journals, including *American Speech, Black World, CLA Journal, Freedomways, Phylon,* and *Readers and Writers*.

Howard Fast

1914-

Howard Fast, 1992

My father, Barney Fast, was a workingman all of his life. He was born in 1869 in the town of Fastov in the Ukraine and was brought to the United States in 1878, aged nine, by his older brother, Edward. Immigration shortened Fastov to Fast, gave it to him as a last name, and so it remained.

In 1897, working in a tin factory in Whitestone, Long Island, my father made friends with a young man named Daniel Miller. Miller's family had moved from Lithuania to London a generation before, and Daniel, one of a family of five sons and two daughters, had made his way to America alone. When the war with Spain began, Barney and Dan and a few other Jewish boys working at the tin factory organized a regiment to fight in Cuba and thereby revenge themselves for the expulsion of Jews from Spain in 1492. They persuaded enough non-Jews to join up to make a regiment of three hundred men, and one of the bookkeepers at the plant, a man in his middle sixties named Charlie Hensen, who claimed to have been a cavalry officer during the Civil War, offered to train the three hundred as a cavalry regiment. That was not as loony a proposition as it sounds, for the war in Cuba was disorganized, with all sorts of citizens getting into the act—as witness Theodore Roosevelt and his Rough Riders.

Hensen collected twenty-five percent of each man's pay, with which he proposed to buy uniforms, sabers, and horses. But after a few months, Hensen and the money disappeared, and Barney never did get to Cuba. He did, however, become bosom pals with Danny Miller, and Danny showed Barney a picture of his beautiful sister. My father fell in love with the picture, began to correspond with Ida Miller, saved his money, sent her a steamship ticket for passage to America, and in due time married her. In 1904 their first child, Rena, was born, and in 1906 they had a son named Arthur, a sensitive, beautiful boy that I know only from photographs. He died of diphtheria six years later. My brother Jerome was born in March of 1913, and I came in November of the following year. My mother's last child, Julius, was born in 1919. My mother died of pernicious anemia in the spring of 1923, when I was eight-and-a-half years old.

We were always poor, but while my mother lived, we children never realized that we were poor. My father, at the age of fourteen, had been an ironworker in the open-shed furnaces on the East River below Fourteenth Street. There the wrought iron that festooned the city was hammered into shape at open forges. As a kid, Barney had run for beer for the big, heavy-muscled men who hammered out the iron at the blazing forges, and there was nothing else he wanted to do. But the iron sheds disappeared as fashions in building changed, and Barney went to work as a gripper man on one of the last cable cars in the city. From there to the tin factory and finally to being a cutter in a dress factory. He never earned more than forty dollars a week during my mother's lifetime, yet with this forty dollars my mother made do. She was a wise woman, and if a wretched tenement was less than her dream of America, she would not surrender. She scrubbed and sewed and knitted. She made all of the clothes for all of her children, cutting little suits out of velvet and fine wools and silks; she cooked and cleaned with a vengeance, and to me she seemed a sort of princess, with her stories of London and Kew and Kensington Gardens and the excitement and tumult of Petticoat Lane and Covent Garden. Memories of this beautiful lady, whose speech was so different from the speech of others around me, were wiped out in the moment of her death. I remember my father coming into the tiny bedroom where I slept with Jerome, waking us gently, and saying, "Momma died last night." Although I was very young, I must have known what death meant—my mother had been sick for over a year—for at that moment my mind had to choose between memory and

madness, and forgetfulness and sanity. My mind chose forgetfulness so that I could remain sane. The process is not uncommon and is called infantile amnesia; it was not until years later that my memories of my mother began to return.

Because my memories of my mother were wiped out in a flash, the dark-haired woman who lay in the open coffin in our tiny living room—packed with family and curious neighbors—was strange to me. I wept dutifully. My mother's brother Gerry, a young physician and the only solvent member of the family, pressed a silver dollar into my hand, and it quieted my tears. I had never seen anything like it before.

All the dismal business of a death in poverty, of the tragedy of my poor father left with three small children and a nineteen-year-old girl who had been coddled and treasured by her mother to the point of becoming a spoiled child, shattered by her mother's death, does remain in my memory. For a few months after my mother's death, my sister tried to keep the family together, but more and more she saw herself trapped, doomed to spinsterhood by the responsibility of caring for three little boys. So acute was her fear that she plunged into marriage, compounding the tragedy and leaving my bewildered father to take care of the three small children. Jerome and I hated the man she married. His only virtue in our eyes was that he was British, somehow distantly related to us by marriage, but he was insensitive and stupid.

I loved my sister—and did so to the day of her death—but my father was shattered by her departure. My maternal grandmother—I never saw my father's parents—took my brother Julius to live with her in Long Island. He was only four years old, and there was no way my father could take care of him. Indeed, there was no way my father could take care of Jerome and me.

My father was a dear and gentle man, a gentleman in every sense of the word, but his own mother had died when he was seven years old, and the death of his wife threw him into a deep depression. I know that several women loved him, but he never married again. If he had, possibly my life would have been different, but as it was, my brother and I were left from morning to night on our own, with no one to turn to, no one to care for or feed us—with a father who was depressed and disoriented and often did not come home until well past midnight, plunging Jerome and me into periods of terror that were to be repeated again and again.

The years that followed provided an experience in poverty and misery that was burned into my soul. In time, nothing much changed in the scheme of poverty; what did change was my ability to face and alter circumstances. I ceased to be wholly a victim. The place where we lived was a wretched slum apartment, made lovely by the wit and skill and determination of my mother; but after her death and the departure of my sister, the place simply disintegrated. Jerome and I, two small boys essentially on our own, had to be mother and father and brother to each other. Jerome cared for me; to the best of my ability, I cared for him. My father disappeared each morning at 8 A.M. and rarely did he return until after midnight; periodically, he was out of work. We made some efforts to keep the apartment clean, but that's not within the scope of small boys. The apartment became dirty; the cheap furniture began to come apart; trash accumulated. In his depression, my father seemed unaware of what was happening. We had holes in our clothes, our shoes were coming apart, and Pop made only an occasional effort to rectify things.

In actuality, we had no childhood; it slipped away. When I was ten and Jerome was eleven, we decided to take things in hand. My brother was like a rock, and without him I surely would have perished. We needed money, and Jerome had heard somewhere that you could make money delivering newspapers, in particular the *Bronx Home News*, which existed entirely on home delivery with a system worked out by a man named Keneally. I don't recall his first name, and there's no way I can find it, but I remember him with great fondness. He had an office in Washington Heights, and one day after school, Jerry and I made our way there and presented ourselves to Mr. Keneally, a tall, lean, long-faced man.

I can imagine how we appeared to him, two ragged kids with long, shaggy hair, holes in our shoes, holes in our stockings. "We can do it!" Jerry pleaded, and Keneally said okay, he'd give us a chance, even though we were too young to do a proper route. But one of his boys had left, and maybe the two of us together could do one route. He was very kind. He was of the generation of Irish who had fought their way up from the starkest poverty, and he understood. We were given a book of some ninety customers who took daily papers, including Saturday and Sunday, and each week we had to collect twelve cents from each customer. We paid a straight price for our bundle, and it amounted to about two out of every twelve

cents—a price we paid whether we were able to collect or not.

So my working life began, at age ten, and from then until I was twenty-two years old I had one job or another: for three years delivering the *Bronx Home News*, then working for a cigarmaker on Avenue B on the East Side, then a hatmaker on West Thirty-eighth Street, then making deliveries and cleaning at an uptown butcher shop, and then at the 115th Street branch of the New York Public Library. When I left the library, I worked for a year in a dress factory, first as a shipping clerk and then as a presser—at least a presser in training. Meanwhile, I finished grade school, went to high school, got a scholarship to the National Academy of Design, and worked there for a year. I gave it up when, at the age of seventeen, I sold my first short story.

The first toll poverty takes is human dignity, and no family in abject poverty lives like the Cratchits in Charles Dickens's *A Christmas Carol*. He was faulted on that, and he wrote *The Chimes* to show the other side of the coin, but he left out the sense that every poverty-stricken family has of a world put together wrong. It was particularly evident in New York, where the poor lived cheek by jowl with the rich. The rich were always evident, the people I so catalogued then, those who lived on Riverside Drive and Fort Washington Avenue. They were middle-class people, but we had nothing, and to us they were wealthy in the only way we knew wealth. In those days of the 1920s, there was no safety net beneath the poor, no welfare, no churches handing out free dinners. Survival in poverty was your own affair. I have tried to explain this to people who expressed indignant wonder at the fact that I joined the Communist party. The absence of unemployment insurance is educational in a way that nothing else is.

One of the main reasons, perhaps, for our survival as a family unit was the place where we lived. The anti-Semitism that prevailed was maniacal; there is no other way to describe it. And this crazed Christian sickness forced Jerry and me at first, then Julius with us, into a closed, defensive unit. Aside from my uncle's family in the summer, no relative held out a hand to us. Some of them were well-to-do; all of them lived comfortably, but my father's pride forbade his asking for help, and none was offered. They were a lousy crew, and I'll say no more about them.

We didn't complain, Jerry and I, and in a sense the challenge of keeping the family alive was a game we played. We lived in two worlds, the wretched world of reality and the marvelous, endlessly exciting world of the books we read. In those days, bread, milk, and cheese were delivered very early in the morning to the doors of the prosperous. When we had no food, we'd be up at six in the morning to find bread and milk and cheese that would keep us alive. We did not consider it stealing; we never questioned our right to remain alive. Once, we appropriated—a better word—an entire stalk of bananas from a truck. Some we kept for ourselves, eating bananas until we could not face another. The rest we sold for a nickel a hand. When we were utterly penniless and my father was unemployed, we scoured the neighborhood for milk bottles, a nickel for each returned. We knew the back way into every house in the area; we knew the rooftops.

When I turned fourteen, in 1928, I reached an age of maturity, the difference from childhood being, to my mind, the difference between being a victim without recourse and a sort of adult with recourse. My brother and I had arrived at an age where we could change things. Filth was no longer a permanent part of our existence; it could be dealt with and done away with. We were working and Barney was working, making fifty dollars a week, the most he had ever earned per week in all his life. Julius was living with us now, aged nine years old, and both Jerry and I felt a sense of responsibility toward him. We informed Barney that we were going to move out of that miserable slum apartment, and when he put up a storm of protest—he was incapable of altering his living place—we said that we'd move without him. Jerry and I were both working for the New York Public Library at that point, paid thirty cents an hour, a sum that was reduced to twenty-five cents an hour after the great stock market crash; and with extra time on Wednesday and Saturday, I took home nine dollars a week and Jerry eleven. Twenty dollars was not to be sneezed at—indeed, in our world it was a princely sum—and it bought us food and clothes. With Barney's fifty dollars added to our twenty, there was an income of seventy dollars a week, unimaginable riches. It did not last very long, but long enough to get us out of 159th Street and up to Inwood at the northern tip of Manhattan.

I began to think. From the time when the street became my life, I had plotted, schemed, maneuvered, manipulated, cozened, and, when the need arose, pleaded; and these are all mental activities, but by thinking I mean putting one fact against another and trying to measure the result. This kind of thinking is a very special thing.

The winter of 1929–1930 I worked at the public library in lower Harlem, at 203 West 115th Street. I was poorly paid—down to twenty-five cents an hour that winter—but I loved working in the library. The walls of books gave me a sense of history, of order, of meaning in this strange world, and I could easily pick up two, three, sometimes four hours of overtime in a week. I worked from four to nine, closing time, for five days and on Saturday from nine to one. Since we did checking and arranging on Saturdays, I could pick up the overtime there, and I could always slip down to the closed reference shelves in the basement to get my homework done. My wages averaged between seven and eight dollars a week, but in the shattered prices of deflation, that was decent money. The important thing was the world of books around me. I read everything without discrimination—psychology, astronomy, physics, history, and more history—and some of it I understood and some of it I didn't.

And I began to think.

The subway ride I took to my home was a nickel. At the uptown end of the subway, where I left the train, a man in a blue serge suit, jacket and vest and tie—a man of some fifty years—stood out on the street and sold apples for a nickel each. Every night on my way home I bought an apple, a large, shiny Washington State Delicious apple. I bought the apple because I was hungry, because the man touched something very deep inside of me, and because I had begun to think. This went on for several weeks. I was a kid with a job; he was a mature man, a businessman or an accountant or something of the sort to my guess. I thought of my father. Barney was a workingman; this was a middle-class educated man, and one night he stopped me.

"Hey, kid," he said, "what's your name?"

"Howard Fast."

"That's an odd name," he said. "Do they call you a fast worker?"

I stared at him without answering, and then I blurted out, "Do you have kids, mister?"

Now he stared at me, and then he began to cry. Tears—real tears. I don't know whether I had ever seen a grown man cry, and it remains in my memory as one of the most woeful moments of my life.

I grabbed my apple, pressed a nickel into his hand, and ran. I ran all the way home. He was gone the next day, and I never saw him again. There are theories that the level of consciousness varies from time to time and that most of our lives are lived at a very low level of consciousness, almost like a walking sleep. Memory is sharpest when it recalls the highest moments of consciousness; I believe this, and that moment scared my mind.

Other things were working on my personal mental schematic. I had seen my father on strike; I had seen him locked out; I had seen his head bloodied on a picket line. I had watched the economy of my own country collapse; I had seen the packing-crate villages grow on the riverfront. I did not have to be instructed about poverty or hunger; I had lived them both. I had fought and been beaten innumerable times, not because of my religion—Barney never imposed religion on us, for which I am eternally grateful—but because I was Jewish, and all of it worked together to create in my mind a simple plea, that somewhere, somehow, there was in this world an explanation that made sense.

That was my way. I never faulted the other ways. I knew kids who were arrested, who turned into thieves or ran with the gangs—it was the time of Prohibition—and I understood this, and often enough I said to myself, "There but for the grace of God goes Howard Fast." I was lucky. One of the kids ended up in the electric chair. Oh, I was damned lucky.

Jerry found a copy of *The Iron Heel* by Jack London. At that time, Jack London stood first among our literary heroes. Today, I find his prose flowery and too mannered, but our taste was less demanding then, and we read and reread every book of his on the library shelves—except for *The Iron Heel*. We never could find a copy in the library. The head librarian at 115th Street was a Mrs. Lindsay, a very dignified and tall woman, a distant relative I think of the man who was to become our mayor. I got up the courage to ask her why we didn't have *The Iron Heel*, and she informed me that it was considered a Bolshevik book. She had never read it, and she hoped I was not interested in such things.

How could I not be interested? *Bolshevik* was a wild word at that time; it was not so long before that the Bolsheviks had burst into history. You couldn't pick up a copy of the *Daily News*, the *Mirror* or the *Graphic* without having the infamies of the Bolsheviks scream at you from the front page. The word, Russian for "majority," has gone

The author in 1946

out of use today, but then it was the number one synonym for evil.

The Iron Heel was my first real contact with socialism; the book was passed around among the kids I knew at high school. If I had lived on the Lower East Side or in one of Brooklyn's immigrant enclaves, I would have had a taste of socialism with my mother's milk, but in this solidly Irish-Italian block there was no hint of it, and at that time George Washington High School was middle-class, filled with well-dressed boys and girls who had allowances and money for a decent lunch in the school cafeteria. Against this background, *The Iron Heel* had a tremendous effect on me. London anticipated fascism as no writer of the time did; indeed no historian or social scientist of the time had even an inkling of the blueprint Jack London laid out, which came into being a few decades after his death. In it, he drew the struggle against fascism by an underground socialist movement, and he did it so convincingly that we were not quite sure that what he wrote of had not already happened.

It was the beginning of my trying to understand why society was structured as I saw it to be structured. Communist bashing became so pervasive in the 1960s and 1970s that few people even attempted to understand or inquire into the forces that produced socialist thinking and, out of it, the Communist movement.

And then, one day, arranging books in the library, I came upon Shaw's *The Intelligent Woman's Guide to Socialism and Capitalism,* and the die was cast.

I think I read somewhere that Shaw had so named his book to excite the curiosity of men, and I had also heard that he believed women to be more intelligent than men—a belief I share. In any case, *The Intelligent Woman's Guide to Socialism and Capitalism* is the clearest exposition of the subject I know of. I was then sixteen, and the book provided me with a new way of thinking about poverty, inequality, and injustice. Shaw had opened an enormous Pandora's box, and never in my lifetime would I be able to close it. The book also set me off in a new direction in my reading, and in quick succession I read Thorstein Veblen's *The Theory of the Leisure Class,* Bellamy's *Looking Backward,* and Engels's *The Origin of the Family.* My mind exploded with ideas. I hurt dear Hallie Jamison, my wonderful high school English teacher, by engaging her in a discussion of whether any nation involved in World War One had been fighting a just war—her beloved having died on the western front—and I made a general nuisance of myself because of my obsession for knowing everything there was to know. In his novel *Martin Eden,* Jack London had stated unequivocally that a writer must have a total knowledge of science. I believed him and set out to gain just that, even reading a bit of Herbert Spencer—recommended by London— in the process. Still in high school, I found psychology, read the Watsonians and rejected them, read the Gestalt theorists and liked them a little better, read the Binet-Simon book on testing, gave intelligence tests to everyone I could corner, and thereby washed myself out of the process, for when it came time for me to be tested at school, I explained that I knew the tests forward and backward. Result—I never knew my own IQ and took comfort in that.

I decided to become a writer. There was no problem in making this decision. It was the only way of life I ever considered, from as far back as my memory goes. I decided to be a writer, to write stories and books, and to illustrate them myself. I had no desire to become an easel painter—only to be able to illustrate what I wrote in the manner of Howard Pyle and N. C. Wyeth. They were my idols; the marvelous illustrations they did for books and magazines constituted my approach to art.

We had pulled the family together and out of the wretched morass of poverty and misery. Jerry and I were earning enough to keep the family going on a decent basis even when Barney was out of work. You didn't need much to get by in the early thirties. Jerry rooted jobs out of everywhere and nowhere, and when I graduated from high school I was earning nine dollars a week as a page at the 115th Street library. The Morris Plan gave small loans on the strength of co-workers, without collateral. Their interest amounted to twenty-seven percent, but we somehow got Jerry through his first year of college and paid back the loan. I applied to both Cooper Union and the National Academy, then a sprawl of old-fashioned studio buildings at 110th Street, just east of the Cathedral of St. John the Divine. The waiting list at Cooper Union was years in length; the National Academy accepted me for immediate entrance.

I enrolled at the National Academy. By God, I had done it. I was seventeen years old, and I was alive and healthy, when by all the odds I should have been either dead or hopelessly weak and sick. With my brothers and my father, I had a clean, proper home, a bed without bedbugs—as a kid they had made my life in bed a nightmare—books of my own, shoes without holes, a warm winter overcoat, and above all, I was a scholarship student at what was then the most prestigious art school in America. And as yet, I had done no time in jail, and that was not the least of my accomplishments, for I was not a quiet or contemplative kid, but one of those irritating, impossible, doubting, questioning mavericks, full of anger and invention and wild notions, accepting nothing, driving my peers to bitter arguments and driving my elders to annoyance, rage, and despair. I probably had some good points as well.

And I was innocent—not simply unsophisticated, but innocent in the sense that I was free of hate. That applied to both of my brothers too; we were without hate. As far as sophistication was concerned, that was a quality you had to pick up along the way.

I had become a writer and I would remain a writer. The question of ever being anything else never entered my mind; there was only one thing I could be in this life and that was what I was. Each morning I arose at six and wrote. Two hours later,

*Recipient of the International Peace Prize, with daughter, Rachel,
and wife, Bette, 1951*

I left for the National Academy, where I practiced cast and figure drawing in the severe and tedious classical manner. I completed a story every few days and as promptly dispatched it to one magazine or another. It's hard to recall and believe in my own naïveté, for all those first stories were handwritten in ink, and my altered handwriting—I was left-handed—was not easily read. After sending out about a dozen stories, I happened to mention to one of the librarians what I was doing, and to my dismay she informed me that no magazine would bother to read a handwritten story. Either I typed out my stories or forgot the whole matter.

We had a family discussion. After all, since I read each story aloud to my brothers once it was done, they had a sort of vested interest, and it was agreed that we would put out $1.75 to rent a typewriter for a month. I had to learn to use it, and while I made a few attempts at touch typing, I soon gave that up and settled into the two-finger method, which I continue to use. I kept the typewriter for a second and then a third month, and then, incredibly, I sold a story.

Looking back, I find it astonishing; at the time, I felt it to be a miracle. It was not that I had no expectations of selling stories—I was supremely confident that one day I would—but it was a date in the indefinite future, and here, miracle of miracles, it had happened. The story was titled "Wrath of the Purple," and the purchaser, for thirty-seven dollars in honest American money, was *Amazing Stories* magazine, the first of the science-fiction magazines.

In 1931, thirty-seven dollars was a substantial sum of money—at least at my level of society. I was still working at the library, going there directly from the academy, but the best I could do at the library, even with all the overtime I could squeeze out of the job, was nine dollars a week, and here one story had brought me more than a month's pay. Now that I had reached my full height of five feet, ten-and-one-half inches, my work at the library changed. Rather than rearranging books, putting returned books back on the shelves, and seeing that all the reference numbers read in proper sequence, I was put to the business of tracking down overdue books, going to the apartments of the people who had borrowed them, and reclaiming them—and if possible collecting the fines. The fine, I recall, was two cents per day per book.

I wrote my first novel when I was sixteen. I had never heard of anyone having a novel published at sixteen, but I said to myself, "Why not a first time?" I finished it, read it through, and decided that it was so bad the best thing I could do with it was consign it to the trash can. The second novel dealt with my year at the academy. It was titled "To Be an Artist." I brought it by hand to three publishers; each one asked me to come and get it—without comment. I was not deterred. I sold a story to a pulp magazine, and it brought me forty dollars.

I wrote my heart out every morning, and I went to work for the hatmaker. As the months passed, I discovered something that I had suspected for many years but had been unable to come to grips with: that the most wonderful, beautiful, and desirable of God's creatures was called a woman. To a boy of seventeen, this phenomenon is shrouded in frustration and ineptitude. I fell passionately in love with a girl named Marjorie. The problem was that, what with working at a job, writing, trying to educate myself, and sharing in the housekeeping, cleaning and cooking, of our male ménage, I had no time to deal with young love.

I learned about the bookstalls on lower Fourth Avenue (now Park Avenue South), hundreds of open stalls, thousands of books, and for forty cents I bought a battered copy of *Das Kapital* by one Karl Marx. Not too many years before, I had regarded books as things that existed only in the New York Public Library; now I was creating my own library, but as far as *Das Kapital* was concerned, I fought my way through two hundred pages or so and then surrendered. George Bernard Shaw did much better with explanation. *The Communist Manifesto,* which I bought for ten cents, a worn pamphlet, was full of brimstone and fire and much more to my taste. I fell in love with a girl named Thelma. I fell in love with a girl named Maxine.

When someone asks me how and why I became a Socialist and a Communist, the answer is always inadequate. Intellectuals deal with ideas and abstractions. Never having had enough education to become a proper intellectual, I have spent my life dealing with facts and events, and this journey has burned itself into my memory. I have tried to write these events as I experienced them, with no broader perspective than I had at the time and without giving them too much importance. I left home and spent a month wandering through the South, looking for work, seeing a land as different from New York City as night from day. I journeyed through a society in disintegration, saved from inner destruction by World War Two, still six years in the future. And through all this, I never whimpered or turned a thought against this land which I had come to love so, nor can I ever think of the South without recalling not the jails and the guns but the wonderful slow wagon ride through the Peedee Swamp, arguing the Civil War with the Southern kids. But I had reached an age where the innocence, born not of faith but of intolerable poverty, was beginning to crumble and where I began to understand that society could be planned and function in another way, called

Howard and Bette Fast with their two children, Jonathan, five, and Rachel, nine, winter 1953–54

socialism; and because I came to believe that the only serious socialist party in America was the Communist party, I was bitterly attacked and slandered for fifteen years of my life.

I went to work. I found work as a shipping clerk in a dress factory in the heart of the garment center, and I wrote, morning and evening, six, seven, eight hours a day. I had written three complete unpublished novels before I took off for the South. I wrote two more in the few months after I returned. Five novels—one a five-hundred-page opus. They are best unremembered. The sixth novel, which I called *Two Valleys,* found a publisher.

This first publisher was the old original Dial Press, and the man who accepted the book was the editor in chief of that distinguished publishing house, a gentleman by the name of Grenville Vernon. I received a one-hundred-dollar advance, and the book was sold to the British publishing house Michael Joseph. The fact that the author was not yet nineteen was made much of, and while the novel was no great work of art, it was a gentle and readable book, a love story set in Colonial times in the mountains of what is today West Virginia. The reviews were decent and kind, with many bows to my age, but sales were inconsequential because the owner of the company, Lincoln MacVeagh, had put the house up for sale. For all that, I was recognized as a bright new hope on the literary horizon. I was given a Bread Loaf Award, and I spent two weeks at that lovely spot in the Green Mountains eating marvelous food, learning the finer points in the use of knives and forks, watching the critic John Mason Brown and his colleagues drink more martinis than I had ever imagined human beings could consume and make sense, and falling moderately but romantically in love with Gladys Hasty Carroll, a very popular and beautiful writer of the time and about ten years older than I. I actually gathered the courage to tell her I loved her before the session finished, but that was as far as it went, and I never saw her again. She was very kind to me.

Suddenly everything dried up and I stopped writing. Months went by and I wrote nothing. I continued to work in the garment factory. I trundled trucks through the streets and packed cases and learned to use a pressing machine and a felling machine, and worked my way up to twelve and then fourteen dollars a week, and dated a beautiful girl who worked in a publishing house; we parted because beyond subway fare to work and back, a nickel each way, and fifteen cents more

for lunch at the Automat, brown beans and coffee, I had nothing, not even a decent pair of pants. Jerry was in his third year of college—we managed that somehow—and Julius was in high school, and everybody worked, and our need to hold the family together, now that two of us were adults and my younger brother was pushing adulthood, was almost demonic. Barney could rarely get better than the lowest paid job, but we managed, with a kind of crazy pride that we took no welfare or outside help of any kind. Interestingly, my father, a loyal Democrat and for years a county commissioner who worshipped Al Smith, was always reminded by the local Democratic boss that if worse came to worst, the party would step in. I think of how many times he came around to check Pop's vote, have a shot of bootleg gin, and say to him, "You know, Barney, that the party will never let you or the kids go hungry." Well, there were times when we were hungry, but we never dunned the party, and Barney always rejected their annual turkey, with instructions that they give it to some poor family.

And then I went back to writing. Up each morning at six, dress, chew a sweet roll, drink a glass of milk, and write. Two more pulp stories were sold, and I paid a semester of Jerry's tuition. On and off, as I would hit a short-story sale, I would pay tuition. I fought for my writing now, so the two hours before I went to work were daily agony. More and more deeply aware of my own position, I struggled to write about myself. I put together a story about a little boy, living in the street I lived on, whom I called Ishky. I coined the name because it sounded very Jewish, and I had his mother speak only the most broken English; but when his mother's Yiddish was translated formally, it emerged as classical English, full of *thee*'s and *thou*'s. I got the idea from Henry Roth's wonderful book, *Call It Sleep.* Ishky had one friend, a little Italian boy, my friend then, who played the fiddle and who, because he was a shoemaker's son, we called Shoemake. The body of the story concerned the lynching of a black kid. My story would be called *The Children,* and I wrote and rewrote, and tore up what I had and wrote it again, and drank coffee and smoked. Drink had no allure for me; nicotine had.

But cigarettes cost money. The factory where I did my eight or nine hours of survival work each day had a solidly Jewish-immigrant working force—cutters, machine operators, everyone—and the chatter and gossip that never stopped were carried on in Yiddish. On my first day there, when

I had to have orders translated, they named me *goy,* Yiddish for Gentile. I had picked up the cigarette habit from a waiter I worked with one summer, but brand cigarettes were twelve cents a pack—even the lowly Wings were eight or ten cents a pack, depending on where you bought them—and this cut into food money. Therefore I bought one pack a week, treasured it at home as a crutch for writing, and depended on my bumming talents for daytime smoking. And since I never smoked more than two or three cigarettes during working time, and since practically everyone in the factory smoked, I could always find a butt. But only if I asked for it in Yiddish, and thereby my first Yiddish word was *papiros,* Yiddish for cigarette. Whatever my question, the workers would fling back at me, *"Freg mir in Yidish"* (Ask me in Yiddish).

Then a day came when I decided that *The Children* was as finished as it would ever be. My two published books and my handful of sold stories had persuaded a literary agency to accept me as one of its writers. The agency was McIntosh and Otis and was run by three pleasant ladies, Mavis McIntosh, Elizabeth Otis, and Mary Abbott. They were middle-class literary types, good agents, and to me characters out of an Edwardian novel. An additional attraction for me was that on the little table in their waiting room they kept a wooden box of cigarettes. I gave them *The Children*—forty-five thousand words of it—and washed my hands of it. I decided that I would continue as a writer, but there would be no more about myself and my childhood. It was too close, too confusing, and too filled with pain.

Whit Burnett, publisher of *Story* magazine, bought *The Children* and published it. *Story* was the most distinguished magazine of the short story in America at a time when the short story was at its peak as an art form internationally and when American short stories were read and admired the world over—which says nothing for the finances of *Story.* Burnett paid fifty dollars for forty-five thousand words, by word count—still the practice at the time—one tenth of a cent per word. I was absolutely enraged when Mary Abbott telephoned to give me this offer, and I fumed and ranted until she convinced me that Whit Burnett published at a loss and that such was the reputation and distinction of *Story* that it could only profit me even if he paid me not a penny. Mary felt that it was a very good thing for young writers to struggle and make do, but the young writers she knew came from proper middle-class families and good universities

with fallback. I had no fallback whatsoever. Nevertheless, she convinced me that *Story* was the proper place for the short novel I had written. I told her to go ahead, but it would have to be one hundred dollars. On and off, I had put a year into the book, and even as a newspaper delivery boy at the age of ten, I had not worked for two dollars a week. Also, since I had received an advance of one hundred dollars for each of my two published books, I might as well keep my price up. (That's a joke; I would not want it misunderstood.)

The Children was published in the March issue of *Story,* a year and a half after Bette, my wife to be, and I met. Since it was so long a piece, it took practically all of the magazine. James J. Fee, the police inspector of Lynn, Massachusetts, was put onto it, and he read the first copy of *Story* he had ever read, and probably the first book he had ever read. He proclaimed that *The Children* was "the rottenest thing I ever read!" Only two copies of *Story* went to the local news dealer, and Inspector Fee immediately confiscated them. The next day it was banned in Waterbury, Connecticut, and an order for six hundred extra copies promptly came in from news dealers in that town. Whit Burnett danced with delight, and Mary Abbott called to congratulate me, telling me that I was so lucky, since having a work banned was the best thing that could happen to sales, and if only it was banned in Boston, sales would skyrocket. It was banned in Boston and in six other New England cities, and *Story* had the largest press run in all its history. The book was hailed as a small masterpiece and lauded to the skies, and Whit Burnett said that *The Children* saved *Story,* at least for the time being. But saving Howard Fast was another matter, and when my agent suggested to Burnett that he let me share in the prosperity by adding another one hundred dollars to the sum he had paid, he turned her down flat.

A writer is a strange creature. He is a delicate sheet of foil on which the world prints its impressions, and he is self-serving and self-oriented and yet utterly vulnerable, and when I say "he," I mean "she" as well, and for a woman it holds true even more painfully, for whatever a man suffers, a woman suffers more and feels more deeply; and though everyone may believe that he or she can write, in these United States of over two hundred and fifty million people, only a handful can claim the title of writer in its highest sense. I married a gifted, beautiful woman who would one day be one of the finest sculptors we have, and she put aside her own need for my need. I don't know whether it was worth it, or how wise she was to follow me down the paths I took. If one grows old and a little bit wise, all the symbols of greatness and importance and glory shrivel to almost nothing.

By the time Bette and I married, I had finished *Place in the City,* and the book had been published with less than earthshaking results, selling perhaps five thousand copies; but now I was selling short stories for anywhere from five hundred to one thousand dollars each. Such sales every six months, though, did not pay the rent, and we filled in the low spots every way we could. We wrote term papers for college students who had money and no brains; I did pulp stories for fifty dollars each—anything, since once I married I gave up factory work to be a full-time writer.

Bette and I had invested in a 1931 Ford convertible, which cost us forty dollars. Not only did it run, but the clutch was so worn that no one else could start the car. A semimagical way of working clutch and gas pedal allowed me to put it

into motion, and even though one of the tires had a hole the size of a fifty-cent piece, through which the inner tube protruded in a threatening bubble, we ran it for thousands of miles with no trouble. When something broke, it never cost more than a dollar to replace. We parked it on the street, and of course no thief in his right mind would have touched it.

We drove it everywhere, and on one of our journeys we went to Valley Forge in Pennsylvania and spent one afternoon there, moved deeply by the reconstruction of the old revolutionary war encampment. I decided then and there that I'd write a book about the army's winter in Valley Forge, and for the next six months I read American history and wrote the book I would call *Conceived in Liberty;* it became my first real breakthrough as a novelist.

With Sam Sloan, my editor, gone from Harcourt, Brace, and with his replacement there less than thrilled with the sales of *Place in the City,* Mary Abbott sent my new novel to Simon and Schuster.

Fast as candidate for Congress, twenty-third congressional district,
New York City, 1952

Bette Fast in sculpture studio, 1972

They accepted it immediately, published it, and sold fifteen thousand copies, a decent record for my writing. The book, which dealt with the American Revolution somewhat in the realistic manner of Erich Maria Remarque's novel *All Quiet on the Western Front*, about World War One—a treatment never before applied to our revolt—was received with great enthusiasm by the critics. James T. Farrell reviewed it for the *New York Times*, kindly and constructively, and I was unusually thrilled by his guess that when I got the "lightning bugs," as he called them, out of my writing, I might become a very important writer indeed.

During the years between 1937, when I got married, and 1942, when I took over the Voice of America at the Office of War Information, I withdrew completely from active political involvement. For the first time in my life, I was tasting financial security, minimal but actual. Our first year was difficult. I had read bits and pieces, never a full story, of the magnificent running battle and flight to freedom of Chief Little Wolf and his Cheyenne Indians. I wanted desperately to write about it, but the only way I could do so would be to go to Oklahoma, where the old Cheyenne reservation had been, and talk to some of the old Cheyennes still there. Also, in Norman, Oklahoma, at the university, there were Indian students and, on the faculty, a man named Stanley Vestal, who knew more about the Cheyennes than any white man in America. I told the story to Simon and Schuster and talked them into paying me one

hundred dollars a month for an entire year. We had two hundred dollars in our bank account. Ninety dollars bought us an ancient Pontiac to replace our Ford, and with $110 to live on, we set off for Oklahoma. It was a wonderful trip; the Pontiac was fine as long as one didn't push it too hard, and the world of the Great Plains was an incredible change for this survivor of the city streets.

Back in New York, we were dead broke once again, but with the guarantee of one hundred dollars a month from Simon and Schuster. It took nine months for me to write *The Last Frontier*, and when I finished it, neither Bette nor I was particularly thrilled with the result. The editors at Simon and Schuster were less than thrilled, and they returned the manuscript with a note that cancelled the unpaid two hundred dollars of my advance and let me understand that the prompt repayment of the ten months' stipend already spent would be expected. But none too soon, I assured them, since our next meal was the major problem.

Meanwhile, Sam Sloan's new publishing house, Duell, Sloan and Pearce, had begun to function, and when I told him that Simon and Schuster had dumped *The Last Frontier*, he asked to read the manuscript. He read it promptly and asked to see me, and the first thing he put to me was whether I knew how I went wrong. I didn't know, and then he explained, gently, that I had tried to tell the story from the Indians' point of view. "You can't," he said. "You can't get inside Little Wolf's head, and you can't translate Indian speech into English and make it believable." Then what to do with what I had? That was when Sam told me to throw it away and begin again and tell the story from the white man's point of view. When I explained that I had carfare home and not much more, he immediately gave me a check for two thousand dollars as an advance.

The publication of *The Last Frontier* marked the end of our time of poverty and intermittent small riches. Suddenly, Bette and I had enough money for all our modest desires, and I was hailed as a bright new star on the literary horizon. Carl Van Doren, writing a lead review of the book, said, "*The Last Frontier* is an amazing restoration and recreation. The characters breathe, the landscape is solid ground and sky, and the story runs flexibly along the zigzag trail of a people driven by a deep instinct to their ancient home. I do not know of any other episode of Western history that has been so truly and subtly perpetuated as this one. A great story has been found again, and as here told promises to live for generations.''

Of course it was all too much. The literary world is never restrained in either its praise or its condemnation. There were no bad reviews, nor would there be any bad reviews for my next book, *The Unvanquished*, which I wrote and completed in the months between my giving the manuscript of *The Last Frontier* to Sam Sloan and its publication.

Years later, when I complained to my Zen teacher that my being a member of the Communist party had thrust me into literary obscurity and made me the hate target of the literary elite who ruled the weekly book section of the *New York Times* and other such reviews, he looked at me with contempt and said, "You dare to complain of something that saved your own soul!"

Perhaps he was right.

As for my books, they were reviled once I became a Communist, but they were read and read, and at no time during the fifty-six years that followed the publication of my first novel did efforts to suppress them actually succeed.

Pearl Harbor had happened, and the world was at war, and the United States joined the forces that faced Adolph Hitler and his fascist allies. It was 1942, and in the desperate rush by America to turn a peaceful nation into a war machine, many things were quickly if loosely put together. One of these was a propaganda and information center, something that the country had done well enough without in the past but that now was a necessity in this era of radio. This propaganda and information center, so hastily thrown together, was called the Office of War Information, or OWI; and feeling that the only available pool of talent to man it was in New York City, the government took over the General Motors Building at Fifty-seventh Street and Broadway. In the first few months after Pearl Harbor, the government set to it in a sort of frenzy to remake the building according to its needs, staff it, and somehow learn the art—if such it was—of war propaganda.

Howard Fast, meanwhile, was living the ultimate fulfillment of a poor boy's dream. At this point, 1942, I was sitting right on top of eighteen pots of honey. My novel *The Last Frontier*, published a year earlier, had been greeted as a "masterpiece," praised to the skies by Alexander Woollcott and Rex Stout, and chosen as a selection by the esteemed Readers Club; and my new novel, *The Unvanquished*, just published, the story of the Continental army's most desperate moment, had

been called by *Time* magazine, who found in it a parallel for the grim present, "the best book about World War Two." I was twenty-seven years old, about to turn twenty-eight, and five years earlier I had married the wonderful blue-eyed, flaxen-haired Bette, an artist by every right, and still my wife and companion fifty-three years later. We had survived the first hard years nicely enough, and we had just put down five hundred dollars for an acre of land on the Old Sleepy Hollow Road near Tarrytown, in Pochantico Hills.

At Sears, Roebuck we purchased for twelve dollars a set of blueprints, and with a mortgage of eight thousand dollars and one thousand dollars in cash, we built a small, lovely two-bedroom cottage. Bette became pregnant, we acquired a wonderful mongrel named Ginger, and I finished writing a book I would call *Citizen Tom Paine*. I cleared the land myself, Bette learned to bake and cook and sew small clothes, and I saw a rewarding, gentle future, in which we would have many children and Bette would paint and I would write my books and earn fame and fortune. And then came the war, and it all turned to dust.

In quick succession, my father died; my younger brother, close to me and my dearest friend, enlisted in the army; I drew a low draft number; and Bette miscarried our first child and sank into gloom. The future that we had planned so carefully was cast aside; Ginger was given to my older brother and promptly ran away and disappeared; the house was put up for sale; we moved into a one-room studio in New York; and Bette, convinced that my orders would be cut in a matter of weeks at the most, leaving her to face the possibility of years alone, joined the Signal Corps as a civilian artist making animated training films.

When I argued with my wife that it made more sense for me to enlist, as my brother had, then to wait around for a summons by the draft board, she strenuously and angrily objected, guided by the sensible feminine hope that the board would somehow miss me. Then one midday, on West Fifty-seventh Street, I met Louis Untermeyer, and my life changed and nothing would ever again be what we had dreamed our lives might be. Whether it works that way, where a chance meeting can turn existence upside down, or whether what happened to me would have happened in any case, I don't know.

Louis Untermeyer, at that time in his middle fifties, had a national reputation as a poet and anthologist. His knowledge of poetry was encyclopedic, his critical sense wise and balanced, and his wit delightful. He would become a major figure in my life, a beloved friend as well as surrogate father, but at that time I knew him only slightly.

On this day in 1942 I greeted Louis Untermeyer as my savior and eagerly accepted his invitation to lunch. Any meal with Louis was a delight. He would bring a gourmet's appreciation to a boiled egg, and his wit was so much a part of him that he had no existence without it. During lunch I poured out my tale of boredom and frustration, and he offered a solution. The solution was the Office of War Information, and it was located down the street, two blocks from where we were eating.

Elmer Davis, newly appointed head of the Office of War Information, was trying to whip a massive, shortwave radio operation into shape, setting up speaking and translation units for every country of occupied Europe. The feeling at the State Department and the War Department was that we must somehow reach the medium-wave receivers in European households, and since the only part of the European community that was free and allied to us was Great Britain, our people cast their covetous eyes on the British Broadcasting Company. The British were none too happy at the thought of the Yanks putting their grubby fingers on the precious BBC, but their dependence on these same Yanks was enormous, so there was no way they could shunt our demands. Elmer Davis, a one-time correspondent for the *New York Times* and later a radio news commentator, was at that time the most respected man in the field of radio news transmission. Joseph Barnes, a veteran newspaperman, talented and respected, was brought in by Davis to work with him. Both of them understood the importance of medium wave as opposed to shortwave, and they persuaded our government to lean on the British; the result was that the British agreed to turn over their BBC medium-wave transmitters to us for four hours a day, from 2:00 A.M. to 6:00 A.M. our time, which was 7:00 A.M. to 11:00 A.M. London time. AT&T set up a triple transatlantic telephone transmission to London; it would take our voices across the ocean with practically no loss in quality.

So now we had it, a transmitting facility that would cover Europe with our propaganda and could be tuned in by every home on the continent. Now it remained only to find someone to prepare the basic fifteen-minute program that would be translated into eleven languages and repeated several times in French and German. My knowledge of what happened in this search came from

John Houseman, who headed up the shortwave operation—dramatic radio propaganda—and whom I later came to know and like enormously. John—or Jack as we called him—had given up his work as a successful producer to come to the OWI, and according to him, three men were hired in succession to be BBC anchor writer, and each of the three served from a week to two weeks and then was fired. One was the head of the second-largest ad agency in New York; the other two were newspapermen.

During a meeting with Houseman on another subject, Davis and Barnes raised the question of whom to hire for the BBC and where to find him. They told Houseman how desperate they were and what a letdown the three candidates had been, all of them highly recommended and men of experience. There were other men—it was before the time when they might have turned to women—whom they wanted, men in good positions who would not give up their careers even for the OWI. Houseman asked Davis and Barnes exactly what they wanted, to which they answered someone who could write clean, straightforward prose, someone who was literate yet simple and direct.

To this, Houseman answered that he had just read the proofs of a book called *Citizen Tom Paine*, clean, colorful political writing by a kid name of Howard Fast. And how old was this kid? Twenty-seven or twenty-eight. And how do they get in touch with him? He's right here in this building, top floor, writing a pamphlet about the American Revolution. And what in hell was he or anyone else doing sitting up there and writing a pamphlet about the American Revolution? Didn't anyone up there understand that this was World War Two, and not the American Revolution? A few minutes after this discussion, the head of the pamphlet department came to my desk and told me that Elmer Davis, chief of the operation, wanted me downstairs in the radio section.

In Elmer Davis's office, Davis and Barnes and Houseman awaited me. I walked into the room, and the three cold-eyed, hard-faced men stared at me as if I were an insect on a pin, and then Elmer Davis asked, "Are you Fast?"

Of course, they were not hard-faced or cold-eyed, but I was scared and unsure of myself and convinced that I was to be fired for some awful foul-up in my pamphlet, which must have been brought to them as proof of my culpability. I can recall the conversation that followed fairly well, by no means exactly after all these years. Jack Houseman, my entry angel into this strange new world,

Celebrating Louis Untermeyer's ninety-second birthday in Weston, Connecticut.
Top row, from left: Bette, Jon, and Howard Fast, Untermeyer's son.
Bottom row: Brynn Untermeyer, Louis, Erica Jong Fast.

began by spelling out the nature of what would be called from then on simply the BBC, how the deal with the British had come about, and what it was intended to do. Then Elmer Davis picked up and said to me, "That's why you're here, Fast. Jack says you can write."

They were all standing. Suddenly, they all sat down. No one asked me to sit down, so I remained standing. They kept looking at me as if I were distinctive in some way. I wasn't. I was five-feet, ten-and-a-half inches. I still had plenty of hair, and I had round cheeks that embarrassed the hell out of me because they turned pink at my slightest unease. Brown eyes and heavy, horn-rimmed glasses completed the picture.

"Do you follow me?" Davis asked.

I shook my head.

"What he means," Houseman said kindly, "is that he wants you to take over the BBC and write the fifteen-minute blueprint every day."

I shook my head again. If I had unclasped my hands, they would have been shaking like leaves. I was not being fired. This was worse.

"I can't do that," I said.

"Why not?"

"I just don't know how. I never wrote for radio. I never wrote for a newspaper."

"We're not asking for references," Barnes said. "Mr. Houseman here says you can write simply and well and that you can think politically. We're asking you to write a fifteen-minute news program that will tell people in occupied Europe how the war goes, what our army has done, and what our hopes and intentions are. We want you to do it plainly and honestly, to tell the truth and not mince words. You are not to lie or invent. You will have a pool of some twenty actors available, and you will choose three each night to speak your words for the English section. Other actors will speak the foreign translations."

"It's no use," I pleaded. "I'm going to be drafted. I have a low number."

Elmer Davis came to me and lifted off my glasses. Staring at them, he said, "You're technically blind in your right eye, aren't you?"

The author in 1980

"Oh, no," I said. "No. I see quite well out of that eye."

"You won't be drafted," Elmer Davis said.

"Suppose I botch the whole thing?" I said.

"We'll give you a week, and if you botch it, we'll dump you."

"And if you're drafted," Barnes assured me, "you'll be back here in a uniform—unless we toss you out first."

They didn't fire me. The weeks stretched into months, and they didn't fire me. My number came up a few weeks after my BBC job began, and I was still of the belief that if you were going to fight fascism, the way to do it was with a gun in your hands. I wasn't worried about my bad right eye, because during the physical, standing on line to have my eyes examined, I simply memorized the chart. When my turn came and I handed my papers to the eye doctor, he studied them a bit longer than he had to and then consulted some notes on his desk.

"Fast?" He handed me a card to cover my right eye. No problem there. "The other eye now." I began to call off the chart, and the doctor

grinned and held up three fingers. "Forget the chart. How many fingers?"

I guessed two.

"Actually, three. Come on, mister—go back to where you were."

"They set me up, didn't they? Who was it? Barnes? Davis?"

I stomped out of there in a fury and went back to the nightmare that they called the American BBC—and a nightmare it was. I had never driven myself like that before or since, and I was no stranger to hard work, physical or mental. I would get into my office at eight in the morning, usually to find someone from some branch of the government waiting for me. The White House wanted to stress the numbers of tank production because the Germans were saying that in no way would we ever match their numbers. Or Whitehall wanted us to play down the invasion of the continent. Or why wasn't I putting more emphasis on food production? This gentleman is from the Department of Agriculture. I could plead that he didn't have to come up from Washington in person and kill a precious hour of my morning. The secretary so instructed him. The secretary felt that I did not understand that a war was fought with food as well as bullets. The people on the continent were starving. Did I understand what it meant for them to know that there would be ample food? Nobody made appointments with me; they just poured in. The Chamber of Commerce—how on earth did the U.S. Chamber of Commerce know what I was writing? No one publicized that we had four hours of BBC each morning, but everyone appeared to know. Ordnance has this new carbine; eight in the morning, they're there with the carbine. What in hell am I to do with a carbine? How did I get here? I'm a kid, and I know practically nothing about anything. Ten P.M. I get back to my office, and a distinguished-looking gentleman tells me that he has been waiting two hours. He represents the shipyard owners of America. Do I know what shipyards mean in this war? Do I understand that without ships we would lose this war?

So much for the first thirty years of my life. As with any truncated autobiographical memoir, this account deals only with bits and snatches of my life. One searches one's memory for mileposts, so to speak, for moments of decision that point to one or another of the paths that might have been taken. My tenure with the Office of War Information was finished in 1944, when the entire operation of the new Voice of America, which I had created and brought to fruition, was moved to North Africa. I desperately wanted to go with it, but J. Edgar Hoover decided otherwise—by informing my superiors at the OWI that I was a Communist, which at that time I was not. I was offered another post in the organization, an assignment to write a pamphlet on American history. I refused it indignantly and resigned. I had only one purpose in mind, to go overseas and play some part in the war—if only to report on it.

My wife had become pregnant, and our first child, a daughter, was born that year. At the same time, I took two steps that were to change the course of my life. I joined the Communist party, and I went overseas to the China-Burma-India Theater of Operation as a correspondent for the magazine *Coronet* and for the newspaper *P.M.* My journey overseas and my experiences in North Africa, Saudi Arabia, and India resulted in little of major importance for either the war effort or the periodicals that had engaged me, but indeed they were very important in my education and development as a writer and observer of the tragedies and obscenities of the human race. I had a firsthand look at the waste and horror of war, and of the crime that mankind inflicts upon itself.

My part as a reporter overseas was short-lived; my membership in the Communist party, on the other hand, extended from 1944 to 1956. It changed my life, and even to the date of this writing, in April of 1993, almost forty years after leaving the party in sorrow and anger, its effects upon my career still continue. My reasons for joining the party are too complex to put down here. I have spelled them out in great detail in a memoir called *Being Red,* published by Houghton Mifflin in 1990. Suffice it to say that during my time at the OWI, I watched and wrote of the Soviet Union's struggle against the armies of Adolph Hitler. I worked with Communists, among others. I met Communists whom I admired. In the 1930s, almost every American writer or artist or musician whom I admired was either a member of the party or a friend of the party.

But for myself and my family, those twelve years became an unending parade of persecution and isolation. *Freedom Road,* a story of the struggle of the newly freed slaves after the Civil War, was the last book of mine to be published before it was generally known that I was a Communist. It appeared in 1944 to a chorus of critical praise such as few books have ever received. It sold more than a million copies worldwide, becoming during the next ten years perhaps one of the most widely read

serious novels of the time. But that was the end of the critical praise. My next novel, *The American,* was denounced as Communist propaganda, the fate of book after book as the years of my party membership continued.

With the writing of *Spartacus,* things came to a head. The manuscript was submitted to my then publisher, Little, Brown and Company, welcomed and highly praised by my editor, Angus Cameron, then vice president of the company, and scheduled for publication. J. Edgar Hoover, head of the FBI, then decided to intervene personally, sending an agent to Little, Brown and Company with a decree that they were not to publish the book. Similar instructions were sent to every other publisher to whom the book was submitted. After seven leading publishers had declined the book, I published it myself. It sold forty thousand copies in hardcover and another million in paper reprint—but those reprint sales took place after I had left the party, as did the making of the motion picture.

In the course of those years in the party, every book I wrote was viciously attacked and denounced, a situation that reversed itself to a degree after I resigned from the Communist party in 1956.

In those Communist party years, I was sent to prison for three months for contempt of Congress, the act of refusing to surrender lists of names of people who had supported medical aid to Republican Spain.

In 1952, I was a candidate for Congress in the twenty-third congressional district in New York. I ran on the American Labor party ticket—a ticket denounced as pro-Communist—and I was soundly defeated.

When I look back on the years I spent as a member of the Communist party, I am torn between a sense of twelve years of frustration and repression, and a sense of twelve years of struggle and growth in social understanding. I don't regret them, but I deeply regret that I lacked the understanding that would have allowed me to balance my passion for social justice with a clearer judgement of the Communist party, which, instead of bringing us closer to socialism, turned a generation away from it.

When I left the party in 1956, after the monstrous revelations of Joseph Stalin's maniacal cruelties, I had a raging anger against a movement I felt betrayed by. I put some of my feelings into a bitter book called *The Naked God,* published in 1957, and subtitled *The Writer and the Communist Party.* But this feeling of rage and bitterness soon passed, eased by the fact that the world I once knew as a young writer opened up to me again. Two of my books, written under the shadow of my party membership, were immediately bought by film producers. *Spartacus* became not only an enormously successful film, but a best-selling novel ten years after its initial publication, and the novels written after leaving the party found a new generation and a new audience.

For my wife, my daughter, and my son, it was the beginning of a new life, a life without constant fear and persecution. In a nation where so much is easily forgotten, where history is almost meaningless, the years of the witch-hunt are hardly remembered at all, but they were agonizing years, not only for myself as an actual party member, but for liberals as well.

During the years of the blacklist, I decided to do what so many other blacklisted writers had done, to write under another name. My first attempt was a book called *The Fallen Angel,* which I published under the pseudonym of Walter Ericson. It was subsequently made into a film called *Mirage.* Later, my new agent, Paul Reynolds, suggested the name of E. V. Cunningham. I wrote twenty books under that name, published here and immensely successful in Europe.

Indeed, my release—it can be called that—from the party resulted in an explosion of repressed creativity on my part. Only the first of the

E. V. Cunningham books was written during the blacklist; however, the pleasures of writing half-serious suspense stories became so captivating that I wrote, as I said, nineteen more. Nor did I limit myself to the novel. I had always loved California, and in 1974, we moved to Los Angeles, where my wife and I lived for six years. I did screenplays for three films, only one of which was produced. I turned my novel *Citizen Tom Paine* into a theatrical play, done first in Williamstown and eventually in Kennedy Center in Washington, D.C. I wrote a play based on the life of Jane Austen, called *The Novelist.* It was done at Williamstown, at Theater West in Springfield, Massachusetts, in Mamaroneck, and for a short run in New York.

While living in California, I decided to write a book about a woman whose life and experience would parallel my own, having her born the year and month of my own birth, namely November in 1914. I enjoy writing about women. I called her Barbara Lavette, and eventually the story of Barbara Lavette, from her birth to her sixty-eighth year ran to five books that sold over ten million copies.

No matter what direction my writing took, I could never give up a social outlook and a position against hypocrisy and oppression. This has been a theme that runs through all of my writing. Some five years ago, I undertook a weekly column for the New York *Observer.* Selections from this col-

The Fast home in Connecticut

*Howard and Bette Fast with two of their three grandchildren,
Mollie and Benjamin, 1984*

umn were published in a book of essays called *War and Peace*. The book was published by M. E. Sharpe.

All in all, I have lived the life of a writer, a man of letters, a life I chose and which I followed doggedly through the seventy-eight years of my life. I have been fortunate and unfortunate—but more fortunate than unfortunate. I have been married for fifty-six years to a wonderful woman, with whom I fell in love at the age of twenty. We have two children and three grandchildren, and we live very quietly in Connecticut, a place where we have lived for many years and which we love dearly.

I cannot close this short survey of my life as a writer without mentioning a book I wrote called *April Morning*. I wrote this book in 1960, the story of a young adolescent who was witness to the battles of Concord and Lexington at the beginning of the American Revolution. Quietly published by Crown Books, without fuss or fanfare, it went through almost fifty editions in hardcover and literally millions of copies in softcover, mass-mar-

ket reprint. Generations of middle-school children have read this book, which is used as a text in most of the fifty American state school systems, and have taken from it a deep feeling of what America is and how it came into being.

Portions of this essay are excerpted from the author's memoir, *Being Red*.

BIBLIOGRAPHY

Novels:

Two Valleys, Dial, 1933.

Strange Yesterday, Dodd, 1934.

Place in the City, Harcourt, 1937.

Conceived in Liberty: A Novel of Valley Forge, Simon & Schuster, 1939.

The Last Frontier, Duell, 1941.

The Tall Hunter, Harper, 1942.

The Unvanquished, Duell, 1942.

Citizen Tom Paine, Duell, 1943.

Freedom Road, Duell, 1944.

The American: A Middle Western Legend, Duell, 1946.

The Children, Duell, 1947.

Clarkton, Duell, 1947.

My Glorious Brothers, Little, Brown, 1948.

The Proud and the Free, Little, Brown, 1950.

Spartacus, Blue Heron, 1951.

Silas Timberman, Blue Heron, 1954.

The Story of Lola Gregg, Blue Heron, 1956.

Moses, Prince of Egypt, Crown, 1958.

The Winston Affair, Crown, 1959.

Power, Doubleday, 1962.

Agrippa's Daughter, Doubleday, 1964.

Torquemada, Doubleday, 1966.

The Hunter and the Trap, Dial, 1967.

The Crossing, Morrow, 1971.

The Hessian, Morrow, 1972.

Max, Houghton, 1982.

The Outsider, Houghton, 1984.

The Call of Fife and Drum: Three Novels of the Revolution (contains *The Unvanquished, Conceived in Liberty,* and *The Proud and the Free*), Citadel, 1987.

The Dinner Party, Houghton, 1987.

The Pledge, Houghton, 1988.

The Confession of Joe Cullen, Houghton, 1989.

The Trial of Abigail Goodman, Crown, 1993.

"The Immigrants" series:

The Immigrants, Houghton, 1977.

The Second Generation, Houghton, 1978.

The Establishment, Houghton, 1979.

The Legacy, Houghton, 1980.

The Immigrant's Daughter, Houghton, 1985.

Novels under pseudonym E. V. Cunningham:

Sylvia, Doubleday, 1960.

Phyllis, Doubleday, 1962.

Alice, Doubleday, 1963.

Shirley, Doubleday, 1963.

Lydia, Doubleday, 1964.

Penelope, Doubleday, 1965.

Helen, Doubleday, 1966.

Margie, Morrow, 1966.

Sally, Morrow, 1967.

Samantha, Morrow, 1967, published as *The Case of the Angry Actress,* Dell, 1984.

Cynthia, Morrow, 1968.

The Assassin Who Gave Up His Gun, Morrow, 1969.

Millie, Morrow, 1973.

The Case of the One-Penny Orange, Holt, 1977.

The Case of the Russian Diplomat, Holt, 1978.

The Case of the Poisoned Eclairs, Holt, 1979.

The Case of the Sliding Pool, Delacorte, 1981.

The Case of the Kidnapped Angel, Delacorte, 1982.

The Case of the Murdered Mackenzie, Delacorte, 1984.

The Wabash Factor, Doubleday, 1986.

Novels under pseudonym Walter Ericson:

The Fallen Angel, Little, Brown, 1951, published as *The Darkness Within,* Ace, 1953, published as *Mirage* (as Howard Fast), Fawcett, 1965.

Short-story collections:

Patrick Henry and the Frigate's Keel and Other Stories of a Young Nation, Duell, 1945.

Departure and Other Stories, Little, Brown, 1949.

The Last Supper and Other Stories, Blue Heron, 1955.

The Edge of Tomorrow, Bantam, 1961.

The General Zapped an Angel: New Stories of Fantasy and Science Fiction, Morrow, 1970.

A Touch of Infinity: Thirteen New Stories of Fantasy and Science Fiction, Morrow, 1973.

Time and the Riddle: Thirty-one Zen Stories, Ward Ritchie Press, 1975.

Nonfiction:

Haym Salomon, Son of Liberty, Messner, 1941.

Lord Baden-Powell of the Boy Scouts, Messner, 1941.

Goethals and the Panama Canal, Messner, 1942.

(With Bette Fast) *The Picture-Book History of the Jews,* Hebrew Publishing, 1942.

The Incredible Tito, Magazine House, 1944.

Intellectuals in the Fight for Peace, Masses & Mainstream, 1949.

Literature and Reality, International Publishers, 1950.

Tito and His People, Contemporary Publishers, 1950.

Peekskill, U.S.A.: A Personal Experience, Civil Rights Congress, 1951.

Spain and Peace, Joint Anti-Fascist Refugee Committee, 1952.

The Passion of Sacco and Vanzetti: A New England Legend, Blue Heron, 1953.

The Naked God: The Writer and the Communist Party, Praeger, 1957.

The Howard Fast Reader (includes *The Golden River*), Crown, 1960.

The Jews: Story of a People, Dial, 1968.

The Art of Zen Meditation, Peace Press, 1977.

Being Red (autobiography), Houghton, 1990.

The Novelist: A Romantic Portrait of Jane Austen, French, 1992.

War and Peace: Observations on Our Times, Sharpe, 1993.

Books for young readers:

The Romance of a People, Hebrew Publishing, 1941.

Tony and the Wonderful Door, Blue Heron, 1952, (illustrated by Imero Gobbato), Knopf, 1968, published as *The Magic Door* (illustrated by Bonnie Mettler), Peace Press, 1979.

April Morning, Crown, 1961.

Plays:

The Hammer (produced in New York, 1950).

Thirty Pieces of Silver (produced in Melbourne, 1951), Blue Heron, 1954.

George Washington and the Water Witch, Bodley Head, 1956.

(With Dalton Trumbo) *Spartacus* (screenplay; motion picture directed by Stanley Kubrick, produced by Universal Studios, 1960).

The Crossing (produced in Dallas, Texas, 1962).

The Hill (screenplay), Doubleday, 1964.

David and Paula (produced by American Jewish Theater, New York, 1982).

Citizen Tom Paine: A Play in Two Acts (produced in Washington, D.C., 1987), Houghton, 1986.

The Novelist (produced in Williamstown, Massachusetts, 1987).

The Second Coming (produced in Greenwich, Connecticut, 1991).

Other:

(With William Gropper) *Never Forget: The Story of the Warsaw Ghetto* (poetry), Jewish Peoples Fraternal Order, 1946.

Korean Lullaby (poetry), American Peace Crusade, n.d.

(Editor) *The Selected Works of Tom Paine,* Modern Library, 1946.

(Editor) *The Best Short Stories of Theodore Dreiser,* World Publishing, 1947.

(Contributor) Richard Burrill, *The Human Almanac: People through Time* (includes Fast's *The Trap*), Sierra Pacific Press, 1983.

More than ten of Fast's novels and stories have been adapted for production as motion pictures, including *Spartacus,* based on his novel of the same title, 1960; *Man in the Middle,* based on his novel *The Winston Affair,* 1964; *Mirage,* based on a story he wrote under the pseudonym Walter Ericson, 1965; *Penelope,* based on his novel of the same title, 1966; *Jigsaw,* based on his novel *Fallen Angel,* 1968; and *Freedom Road,* based on his novel of the same title, 1980. *The Immigrants* was broadcast as a television miniseries in 1979.

Author of the play *The Hessian,* based on his novel of the same name, 1971; and television scripts *What's a Nice Girl Like You . . . ?,* 1971, based on his novel *Shirley; The Ambassador,* 1974; *21 Hours at Munich,* with Edward Hume, 1976.

Author of weekly column, *Observer,* 1989—. Fast's manuscripts are collected at the University of Pennsylvania, Philadelphia and the University of Wisconsin, Madison.

Laura Furman

1945-

Laura Furman, Austin, Texas, 1991

I

When I was nine months old, my parents bought a brown-shingle house, an abandoned one-room schoolhouse, and seven acres in Long Valley, New Jersey, in what my father called dairy country, about two hours from New York City where we lived. We spent every possible weekend in the country, all summer (my father commuted on weekends), and holidays. I played with my sisters and other friends whose families spent the summer nearby, and I was allowed to explore the lawn, the playhouse, even the woods alone. The time I spent alone was one of the great gifts my mother gave me. The capacity for solitude, cultivated early, has stood me in good stead as a writer.

The Drakestown schoolhouse was across the field where we picked wild blueberries in summer.

189

I pumped the dusty organ, making it groan its few remaining notes, and read the sums and salutations of the last class. The schoolhouse had closed so long before we came upon the scene that the chalk marks could not be erased from the slate boards. On the other side of our house was a brook; beyond, our farmer neighbors, the Skinners. The brook was later enlarged to a pond that reflected the trees and sky beautifully but leaked constantly. Once when I was playing on the driveway, my sister released the emergency brake of our car and it—carrying Emily, missing me by inches—rolled backwards into the pond. Our neighbor Harvey Skinner came to the rescue with his tractor. Behind the house were the woods where I traced my path to the old spring which was covered by a rusted iron cone. If I stood on tiptoe and leaned against the corroded metal I could see the spring water far below; it looked like it was the cleanest thing in the world and the coldest. A hump on the lawn ran from the playhouse (formerly a giant doghouse) across to the red barn that was crowded

with tools, my father's workbench, his canvasses, his skis, our bikes, our junk. Near the barn was an ancient apple tree that I napped under as a baby, on a pink satin quilt that is one of my earliest memories—a quilt faded and dulled with washing, stained by rotted apples. The tree was lost in a hurricane, along with a maple that was taller than our house. One winter there was a memorable storm, and my sister Emily and I (Hester was not yet born) dug tunnels in the snow that had piled up on the lawn.

The hump on the lawn marked the boundary between the original lawn and a place where someone had added topsoil to make a real lawn, better than a mowed pasture. The hump marked the edge of our croquet games and made a place to roll somersaults; when I lay dizzy, I could rest my head against it. Beyond the treetops, I tried to locate the center of the sky and to read in the hieroglyphs of clouds what my fate would be. By this I meant what story I would be heroine of, for I was convinced that I would live a life that would be

*"Three generations of Furmans. My grandfather, Louis M. Furman,
is standing to the left,"* about 1905.

like a story. When I was a child I was often afraid, though I thought I would be brave if called upon to be so.

Only in rare moments did the city rival the country. Sometimes when we were on a bus going through Central Park in the rain, the trunks of the trees, the rough stones of the tunnels and walls, the empty benches shone something like the shine of sky, apple tree, barn, green lawn—the shine of the country.

There was no place like our apartment, when my father was at work and my sister at school, when there was no one at home but my mother and I. To this day, being home in the middle of the day feels luxurious to me. Then being home was a luxury to be earned only by sickness. Some of my happiest childhood memories coincide with illness—chicken pox, endless sore throats, fevers unattached to names, sniffles. Mornings when I was home sick, I listened to my mother cleaning the house, vacuuming, dusting, sweeping, washing dishes, until in my sick room I smelled the harsh familiar detergents and polishes. At noon we'd have lunch, I in bed if I were sick enough, otherwise at the kitchen table, and after lunch I'd return to bed and sleep on and off until the evening when the quiet and my sole possession of my mother would end. I took myself to the living room and curled into a corner of the high-armed couch, and there I hid, still listening for my mother, still savoring the day. I can sometimes recapture the feeling when I am reading and the house is quiet; more rarely when I am writing and become unaware of my actions or thoughts, as absorbed as if I were hearing a good story.

Apartment living, and living in the city in general, meant being aware of people other than my family. The steam pipe in the bathroom carried voices from the apartment below. When I took the elevator and it stopped at another floor, I could catch the ragged end of familial talk ("Later! I've got to go! I told you already!"), the slamming of a door, and the startled look of the person who hadn't realized I was in the elevator, hearing it all. In the mosaic-tiled halls of our building, I saw umbrellas and boots, I caught glimpses of apartments through half-opened doors, and sometimes heard screams and arguments, oblique clues to the interior life. One of the first works of literature I read that matched and illuminated my unexamined experience was John Cheever's short story "The Enormous Radio," which features a radio that can be tuned from one apartment to another, exposing the cruelty and the generally miserable

lives within, and the masks assumed in public. These differences—private and public, city and country—have defined my interests as a writer.

My father, Sylvan S. Furman, grew up in Brooklyn, in a Bensonhurst then filled with prosperous houses and respectable apartment buildings. He was the oldest of four children; he had two brothers and one sister who died when she was eleven. My grandfather, Louis M. Furman, was an immigrant tailor who had built a men's clothing business and who before the Depression had stores in Brooklyn and Manhattan. In the 1930s my grandfather lost the stores, and he moved with his younger sons, Dan and Paul, and his wife, Dora, to Florida, first to Daytona Beach and then to Miami Beach, and established Furmly's, a men's clothing store, eventually located on Lincoln Road in Miami Beach. Later there was a branch in Coral Gables. When my uncle Paul sold Furmly's in the late 1980s the Furmans were finally out of the retail business.

My father called my grandfather's "the heroic generation," for they came to America, often as little more than children, with nothing, and within a generation were established. Indeed, my father went to Columbia College and earned a bachelor's degree there, later two master's, one in psychology and one in psychiatric social work, a far cry from Ellis Island or shortening pants. (He had a long career as a social worker, but his avocation was painting.) My father used a saying of my grandfather's, "Never show a fool a half-finished garment," to comfort me years later when I was having trouble selling a novel, and I grew up hearing that the customer was always right. I didn't meet the Florida Furmans until I was twelve, though I saw my grandfather once a year, when he came north each summer on a buying trip and visited us in New Jersey for a few days. His passage from Ukraine, the large-familied and populated life in Brooklyn, seemed to me to have happened so long before my birth that it had nothing at all to do with me or my immediate family. There were Furmans and Goldbergs who were our relatives in New York and the surrounding area, but we rarely saw them.

I knew even less about my mother's family, aside from my aunt Molly who lived in the Bronx with her husband and two daughters. My mother was born Minnie Airov in the Cambria District near Pittsburgh, Pennsylvania, in a coal-mining town where her father owned a little grocery store.

Parents, Minnie Airov and Sylvan Furman, about 1938

They were the only Jewish family in town. My mother had an older half-brother Sam, and two sisters, Molly and Sophie, and a younger brother, Joe. The family story I grew up with was that come the Depression they moved to Atlanta because there were relatives in Chattanooga. It wasn't until I looked at a map and saw the distance between Atlanta and Chattanooga that I questioned the story.

My maternal grandfather, Morris Airov, suffered from Huntington's chorea, which was at first mistaken for insanity. My grandmother Ida (whom I never met nor did I meet my mother's father) kept the family together somehow, and my aunt Sophie married a gentle person named Israel Zimmerman, who owned a grocery store in a black neighborhood in Atlanta. He supported the family, according to what I heard, until Sophie's sisters were grown and gone, and Joe was educated and gone. (Joe became a professor of economics at Emory University, another immigrant leap.) I didn't meet the Airovs and Zimmermans until I was twelve, when my mother and sister Hester and I went to Atlanta for my cousin Hannah's wedding.

My parents might have wondered if they saw their families in Florida or Georgia as often as they should, or if my sisters and I needed to see more relatives. Maybe they'd grown up with plenty of relatives and figured they were doing us a favor. On rare occasions, my father told about a favorite aunt or cousin, and the stories sounded as if the people he spoke of were in another world, not just Brooklyn or Florida, because they were, to him, in another and finished life. Even at the end of his life, at a time when many people become intensely nostalgic, my father was not interested in returning to old scenes. He had remained friends with several of his college classmates, but passed up going to his sixtieth college reunion, saying, "Who would I know there?" He did think about the past, and told me that after a point it is all one long remembrance.

Of course, my parents' money was limited, and their time and energy filled by their lives in the city and the country and by our demands. I don't know if my mother went back when her mother and father died. In my memory it wasn't until the summer of Hannah's wedding that she returned at all to Georgia.

She'd left Atlanta one year after high school and worked in New York as a secretary. She met my father at the Lavanburg Corner House, a home for Jewish orphan boys where she was secretary to the director and he was a young social worker. They both lived there; room and board was part of their salaries.

On the wall of the room I write in, there's a portrait of my mother painted in 1939 by my father when she was twenty-seven. (They married the next year.) The colors of the portrait are mustard yellow, faded apple green, and maroon. Of all my father's paintings, the portrait is my favorite. It is much influenced by Matisse in the simplification of shapes, the patterning of the drapes behind her, the chair she sits on, the simple lines of her blouse. Her oval face resembles one of Matisse's odalisques, but she is recognizably my mother.

Oil portrait of Minnie Furman
by Sylvan Furman, 1939

The summer before she died, when she went back to Atlanta, she was blooming. In the wedding photos she looks stockier than in the portrait but more animated and happy. In the portrait, she is self-contained, and she looks off to one side, away from the painter.

The wedding was held at a country club, a white building with columns and a swimming pool, decorated in a tradition I'd never seen before, with lots of cream, soft greens, and pink. This was in contrast with the Danish modern or German immigrant homes of my friends in New York, or the worn chintzes and stiff Sears furnishings of the country places. We stayed in the bungalow where Uncle Izzy and Aunt Sophie lived, where my mother had lived before she left for New York twenty-five years before. The small house was packed with people there for the wedding, and gifts lay on every surface, clothing hung from every door. An old black woman stood in the narrow hallway the whole time, pressing and starching clothing until each piece could stand on its own. It was confusing that the bungalow and country club were in what everyone was calling a city. Miami Beach, where I'd been a few weeks before to visit the Furmans, was slightly more urban, that is, more like New York, despite the sunshine, palm trees, and stucco houses. My mother and little sister came to Florida to pick me up, and we flew to Atlanta together. Aunt Sophie waited for us at the plane, and she embraced my mother and cried. I was amazed that there was a person in the world so attached to my mother that she'd cry at the sight of her, yet I hadn't seen this person before. She looked like my mother and didn't, with sharper features and a more oval face. The sight of my mother with Sophie, her older sister, made me see my mother as younger and more fragile, more like myself. But my mother was at the top of her form that summer, and so was Sophie, busy and happy directing her daughter's wedding.

My mother died of ovarian cancer the following May, when I was thirteen. Sophie, Molly, and Joe died of Huntington's (in Sophie's case, her death was complicated by lung cancer). I returned to Atlanta in 1980 and visited Sophie's bungalow. It was built to catch the breezes, with a wooden entry porch big enough for two rockers. It isn't far from the cemetery where Sophie is buried. There wasn't much for me as I stood looking at the yellow bungalow except the realization that in moving to Texas (where I'd been for two years), I'd come to

With her mother, Minnie Furman, about 1950

live in a place where such bungalows were common.

Fourteen years after my mother's death I was on a tourist bus in Kenya, and the guide announced that the scene before us—the world halved—was the Great Rift valley. Here spread before me was a vast geographical expression of my small history.

I date all my childhood memories with the before and after of her death. The apartment remained the same. No furniture shifted. We did not change outwardly. My older sister and I still quarreled. The room I shared with my younger sister was more often than not a battleground. My father still went to work in the morning and returned at night, made himself a drink, sat in the living room, waiting for dinner. But when I came home from school in my mother's place at the kitchen table was a large black woman with a shining necklace of a scar that reached from one side of her throat to the other. She didn't like us very much, and I became aware for the first time of the need to be liked in order to get taken care of, not to be loved but simply to be fed and clothed. No act of kindness or love, given or received, was automatic for me ever again.

After my mother's death, I felt diffident toward the past, too polite to search my own memories, and afraid to reminisce. I didn't understand my mother's illness, her treatment, or her death. She and my father chose not to tell us that she would die, though this outcome was clear from her operation in October. My only hope while she was dying was to ignore what I saw, what I heard, what I felt. In practicing obliviousness, I was trying for a miracle. I was trying to keep her alive, and the effort continued after her death.

My life went on: from seventh grade through twelfth grade I attended Hunter College High School. My father remarried two years after my mother's death, and he and my stepmother were married for almost thirty-one years, until his death. In time, I went to college, choosing Bennington College in Vermont, taking the part of the country and beauty over the city where she had died. I tried to forget in that I didn't remember. Yet I don't believe that I've ever written a word that has not been informed by my mother's absence and my loss. In writing, I come closest to remembering her and recognizing the loss. The impulse to write, to capture and create the private moments in my characters' lives that are deeply concealed in their public time, derives from my long vigil at my mother's absence.

II

If I wanted to be anything as a teenager, I wanted to be a writer; but it is more precise to say that by being a teenaged writer I found companionship—mostly in books, but also from a few friends—and a place where I could be comfortable and where I could lose myself. Being a writer then meant writing everywhere—in class, in coffee shops, on the bus and the subway, sitting on my bed at home; and on anything—napkins, class notes, textbooks, any paper would do. Words and sentences sprang to my mind, and images of myself that I transferred automatically into narrative. Writing was a way of telling the world, making it into a story I could understand or at least consider. One friend gave me a copy of *To the Lighthouse*, for Christmas 1961, inscribed, "This is where I hid until four one morning in June, coming to school baggy-eyed and ecstatic . . ." The book was a revelation, a romp of words and characters that I rolled in happily. It wasn't until years later that I realized it was all about the death of a mother.

When I think of myself without words I think of being late to school, leaving the apartment late because I couldn't find clothes to wear, missing the crosstown bus, standing on the corner of Ninety-sixth and Lexington, trying to decide as the minutes ticked by whether to take the subway, which I hated and was always packed at that hour, or to wait for the bus; then arriving at Hunter, worrying that I would go to the wrong classroom. By the time I was in the building my worrying was such that my vision was darkening and closing in, and I could barely see my way to the right room. Or I would get to class on time, then dream my way out of it, until, called on, I'd rush back from wherever I'd been, most likely just the other side of the window.

My favorite class was Latin, and my six years of Latin at Hunter probably gave me the most important foundation for reading and writing. My excellent English teachers brought such passion to literature that I heard Keats, Chaucer, Shakespeare as voices speaking to me. But Latin, which we were taught very slowly—the first year being divided into two—gave me a firm foundation in grammar and let me discover the satisfaction of seeing how sentences are put together, the words working to make a whole that followed the rules and that I could name and understand. One of the most satisfying things I learned in Latin was the past perfect tense, which expresses an action before the past of the narrative. When I understood the past perfect, a rich world of time opened for me.

It was not Latin itself that gave me so much, for surely Latin can be taught boringly. My teacher was Irving Kizner, short, portly, with a comic nose. The classroom my first year of Latin looked east over Lexington Avenue, and during morning class the room was often flooded with so much sunshine that Mr. Kizner had to pull down the enormous shades. Even without the darkness, there was a dreamy quality to the class. He was a born teacher, and his class was one of the few occasions during the school day when I wasn't distracted by my fears. When I didn't know the answer to a question, he helped me find it. When I knew the answer, it was exciting, not for the grades I earned but for the understanding, which felt like a steady place to stand. Until then my life at school had consisted of one terrible hurdle to be jumped after another. Our Latin textbook was full of stories about *puĕllae*, using the verb *esse* in multiple ways. After the daily grammar and vocabulary quiz, after our stumbling translations of the simple

text, Mr. Kizner often told us a new chapter in his continuing tale about a GI who was lost in the middle of Italy during World War II. The soldier was a New Yorker, a native of the Bronx (Mr. Kizner lived in the Bronx and took the Lexington Avenue subway to school; I sometimes saw him on it). The soldier was separated from his unit and wandered in the Italian countryside (possibly Cumae) until he took shelter in a cave and found an old woman. She was incalculably old; she was a sibyl. Neither of them spoke modern Italian, and she no English. The only way they could converse was in Latin, which luckily the soldier had studied in high school and college. The soldier's story took on a life for me apart from the pleasure of understanding what he and the sibyl were saying in their simple Latin. The soldier was alone in a strange country, unable to speak the language; he wandered into a dark place and there found someone he could understand and who could not only understand him but also protect him by seeing the future. My whole life seemed like a

Laura (left) and her sister Emily, playing croquet, New Jersey, about 1952

Laura Furman, 1965

riddle then—past, present, and future—but I felt that the answer was there, waiting to be heard, if only I could understand its language. Maybe I would wander into a cave, perhaps one of the tunnels in Central Park, and meet a sibyl who would tell me what would become of me.

Five years later, at college, I found another teacher who opened up a world of reading and understanding: Stanley Edgar Hyman. Mr. Hyman was a critic who taught two courses at Bennington, as I recall: Language and Literature, and Myth, Ritual, and Literature. The first was the beginning literature course that he divided into the study of four forms: drama (Shakespeare's *Antony and Cleopatra*), prose (Thoreau's *Walden*), poetry (various poets), and fiction (Joyce's *Portrait of the Artist as a Young Man* and an excursion into *Ulysses*). Mr. Hyman showed, through careful understanding of the words, sentences, paragraphs, and sections of the text, that a large form echoes throughout a work, amounting to the secret reason for a work's emotional impact and integrity. My new acquaintance with the idea of form, of a formal backbone to works I loved, changed reading for me, or rather made two kinds of reading out of my former experience of immersed loss of consciousness. I still preferred being lost in a work (to this day I find it hard to stick with writing that doesn't capture me), but now there was another

possible level: I could take apart a text and find its secrets, chart its course, discover its landmarks, and retell its story as my own. Of the books that I have loved and taught (an activity that forces understanding beyond the first romantic liking of a text), the ones that stand up to close scrutiny are also the ones that surprise me time and again. A really good book always keeps some of its secrets, and shows them only on the next reading, perhaps when the reader brings something new to the text. I think of William Maxwell's *So Long, See You Tomorrow* in this way, and I don't worry any longer that I will wear it out or use it up by repeated reading or teaching.

At Bennington I received my only formal training in writing fiction. I took one semester with Saul Maloff, a critic and novelist, and one with Bernard Malamud. In Mr. Maloff's class I mostly enjoyed approval. In fact, I basked in it. Mr. Malamud's class I took two years later, after a year away from Bennington. He required that we submit work to him before we were allowed to take the course, so I assume that the other students felt as I did when admitted—confirmed in some way and also frightened. I had submitted the little work I'd been able to do while working full-time at Harper and Row (as it was called in 1964) and living on East Eleventh Street between Avenue B and Avenue C with my boyfriend, also a college dropout. I'd set up a desk in one of our two rooms that I didn't use very often, not for lack of time but for lack of knowing how to go about writing.

I wish I could repeat lessons Mr. Malamud taught about fiction but I remember very few of his exact words in the classroom. What I do remember is the sense he gave that every word had to be chosen carefully, not just to make a pleasing sound or even to communicate information or a subject, but because the choice had a moral dimension. He brought to writing and to literature a strict and serious devotion that was almost religious in intensity. He once told me that to become a writer, you sacrifice your twenties—and then he went on with a sad litany of what happened to the other decades. He himself had undertaken to become a writer as a mission, not as a career or an opportunity for a certain kind of life. When he was my teacher he was already acclaimed. He had a keen interest in his work being counted among the best of his time. He praised freely writers he admired (such as Flannery O'Connor). Mr. Malamud set a standard that was very high and that, he let us know, was the one thing worth aiming for as a writer.

In class I kept track of who was getting more praise, who was better, who might get published, who was a real writer. I don't know if other students did the same, but it soured me on writing classes. Malamud's class was the last I was in as a student, and for years it influenced the way I taught. My first desire as a teacher of writing was to protect the feelings of my students (which I imagined to be identical with my own as a student), and to create a noncompetitive, helpful atmosphere in the classroom. At Bennington, senior literature majors wrote a senior thesis, an extended term paper, really. I wanted to write a creative thesis but was judged not to have enough feeling for fiction. Instead I wrote on the idea of friendship in F. Scott Fitzgerald and Ford Madox Ford. Students for a Democratic Society was just coming into the news, along with the Vietnam War, and my tutor upbraided me at every session: "Look what your friends are doing!"

At Bennington, I gained two lifelong friends, and I learned a trade. This I did by dropping out of school for a year and working in the college text department of Harper and Row. Once I returned to Bennington, I worked during each nonresident term and during the summer vacation at a publishing house, improving my skills in book production and copyediting. It was as a copyeditor that I made my living from 1968 when I graduated until 1974, when I had my first full-time teaching job.

When I graduated from Bennington, I wanted to be a writer but had no idea how to go about it. I knew that I had to earn a living, and there was a job waiting for me at Grove Press in Manhattan. I went down to the city, found an apartment, and began to work. My apartment was on Bleecker and MacDougal. I think I was the only non-Italian in the building. Before I moved in— I'd left a few suitcases in the apartment—I was robbed of most of my jewelry. This period of living in New York and working first for Grove and then as a free-lance copyeditor for other houses was fruitful for the stories I later wrote (such as "Watch Time Fly") but essentially miserable. I had broken up with my college boyfriend and was seeing first a medical student and then a graduate student in anthropology at Princeton. Each I assumed I would marry; neither lasted very long. Days I worked and intended to write at night but I rarely did. At Grove Press I had a good example of a working writer in Gilbert Sorrentino, who was an editor there. Gil woke up early and wrote for several hours before coming to work. He was an example, like Malamud, of a fiercely dedicated writer.

Every few months my aunt Molly came down from the Bronx and we went out to lunch near Grove Press. She talked about my mother's death as if it had happened yesterday, but it seemed to me to be so long ago that I had forgotten it entirely, and forgotten the rest of my family as well. I wasn't engaged by my family story but by the future in which I would be living in the country, married, writing, and in a quiet and peaceful state that had nothing to do with living and working in New York. If anyone had asked me if I were waiting for marriage, country life, writing, I would have denied it hotly. The times were so noisy from 1968 to 1973 that the life I wanted—an echo of my happiest time as a child— seemed not only outmoded but inaccessible, as if the world in which one might be happy had come to an end. The noise came from the Vietnam War, and the antiwar movement, then from the women's movement, and from the more amorphous movement of many people my age to find new ways of living together. Social and political forces combined to such an extent that even those I knew who were primarily concerned with their own ambition and psychotherapy felt that their self-improvement was a political act. Everything was up for grabs. Everything could be reinvented. I imagined myself then as knowing and conscious, but I was blissfully unaware of much that would come back to haunt me and my friends: madness, drugs, jail terms, and for some a final disappearance into the underground political world. I wanted out but I didn't know where to go.

A break in the noise came on some weekends and in the summer when I and other friends went to upstate New York, just over the border from Vermont. I tried to write and to extend my ability to concentrate by following some advice from Susie Crile, a painter and friend from Bennington days, whose farmhouse slowly became the center of my life for years to come. She suggested that I sit at the typewriter for five minutes until that amount of time became bearable—not necessarily to write, just to sit—and extend that in small increments until I could stay there and work. The result of the exercise was that I grew used to being restless and nervous, and continued to work despite myself.

Susie's house is a turn-of-the-century farmhouse, not remarkable for itself—white asbestos siding, blue trim, big porch on two sides—but for its setting at the top of a hill overlooking other, smaller, rounded hills. Her land is mostly fields (half of them untillable for being wet or steep) that stretch to a wood. Especially in Susie's farmhouse and in a rambling stone mill that another friend had turned into a pottery factory/commune, I found a different life, still turbulent but quieter. I felt protected by the landscape, the isolation, even by the calm architecture of the Federalist and Greek Revival houses.

I quit my job at Grove Press because I didn't like working in an office, and began working as a free-lance copyeditor on *Sisterhood Is Powerful,* an anthology of the nascent women's movement, edited by Robin Morgan for Random House. I moved back to the Upper West Side and was lucky enough to find work from other houses. The manuscripts I copyedited were varied: Hemingway's *Islands in the Stream, The Greening of America,* mysteries, and novels. Copyediting was an important part of my education as a writer; in fact it was a superior kind of reading in which I had to be able to recall a quirky spelling from hundreds of pages back and to organize a manuscript into the particular style of the house. Through one of the smaller houses I worked for I was given an introduction to Dominique de Menil, the art patron and collector who lived in Houston and New York. Mrs. de Menil needed a copyeditor for a large catalogue she was doing for a show of Greek and Roman art from Texas collections. When all the material for the catalogue was ready I went upstate for the summer. Susie's farmhouse had been badly damaged over the winter by burst pipes, and so Susie and I rented space above a drugstore in a nearby town. She set up a rudimentary painting studio and I made a big table area for all the entries which I then laboriously organized and styled into a manuscript. The catalogue entries were dry and technical, and I kept my radio tuned to the Watergate hearings, which were also dry and technical but with secrets and passions running underneath. The dull serenity of the catalogue's language was a reproach to my life in New York, which had begun to feel impossible.

At the end of the summer, the manuscript was sent off to the printer, and I was asked to go to Hamburg when the proofs were ready. It was my first trip to Europe. Once I'd completed my work in Germany, I took advantage of the open air-ticket and went to visit friends in Sweden. He was an American doctor who had left the army (a VA hospital in Staten Island). His wife was a friend from summer camp. They were living just outside Stockholm in a neighborhood called Solna, in a

district called Hagalund whose gingerbread cottages were being torn down to make way for giant apartment blocks. My friends and other Americans I met were involved with the deserter/resister community in Sweden.

Hagalund was anything but noisy. It was a grinding halt, in fact. I stayed on for no apparent reason but passivity and an inability to decide to leave, which included not knowing what I would do if I left. I tried to write a story about my friend who made lists and transferred to each day's list that which was unaccomplished the day before, but I didn't get much past a stark beginning. My paralysis was broken by a letter from Dominique de Menil asking me if I would care to begin work on a project called "The Iconography of the Black in Western Art." This supposedly temporary free-lance job would be my support for more than five years.

My winter in Sweden was the basis of my first novel (unpublished) "Talking about the Weather," a short story called "A Long Conversation," and now a long story "Hagalund," completed in the summer of 1992. After twenty years of trying to write it, I am finally content with the story.

III

I returned to New York knowing that I had to start writing in earnest, and indeed within a year I had completed enough of a short novel to apply for and be accepted for a stay of several months at Yaddo in Saratoga Springs. What the summer at Yaddo showed me, aside from how long a day can be when all one does in it is write, was that I had finally begun to work. No one at Yaddo—other than I—questioned my right to be there, though I had never been published and had written little. I was treated with respect and friendliness. I met others who were further along the road and had been battered by the journey. I thought that I would never feel bitter or neglected, nor would I ever share in shoptalk as if we were all plumbers or accountants. I assumed, as the young assume of aging, that these things happened to other people.

Most importantly, Yaddo gave me a model for a quiet life of concentration and work, a life stripped down to essentials. That it was a model with built-in distortions didn't take away from its lesson. I returned to the city, to my harum-scarum social life and to my friends who were at loose ends or worse. New York was by then a source of constant irritation. I never took the subway, only the bus or my car, and this meant that it took forever to get anywhere in the day and that I had to be home before eleven o'clock when the garage closed or risk walking on the street alone at night, which terrified me. I distrusted the water and the air. I took the city personally. The moments that were happiest to me were on the West Side Highway heading north for the country, and when I passed over the bridge into Bronxville I felt as relieved as if I'd escaped wolves snapping at my VW's tires.

In December 1972 I returned to Yaddo for another, longer visit. There were very few guests, and the mansion was closed so most of us were in West House. I preferred Yaddo with fewer people and with the lawns and woods covered by snow. The beauty of the landscaping was starker and easier to see, and the place just seemed more peaceful to me than in the summer and still does. There was a little of the feeling of being at an orphanage over the holidays, but it was for the most part a congenial group. I met Robert Towers during that visit, the critic and novelist who with his family became part of my life in upstate New York. One fond memory I have is of New Year's Eve when we all sat around on the rather uncomfortable chairs in the library above the Garage and passed the time by telling stories. The best storyteller was Curt Harnack (then director of Yaddo), who told of a friend's drowning that he'd always suspected was a murder. I learned more about the difficulties of being a writer when I saw the near-homelessness of one old poet who wandered from colony to colony, nearly destitute. I felt my own loneliness at my self-imposed exile from New York. But my writing each day made up for it, or almost did, and in any case there was a balance that I had to make or else the rootlessness of a Hagalund life might repeat itself on a permanent basis.

In February 1973 I moved to Susie Crile's farmhouse. Taking all the good of my time at Yaddo and putting all the bad of my recent life on the city, I decided to see if I could live alone and write in the country. My friends said I was brave, but I felt as if I had no choice.

I tried to maintain the Yaddo quiet and the Yaddo schedule. I soon discovered that if I didn't have a measurable goal for the day's work, the day and the work stretched interminably. Also that even the small but regular sociability of Yaddo had so cut my loneliness and my anxiety that I could work ten times better there than alone in the farmhouse. But Yaddo wasn't a possibility for a real life and this was. I persevered and made rules for myself: I wasn't allowed to leave the house until I had done X amount of work; I wasn't allowed to go to town for the paper until I had done X amount of work; I wasn't allowed even to telephone anyone until I had at least started to work. Then and now, getting down to work is a maddening combination of hacking away at a jungle of annoying tasks and volunteering to do any small and petty job to avoid work. I read once that John McPhee ties himself to his chair with an old bathrobe belt and it seems like a sensible idea. Once there in your chair, why fool around?

Alone in the farmhouse on top of the hill, I did a lot of writing, and I began to make country friends. A painter, Constance Kheel, whom I'd gone to Bennington with lived nearby with her husband and baby; a potter from the mill had bought a farmhouse on the next road where she lived with her husband and daughter. Nearer to Greenwich (the next town) lived two artists, Gerald Coble and Robert Nunnelley, whose house I wrote about in a short story "Listening to Married Friends." When my first story was published and Gerald said it was as good as anything, I felt that I had the best praise I could want. He is a rare person who brings to all his tasks—gardening, cooking, working on his house—the patience, concentration, and integrity necessary to make art. When spring came along I was still in the country and still involved in the test that living there meant to me: could I survive on my own, could I survive and write in the quiet? I had the world polarized to that small part of New York State or New York City. I couldn't see beyond those two possibilities. I had embarked on another novel, one that was never published, that I called "Terrible Algebra," from a letter of Henry James's in which he wrote that when one is tempted to criticize the terrible algebra of another's life, one should consider the awful geometry of one's own, which now reads clearly as a plea for tolerance. Then it seemed to be a statement of the equal messiness of all the lives in my novel.

My potter/neighbor mentioned that there was a little house down the road for sale. I had been exploring the possibility of fixing up an eighteenth-century house in a nearby village. The white clapboard house I eventually bought was hidden from the road at the end of a dirt lane. It was in the brow of a hill, down the back of Susie's hill, and the small piece of land (about nine acres) ended in the woods that joined Susie's. There was

Interior, Fly Summit, 1976

a shed that the owner called a pig shed, a small barn, and a large hay barn with room below for cows or (as it turned out) for ewes and lambs. The owner was a musician whose wife had left him. The house was a mess. He'd decorated the living room with a poster of Jimi Hendrix with bicycle chains crossed over it. When he showed me where he and his wife had had their vegetable garden, he said, "It's a dream gone by," and I felt the same ten years later when I sold the place.

There was a lilac hedge along the drive, hydrangea next to the little barn, a red lilac bush in the corral, and a view down the descending hills all the way to the Berkshires—or so I thought. The small piece of land was triangular, with a neglected apple orchard, a swampy front field, and a sloping hay field behind. My address was Fly Summit Road. With no savings in the bank, no job guarantee, and no reason to be there, I bought the house. (Before approving the mortgage, the local bank asked for a letter explaining why a young unmarried woman would want to bury herself in the country.)

The first summer I continued to live at Susie's while I and others worked on the house. By the fall I was living in my own house, getting ready for another winter. I had carved out a bedroom, living room, kitchen, and bathroom. By the time I left Fly Summit there was another room and the upstairs was waiting for walls. The responsibility of owning the place, the beauty of the setting, and the severity of my situation made me at times ecstatically happy and at other times despairing. I was lonely all the time. But I also became more able to rely on myself. It didn't occur to me until years later that I was trying to recreate our house in New Jersey where I had been happy as a child, and that I was trying to recreate my mother's presence by involving myself in the activities she loved: fixing up an old house, gardening, cooking. What was missing was a family. What I had was my writing which I made into the only cornerstone I had.

Wendy Weil became my agent the summer I bought Fly Summit and she remains my agent and friend. I finished "Terrible Algebra" at Fly Summit and survived its being rejected for several years until Wendy and I finally gave up. I had begun writing short stories on Wendy's advice, and five years after I began to write seriously the *New Yorker* bought "Last Winter." When my job with Mrs. de Menil ended, I was thirty years old, living alone in an old and unfinished farmhouse with two cats, a mortgage, and no steady means of support. I might have sold the place and moved back to New York, gotten an editing job, anything other than staying put, but staying put and surviving had come to be synonymous to me. For the next few years I lived month-to-month on a small grant from New York State, a one-term teaching job in Wilkes-Barre, Pennsylvania, research work for a friend's father, and, occasionally—the best of times—selling stories.

My editor at the *New Yorker* was Fran Kiernan, who had attended Hunter briefly. I had read the magazine since I was a child, and my idea of a *New Yorker* editor was a glimpse I once had of Rachel MacKenzie—white hair, fragile, white gloves. Fran, it turned out, was only a year older than I— pretty, blonde, funny, and sharp. Working with her for the next twelve years until she left the *New Yorker* was the education that I see students wanting from graduate school. She was (and still is) in many ways my ideal reader, able to understand my intentions and inferences. She asked the right questions that helped me open up a story. Fran and William Shawn were the best readers I've ever known, the most sympathetic, sensitive, intelligent, and tireless. Fran is my model as an editor in my relations with the writers whom I publish in *American Short Fiction,* the quarterly I founded in 1990.

Summers at Fly Summit went by too quickly, as summers do in the East. During the winters, I read and wrote, jogged or walked or tried to ski in the hay field, chopped wood, cooked, saw friends, hoped for visitors, and waited for spring. I read and re-read Anthony Powell's *A Dance to the Music of Time.* I'm not sure why. It was not the specific English subject matter of his masterpiece that fascinated me, but his accomplishment in expressing change as it takes place over time—change of personality, change of scene, and also the unchanging nature of character. The relaxed skill of Powell as narrator allowed me as a reader and as an apprentice writer to connect to his work. When I think of peaceful winter times at Fly Summit, I think of afternoons when my own writing was finished for the day, and I read on the extra-long orange velvet couch that friends had given me, twelve feet from my busy woodstove. I have never recovered from the nervous anticipation I devel-

oped during those years about the mail. My mailbox was a half-mile away, at a neighbor's farm, and I had to decide each day whether to walk, jog, or drive to it, guessing if the mail truck had been there yet or not. I had the feeling that anything could come in the mail, and that something might change my life.

By 1978, I was ready to leave Fly Summit. I did not think of it this way. I thought that I simply had to find a more stable way to make a living. I was spending so much time worrying about money that what I was supposedly gaining by living in the country—peace and quiet and a lack of distraction—was destroyed. I interviewed for jobs at two universities and, by chance, also talked to a friend in Houston who was starting a magazine and who needed a copyeditor. Though I felt then as if I were being expelled from the only appropriate life and place for me as a writer, I view leaving that beautiful place as one of the first wise moves I've ever made, also my choice of a magazine job in Houston, Texas, rather than either of the jobs I

*The author at the Paisano Ranch,
near Austin, Texas, 1981*

was offered in small university towns. In October 1978 I drove from upstate New York to Houston in my blue Pinto station wagon that was loaded with everything I could cram into it, and settled into an apartment in a neighborhood across from the eventual site of the Menil Collection. The people I worked with at *Houston City Magazine* were young and bright. There was an improvisational air to the magazine. I found myself with energy for more work, more friendships, more activity than I'd seen in years. I woke early in the morning and wrote for two hours until it was time to dress for work. At night I went to concerts, attended the opera for the first time in my life, and had dinner with friends. My first book was accepted for publication by Viking Press that fall, and the publication felt like a full-circle achievement to me. I had begun the title novella *The Glass House* as a short story called "Four Way Stop" after an extended period of work in Houston for Mrs. de Menil, and I had finished it my last year at Fly Summit.

At first I viewed my time in Houston as temporary. I planned to return to Fly Summit as soon as I could. But I was offered a teaching job the following year at the University of Houston and I stayed on after a summer visit East. My staying on has continued for fifteen years.

My discovery of Texas happened over time, as did my slow but lasting love for it. It never occurred to me that I would stay in Texas, partly because I had come from a beautiful landscape and Houston, for all its virtues, doesn't offer much in

"My house in Texas," 1986

the way of physical beauty. But it offered people I liked who seemed delighted that I was here, and then it offered interiors with a beauty I hadn't seen before. Sooner or later, my eye began to adjust and instead of looking for the sights I was used to, I was able to enjoy the quirkiness and individuality of the new place. I have changed too much to be comfortable living in the East again. Sometime when I wasn't noticing, my sense of proportion altered. The sky in the East looks too small, the horizon too crowded.

I saw pieces of Texas during my first three years—Galveston, Port Aransas, Lake Whitney, Dallas, Austin—but it has taken me years to understand and really be able to distinguish the different zones and landscapes. My first Christmas in Texas, my younger sister joined me and we drove to a friend's house on Lake Whitney. We cooked out Christmas Eve over a wood fire and congratulated ourselves on being warm for a change at that season. When we woke up the world was covered by two inches of ice, there was no power for miles around, and I had to chip at the lock to open the Pinto. I took this bewildering experience as an aberration rather than as a Texas rule. Changed as I am, I still wait for northern weather that stays the same for months at a time. Here in Texas I can't date memories by remembering the weather and knowing it is spring or winter. I have never gotten used to the fact that cold doesn't last here but warmth does.

I met my husband, Joel Warren Barna, in January 1979 when he started as a writer for *Houston City Magazine.* We married two years later during a snowstorm in Westchester County at our friends Michael and Elinore Standard, and a few weeks later I took off for the Paisano Ranch, near Austin, while Joel stayed in Galveston to edit the magazine of which he was then part owner. For the six months I had the Dobie Paisano Fellowship, I lived alone (with our dog Blanche) at the 240-acre ranch outside of Austin, and Joel and I were together on weekends, either at the ranch or in Galveston. My father visited me at the ranch, a visit I remember fondly, and other friends from New York and California. But mostly I was alone and I had a chance to work and to explore Barton Creek and the land. I wrote most of my second book, *The Shadow Line,* on the ranch, and I set my fourth novel there, "The Stars at Night." I came to love the ranch and to see it as the heart of Texas, though Texans from other regions might disagree. It was a hardscrabble place, never grand or prosperous, and being there was an initiation into feeling at home in Texas.

After the ranch, my husband and I moved to Dallas briefly, then to Austin, where we lived in a hand-built stone house on a cliff on the outskirts of the city while I worked on *Tuxedo Park* and enjoyed a Guggenheim Fellowship. In 1983 we moved to the small town south of Austin where we still live in an old house that little by little we have made comfortable. I sold the house in Fly Summit a few years after we moved.

In 1983, I began teaching at the University of Texas at Austin. I never expected to become a teacher, though it is a logical and often convenient job for a writer. When I graduated from Bennington I had a feeling of triumph that at last I had escaped and that I would never again have to enter a classroom. Given such a feeling, my first few years as a teacher were predictably rough. I doubted that what I was doing was either honest or honorable. I didn't know what I could teach to the undergraduates who were sure that they were writers or to those who were looking for an easy *A.* Although each year I found one or two students whom I liked teaching, it wasn't until I had the kind of good graduate students that I have now at the University of Texas that I realized what I have to offer. I have my skills as an editor, my experience as a writer, and whatever patience and wisdom I possess. If I am able to do anything as a teacher, it is to convince students that writing is its own reward, and always will be. If I can interest the students in the process of writing and help them to understand how to work past a promising (or even unpromising) first draft to a story's final form, then I've done what I can do. After almost ten years of teaching, I sometimes even enjoy myself. I have started to teach literature, and I've had to work hard to learn this new skill. Partly through teaching a graduate course in nonfiction by fiction writers, I've begun to write a memoir about my adolescence, a shift that surprises and interests me.

In 1989 my husband and I adopted a baby, and since then my life has been changed more than by any other event, with the exception of my mother's death. The happiness I had before was incomplete, and I still thought that my work as a writer was the most important thing I would do in my life. Now my work as a writer, though crucial to me, can take its place in a more balanced life. Often when I'm with my husband and son, I remember Fly Summit and I see that they were what I was missing in my idyllic setting and my life

Laura Furman's husband, Joel Warren Barna, and their son, Solomon, Austin, Texas, 1990

devoted solely to writing. With more external demands on my time and energy than there have ever been before, I am working on the sequel to *Tuxedo Park.* In an interview, Anthony Powell said that when, after the war, he had to decide what fiction to start writing, he chose a series of novels with the same characters because all writers use the same characters over and over, giving them different names and locations, so why not use the same ones?

I always wish the day were longer but I no longer feel that I must work quickly before disaster overtakes me, as I did when I was younger. The balance between a full life of family and a job on the one hand and my writing on the other often seems impossible to achieve. At the best of times I forget to try to balance and I find myself midway across the tightrope, not looking down.

Copyright © Laura Furman, 1990

BIBLIOGRAPHY

Fiction:

The Glass House: A Novella and Stories, Viking, 1980.

The Shadow Line (novel), Viking, 1982.

Watch Time Fly: Stories, Viking, 1983.

Tuxedo Park (novel), Summit Books, 1986.

Contributor:

Sisterhood Is Powerful, edited by Robin Morgan, Random House, 1970.

Her Work: Stories by Texas Women, edited by Lou Halsell Rodenberger, Shearer (Bryan, Texas), 1982.

Fiction 100, 4th edition, edited by James H. Pickering, Macmillan, 1985.

Prize Stories of the Texas Institute of Letters, edited by Marshall Terry, Still Point (Dallas, Texas), 1986.

Mirrors: An Introduction to Literature, edited by John R. Knott, Jr., and Christopher R. Reaske, Harper & Row, 1988.

Also contributor of stories and essays to *Fiction, Gentlemen's Quarterly, House & Garden, Mademoiselle, The New Yorker, Redbook, Southwest Review, Texas Humanist,* and *Vanity Fair.* Founder and editor of the quarterly *American Short Fiction,* 1990. Work in progress includes "The Stars at Night" (a novel set in Texas), "The Natural Memory" (a short-story collection), "Content Farm Road" (a sequel to *Tuxedo Park*), and a memoir.

Josephine Jacobsen

1908-

What do I remember, and what is worth remembering? It is important to know the difference. Too often what persists most sharply is something small and intense, while large changes stay merely as cumbersome facts.

My father died when I was five. What do I—except for facts—remember of him? Earliest, his running down the stairs, shooting his cuffs, full of some sort of intent. Until he lay permanently in bed, I remember him always in motion—running downstairs, balanced on a ladder against the house, trimming a mass of Paul Scarlet Climbers, magically lifting me high.

Later, I knew that he had been a small, asthmatic boy. He was by nature an athlete—a rock climber on mountains, a strong swimmer; at Heidelberg, where he went to college, an expert fencer, proud, in the weird mind-set of the day, of his slashed cheek. He was gregarious and ebullient, which was just as well, since he was sent early to boarding school by his parents. Both were dead when at fifty, a widower, he married my mother, a widow with an eleven-year-old son. His family had lived by choice in Italy, and after he graduated from Heidelberg he took his medical degree in Bonn, finally coming back to family roots in Cincinnati, where he practiced. He did well, and, strong on the pleasure principal, retired at fifty, spending winters at Shepards hotel in Cairo and summer weeks in Coburg, Canada, where he met my mother, and where I was accidentally born, precipitating myself into what had been supposed to be a peaceful preparturition holiday. I weighed an unpromising two and a half pounds, in a time when survival of such miniatures was rare. I remember the humiliating information that I was put in an incubator and fed with a medicine dropper. My mother was told that I wouldn't make it, but never one to be dictated to in any manner whatsoever, she and the black woman who was a second mother to my childhood and the beloved friend of my life somehow forced me to face up to what has been a very long journey indeed.

In his forties, my father had strained his heart at Viareggio, having swum so far out that he barely

Josephine Jacobsen, 1987

made it to shore. That first heart attack did nothing to slow him down. The second and ultimately fatal one came when he impatiently seized the handle of a heavy lawn roller from the more sensible twice-a-week gardener Tony and rushed it up a steep bank. This time the stroke left him paralyzed and he lay in an immense carved bed to which I was brought for visits. His mind was clear until his death two years later. His immense vitality must have made those years intensely bitter. His energy was strong and his interests were varied. He was a good amateur Egyptologist; I still have a scarab which was given him as a young man by de Lesseps, a friend of his father's. He loved travel, poetry, the opera, dancing, gardening. He had a gift for happiness.

"The wedding of my parents," Raleigh, North Carolina, 1907

My mother's temperament couldn't have been more different, though she too was capable of great gaiety when the swing was up. But she was mercurial, strong in likes and dislikes, impatient, impetuous, unreasonable, loyal, and scornful. She had a fine mind, which in the mode of the day was never trained, except by herself. She went to the classic finishing school, married very young, lost her husband when her son was five, and remained a widow, by no means of necessity, for seven years.

She read enormously and experimentally, one book leading to another: fiction, biography, philosophy. She worshipped Emerson so that, with a daughter's perversity, I never read him until I was forty. She was an extremely beautiful woman and, in the flowery Southern comment of that day, was known in her native Raleigh as "the beautiful Miss Winder." In her early twenties, she became a Roman Catholic, partly for the characteristic reason that people dressed in their best for the Episcopal church to which her family had been wedded for generations. She felt that the simple people in their homely clothes were more appro-

priate to a Christian service. This, of course, was her first, not her only, impulse toward Catholicism. She always had a stormy relationship with the Church, being far ahead of changes she would have appreciated. She had two good friends among the Catholic clergy, who patiently struggled to persuade her of the existence of hell, a state she indignantly refused to acknowledge.

To her, reading was a necessity, not a pastime, and my own curious education or lack of it, stemmed directly from the ocean of books that surrounded the small floating island of our peripatetic home, or homes. I read early, and was read to earlier still. Mother had a somewhat reckless scorn for the concept of formal schooling, considering the long years a shocking waste of time. Her conviction that when I finally got to school—no hurry about that—I would have no problems was not shared by me. That it turned out to be true was simply one of those untrustworthy results which confound the rule.

After my father's death, we moved a great deal. My half brother—whom I thought of always as a whole, not half—went to boarding school and college as a matter of course. Mother's travels were part restlessness and part optimism, to which she was prone, as she was prone to despair. My entire childhood took place more or less en route, with occasional stops of a year here or there.

Our home on Long Island was rented after my father's death, until it was finally sold when I was twelve. Basically, we lived in New York, in an apartment on Eighty-sixth Street, but that too was frequently rented while we bivouacked in Pinehurst, North Carolina, or Sharon, Connecticut, or (in winter only) in Atlantic City at the long-lost Dennis.

I had no friends, merely good brushes with acquaintances, and I suppose I should have been lonely. But I don't remember being so. Not having had a rooted habitat, our seminomadic life seemed to me perfectly normal. I supposed most people lived this way. Mother was a constant; my black nurse, Alice, was a constant. Wherever we were, Mother seemed to have relations with a certain number of people.

Especially, I loved our months at the Dennis. There were wonderful movies on the boardwalk, of which Alice and I were a carefully vetted audience. And wonderful things happened. I saw Pola Negri and Gloria Swanson, the Talmadge sisters. I saw Conrad Nagel, in a pit of crocodiles, and John Gilbert, expressly spilling soup on Mae Murray's dress on a snowy evening. And there was an even more wonderful live world at the Apollo Theater, where with my mother I saw Jane Cowl, Holbrook Blinn, Ethel Barrymore, Fred Stone. My very earliest theatrical experiences were Pavlova, a blown ghost, and Maud Adams, soaring (well, more or less) as Peter Pan.

There are two questions which I suppose all poets are most often asked: When and why did you begin to write? It is more difficult than it sounds, though I think the answer to the latter is almost always the same. It is the curious tension between something which must be said, and the inability to say it. It is as though some strange object has been discovered, and there is no word for it. It must be named, and no known word applies. Only much later does its confounded discoverer find that the anonymous newness lies, not in the word, but in its use; that there is no "poetic vocabulary" in the admonition to "tell the truth, but tell it slant." This occurs not like a clap of thunder, but in a usually painful and forever uncompleted struggle with the customary and

inaccurate, a struggle always to some degree lost or uncompleted.

That is still a long, long way ahead. At first some unrecognizably distorted speech will emerge, usually forced into rudimentary rhyme, propped up by an arbitrary form.

This weird compulsion hit me when I was eight or nine. I have no more idea of first words chosen and discarded, chosen and naively accepted, than of the day's weather. But I can pin down, very clearly indeed, the exact moments in which I lost, once and for all, my poetic innocence, and, terrified and vainglorious, looked on what I had done. I tried to describe that initiation in another essay.

> My initiation into one of the great processes came, in a matter of minutes, when I was ten, when I had that loss of innocence which can never be repeated. I saw a poem of mine published. Printed. In a magazine. For sale. Being bought by readers.
>
> This event took place on Lexington Avenue and 86th Street, at a kiosk. *St. Nicholas* was then the solitary magazine for children which did not bleat at them, or condescend, and I worshipped it. I had sent off a poem . . . [with] next to no hope, but a clawing excite-

Josephine Jacobsen, age five, with her mother Octavia Boylan

ment. Then I got a *letter* from the magazine, congratulating me, and naming the unbelievable issue. I knew the day, if not the minute, when *St. Nicholas* arrived at the kiosk; but I had not been allowed on a New York Street alone, and I needed to go by myself. After endless arguments, pleadings, pleadings, I could go—though, releasing me, the doorman was dubious.

There it was. I paid for the experience which comes only once and held the shiny cover in my hands. It was there. So immense was the shock, so penetrating to my innocence, that I can no longer remember the title, *or the subject matter*, though I can recall the dismal nature of both in the case of two subsequent poems published before I reached the disqualifying age of twelve.

I stood on the sidewalk, obstructive, stunned, looking at my words, naked, displayed to the world, and happily, I did not know that this deflowering would be a climax never reached again. For I was purely satisfied. . . . I believed, on the sidewalk of Lexington and 86th, that I had reached it, beyond all failure; and not even when a silver and then a gold badge fell upon me without recreating that initial ecstasy did I understand the truth.

The insidious quality of that moment has remained in my mind. The poem itself appeared to me differently: enhanced, anointed. The tiny creative act, dubious as it was, was buried in the satisfaction of an even more dubious proof. I did not know Emily Dickinson's frog, the Somebody who told his name all day to an admiring bog; but the kiosk rises before me regularly, as I watch the slide down the slippery slope from poetry, to publication, to prestige, to publicity, to . . .[1]

Fiction made a later and less defined attack. Stories were all around me—I lived in a welter of small events, which I knew, without understanding that I knew, had roots that ran in unexpected directions. I am sure that my early, and continuing, passion for the theater, for the drama of actions and its internal and external development, so affected my sense that in both poetry and fiction, a radical change, some vital shift in perception was, always, taking place within the creative act. But at that stage the reverse was true: it

seemed to me that it was the triumph of the printed product that ensured my identity as creator.

And a hardy annual question: Which were your early poetic influences? In my own case, they lack all coherence. I blundered about between Robert Service, Swinburne, Kipling, and Keats. I suppose there was a deep satisfaction in the actual pulse of poetry, its beat, its advance and deflected return.

I can—but happily don't—recite verse after verse of Sam McGee's chill; of the miner (dog-dirty and loaded for bear) who recognized at Dangerous Dan McGrew's the watching Lady—who's known as Lou. By the time I had graduated to the more complex "the young recruits are shaking, and they'll want their beer today / after hanging Danny Deaver in the morning," I had already returned again and again to the elfin grotto where the beautiful and merciless lady wept and sighed full sore . . . I had small discrimination, but immense appetite.

Having had a taste of communicating my private discoveries to people I had never met and would never see, I was stymied. Before twelve, I was subjected to my first experience of this marvel of communication; and happily it never occurred to me subsequently to send out my weary and malformed discoveries to any adult publication.

Though wherever we were there were always books, life was too chaotic, and on the whole too engaging, for me to have the least sense of direction. If I had been asked the adult's favorite and inane question "What do you want to be when you grow up?," as simply as a small boy's "I want to be a fireman" I would have responded, "I want to be an actress." It seemed to me that both poetry and fiction fell within my possibility.

We were in Atlantic City—as ever at the Dennis—when America entered the First World War, and my memories of that time are totally tangled in the confusion of emotional highs; straight out of school my brother volunteered for the navy and was shipped overseas. Desperately patriotic, I knitted first, with a sort of coarse white string, lumpy and asymmetrical washcloths with which unknown doughboys would scrub their shining faces; then, when the thin steel needles proved a misery, endless yards of khaki mufflers with which they could protect their throats from inclement weather.

With fervor and misery, I sacrificed a third of my daily allowance to insert a dime in the slot of the cards for Liberty Bonds which a series of pretty

---

[1]Josephine Jacobsen, "Lion under Maples," in *The Confidence Woman: 26 Women Writers at Work*, edited by Eve Shelnutt (Marietta, Georgia: Longstreet Press), pp. 64–65.

girls, perched high on a stranded tank on the boardwalk, sold to the strains of "Over There."

My mother, who for years had a file of suitors in whom she took a sort of mild and purposeless interest, had as a friend a German who had left his home to become an American. He hated the Prussians and had applied to, and been rejected by, the U.S. Army. But his fate was similar to those of the stoned dachshunds and the blackballed Fritz Kreisler. He lost his job and was the recipient of several white feathers. Then my mother received a cable telling her that my brother was a "serious" pneumonia case in a Brest hospital. He recovered, and the German American disappeared. But a shell had been broken in my protective armor, and I dimly understood the ominous contradictions of emotions. A dozen years later, I wrote a line which I still stand by ". . . the tissue paper between the foot and the plunge . . ."

At the age of three, I had been entered in a very special boarding school for my sixteenth year, and, by the time I was thirteen, Mother began to feel that perhaps I should put down some geographical roots. My only extant relatives, beyond my mother and brother, were an aged aunt still in the South and a niece of my father, the widow of a Portuguese exiled nobleman, living in Italy with two sons. The vague image of this branch of the family constituted my sole connection with glamour. We had, however, family roots in Baltimore, and when I was fourteen, we moved there. As a sort of initiation rite to normal living, I was enrolled in Roland Park Country School.

It should have been a disaster. I had never had contact with anyone my own age, except for the briefest glimpses; technically, I was uneducated, never having studied anything, and had the smallest athletic experience, since Mother had a conviction that a gym and all its works were unnecessary, if not dangerous. Four months before our arrival in Baltimore, she engaged a patient gentleman—I can still see his earnest gold-rimmed glasses—to tutor me in the absolutely virgin territory of arithmetic. This, it turned out, was my meat. We advanced by plunges. Some true relationship to the controlled leaps of poetry, its supremely satisfying sensations, made those four months magic. I felt an unidentified craving for the justice of form satisfied, and in school arithmetic—and then, far more satisfying, algebra—remained my favorite subjects. In English, I had a certain experience of déjà vu but in mathematics I was happily shepherded through nonsubjective processes.

From the first moment, and embarrassingly in contrast to the history of creative souls, I loved school. It was a perfect cornucopia. Though I hadn't honestly been conscious of any basic loneliness, I swam happily in a tide of adolescent instant friendships. I skipped a class, thus multiplying the number of people to whom I was exposed. I acted in the plays. I toiled proudly as assistant editor of *Quid Nunc*. The most dismal event imaginable was a day when I had to miss school. This is mortifying to report, but I have grown so accustomed to the unsuitability of my background as a writer that I have become callous in this regard.

When, a few years later, I first began to publish, I was completely dashed by the biographical notes of other writers. They all seemed to belong to one of two classes, those of complicated and impressive provenance, or those—infinitely more enviable—who could list a seductive variety of identities: sandhog, itinerant laborer, sailor third-class, circus roustabout, gandy dancer, painter in Paris. What, in heaven's name, had I to offer?

Josephine as a senior at Roland Park Country School, Baltimore, Maryland, 1926

After my shameful joy in school, I could at least console myself that my solitary years and the long-awaited boarding school were a mild disaster. I hated the august and dated regimentation and restrictions of the latter: letters to be laid, unsealed, on the principal's desk; total silence in all halls; no speech with any male (including the postman, or relatives of other boarders). Whether as a result is not clear to me, but I managed to come down first with whooping cough and then influenza and retreated happily to my day school, from which I reluctantly graduated before my eighteenth birthday. I was still going to be an actress, but this was to be combined with a distinguished career in poetry. College simply never arose, or rather it arose early on and was dismissed. As a matter of course, my brother would go to college; as a matter of course, Mother assumed that I would not.

It was while we were living in a New York apartment that I possessed and lost two things valuable to me—a thoroughbred Russian wolfhound and, in a brief summer interlude, a Shetland pony. The former was suddenly given me by the wealthy and benevolent father of one of my brother's friends, who raised this photogenic and, to me, exotic breed on his estate in New Jersey. I was shown a photograph of an adult Borzoi, gorgeous and alert, apparently about to give chase to his natural enemy. Devastated by pleasure, I received a small and shivering replica, complete with formal pedigree. Mother, always stronger on generous impulse than foresight, had never in her life possessed an unhousebroken puppy, let alone on the seventh floor of a New York apartment. For days, Alexi spent much of his time, punctuated by disastrous exits, shut in a bathroom where he shivered and made small noises. That he was in a fatal milieu was instantly obvious, but I clung to hope for close to a week before he was returned to the normalcy of New Jersey and his peers. For years I kept his regal photograph.

The Shetland pony, equally patrician, named Harvester, came to us during a summer in Coburg, complete with a small shiny black buggy pricked out in red lines and with a collapsible leather top. There was also a saddle, which Harvester disliked. He was opposed to friendship and imaginative in hostility. I humbly adored him and rapidly learned to throw my right leg over the saddle to the left, as coming home he consistently swerved in a dogged effort to jam my knee against the rock wall of the entrance. I thought him, the buggy, the saddle, and my own good fortune perfect in every way,

and when the apparently unforeseen problem of his days and ways in New York loomed in the autumn and he and his were returned to Virginia, I understood loss in a far from superficial way.

Now I have salvaged the realization that it was in many ways valuable to have sharp contact with two of existence's aspects—impermanence and loss. They seem so often to come as total shocks to older people. It is the very stuff of fiction, and certainly of poetry.

Mentally sophisticated, and often critical of surrounding assumptions, Mother would suddenly exhibit roots deep in the grounding of self. She had a subconscious bias: for young girls, college was the respectable refuge for lives which threatened to be devoid of those whom Tennessee Williams immortalized as Gentlemen Callers. This not being any particular menace in my case, Mother simply assumed that a debut, a period of travel if financially possible, and ultimate marriage was the normal progress, so that the matter of college never seriously arose. I was reasonably bright, and in mental and literary matters rather sophisticated, but it would be difficult to overestimate my naiveté in any major choices.

Regularly, every year, Mother was called out to my school by its kind and conscientious headmistress, Miss Castle, who earnestly repeated the same conclusion: this student is college material. Mother, with perfect courtesy and equal patience, fended off this proposition, courteously refraining from showing any amusement that the question should be *could* I rather than *should* I. Another notion of Miss Castle's was that I should take remedial Latin, a language of which I knew not one word, with the exception of those in the Catholic Mass. This campaign Miss Castle also lost, and of the two it is the one I decisively regret; the matter of college, as things turned out, is one about which to this day I am of two minds. There were irreplaceable things which I lost in its absence, but I am not totally sure, given my future profession, that my lopsided preparation for it was wholly unfortunate. It is a complicated up-and-down matter. I lost all early connection with the world of writers, but I think my work's total self-definition has its roots, for worse or better, in the solitude of my learning. With absolutely no connection with the world of writers, or that of academic criticism, I was forced, laboriously and with many stumbles, to mine deep, discover and discard, and, finally, to develop a sense of my own intention.

At the present date, it seems strange to the point of the unlikely that out of the seventy-two girls who made their debuts in Baltimore in 1926 exactly three went to college.

At just under eighteen, I was avid to emerge into "real life," which to my mind did not entail further classes, or strictures, or indeed any other directed period, and I accepted happily enough the prospect of my debut as a preliminary to that freedom. I thoroughly though inexplicably enjoyed an exhaustive and repetitive ten months of activity as rigid as a monastic schedule. I knew no better than to enjoy it, and much of it I enjoyed very much indeed. A very few years later, I tended to become secretive about this period, and by the time I began, tentatively but doggedly, to enter my profession, went through years in which I concealed from anyone whom I regarded as my literary betters (and obviously that included any writer I met) this brief period of my shame, much as a Victorian heroine might guard the secret of an illegitimate birth. And yet I learned a good bit from that period, including my inkling of the nature of a large city, which had been limited to the charted areas of familiarity. True, in a Red Cross uniform, I drove a miniature truck for the Junior League, filled week after week with the detritus of years (the League was moving its quarters), to the town dump, my white gloves bright on the wheel, to the hilarious comment of normal truckers bound for the same objective. But I also went into the vast ethnic variety of a major port, strange to me as a new country, where I transported very old or very ill people to Johns Hopkins Hospital. I remember walking into a third-story bedroom, empty of all furniture except for a metal bed, in which a pretty and terrified-looking black girl, fully dressed in preparation, fixed me with enormous eyes. That moment competed very well indeed with any curriculum.

At the same time I experienced the fringes of another profession which was pure pleasure, punctuated by terror. I was admitted into the company of the Vagabond Theater.

In the late twenties, the Vagabonds were arguably the best semiprofessional little theater in the country. Enchanted as I was to have any part whatsoever in its affairs, it wasn't until I visited California that I realized that the Vagabonds had a national reputation among aficionados of the theater. It was a group of talented and very varied men and women who for years had worked together. They produced half a dozen plays a

In Baltimore, 1933

season, which naturally varied in quality, but which never fell below a fairly high level. My brother, a very talented actor—who was subsequently on the professional stage—was one of their stars, and through nepotism on his part and passionate desire on mine, I graduated from a bemused member of their audience to speechless appearances as a tray-ladened maid, a neighbor, a crowd member. I had a love for the theater which was real and permanent, never limited to my own aspirations; and as I finally walked before those lights with a word or two to utter, or later stood in the wings, seasick and icy with panic as my brain blanked out any word whatsoever (miraculously restored on stage), I learned lessons personal and professional. We had a number of members who subsequently became names on what was to us the mythical shrine of Broadway—I think especially of Evelyn Varden and Mildred Natwick—and there was a level of nonpompous and serious effort which often produced impressive results.

I worked with the Vagabonds until their schedule of three weeks of nightly rehearsal (all of the men and most of the women had jobs) and two weeks of nightly performances became obviously impossible after my marriage.

I remember distinctly my personal high and low spots, the first coming when the Vagabonds celebrated their twenty-fifth anniversary by putting on, for a week each, two plays at Ford's theater, then at its glittering height, and I—admittedly because I had the single feminine part in *The Truth about Blades*—was assigned the star actress's dressing room, with an actual star on the door and filled with flowers from envious friends. The low occasion was at the end of my first year, when a sort of rough frolic was put on by the company. I was allowed into a Hawaiian number as a chorus member, but my mother refused to permit me to participate when she learned I was to wear a grass skirt, an appearance she found in equal parts ridiculous and indecent. My passionate and repeated explanation that beneath our grass exterior we would be fully clothed shattered on my mother's logic: if that were obvious it would be ridiculous

"With my (whole, not half) brother, John Skinner, in New Hampshire," 1959

and if it were effective, far worse. I was eighteen. I came as a furious member of the audience.

Shortly before this I had published, at my mother's expense, a small collection of poems which, eighteen months later, I would happily have shredded, except for one badly flawed poem about a marble satyr I had seen in Rome. I had grown up with the bronze copy of the Dancing Faun of Pompeii, which my father, as a young man in Pompeii, had had cast in bronze. It stands now on our small stone porch, a shape of pure strength and joy become intimate. Very early in the morning it grows gradually out of darkness, carrying its hundred-odd years as lightly as it carried them past sunlight before I existed, balanced as its original predecessor; and long, long after I do not see it, it will stay tilting in its dance.

Learning to distrust my book was not the only change of that time. It still seems odd to me that I should have gone, with a rather dreary date, to the home of a friend, looked at a stranger, and thought, so this is the person with whom I wish to spend the rest of my life. But that is what happened. I am far from sure that my experience was totally duplicated. We were not married until almost three years later, one of which I spent distractedly in California, wondering what I needed to write, and hopelessly apprehensive of irreparable loss.

We had a brief engagement of two or three months and were married in a friendly living room, with immediate family and three unrepentant gate-crashing friends of my new husband. My poetry, like my personal life, changed completely.

That was the year of the Great Depression. With the callousness of joy we lived through it, working over the 125-year-old house we had been able to acquire only because the owner had been forced to sell. That was the spring when Roosevelt closed the banks, and we were stranded on a business trip to New Orleans, with money enough for one berth on the way home. We slept in it, scared of rolling into the aisle in our sleep, waking massively hungry, to be tormented by the smells of chocolate and oranges being consumed by more far-sighted passengers. The basic protections made the trip interesting rather than distressing, and like a later experience in Barcelona, it belonged to the not unpleasurable *frisson* of a brush with escapable danger as opposed to the yawning gulf below the truly vulnerable.

In Barcelona, a check, carefully planned to arrive just before our departure from Spain, had come to our Barcelona hotel before us and was promptly buried somewhere in the disorder of papers. We got it back months later from the embarrassed hotelier. Close to the end of our money, we waited day by apprehensive day. We stopped our happy practice of going out for meals, eating cautiously where our meals could go on our swelling hotel bill. We bought no gasoline for our little Beetle, stored away in the depths of the hotel garage; we wandered through the blaze of bloom in the Ramblas, unable to buy a petal. By the time—after a frantic overseas call—a duplicate check arrived, the day before we would have had to leave Barcelona in order to board our Genoa ship, the hotel's Swiss manager, having twice presented us with a bill, developed a manner partly hunted and partly hostile, and I have never forgotten the incredulous look on his face the morning we hastily and triumphantly settled our account and demanded our car. (You have a *car? Here? Assets*—there were always assets!) Those temporary deprivations were like the shallow hardship of a couple caught in an ice storm on the last block toward a lit house and a sturdy fire. They brought a faint message of the true, pitiless disaster, of the immense vulnerability in which we all are cousins. Like the trivial losses which in childhood are immense, like the lighthearted rootlessness which is so distant from the homeless, those experiences were quite other in poetry.

If there is little trace in this account of early days of the things which are darker, of pain and loss, it is never because these things were nonexistent, but because they are in the very texture of writing, where they belong. The loss of a father, a mother, a brother, a baby, a twenty-two-year-old grandson, all are there, not to be described, but to be present in poetry, in fiction, as part of what both try to communicate.

I have spent a disproportionate length of time on my early years for a reason. I believe that for any writer it is these years which are the true seed, however disguised, of the subsequent work—strained through the mesh of time, colored by a growing perception of depths and alchemy, but already determining the texture and direction of the work. It is not wisdom or maturity or skill which they have brought; these will, or will not, come later, as all the developments and surprises and experiments will come. But the seed will bear its inevitable fruit. Most of the rest of the writer's professional career will have all the familiar aspects and concerns—publications, revisions, lectures, reading, awards. It is really, as Mr. Berra so wisely

observed of something else, déjà vu all over again. There are moments, and people, and happinesses which arise sharply out of the full tide of memory but the long path—which in my case has been very long indeed—leads past the familiar signposts.

There is one thing which constantly changes place, infuriatingly, and of necessity. Once, when I was talking to a truly fine writer about that sense of creative satisfaction one always imagines one step down the road, he said to me, "They keep changing the goalpost." How right he was. And if the goalpost isn't changed, if you reach it and it stays there, you are ill, if not dead, as a writer. You may march in place and write and write (and publish and publish) but your work as a writer is over. The importance is in the frustration—you must imagine that point to be obtainable so strongly that it just eludes your touch. It is now a cliché to say that the work is never completed, only abandoned.

There are those early friends, my first among writers, who gave me the initial, heady delight of that particular kind of friendship: Archie Ammons, Elliot Coleman, Julia Randall. Then the list becomes unmanageable. If I had few friends as a child, what riches were waiting for me. Kenneth Rexroth once said bluntly, "The truth is, writers are not very nice people. The trough is too small, and there are too many pigs." Certainly there are fringe areas of pomposity, ferocious competition, bloated egos. But speaking from one writer's experience, I have found such a quantity of courage, perception and, above all, generosity, among the best writers I have known that I sometimes marvel that an occupation so based on vulnerability and intimacy of purpose can produce such qualities. Two areas of experience in which I have found this especially true were my two years as Poetry Consultant to the Library of Congress and my many stays at the MacDowell Colony, and at Yaddo. Most of the writing I have done has been done in those two superb refuges. People who know that a writer has been to both ask again and again, which did you prefer? Impossible question. Both places, so different in many practical ways, are so alike in what they offer: the deep sense of security as to time, privacy, the sense of a common purpose, and a deep respect for work. MacDowell, with its wonderful ramshackle common room, its studios scattered throughout the woods, its sunny fields and sense of informality; Yaddo, with its rather somber beauty, its other-time-and-other-place Mansion, its rose gardens, fountains and

"In my attic workroom," 1971

giant trees. . . . This writer's gratitude to both places is without bounds.

Most of my work is due to those paradisal havens. When I read applications for art colonies—the passionate need of writers struggling with time, money, and jobs to get to a place where their own work is the *raison d'être* of the day, where everyone around them takes seriously what they are doing, and where so much privacy, scrupulously preserved, surrounds them—I feel a total identity with each applicant, talented or not.

My own routine has been such a curious one. At home, I have never had a studio, or a tightly kept schedule. Time has been full of the people closest to me—my immediate family—my intimate daily concerns. Somehow, it has occurred that during all this I have stored up that special energy caused by the need to write, so that when suddenly surrounded by precious hours and hours in ideal surroundings, I have been able to do in weeks the work of several months. I doubt if this would be possible for the novelist, but for the poet or short-story writer, those practitioners of the compressed,

the connoisseurs of elimination, these relatively short periods of concentrated work can be ideal.

When I took up my job as Poetry Consultant to the Library of Congress, I had assumed that it would temporarily cut off my own work, and certainly leave no time for fiction. But during all those months, I wrote as much poetry as before I went. A hotel room at night in a city not one's own is not a bad opportunity.

And the constant sense of the daily and permanent value of poetry flowed through the Poetry Office. There have been endless discussions of the nature of the position of Consultant—now known as Poet Laureate. What is its relevancy? There have been as many answers as Consultants. For me, my two years there had many aspects. There was the sense of being part of one of the great libraries of the world, and the special sense of its connection with the world's poetry. Month after month, poets, students of poetry, turned up in that small and lovely room: from France, from Africa, from England, Rumania, Russia, and Japan. On and on, in a country in which, for most people, the poet is a curious and mentally ornamental creature, largely irrelevant except to his own concerns. That great rooted sense of the vital importance of poetry was a marvelous feeling. The audiences which came, rain or snow, for the poetry readings were special audiences, both as to enthusiasm and knowledgeability.

My special interest as Consultant was in bringing Black poets to give readings or to make recordings. Among those who came in my eighteen months of actual presence were Sam Allen, June Jordan, May Miller, Leon Damas, Sterling Brown, and Lucille Clifton.

But I agree wholeheartedly with James Dickey's statement that the most valuable thing about the Consultantship was its recorded collection of poets reading their work. To imagine for one moment what such a thing would have meant in the history of the poetry of the past is breathtaking. The net has been flung wide, and obviously there will prove to be much expendable work; but the solid, priceless stuff is there. True, a number of poets are very bad readers, but a good delivery is only a part of the relevant joys. Think of hearing Keats, or Marlowe, or whomever you choose among your personal giants.

The caliber of the people with whom I worked at the library was perfectly extraordinary, among them Roy Basler, John Broderick, and in the Poetry Office itself, Nancy Galbraith, and Jenny Hudson. I loved Washington, by which I mean the Washington of my especial field. There was Washington, beautiful world. Washington, murder capital of the world. Washington, where the poet could find stimulation. And companionship.

When the Carter administration gave its White House party for poets, I think many of us had a somewhat ambiguous reaction—would it inevitably be a little pompous, a little political, a little irrelevant? I think most of us found it the reverse. Its structure was simple and expert—Rosalynn Carter and Joan Mondale managed to give the afternoon a sense of their personal involvement. The strategy of having the twenty poets read, two or three to a room, simultaneously, kept away the sense of the confused and prolonged. I had the good fortune to read with Stanley Kunitz and Robert Hayden, whom I admire as men as much as I admire them as poets. Reading to an audience filled with poets is a very special and sometimes intimidating experience. It is also especially rewarding. The gathering was during the last of the endless hostage crises, and Mr. Carter, looking exhausted but determined,

took time out to greet each of us. It seemed to me as suitable as it was atypical to see the White House swarming with a hundred poets.

There are the lists of the publications, the reviews, the awards of this year, that year, but it is the periods marked by their relevance to work which stand out. They are thick strands, periods of the writer's life meshed with the poems, or stories, or that effort truly to comprehend which is criticism.

From childhood on, I wrote stories because I wanted to. They were not a necessity to me, as poetry was. They were a joy and a magic of multiple lives. How I learned to write stories, instead of the little tales I believed to be stories, is imperceptible to me. Early on I wrote a dozen or more stories which an exemplary agent thought good enough to handle. Patiently she sent them out, garnering a cordial, almost effusive, series of rejections. She was bidden to keep an eye on me, on the editor's behalf—he or she didn't want my next effort to slip by. For five solid years, with the generosity of an angel and the persistence of a fly, she kept this up, undiscouraged by the combination of praise and implacable resistance.

I stopped writing stories.

Almost twenty years later, with three books of poetry and one of criticism behind me, I suddenly realized that I wished to write stories. This time I felt quite differently. Suppose I never published a story—what on earth was wrong with writing one for my own satisfaction? I began again, and no story I wrote after that has gone unpublished. The first of this second batch, "On the Island," appeared in the *Kenyon Review*, and subsequently the next year in both the *O. Henry Prize Stories* and *Best American Short Stories*—something I vaguely feel is not supposed to happen, but which did. The story has since been anthologized seven times. I tell this Cinderella tale specifically to persuade people who passionately want to write short stories but flag along the path of rejection to remember that there really are true Dick Whittington stories, and to express my conviction that if that agent, Elizabeth Otis, hadn't had her stubborn confidence in the work, I'm not totally sure that I should have ever gone back to the form.

What I learned, and how I learned it, in the interim between the early and later stories, I have no idea. I think that the most important thing I learned was what not to do—how not to cripple or weaken or distort the intention I had been given.

Then the editors of the Jackpine Press, whom I had barely known but who are now close friends, wrote that they would like to bring out a collection, and *A Walk with Raschid* was followed by *Adios, Mr. Moxley*. Eventually, Joyce Carol Oates and Raymond Smith suggested that Ontario Review Press publish selections from both books, with new stories added. In 1989 this appeared as *On the Island* and became one of the five nominees for the PEN Faulkner Award of the following year.

I found this progression exhilarating. The stories were to me more real than many daily events, and writing them gave me the immense satisfaction of someone enabled to lead an extra life. Indeed, they were so real to me that even those aspects of their physical setting which would never appear in the story were so exact that I could have described each in detail: I know the texture of the concrete rail Henry wretchedly leaned against as he told of Alexis's disaster—the shape and size of the window through which James stared out over the sleeping Medina. I know them because they are there.

I have quite often been accused of grimness in my stories—interestingly, never by critics but by bemused friends. I think of the lady who asked Flannery O'Connor why she never wrote "any-thing that would lift my heart up," to which Miss O'Connor replied, "Madam, if your heart were where it is supposed to be, it would be lifted up." Certainly, in the case of my own work, I have no such assurance. But I do know that what may be read as pessimism or grimness is my honest attempt to explore the ambiguities and surprises of human actions. My stories must continue beyond the end of the storyline, and the story life must have had a beginning long before the first word; the stories intercept something at a definitive moment.

I have often had comment of the differences between the stories. Some of the contemporary writers whose work I admire—Peter Taylor, Eudora Welty, Ann Tyler—have set their work squarely where region is a basic part of their characters' existence. As I have said, a childhood, an adolescence, tends to dictate whether the mode shall be mining or voyaging—both offering endless opportunities.

As for poems, necessarily a poet discusses her poems with such inaccuracy that I sometimes wonder if the process is respectable. When I already had so much that was new to me—a husband, a small son—I began to feel that another powerful thing had overtaken me. I felt as though, stepping into bright water, imperceptibly my foot-

Library of Congress Consultants in Poetry, March 6, 1978: (from left, seated) William E. Stafford, James Dickey, Josephine Jacobsen, Elizabeth Bishop, and Daniel Hoffman; (from left, standing) Reed Whittemore, Richard Eberhart, Robert Hayden, William Jay Smith, Stephen Spender, Stanley Kunitz, Karl Shapiro, and Howard Nemerov

*With best wishes
to Josephine Jacobsen*

Jimmy Carter 1-80

With President Jimmy Carter, 1980

ing was gone, and I was suddenly swimming toward what I could never really ever touch. When at that time I dropped some poems into the corner mailbox, addressed to *Poetry,* I did so with as much confidence as I felt in pushing my son's note to Santa Claus up the chimney. Harriet Monroe accepted two of the sonnets, plus a small lyric, and I knew that the water was deeper than I thought, and that I must constantly swim more strongly. My life seemed to me already so crowded that I couldn't conceive how this vital necessity was to be added without disaster.

There was never a real answer to that integration. Our son as a small child had asthma, honestly inherited on both sides of an allergic family, and because of this we acquired an old house in the White Mountains, for a sum inadequate to a contemporary cruise. We lived in it for fifty-five summers packed with family, extended family, friends, and grandchildren, friends of grandchildren. It had twelve rooms and four perfectly extraordinary baths, one a sort of goldfish bowl, one designed for a midget, and one in discrete halves. It always needed repair, had great charm of

personality and was overloved, and finally abandoned long after it had become a burden and no longer a refuge. I had at first a small shack behind the pines of the driveway; but after winters of invasion by red squirrels and gourmet porcupines, it ended as a dumping ground for tools and fertilizer—which are, after all, agents of creativity. Most of our New Hampshire friends regarded my poetry as a perfectly harmless and legitimate amusement.

In Baltimore, I first began to meet writers. Mary Owings Miller, herself an excellent poet, who, by some legerdemain none of us really understood, had managed to found and edit first a small but excellent magazine—*Contemporary Poetry*—and then, under the same title, a series of poetry collections, small, but of high professional standards. In my late twenties I had met friends who would remain important to me all my life: Elliot Coleman, then head of the Johns Hopkins Writing Seminars, teacher, poet, and loyal and exciting friend; Father Joseph Gallagher, priest, poet, essayist, and unlabored wit; Julia Randall, already a rare metaphysical poet; William R.

Mueller, educator and writer, who became almost a brother and with whom twenty years later I would have the joy of collaborating on two books of criticism. A. R. Ammons, still isolated from what would be a major career as poet; John Dorsey, distinguished art critic and sustaining friend. Life pulled in so many directions I felt a sort of exhilarated panic. Later, when she wrote her Ph.D. thesis on my work, Evelyn Prettyman became one of a new and highly congenial group.

Mary Owings Miller did more for my courage and confidence than she probably ever realized. In her series, she published *For the Unlost* and *The Human Climate,* and it was then that a few reviews began to trickle in.

As I published more and more, I became more and more aware of the dangers of an assumption of progress, of the fact that the poet, perpetually, starts from a new beginning.

Though I had a fairly solid selection of work behind me, I was far from widely known outside the circle of poets when I was invited to become Poetry Consultant at the Library of Congress. I had by then a degree of inner confidence—except when I sat down to a blank page; but I still remember how I enjoyed a head-on comment, in the city of diplomacy, when Fran Taylor, in response to my confession, "You have no idea how surprised I was when I was approached by the Library!" said cheerfully, "*You* were surprised! What do you think *Washington* was?" She was so right.

By my second term I was more confident, and, I believe, more effective.

Any publicly supported position for poets trembles always on the brink of disaster. The opposite distress is the assumption that in a great nation, poetry is a peripheral occupation. From long before Plato, poets have been quite correctly regarded as dangerous. They are, indeed, and without that danger the bland grip of complacency tightens.

As my husband retired, we began the travels we had never been able to take. We did it unluxuriously, and without benefit of travel agent or formal agenda, by freighter or in our Beetle, in which we once drove from Baltimore to Guatemala

"Our son and youngest grandson," Plainfield, Vermont, 1978

City without marital rupture. We went to Italy (five times), to Spain, Portugal, Greece, to Mexico (five times), to Trinidad, up the Orinoco; to Morocco, to Kenya, Tanzania. We slept in posadas and paradors and, in Ireland, in farmhouses. We went to wonderful islands: Haiti, Rhodes, Grenada.

With such haphazard methods, and often in relatively remote spots, we should have had a few disasters, but we didn't; a few washed-out roads, a few torrid and chilly nights, and two hair-raising drives—to Rhonda, in the days when the road pushed wheels to the road's edge when two cars met, and an even more terrifying one when we naively took the road to Chichicastanango after dark. But these drives taught me what lights and food and shelter meant when it seemed improbable that they would be reached.

We saw the giant sunset combers towering in on the beach at Pied de La Questa. We saw the butterfly meadow on the way to high Lindos, and we talked to a Mexican artist in Tepotzlan who affirmed, and I think believed, that at midnight and dawn respectively he—and others—had seen men turn into *loups garous* and back, in that area famed for werewolves.

I did not write poems describing these places. Like the personal high and low spots of my life, they went into my eyesight and my ears, into my writing reflexes. I have written scarcely any purely descriptive poetry, though I often enjoy reading it. What I cared most about, and what most affected my work, was the wonderful sense of strangeness—the feeling of being physically and mentally present in a scene of culture, a place, with its colors and smells and weather and voices, which was totally other. I think that as many writers draw strength from contact with their geographical roots, I drew it from the differences: from the very precious strangeness of where I was.

We often learned, in the lovely spots in which we would stay, that a radiator—if there was one—could often chill our fingers. But, what wonderful places: the giant stands of marguerites outside the palace in Obidos; in a frigid bedroom in Ajijic, the welcome magic of a blaze in the fireplace; and after the terrifying climb to Chichicastanango, the sudden miracle of the Mayan Inn. In Erice, how we clung together for warmth, clutching a wine bottle of hot water hourly replenished. The day at Revolcadero Beach when my husband, as usual unwilling to be directed, swam beyond the ropes and was caught in a deadly undertow, to be rescued by two Acapulcan lifeguards, while I,

nearsighted and high on the beach, read, blissfully unconscious of what all the bustle was about.

But nothing, nothing had the magic of the two nights in Africa, one at Treetops, one at Kilimanjaro. When we, my husband and I and our fifteen-year-old companion, reached Treetops, the white hunter was keyed up. They had had very few elephants recently, he said, but there was word of a large herd coming in. He told us to talk quietly, walk quietly, and make no loud noises. That night, as we three knelt at our windowsill, 103 elephants, silent, immense in the moonlight, gathered by twos and threes, and then by dozens, putting their huge feet like plush, shifting, and rocking around the water hole, where the green of the hyena's eyes stared from a distance, as the herd shot water over each other, curled up their trunks, and hugely assembled. That was just before Christmas.

On New Year's Eve, we were at the base of Kilimanjaro; we knew that the summit was almost always shrouded in clouds and true, we went to bed seeing only the dark gigantic shape under a full moon. Fast asleep, just before midnight, we heard pounding on the door. It was our grandson, wild with excitement. "Come out! Come out! *Quick!*" We flung blankets around our shoulders and stepped out into the cold air.

The summit of Kilimanjaro was bare to the moon, round and white in a circle clear of stars. The snows, untouched, untouchable, shone under that brilliant eye. We stood there together, the three of us, dazed, hypnotized, as the new year crossed our uplifted faces. It is something we live over and over.

Then we discovered the Caribbean.

The first Caribbean port I ever saw I saw as I came, alone and exhausted, to Haiti. My mother had died after a long illness, my husband could not leave, and I went alone to Port au Prince. I remember the strange sense of homecoming I had as I stood on the deck and saw the colors, felt the touch of the Caribbean air. I haven't understood why it is the Caribbean in which I have, always, that sense of familiar comfort. Heaven knows Haiti was a sad and violent place (though nothing like what it later became), but its magic, its colors, its voices, the night scent of flowers were new to me. I spent a month there alone in the Ibo-lele, that light-filled hotel high in the mountains beyond Petionville, and through good luck and friends made there, I went to the studios of the Haitian artists who had suffered much and were to suffer more. A year later, on a freighter trip, I came back briefly with my husband. The change was already chilling, and I remember looking at the almost savage beauty of the island and saying to myself aloud, I will never see this place again.

Haiti, Trinidad, Barbados, Tobago, Martinique, Grenada. And it was Grenada that became a second home. Twenty-two times we have returned and, as I write, we still hope, each year, for one more visit. A full third of all the work I've ever done was done in Grenada and was the result of its experience.

Except for the shelter of Yaddo and MacDowell, I have never worked so well as in the Caribbean. It has profoundly impregnated my work, and I hope I have written always as a familiar stranger, coming back and back, yet always aware that I saw with a fresh eye of strangeness, and never presuming to explicate, or to assume a native air.

Now that travels, even here in the States, are pretty much off-limits, I do miss the readings, partly because one learns so much from regularly submitting one's work to that particular discipline, but mostly because of the rapport between audi-ence and reader; that variable, testing, exciting relationship which is defined without words, which draws out common adventure. At its best, it is like nothing else, and certain hours and certain places remain as real as the pen in my hand. Having just survived, if not celebrated, my eighty-fourth birthday, one hundred thousand words could not possibly contain what has happened to me and within me in the practice of my profession, what Eliot sternly calls "the poet's gigantic days and nights." But I still believe that the knowledge that produces poetry, discovery of self, discovery of the sense of triumph in a word, of loss, minor or overwhelming, is learned in its essence early, and that its variations only tell what in some inner sense the poet already knew.

It may seem odd that, in looking back, I have spent so much time on the first twenty-five years of my life; but I realized some time ago that it was these formative years which set in motion everything else: who I was, where I came from, what I wanted. The rest is the development of that seed.

"At home in 1984: Eric and I were quite unaware that we were being taken"

I have had a great many solid joys in my life and, inevitably, a few of the tragic losses which are the result of loving other vulnerable human beings. These, like the quality of a marriage which has made everything good possible, are personal and related to my work only as all important experiences are reflected in one way or another in whatever the writer produces. So it is with my fortune in a congenial and exciting family, three of whom are themselves writers.

*

I continue to believe that it is the first three decades which seed everything; the seed may be cultivated, grafted, may produce unexpected bloom, but it is all there. Childhoods are widely different, different even under similar circumstances: the staples of adult professional life are fairly constant—publications, reviews, anthologies, collections, awards, recordings, readings, lectures. As my disgusted and ephemeral French governess constantly repeated, in describing the variety in actions, and similarity in wickedness, of my misdemeanors, "*Plus ça change. . . .*"

BIBLIOGRAPHY

FOR ADULTS

Poetry:

Let Each Man Remember, Kaleidograph Press, 1940.

For the Unlost, Contemporary Poetry, 1946.

The Human Climate, Contemporary Poetry, 1953.

The Animal Inside, Ohio University Press, 1966.

The Shade-Seller: New and Selected Poems, Doubleday, 1974.

The Chinese Insomniacs: New Poems, University of Pennsylvania Press, 1981.

Adios, Mr. Moxley, Jackpine, 1986.

The Sisters: New and Selected Poems, Bench Press, 1987.

John Wheatcroft, editor, *Distances*, Bucknell University Press, 1991.

Short-story collections:

A Walk with Raschid and Other Stories, Jackpine, 1978.

On the Island: New and Selected Stories, Ontario Review Press, 1989.

Other:

(With William Randolph Mueller) *The Testament of Samuel Beckett* (dramatic criticism), Hill & Wang (New York), 1964, Faber (London), 1966.

(With Mueller) *Ionesco and Genet: Playwrights of Silence* (dramatic criticism), Hill & Wang, 1968.

Selected Poems (recording), Watershed, 1977.

Wheatcroft, editor, *Our Other Voices: Nine Poets Speaking* (interviews), Bucknell University Press, 1991.

Contributor:

The Way We Live Now, Ontario Press, 1986.

Substance of Things Hoped For, Doubleday, 1987.

Eve Shelnutt, editor, *The Confidence Woman: 26 Women Writers at Work*, Longstreet Press, 1991.

Work represented in numerous other anthologies, including *Best American Short Stories*, 1966; *O. Henry Prize Stories*, 1967, 1971, 1973, 1976, 1985, and 1993; *Fifty Years of the American Short Story*, 1970; *A Geography of Poets*, edited by William Field; *A Treasury of American Poetry*, edited by Nancy Sullivan; *Night Walks: Short Stories*, edited by Joyce Carol Oates; *A Treasury of American Short Stories*, edited by Sullivan; *Pushcart Prizes Six;* and *Belles Lettres*, 1986.

Charles Johnson
1948-

Charles Johnson, 1989

Sometime in the 1920s my great-uncle, William Johnson, left the home of his family in South Carolina to live in Evanston, a northern suburb of Chicago. He was a young man then, dark-skinned, tall, good-natured, pious, industrious and, I suspect, a product of Booker T. Washington's "boot-strap" philosophy of racial uplift. Once North, he married, and started his own milk company, which served the black neighborhoods in my hometown. The Great Depression brought his company to an end, but by the 1940s Will Johnson had started another business—the Johnson Construction Company—that would be profitable for decades and result in the creation of numerous churches, apartment buildings, and residences not only in Evanston but across other suburbs of Chicago. His success made him the patriarch of my family. And, most important of all, it allowed him to offer jobs to his relatives still living in South Carolina.

One man who accepted his invitation for work in the North was Benny Lee Johnson, my father, who was the "middle" child in a family of twelve children. Six boys. Six girls. My father was, in fact, sandwiched by birth between two girls, and thus was a bit to one side, a bit adrift from his siblings on my grandfather Richard's farm outside Abbeville. He was always, I believe, a proud man, responsible but shy, a person who valued regularity, enjoyed churchgoing, and measured himself by the quality and quantity of his labor. In all the years I've known him he has never uttered an oath stronger than the word "Shoot!" when he was angry. If Benny Lee identified with anyone, it was *his* father, who in addition to being a farmer was also the local blacksmith and a carpenter. There can be no question that my father loved life down South—hunting in winter, the rhythm of life close to the land, a tightly knit family that worked together—and, as a boy, he had fresh ideas for how to help Richard get crops in early, and for expanding his sideline as a blacksmith. If you have seen the character Hoke, played by Morgan Freeman in the film *Driving Miss Daisy*, then you have seen my father. He could have stayed in South Carolina forever, he tells me, but when life became economically harder on the black family farm in the 1940s, my father had to find work elsewhere. My aunts, his sisters, say he cried the morning he left them to join his Uncle Will in Illinois. He was twenty-five years old that day, and his plan was to make a little money and return as soon as he could.

Doubtlessly, my father would have gone back to that life he often described to me as idyllic (if you ignored racism, which his family generally did because they seldom had to interact with white people). But once he reached Evanston he met a woman five years his senior, Ruby Elizabeth Jackson, the only child of an only child (a maternal grandmother I always knew as Nana) who had lived in Evanston since age twelve and was *glad* her parents—Charles and Beatrice Jackson—left Georgia. This woman, my mother, was most suited for cities. Not that she was a woman familiar with nightclubs or a fast life. On the contrary, she was a church-girl, a virgin and proud of it (my father would have been attracted to no one else) but one with a wide interest in everything novel, which the Chicago area offered in abundance. I know she loved her father, a dark, handsome man who worked as a mechanic and was dead at age fifty from a heart attack before I was born; and she and her mother, whom she called "Bee," were more like mutually dependent sisters than mother and daughter. Both had an artist's eye for the beautiful, the unusual, the eccentric, and loved gardening. And in my mother's five-feet-four-inch frame there dwelled just a bit of the soul of an actress—a playful knack for saying or doing things simply for the effects they might create on others. Her hope had been to be a schoolteacher, a dream she never realized because she had a severe case of asthma that dated back to her childhood.

In many ways my father and mother seemed as different as two people could be: he was a quiet, deeply conservative, pro-black man with a fifth-grade education, who until the 1960s voted Republican ("I can always find work when they're in office," he said); yet she was emotional, moody, a high school graduate who believed in integration, belonged to three book clubs, and always voted for Democrats ("They do more for our people," she said). But in fact they actually complimented and completed each other. He *listened* to her; she relied, physically and emotionally, on *him*. And both were, like so many in that first wave of black southern immigrants to Evanston, children of the black church. Given her health and age, my mother would only have one child, who arrived a year or so after she met Benny, which meant he had now a family of his own in the North and would never live on the farm again.

And so I was born on April 23 (Shakespeare's birthday), 1948, at Community Hospital, an all-black facility. That place, and the remarkable person behind it, Dr. Elizabeth Hill, deserve a mention in this memoir because prior to its creation, Dr. Hill—one of the area's first black physicians—was barred by segregation from taking her patients to all-white Evanston Hospital. Instead, she was forced to take them to a hospital on the south side of Chicago, and quite a few of her patients died in the ambulance on the way. Almost single-handedly (so I was told as a child), Dr. Hill organized black Evanston (and some sympathetic whites) to create a black hospital. My Uncle Will would go nowhere else for treatment, even after Evanston Hospital was integrated. My father's sister and other black Evanstonians found life long work there before its closure in the late 1970s. And every black baby born to my generation in Evanston came into the world there—my classmates and I all had in common the fact that we had been delivered by Elizabeth Hill, who never married and considered all of us to be her "children." Even when I was in my teens she knew me on sight and would ask what I'd been up to since last I saw her.

Predictably, then, I grew up in a black community in the 1950s that had the feel of one big extended family. Ebenezer A.M.E. Church, where I was baptized (and later my son) and married, was a central part of our collective lives. Naturally, Uncle Will was a big church donor and one of its elders. (By the time I knew him he was a bald, bullet-headed, pot-bellied man who wore suspenders, studied the evening news on television as if it were an oracle, and smiled down at me from his great height with all the affection he gave the children of his nephews and nieces. Because no one in our family had yet gone to college, he'd tell me, "Get an education, that's the most important thing you can do," and I'd say, "Yes, *sir,* Uncle Will. I *will* get an education.") But my parents and relatives—all quietly pious since we were all Methodists, remember, so "shouting" and "getting happy" were frowned upon—and neighbors also had significant roles at Ebenezer: my mother sometimes taught Sunday school, my cousins sang in the choir, I was an usher. In an atmosphere such as this, where my Uncle Will had built the very structures black Evanston people lived and worshipped their god in, where everyone *knew* their neighbors and saw them in church on Sunday, it was natural for grown-ups to keep an eye on the welfare of their neighbors' children—I'm referring to my earliest playmates—and to help each other in innumerable ways. In short, Evanston in the 1950s was a place where, beyond all doubt, I knew I was loved and belonged.

There were never any days when my family missed a meal. This was due to my father's occasionally working three jobs (a day job doing construction, an evening job as a night watchman, and helping an elderly white couple with their chores for a few hours on the weekend). So no, we weren't as poor as some of my friends who had no father at home. But neither were we wealthy or middle-class. Ever so often my mother took a job to help make ends meet. One of these was as a cleaning woman for Gamma Phi Beta sorority at Northwestern University, where my Nana was already working as a cook. And she brought me along with her since she couldn't afford a baby-

The author's parents, Ruby Elizabeth Jackson and Benny Lee Johnson (center), at their wedding, Evanston, Illinois, 1947. Also pictured are his uncle David Johnson and great-uncle William Johnson (standing), his aunt Pearl Johnson and cousin Tave (right), and (from left) a guest, his aunt Octavia Johnson, and his maternal grandmother, Beatrice Jackson

"Me (far left) with my cousins on my grandfather Richard Johnson's farm in South Carolina in the 1950s"

sitter. I remember her telling me that the sorority's chapter said no blacks would ever be admitted into its ivied halls. There are two great ironies in this story. The first is that my mother brought home books thrown out by the sorority girls when classes ended, and in those boxes I found my first copies of Shakespeare's tragedies. The other irony is that decades later in 1990 Northwestern's English department actively (and generously) pursued me for employment by offering me a chair in the humanities, which I declined.

Along with those books from Northwestern University, my mother filled first the aged apartment we lived in before 1960, then my parents' first home with books that reflected her eclectic tastes in yoga, dieting, Christian mysticism, Victorian poetry, interior decorating, costume design, and flower arrangement. On boiling hot midwestern afternoons in late July when I was tired of drawing (my dream was to be a cartoonist, which I shall discuss in a moment), I would pause before one of her many bookcases and pull down a

volume on religion, the Studs Lonigan trilogy, poetry by Rilke, *The Swiss Family Robinson,* Richard Wright's *Black Boy,* an 1897 edition of classic Christian paintings (now in my library), or Daniel Blum's *Pictorial History of the American Theatre 1900–1956,* which fascinated me for hours.

As an only child, books became my replacement for siblings. This early exposure to so many realms of the imagination can only be the reason why I came up with the idea of making myself read at least one book a week after I started at Evanston Township High School, from which, by the way, my mother had graduated in the late thirties. I must confess that before high school I was an avid science fiction and comic book reader, my collection of the latter reaching to about 2,000 comics. My self-imposed schedule of reading one book per week saw me start with all the James Bond novels and end with Plutarch's *Lives of the Noble Grecians.* I spent hours each week at a newsstand selecting "that" book I'd spend seven days of my life with. And, as might be expected, it happened that one week I finished early—on a Tuesday, I recall—and I thought, "God, what do I *do* now with the rest of the week?" So I read a second book and discovered, "Gee, I read *two* this week and my head didn't explode or anything." Then it became easy to make it three a week, and I *did* think—but only once—that someday it might be nice to have my name on the spine of a volume I'd written.

Mother's slim volume on yoga also helped me make the first, tentative steps on a path that would later prove invaluable for my life and literary interests. It contained a short chapter on "Meditation." Although the book's hatha yoga postures struck me as being excruciatingly hard, I decided to try out the author's instructions for clearing the mind. After half an hour of this—the most tranquil thirty minutes I'd ever known, one that radically slowed down my sense of time and divested me of desire—I felt both deeply rewarded and a little scared, as if I'd been playing with a loaded pistol. As much as I'd enjoyed this first pass at *dhyana*, I suspected (and rightly) that if I kept it up, I'd become too dispassionate, too peaceful, and would lack the fire—the internal agitation—to venture out into the world and explore all the things, high and low, that I, as a teenager, was burning to see, know, taste, and experience. Quietly, and without telling anyone what I'd done, I put her book back on the shelf and promised myself that someday—someday!—I would investigate this marvelous thing more deeply after I'd sated myself on the world that called me so powerfully.

And so, again, ours was a house of not just provocative books but also inexpensive art objects that Mother found at flea markets and rummage sales. When she couldn't find them, she *built* them—for example, bookcases made from old cigar boxes, which I helped her resurface and paint. We'd read the same books together sometimes, Mother and me, and discuss them (I think she relied on me for this, even raised me to do it, since my father had little time for books), and when I was twelve she placed the most unusual book of all in front of me. A blank book. A diary. "Some people write down what happens to them every day in books like these," she said. "You might enjoy this." Enjoy it? Oh, she knew me well! Like any kid, I enjoyed receiving gifts at Christmas and on my birthdays, but from my earlier years of being praised for my drawing ability in elementary school (art class was the one place where I excelled), the things I wanted *most* invariably turned out to be the things I had to make myself. Once I

started writing on those pages about my feelings, about my friends and relatives, and once I saw how I was free to say *anything* that came into my head about them, I was addicted. But remember what I said—Mother was a shrewd woman. I realized why she'd given me that first diary when we all sat one evening at the dinner table. She looked up from her plate, and in the most casual of voices asked, "Why don't you like your Uncle George?" I stopped chewing. I couldn't swallow. For maybe five seconds I thought she was psychic, a mind-reader. Then I remembered the diary. She'd been *reading* my entries. But what could I do? I didn't want to stop spilling my thoughts out, or give up the pleasure that came from seeing them externalized and in some strange way thereby made more manageable. No, my only choice was to hide it, which I did—behind my dresser, under my mattress, wherever I thought she wouldn't look. Since that day I've filled up probably a hundred diaries, journals, and writer's notebooks. Crates worth of them containing poetry, essays to myself, whatever was in my head at that time—most of them are gathering dust in my father's garage because after filling up one I seldom look back, though if I wish to, I can reach behind me twenty years to this very day and read you an entry. (If nothing else, a journal or diary teaches us how silly we were, in retrospect, to be so upset about things that occupied us two decades ago.)

Like so many things I owe to my mother, I am indebted to her for seducing me with the beauty of blank pages. But this was by no means a new infatuation. As with books, it was into drawing that I regularly retreated as a child. There was something magical to me about bringing forth images that hitherto existed only in my head where no one could see them. I remember spending whole afternoons blissfully seated before a three-legged blackboard my parents got me for Christmas, drawing and erasing until my knees and the kitchen floor beneath me were covered with layers of chalk and the piece in my hand was reduced to a wafer-thin sliver.

Inevitably, the passion for drawing led me to consider a career as a professional artist. From the Evanston Public Library I lugged home every book on drawing, cartooning, and collections of early comic art (Cruikshank, Thomas Rolandson, Daumier, Thomas Nast) and pored over them, considering what a wonderful thing it would be—as an artist—to externalize *everything* I felt and thought in images. Some Saturday mornings I sat on the street downtown with my sketchbook, trying to capture the likeness of buildings and pedestrians, who were probably amused to see a black kid studying them out of the corner of his eye, then scribbling furiously. And I made weekly trips to Good's Art Supplies to buy illustration board with my allowance and money earned from my paper route (and later from a Christmas job working on the assembly line at a Rand McNally book factory in Skokie, and from still another tedious after-school job cleaning up a silks-and-woolens store where well-heeled white ladies did their shopping). Good's was a tiny little store packed to the ceiling with the equipment I longed to buy. The proprietor, a fat, friendly man, tolerated my endless and naive questions about what it was like to be an artist and what materials were best for what projects; he showed me a book he'd self-published on his own theory of perspective (I never bought it), and after he'd recommended to me the best paper for my pen-and-ink ambitions, I strapped my purchase onto the front of my bicycle and pedaled home. (For a Christmas present my folks finally did

Charles with his father

buy me one of Good's drawing tables; I moved back furniture in my bedroom and set it up like a shrine. When I went away to college, it went with me, like an old friend.)

But if drawing brought me my deepest pleasure and my first sense of my own talents, it also led to my life's first real crisis. By my early teens I was determined to be nothing *but* a commercial artist. I told my father so. Without thinking this through, and without ever having known any black artists, he told me with the gravest concern for my economic future that, "They don't let black people do that. You should think about something else." I pleaded with him that I didn't *want* to do anything else. But Dad would not budge. For days after this conversation I was gloomy, crushed, and directed many an evil thought his way. A future without art? I would rather have died than not pursue drawing and self-expression as far as it could take me.

By some stroke of luck I was at that time a reader of *Writer's Digest,* mainly for their profiles of famous cartoonists who were my idols. One issue featured an advertisement for a correspondence course in cartooning taught by Lawrence Lariar, a man who'd published over one hundred books—both as a mystery writer and cartoonist—was cartoon editor for *Parade* magazine, a former Disney studio "story man," and each year served as editor for *The Best Cartoons of the Year.* My anger at my father's lack of faith in my future as an artist prompted me to write to Lariar, saying, "My dad tells me I won't be able to have a future as a cartoonist because I'm black, and I just want to know what you think." Lariar, a true liberal—a Jewish man (he changed his name decades earlier) who once took gleeful pleasure in his neighbor's anger when he invited a group of black artists to his Long Island home to give them instruction—fired back a letter to me within a week: "Your father is wrong," he said. "You can do whatever you want with your life. All you need is a good drawing teacher." I read this letter to my father. He hated to *ever* admit he was wrong, but he shrugged his big, tired shoulders and gave me a headshake that definitely meant, "Okay, what do *I* know about this?" I wrote Lariar back, asking, "Will you be my teacher?" His reply was all right, but I'd have to pay for his two-year course. No free lunches here. After a long talk with Dad he agreed to make the monthly payments for me.

I was by this time a high school student *hungering* to publish *any*where as a cartoonist. For two years I dutifully performed the cartooning exercises Lariar mailed me, sent them back, then studied his remarks and revisions. Since my family has relatives everywhere, I made a summer trip by Greyhound to Brooklyn, where our relatives put me up on a roll-away bed. In New York I made the journey out to Long Island to visit Lariar, shop talk about drawing (he loaded me down, dear man, with original art from syndicated strips of his own), then I carried my "swatch" (a cartoonist's portfolio of samples) all over Manhattan, pounding the pavement as I went by the company that published Archie Comics ("We'd hire you but all our illustrators live in New York") and every cartoon editor's office that would let me inside the door. No sales, then. Still, I was encouraged enough by the time I completed Lariar's lessons—I was then seventeen—to approach the editor of my high school paper, the *Evanstonian*, with an offer to illustrate their articles. Reluctantly, he agreed. He let me try a cartoon about a rock-and-roll group that looked like the Beatles. And I guess he was satisfied with my effort because he kept giving me assignments. Around this time I heard from a white classmate who also drew, Tom Reitze, about a Chicago company that manufactured magic tricks and was looking for illustrators (Read: cheap labor) for their catalog. I was at their door the next day. They gave me six tricks to draw. They paid two dollars per illustration. But I *was* paid for the first time and, so not to forget the day I became a "professional," I framed one of those dollars. It hangs right now on my office wall.

Something you must understand about Evanston in 1965 is that, unlike many places, the public schools were integrated. From the time I started kindergarten I was thrown together with kids of all colors, and so I found it natural to have friends both black and white. As kids, we thought bigotry was atavistic and—even worse—just not cool. Evanston Township High School, we constantly heard, was rated in the mid-1960s as the second-best public high school in the nation, right behind our competitor, New Trier. It was a big school, almost like a small college—my graduating class had 1,000 students; black students made up 11 percent of the population. In its progressive curriculum we found a first-rate education provided, clearly, by the wealthy white Evanston parents who sent their children there. My friend Reitze went on to Harvard; the much-celebrated Los Angeles installation artist, Franklin "Buzz" Spector, was my classmate (he wanted to be a poet then) at ETHS, and later at Southern Illinois University.

"My mother in Chicago in the mid-1950s"

True enough, white Evanstonians may have funded all those art and photography classes for their kids—but I took advantage of them too, and ran myself ragged playing soccer one year, and dreamed up with Reitze a comic strip for the school paper. Loosely based on the then-popular character "Wonder Warthog," ours was called "Wonder Wildkit" (the wildkit was the symbol for our football team). Reitze wrote, I drew. It ran the year we were seniors and, to my surprise, won a journalism award in national competition (along with a single-panel cartoon I'd published) for high school cartoonists. Truth is, until that moment I was unaware that such an award even existed.

And to its credit, ETHS offered a yearly creative writing class taught by short-story writer Marie-Claire Davis. At the time she was publishing in the *Saturday Evening Post*. As a cartoonist, I thought writing stories was fun and I came alive in my literature classes, where we read Orwell, Shakespeare, Melville, and Robert Penn Warren, but writing wasn't the kick for me that drawing was. Regardless, I let a buddy talk me into enrolling in Marie's class with him. We talked to each other the whole time and barely listened to poor Marie. (But she put Joyce Cary's lovely book *Art and Reality* in front of us, without discussing it in class, and with the hopes that we might read it on our own, which I did, and something in me so enjoyed his essays on art that I thought, yeah, someday I'd like to do a book like this too.) When I turned in my first story, "Man Beneath Rags" (about homeless people), Marie took it to the *Evanstonian* and published it. Then she did another, "50 Cards 50" (about racially directed Christmas cards), and a third, "Rendezvous" (a science-fiction satire). All this pleased me to no end, but my only obsession, as always, was with comic art.

So my "swatch" had grown. I was prepared senior year to attend an art school just outside Chicago (my father had driven me to the interviewer's motel because I missed him at school and, though fatigued-looking, he seemed pleased with my samples). Providence, however, had something else in mind. During the waning days of May I sat talking with my art and photography teacher, a gentle but gloomy man who said to me in all candor, "Chuck, an artist has a tough life. If you're going to be a cartoonist, it'll be even harder. I think you should go to a university, not art school, and get a professional degree." Looking back, I *know* he was saying the artist's life had been hard on *him.* Nevertheless, his words bothered me—I couldn't afford to blow my one shot at college when my whole family was counting on me. I tramped upstairs to my advisor's office, told her what he'd told me, and said, "It's so late in the year. Are there *any* schools still accepting applications?" She looked through her big book and came up with Southern Illinois University in Carbondale. "You could major in journalism," she said. This was not my first choice, I can assure you; it had the reputation of being a "party school." My advisor shrugged when I said this. "You can always transfer after the first year, if you like, and finish at the University of Illinois."

Thus, I went to SIU in the fall of 1966 with the plan of transferring later. I was among a wave of Illinois black kids who enrolled that year, most of them pouring into "Little Egypt" from the Chicago area. I cannot speak for how those other students felt, but I know I arrived as eager for education and naive as any young man could be. "College" was a nearly mythic place, I thought, where one was supposed to pursue and achieve "wisdom." After arriving in Carbondale I soon

learned that few (if any) students and faculty were there for that lofty, transcendent reason. Most of the students I met said, bluntly, that they "just wanted that piece of paper" so they could get a good-paying job and leave school as soon as they could. I listened. I understood their feelings, but that wasn't how I felt. My overriding concern in those days was with acquiring new skills. As many skills as I could in as many disciplines as possible. Nor was I alone in this desire, for another journalism major I met—a Ghanaian student named Fortunata Massa—remarked to me, "The thing I like most about America is that no matter what you want to learn, there is someone here who can teach it to you."

In effect, we were both skill-junkies, technique-junkies in 1966. My belief was that if you gave me a good teacher I could put what *he* knew together with what *I* knew and the product of this fusion would be greater than its two original parts.

Within a few days of unpacking in my dormitory room I found my way to the campus newspaper, the *Daily Egyptian,* and showed them my "swatch." They hired me that day (and for pay). It probably helped my case that I was a journalism major because the *Egyptian* was a product of the School of Journalism, founded by a seasoned newsman named Howard Long, who during my undergraduate years enjoyed my draftsmanship and kindly took me under his wing. For the *Egyptian* I drew everything—illustrations, panel cartoons, and two comic strips I coauthored with a dormitory friend and English major, Charles Gilpin, who was devoted to being a novelist and told me enthusiastically about his classes with a young professor named John Gardner. Sometime later that year I wheedled my way onto the town paper, the *Southern Illinoisan,* as a political cartoonist. And I sent copies of every published drawing to my parents and Lariar, with whom I kept up a spirited correspondence. College, as it turned out, fed my creativity. New ideas in an open, intellectual environment became raw material for my pen.

All journalism majors were required to take a class in philosophy. I chose a huge lecture course taught by a brilliant professor, John Howie, on the pre-Socratics. Somehow (I don't know how), and with some gift he had (I don't know what), Howie was able to *sing* the ethical problems Empedocles and Parmenides wrestled with in such a way that I—sitting there in my seat among a sea of students—felt in my depths that these were *my* problems today, matters I had to come to some conclusion about. My imagination had not been so stimulated, I felt, since the day I first discovered drawing; my mind had never been engaged so thoroughly in the process of questioning the world around me. Right then and there, I knew I had to do *more* of this; I decided quietly, with certainty, that I had to live close to philosophy for the rest of my life—for the very sake of my intellectual life. Yes, I kept taking journalism classes, but I took just as many in philosophy and was but five credits short of having that as my undergraduate major.

Something else I learned at SIU that first year was the meaning of loneliness. For the first time in my life I was separated from the extended family of blood relations and neighborhood friends I knew in Evanston. And this *was* a party school. But I'd never been a party person.

Friday and Saturday nights, therefore, were times when I felt most alone at college that first year. The usually raucous dormitory was empty as a tomb—everyone, it seemed, was out dating or partying on Greek Row. (They'd fall in by daybreak, leaving puddles of vomit down the stairwell; and I recall writing freshman composition papers, ten dollars each, for some of the guys so they could have the night off to get loose. I would also do for free handwriting analysis for them because for some reason I'd gotten interested in the pseudo-science of grapho-analysis; and writing those papers for pay wasn't so much a task as it was fun since writing came easily to me.) In those days Morris library was open all night. Adrift in my loneliness, I saw its lights as you might a beacon. I went there after I finished my homework and whatever drawing assignments I'd nailed down for the week. As might be expected, the library was nearly as empty as my dorm. Only clusters of Asian students sat studying together, a fact that deeply impressed me then as it does now when I think of my Chinese and Vietnamese students and how difficult it must be for them to pull straight *A*'s in a foreign country and when English is their second language.

Most of the night I drifted among the stacks, pulling down whatever titles caught my eye: obscure poetry, works of Western and Eastern metaphysics I hadn't yet read, every oversized book on art the library had, and novels by Sartre, London (*Martin Eden*), all the "philosophical" fiction writers. With about thirty books in front of me, I'd sit down and start flipping through them, sampling each. After a few more hours I'd have six or seven I wanted to live with for the week, and at 3:00 A.M. I'd check them out and return to the dorm to spend the rest of the week reading between classes.

Those were solitary but productive days, and unexpectedly rewarding on a personal level. I made several lifelong friends, among them Scott Kramer, another philosophy major from Chicago. When not in philosophy classes together, we'd play chess, or exchange literary works we'd discovered (it was Kramer who put Herman Hesse's *Damien* in my hand, which led me to read *Siddhartha*, a work I felt I had to respond to one day, and did in *Oxherding Tale*, my second novel); or we'd go to an off-campus movie with a beautiful, deeply spiritual girl we knew—a religion major named Jill Walter (she is now Chaplain Jill Walter-Penn and recently had the honor of being invited to NASA to deliver the official prayer for the astronauts who went up in the resurrected Challenger space shuttle); or Kramer and I would coauthor dreadfully didactic metaphysical plays—one is called "The Transcendental Descent," and Kramer, who now teaches philosophy at Spokane Community College, threatens to someday publish this drek we dashed off on a night we were bored. Or we'd sit together, smoking and drinking beer, through each and every episode of "Star Trek's" first season on the dorm's TV—we were, I should add, fans from the start. We were also, I guess, pretty typical of alienated, dreamy intellectual and artistic wannabees, the sort of "serious," brooding young men who quoted Plato, argued about existentialism, and ever so slightly began to ease into the dress and life-styles appropriate for hippies by 1967. The other kids in the dorm (business and agriculture majors) doubtlessly had good reason to think we were strange, particularly after our corner of the dorm and circle of associates began to attract other nonconformist personalities—would-be musicians who idolized Jimi Hendrix and the Rolling Stones, and fledgling writers devoted to Richard Brautigan and Kurt Vonnegut.

That next summer of 1967 a surprise awaited me in Evanston. On the evening of my first night back home, my father announced that, "You have to get up early tomorrow. I got you a job for the summer with the city. You're going to be a garbageman." He'd volunteered me for the last job in the world I would have chosen. But I knew, as he knew, that I couldn't just sit idle for the summer, so I set my clock early and rode with him down to the city yard—he was employed as a night watchman those days—at 6:00 A.M.

As it turned out, the older men I worked with on the trucks that summer knew and respected my father, and they gladly extended their friendship to "Benny's boy." Naturally, the work was hard. In those days garbagemen walked from house to house with a huge, plastic tub, which they filled to the brim with waste, then swung on their backs as they tramped down alleys in ninety-degree heat. After a few weeks of getting used to maggots at the bottom of cans, my clothes soaked by sewage, and stumbling on the occasional dead rat, I began to enjoy this job. I was outside doing physical work—not cooped up in an office—and I certainly didn't mind getting off work in the early afternoon. If we finished too early, we'd buy some brew, park the truck in the shade, then cool off and shoot the breeze until quitting time.

It was on one of those afternoons that another SIU student working on the garbage trucks told me about his friend who'd enrolled in a martial arts school in Chicago. He told me that at this place, Chi Tao Chuan of the Monastery, the teaching was so wickedly effective that when his friend was attacked on the street after only two weeks of studying at the "kwoon" (training hall) he responded with moves that killed his assailant on the spot. I opened another beer and listened carefully to everything he said. I'd long wanted to systematically study a fighting art, partly because what I'd seen of Japanese karate impressed me (one high school friend started before we graduated), and partly because the Chicago area in the late 1960s was a pretty dangerous place for blacks and "longhairs" like my friend Kramer, who was once briefly hospitalized by a group of blue-collar toughs who just didn't like his looks.

Later that week I called the kwoon and asked for an interview. The voice on the other end, that of the school's junior-level instructor, warned me, "You should be prepared for the unexpected. The person you think is the master here may not be; the one who looks like a beginner might be ahead of everyone else." Two of my best buddies from high school, Luther and Napolean, agreed to visit the school with me. It was, if I remember rightly, something of a trek from Evanston—first a bus ride into Chicago, then an "El" trip over to the west side, and finally a bus ride into a neighborhood that looked so run-down and rough I figured you needed to be a martial artist of something just to make it to the school's door.

We knocked and a young instructor peered through the shade over the window and invited us inside a darkly lit, below street-level room. No other students had yet arrived. He asked us to wait for the school's master. As we sat quietly on the floor, just inside the door, my eyes tracked the

room, moving from the training equipment—heavy bags and a wooden dummy—to the small, elegant Buddhist shrine where all who entered were asked to say a prayer, and on to the array of traditional Asian weapons mounted on one wall: flexible instruments such as staffs and spears, broadswords and farm implements the Chinese had found a way to use as weapons. The *feel* of this place, so meditative with its faint traces of incense in the air, so simple in its stark furnishings, struck me as exactly right for what I needed at this juncture in my life: a discipline of the body that also required an ongoing testing of the spirit.

After a few moments the school's master arrived. He was a Westerner. A middle-aged, unshaven white man dressed in a worn, black trenchcoat. He carried a wrinkled shopping bag close to his body. You might have mistaken him on the street for a homeless person. You might have thought the bag contained a bottle of Thunderbird. His student told him we'd come for an interview. He nodded, then sat down beside us. Right then I noticed that the fingers on his left hand did not bend—they'd been broken so often, he told us, that hand was useless now except as a weapon. From his bag he withdrew a long knife—I'd never seen so huge a blade before—and kept it in full view as he explained how beginners in this school *started* with black sashes to show his contempt for karate systems, where black belts symbolized achievement. After their first promotion, each of his students specialized in the fighting techniques of one of the traditional Chinese animals—tiger if you were a big guy, black panther if you were smaller but had the tiger's spirit (this was to be my style), crane if you were tall and angular, and snake if you were small, cowardly, and needed to understand how to inflict pain on others by first absorbing large doses of it yourself. The school also offered firearms and knife training taught by one of his instructors just returned from a tour in Vietnam. Something else he said, half-jokingly, was that, "You don't have to be a Buddhist to get good at this system, but it *helps.*" Napolean sat as attentively and absorbed by all this as I did. But Luther, our group's six-feet-four funny man, displayed a bit too much lip and sass that day ("I'm a lover, not a fighter" was his favorite saying), and the master interrupted his lecture without warning, and barked, "You can't train here. Get out!" Shocked as thoroughly as if he'd been slapped, Luther looked at us, then scrambled to his feet and was out the door in the time it takes to read this sentence. "You two are fine," the master said.

"You can start on Tuesday." After the interview we stepped back outside into the noise and stink of the street, and found Luther waiting for us. He was visibly sad and angry—he wisecracked all the way home about the school's master, but he was pleased Napolean and I would try this out together. Unfortunately, on Tuesday when the instructor led us through muscle-banging calisthenics and introduced us to a "horse-riding" stance that sent waves of pain through muscles in our bodies where we didn't even know we *had* muscles, Napolean decided kung-fu (the word means "hard work") was not for him and dropped out. Thus, I was alone. I decided, however, that since I'd started I'd see this through.

That summer saw me hauling garbage every morning until my back begged for mercy. Nights, I'd make the trek to the kwoon. In every respect, it was an early martial arts studio, one that predated the rules of safety found now in most schools; it was devoted less to learning elegant forms and tournament competition than to animal-like fighting that involved its practitioners forcing themselves into a nearly trance-like state. I remember learning stances, the proper ways to strike and kick, and an exercise that required us to throw 45 punches to the front, side, and back in the space of 10 seconds. The master lectured often on principles of fighting and, just as often, on what he thought genuine manhood was all about. No one sparred with safety equipment. We were told that if an intruder came into the school and wouldn't leave we should kill him—we were within our legal rights to do so since he would be trespassing. There, in that studio, the students had the seriousness of monks (some of them planned to start a monastery for the school in South America), and the master expected total commitment of one's life to the school. Often I wondered if I'd exit the studio alive. For example, I stuck around one evening after class to watch a promotion test. The students up for promotion fought their instructors at sparring time. I watched one beginner after another struck down—and one knocked unconscious—when they got a little too eager to score against those superior to them in rank. And I knew, with growing anxiety, that my own promotion test was only two months away in the fall. I was dead certain I'd be injured. Returning to SIU in September, I swore to do everything I could to prepare myself for that night.

I barely remember the start of my second year in college. What I *do* recall is leaving my fourth-floor dormitory room late each evening, slipping down into the basement with a towel, and clearing away furniture to work out in a musty storage room. Every night I religiously went through my routine—offensive and defensive techniques—until I was drenched with sweat. I systematically worked on that exercise of throwing 45 punches in 10 seconds by checking myself against a stopwatch, and brought down my initial speed from 15 seconds to 2 and at last 3 seconds *below* what was required a week or two before the promotion test was scheduled. I felt ready when I returned to Evanston. I slept at my parents' home the night before, then lugged my suitcase down to the kwoon, intending to catch the last train to Carbondale by 10:00 P.M. after the test was over—that is, if I was in any condition to catch a train.

By some great, good fortune the school's master had rethought these tests after the injuries that occurred two months earlier. This time beginners fought beginners. My memory may be tricking me, but it seems we fought *all* evening long for the master's pleasure; he wanted everyone to try out everyone else. We sparred two against one; we kept going until nearly every student was too tired to stand. Apparently, he liked the way I moved—"Pa Kua!" he shouted, winking at his instructors (he was referring to another fighting system I knew nothing of at the time)—and when at last we sat in a circle, dripping sweat, working to steady our breathing, he awarded me and another SIU student the only "double" promotions to blue sash given that evening.

I'm at a loss to explain how I felt, at nineteen, as we received our membership cards and congratulations. The room was aglow. Though tired in every cell, my body felt transparent; my mind, clear as spring water. I couldn't have cared less if I missed my train and spent all night roaming downtown Chicago—I just *wanted* someone to jump me—before the night train at 8:00 A.M. I count this as one of the best nights of my life, a rare kind of rite-of-passage that showed me, as a young man, something about my capacity for discipline, enduring pain, and pushing myself beyond my expectations.

During holidays I returned to Chi Tao Chuan of the Monastery for lessons. The master started me on a 1,000-move set, one I could work on when I was away at college. But the 300-mile commute made training there difficult. Slowly, I eased into working out with a karate club on campus, won promotions easily, and decided to change styles because this one was nearby. As with the previous

Gee, I'll bet you're glad to be out of the ghetto.

They're really a bunch of great fellers.

Pleased to meet you. I'm being treated for
a Toussaint L'Ouverture complex.

A sampling of unpublished cartoons

year, drawing and philosophy absorbed virtually all my free time when I was not in class.

My second summer home found me again working the garbage trucks in early June. A few days after being back in Evanston, as I was reading Nietzsche's *Beyond Good and Evil,* Luther and Napolean dropped by to razz me for not having a date. But I knew something else was on their minds—they were grinning and acting goofier, it seemed to me, than usual, as if waiting for the other one to spring a secret on me. After several evasive looks and elbowing each other, Napolean said, "Have you met Joan?" I shook my head, no. "Who the hell is Joan?" They traded off telling me the story of the latest "fox" they'd found. Joan New was a student at National College of Education in Evanston and was staying over the summer with Luther's two cousins, Josephine and Martha, girls I'd gone to high school with and loved like family; they rented the apartment above Luther's family. Naturally, Luther had made his suavest play for Miss New. She iced him instantly. *That,* I thought, spoke volumes about her character. I put Nietzsche aside, and decided okay—okay, since they were pulling me toward the door, I'd meet Joan for their sake and so they'd leave me alone. Really, all I wanted that evening was to say hello to Luther's cousins.

We traveled the few blocks to Luther's house. I walked in behind my two oldest friends. His cousins squealed when they saw me, "Chuckie!" We did our round of hugs. Just off to our left, sitting on the sofa, was a woman whose smile was brighter than a sun going nova. Oh yes, I tried to stay calm. I tried to act casual. But something way back in my brain said, *This is it. You don't have to look anymore.* Before the evening was over I'd asked her out. However, as luck would have it, my first car—a Corvair convertible my father bought secondhand for me—was in the shop. I cancelled that first date and made another. Somehow *that* fell through, too, and I was certain this girl was going to give up on me as being hopelessly disorganized. By the third attempt we were, thank heaven, in each other's company. In fact, we spent nearly every night that summer going to movies and art museums in the Loop, gospel concerts (her idea, not mine), picnics, and parking on the beach near Northwestern University.

I've always felt there was more than coincidence to our meeting in the summer of 1968. We were both twenty. Furthermore, we were born exactly seven days apart (I'm older by a week). For all I know, we were conceived at exactly the same moment only forty minutes from each other, though Joan's south Chicago—Bigger Thomas country—was far different from my sleepy, suburban Evanston. She and her two brothers and three sisters lived in Altgeld Gardens, a housing project where murder and theft were, she told me, too ordinary to get overly excited about. Her mother died when she was six, thus Joan never knew her. Instead, her grandmother, a devoutly Christian woman who lived in a walk-up apartment with no water, raised Joan and her sisters into young women who were all the more stunning and mature to me because they, as a family, had remained strong and loving in an environment that can only be described as an urban battlefield. She didn't drink or smoke, curse or screw around. When we met she'd almost given up on black men and was settling into the thought of being single for the rest of her life. She was educated, extremely independent and, though kind toward everyone, had one of Hemingway's "built-in shit detectors." More than anything else that summer—and I didn't know if we had a future beyond one summer—I wanted to make her happy, to see as often as I could her disarmingly gentle smile, and hear her easy laughter (her sense of irony was comparable to my own). My parents took to her immediately, especially my father, who seemed to see in Joan something of himself—frugality, a lack of pretense and, yes, unshakable morality.

I missed Joan sorely after I returned to school. In her absence, I wrote poetry for her (which Kramer put to music for me), managed to sneak her image or name into the cartoons I published that year, and for her birthday I did her portrait in oil. "It looks like a big, color cartoon," my friends observed. And they were right.

That same year I attended a public reading at SIU by Amiri Baraka (né Leroi Jones), the poet and principal theoretician for the Black Arts Movement. He appeared onstage in a dashiki, flanked by two scowling attendants who watched the crowd as closely as if they were members of the Secret Service. For nearly an hour Baraka read poetry and lectured. He took no questions from whites in the audience, and he repeated a message that hit me as forcefully as John Howie's lectures had two years earlier. He said, "Take your talent back to the black community." At that moment I thought he was talking to *me.* I had been publishing as a cartoonist/illustrator for three years, but in late 1968 I was starting to feel that my work was growing stale; the excitement and thrill of discovery was missing—I was only doing "assignments" for others, selling one-page scripts to a company called Charlton Comics (they bought my high school story "Rendezvous" and had their own artist illustrate it), and teaching a cartooning class at SIU's "Free School." I wondered: What if I directed my drawing and everything I knew about comic art to exploring the history and culture of black America? In 1968 we had only a handful of black cartoonists at work—Ollie Harrington, who was then living in east Berlin; Morrie Turner, who did "Wee Pals"; and Walt Carr, a staff artist at Johnson Publishing Company in Chicago. But no one was generating books about black cultural nationalism, slavery, or African-American history.

I walked home from Baraka's lecture in a daze. I sat down before my drawing board, my inkwell, my pens. I started to sketch. I worked for a solid week, cutting my classes. The more I drew and took notes for gag-lines, the faster the ideas came. After seven days I had a book, *Black Humor*. My only problem was I didn't know where to send it. In the spring of 1969 I showed it to the editors at the *Daily Egyptian*, but they were as baffled as I was about who might want this work. On the other hand, they did have something to offer me that year—an internship as a reporter on the *Chicago Tribune* for the summer.

And before the end of the school year something else came along that broke my spell of "dryness." During spring term on a day when I was bored, I wrote a letter to the local PBS station, WSIU-TV, asking if they'd be interested in my hosting a "how-to-draw" series for them. I never expected them to reply. Yet, they did, and asked me in to talk about this project. WSIU, a small station, was looking for an inexpensive series it could feed to other PBS stations around the country. This idea, they said, looked like a possibility. All they needed was two cameras, a drawing table, and me behind it. Scott Kane, the director, came up with a title for the show, "Charlie's Pad," which I wasn't exactly crazy about, but I thought, what the hell, it's cute.

Regardless, I *was* nervous about appearing before a camera for the first time. Kramer, who'd moved out of the dorm and had his own apartment, agreed to let me use it—and his expensive tape equipment—one weekend when he was out of town. I holed up at his place from Friday night until Sunday afternoon, living on egg sandwiches and coffee, and reading a text I'd written over and over into his tape machine; I replayed it, studied my mistakes, then kept going over it for thirty hours until I felt I sounded smooth enough to pass the audition WSIU-TV wanted me to do. Although that test was choppy, they felt I'd be communicative enough to pull off fifty-two fifteen-minute installments on every aspect of cartooning from composition to perspective. My "bible" for the series was Lariar's old lessons from my high school days. "We'll start shooting next fall," Kane told me, "when you come back from summer break."

At the *Chicago Tribune* I worked on that newspaper's "Action Express" public service column under editor James Coates. The column had a big, white van that we drove around Chicago, stopping in places like the south side, where I (being only one of two blacks on the *Trib*), would ask neighborhood people, like members of the Black Stone Rangers, what problems they had and how the paper might address them. Oftentimes, though, we invented our own questions for the column when readers didn't provide the kinds of queries that interested us. For example, I dreamed up a few about black history ("What can you tell me about Marcus Garvey's back-to-Africa movement?"). All in all, this was a great summer: evenings with Joan as we flew around the city in my Corvair, and days on the newspaper (instead of hauling garbage), where I had an eventful discussion with their book editor, Bob Cromie.

His office groaned with stacks of books sent to him for review. How I wound up there, I can't say, but I found myself standing beside him with the manuscript for *Black Humor*, asking his advice about where to send it. He suggested John H. Johnson down the street at *Ebony*. With his recommendation, I dropped off the book, and before the summer was over they'd accepted it for publication in 1970. What do I recall from that trip to his company? Only fragments come to me—Mr. Johnson, a trim, polished man, treating me kindly in his office overlooking Michigan Avenue, and laughing out loud at some of the cartoons. Oh, and this: the odd feeling that five years after dreaming about seeing my name on the spine of a book it was actually about to happen.

All my drawing between 1966 and 1969, and the moving back and forth between two departments—philosophy and journalism—made it inevitable that I would need a fifth year to graduate. However, Joan was ready to finish in June 1970. I nervously proposed, a sort of proposal-in-reverse. We'd both be twenty-two years old and penniless, I said. But I wanted to get married. Yet, and yet:

"I'm determined to be an artist," I said, "and that means I'm probably going to have it rough, and I don't want to take you through that. Maybe we should wait until I'm more secure." And her reply?

"But if we wait until you're successful, we may *never* get married."

I had to admit that she had a point. We decided to plan for a June 14 wedding, two days after her graduation.

Back in Carbondale, I resumed classes and started the work of shooting three installments (once a week) for "Charlie's Pad." More publications followed, plus I was invited by a friend in philosophy, a black master's degree student named Tom Slaughter, to serve as a discussion-group leader for a black history survey course offered by the newly formed Black Studies department.

And then came the U.S. action in Cambodia.

Demonstrations were everywhere on campus that year. My political cartoons for the *Egyptian* had grown so archly political in their call for revolution that my editor cancelled a series of panels and told me to "concentrate on everyday things." By spring war protesters took to the streets, their special target on campus being the Vietnam Studies Center, which some people believed was doing research for the government. A curfew was established, one I broke with three friends, and for my trouble I received a lungful of tear gas thrown by the Carbondale police. A few days later SIU's vice president cancelled classes before the violence led to fatalities.

With the school shut down, I caught a train to Chicago and filed a story about the demonstrations at the *Tribune* (they'd made me a correspondent after I returned to school). Then I went to my parents' house to make preparations for marriage.

We had, of course, nothing in those days. Joan borrowed a wedding dress. We jerry-rigged the entire ceremony at Ebenezer A.M.E. Church. Luther was my best man; Jim Coates took pictures for us. And lots of family and friends covered the gift table four feet deep with everything they thought we would need. After the ceremony we caught a train back to Carbondale. There was no honeymoon; we both started work the next day.

Joan commenced teaching elementary school in DuQuoin, Illinois. I went to work part-time on the *Illinoisan*, where I did *every*thing to earn fifty dollars a week—news stories, interviews, wedding and obituary announcements, farm news, the police report, a column, political cartoons, and on

In a publicity photo for the "Charlie's Pad" television series, 1970

Saturday night I proofread the Sunday morning edition.

And it was at this time that I began to seriously devote myself to writing fiction.

With my emotional life focused on marriage, one published book behind me, another, *Half-Past Nation-Time*, accepted for publication, and the "Charlie's Pad" series starting its broadcast life (it would run for ten years, even in Canada), I decided to venture into another field—the novel. Over the last year a novel idea had been intruding upon my thoughts, a story about a young black man who enrolls in a martial arts school like the one I attended in Chicago, but in this story I intended to bring forth all the Eastern philosophy embodied in that experience. Because the idea would not leave me alone, I wrote the book that summer. My rate of production was ten pages a day. It was the first of what I call my "apprentice novels." And it was not good. On the other hand, I'd never organized 250 pages of anything before in my life, so I said, "Alright, I know I can always produce 250 pages. Let's try another book and in this one improve character, then plot, description, and the fusion of ideas and events."

In two years I went through six books this way. SIU was at that time on a quarter system. A quarter lasts ten weeks. For years I'd been comfortable with organizing my life in ten-week blocks. You start a class in January; you're done by mid-March. I really saw no reason why one couldn't write a novel—three drafts in all—in that time. The second novel was about the "middle passage," but in that version, which I researched while taking a course in African-American history, the white captain tells the tale in his ship's log (therefore, I was never able to get him close enough to the Africans on board to understand them). The second book was about a young black militant's conflict with his family's conservative (to him) values. And the last three novels comprised a trilogy that traced the life of a black musician from childhood until middle age; I'd intended for it to be 1,000 pages, but when I reached 949, Joan—who was having difficulty adjusting to the long hours I put in at the typewriter on our kitchen table—said, "We have to go out today and *do* something!" I agreed with her. I killed off my character on page 950, then we went out to one of Carbondale's better restaurants and had a nice meal.

By the end of the sixth book I was still working part-time on the *Illinoisan,* and preparing in the fall of 1972 for my written examinations for the master's degree in philosophy (I memorized the positions of eighty philosophers from Thales to Sartre). I was also planning a seventh novel, which I knew I wanted to be different from the first six, which were in the style of naturalistic black authors I admired: Richard Wright, James Baldwin, and John A. Williams, and also influenced by black cultural nationalism. From the start, the "philosophical novel" interested me more than any other literary tradition. My personal taste ran toward Sartre, Malraux, Herman Hesse, Thomas Mann, Ralph Ellison, Voltaire, and Herman Melville—the world-class authors who understood instinctively that fiction and philosophy were sister disciplines. Yes, there were the existential stories of Wright, the Freudian adventure of Ellison, and the beautifully transcendental fiction and poetry of Jean Toomer, but beyond these three I found little I was willing to call genuine philosophical black literature. Filling that void was what I decided to devote myself to as a writer; I had no interest in just "publishing books" because as a cartoonist with so much work in print I'd exhausted my interest in just seeing my name on things.

Nevertheless, I knew that for this new book I needed a good teacher. I'd read John Gard-

The author's wife, Joan, on the day of their wedding, June 14, 1970

ner's perennially magical *Grendel,* so one afternoon when I was skimming the *Illinoisan* and noticed an ad for his course "Professional Writing," I didn't hesitate to phone him and squeeze myself into his class. I attended that class only once. The other writers, I noticed, were all beginners, and I walked into Gardner's home, where the class met, with six book-length manuscripts under my arm. We agreed that I would simply meet him in his office when I had new chapters to show.

To shorten a long story I've told many times in other publications, John was the mentor in fiction I was looking for. He sometimes referred to himself as my "literary father" because for the first few years of our ten-year friendship I accepted his word on literature as law. And why not? No literary novelist I've known has demonstrated Gardner's dedication to the theory and practice of great fiction. He was steeped in Greek, medieval, and contemporary philosophy (unfortunately, his knowledge of the East was slight, and on the subject of Buddhism we argued hotly); a man who knew twelve languages, wrote in seventy-two-hour stretches without sleep and, given the fact that he'd been ignored as a writer for fifteen years, devoted himself to encouraging young writers everywhere. Art for him was—as it was for me—a matter of life and death; beauty was a queen we both longed to serve. With Gardner looking over my shoulder and scolding me whenever I started to go wrong, and after reading eighty books on magic and folklore, I wrote *Faith and the Good Thing* in nine months, which I thought was an incredibly long incubation period for a book. It was Gardner who slowed me down, helped me understand that 90 percent of writing is revision, and that, "Any sentence that can come out *should* come out."

I continued marketing cartoons, selling what would be my last professional drawing to *Players* magazine in 1973. I completed my master's degree with a fifty-page thesis written in a week, entitled, "Wilhelm Reich and the Creation of a Marxist Psychology." Marxism was my passion and political orientation throughout graduate school. It provided a pathway to the style of philosophy I would concentrate on for three years at the State University of New York at Stony Brook: phenomenology. As Joan and I were packing to travel to Long Island, the Gardners were leaving southern Illinois for Vermont. We would see them at different times around the country, and I would write him long, essayist letters on the nature of art until his death in a motorcycle accident in 1982, but we would never again work as closely as in those early SIU days.

By the time *Faith* was published in 1974 I was immersed in studying literary theory, and German and French phenomenology at Stony Brook, teaching a class called "Radical Thought" (everything from Marx's "1844 Manuscripts" through Mao Tse-tung), then courses in "Third World Literature" and "The Black Aesthetic" (the worst course I ever taught). I studied with professors Don Ihde, Homer Goldberg, and Jan Kott, and at night—over a period of four months—went through each word in Webster's 2,129-page *New Twentieth Century Dictionary* to build my own personal lexicon for writing. I trained at an Issinryu karate school, and began wrestling with early drafts of *Oxherding Tale*, the book I sometimes refer to as my "platform novel." The reference is to the Platform Sutra of the Sixth Patriarch, a foundational work of Buddhism. For me, *Oxherding Tale* was to be similarly foundational in that I hoped to lay the groundwork for my future fiction. After teaching, I speed-read every book in Stony Brook's graduate library on slavery, for this was to be a neo-slave narrative for the second half of the twentieth century, a fiction that would explore bondage and freedom not merely in physical and legal terms but also in ways psychological, phenomenological, sexual, and spiritual. I wanted it to be a reply to Hesse's *Siddhartha*, which I loved, and to realize my plans to thematize Eastern thought vis-à-vis the black experience, which I had not successfully done in my first "apprentice" novel.

It was the most ambitious book I had ever undertaken. On Long Island I began generating the first of 2,400 pages I would throw away to realize the 250 pages of the final manuscript. Added to which, and most important of all that year in 1975, Joan gave birth to our son, Malik. His birth was a blessing; fatherhood was a role I'd long wanted to enter into. But we were living on my $4,000 teaching assistantship! I needed a job, badly. And in philosophy during the mid-1970s jobs were becoming scarce. So when the English department at the University of Washington called to ask if I'd apply for an assistant professor position in creative writing (they'd read *Faith*), I said, yes. Before leaving Stony Brook in 1976 I passed my exams and had my dissertation topic approved—a book of phenomenological aesthetics applied to black American literature.

From the moment we arrived in Seattle I felt I'd found the region, the landscape, and the lifestyle I'd been looking for since I left Evanston. I fell to teaching those first few years with a passion for the profession I'm certain I acquired from Gardner; I split my short-story writing classes in half if too many students signed up, and taught the second class for free. Because UW's first classes for me were on the art of the short story, I found myself writing short fiction in the evenings after work—*Oxherding Tale* was still giving me trouble—as well as aesthetic essays on black fiction, articles on Gardner, and book reviews.

Then in the winter of 1977 I wrote my first docudrama for PBS, "Charlie Smith and the Fritter Tree," broadcast as the first program in the last season of the *Visions* series in 1978. The call to script this came from Fred Barzyk at WGBH's New Television Workshop in Boston. After doing a documentary on the life of the oldest living American, Charlie Smith (he died in 1979 at age 137), he needed a black writer capable of comedy set in the slavery era and the Old West, where Smith had been a black cowboy. I wrote the teleplay during the summer of 1977 and by December, we were shooting on location in New Orleans (Smith was sold there at age twelve to a Texas rancher) and little cowtowns in Texas, with actors Glynn Turman and the late Richard Ward playing Smith. This would be the first of many

Son, Malik, and daughter, Elizabeth, 1991

PBS historically based dramas I'd be called on to write in the late seventies and early eighties, among them "Booker," the first show in the *Wonderworks* series—it received both a 1985 Writers Guild Award for best script in the children's show category and an international Prix Jeunesse award. Barzyk and I would continue to do PBS projects over the years. Our most recent effort was "Fathers and Sons," a ten-minute monologue on the plight of young black males performed by John Amos as a segment for *Listen Up!,* broadcast in March 1992.

Back at Washington after the Smith show, the English department gave me early tenure in 1979. I hunkered down to work again on *Oxherding Tale* and finished it in the summer of 1980. Although I had realized all I'd hoped for in this book, New York publishers simply could not understand it. The notion of what a "black" novel was in the early 1980s was very limited indeed. Protest fiction, the overtly "political novel," or all too familiar "up from the ghetto," naturalistic fiction was in vogue and defined a narrow range of

acceptable—and commercial—black fiction. My agents, Anne and Georges Borchardt, sent it to over twenty-five publishing houses before John Gallman at Indiana University Press accepted it; to this day, Anne says that selling this difficult book—it appeared in 1982—was one of the triumphs of her career.

Once finished, though, I put that book out of mind. I took my first sabbatical, using the year away from teaching to work as one of two writer-producers for *Up and Coming,* a dramatic series about a black family produced at KQED in San Francisco by Avon Kirkland. (His most recent work is "Simple Justice," broadcast January 18, 1993, on PBS). On that production, which lasted six months, I made one of the best friends of my life, screenwriter Art Washington, who came on as the other writer-producer. (His latest picture is a black boxing drama, "Percy and Thunder," for TNT's prestigious *Writers Cinema* series.)

And it was in San Francisco that I began to train religiously again in kung-fu. I enrolled in grand master Doc Fai Wong's choy li fut studio, working out after my KQED workday was over; I began lifting weights then too, having lots of free time since Joan and Malik remained in Seattle while I holed up in an efficiency at John Muir Apartments. After more than a decade of avoiding the practice of meditation and making only a scholarly commitment to Buddhism, I fully surrendered to both in San Francisco. That decision came none too soon. While I worked on *Up and Coming,* my mother, who'd gone into Evanston Hospital for an operation, died. On top of that, Joan announced to me long-distance that we were going to have a second child.

Through that period meditation was a rock and refuge. I wrote and read a tribute to my mother at the funeral, explaining to a church packed with her friends and family how she had pointed me on the path to art. This was the only time I have seen my father cry. He is now seventy. He has never remarried. Her absence is something we have felt palpably since 1981, and it has made us closer as father and son.

I returned from the funeral to complete my time at KQED. For two weeks I was simply too gloomy and grief-stricken to do much except meditate, train at Master Wong's studio, and brood. Washington talked me through those days right up through the show's wrap-party in December. I returned to Seattle just three days before

Joan gave birth to our daughter, Elizabeth, who is named after my mother.

I shifted my choy li fut training to the recently opened Seattle branch of Master Wong's school, which kept its doors open for four years. When *Oxherding Tale* was published the English department gave me another early promotion, this one to full professor. The next summer, 1983, I began work on *Middle Passage,* reaching back to my second "apprentice" novel with the intention of doing it right this time. Over the years I'd accumulated all the research I needed on slavery. What was missing was knowledge of the sea and its literature. As I wrote the first draft over the next nine months I read everything I could find related to the subject—Homer, *The Voyage of Argo,* the Sinbad stories, all of Melville and Conrad, ships' logs from the nineteenth century, slave narratives composed by Africans who'd come to the New World on those boats, nautical dictionaries, and even one study of Cockney slang in order to individuate the voices of the sailors on board ship.

But the first draft needed more work, according to Anne Borchardt (who is always right). I suggested to her and Georges that while I redrafted the book they might offer the stories I'd been publishing since 1977 as a collection. They sold the collection, *The Sorcerer's Apprentice,* to Atheneum in 1985. As it went into production, I left Seattle for one semester to accept a visiting distinguished professorship at the University of Delaware and, since I would again be living alone for a few months, commenced work on a new book, a philosophical study, that publisher Gallman was urging me to write.

After the publication of *Oxherding Tale* I gave a reading at Indiana University. Gallman had a dinner for me, one that included some old friends, like writers Scott Sanders and John McCluskey, Jr. During dinner Gallman said that what he *really* wanted to publish was a critical book on black writing since 1970. Would *I* do this? he asked. The thought of such a book made me nervous. I toyed with the food on my plate. An unspoken rule of the book world, I knew, was that a writer shouldn't say what he honestly feels about his contemporaries, as John Gardner discovered when he published *On Moral Fiction* and angered dozens of writers with his judgments of them. But, then again, I had read the bulk of black fiction since the late 1960s. 'Tell you what,' I said. "If you'll let me write a theoretical opening, a phenomenological overview that I started when I was at work on my dissertation, I'll do the second part as a survey of black

writing. I'll provide analysis, titles, and authors for anyone who mightn't have read these works and would be interested in reading black authors other than the two or three black women being promoted right now to the exclusion of everyone else.''

Thus was conceived *Being and Race: Black Writing since 1970.* Gallman provided me with the opportunity to resurrect the two drafts I'd written after leaving Stony Brook *and* create something unusual in African-American letters: a phenomenological literary manifesto. I must confess, too, that I used the occasion of this book, which took a year and a half to write (it appeared in 1988), to provide a theoretical extension for the aesthetic position represented by *Oxherding Tale.*

If I had not been completely inundated with work before, after returning to Seattle from Delaware I found myself constantly buried. The French publisher Flammarion flew me to Paris for a week of book promotion when their edition of *Oxherding Tale* appeared in February of 1986. *The Sorcerer's Apprentice* was published that same year and became a runner-up for the 1987 Pen/-Faulkner Award (the prize went to my good friend Richard Wiley for *Soldiers in Hiding).* Added to all this, grand master Wong gave me and a longtime friend in the martial arts, Gray Cassidy, permission to resume choy li fut classes in Seattle after the demise of our original school. He named our studio "Twin Tigers." We started classes in my backyard, my carport (in winter), then secured a space at a neighborhood center, where we remain today (we have since renamed the studio "Blue Phoenix Kung-fu").

In 1987 I accepted a three-year appointment as director of the creative writing program at UW. Plus the job of serving as one of the fiction judges for the 1988 National Book Award (our choice was Pete Dexter for *Paris Trout).* It was a hectic period, these last few years of the 1980s. I worked on finishing *Middle Passage,* did interviews after the publication of *Being and Race* (and an essay based on it for *Dialogue,* a publication of the U.S. Information Agency), kept on practicing kung-fu, and made a lecture sweep for the government's Arts America program through Eastern Europe, lecturing on my work and multiculturalism. I was also one of ten writers producing a monthly book review for the *Los Angeles Times,* and now and then for the *New York Times Book Review* and the *Washington Post.*

Come summertime of 1989 *Middle Passage* was finally completed. While in Evanston visiting my father, I made a trip to my mother's grave and placed fresh flowers there. I remembered how in 1969 I'd visited a fortune-teller in Carbondale at the urging of my roommate, who swore by her—an elderly, white-haired woman named Ella Tweedy. In her home, sitting at her table on which rested a crystal ball, she'd read my palm, and said, "You have a mission. You're protected—and everyone associated with you—until it's done. It involves writing. You'll have two children, be well known for what you do, and have lots of money." At the time she said this I'd laughed. Writing? I was a cartoonist—it was all I ever thought about. But twenty years later, there at Sunset Cemetery where many of my relations were buried, I decided to commune with them for a little while: my Uncle Will, who died at age ninety-seven, my mother, and her parents. I asked their blessing for this third, difficult, philosophical novel I'd produced.

I genuinely believe my ancestors heard this prayer. The following year, as I was winding up my time as director of the creative writing program, Northwestern University courted me heavily with a job offer. My own department counteroffered with an endowed professorship, the first in the history of writing at UW. Since Johnsons have a tendency to be doggedly loyal to whoever has supported them, my family and I decided to remain in Seattle.

Two months later *Middle Passage* was nominated for the National Book Award. Contrary to what some might believe, its appearance on the "short list" did not surprise me, since I had been a judge in 1988 and had some idea of how the nominating process worked for this prize; I felt, in short, that it *had* to be nominated after the reviews the book received. Another factor was this: I felt, as many critics did, that the reading public and academic establishment was again becoming interested in that long-forgotten species, black male writers. During the late 1970s and early 1980s we had been systematically ignored. It was time, I believe many people felt, for black male novelists to be awarded a degree of recognition.

So I came to the award ceremony prepared to win. In my (rented) tuxedo pocket was a tribute to Ralph Ellison, which I told his wife Fanny I intended to read if I won. At our table, sitting with me, was my publisher and friend Lee Goerner; my agents of sixteen years, Georges and Anne; and critic Stanley Crouch. This was my way of saying thanks for the insightful *Village Voice* review he'd

written for *Oxherding Tale* in 1983, a two-page analysis that led directly to the book's purchase by Grove Press for a paperback edition. In New York, on that evening of November 27 in the Plaza Hotel—the fortieth anniversary of the NBA—the air was full of excitement in a room packed with people I'd long admired: my first editor, Alan Williams, Russell Banks, Gloria Naylor, Saul Bellow, fiction judges Catherine Stimpson, William Gass, and Paul West (who caused an unnecessary stir when he complained to the newspapers about too much ethnic diversity in the books nominated), and Terry McMillan; and the other fiction nominees: Joyce Carol Oates, Jessica Hagedorn, and Elena Castedo.

Strange to say, there was only the slightest suspense for me that evening. It seemed the ceremony had barely started, and all the nominees had walked to the stage to receive their plaques, when Stimpson announced, "The winner is *Middle Passage.*" Lee Goerner threw his napkin straight toward the ceiling. I heard Terry McMillan shout from across the room. Two chairs away from me, Crouch said, "Charles!" and gave me one of his winks. But by then I was moving toward the stage, shaking hands, pulling the tribute from my tuxedo. I asked Stimpson, "Can I have five minutes?" She

"My wife, Joan, and our pup, Casey," 1992

had no idea what I was planning to do, but said, "All right."

For an instant I was tearful and choked up while reciting the names of people I knew I had to acknowledge—my agents, my publisher, and John Gardner. Then I settled back into my teacher's mode and read the Ellison tribute. Later I learned he was pleasurably shocked by this. But there was no way I could stand before the world after receiving a prize like the National Book Award, and as only the second black man in thirty-seven years to be so honored, and simply talk about *myself.* That would have been a clear violation of Buddhist ethics. The tribute to Ellison, as I saw it then (and now), was a once-in-a-lifetime opportunity to celebrate one of the greatest authors of this century, and to remind the audience that his aesthetic vision in *Invisible Man,* so rich, so original, and inventive, is the standard by which black fiction in the future must be judged. Like the day of my marriage, the days my children were born, and that night of my first martial-art promotion, I count the experience of reading that tribute to seventy-six-year-old Ralph Ellison as one of the finest moments of my life.

It is now three years since that ceremony. For a long time I was busier than any human being has a right to be—on the road doing book promotion and lectures in America and Asia for fourteen months, sitting for over one hundred interviews, fielding more requests for writing assignments than I should have been able to handle, turning out television and motion-picture scripts, and teaching, teaching, teaching. So many people have asked me, "Has your life changed?" When I reply, "Not really," they're usually disappointed, though that is the truth. Quantitatively life changed, for my workload increased about tenfold. Qualitatively, though, it is the same life and labor—that of devoting myself to a genuinely philosophical black American fiction—it was two decades before.

Charles Johnson with Ralph Ellison at the 1990 National Book Award ceremony

BIBLIOGRAPHY

Fiction:

Faith and the Good Thing (novel), Plume, 1974.

Oxherding Tale (novel), Indiana University Press, 1982.

The Sorcerer's Apprentice: Tales and Conjurations, Atheneum, 1986.

Middle Passage (novel), Plume, 1990.

Other:

Black Humor by Charles R. Johnson (cartoons), Johnson Publishing Co., 1970.

Half-Past Nation-Time (cartoons), 1972.

Being and Race: Black Writing since 1970 (criticism), Indiana University Press, 1988.

Also author with Ron Chernow of *In Search of a Voice,* in "The National Book Week" lecture series.

Frederick Manfred
1912-

BRIEF SKETCHES OF THOSE
WHO HAVE HELPED ALONG THE WAY

One summer day in 1916 my aunt Kathryn invited me to come along with her to the northwest corner of our grove and to go sit in the shade of a huge cottonwood tree. Something was going on in the house which I was not supposed to witness. Soon we were sitting on the green grass. There was a soft breeze coming in from the west, and it was soothing for both of us. Aunt Kathryn had taken her little canvas work satchel with her, and soon she took out some tatting she was working on and began adding to a piece of delicate handmade lace. Holding a web of thread with outspread fingers of her left hand, she began weaving an ivory shuttle in and out of the web.

Left to myself I was soon lost in exploring the world around me. I was one of those who liked looking into things, in the trees, in the bushes, in the grass. I noticed an ant emerging from a small hole in a tiny mound of dried dirt curdles. I followed it through the grass, watched it climb up the cottonwood tree, watched it come down with a shining drop of sap held in its mandible, saw it vanish down into the hole in the tiny mound of dirt curdles.

Aunt Kathryn had apparently watched me the whole while and, letting her tatting down in her lap, she remarked, mostly to herself, "I wonder what's going to become of you, Freddie." And she shook her head to herself with a little smile. I was her first nephew.

Aunt Kathryn was living with us at the time. She taught all eight grades in a small country schoolhouse a quarter of a mile away. She'd graduated from the Iowa State Teachers College in Cedar Falls, Iowa. She'd also had some poems published in Sioux City, Iowa, in green leather with gold lettering: *Poems* by Kathryn Feikema. My mother Alice was proud of being related to a writer, and she'd placed the green book on our parlor table. It sort of made up for the fact that my

Frederick Manfred

father, Feike Feikes Feikema VI, usually known as Frank Feikema, couldn't read or write. (We later discovered he had dyslexia. Yet he was a fine musician, playing the fiddle and the accordion at square dances.)

When I next watched several red ants attacking a white grubworm, she turned to me again and asked, point-blank, "Really, Freddie, what do you want to become some day?"

I had vaguely thought of becoming an engineer on a train, and a great baseball player, and

245

maybe even a farmer. I was only four years old so what did I know. So I asked, "What's the best thing to be?"

She tatted on a few moments. Then finally, sighing, she said, "Well, I'd rather be a poet than a president."

That remark of Aunt Kathryn's has haunted me all of my life. How wonderful. Who was president when Homer composed the *Iliad* and the *Odyssey?* Who was president when Cervantes wrote *Don Quixote?* Who was president when De Camoëns wrote *The Lusiads?* It turns out Aunt Kathryn was wonderfully right. Systems of philosophy, of religion, of politics, etc., may come and go, but a good poem and a good story have a chance to last the human forever.

In the evenings Aunt Kathryn read to me from *Mother Goose's Tales, Tom Thumb, Peter Pan, Cinderella,* and Hans Christian Andersen's *Fairy Tales.* After a while, watching where her eyes were looking at the page, I began to make out what the letters meant and soon I was reading ahead of her. I had to be careful not to let her catch on that I was beginning to read or she'd quit reading to me.

Sometimes my mother Alice, when she wasn't too busy cooking, darning, cleaning house, feeding the chickens, or minding my younger brother Edward, read to me too. Several times she read stories in Dutch to me, and the one I liked best in Dutch was *Hans Brinker; or the Silver Skates.*

All those stories woke up my father, and he began regaling us with stories about when he was a boy, moving to all sorts of places in America because of the wanderlust nature of his father, my grampa. Once, he said, when they really were broke in Missouri, he and Aunt Kathryn, when they were little children, had to take a sack and go scrabbling through the garbage cans of the rich for morsels of food; possibly even discarded clothes. He said that once he and Aunt Kathryn ran into a hoop snake and that they were lucky to get away alive. As a little boy I had trouble believing that story, especially "the hoop" part. To emphasize the point, Pa said the hoop snake takes its tail in its mouth and then, instead of crawling toward one, it rolls toward one and only the fast runners can get away. When I looked at Aunt Kathryn to see how she was taking that tale, she, with a little insider smile, nodded, yes, it was true.

When I was five going on six I started going to a country school a mile and a half away. Because I could already read a little, my first teacher had me take both the primary grade and the first grade at the same time. Her name I've forgotten. But I did

"Wedding picture of my parents, Frank and Alice (née Van Engen) Feikema," 1911

notice years later that she wrote in a note to the school superintendent of Lyon County, Iowa, that number sixteen (Fred Feikema) had not only read all the stories required in those two grades, but also all the stories in the second and third grade readers.

The next year Aunt Kathryn came to teach in that school, and she in turn also brought various books to school for me to read over and above class requirements: *Black Beauty, The Rover Boys, The Speedwell Boys.* By that time she also felt I was ready for Lewis Carroll's *Alice's Adventures in Wonderland.*

I got along pretty well with Aunt Kathryn until the day I overheard her tell my father and mother, "What we've got to do is push Freddie down and Eddie up, to make them even smart." Well, I loved Eddie, he was my first playmate. But he was a slow learner. And it wasn't until many years later it developed that he, like Pa, had dyslexia. Edward too had a lot of music in him—for years he sang baritone in a yearly rendition of Handel's *Messiah*. So in a way Aunt Kathryn was right in wanting to push Eddie up. Teachers of those days hadn't learned how to handle students with that learning disability.

When I was in the fifth grade my mother decided that her children should get instruction in the Christian Reformed Church grade school. So we moved closer to Doon, Iowa, our hometown. Pa bought us a horse and built a cab on the running gear of an old buggy and we, Eddie, my next brother Floyd, and I, started driving to school every day. Then in the sixth grade I came upon one of my finest teachers, a man, Principal Onie Aardema, a college graduate. He soon saw that I could finish off the class assignment in a few minutes and then sit there restless. He caught me once dipping the blond pigtail of a Henrietta in my inkwell. Instead of punishing me, he asked me after school one day if I liked to read. Of course I said yes. And then he too began bringing books to school for me to read: *The Clansman, The Arabian Nights, What Every Boy Should Know about the Stars*, various novels of Zane Grey, *Girl of the Limberlost*, and *When a Man's a Man*.

One day in late April of 1924, the entire upstairs room of the sixth, seventh, and eighth grades decided that Principal Onie was too strict, and they rebelled, and en masse left the school grounds and ran off to an abandoned gravel pit a quarter of a mile to the west. The boys shouted that they were going to play games like dock-the-rock and tin-can football. The girls claimed that now they were free to gossip about all the scandals in their church.

All but Freddie Feikema. I decided to stay in the classroom with Principal Onie and read the books he'd brought me.

Principal Onie was somewhat upset though he did manage a pinched smile. He asked me, "Are you sure you don't want to join your friends in their revolution?"

I shook my head. "I don't see any fun in throwing stones at tin cans. Or eating slumgullion with the railroad bums who've made their home in the abandoned sandpit."

"Well, there's no use holding the classes you were in. So what are we going to do with you here with me?"

"I'm gonna read. I can finish Grey's wonderful baseball story *The Southpaw*. And then I can start *The Riders of the Purple Sage*."

"Your friends are going to hate you."

"Teach, they've already started doing that. They're jealous that I can hit so many homeruns during recess. And they're mad at me for finally raising my hand when you ask tough questions."

"Why do you suppose they have that attitude?"

"They get it from their pa and ma. Who don't read."

"How do you know that?"

"When we visit them I always look around in their homes to see if I can find a good book to read. And they never have any books at all."

"And your folks do read?"

"Pa don't. He can't read. But Ma reads for herself and she reads for Pa. Every Sunday evening."

"Ah. Now I know how to handle the school board when they meet to deal with this school-kid revolution."

"Another thing, Prof. You spent a lot of time praising the Americans for revolting against King George of Great Britain. Especially when you told us about that wonderful Boston tea party."

"Yes, I guess that had something to do with it."

Later on that summer, I got around to where I admired the spunk of those three classes to revolt. Christian Reformed Church kids were always expected to be very obedient. "No complaints now!" "Shut up!" "Behave yourself!" "Don't serve the Devil!"

In May just before five of us, Nellie Brower, Ruby DeJong, Mynard Van Tol, Jessie Zylstra, and myself, were to graduate from the eighth grade, Principal Onie visited my father and mother to tell them that it would be a sin if they didn't make sure I went on to high school; if not to the Doon High School, then to the new church-supported Western Academy in Hull, Iowa. I was too gifted, he said, to be lost just working as a hired man somewhere for some illiterate dolt of a farmer. He said God could use their young boy somewhere in the Christian world. With an apologetic look at my father, my mother agreed. Ma said, "Perhaps he can be a Christian schoolteacher like you, Mr. Aardema."

"Or a *domeny*," Pa said, "pounding the dust out of the Bible on the pulpit."

I didn't say much at the time. Teacher? Never. Preacher? That was even worse. By that time I'd pretty well made up my mind to be a poet

*Kathryn Feikema, the author's paternal
aunt and early teacher*

or a writer of some kind. I never told the folks how
on several occasions Teacher Onie had intercepted
little ditties I'd written to the pretty girls in the
three top grades: Irene Levering, Nellie Brower,
and Nellie's younger sister Elizabeth, who in the
game of pom-pom-pull-away could outrun everybody. Elizabeth was always the one we couldn't
catch. I was following in the footsteps of my poet
aunt Kathryn.

Principal Onie also told my folks that he was
entering my name for a scholarship that Western
Academy was offering to bright grade-school
scholars in the church. So they wouldn't have to
pay tuition the first year.

Within a month of attending classes at Western, I discovered another wonderful teacher
in Garritt Roelofs. It made up for how lonesome I
felt for my younger brothers in faraway Doon

some eight miles away. Here I was twelve years old
in the freshman class where the average age was
fifteen. Many of them were young men who
decided they'd rather go to school, learning algebra and public speaking, than pitch hogshit out of
pig barns. And there were several older women
who saw that they were headed for the life of an
old maid, and they'd rather turn out to be a
respected country schoolteacher somewhere.

Roelofs had also graduated from Calvin College in Grand Rapids, Michigan, and he taught
history. My first class with him was Ancient
History. Besides being a well-read man, he was also
an excitable man. We used to talk among ourselves
about how suddenly the place was full of electricity
when he entered his classroom. Even before he
leaned against his blond oak desk, he was describing life in Athens for us. Many was the time, when
listening to him, I was suddenly transported to the
streets of Athens, and I could see people walking in
their sandals, and could smell the olives they'd
been eating, and could see the sweat pouring down
the faces and bodies of the marathon runners, and
could see Pericles hugging his love Aspasia after
he'd defended her for impiety with tears in his
eyes, and could see squat ugly-headed Socrates
quietly demolishing the theories of Alcibiades and
how the Spartan king Leonidas with a few hundred
men defeated the vast Persian army of Xerxes at
the Greek pass of Thermopylae. When we left the
class, all of us were exalted enough to float along a
half a foot off the floor.

In my junior year at Western, 1926–1927, I
had to take a job for my board and room. I went to
work for Henry Westra, who owned a dairy on the
south edge of Hull. Every morning, starting at five
o'clock, hired hand Peter Van Batavia and I began
milking twenty-six cows. The milking machine still
hadn't been invented. Pete and I each milked
thirteen cows by hand. Westra, the boss, hovered
nearby to make sure that I at least milked the cows
dry. Sometimes he got himself a milk stool and
checked my cows by stripping them dry between
his thumb and forefinger. If a cow wasn't emptied
completely, she soon quit producing milk. The
first month I had very sore forearms; this became
especially true when several times I milked all
twenty-six cows alone because Pete and the boss
got involved in putting up alfalfa hay before it
rained. After two months my forearms began to
resemble the forearms of Popeye the Sailor Man.
(Even today when I shake hands with men, I have
to be careful not to hurt them with my grip.)

In the afternoon, the moment school let out, I had to hurry home across town to start the milking again. It took an hour and a half to finish the milking and bottle all the milk.

Every morning at seven o'clock, having finished the bottling and a hurried breakfast, Westra and I began delivering the milk around town in Hull. We tried to finish by eight-thirty so I'd have time to change clothes and hurry off for the Academy.

Saturdays, between the morning and evening milkings, we hauled manure into the nearby fields, fixed fences, put up silage in the silos, and curried the cows. Sundays we were expected to go to the two church services between the milkings. There was never any time off. Fellow students almost became strangers to me. The worst was, my marks suffered. There never was any time for assigned outside reading. And never any time for reading just for the fun of it.

Finally Professor Roelofs stepped in. One Saturday he drove out to see my father and mother. He wanted to know if my parents were serious about my education. Of course they were serious, especially my mother. "In that case," he said, "you better take that boy away from Westra. Not only has your Fred's marks been going down, he's in danger of flunking all his classes. Furthermore, you better think of your son's health. Mr. Westra is overworking him. Your boy is only just fifteen years old, yet Mr. Westra expects him to do the work of a man in his twenties. Or thirties. Fred is just a boy. Not that he has complained. He's tough. But it's wrong to let him stay there with Westra any longer. Can't you borrow some money somewhere for his board and room so he can concentrate on his studies for the rest of this year so he can bring his marks up and not flunk any of his classes?"

It was done. Pa drove over and peremptorily removed me from Westra's dairy. All Pa said was, "I want my kid to have an education and not just to learn how to become an overworked hired hand." Pa found a place for me to live in town. It was next door to where Professor Roelofs lived. And it wasn't long before I began visiting him. Some nights I became the Roelofs's baby-sitter, and after I'd finished my class assignments I began to browse through his wonderful library. When he learned that I loved to read, he began to pick out certain books that I should know. One of them was John Lothrop Motley's *Rise of the Dutch Republic.* Every time I finished one of his books, Professor Roelofs would ask me in a gentle yet firm inquiring

way what I got out of it. "Fred, my boy, once you've read a book with some intelligence and with some attention, what's in that book will belong to you forever. They can stick you in jail but they can never take that away from you. It's yours."

A couple of times I was invited to have supper with the Roelofs family. One time, after Mr. Roelofs had closed the meal with a prayer of thanks, his son asked, "Who's this Inspireus, Dad? Is he one of those Greek heroes you talk about?" A wonderful, excited smile warmed over Professor Roelofs's face. "No, son. Yes, I guess it does sound like the name of a Greek hero. But the words 'inspire us' mean that we ask God to guide us into doing good deeds."

Some years later Roelofs ran for state senator and won. Then still later he became the secretary for Henry A. Wallace, U.S. Secretary of Agriculture in Washington, D.C. And then, still much later, as my various novels started to appear, he wrote me many fine notes about how pleased he

"With three of my brothers: (from left) Floyd, Ed, me, and (in front of Floyd) Tommy"

was that at least on me his teaching hadn't been wasted. Garritt Roelofs was a man to inspire many of us.

After graduating from the twelfth grade in 1928, my mother decided that I was too young to go live in Grand Rapids, Michigan, where our church college, Calvin, was located. "Son, you're too young for the fleshpots of the big city. Also, your father has moved us to a large farm, a half section, and he'll need your strong back until your younger brothers grow old enough to help him."

During the next two years, I added almost six inches to my height, from six-two to six-eight; I joined the Christian Reformed Church at my mother's urgent request; then my mother died because of rheumatic fever; and I found some books to read in our doctor's home, Jack London complete and James Fenimore Cooper complete.

It seemed to me that Cooper mistakenly had the idea that the use of polysyllabics and complex sentences made for good writing. I found that if I began his novels some hundred pages into the text, they then became readable. His style became simplified when he began to describe scenes of action, of war, and love. And it seemed to me that London, though more readable, still didn't give me what I then called "the really real." Really good writing should be so real that one should actually be able to smell sweat, and manure, and wild roses. I had continued to write ditties to my beautiful cousin Alice, and it came to me, since we Feikemas were natural storytellers, that I should try to write stories in which I'd give the reader the "really real" of life on the farm as well as in small towns.

I knew my father didn't like the idea that I wanted to be a writer. He already complained endlessly that I was wasting my time reading Cooper and London, as well as reading the *Complete Shakespeare* in a limp red leather edition (which I'd bought with cornpicking money earned working for a week at a neighbor's). So I constructed a crude desk up in the haymow near a small window, out of sight of anyone in the yard. But the trouble was my handwriting was wretched, almost unreadable. It happened that the third baseman on our town team learned about my dream of becoming a writer. He was the agent at the Great Northern depot and he had a typewriter. He offered to let me use the typewriter. Using the hunt-and-peck system I slowly typed up the stories. Larson gave me some old manila envelopes and I began sending the stories off to the *Saturday Evening Post* and *Collier's*. Of course they came

back to me when I included return postage, and always with a formal printed rejection slip.

Some of my former student friends at Western Academy, remembering that I'd always dreamed of going off to Calvin College with them, got in touch with me in the summer of 1930. I had a ride if I wanted it for five dollars. Edward Bierma, pre-law student, had bought an old Ford sedan for one dollar, and dozens of old tires for another dollar at the Sioux Center dump, and he had rewired the engine and put in new spark plugs.

My father had remarried but his new wife was totally against my going to college. She felt that I should help my father make a lot of money on the half section of land. But for once my father approved of me going. He brought me to Perkins Corner where Bierma and three others were to meet. He greeted the fellows, started to laugh when he saw all the tires and suitcases tied on top of the ancient gray sedan, and then, shaking hands with me, he said, "I was always hoping you'd use your brains to show me how to really farm. But I see you have your heart set on better things, so I'm letting you go." I noticed something odd and crinkly in the palm of his calloused hand, as well as noticed it was a peculiar kind of handclasp. Ah. There was something he was giving me which he didn't want the other four fellows to see. A couple of hours later, stopping for gas and a pit stop, in a country privy behind the gas station, I had a look at the crinkly thing. After the handshake, I'd thrust my hands in my pants pockets, which was typical of farm boys who don't know what to do with their work clumsy hands, and I managed to leave the thing hidden in my pocket. Well, well. Pa had given me a fifty-dollar bill. I'd never seen one before. Somehow Pa had managed to sneak it out of the house after getting it from the local Doon banker, who was all for me going to college.

It took us three days to drive eight hundred plus miles to the Calvin College dormitory in Grand Rapids, Michigan. We couldn't go much faster than thirty miles an hour. Also, we had a half-dozen flat tires, lost one wheel once going down a steep hill near Dubuque (the wheel actually beat us to the bottom of the hill); somehow with a pair of pliers and bailing wire and an old crescent wrench we got the wheel back on.

Luckily for me, with us in the old wreck of a car was a pre-seminarian senior, Chris Gesink, who saw how lost I suddenly was in the big city. He offered to help me with my class schedule. He saw to it that I'd get rid of half of my prerequisites the

Eighth grade graduation picture of the Doon Christian School: (from left) Jessie Zylstra, Nellie Brower, Frederick Feikema, Principal Onie Aardema, Ruby DeJong, and Mynard Van Tol. "I was twelve; the rest were fifteen years old," 1924.

first year. But there was one class he insisted I had to take the first semester. It was Logic with Professor W. Harry Jellema. "Most Calvin students become fiends with their logic. And if you don't take it, they'll beat you in argument every time. Also, logic will help you come to grips with the study of history, and German, and poetry . . . with everything that the human mind creates."

Logic with Jellema was tough. All those days on the farm and jollifying uptown in Doon, I'd never heard such language as I found in my logic textbook, or for that matter what Mr. Jellema used in class. It was almost a foreign language for me. It was when I began to use syllogisms to explain a problem such as how to repair a broken cultivator or an evener on a wagon tongue that I began to catch on. Soon too I saw the difference between induction and deduction. Deduction could be a hardheaded business, but induction often involved crafty, specious, subtle ways of going at a problem.

Taking that logic class the first semester helped me catch on to the main thrust of the study of psychology, which Jellema also taught. Soon I began to hold my own when I began to argue points with pre-law Bierma and pre-seminarian Gesink.

I was sitting late one evening at the piano in the dorm lobby picking out several tunes single-fingered, "Home Sweet Home," "Pretty Red Wing," and some of my own original tunes that reflected the sounds of life back on the Iowa farm of my father, as well as some tunes that my father liked to play on his fiddle and accordion and harmonica. I was *so* homesick for my five brothers, remembering all the games we used to play, war with corncobs, workup in farmyard baseball, wink, etc., when I noticed off to one side that a slim fellow with burning brown eyes and a silver lock had settled in a deep leather chair, listening.

I stopped plinking the piano keys, apologized for not being an accomplished pianist.

He waved that to one side. "It sounded so lonesome I just had to come down to see who was playing here."

We started to talk, about our families, about our classes, about our dreams for the future. He said he someday hoped to be a recognized historian; I said I wanted to be a writer of some kind. Soon we were talking about books we'd read; and books we should still read. And as the days and weeks went by, we both discovered we hated sham, phoney people, liars, bullshit. And we learned to trust each other, that our talks were confidential never to be repeated to others. Together we picked two tablemates for the dorm dining hall; in the beginning John DeBie and Johan Te Velde. And finally the four of us subscribed to the fat *New York Sunday Times* and the *New Republic*. Of course it didn't take long for the pre-seminarian students to sneer at us and call us the Brains Trust, a term borrowed from politics where President Franklin Delano Roosevelt had picked some brilliant men for his Brains Trust. It was from John Huizenga that I learned how to handle the sneers. Ignore them and be quietly indulgent in one's manners with the supercilious sneerers.

When I flunked freshman English, it was he who had the good counsel. "I find your talk lively and earthy. Perfectly grammatical if one accepts the Iowa syntax, just as we must accept the syntax of Mark Twain's Hannibalisms. Surely you've had near disasters on the farm and you learned how to handle them. So sink back into your mind and figure out how to outwit Miss Timmer, your teacher."

I did just that. I wasn't sophisticated enough to convince Miss Timmer that Mark Twain wrote literature so it was foolish of me to convince her that in my way what I wrote was literature too. So I decided to ape her mannerisms and her language in class, and then the moment class was over run to my room and write the next assignment, essay, sketch, poem, in her manner and her language. That worked. She passed me for both semesters. I didn't learn much about how to write my way, but I did learn what made her kind of mind tick. And it is true that if one wants to write in the daughter American language, one had better be able to write quite well in the mother English language. Or if one wants to know what a young girl you're dating is going to look like when she's forty, take a good look at her mother.

For some time I aped John Huizenga too, both his speech and his writings. He had a tendency to use a lot of heavy polysyllabic words. I got myself a

Garritt E. Roelofs, history teacher at Western Academy, Hull, Iowa, 1924

little leather notebook and jotted down all the "big words" he used as well as those I found in the *Times* and in the *New Republic* and in my college textbooks. Each day I tried to use a page of those whopper words in my talk, to the disgust of my tablemates. When John took a newspaper job as a reporter, I noticed that slowly but surely his language turned simple, Anglo-Saxon in nature. And when later I got a job as a reporter, I put aside my big-word notebook. I learned about then that that was a lesson Hemingway as a reporter had also discovered for himself.

At Calvin I ran into another person who had a lot to do with my writing. It was Helen Reitsema, a classmate. We took many classes together; often conferred on our lessons. She was a demure elfin blond beauty. She was five-foot-two; I was six-foot-nine. She was an easy *A* student. She wrote lovely poems for the college paper, the *Chimes;* the one about her deceased mother was especially haunting. She was a much better writer than I was at the time.

I continued to write occasional poetry for the *Chimes*, as well as short prose pieces. But I didn't think much of them; thought them rather fragmentary. I joined the Pierian Literary Club and to my surprise in May of my sophomore year was elected president of the club. Because of the books written by modern America writers John and Helen would mention now and then, I decided that we should write papers about them: John Dos Passos, T. S. Eliot, Hemingway, Faulkner, Edmund Wilson. It meant, besides hearing what my club mates would say about them, that I too had to read them. There was no class in which we could enroll to study them so in a sense we made up our own class requirements and assignments.

The next year Helen was elected president, and she kept up the study of modern American writers, among them Edna St. Vincent Millay. There was really no dating for Helen and myself. She'd already started dating the man she'd later on marry, so I tried desperately to respect her choice. As time went on she began to make comments to me about my effusions in the *Chimes*, none really negative, but all very helpful. She told me what caught her eye. And she told me never to give up my dream of wanting to become a writer. I was also wonderfully tempted to tell her that that dream also included her at my side. That was in vain, of course. But I began to write anguished poems about my sad plight. As I look back at it now it was almost laughable. But at the time it surely wasn't. Huizenga was quite aware of my discomfort at all the teasing I received and told me to laugh it off. "A gentleman always smiles at barking dogs and then proceeds with his evening stroll." Helen, when she became aware of it, told me she was honored with my interest in her.

During my junior year I didn't catch a ride home during Christmas vacation, but remained in the dorm to keep the furnace going and keep the hallways neat. I was the only one to remain there for two weeks, while eighty-three others had their fun at home. One morning after eating breakfast with the house mother, feeling lonesome, I began to think of what had happened the previous summer. I'd taken a job with a nearby farmer for three months. But one evening my farmer boss received a call from my father saying that he didn't feel well, that the Doon doctor said he had a case of the "milk leg," a form of prairie malaria. Could I please come home for a few days and cut down the dead-ripe oats. I did go home at that time and asked my brothers Edward and Floyd to bring me a fresh set of four horses every three hours to pull the binder (combines were invented later). There was a full moon out and I cut oats straight through for some thirty hours. There was no wind though there was a threat of rain in the air. And rain was the problem. A heavy rain would flatten the oats and Pa would lose most of the crop. At night, in the moonlight, it was very beautiful. Where I'd finished cutting, the stubbles had the color of coarse gold; where the oats was still standing, it was like a sea of gently waving tesselated bits of silver.

Sitting alone in that hollow empty dorm, I suddenly felt very lonesome for our farm, so lonesome I was moved to write about that great day of harvesting. I wrote for a full day and finally titled the sketch "Harvest Scene." When John Daling the student editor of the *Chimes* heard about the sketch, he asked to see it. And shortly later he published it.

I was very shy in those days. My best thinking, and my most eloquent dreaming, usually occurred out in the field while plowing, and I did it all with nobody around to interrupt me or to look at me.

Dr. W. Harry Jellema, philosophy professor at Calvin College, Grand Rapids, Michigan

So in class I had to look out of the window while responding to a professor's question. Once "Harvest Scene" was published, I went around behaving like a criminal, trying to avoid anybody from seeing me, slipping into my seat in classes unobtrusively as possible. And I always made it a point to sit near a window. That way I only had to worry about the faces to my right as well as the professor's face.

Early that May, our philosophy professor, Dr. Jellema, came into class one morning, placed his briefcase on his desk, went over and adjusted the ventilation, and from memory called the class roll. Then he went back to his briefcase, pulled out the latest copy of the *Chimes*, and began reading my sketch, "Harvest Scene."

I was instantly aware that everybody had started to look at me. They were all good philosophy students; so what was the professor doing reading a piece of my fiction in his class? I could feel all those wondering glances striking my right cheek. Luckily, I'd quickly frozen the expression

on my face so I wouldn't look like a goof, overweening in my sudden vanity.

Professor Jellema read the whole thing. Then he went on to explain why he'd read "Harvest Scene." "We were talking in our last class about 'prolegomenon,' 'first knowings,' or 'introductory observations.' Here in this story we are given some introductory scenes to help us understand what harvesttime means on a farm. Notice how the author made a story out of quite a complex farm operation and gradually educated us as to what it was all about. One couldn't ask for a better instance of 'prolegomenon.'"

I was astounded, of course. What? Me, a farm boy, now suddenly an embryo philosopher? What I really appreciated was that he didn't mention my name or address me personally before my peer group. High class.

But I did realize something of importance. I could write. And I probably was deeper than I might have known.

When I wrote my final philosophy exam in a blue book that semester, I penned a little note at the end of it. "Professor Jellema, how come you always give me *B*'s and not *A*'s, when I know after conferring with other classmates that I have the right answers?"

When I got the bluebook back, I found his note penned below my note. "Dear Mr. Feikema. Yes, you do have all the right answers. But you arrive at them intuitively, not philosophically. And in this class I have to grade you according to your philosophical ability."

Intuitively. Yes. I was an artist first.

"My great friend, John W. Huizenga, from college days at Calvin," 1936

Some four years later, while working as a reporter for the *Minneapolis Journal*, I visited a class taught by Meridel LeSueur. She was a well-known leftwing novelist. I'd heard that she had a kindly interest in young ambitious writers. She held her class for amateur writers upstairs in the back of Murray's Cafe, on Sixth between Hennepin and Nicollet, at lunch hour. I sat off to one side, listening to her read portions from manuscripts given to her and then making comments on the writing.

When the class was dismissed, she called me over to ask who I was and what it was that I wanted. I explained to her that I'd started a novel but didn't know if it was any good. She told me to bring it to her home. At that time I called it "Of These It Is Said." (Later on I changed the title to *The Golden Bowl*).

About a month later she called me and told me to meet her for lunch at the Stockholm Cafe. It was a joint where unemployed lumberjacks liked to visit. We found ourselves a booth and ordered a beer and a hamburger. She placed my manuscript on the edge of the table. She asked me more questions about my family background, where I was born and to what kind of people, did I have a girl friend, what was I reading, what did I dream of becoming. She was a very beautiful woman, dark hair with an oval face of dusky skin, one of nature's classically formed eternal forms. I was quite overwhelmed by her attention. But I kept waiting for her to say something about the novel I'd tried to write.

Finally, as we were paying for our luncheon Dutch treat, she picked up the manuscript and handed it to me. She said, "I'm not going to talk particulars about this. You don't need my help. You're one of those writers who shouldn't listen to anyone, who will, on his own, work out his own valid criticism. Don't become part of a clique. You are alone. So go it alone. Already your manuscript is as good as John Steinbeck's *Of Mice and Men*. And work hard and good luck."

I don't remember what my good-bye was like that noon. I do remember I walked back to the *Minneapolis Journal* and tried to write about some kind of sports event, but actually I was floating a foot off the ground for the rest of the day.

It was some four years later, after I'd stayed in a sanatorium for tuberculosis for several years, that I helped Hubert Humphrey run for mayor of Minneapolis. He lost by only a few thousand votes. The experience was an eye-opener for me. I decided to write a report on it for the *New Republic*. In it I compared Hubert to Harold Stassen, governor of Minnesota, and predicted that Hubert might possibly become president someday, but Stassen never. Hubert was warm and very bright; Stassen was cold and bright.

Robert Penn Warren, then teaching at the University of Minnesota, read the report and called me one day. He was writing a political novel (which he later entitled *All the King's Men*) and wanted to ask me about Minnesota politics. I agreed to take walks with him, with afterwards a visit to his home where he plied me with hot-buttered rum to loosen my tongue. He wanted to know if I'd ever use what I knew about Minnesota politics in a novel of my own, and I said perhaps I might but it would be a different creation from his own and he was welcome to use whatever would fit what he needed.

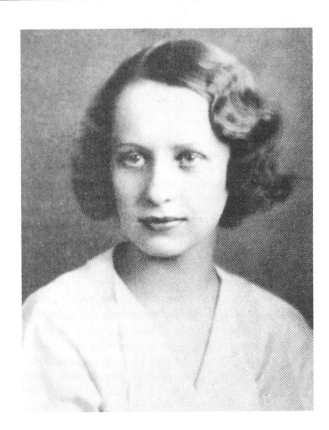

"Helen Reitsema, first love at Calvin College and still my good friend," 1934

Red Warren and I became good friends. He told me many stories about his South. He kept urging me to look up certain writers: Allen Tate, John Crowe Ransom, Donald Davidson, William Faulkner, Kenneth Burke. About Burke he remarked that he was more of a philosophical giant than a literary giant. Because of Warren's remarks about these men, I began with such little money as I had to buy their work.

I had some trouble getting into Faulkner. One noon I had lunch with Red and Russell Roth and Dan Brennan and all those three fellows did that whole noon hour was talk about Old Bill. Russell Roth was the first man to write a thesis on Faulkner which was later reprinted in the magazine *Perspectives,* and Dan Brennan as a very young man had hitchhiked down to Faulkner's home in Oxford, Mississippi, and had stayed with him for a week. There is an item in the Faulkner bibliography called the Brennan Papers. The three men laughed and laughed about some of the Old Bill stories. The one that tickled Red the most was about the funeral of Popeye who'd been shot in the forehead. During the funeral everybody got drunk, and somehow the casket of Popeye was bumped and it tipped over and hit the floor and out rolled Popeye. Warren knew the passage almost by heart:

> Popeye had worn a cap which, tumbling off, exposed a small blue hole in the center of his forehead. It had been neatly plugged with wax and was painted, but the wax had been jarred out and lost. They couldn't find it, but by unfastening the snap in the peak (of the cap) they could draw the cap down to his eyes.

I too enjoyed that passage. But on the way home as Red walked toward his car and I to my streetcar, I asked him how I might get into Old Bill. Red said, "Get Malcolm Cowley's *Portable Faulkner.*" I nodded, and turned back to Powers Book Store and bought the book. And I've been hooked on Faulkner ever since.

Maryanna Shorba Manfred, first and only wife of Frederick Manfred, 1941

On one of our walks I expressed grave misgivings about whether or not I'd ever be a published novelist. Equally grave, Warren assured me that on the basis of how well I'd written the article on Humphrey and Stassen for the *New Republic*, there was no doubt about it. Some fourteen years later, Warren wrote me a card telling me that he'd voted for my *Lord Grizzly* to receive a National Book Award. From a mutual friend I learned that he'd given my book five points and only three points for Faulkner's *A Fable*. *A Fable* won the award.

When Helen Clapesattle of the University of Minnesota Press heard that I was writing novels, she told me to get in touch with Paul Hillestad of the Webb Publishing Company in St. Paul, Minnesota. Clapesattle had written a book about the Mayo Clinic called *The Doctors Mayo* for the Press and it had become a national best-seller. I did look up Hillestad and found out he'd been publishing farm manual textbooks and had been dreaming of becoming a trade publisher of novels and poems for national distribution. By the time I met him, I'd probably had at least a hundred rejections by publishing houses in New York. After a long talk, he suggested that I bring him all of my manuscripts. I did: six different manuscript versions of the novel that eventually become *The Golden Bowl*, an early draft of *This Is the Year*, and a long rambling draft of a book that later on blossomed into *Sons of Adam*.

It took three months before he called me. He first took me to the Covered Wagon where we had a glass of Forrester whiskey and then a luncheon featuring Lake Superior trout. Then we walked back to his office at Webb's. Paul was a short slim fellow with a little moustache. His manners were of the precise gentleman kind. It told me that he would demand a finished manuscript, that he'd be a fiend for proper grammatical structure. For the first time my experience with precise-minded Miss Timmer at Calvin College came in handy.

He first picked up the long rambling manuscript and talked about it some, and finally said that it wasn't ready. Then he picked up the early draft of *This Is the Year* and remarked that it too needed more work, and as it then stood it had the look as if the chapters had been safety-pinned together. It wasn't smooth.

At last he tackled the six manuscript versions of *The Golden Bowl*. One by one he commented that they were all interesting but . . . By the time he finished with the fifth draft, I was sure he would turn the sixth draft down too. Instead, he

Dr. Arthur R. Huseboe, Director of the Center for Western Studies, Augustana College, Sioux Falls, South Dakota, friend and advisor for many years

looked at the sixth a while, thinking to himself, and finally said, "Well, now this is publishable as it stands. But I'd like to suggest something. Could you go over it one more time to make sure it's the way you want it?" Of course! It was going to be published at last!

I took all the manuscripts home with me and set to work on that sixth draft of *The Golden Bowl*. I pared down some of the more flowery passages, cut a few pages, and going at it more confidently (I was going to be published!), I found myself adding several chapters, one in particular about Maury as he sat with some hoboes and bindle stiffs at night along the railroad tracks in Montana. And, best of all, I added an italicized poetic passage which summed up the book.

After I finished, exhausted, I went to bed.

A couple of hours later I was awakened by my wife Maryanna, who kissed me and whispered in the dark, "Oh, Poppie, that's now a wonderful book!"

Up to that point Maryanna hadn't thought much of my writing. She didn't think I had it as a writer of fiction. She was afraid that I didn't have it in me to take that final step that all writers must take . . . know how to shape a finished work of art.

With Maryanna finally solidly in favor of what I was doing, I went back to Hillestad at Webb's. What I learned there was a final difficulty. The owners, Harmon and Klein, weren't sure they wanted to print my realistic work. It appeared they had in mind publishing fiction that was in the nature of the scholarly farm manuals they'd been publishing. But I finally persuaded Hillestad to take a chance. Go for broke. *Bowl* was published in the fall of 1944.

The next spring in 1945 I learned that I'd been awarded a grant-in-aid from the American Academy of Arts and Letters for *The Golden Bowl*. Jean Stafford had been awarded the other grant-in-aid for her novel *Boston Adventure*. Paul Hillestad decided I should go to New York to receive the grant, and Webb Publishing paid for our transportation and hotel bill. There my wife and I met Jean Stafford, Van Wyck Brooks, and other important literary figures. Jean urged me to start sending my work to the *Kenyon Review* and the *Sewanee Review*. And from Van Wyck I learned that it was Sinclair Lewis who pushed for *The Golden Bowl*.

The next January in 1946, the phone rang in our new country cabin while I was frying steak and potatoes for myself. The cabin hadn't been winterized, and Maryanna and I decided that she and the baby Freya would stay with her mother in Minneapolis during the week, and weekends I'd drive in to see them.

"Hello?"

"Feike Feikema?"

"Yes?"

"This is Sinclair Lewis. I'd like very much to meet you. I'm staying at the Leamington. Could you drop by?"

"Yes. I'm driving in tomorrow."

"Wonderful. A great pleasure. I've been looking forward to this. Really. I'm just simply delighted to hear your voice at last and that we'll meet."

Lewis had also invited Ann Chidester, another young Minnesota novelist, to see him at the same time, around four in the afternoon.

When the two of us knocked on Lewis's door, he welcomed us enthusiastically. A pair of luminous gray-green eyes topped by thinning white hair looked up at me. His sharp eyes swept me up and down. It could be seen he was quite surprised by my six-foot-nine height.

"Mr. Lewis? I'm Feikema."

He seized my hand in both of his. "Come in, come in. Take off your things and put them there."

After I'd taken off my tall fur cap and long dark blue coat, he walked around me excitedly, like a basketball coach who couldn't believe his eyes. He turned to Ann and said, "My God, isn't he a big lummox. I thought I was tall, but look at him. He's bigger than Paul Bunyan himself."

Before I'd walked over to the Leamington, I'd stopped in at the Powers Book Store and bought his latest novel *Cass Timberlane* for him to autograph, even though I'd heard he didn't like to autograph his books. I'd also taken along my second novel, just published, *Boy Almighty*. He saw the package. "What've you got in that package?"

"A couple of books."

"Well, are you going to let me see them?"

I handed the package to him. His nervous tic-ridden fingers pulled off the wrapping. He looked at the two books. "Good, good. Here, you fix up your book for me, and I'll fix up my book for you."

I wrote something to the effect that I regarded him as one of those who had shown the way for the younger generation coming in. He wrote a simple short sentence in my *Boy Almighty* which I had trouble believing. "To Fred Feikema, a great man." He could tell that quick? In just one short meeting? At the same time, what he'd written made the blood suddenly roar through my head.

Then, relaxed, he invited Ann and me up to his house in Duluth for a week.

Ann and my wife Maryanna and I drove up in Ann's car. It was bitter cold out and there were great drifts of snow everywhere. He assigned a room near his study for Ann, and we had the next room over.

It turned out to be a heady week for my wife and me. Red Lewis liked to sit at dinner for a long time, sometimes well towards ten o'clock, talking, telling stories, discussing the latest books we'd read. In the background he had a dark fellow play a lot of Delius music on the phonograph. It was as if he was trying to catch up with something he'd been missing. Also in his house the walls were filled with Childe Hassam oils. He seemed to be steeping himself in that too, as if to catch up.

Halfway through the first dinner, as we four sat in red leather chairs around a wonderful long leather-topped table, Lewis picked up a sheet of paper and handed it around. On it were listed a series of titles. Lewis said, "I've made a good start on a new novel about a hero who discovers that he has some Negro blood in him. And also discovers that he has some kingly blood in him from England. But I can't decide on the title. Which one of these titles catches your eye?"

Ann looked at the list first, then Maryanna, and then myself. There were three titles: Kingson, Kingsblood, Kingsman. All three of us chose Kingsblood. The unanimity surprised Red. "Good. I've got the title for my new book then. And now I can relax for the rest of your stay here. Next week I can go at it again." When that novel came out, Lewis decided on the title *Kingsblood Royal*.

Finally it was time to go. While Maryanna and Ann were getting their coats and boots, he had a last word for me. "Look at you. A great big fellow. With your whole life still before you. With the whole wide world still to conquer—when, from that height, it's already at your feet. A lot of world because you stand tall."

I protested. "That tallness could be a hindrance. Some of the short people like to mock it."

"Look. Don't trip over your own strength. Like I did over mine for a while." He punched me lightly in the belly. "Work. Work. Work. And it'll all bend before you."

Late that same year the University of Minnesota Libraries asked if they couldn't eventually have my papers—the manuscripts, letters, and journals. They'd asked Sinclair Lewis for his papers. He told them that he'd already given them to Yale University. "But," he said, "go after the papers of that young Feikema fellow before it is too late." W. W. McDiarmid, University Librarian, worked out the arrangements with me.

Over the years since meeting Sinclair Lewis, there were many others who touched my life meaningfully. Abbott Washburn, public relations man for General Mills, invited me to go along with him and John Dos Passos to Duluth, Minnesota. Dos Passos was writing an article about General Mills and needed to examine their holdings along the shores of Lake Superior. I spent a lot of time with Dos Passos in the Spaulding Hotel. It was fun, and very instructive, to see how Dos Passos interviewed people. He showed me endless patience with people I thought dolts. His best advice was, "Don't let anybody tell you what you should write about and how you do it. If you're any good,

The author writing the first draft of Green Earth, *1972*

you'll eventually be recognized for what you really are."

Still later there was Vardis Fisher who decided with his wife Opal to drive all the way from Hagerman, Idaho, to check me out. The four of us—Vardis, Opal, Maryanna, and myself—got along very well, with our little Freya playing on the floor. Vardis had a keen mind, somewhat caustic, penetrating, and was always wondering what our real thoughts were. He felt what was important was what the final version became, not from where the writer might have got it. Literature first, the feelings of friends and relatives last.

There were two men at the University of South Dakota in Vermillion who saw to it that I was named writer-in-residence there, with the Hill Family Foundation footing part of the bill. Knutson was chairman of the English department and Milton, in addition to his classes, edited the newly established *South Dakota Review.* For years Knutson kept nominating me for the Nobel Prize for Literature in Stockholm. Almost every Monday when I drove down for my three-hour seminar in

writing, he and I had lunch together in the Prairie Cafe. Both Knutson and Milton were very well-read men. The dialogues I had with them were every bit as good as any I had at The Players in New York or at the Pen doings also in New York.

I had one really great editor in New York. He was David McDowell of Random House and Crown. He'd gone to Kenyon College with Peter Taylor, Robert Lowell, and Robie Macauley. David and I got along as he put it "as loose as a goose," even though he came at me with his southern "Fugitive School" training and I came from the Upper Midwest. He often shook his head at my reasoning but finally always accepted it. He had a catholic taste and always asked for the best from his writers. He and his coeditor, Martha Murphy Duffy, were brilliant.

Later I ran into a man who has had a lot to do with my welfare since the early sixties. He is Arthur Huseboe, currently the director of the Center for Western Studies in Sioux Falls, South Dakota. He too has shown endless patience for the way I go at my writing. I may often have written novels and poems and essays, and given talks, that may have offended his sensibilities, but he has always gone out of his way to understand why I write the way I do.

Huseboe is also a wonderful conversationalist on many subjects. Besides literature, we'll talk about such things as anthropology, philosophy, religion, quantum mechanics, and what it means to be an artist. Once he introduced me to Richard Clawson from NASA who'd discovered that good artists have an aura about their bodies which shows up in high tech photography. The aura shows up as a thin outline of shimmering blue.

Afterword

I must make a few final remarks about my wonderful doughty grandfather, my father's father, Feike Feikes Feikema V. Where my father was six-foot-five, Grampa was five-foot-ten. Where my father was tall and lanky, Grampa was broad-shouldered and powerful. His thighs were so thick he couldn't cross them at the knee. All his life Grampa was puzzled that my father couldn't read whereas he himself could.

He was restless almost from the moment he was born. His younger siblings had endless stories about him running away; and finally he did sail before the Dutch mast and then later on for the British mast. He saw a lot of the world.

When it came time finally for him to settle down to have a family, he talked a tall Frisian girl into eloping with him. Her name was Ytje Andringa. She came from an aristocratic family in Franeker, the Netherlands, and of course her family, especially her stepfather, was totally against her seeing Feike the Fifth, even though he could claim that several generations before his great grandfather also came from the same background. The Feikemas had once been landowners of a place called Great Lankum. Also, a street in Franeker had been named after the family, Feikema Street. But Feike the Fifth's claim meant nothing; at the moment he was only an "arbeider," a simple workman with no inheritance. And right after my father Feike VI was born in Taum, a village near Franeker, he talked her into running off to America. From pictures of Ytje it is obvious she was several inches taller than Grampa. And from family legend we've learned that Ytje's father's people were giants, some of them almost seven feet tall; and that's where my father and all his children get their height.

Grampa was an alpha male if there ever was one. When I was six years old he stayed with us that summer. One night we had company who arrived on the yard just as we'd finished supper. I was overjoyed because I could play with the visitor boy, Everett Vanden Heuvel. I completely forgot that I still had to feed the calves some skim milk. But Grampa hadn't forgotten. He was sitting on a stump in the house yard, and after a while he called me over to him. I ran over and just as I got within reach of him Grampa suddenly gave me a biff over the head.

"What's that for?" I cried.

"You've filled your belly but what about your calves?"

Of course he had me there. I backed up several steps and then said, "Grampa, you had no right to hit me. That's for my pa to do, not you."

He was wearing a moustache and was smoking his corncob pipe and he managed to hide the beginning of a smile. "You better finish your chores though, boy."

I called Everett over and together he and I fed the calves.

Later on I overheard him tell my father, "You don't need to worry about our little Feike. He's gonna hold up his end of things."

Copyright © Frederick Feikema Manfred

BIBLIOGRAPHY

Fiction, under name Feike Feikema:

The Golden Bowl, Webb (St. Paul, Minnesota), 1944, Dobson (London), 1947, revised edition (under name Frederick Manfred), South Dakota Press, 1969.

Boy Almighty, Itasca Press (St. Paul, Minnesota), 1945, Dobson, 1950.

This Is the Year, Doubleday, 1947, reprinted (under name Frederick Manfred), Gregg, 1979.

The Chokecherry Tree, Doubleday (New York), 1948, Dobson, 1950, revised edition (under name Frederick Manfred), A. Swallow, 1961.

"World's Wanderer" series:

The Primitive, Doubleday, 1949.

The Brother, Doubleday, 1950.

The Giant, Doubleday, 1951.

(As Frederick Manfred) *Wanderlust* (contains revised editions of *The Primitive, The Brother,* and *The Giant),* A. Swallow, 1962.

Fiction, under name Frederick Manfred:

Morning Red: A Romance, A. Swallow, 1956.

Arrow of Love (short-story collection), A. Swallow, 1961.

The Man Who Looked like the Prince of Wales, Trident Press, 1965, published as *The Secret Place,* Pocket Books, 1967.

Apples of Paradise and Other Stories, Trident Press, 1968.

Eden Prairie, Trident Press, 1968.

The Manly-Hearted Woman, Crown, 1975.

Milk of Wolves, Avenue Victor Hugo, 1976.

Green Earth, Crown, 1977.

Sons of Adam, Crown, 1980.

Flowers of Desire, Dancing Badger Press, 1989.

No Fun on Sunday, University of Oklahoma Press, 1990.

Of Lizards and Angels: A Saga of Siouxland, University of Oklahoma Press, 1992.

"The Buckskin Man Tales" series:

Lord Grizzly, McGraw, 1954.

Riders of Judgment, Random House, 1957.

Conquering Horse, McDowell/Obolensky, 1959.

Scarlet Plume, Trident Press, 1964.

King of Spades, Trident Press, 1966.

Other, under name Frederick Manfred:

Winter Count: Poems 1934–1965, James Thueson, 1966.

Lord Grizzly: The Legend of Hugh Glass (screenplay; based on his novel *Lord Grizzly*), University of South Dakota Libraries, 1972.

John R. Milton, editor, *Conversations with Frederick Manfred,* University of Utah Press, 1974.

The Wind Blows Free: A Reminiscence, Center for Western Studies, Augustana College, 1979.

Dinkytown, Dinkytown Antiquarian Bookstore, 1984.

Prime Fathers: Portraits, Howe Brothers, 1987.

Winter Count II: Poems 1966–1985, James Thueson, 1987.

The Selected Letters of Frederick Manfred 1932–1954, University of Nebraska Press, 1989.

Contributor of short stories to such collections as *Dakota Arts Quarterly, The Far Side of the Storm, Fiction 8,* and *Great River Review.* Also contributor to the following periodicals: *American Scholar, Chicago Sun Times, Esquire, Minnesota Quarterly, New Republic, Saturday Review,* and *South Dakota Review.* Author of weekly newspaper column, "The World Around Us," in *Prospector* (New Jersey), 1936. Manfred's manuscripts are collected at the University of Minnesota.

William Matthews

1942-

DURATIONS

The amnesia that surrounds our earliest life is not only a great human mystery, but also a receptacle into which is poured by the baby's relatives the beginnings of a life story. In later years these relatives can look at the grown child and see their first observations confirmed, for was he not always a curious baby, a cranky baby, a calm baby, what have you? We come into the world swaddled in the beginnings of a story, and by the time we begin remembering and tending it, it already has a shape and a momentum.

When I was born in 1942, my young parents were following my father's naval orders around the country—Bremerton, Washington; Norman, Oklahoma. I spent many of my first months with my father's parents in Cincinnati. There are photographs of me in, of course, a sailor suit. The lawn at the back, or western side, of my grandparents' house had a few huge trees—could they have been oaks?—and I think I remember standing at the edge of that lawn, on a kind of flagstone patio, in the late afternoon light, staring excitedly and contentedly at the effect the tall trees and their long shadows made. The world seemed vast and full of comfortable mystery, and yet I was but a few feet from the safety of the house.

But that would have been later, when I was four, or maybe even six. I stood there often. And of course I've seen photographs of the lawn and house. And maybe I'm recalling some older relative's anecdote about a boy at the edge of a lawn that somehow, inexplicably, has got blended into my own memories, like vodka slipped into a bowl of punch.

My earliest memory seems to be from the backyard of my mother's mother's house in Ames, Iowa. There's a sandbox, a tiny swatch of grainy sidewalk, and—there! it's moving—a ladybug. I have tried again and again to construct a tiny narrative from these bright props—they lie there and gleam with promise but won't connect.

William Matthews, Vermont, 1993

*

The war ended, my sister Susan was born, my father took a job with the Soil Conservation Service in Ohio, and then the four of us were in a boxy farmhouse outside Rosewood, Ohio, for a year, and then moved into a house just outside the city limits of Troy, Ohio.

The smells of that house, that life, those years, I absorbed all unthinkingly, as greedily and easily as breath. Later, thinking back fondly on them, I at first organized them: indoors and outdoors, female and male.

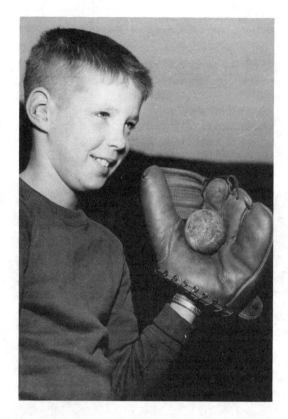

Matthews with his first baseball glove

Coffee, dishwashing liquid, baking are foremost among the kitchen smells, and the braided scent of misty heat and faint scorch that meant ironing. I remember, too, coming home from school during the army/McCarthy hearings to find my mother ironing glumly, fascinated and appalled by what I now know to call the self-righteousness and swagger and mendacity of the whole gloomy circus. Once or twice—I think I remember this correctly—she was weeping a little. A child's world is small. Think how easily I wrote "the war ended" above. I don't remember it myself. In the 1945 I remember, I suddenly had a sister. I saw in the kitchen those puzzling afternoons how the cruelty of the official world—the world history records and by whose accounts I knew to write above that "the war ended"—could come into the house and linger, itself a sort of odor.

The kitchen held also a great terror—the pressure cooker. I must have asked about it, and must have received an enthusiastically scientific description. It was like a bomb, then, I knew instantly. We were only the matter of time, the whole family, the house, perhaps the hapless neighbors. I walked past it like a paperboy skirting a sleeping Doberman. Any day it would bulge and redden and shudder and blow, and we would rise in shards and fall in flecks, and there would be no help for us. How could I warn anyone? A little child shall save them. But if that little child had woken his parents too many times to police the closet and scour the pit beneath his bed, how could he militate defense against death by pressure-cooker shrapnel and broccoli? I wouldn't say a word, and when we were all dead they'd know how right I'd been in what I had not said, and they'd be sad.

The dominant outdoor and male odor was liniment: my father played for (and later, managed) a local amateur baseball team. There was the very soil of Miami County, brought home in smears and small clods on my father's boots from the farms he visited on his job. The smell of the leather of my first baseball glove and the oil I eagerly rubbed into it brings back to me not only that early proud ownership, but also the odors of one of the night games my father's team played: the smell of car engines cooling in the parking lot, a little infield dirt swirling in the night air, sweat and flannel and liniment, and now and then from the stands, signalled by the sound of a church key carving triangular holes into the top of a beer can and a small sigh of released carbonation, the yeasty aroma of beer as the regular spectators settled in for a long game.

Before I started school, my mother taught me to read, and so the smell of newsprint meant to me then the eagerly awaited Sunday comics as surely as bells meant food to Pavlov's dogs. It's that smell that came first to confound the categories by which I'd later organize my olfactory memories. It's an indoor and female smell, in an obvious way, for we read the comics indoors and I revelled as much in my mother's attention as I did in learning.

But reading leads you out of yourself as well as in, and reveals, even in the comics, a world larger than home, more various than Troy, Ohio, and rewards you for the early labors of reading with the increasing knowledge that if you can read, you hold a passport to that world. The borders between indoors and outdoors, between the largely domestic comforts of the "female" world and the harsher, more public strivings of the "male" world, come to seem thin and elastic.

My love of newsprint didn't dim. I delivered the *Dayton Daily News* in the early mornings for years, was the editor of my high school newspaper, and worked two of my college summers for a small community paper in Cincinnati.

But the best thing my newspaperboy days brought me was Spot, the dumpy dog. "Vaguely beagle," as I described her in a poem, she followed me one morning for the whole length of my route. She was waiting for me the next morning, and I was like some inexplicable canine Pied Piper, for dog after dog joined us as I covered my route. Dogs love me, I thought, but in fact, as my parents explained to me, Spot was in heat. We took her in and slowly the blood-stirred males dispersed. She lived fifteen more years, with her faint, persistent smell, in all seasons, of leaf mold and her peculiar way of cocking her head as if someone only she could hear had made an especially apt comment. My parents let me name her, I hardly need to say, and praised me for giving her the best possible name. But one day I found my mother shooing the dog out the back door from the kitchen and murmuring to herself, with a pleased smile, "Out, out, damn Spot."

There was a basket over the garage door and the solitude I didn't share with a dog or a pile of books from the library I spent with a basketball. These are, I now think, the imaginary friends a boy has when he is too old to admit to himself he wants an imaginary friend.

I shot baskets long into the grainy dusk. I shot baskets in the rain, when the slick ball took on an orange-pink tinge and the dirt that gloved my hands and tarred my clothes came not only from the driveway but also from the specklets of dust that raindrops form around. I shovelled snow from the driveway to clear a space to shoot baskets. And now and then on Saturday afternoons when my parents had locked themselves into their bedroom to make love, as I now know, and I could sense that they were, in any case, not thinking of me, I would shoot baskets and take care to have the ball carom off the side of the house beneath their bedroom window with its drawn shade. "Now, now," my young unconsciousness cried out, "none of that."

Troy was a company town, and the company was Hobart, makers of scales and kitchen equipment. Its visible largesse was the Hobart Arena, where Susan would go to practice her figure skating and I to play junior hockey, an activity almost as favored as youth baseball because the arena was home to a minor league hockey team.

Susan became a dancer, a choreographer, and a respected teacher of dance at Queens College in New York City. When I moved to New York in 1983 I asked her to recommend an orthopedist to look at the knees I had gnarled from thousands of hours of driveway and playground basketball. She became, for all the years I spent on the baseball diamond and on basketball and tennis courts, the better athlete, the one who lived the possibility that the body can shape the soul as readily as vice versa. My father was a good football player and wrestler as a young man, and a good catcher for that baseball team in Troy, and an avid though ordinary golfer in his later years. I had neither the body nor the temperament for his sports, but as a boy baseball player I was a catcher. I didn't need to crusade for his affection; he gave it freely. I imitated him from love and admiration and because I wanted to know, I now think, something he knew about physical life. In one of those instructive ironies life so richly and relentlessly provides, my little sister in her frilled and terraced skating costumes was the one who learned it, and my father never played a minute's catch with her in the yard while Spot barked at the balls she failed to catch, nor explained to her the Vardon grip.

I took piano lessons but my attention slackened, and I rode my bike to the library and back, to the baseball diamond—I wore my Williams Meat Market tee shirt proudly everywhere—and back. I mowed the neighbors' lawns for pocket money. I fell in love with unidentical twins, I corrected my fifth grade teacher's grammar and took her just wrath broadside, I hired myself out as a boy caddy to the Hobart moguls at the local country club.

Just before we moved to Cincinnati at the start of my eighth grade year, I took a girl, my spurned piano teacher's daughter, to the movies and then to someplace where we could get a soda or an ice cream. A couple of older boys—I'd played baseball with and against them—couldn't let a chance like this go by. "Is she your honey?" one of them asked me in a low voice just out of her hearing. Didn't I have a girl on my arm, and a beauty at that? Wasn't I a boy of the world? Wouldn't I soon be one of them? "Yes," I admitted. "Well then," he said, and his voice turned clarion, "if she's your honey, why don't you eat her?"

*

Something more interesting by far happened before we moved to Cincinnati. Children's International Summer Villages, a peace organization

The author's parents, William P., Jr., and Mary E. (Sather) Matthews, summer 1960

whose main project was to bring eleven-year-old children from various countries together for a summer month, decided to send a delegation to Sweden from Miami County, and I was chosen as one of the four children who would go.

So in 1954 I spent a month outside Göteborg with kids from seven other countries: happy, curious about the cultures and habits and languages of the other children, playing games I'd never heard of before. And singing, always a hallmark of CISV gatherings, I've learned since.

We had been chosen without any expectation that our families would pay for the trip, and in order to keep the selection process democratic, it was expected that a returning delegation would help to raise money for the next year's. I found myself with a small slide show talking to the Lions Club, the Kiwanis, etc. My presentation, once I'd polished it a little, explained the CISV program, studded the program with a few boyish jokes, and gave thumbnail sketches of the various delegates pictured in the slides. I taught myself, without ever

quite naming the project, to become an effective public speaker.

Meanwhile my father had volunteered to do some organizational and fund-raising work for CISV, and got so involved in it and so good at it that a job offer came to him. Would he run the U.S. office of CISV, located in Cincinnati, where the program had been founded?

Yes, he and Mother decided, and we were off to Cincinnati.

*

A last glimpse of Miami County. It's the 1952 presidential campaign, the last one to use trains for whistle-stop campaigning. Mother has decided to take me to see Adlai Stevenson, and President Truman, who'd been called in to add some force to Stevenson's hopeless campaign against Eisenhower. There were few enough Democrats in the county, and few came out. The train stopped at a train crossing in Troy, the two principals spoke briefly, and the train chugged off. I remember a few women who had, like Mother, brought a child or two, and a few campaign aides, they must have been, wearing suits and carrying clipboards or manila envelopes. Mostly the other kids, like me, were looking around and at each other. This is a little bit of history, their mothers may well have told them, too.

It was probably twenty-five years later that I found myself, for some reason, telling someone at a literary party my impressions of that day. The poet Stanley Plumly, now one of my closest friends, came across the room to tell me he'd been there that day too, from Piqua, with his mother. "I think she had a sort of crush on Stevenson," he said, "well-spoken, worldly, an ironic gentleman."

"Mine, too," I said.

*

Mother had grown up in Missouri and Iowa. She was of Norwegian background, and there was a streak of prairie populism in her family that countered the sometimes gloomy Lutheran solipsism one could find all too easily in such communities. Her mother died not long after giving birth to her, and her father, a professor and passionate liberal, died before I ever met him. When I met her stepmother, she was running an employment agency in Lincoln, Nebraska; I think it catered mostly to women who also needed to apply a steady and routine courage to the problems of daily life. Mother came from a relatively poor family with a staunch belief in education, and the two towns where I visited her stepmother were both university towns. It was in Ames, Iowa, where my parents met. Mother was an undergraduate, on scholarship. Father, a Princeton graduate, was taking an M.A. in organic chemistry to prepare him for work in agriculture.

Father's father ran a farm management company outside Cincinnati, so Father's plan to work for the Soil Conservation Service put him in the same line of work, but not in business. Similarly his first assignment put him some distance from Cincinnati but not a great distance. Many a young man fond of his parents has tried to balance that affection with his own need to break away and be on his own path, and it's hard juggling.

Also, Miami County had a high number of Amish, Mennonite, and Dunkard farmers in it; they were some of the best farmers in America, and in scant need, Father realized early, of advice on scientific farming from a recent Princeton

graduate. Much of the time Father had been muddying his boots in the fields had been spent learning about farming from local experts.

The move to Cincinnati meant taking on the international focus of CISV, and considerable travel. Both my parents must have been pleased and excited with this new momentum, which would carry them, in another ten years, to England, where Father ran the CISV international office for twenty years until his retirement, and where he and Mother hosted visitors from all over the world, and from where they travelled. The promises of their separate early lives and their young marriage began to take enduring shape when they decided to move to Cincinnati.

But to Susan and me it meant terror, as all moves do at first for children. My new school had two thousand students in grades 7–12. I had the monstrous egotism of my age and imagined I was the only one of them rancid with fear. At the time, of course, I didn't think back to the pressure cooker, nor think of the plots of the B-grade horror movies I loved so fiercely in those years.

In such films there's one character who knows that giant, irradiated ants are the cause of all the dead state troopers and the stink of formic acid, and everyone else thinks he's crazy. That radiation was often part of the plot and that Japan and the USA were the two countries where almost all these films were made tells us something about the way history induces nightmares, and also something

The author in high school

about the way the manufactured nightmares of the film industry hope both to exploit and comfort our usual bad dreams, the ones with dank sweat and twisted sheets and not a whiff of popcorn.

But the terrors of those years proved negotiable. I played basketball, not with great distinction, but well enough to disguise myself as a jock, which turned out to be great protective coloration for a bookish and dreamy boy. And I wasn't to be at school in Cincinnati long. I did my last three years of high school at boarding school—Berkshire School, near Great Barrington, Massachusetts. Two hundred students. In that smaller arena I edited the high school paper and the literary magazine, played basketball, collected good grades, and got myself admitted to Yale. Along the way I had some excellent instruction in English from three teachers—Thomas Chaffee, Arthur Chase, and James Durham—who sharpened considerably my skills as a reader and writer. It now began to seem possible that my dreaminess, obsessive reading, and love of words pointed toward writing or editing or teaching or some combination of the three. He was always a chatty baby, the relatives remembered.

Cleanth Brooks and John Hollander were two professors especially helpful to me. I published two poems in the *Sewanee Review* my sophomore year, and married Marie Harris, herself an apprentice writer, at the end of that year. Soon enough we two literary babies had our first child, Bill. Time swirled. I graduated and we headed for graduate school in Chapel Hill, North Carolina; Marie was due, with Sebastian, in late August and the next week my classes would begin. We were in an apartment complex with many young couples; the stunned women, their lives transformed so rapidly and thoroughly by early motherhood, would gather around the sandbox and swings, keep an eye on their toddlers, and compare notes. The men went to classes, and then came home to diapers and colic. We were around for more of domestic life than men who worked 9 to 5, but the distribution of labor was even then so vastly unequal, and discontent simmered between the sexes, all the more complicated for those couples where real love bound one to another.

I was trying to balance family life and my literary ambitions, and uneasy about it because my work—and I could barely call it work, for I was a student—came first, and my family next. Also it seemed clear to me that my work—my studies—was not what I really wanted to do. I could "do scholarship," as the idiom had it, but not with

excellence or passion. What seemed to my fellow graduate students the path *(la via diretta)* to the Ph.D. seemed to me a dark wood *(una selva oscura)*.

I had a crisis of faith. I had won a scholarship on which my family could almost live, and it had been awarded to me with every expectation that I would be avid for the Ph.D. My generous parents were sending us two hundred dollars a month, not a small sum for them in those years, to make up what of our modest expenses the scholarship didn't cover; no doubt my parents had similar expectations. My wife resented—how could she not?—the way I could name an obligation and leave the house to meet it. And so I scarcely relished telling her, and thus I didn't, how little that obligation truly engaged me, day by day.

And like anyone caught in a mess of his own making, I was angry.

As a result I began to write poems seriously. I had written and even published a few poems when I was in college. I cared about them furiously while I was writing them and then I was done. Now I wrote and the poems weren't good enough and I thought about them all the time. I was never done. It wasn't that I wrote poems because I knew that was what I really wanted to do. Indeed, I wrote poems to escape thinking about what I really wanted to do. But I wrote them as if some essential honesty in me were at stake—and I think now, as I did then, that it was—and writing them that seriously led me to understand that what I really wanted to do was to write poems.

I didn't want to devote the time I could spend teaching myself to write poems to write a dissertation. Perhaps I was wrong to think of it as an either/or proposition, but I did. The dissertation was, after all, a prerequisite for a teaching job, and if I let it drift, and every day I chose to let it drift, how would I support my family?

There were jobs teaching creative writing, of course, and as luck would have it I found one, and before I reported for duty I had a book of poems accepted for publication. As well as I had woven that net of likely crisis for myself, I somehow wriggled through it.

So I was feeling pleased with myself the day Marie and the boys and I drove toward our new home and my first teaching job. I'd been to Aurora, New York, for the interview. It was a village of six hundred on the western shore of Cayuga Lake; it grew to twelve hundred when the students were in town. We drove over a brow and there it lay below us, tiny and bucolic. My wife broke into tears.

*

Sebastian had responded to a new home by walking out onto the porch and surveying the territory. "Where are the friends?" he asked. He'd need to ask again in a year, as I moved from Wells College to Cornell. We were there four years. I wrote my second book. The marriage exhausted itself and collapsed. The boys were brave but hurt. They spent two school years with Marie and then came to live with me during their school years and with Marie for summers.

*

By then I was in Boulder, Colorado. I had a house in the mountains with two fireplaces and five acres of rocks, mountain meadowlands and ponderosa pines riddled by beetles, and a dog—the ninety-five-pound, mush-hearted Underdog (You don't name a German shepherd that size Fang). But when the boys arrived, the place came to life.

I taught there five years, and then five years at the University of Washington. Bill and Sebastian both finished high school in Seattle and went to Pitzer College. Bill, a good painter, has settled in Seattle. Sebastian is currently in his last semester in the graduate program in creative writing at the University of Michigan; he's a prose writer.

When Sebastian left Seattle for college, I came to New York. I could almost write "came back," for New York had been the preferred weekend destination from boarding school and then from college. I came for the museums and especially for the jazz clubs. I saw Monk, the great Charles Mingus, Miles Davis, Blossom Dearie, Betty Carter, Stan Getz, Ornette Coleman, John Coltrane, Eric Dolphy, Roy Eldridge, Al Cohn and Zoot Sims, Cannonball Adderly. The large world, which had beckoned to me first from reading and then from the international outlook CISV and my parents fostered in me, had one of its major crossroads in New York. It would take me a while to learn that what is most alluring about a great city is not its sophistication—this is often not much more than a huge concentration of money and goods in the social arena and a certain mandarin swagger in the arts—but the anthology of provincialisms that such a city comprises. The rich linguistic pool excited me—all those languages overheard on the streets, and all the dialects of English! The restaurants seemed to include every possible cuisine, and though I couldn't afford most of them, it pleased me to think they were there, the way I had been excited on my first visits to the public library in Troy. All those books, and I might read any of them.

When I came back to New York, then, in 1984, I first taught at Brooklyn College, where I met John Ashbery's classes when he was briefly ill. I began the following year at City College, where I hold a professorship and where a number of distinguished writers—Don Barthelme, Grace Paley, Adrienne Rich—have taught in recent years. I have now and then taught an extra course for the graduate writing program at Columbia—moonlighting, so to speak, though Columbia holds its classes in the daytime. The program's generous offer has been for me to teach a seminar of my own devising. I've taught a course in the Roman poets, including my beloved Martial; I'm finishing work this spring on a book of translations of one hundred Martial epigrams. I've taught a course called Freud for Writers, and taught Virgil, Homer, and Dante. This happy arrangement has permitted me to continue my own education and provided extra dollars to spend on opera tickets

"William Matthews, Boy Jazz Buff"

*Matthews's sons, Bill (behind the stroller)
and Sebastian, 1966*

and at the jazz clubs, and occasionally at one of those restaurants I can now sometimes afford.

The jazz clubs of my youth, with their blue coils of cigarette smoke and bad "Italian" food, are gone. The Half Note is gone, the Five Spot is gone, the Showplace on West Fourth Street where Mingus fired a dozen pianists every six months is gone. Twice I saw him harry a pianist from the stage in midset. This last year I saw Gerry Mulligan at the Blue Note and Tommy Flanagan, the Mozart of the jazz piano, at the Village Vanguard, and the house asked its patrons not to smoke during the performances. It's not only that smoking is rightly vilified, but it's also that Flanagan has a heart condition and Mulligan the look of a man made wary by the damage he inflicted on himself when younger. Some of the jazz buffs I sat in the clubs with in the early 1960s had in common with fans of stock-car racing a secret desire to watch someone go up in flames. "He's really strung out tonight," they would say to one another. That these disaster-buffs were usually white and com-

paratively secure materially, and the musicians black and on the economic edge, made this prurience all the more repulsive. Some of the use that the more flamboyant jazz musicians and abstract expressionist painters of that period offered to their audience was very nearly the use a throat offers a vampire, and just as gratefully received.

In 1984 Arlene Modica and I were married in New York. Arlene was working as a publicist for Villard, a division of Random House, and then later for Putnam. You could tell from a look at her apartment that she was in publishing; all her books were hardcovers. What she hoped to do instead was to become a psychoanalyst and to write. She entered a psychoanalytic institute and began taking courses, and she started work on a book called, rather ominously, *Why Did I Marry You Anyhow?* Houghton Mifflin bought the book, which did well enough that there was some competition—Scribner's prevailed—to publish her next book, *If I Think about Money So Much, Why Can't I Figure It Out?* (1991). As things turned out, the marriage was brief. We had both witnessed vitriolic and expensive divorces and promised each other to do better. No such parting is truly amicable, but we kept our promises. Today Arlene is a practicing analyst, a proven author; she's remarried happily and expecting, as I write, her first child.

*

In 1989 my father died. My parents had been in the States and I'd scheduled a book party for *Blues If You Want* during their visit, so they could attend. The next day they flew back to England, and my father had a massive heart attack at the luggage retrieval area in the Newcastle upon Tyne airport. He was sixty-nine.

Susan and I flew to England to help Mother with the funeral. My father's father had died when I was in my early twenties; it was the first death that shook me at my center. In the intervening years I've seen the deaths of writers and musicians who'd meant as much to me as family members—Thelonious Monk, Charles Mingus, Vladimir Nabokov, Elizabeth Bishop. In the case of artists like these, whose continued development and invention had produced not only beloved work but a model for the way a life in the arts can be imagined and lived out, the deaths meant an absolute end to the marvelous momentum by which an important body of work is produced. Here were people who seemed able to bring the whole weight of their lives to bear on the next poem or novel or performance, and suddenly that weight was airy nothing.

I felt it again with writers I had some friendship with—James Wright, Richard Blessing. Richard Hugo's death meant the loss of a good friend and one of my favorite poets. It began to feel to me that we spent the first half of our lives saying hello, slowly working our way from the isolations and narcissisms of childhood into a larger world, only to spend the second half of our lives saying goodbye. "Death," Wallace Stevens wrote, "is the mother of beauty." When I was younger, the fluent ease with which the Twenty-third Psalm refers to the span of our lives as "the valley of the shadow of death" seemed to me a great rhetorical flourish; I now think it an achievement of exemplary accuracy.

*

A world in which I cannot share another meal with my father is a diminished one, but the young can fill some of these holes with their expanding presences. The love of a parent and child is the only central love in our lives whose goal is some large measure of separation, and my sons, each in his late twenties, are busy building some autonomy in their lives. All the same, we're in frequent and affectionate communication. Watching them try to build lives in the arts has been a great pleasure to me.

Bill and Rochelle have provided me a grandchild, Raven William, the behemoth baby (twenty-five pounds at nine months). And I think of myself as an honorary grandfather to Rochelle's daughters from an earlier marriage, Alison and Davey.

Other compensations from the young have come from many of my students. A pleasingly large number of them have gone on from their student days to make lives as writers and, frequently, as teachers, too. Their devotion to a difficult craft in a culture which has marginalized poetry speaks well for the rewards of writing; these are seldom worldly rewards, to be sure, but the private and interior ones are great. And of course there's a crucial stewardship these writers and teachers perform for a society that doesn't know enough to value it: the work of exploring and maintaining the mysterious link between our language and our emotional lives.

But the largest compensation is the tang of mortal fear. I have never been more aware that the meter is running and, consequently, never been more vivid, concentrated, happy, or warily hopeful.

*

How might I better embody such cautious optimism than to marry a third time?

Of course the vows, as we pronounced them before Nathaniel Dean, Attorney General of the Bahamas, in Nassau, in early December 1989, said nothing about "cautious optimism," and didn't include Dr. Johnson's famous jape about "the triumph of hope over experience," and didn't allude to Chekhov's wry observation that if you are afraid of loneliness you shouldn't marry. They don't quote Chaucer on "the woe that is in marriage" or mention Madame Bovary, and they were written long before Thurber made his heartbroken jokes and strangled cartoons about the war between the sexes. Jane Austen was not quoted, nor Emily Dickinson:

To make a prairie it takes a clover and one bee,
One clover, and a bee,
And revery,
The revery alone will do,
If bees are few.

Nor was Simone de Beauvoir mentioned.

We were asked, and we had volunteered to be asked, Patricia and I, to say the time-honored and time-abused vows, properly rinsed by feminism of the verb "obey" and other like anachronisms.

We had planned our trip and worked out the bureaucratic details—it was my third marriage and Pat's second, so there was plenty of paperwork—by phone with Mr. Dean's office. And then my father died three weeks before the date we'd set. We'd keep the date, we decided, for what else could it mean to say the words "for better or for worse?" So Pat, in the dress we'd bought the day before, and I in my white suit, wrinkled from being packed, or wrinkled from being worn on the plane to keep it from being wrinkled by being packed, I can't remember which, stood in Nathaniel Dean's office and were married. Pat is a writer and teacher and a beauty in body and soul, a mother of three whose lives I'm happy to be entangled in, and the best of companions.

William Matthews at the Vermont Studio Center, 1993

*

I like to think of myself as by nature a domestic person. I cooked for and made a home for my sons for their junior high school and high school years, in addition to the usual fatherly activities. I'm a reader, a listener to music, a man made happy by kitchen chores and pleased when there are friends at my table. My marital history casts a considerable shadow on this sunny portrait.

It's also true that I have had thirteen domiciles—thirteen sets of change-of-address notices mailed, thirteen massive packings and unpackings of books, thirteen new phone numbers, etc.—since I was first married. How many blenders, extension cords, clay pots for the new houseplants I'd bought, etc., have I bought in ritual tribute to the gods of restlessness? I do not count summer rentals, the sparse comforts of the rooms given to the faculties of summer writers' conferences, writers' colonies, hotel rooms. I only count the ones that counted, and they are thirteen.

Soon it will be ten years that I have lived in New York (three addresses). Already I have been at one address for a record length of time, and taught at the same university for a record length of time. I have finally found a home, I could say with a self-dramatizing flourish. But that would be morally melodramatic, and would obscure a couple of important truths.

One is that I found a way to be at home wherever I lived and taught, with the exception of Seattle and the University of Washington. In those years first Bill and then Sebastian left home for college, and I found myself depressed, more deeply rootless than I'd ever admitted to myself, and ricocheting around like a squash ball. I had, like many a parent, described my life as organized around and given over to my children, and when the ordinary maturation of the boys made that explanation of myself an occasional rather than a daily motto, I had to begin admitting how poorly I knew me. What did I want? I had almost no idea.

The other is that I have loved restlessness, and seen in it and in its most reputable manifestation, travel, a vivid metaphor for curiosity. I have been around because I wanted to go around. I whirled my bike to the Troy, Ohio, library, hoping to be transported, and it worked. Around the world in eighty books, or eighty thousand.

What I want now is to make for that restless imagination a durable home. Hasn't it done as much for me?

BIBLIOGRAPHY

Poetry:

(With Russell Banks and Newton Smith) *15 Poems,* Lillabulero Press, 1967.

Broken Syllables, Lillabulero Press, 1969.

Ruining the New Road, Random House, 1970.

The Cloud, Barn Dream Press, 1971.

The Moon, Penyeach Press, 1971.

(With Robert Bly and William Stafford) *Poems for Tennessee,* Tennessee Poetry Press, 1971.

Sleek for the Long Flight, Random House, 1972.

Without a Mouth, Penyeach Press, 1972.

An Oar in the Old Water (pamphlet), Stone Press, 1974.

Sticks and Stones (drawings by Ray Kass), Pentagram, 1975.

Rising and Falling, Little, Brown, 1979.

Flood, Little, Brown, 1982.

A Happy Childhood, Little, Brown, 1984.

Foreseeable Futures, Houghton, 1987.

Blues If You Want, Houghton, 1989.

Selected Poems and Translations, 1969–1991, Houghton, 1992.

Other:

(Translator with Mary Feeney) Jean Follain, *Removed from Time* (pamphlet, from the French), Tideline, 1977.

(Translator with M. Feeney) J. Follain, *A World Rich in Anniversaries* (from the French), Grilled Flowers Press, 1979.

Curiosities, University of Michigan Press, 1989.

Contributor to numerous anthologies; also contributor of articles and reviews to periodicals. Advisory editor, *Tennessee Poetry Journal,* 1970–72; poetry editor, *Iowa Review,* 1976–77; contributing editor, *Gumbo,* 1977—.

Harold Norse

1916-

Norse's mother and natural father,
about 1917

My mother's family came from Kaunas, Lithuania, and settled in Brooklyn in 1905. My father was a classical pianist who gave piano lessons and played in movie houses, accompanying silent films. Judging from a faded, sepia photograph, my parents were very much in love—but they never got to the wedding. In Pfc. doughboy uniform he is seated beside Mother, both wistfully gazing into the future, his left arm around her shoulder protectively; with his other hand he holds her hand on his knee—a sentimental heirloom, heavy on romance and youthful euphoria. He died in the war, or so I was told. I was born July 6, 1916, at the Lincoln

Hospital in New York, when the Battle of the Somme, the first big slaughter of the war, began.

Mother was "petite," as she called it, and in the photo my father doesn't look much taller. I inherited "petite" genes. I never saw him and she refused to speak about it; it was too painful. An army nurse during the war, she worked later as a seamstress, which she had done from the age of eleven. When she spoke of her father, an accomplished linguist, scholar, and horseman, she cried. He had died at thirty-six of pneumonia and Mother, after a privileged childhood with tutors and servants, which she tearfully recalled, knew only the life of a drudge. My grandmother, swindled by lawyers, lost everything and ended up in a cold-water flat in South Brooklyn, where she brought up seven children and died of asthma at fifty-something.

Thanks to a concerned aunt, during the Depression I discovered I was a "love-child." Hard times and a ne'er-do-well stepfather had radicalized me sufficiently to greet the news with scorn. I shared it with friends who also found conventional morality a joke; the term "love-child" had a quaint, old-fashioned sound unlike the mocking jeer of "bastard," dictated by convention, which had no shock value for working-class youth of my Depression generation. How can society blame and shame the innocent victim and pretend to be fair? Cynical about such social codes (I still am), I felt like the young hero of a proletarian novel, the politically correct literary model of that era. What was traumatic, if not cataclysmic for my Victorian mother, made me scoff. Illegitimacy was a smack at hypocrisy. For Mother, though, it meant pain and disgrace, and out of respect for her feelings I avoided the subject.

Nothing in my early life was clear-cut, precise, orthodox, or "normal." There were so few facts that I had to do research just to find out what others took for granted: name, rank, serial number. My ID (like my id) remained an enigma. Who was I? Aunt Mary Pitts from Nova Scotia enlightened me, not out of malicious gossip but genuine concern. If I didn't take a name and legalize it, she said, I'd have trouble with the law and jobs: "Legally you don't exist!" My stepfather, Max, hadn't adopted me so I could shed his name and choose my own. I anagrammed Norse from a family name. It had a mythic ring.

My gracious aunt Eva, Mother's younger sister and everyone's favorite person, was responsible for my only religious exposure. Beautiful, loving, and the family peacemaker who never lost her temper, she turned down a career with the Ziegfeld Follies (Grandma didn't approve), became a Catholic to marry the mayor of Scranton's nephew, the dullest man I ever saw, and had a home in Scranton on North Hyde Park Avenue. Childless, she lavished her affection on me. Mother worked in factories, leaving me with old, German, female relations and Irish nurseries in Brooklyn for the first six years of my life. Aunt Eva's brief visits were the bright spots at a time when I felt like an orphan. When I was five she took me to church, splashed me with holy water from the baptismal font, and made the sign of the cross. The incense, icons, and stained-glass windows fascinated me. As the organ droned, she hung a gold chain and gold cross around my neck and I felt safe and protected. In some mysterious way I still feel it whenever I enter a Catholic church: the power of magic. But Mother removed the cross, forcibly, I think, and I never saw it again. Though Jewish and God-fearing, she had never been exposed to religion.

In our family, intermarriage was the norm; two of her three sisters and all three brothers married German, Irish, and French-Canadian Catholics, and converted. My father was German-American and I thought being American was the solution to perplexing questions of identity as we melted like butter into the big New York pot. But then the Big Liar, Hitler, made Jewish blood a crime punishable by death. Empathizing with Jews in World War II, I believed, was a moral imperative if you were spiritually honest. A Jesuit priest once said I was technically Catholic because of the lay baptism, but I knew I was equally Catholic, German, Jewish, and American. Religion in my family did not cause hostility, it caused laughter, and as a result, perhaps, I am an agnostic.

Mother, who could barely read and write English, was determined that I should have the education she lacked. As a boy my goal was to be a writer and English teacher. Thanks to her I took degrees in English literature, at Brooklyn College and New York University. But, to secure our future, she thought this could best be achieved by

Norse, at age two, with Irish and German aunts; his mother is at the upper right with her hand on Aunt Eva, who is seated, about 1918

marrying a man who knew the value of education. She couldn't have chosen a more shiftless one.

I remember looking up at a barred window behind which sat a bespectacled county clerk at city hall in Coney Island. The man paid the clerk two dollars and got the marriage license. He was twenty-three, she was twenty-nine, and I was six, and we hated each other, he and I, at sight. I was a born-again Oliver Twist and David Copperfield, and still get emotional at cruelty to children, adults, and animals. At seven I read and wrote fables and poems, escaping into fantasy from a dysfunctional family. My stepfather (then still a youth) asserted male supremacy with periodic outbursts of violence, while I fantasized how I would take revenge when I grew up. After years of enduring verbal abuse I had a strong pent-up desire to strike back. At thirteen, seeing him slap my mother, drawing blood, I went berserk. I seized a bread knife and stuck it against his paunch in a blind rage. He froze, not daring to move, and I could see that the bully was a coward. Thus ended the wife-beating, the taunts, the jeers of "sissy," and my feeling of victimization (see *Memoirs of a Bastard Angel*). This was also recorded in my poem "True Confessions" (in *Hotel Nirvana*). It was a turning point, a rite of passage. I was becoming a man.

If I haven't described the houses and locales we lived in it's because I can't. There were so many that they were a blur in my memory. All the single, furnished rooms were drab—with dripping taps; bare, twenty-watt light bulbs; mice; shabby, broken furniture; vermin; noisy neighbors; foul odors. But once, I recall, we had a sunny, cheerful apartment, with our own new furniture. My stepfather had become an accountant at the Hotel Waldorf-Astoria. He wore rimless pince-nez specs, neat suits pressed by my mother, for whom neatness and cleanliness were a religion, and looked distinguished, she said. We had moved into middle-class respectability in Bensonhurst, on the top floor of a redbrick apartment house in the Bay Ridge section, at 1770 Seventy-fifth Street, near what is now Bay Ridge Parkway. It had an elevator and garbage disposal in the hall and we enjoyed the comforts of petit bourgeois life. We bought our first radio, a Garod, I think, and for the first time I had a room of my own. I remember the cheerful songs of prosperity on the radio, like "Blue Skies" and "Blue Heaven" (also "Amos 'n' Andy," the stereotypical Negro comics that were played by white men). I sang the upbeat songs, but it didn't last; the stock-market crash wiped out Blue Heaven and it was "Brother, Can You Spare a Dime?" We were back in the roach-infested hell of furnished rooms; my anguish at losing friends and teachers was terrible as I had to face new bullies each time we moved.

Max was a beer-drinking, barrel-bellied, cigar-smoking petty gambler and confidence trickster. He was completely irresponsible, the shame of his hard-working Jewish family. There were, however, brief, pleasurable interludes when he sang duets with my mother, whose coloratura hit high C and tinkled like a bell; he'd harmonize in a sweet tenor voice and I'd join in with my boy soprano in sentimental ditties like "A Bicycle Built for Two." He also played the violin, after which he'd open his eyes dreamily and quip, "Where am I?"

As a budding writer I was good at thunderstorms, animals, and the sea, but formed some bad habits, like verbosity and sentimentality. Teachers weren't much help; they were incapable of giving instruction on style, tone, and form. They said "avoid adjectives" and spoke about an objective point of view when I had only one, my own. When I was twelve, Max brought home a coworker called Victor Carducci, a grandson of the famous Italian poet Giosuè Carducci, who won the Nobel Prize in 1906 and died the following year. When Victor asked to see my writing I presented some poems and nervously awaited the verdict. He said I had talent and encouraged me to develop it, but didn't say how. Nothing could stop me from writing, however, and at thirteen I published my first story in the *Lincoln Log*, the high school literary magazine, and came out second on the Sanford-Binet IQ test. Max was impressed, which was good for my damaged self-esteem that he had worked so hard to undermine. My first publication was a poem at the age of nine, in Walt Whitman's old newspaper, the *Brooklyn Daily Eagle*.

Despite the grimness of my childhood I was a remarkably resilient, energetic boy, prankster and clown, full of fun, laughter, mimicry, and foreign accents, the one who thought up new games and make-believe dramas to act out. I took dares and jumped off roofs, fences, and so on, getting bruised and cut. Best of all, in summer I often got to visit my uncle Mike, the bootlegger, in East Hampton, Long Island, where he had a training camp for boys, and taught them to box. He was a big, muscular man in the heroic mold, my only role model. His wife, Mary Pitts, was from Montauk, where her parents had a tiny house by the sea. They were simple folk who had emigrated from Nova Scotia. Mr. Pitts, a fisherman, took me with him before dawn on his motorboat full of slithery fish, caught as he monitored his lobster pots. It was wonderful at sea in the dark, cold dawn. I got my sea legs at eleven, on my first trip, and have loved the sea ever since. I enjoyed hearing "canuck"— French-Canadian—and they laughed at my French pronunciation.

I was small but sturdy and when I was fourteen my uncle taught me to box, throwing me into the ring against older boys and shouting, "Fight!" I was so scared that I fought like a wildcat and came out shaky but unbowed. This gave me the courage and confidence I lacked. I guarded my turned-up nose carefully because it was cute. Uncle Mike Rogers (anglicized from the original name, Rognitsky) had a large, two-story, white clapboard house, a garage, and three cars. I'd baby-sit Cousin Georgie, their only child, feeling part of a close, loving family, and I longed to live with them. My uncle was warm, extroverted and generous, but he was also hot-tempered and tough. He neither smoked nor drank, and was liked by all, even the cops. I have a snap of myself on the lawn at East Hampton with his younger brother Lou, a shy, silent man, and little Georgie.

The summer I turned fifteen Uncle Mike had a hired hand called Earl, a blond country boy with muscles that he flexed for my benefit. We shared a room and a cot barely big enough for two. The first night I woke suddenly at dawn: Earl's hands were all over me, and he was trying to remove my bathing trunks. When he saw I was awake he said, "When are we gonna finish this business of gettin' married?" Sitting bolt upright I squawked, *"Married?! Whadda ya mean, married?"* Without waiting for a reply I jumped out of bed and ran in terror to the bathroom. When I got back Earl was dressed. "Don't say anything to your uncle, okay?" he said. I knew that if Uncle Mike found out he'd thrash Earl and fire him, but mostly I was afraid of his anger, his contempt. I knew what Earl wanted and if he hadn't stupidly used the word "married"—shocking in its literalness—he might have succeeded. I'd had sexual fumblings with girls and boys at the age of five, nine, and twelve, but at thirteen my need for tenderness and touch was obsessive. I was a textbook case of Freud's "polymorphous perverse," but I wasn't at all perverse, just completely natural, as he defined it for puberty. Since strict taboos inhibited open behavior I suffered in silence, keeping my desires hidden, a victim of false mythology, lies, and sexual stereotyping. I remember trudging the streets of Brooklyn tirelessly, without appetite or interest in anything but to satisfy my desire for love; night and day I wandered about, hoping to run into a boy like myself, longing for a brother, lover, friend. Nothing came of it. I was so frustrated that at sixteen I tried cutting my wrist with a razor in the bathroom—luckily the wrong way, but I bore thin scars that, like me, became invisible. I hid my nature, my overwhelming need, even from boys who shyly and tensely signaled their interest; but we made no move; the shame of being called a "fairy" prevented us from anything but eye contact.

This unrelieved tension affected my studies, and probably my IQ, for concentration was impossible. Yet, miraculously, I graduated from Lincoln High in Brighton Beach with the four-year gold medal in English that I won for an essay. And in my first semester at Brooklyn College I won first prize for a poem in the *Observer* contest, normally won by seniors. The poem, "Scranton," was based on childhood memories of miners and coal mines, and was a big hit in the Depression years, establishing me, at seventeen, as the new literary celebrity. In my senior year I became editor in chief of the *Observer.*

A memorable psychology course, in which I hoped to learn about sex and behavior but didn't, was taught by a young instructor (before his well-

deserved fame) called Abraham Maslow. He assigned a term paper of any length, the subject of which was our life story. Just what I wanted: to write my *cri de coeur.* My first autobiography—130 tormented pages of *Weltschmerz*—was the essence of romantic discontent. I had read Irving Stone's *Lust for Life* and identified with Van Gogh, the artist as madman, victim, saint, Christ-figure crucified by society, who said, after his first sexual experience at twenty-eight with a whore, "Sex lubricates the machinery of art," or something like that. For about a year or two I experienced a sharp, prickly pain in my scalp that, I thought, was like a crown of thorns. It also ran down my sternum like a row of knife points. Definitely a hysterical symptom. To my surprise, Maslow did not call the men in white jackets but singled it out as the most remarkable document he had seen by an undergraduate, praising its honesty and insightful grasp of my predicament. He asked if he could keep it. For all I know, it is still languishing in his archives, where I hope it remains. I think he graded it *A+* but I recall it as turgid, pathological, adolescent introversion.

For me the most important event at college was meeting a sixteen-year-old freshman called Chester Kallman, a pale blond with large blue eyes and dark circles of dissipation under them. He stood in the doorway of the *Observer* office like Garbo in *Anna Christie* and I had the strongest déjà vu in my life. We stared as if hypnotized, completely spellbound—the start of a passion that would last ten years, interrupted only by three towering events: Pearl Harbor, World War II, and W. H. Auden. Of the three Auden loomed largest.

On April 6, 1939, we went to hear Auden, Isherwood, Louis MacNeice, and Frederic Prokosch at the Keynote Club in New York, on West Fifty-second Street, four blocks from my first independent room on West Fifty-fifth Street and Sixth Avenue. Afterwards, Auden rebuffed us backstage, but Isherwood gave me his calling card, saying, "I hope you'll visit us." Chester asked for the card with the excuse that he wanted to show it to his father but never returned it and visited them alone. Auden was enchanted and, on a second visit, smitten. How did I feel about Chester's first betrayal? It was a rotten thing to do; but I was too shy to see them alone, lacking Chester's confidence. He had poise, wit, and conversational skill, whereas I was shy and insecure. Auden was hooked and I feared losing Chester. What the biographers don't say, or know, is that Chester was unfaithful from the start. He had never been attracted to

Auden and had remained promiscuous from the age of twelve.

Influenced by Auden and Spender, we quoted their poems by heart and read their books avidly. Spender's poem beginning "O young men, O young comrades" was a call to arms in more ways than one. Auden's early poems, even when unintelligible, fascinated us. The language, imagery, and rhythms were the most forceful we'd known since Hopkins, Crane, and Eliot. His poems of the thirties with their private allusions, though obscure, mesmerized us. We didn't need to understand them to feel like members of an intellectual elite. In 1939 I coined a word for it, the *Homintern* (Homosexual International, after Comintern, the Communist International), which Auden appropriated and used until his final years, without crediting me. It was, in fact, his favorite portmanteau word; his stated ambition was to get it into the *Oxford English Dictionary,* with his own neologisms, but as far as I know he never succeeded. If it does make it to the *OED,* I proudly proclaim my paternity. There was no such organization, of course. Auden and Spender implied a communistic love for young men, a deep male bonding of the flesh but, as in Crane, Hopkins, and Whitman, it was cryptic, coded, still the love that dared not speak its name. Disclosure meant persecution, disgrace. And since support groups did not exist, it was *sauve qui peut,* an act of desperation. The toll of self-censorship on the nerves and emotions was incalculable. When I hear the terms "sexual preference" or "choice" I am appalled at such ignorance. Who would consciously choose to suffer the dangers and indignities of a despised way of life, exposed to hatred and contempt, the victim of verbal and physical abuse, even murder? Sex is not a preference but a primal drive, an irresistible force of nature. Whether gay or straight, or in between, it is the same drive, neither more nor less intense.

In the fall of 1939, when Auden moved to 1 Montague Terrace from 7 Middagh Street nearby, I became his secretary. Jane Bowles had performed that function when she and her husband, Paul, lived at Middagh Street with Carson McCullers, Benjamin Britten, Peter Pears, and a trained chimpanzee. Auden was a strict disciplinarian and ran the house, which fascinated Jane but not Paul. Brooklyn Heights was a quiet residential area, the site of literary history, that I called the "campus," a few blocks from Brooklyn College when it consisted of five dilapidated office build-

Norse, college graduation photo, Brooklyn College, New York, 1938

ings downtown before it relocated to its present site in 1937. Auden lived near Hart Crane's old residence, 110 Columbia Heights, where Crane wrote *The Bridge,* a few doors from where Thomas Wolfe wrote *Look Homeward, Angel,* and Walt Whitman, in 1855, handset the type for *Leaves of Grass* on Cranberry Street. All had bronze commemorative plaques. The Auden Society (of which I am an honorary member) recently informed me that a bronze plaque would soon be put up for Auden.

At seventeen I visited Hart Crane's old apartment, then occupied by an English professor. Before Crane, the engineer who built the Brooklyn Bridge, Washington Roebling, had lived there, supervising construction from the rear windows on the East River.

If spirit of place means anything, a case can be made for a literary line of succession that links Whitman, Wolfe, and Crane in a family of rhapsodic, visionary writers established there. I had found my literary place. There was another link, the manly love of comrades (even about the lofty head of Wolfe hovered hushed rumors), or the "adhesiveness" of brotherly love, as Whitman called it. My initiation into this brotherhood began there. I was inducted by "David Blake."

(From *Memoirs of a Bastard Angel*)

Auden was not impressed by American writers. He thought Crane was "lousy" and Wolfe and Whitman not much better. American writers, he believed, did not equal the great Europeans. Even Chester regarded Whitman as a bore though he loved Crane.

David White ("David Blake") was the English professor who "brought me out" in his flat at 138 Columbia Heights. He was in his mid-thirties, bald, emaciated, and the scion of a midwestern family with major oil interests. His father had been governor of his state, but David was a Communist and aesthete. He had a library of first editions, mostly modern poetry, which I borrowed and read, a huge record collection, rare wines, whiskey, liqueurs, and old prints. I was seventeen when we met in the *Observer* office where I had presented myself as winner of the poetry competition and he was faculty advisor of the magazine. He gave me a job cataloguing his record collection, but it was really a liberal education in life and the arts. One of the records was Billie Holiday singing "Strange Fruit." For me she became an instant icon.

By the time I was twenty-one, in the climate of trust and love David provided, I could comport myself well in any company but couldn't live with him, which he wanted, as his boyfriend. I couldn't reciprocate his feelings. He was kind, considerate, courteous, and never argued; students and faculty equally admired him. Even Auden found him "a lovely man, a real charmer," when we brought him to David's flat. But both Auden and I wanted Chester and when he stopped sleeping with Auden, less than two years after they met, Auden was even more miserable than I. In a letter dated November 1, 1941, from Ann Arbor, Michigan, where he was teaching at the university, he wrote:

Dear Harold, Chester [has] gone to California to find his own life. What being without him is like for me, I think you can guess. I feel as if I were scattered into little pieces. And if the Devil were to offer him back to me, on condition that I never wrote another line, I should unhesitatingly accept.[1]

As Auden's secretary I typed his correspondence, domestic and foreign, and his long poem "New Year Letter," which he finished in April 1940. I was a fast, expert typist, but when I made one mistake, inadvertently omitting a line, Wystan began screaming. I could have retyped the page but I left in a huff. The whole thing, however, was soon forgotten. Auden's rudeness was legendary and his tantrums notorious, but he was also very caring and open-handed with those he felt close to, and we were close. Chester and Wystan had violent screaming fights but Chester and I had never quarreled seriously until Auden appeared, when I felt left out. Then, sometime in late 1940 Chester became enamored of a young English aristocrat, an admirer of Auden. Jack was really handsome and attractive and Chester conducted the clandestine affair for some time before disclosing it to Auden, announcing that he would never sleep with him again. In a violent, jealous rage Auden attempted to strangle Chester in his sleep. Then, guilt-ridden at his own behavior, he became reconciled on Chester's terms.

Earlier, in 1939, Wystan wrote me a Christmas letter when he thought he and Chester would be together forever. I considered myself lucky until this bombshell letter. He acknowledged that I must feel "a little bitter," as he put it, about his "having taken Chester away" from me. I felt worse than that. He went on to compare my disadvantaged state with his privileged one, listing his advantages: loving parents, luck, "the best education that money could buy . . . knowing the Right People, and living at exactly the right time for my work to receive notice as the new poetic model, one in fact for whom everything possible has been done to make his life easy." He imagines me comparing my lot with his as the world shrugs its shoulders saying,

"Unlucky chap. Illegitimate, you know. Frightful home life . . . no money . . . quite talented . . . but not enough. Ersatz ambition, I suspect, for the desire to . . . belong to the same class as his father who cheated him out of his birthright." That is just the sort of thing the world does say, Harold

---

[1]All excerpts from the unpublished letters of W. H. Auden printed with permission. Copyright © the Estate of W. H. Auden.

dear, please realize this. . . . The world is right in worshipping Success and despising Failure, but its conception of what these are is so distorted, that it usually fails to recognize either. There is only one reason . . . why the world's judgments and prophecies seem so often to be confirmed, and that is because people accept its values. . . . If you accept them you will fail. . . . Luck, says the world, is money, birth, beauty, brains. The useless is suffering . . . negative . . . barren and vulgar. This is a lie, Harold, a bloody lie, and because they believe it, thousands of people are destroyed every day, either by trying to run away from their suffering into phantasy, drink, or lechery, or . . . they are consumed by the wish for revenge and go down into the Night of hatred and envy.

Accept suffering, he says, it is a greater gift than all of the above, "more precious than a substantial income or an Oxford education." I was appalled at this portrayal, which I could not accept—he was stacking the deck. It concludes:

> . . . all you have suffered is gathering inside you and crying out to be recognized as a great talent, all the doors that have been shut in your face and locked are trying to urge you towards your true direction . . . i.e., to be a saint, one of those rare beings whom, when they die, the people who knew them remember . . . for their existence . . . whose presence is enough to make others convinced that human life has not been an entirely vain experiment.

I thought the letter, though sincere, was a rationalization, a cover-up for guilt at "having taken Chester away" from me, and the argument about suffering as a great gift was absurd. This was the preachy message from the clergy to the poor and oppressed everywhere. Auden was playing God. It sounded like a religious justification for social wrongs. I couldn't accept it. Compassion, yes; resignation to misery, no. As for talent, he thought little of mine or Chester's and, like "the world" he was personifying, he would have said the same of Whitman, James Baldwin, Tennessee Williams, Allen Ginsberg, and Jean Genet at twenty-three. He had just written "Refugee Blues" and "September 1, 1939," the latter after Chester and I had directed him to a gay bar that inspired it. There is no acceptance of suffering in these poems but, appropriately, outrage at the suffering and dying caused by a "psychopathic god," a mad-

man's lies, whims, and delusions. But when he got religion he turned against the "September" poem. His earlier poem, "About suffering they were never wrong, / The old Masters," also chose a safe viewpoint: *he* isn't the one who suffers. His fatalistic assumptions about my life were false and I was determined to prove him wrong. He was pontificating, like the preachers who plunder the alms box and bed the virgins while feeling righteous in their faith. Nor was he free of hatred or envy or the desire for revenge, which lent his words a sanctimonious tone. He hated and envied rivals like Dylan Thomas.

As the years passed I achieved a modest success, attracting the attention, in 1951, of another major figure, William Carlos Williams, who singled me out from a group of little-known poets that included Paul Blackburn. He wrote: "I admired your poem, "The Railroad Yard" . . . the thing that struck me most forcibly was the language . . . I was very moved." March 26, 1952, I made my debut to a packed house at the New York Museum of Modern Art with the long poem

Portrait of Norse taken in New York, 1940

he admired. The museum had initiated a "discovery" series for which an established poet, in this case Williams, presented some younger poets for their first public readings (Kenneth Beaudoin and Eli Siegel were in our group). I was the hit of the evening. The previous presentation, some months earlier, was made by Auden who, not surprisingly, introduced Chester. Ironically, my poem was about my childhood year in Scranton, the suffering "transcended and transformed into art," e. e. cummings told me after the reading, inviting me to visit him, which I frequently did. The poem appeared, under another title, in James Laughlin's *New Directions Anthology Number 13*.

After Pearl Harbor I joined the U.S. Maritime Commission, building Liberty ships in Mobile at the Alabama Drydock and Shipbuilding Company. I considered shipping out to Murmansk, the highest risk and highest-paid trip, but it was risky enough in Alabama. I helplessly watched as an old black man was beaten to death in the shipyard by hundreds of whites while we were supposedly fighting racism. No newspaper in Mobile would publish my eye-witness account of the atrocity. On trial runs in the Gulf of Mexico I saw the periscopes of German U-boats which were sinking Liberty ships. Then suddenly my appendix burst in the sheet-metal yard and, thanks to the experienced supervisor who recognized the symptoms—I was cold and shaking in the heat and clutching my side—my life was saved. He raced me to the hospital and within minutes I went under the knife. "Son," said the surgeon, staring at my abdominal muscles, "I hate to cut into such a fine body. It's like cutting into a statue." The McBurney incision was the dividing line between my past and future. I had faced death and wanted to live each moment fully, as if it were my last, as Auden had said in a letter. But I needed to recuperate. With savings from the wartime job, I returned to New York at the end of 1942, staying at the West Sixty-second Street Y. I was twenty-six and virtually unpublished.

Then *Poetry* took a long poem, *Accent* took two poems, and from that time I appeared in the "littles" and anthologies, getting a reputation in New York. I moved to a tiny room in Greenwich Village on Horatio Street, near a slaughterhouse, and plunged into Village life. One dark glacial dawn in the winter of 1943, as I was about to enter a cafeteria on Fourteenth Street with a friend called Harry Herschkowitz, a protégé of Henry Miller, we ran into a small, thin, black youth

shivering in a sweater full of holes and a navy watchcap pulled down over his ears. His eyes bugged out and he looked desperate. Harry introduced me to James Baldwin, age nineteen. Auden would surely have told him to forget writing—he had less of a future than I, was also illegitimate, with a violent father who was a Baptist minister, and a squalid, poverty-stricken home life in Harlem. Staring into mirrors he'd moan, "What's going to become of me? I'm poor, black, ugly, and queer!" His father knew the answer: he wanted him to be a saint! Having so much in common we quickly grew close; in fact Jimmy fell for me. Mutually protective, we solaced and supported each other. I read the manuscript of *Crying Holy*, his first novel that would take ten more years of revision before it was published as *Go Tell It on the Mountain*. He visited me often and we sat huddled in the cold before the little fireplace, discussing books, racism, being gay. Another visitor was Tennessee Williams, with whom I had shared a cabin in Provincetown the summer of 1944 when he was completing *The Glass Menagerie*. He was thirty-four, another short, slight, penniless writer, with a sad, forlorn look. He was no talker. Jimmy could liven up a conversation, Tennessee could deaden one. Then one evening in a state of excitement he announced that Eddie Dowling, the actor-director, had taken the play. He had made it.

About 3:00 A.M. one morning I met a youth of eighteen in the subway and brought him home. When he showed me his rhymed quatrains I knew Auden wouldn't have put money on him, either. He was shy, quiet, timid, and lonely. His name was Allen Ginsberg. It's truly amazing to compare Big Names with their Humble Beginnings. Those early years of doubt and despair play no part in the public image, which is always fictitious, with little resemblance to the person. Fame distorts the personal record.

Jimmy brought me to meet Paul Goodman, who was married but always surrounded by handsome young men, many of whom, like George Dennison and Irving Feldman, were incorrigibly straight. Paul loved "young fellows" but if rejected became rude. After we met he kept asking Jimmy about me. When I showed up alone he made a pass that I rebuffed. I had to put up with his catty remarks after that but we remained friendly for years, critiquing each other's latest poems at my flat or his. He respected me as "a talent" but I found his style, though daring in its homosexual content and vernacular, too conventional. William Carlos Williams believed Auden was a brilliant

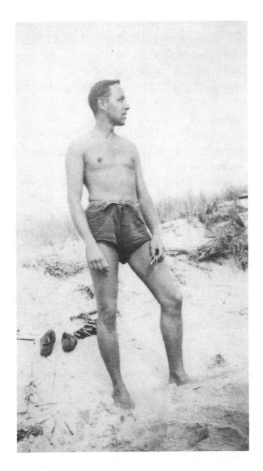

"Tennessee Williams on the beach, at the time he was writing The Glass Menagerie," *Provincetown, Massachusetts, 1944. Photo by Harold Norse.*

technical virtuoso whose revival of traditional forms and styles perpetuated sterile formalism and discredited experimentalism, and I felt the same way, without having worked out an alternative of my own. But I thought, and still do, that had Goodman been as iconoclastic in style as he was in his political anarchism, he might have turned out to be our Genet, who influenced him.

Once again David White asked me, after so many years, to live with him in his new apartment on Clark Street, but I refused as gently as I could. Within a year he died of a heart attack and, at twenty-eight, I felt my boyhood had finally come to an end.

I'd had a novel accepted, then rejected, and decided I was not a novelist by conventional

standards. When Baldwin suffered a similar reversal I said I was in the same boat. "Oh no, baby," he responded, "we're in different boats! You're *white!*" This was one nuance of despair I couldn't top, but I felt it *was* the same boat—call it class—though segregated. Still, we had common cause and he agreed that being black, Jewish, or gay meant that we suffered from the same bigotry and intolerance.

I found a cold-water flat on the top floor of a brownstone tenement at 28 St. Mark's Place. The bathtub was an ancient claw-foot specimen raised on a wooden platform, like a Duchamp ready-made, dominating the kitchen. My poetry and reviews were appearing in the *Saturday Review,* the *Nation, Poetry,* the *Kenyon Review,* etc., and on the basis of my publications I got a job teaching in the humanities department at Cooper Union, where I stayed for three years, and matriculated at New York University for an M.A. When I walked into my first class at NYU I was amazed to see a poem of mine, from the *Sewanee Review,* on the blackboard. Our professor, Margaret Schlauch, a distinguished linguistics scholar, devoted the entire session to a study of the poem.

Jimmy Baldwin introduced me to a twenty-two-year-old composer, Richard Stryker. My journal for November 1948 records: "Not since Chester have I had such a full relationship . . . this time monogamously reciprocal." Jimmy, who had also been enamored of Dick, having met with no success sailed for Paris on a Saxton grant to work on his novel. Meanwhile I collaborated with Ned Rorem on a song cycle called "Penny Arcade." In a flurry of postcards he outlined his needs, giving me only a day each for six lyrics. With a heavy teaching schedule, plus graduate work, the pressure cramped my style. I thought the hastily dashed off poems were awkward but Ned set them with equal haste and on May 19, 1949, it was performed with mezzo-soprano Nell Tangeman and Ned at the piano, at the MacMillan Theater, Columbia University. Years later Ned wrote: "Much of the musical material used therein I incorporated into later works." During 1948–49 he set other poems of mine. At this time I moved to 573 Third Avenue where for twenty-two dollars a month we had the top floor of an antiquated four-story building with the El thundering below. On the street level a family of German-Jewish refugees had a diner, about which I wrote a short story published in *Commentary,* then a leftist Jewish magazine edited by Robert Warshow, whom Baldwin credited with having taught him about writing at just the right time. Warshow published his early essays and my poetry, reviews, and short fiction. He solicited a review of Auden's *Nones*, about which I was laudatory, but made the point that, though using the canonical book of the hours for theme and structure, Auden showed he was not a mystical or spiritual poet but a worldly hedonist. Auden took it badly and I was never forgiven, though I still saw Chester.

Through Dick I met John Cage, Lou Harrison, Alan Hovhannes, and many performers. Dick studied composition with Ned and Lou, and wrote the score for Kenneth Rexroth's *Beyond the Mountains* for the new Living Theater. Through Tennessee I had met Julian Heck in Provincetown when he was nineteen. After his marriage to Judith Malina we all grew very close. Our lives were a series of concerts, theatre, films, art galleries, bars, and parties. At one party I met a millionaire art collector, Dwight Ripley, who offered me anything I wanted. Thinking this mere drunken whimsy, I said airily, "A Picasso!" Four days later a chauffeur rang our doorbell and delivered a 1923 Picasso gouache!

Dwight bought the Tibor de Nagy Gallery and Johnny Myers became its director. They published Frank O'Hara's first book, *A City Winter,* and I declined an offer from Dwight to publish mine since his interest in me was more than literary, and I gave him no hope of sexual favors. But I dined with him at French restaurants, like the Chambord and Pavillon, and rode in taxis and accompanied him to the Plaza Hotel (where he was born) and at the Hotel Chelsea, his "Bohemian digs." Dick threw violent scenes and when I discussed it with Goodman he said, "He's consumed by envy and jealousy. He once thought he was a genius, but now he isn't so sure." Lacking faith in himself Dick also had writer's block, and though my feelings hadn't changed he accused me of infidelity. Thinking a few months of separation might clear the air, to which he agreed, I decided to sell the Picasso and leave for Europe. A poet I knew, who was so broke he bummed bus fare, offered to act as agent, being experienced with art dealers, and I foolishly gave him the Picasso. I got less than a hundred dollars in small installments and put off the trip to Europe. Eventually he grew very rich as an art dealer notorious for fraud, theft, and deception.

Another chance of a lifetime dropped into my lap when a friend told me of a colonial farmhouse in Canterbury, Connecticut, going for a thousand dollars. It was a fixer-upper built in 1809, with one hundred acres of woodland and some arable land.

My mother put up the money. It had a vast variety of trees, plants, ponds, wild game, and birds. Here was my dream estate, an escape from the city that I'd share with Dick and the Becks—but we never lived there. Dick feared isolation and the house became a burden. (A few years later I sold it for three thousand dollars.) Dick was drinking heavily and chain-smoking three packs of cigarettes a day. I too smoked nervously. Once I found him on the floor weeping drunkenly among cigarette butts and ashes, his hand bleeding. "Call Bellevue!" he wailed (the mental hospital). He had deliberately smashed a glass ashtray in his hand. He also poisoned the atmosphere between me and the Becks, complaining that they owed him money while rehearsing Rexroth's play. He was so resentful that I confronted them and what followed was a mad scene of backstage hysterics, everyone shouting at once.

Time doesn't heal wounds, it just covers them with scar tissue. They can hurt a lifetime. Dick went to live with the Becks, airing his resentment of me, repeating the same behavior in all relationships. He had served three years in prison as a conscientious objector and emerged as a violent, conflicted pacifist.

Spring 1951: I received the letter from William Carlos Williams praising my poetry; Chester Kallman invited me to a cocktail party at the Gotham Book Mart for his chapbook *Elegy;* and I participated in a performance of John Cage's "Imaginary Landscape No. 4," a musical collage of chance sounds for twelve radios (the only instrument I could play) and twenty-four players, including Dick and me, with Cage conducting—one turned on and off on cue, the other regulated volume. Eight years later I would use aleatory techniques in cut-ups with William Burroughs in Paris. Since 1941 I had experimented with accentual and free forms, natural speech rhythms, line breaks, and associative techniques but no one would print the results.

On subsequent visits to Williams in Rutherford he encouraged me to collect my first volume, *The Undersea Mountain,* reviewed favorably by the *New York Times* and *Herald-Tribune,* and also *Poetry* and the *Hudson Review*—mostly formalist poems, admired by Allen Tate and John Crowe Ransom. But in the end Williams was right. My true path lay in the direction of experimental verse. My book caught the eye of Anaïs Nin, who had the same publisher, though no one else would touch her work. Kimon Friar brought me to her Village penthouse at 215 West Thirteenth Street and, like Williams, she received me warmly, presenting me with inscribed copies of *A Spy in the House of Love* and *House of Incest.* "Americans are afraid of feeling," she said, "of expressing it. You do it wonderfully." She wrote in *Diary 5:* "I met Harold Norse, a poet who has great emotional power in a beautiful, disciplined form."

On August 3, 1953, I sailed for Europe with sufficient funds for three months and stayed fifteen years. In Italy, Greece, France, and Morocco I found sex in all its manifestations freely expressed, as it doubtless had been in pagan times, without persecution, rightly regarded as self-evidently natural, which made life worth living. Such civilized attitudes liberated me from sexual tensions and stresses that undermine and enervate the life force in puritan societies like ours and Britain's, with their crippling anti-sexual bias and hypocrisy. Senator Joseph McCarthy and J. Edgar Hoover, both later known to be homosexual, turned the U.S. into a penal colony, persecuting gays and liberals in their witch-hunt for Communists and dissidents, buzzwords for intellectuals and freethinkers. Though I had little money, I was happy to escape the atmosphere of paranoia and police-state oppression during the fifties, and remained as long as possible in the Mediterranean world where, at least, one could live cheaply in a warm climate of beauty and sensuality.

I spoke fluent Italian, passable French and Spanish, basic German, and demotic Greek after spending six years in Italy, three in Paris, three in Greece, and a year each in Morocco, Germany, and England, with brief trips to Switzerland, Spain, and Holland. Those were the happiest years of my life. In 1954, during my first summer in Italy, I hitchhiked around the country, writing a travel book and poems for the occasion, and publishing excerpts and poems in *Art News, Poetry,* and other mags.

I taught English at British and American schools, but was freed to write on small stipends from a patron—the patronage system had not died in Europe. Through media attention I became a celebrity and met distinguished Europeans in the arts. While learning Italian I began translating the early nineteenth-century Roman poet Belli, astonished that his sonnets, written in the vernacular, were so similar to New Yorkese, with the spicy irreverence of slang and gutter language. Each sonnet was a comic drama from the mouths of working-class narrators, anti-papal in sentiment during the corrupt regime of the papal state. It was

a daring undertaking since Belli had never been translated and the raw language was unprintable. Scholars and writers said it was impossible to translate: James Joyce and D. H. Lawrence had tried and failed. I responded that it could be done in New Yorkese, and translated about sixty sonnets. I showed them to my friend Alberto Moravia, who was so impressed that he wrote an introduction and Williams wrote a preface.

Through Moravia I met Pier Paolo Pasolini at Rosati's, a café in the Piazza del Popolo. He was skeptical that an American press would print it because of its obscenities. He was right, but I said a small press might do it. Then the *Hudson Review* accepted half of the lot and when the printer refused to typeset them because of the anti-papal sentiment and foul language, they waited until the contract expired, got a new printer, and twenty-six sonnets with my introduction appeared in the April 1956 issue with Pound's last translation, Sophocles' *Women of Trachis.* This was a coup. I was elated. The Italian press wrote me up in articles and interviews, as did the *London Times, New Delhi Times,* and *Figaro Littéraire* in Paris. I was mentioned on RAI, Italian radio. The scholars were astonished. During my brief visit to New York in the summer of 1958, Jonathan Williams, poet and publisher of Jargon Books, offered publication. It came out in 1960, while I was living in Paris at the Beat Hotel, 9 rue Gît-le-Coeur, with William Burroughs, Brion Gysin, and Gregory Corso. At my book party at the Librairie Anglaise, 42 rue de Seine, I met William Saroyan, who wanted a signed copy.

I often saw Anaïs Nin in Paris and was photographed with her at the Librairie Anglaise book party for her novel *Seduction of the Minotaur,* summer 1962. My arrival in May 1959 had led to my third most vital literary liaison—with William Burroughs. It happened through a chance meeting in Naples, where I taught at the U.S. Information Service School. I met a middle-aged American heiress, Julia Chanler Laurin, of the Astor family, who was a great talker and very well-read. One day she said, "Answer without thinking: What city would you choose to live in more than any in the world?" "Paris!" I said without hesitation. "You have an apartment waiting for you there!" she said.

The apartment had a private entrance in a sixteenth-century house on rue St. Louis en L'Ile, a block from James Jones, the novelist, who became a friend and drinking buddy. At the newsvendor shop across the street I chatted with Marc

Norse (right) with James Jones at an exhibition of Norse's ink drawings called "Cosmographs," Paris, 1961

Chagall, which inspired a poem about us in *Mysteries of Magritte.* Through Julia I briefly met Blaise Cendrars and Max Ernst, both of whom had had a crush on her in her youth, when she was immersed in the literary-art world of the twenties in Paris, where she was born and raised. Early in 1960, when Julia needed the flat, I moved into the Hotel Univers and began to paint, throwing Pelican inks on Bristol paper and washing them in the bidet with startling results: they were maps of inner space, which I called "Cosmographs," jokingly referring to myself as founder of the Bidet School. Sure enough, a school of young painters, calling themselves Cosmographers, imitated me. After a month at the Univers, I moved into the Beat Hotel at Burroughs's urging, in March. I was offered shows by three galleries a year later but chose the Librairie Anglaise, where the Greek sculptor Takis hung my paintings on the walls and ceiling (in space), suspended by wires and magnets. Burroughs wrote the introduction, saying that the random principle revealed unexplored psychic areas; *le tout Paris* turned up, with Allen Ginsberg, Corso, Henri Michaux, and established painters. *Life* did a story with photos (bumped in New York) and the French press covered it: *L'Exprès, Paris Match, Figaro,* etc. It sold well and I bought a used Fiat 600. The remaining Cosmographs are still in my possession. John Ashbery, then art critic for the international edition of the *Herald-Tribune,* reviewed the show, March 22, 1961: "Harold Norse, Beat American poet, shows his highly attractive 'Cosmographs' at the English Bookshop. Painting with colored inks on wet paper, Norse produces fantastic webs, maps, or labyrinths, and strange combinations of iridescent color." Ashbery said they inspired him to paint, which he had always wanted to do. When I said that like my cut-up fiction and poetry it was based on aleatory techniques, he exclaimed, "I've been doing that for years!" He picked words at random from dictionaries, books and magazines and strung them together, he said.

I met Burroughs in June '59 when he was still addicted to heroin, and introduced him to Ian Sommerville, a Cambridge physics student who became his nurse, companion, and collaborator. Burroughs underwent his first successful cure, and I began writing cut-up prose early in 1960, feeling like a medium controlled by subconscious forces. Burroughs and Brion Gysin were wildly enthusiastic. Gysin, an American painter, discovered the technique by chance at the hotel when he accidentally sliced through newspapers while making a mat for a painting, then read the fragments pieced randomly together and burst out laughing. They were like messages from a witty trance medium. He called it cut-up writing. Chance techniques were first explored by Dada and Surrealism, and Burroughs used cut-ups in his novels. For three years we saw one another daily, dining together and discussing cut-ups as an expanded consciousness technique. It began to influence the new psychedelic drug culture through rock stars like David Bowie in the sixties. In his preface to my cut-up novel, *Beat Hotel,* written there, Burroughs said I played a "pivotal role" in developing the cut-up technique. My novel became a Beat classic.

The Beat Hotel, now a posh shrine for devotees from around the world, was called by the *Time* reviewer who panned Burroughs's *Naked Lunch* "a flea-bag shrine where passers-by move out of the way for rats." *Time* has changed its tune.

My third book of poems, *The Dancing Beasts,* containing some of my best work in the formalist mode, came out in 1962 while I was at the hotel. The reviews were very favorable but since I was producing experimental, open form, and cut-up writing, to me the book seemed anachronistic. Now, in 1992, I can see the merits of some of those poems, which Robert Graves so much admired when I visited him in Deyá, Mallorca, in the summer of 1962, on my way back to Paris after Tangier. Graves said, "Very, very honest, very, very good, no cheat. You will go far."

Nineteen sixty-three was the year William Carlos Williams died, the hotel was sold, and we dispersed. I left for Greece, where I felt like Ulysses among the lotus eaters. On the island of Hydra I introduced the cut-up technique, via my *Beat Hotel* manuscript, to the Canadian poet Leonard Cohen, which influenced him to write some extraordinary pages that he showed me a few days later, of his novel *Beautiful Losers.* I contracted hepatitis in Hydra in 1965 during an epidemic and ended up in an Athens hospital. After I departed for Switzerland for a cure, the Greek fascist junta staged a coup and I lost most of my possessions and my Dutch lover, who liberated my belongings—from me. I never returned. He married into wealth and still thrives on chicanery.

In Gstaad, in the Swiss Bernese Oberland, thanks to my patrons, I recovered after a dull but peaceful winter drinking fermented beet and carrot juice, a natural cure. I listened to Krishnamurti's talks in Saanen, went to Germany for a year, fell ill again, back to Gstaad, then London, where I got a flat on St. Marks Crescent in Hampstead for a year, where I was visited by Stephen Spender. My wanderings reminded me of Rilke's feverish travels, rushing around Europe in frenzied angst, unable to settle anywhere or find peace. My weight had gone from 150 to 120 pounds and I had lost my energy, but I wrote long disjointed poems reflecting the melange of places, languages, and states of mind, collected in *Karma Circuit* and the Penguin book. In London a psychic told me I was

Norse and Anaïs Nin in the English Book Shop at her book party for Seduction of the Minotaur, *Paris, 1962*

Harold Norse with William S. Burroughs at the Naropa Institute, 1980

suffering from grief over a broken affair, and that the liver would heal if I let go. He was right. I visited Burroughs, who was living at Duke Street, St. James, and he roped me into Scientology, believing it would solve my problem. But the auditing didn't work and he soon gave it up himself.

On repatriating in September 1963 I lived in Venice West for three years, at 15 Paloma Avenue, where my mother, having left New York, found a warm, cheap place by the sea. I had a two-room apartment with a wall-bed, a block from the Pacific. The apartment, which I called "the clinic," was white and sterile. I couldn't write there. I saw that if I was to go on living and writing, I had to find a natural cure. What better place than Los Angeles, California, where "organic," "karma," and "energy" were buzzwords?

The sun, the semi-tropical languor, the smog-free sea air, with its bracing negative ions, the organically grown fruits and raw vegetables, plus deep breathing and brisk walking, restored my health completely. My liver regenerated; I began jogging along the shore, rode a bicycle, and lifted weights at the original Gold's Gym two blocks away, where I got to know Arnold Schwarzenegger, age twenty-one; we jogged and joked together. In less than two years I had solid muscle and no flab. At fifty-four I looked and felt thirty-eight. It started with an elderly chiropractor in West L.A. who knew I had to kick my thirty-year addiction to barbiturates, which doctors kept prescribing for insomnia. So in my white clinic apartment I clawed the walls for twelve days, eating grapefruit and taking enemas. It was harder to kick than heroin, she said, but it worked. I've been a vegetarian health-food freak ever since.

I never told my mother about my illness—she would have made it worse. Her grip on reason at best was never too firm, but now—well, when she read a telegram from a youth in New York asking to visit me (we met at the Y), she bitterly accused me of concealing a wife and son from her. What I concealed was my libido. Then for three days she wept because of a smudge on my bed sheet which she mistook for cigarette ash, convinced I'd burn down the house because I was smoking in bed. I had quit five years before but she didn't believe me. She never believed anybody or anything except her own fantasies, projections, and misconceptions, and she grew worse with age. I couldn't communicate with her. Her life was a blur of anxiety, worry, and old memories. She agonized over imaginary problems of her own invention.

I had a three-year friendship with Charles Bukowski, during his depressed, alcoholic, postal-clerk days, and with Lawrence Lipton, who wrote a long article on me in the *Los Angeles Free Press* in 1969. That year volume thirteen of the *Penguin Modern Poets,* a three-poet series (Bukowski, Philip Lamantia, and me) came out. I'd been approached in London by the editor and brought them aboard. It was Bukowski's first international exposure. Then one day in Santa Monica I spotted Paul Bowles on the balcony of his hotel room and we had a pleasant reunion six years since my year in Tangier, which he and his wife, Jane, made unforgettable by their inimitable personalities (see *Memoirs*). Isherwood appeared and behaved distantly because of an imagined slight in New York twenty years earlier. Paul was teaching for a year as Distinguished Professor at San Fernando Valley State. But, unable to write, I grew bored with the beach community. From time to time I visited Anaïs at her Frank Lloyd Wright home in Silver Lake. Stimulated by her confidence in me, and having regained my health, I felt compelled to leave, despite my guilt about deserting my mother, who never stopped nagging, criticizing, and ordering me around, knowing no other way to relate. She drove me away and then complained that I abandoned her. Ironically, though her chief concern was health, she produced constant emotional stress.

On December 29, 1971, I departed for San Francisco, intending to spend a year (twenty-one years later I'm still here, in the Mission District, after a rural interval at Monte Rio in Russian River). I began writing and publishing extensively in a downtown flat near the East Bay Bridge—which I took over from a friend who had gotten married—and taught creative writing at San Jose State for five semesters. I also found myself on the poetry circuit reading to capacity audiences, at the Poetry Center of San Francisco State, San Jose State, Cabrillo College, and many other venues. At Anaïs's last reading, a three-day celebration of her work at UC's Zellerbach Hall in Berkeley, before two-thousand people, I read my chant "I Am in the Hub of the Fiery Force" and got a standing ovation. Anaïs hugged and kissed me onstage and afterwards I was mobbed like a rock star. Youths reached out to touch me reverently. The same thing happened in San Francisco at Fugazzi Hall, where I read with Kay Boyle and Lawrence Ferlinghetti, who requested a selection of my poems, which became *Hotel Nirvana*, my City Lights Pocket Poets book, nominated for a National Book Award in 1974, the year I got a National Endowment for the Arts poetry fellowship. From 1972 to 1974 I edited my magazine,

Bastard Angel, receiving an NEA and de Young Museum grant for two issues.

The museum curators did a one-hour documentary film interview in my flat and the third issue served as the museum catalog featuring the Beat Generation poets. For three consecutive nights we read to overflow audiences in the museum theatre (Ginsberg, Snyder, Whalen, Ferlinghetti, McClure, Duncan, and myself). Our portraits, notebooks, worksheets, and books were on exhibit for four months. In the late sixties and early seventies, after the Summer of Love, the hippie/beat counter-culture was cresting and my poetry, with its psychedelic, erotic, and social messages, reached young audiences internationally. At each reading, in a life-giving catharsis, I experienced a surge of energy in the interchange between poet and audience. When I read with Allen Ginsberg at the Fritschman Theatre in Los Angeles to over a thousand people, again I was mobbed. The young audience lingered on and on, staring straight into my eyes meaningfully, expressively.

John Cage, using the *I Ching*, selected notes at random for his scores, which are really musical collage. The ancient Chinese viewed life in random not causal terms, and collage, like life, reflects this by producing the unexpected. The element of

Norse reading, with Allen Ginsberg (far left) and Peter Orlovsky, at the Naropa Institute, Boulder, Colorado, 1980

chance was notably lacking in mainstream American poetry, dominated by reason and realism. In writing, cut-ups reflect the aleatory nature of events, the mosaic pattern of reality, of the mind operating in different time frames and places simultaneously, with random associations and stimuli included, not edited out. Dada and Surrealism explored this through automatism, which has always fascinated me. The surrealism of daily life—fortuitous juxtapositions and events, synchronicities that defy reason—boggles the mind. *Karma Circuit* reflected this principle.

Anaïs Nin specifies that poetry and dream are not under "the command of reason" but of the psyche. She saw this in my first book, the union of physical reality with the dream life: symbols, feelings, associations. These elements joined most forcefully in *Carnivorous Saint*, 235 pages of homoerotic poems, from 1941 to 1976. The mainstream ignored it, the gay press was unanimous in its praise. Even Isherwood broke a thirty-year hostile silence in a note to me, saying he had read it from start to finish "with great admiration and enjoyment," and then snubbed me again at a talk he gave! Praise from an enemy is the sincerest kind.

A year later the first volume of *Gay Sunshine Interviews* with a dozen writers came out, including Genet, Ginsberg, Burroughs, Isherwood, Vidal, Tennessee Williams, and myself. Ginsberg called it "a revolution of manners . . . unheard of in previous . . . centuries." He was referring to the candid self-revelation of the interviewees about their sex lives, which characterizes *Carnivorous Saint*, a book that helped break the ground. I'm contemplating an updated volume of *Saint*—fifty-five years of homoerotic verse. It would actually be the third edition, new and revised, since a second appeared with the title *Love Poems* (1940–1985), which the publisher assigned. I disliked the title and the production—small typeface, cheap white paper, and typographical errors. *Booklist* called it "a major work of gay literature" and *Library Journal* said I was "an elder statesman of homoerotic verse . . . making this . . . an important addition to poetry collections."

In the emergence of liberation movements in the sixties—black, women's, and gay—writers have played a major role, among them my friends Baldwin, Nin, Ginsberg, and Burroughs. In San Francisco the sexual freedom reminded me of enlightened European countries. Then AIDS dealt the gay civil rights movement a death blow, temporarily, with a violent backlash from funda-

Harold Norse at the City Lights Bookstore reading and book party for The American Idiom, *San Francisco, California, 1991*

mentalist fanatics. I began to practice abstinence and now, unwillingly, I'm celibate or careful as I watch my friends die of AIDS and cancer. Baldwin's preface to my memoirs appeared posthumously; we spoke by phone four months before he died of cancer. Anaïs had seen and extolled early sections of the memoirs just before her death, also of cancer; but the death of my mother in 1982 was the most shattering. With the loss of so many close friends in one decade, and then the economic pressures of the '90s, and my own aging, with an increased sense of mortality, and an *oeuvre* yet to be completed, my life took on a new note of urgency. More than ever before, writing was my reason for living.

As for the memoirs, the press was divided between high praise and mean-spirited grumbling about "name-dropping" ("They weren't names when I knew them," Anaïs used to say). The names I drop are of friends, mostly, whose lives were intimately connected with mine. "Name-dropping," by definition, applies to those who wish to give the impression of familiarity with famous or important people though their contact may have been superficial or fleeting. But many reviewers raved: the *Washington Blade* said, "It belongs with the 'greats' of 20th century American literature." And Burroughs, very impressed, wrote: "Magically evocative and visual . . . fascinating. It can be read as a picaresque novel . . . horrific and hilarious." Since I knew very well that he wrote only what he believed, or not at all, this meant a lot to me. The *Advocate* called it: "An important, moving testament . . . by an original talent and cornerstone of both the gay and beat literary traditions." It actually made the best-seller list of *Christopher Street*, the *New Yorker* of gay literature, which featured excerpts and ran a cover photo of me; and it was among the five finalists nominated for the Lambda Book Award. British, French, and German publishers took it, but in the U.S. it was remaindered. Warehousing tax laws, which should be abolished, leave no choice for mainstream publishers to stock any but big best-sellers. Yet the first German printing sold out in five months. The American publisher did no promotion but I keep getting letters and phone calls from the U.S. and abroad from enthusiastic readers. Clearly, it would sell in a reasonably priced paperback, small-press edition. I also received a Lifetime Achievement Award in 1991 from the National Poetry Association and am now working on my collected poems, short stories, and revision of the 1954 travel book about Italy.

BIBLIOGRAPHY

Poetry:

The Undersea Mountain, Swallow (Denver, Colorado), 1953.

(Translator) Giuseppe Gioacchino Belli, *The Roman Sonnets of G. G. Belli*, Jargon, 1960, Villiers Ltd. (London), 1974.

The Dancing Beasts, Macmillan, 1962.

Olé, Open Skull, 1966.

Karma Circuit: 20 Poems & a Preface, Nothing Doing in London, 1967, Panjandrum, 1974.

Christmas on Earth (broadside), Minkoff Rare Editions, 1968.

Penguin Modern Poets 13, (poetry of Charles Bukowski, Philip Lamantia, and Harold Norse), Penguin (Harmondsworth, England), 1969.

Hotel Nirvana: Selected Poems, 1953–1973, City Lights, 1974.

I See America Daily, Mother's Hen (San Francisco), 1974.

Carnivorous Saint: Gay Poems, 1941–1976, Gay Sunshine, 1977.

Mysteries of Magritte, Atticus, 1984.

The Love Poems (1940–1985), Crossing, 1986.

Seismic Events, Contact/II Publications, 1993.

Prose:

Beat Hotel (novel; translated into German by Carl Weissner), Maro Verlag (Augsburg, West Germany), 1975, (published in original English), Atticus, 1983, (translated into Italian by Giulio Saponaro), Stamperia della Frontiera, 1985.

Memoirs of a Bastard Angel (autobiography), Morrow, 1989, Bloomsbury (London), 1990, (translated into French by Richard Crevier), Editions du Rocher, 1991, (translated into German by Carl Weissner and Walter Hartmann), Rogner und Bernhard, 1992.

The American Idiom: A Correspondence (with William Carlos Williams, 1951–61), edited by John J. Wilson, Bright Tyger (San Francisco), 1990.

Contributor:

New Directions Anthology Number 13, edited by James Laughlin, New Directions, 1951.

New World Writing Number 13, edited by Reed Whittemore, Mentor Books/New American Library, 1958.

City Lights Journal, edited by Lawrence Ferlinghetti, City Lights, *Number 1*, 1963, *Number 4*, 1978.

Acid Anthology, edited by Brinkmann and Rygula, Maerz Verlag (Darmstadt, Germany), 1969.

Best Poems of 1968: Borestone Mountain Poetry Awards, edited by Hildegarde Flanner, Lionel Stevensen, and others, Pacific Books, 1969.

Poems from Italy, edited by William Jay Smith, Crowell, 1972.

The Male Muse, edited by Ian Young, Crossing, 1973.

185 Anthology, edited by Alix Geluardi, Mongrel, 1973.

Panjandrum Anthology, edited by Dennis Koran, Panjandrum, 1973.

City Lights Anthology, edited by Lawrence Ferlinghetti, City Lights, 1974.

Angels of the Lyre, edited by Winston Leyland, Gay Sunshine, 1975.

Poets West, edited by Lawrence Spingarn, Perivale, 1975.

The Beat Diary, edited by Arthur and Kit Knight, TUVOTI, 1977.

A Geography of Poets, edited by Edward Field, Bantam, 1979.

Orgasms of Light, edited by Winston Leyland, Gay Sunshine, 1980.

The Penguin Book of Homosexual Verse, edited by Stephen Coote, Penguin, 1983.

(And illustrator) *The Maverick Poets,* edited by Steve Kowit, Gorilla Press, 1988.

An Ear to the Ground, edited by Marie Harris and Kathleen Aguero, University of Georgia Press, 1989.

Contributor to periodicals, including *Antaeus, Art News, Beat Angels, Christopher Street, City Lights Review, Commentary, Evergreen Review, Exquisite Corpse, Harpers and Queen* (U.K.), *Hudson Review, Kayak, Kenyon Review, Nation, Paris Review, Poetry, Poetry Now, Saturday Review, Sewanee Review,* and *Transatlantic Review.* Editor and founder, *Bastard Angel* (nonprofit literary magazine), 1972–74.

Norse's work has been translated into numerous languages, including Arabic, Danish, Dutch, French, German, Greek, Italian, Norwegian, Portuguese, Spanish, and Tamil (a language of India). Norse's manuscripts are collected at Lilly Library, Indiana University at Bloomington.

David Pownall

1938-

I was born on May 19, 1938, in Walton, Liverpool. My father was a labourer. Most of my family on my mother's side were dockworkers and of Ulster extraction; on my father's side they were English and a little more genteel. My father was conscripted into the army in 1940, and when the heavy air raids began on Liverpool in May of that year my mother went to live with her parents on the Wirral peninsula. There we remained for the duration of the war, during which my father was killed in North Africa and my mother bore him a second, posthumous, son: my brother John Barry.

After the war my mother tried to become independent of my grandparents and took a job as a cook in a country house. I was then seven, and the change to the Cheshire landscape and the large gardens of the house had a lasting influence. We lived in servants' quarters, my mother having to learn many things—the man of the house was an ex-Indian Army colonel and sportsman who was always bringing home deer and salmon—and my memory of these times is essentially happy, although I knew that my mother's grief was strong and bitter.

Eventually we had to return to the house of my grandparents on the Wirral. My grandmother had reached the point where her husband's heavy drinking was making her life unbearable, and she needed us to be with her to make existence worthwhile. My grandfather had been gassed during the 1914–1918 war and had returned vicious and ill. By 1948, although he had a good job as a superintendent of warehouses, he was a sick, sour, old man. My presence in his house was made provocative because he had not liked my father—who had been an easy-going, good-natured man whose only addictions were my mother and dancing—and he was incapable of living with our grief, which though not displayed was steady and still running strong five years after the event.

Within months it was obvious that I could not remain in the house with him on a permanent basis because his dislike of my father was transferred to me and returned with interest. But my mother and

David Pownall

grandmother had formed a system of mutual support. My mother worked, and my grandmother helped to bring up my brother and me. This interdependence went much deeper, both women sharing their grief over their dead, one of whom was still living. This is not to say that they were unhappy in this. My mother was straight, tough when it was needed, and my grandmother, Maud, was the street comic. When my grandfather was away or in hospital there were always parties.

My bad relationship with my grandfather got to the stage where plans had to be made to have me moved. As he was still master of his own house and divorce a total impossibility in my grandmother's mind, I was entered for a scheme whereby I would receive a free boarding-school education, my qualifications being the loss of my father in the war and passing an examination.

So I left home. Although I returned for holidays it was never to the original hearth. My mother and grandmother did everything they could to maintain my place in the family, which was large in the extended form with many aunts and uncles, but being away in the south and being given a better chance of a good education than any member of the family had ever had both freed and fixed my future. I could never be at the heart of what went on in that war-shadowed household, nor would I ever be able to forget it. Themes of loss, grief, magic, illusion, and the theatrical, all stemming from the struggle to bind together what is broken, have run through many of the stories, novels, and plays I have written; most of them marked by a humour that I inherited from my much-adored grandmother, which was also engraved by my mother's sense of sardonic realism.

The school that I was sent to at the age of eleven was on a twelve-hundred-acre farm estate of chalk Hampshire downland, well-wooded and full of tracks. The loveliness of the landscape went a little way toward offsetting the ugliness of the régime. The staff favoured corporal punishment as a means of both learning and discipline, and the society of small boys which existed beneath it was brutalised even further than Nature would have it. I was a big, robust lad by the time I went to Lord Wandsworth College and not willing to accept the initiation rites that a *newt* was expected to cheerfully endure; I got frequently embroiled in fights, often thrashed by masters with sticks, rope ends, anything that came to hand, and ended up within a year as a hard case who would rather take a beating than do detention. Many boys ran away. I never bothered because I knew that it was pointless. There was nowhere to run to.

This state of affairs continued for two years, and I failed my probationary period four times. But I was kept on, probably because of my mother's pleading. At one time, when things were blackest, it was decided that the only experiment left in my case was to give me responsibility and see if that would bring me round. Accordingly I was made a house captain. Within a month I had this taken from me and was declared to be uncontrollable. It was now, I believe, that a man who has had a great influence on my life, and is still my friend and mentor forty years on, must have spoken up for me. He was Bill Fryer, a young history teacher

"My mother and father," 1936

not long down from Cambridge, and he must have defended me.

At the centre of this conflict was the housemaster with whom I shared a mutual loathing. He was an ex-army captain from the Great War and had lost a leg. Grief and my grandfather. Pain and dismemberment. Whether I was fair in my hatred of him, or of my grandfather, is a re-trail which I often make in memory. The pity of war was lost in its living scars. Whether my father, if he had survived, would have come back the same happy-go-lucky young man was a speculation woven into my family's myth. From the evidence I had to deal with, there was no proof that the survivors of war ever dispensed happiness.

At the end of this fractious time I moved to a senior house, and things quieted down. It was almost as if adolescent fury had spent itself by the time I reached my thirteenth birthday. From then on I was more interested in survival, sport, the land, girls, and literature. With Bill Fryer's help I started a magazine, *Mycetes* (laughing monkey), and filled it with my own poems. As time went by I found other boys at the school who wanted to have work published.

Juvenilia has its own criteria. On reading mine now I am impressed by the inanity of the expression and the old-fashioned ring that it has. But the subject is always power and the destiny it fashions. I did not write about war—as many boys did, the end of the last one being not too long before—nor did I use imagination on the horrors being loosed on us by special compulsory film shows of the Nazi death camps. What I seem to have concentrated upon was the great natural force that produces death and delight in an evenhanded way. In it I can find neither redemption nor despair.

By the time I was fifteen I had decided that I was going to be a writer. There would be a long apprenticeship; that much I knew. With Bill Fryer's sensitive guidance and the support of my mother and grandmother, also my brother's determination to follow me to Lord Wandsworth College (and they took him, which betokens something), I decided to try for a university place to study English and history, if I could. This, in 1954, was a high ambition indeed for a boy of my background. Although it was part of the national aspiration that working-class children should have higher education opened up to them, it was still more of a dream than a reality to those without private means. The pressure to start work and earn was always there, but this was kept off my shoulders. Between Bill Fryer and the two good women who had brought me up, I was made to feel that self-fulfillment was no sin: a useful protection for anyone drawn to writing as a means of livelihood.

If I look back on my first fifteen years, employing all my limited powers of analysis and criticism, I see how close to out-and-out rejection of that shattered, stumbling society I had come. Born into destruction, the times full of madness, extreme images of cruelty and death everywhere, I seem to have zigzagged towards a secure place of healing. One that offered itself was Christianity. I was a choirboy and spent hours in church absorbing far more than I was aware of between the ages of eleven and thirteen. At fifteen, having been cast out of the chancel because my voice had broken, I began yearning to return. I studied for my confirmation in the faith of the Church of England, but once the trembling hand of the ancient Bishop of Winchester had touched my head and it was done, the need faded, and I was left with a lasting love of

that music and language but a preference for the questions rather than the answers.

The influence of that village church in Long Sutton has been very profound, strengthened by the faith of Bill Fryer who was then, as he is now, a Christian of medieval temper. Out of that thirteenth-century church, built on a Saxon foundation, has come some of my best imaginative work: the novel *The White Cutter,* the play *Richard III, Part Two,* also my abiding involvement with the inarticulate expressed through music and the land, and the comedy of the Christian paradox.

Another strong association with England's long-rooted past that was at work during these years came through a school friendship. Dale Sanders had lost his father in the war and ended up at Lord Wandsworth College for the same reasons I had. His mother had married a Polish pilot who had settled in Yorkshire and started a garage. He had managed to buy a semi-derelict, nineteenth-century priory which stood on a hill opposite the great Norman keep of Conisborough

"At two-and-a-half years old, with Maud, my grandmother"

Conisborough Castle, Yorkshire

Castle of *Ivanhoe* fame in which he housed his wife's parents—a doughty couple from the coal-mining community—other relatives and children (some of them illegitimate and to me of hazy parentage in the mêlée), plus a host of boarders, fellow-Poles, men from the Dutch East Indies, and, finally, the friends of his stepson, amongst whom I was numbered.

This marvelous place, with its overgrown gardens full of rusting vehicles, was my second home. It was still not possible for me to live under the same roof as my grandfather for more than a few weeks, so I needed somewhere to go. This grey, old, Yorkshire hill town with its massive castle, steep streets, and the coal mines at its foot made its mark as a place of exile and welcome. They were a passionate, tumultuous crowd, always at war with each other, and I was hardly noticed— but *I* noticed, and with great enjoyment. I never went to Conisborough without being glad to go, or left without regret, and my mother and brother became visitors also, such was the level of hospitality at the Priory.

This odd situation—having not a surrogate family but one running in parallel—transfigured the nature of the actual ties but intensified the loyalties. If this had not happened then, all might have been lost. Because I could not live in my own home, my regard for it in terms of the affections of my grandmother and mother (my grandfather loved my brother for a reason that could only have to do with guilt and resurrection—he was born

after my father's death and therefore a second-chance child; the first, my childlike father, having been swept away) grew greater, focussed on the courage of these two strong, unfortunate women. Often I have searched myself for any resentment for my exile and found none. Somewhere, therefore, I had found an understanding that was not mere resignation but an active force, and I believe it to be part of whatever authorial strength I have.

My final years at school were restless ones. No amount of seniority and privileges could allay the irksome restriction, and things turned sour. This was due to my own impatience to be away and free of the place, and also that the school itself was going through the toils of change. It had been run in a prewar style by a stern Scot who understood himself even less than the two hundred and fifty boys who were ruled by him. Dry, acerbic, passionate only about rugby, he was nevertheless a challenge. Cliché cannot deal with him. God knows where he got his ideas about education—from the military and John Knox one suspects—but his closest friend, Richard Seaton, was a lively, flamboyant, theatre director who came and produced a Shakespeare play with us each year. In 1954 this peacock, with his wings of blue-rinsed hair, his twisted left hand (the result of a stage-fire) held to his breast, and his lisp, hypnotised me into the part of the second gaoler in *The Merchant of Venice.* Those few lines were enough, and I became his devotee, sharing the common panic as he fainted during each of the rehearsals in the last week because, as he put it, "I couldn't bear the shame of failure, boyth." He took me to local productions, as did Bill Fryer, and I visited his house in Basingstoke where he lived with a silent, benign partner in rooms lined with posters and photographs of his great days in London's West End. He was a man of the wiliest nature, out to impress me with the depth of the theatre, how seriously it could be taken, how much it could be an essence rather than a sham. By the time I had done Hotspur and MacDuff for him, the theatre was awake in me but in a majestic, historical form, and very much to do with the pride of making things in the imagination. I have no doubt that Richard Seaton put as much into the work he did with us as he did in his professional life. However, his greatest mystery remained unsolved—how he was such a close friend of the headmaster—and pondering upon it has only produced the strangest, poetical answers.

To be fair to one's own past is hardly a writer's priority. History is there to be exploited, and the more subjective it is the more it is up for pillage. But the need to assess how my life would have turned out if I had not been sent away was made important to me by my mother, who always suffered great guilt because she had not been able to survive independently and thus made my exile necessary. In many ways this unmade accusation dominated our relationship, and although I never made it (though my actions might have indicated that I felt it), she always sensed that it had been the means by which we were so closely bound. Upon her death I stopped seeing her as the old bronchitis-racked woman of the hospital actuality and replaced that image with the young woman before the war—someone I cannot possibly remember—a girl, large-eyed, most alive on the dance floor, hoping that her romantic dream would last.

My choice of university was straightforward. In 1956 there was only one place that I could get into that would allow me to read English and history without matriculating in Latin (one of my intellectual failures at sixteen), and that was the University College of North Staffordshire, now Keele University. This college based its system on an experiment advocated by the educational philosopher Lord Lindsay whereby all students must do a common foundation year on Western civilisation seen from the viewpoint of every academic discipline and then choose any two-subject degree with two subsidiaries, one of which being a science if one was studying arts, and vice versa.

The intention behind the Keele experiment was to challenge overspecialisation, also to create a college that had very close staff/student relationships with all the traditional barriers removed. Add to this the location—an estate out in the country with a splendid, red sandstone Jacobean hall at its heart—the vestiges of a displaced persons camp (my first room was in a Nissen hut where a refugee had hanged himself), and a strong military presence in the shape of older students who had done their National Service (I had been deferred), and the unavoidable parallel with the school I had just left is made. However, it was different by virtue of this similarity: because the laws were different, the freedoms were different. It was as if the school had been opened out, civilised, made humane, then projected into the world of the Female.

Until then I had lived in a Male world (the school), and a Female one (my family where the only man was a ruin—pitied, feared, and tolerated by women). Now this artificial division collapsed,

and, delighted with the change, I promptly fell in love. Within months my grandfather died as a result of falling down the stairs when drunk. All in all these were exhilarating times. I wrote through them, poetry that was an alarming blend of medievalism, lyricism, sexuality, and outbursts of religious energy. These were showered upon my beloved, a beautiful but conventional girl from Bolton, well used to boys, pragmatically brought up in dour Northern surroundings, and she did not understand a word that I wrote—which made it all the better.

My first year at Keele was spent in explosions of liberty, sensuality, and idiocy. By the end of it I was lucky to scrape through my examinations. I had drunk much of the wines of western civilisation, been shown the sheer size of music, driven my first love away in exasperation, talked away many nights. It had been the perfect time for someone let out of prison. However, the shock of nearly losing my place and fear that the intoxicating happiness would disappear were sharp. I went off to work in the warehouses of the Liverpool docks (where my grandfather's ghost still haunted) and immersed myself in the drudgery of stacking bales, recording conversations, being part of a world that I sensed was on its way out as the great port failed to come to terms with the postwar shifts in trade.

It was a salutary lesson. My grandfather's death had removed the family's main source of income, and he had left nothing. What my mother earned as a shop assistant plus the derisory pension given to my grandmother was all there was. If my brother and I had not been in free education family economic survival would have been doubtful, and both of us would have had to leave and start work. Taken with the mood on the docks and the mounting industrial tension between union and management as postwar euphoria died completely away, it was suddenly a grim time. This contrasted acutely with the half-guilty joy of liberation in our house as the last spectre of the living wars went to his grave. Now I could go home and stay home, be a part of it as I had never been before.

In this new period of peace there was the irony at work whereby the past insists upon its rights in the future. For my brother and myself the change had come too late. We had grown away from everything that was most precious to us and would only be able to return with that conscious effort that is no substitute for what is natural. What made it harder was the continuous selflessness we had to encounter: a refusal to make us share the financial hardships except when we could earn money in the vacations and an almost blind, unquestioning support for our ambitions. No matter what I may have said I wanted to do—including writing—my mother and grandmother would have agreed, because *I* wanted it. There would have been no argument, no show of resentment. However, their dreams were more honest. Maud dreamt that she saw me rowing for Oxford (a postgraduate degree obviously) and in a boardroom "with a lot of distinguished-looking men."

To plan to write for a living after graduation was impossible: too cruel, too selfish. In many ways it was a relief to dispose of the immediate need to look upon it as my career. When I returned to university I began to write in earnest—poems, short stories—and I became the sports editor of the student newspaper. None of this work was remotely about my loves of those years but groped for plot and character. I published in college magazines, had a few poems accepted by the BBC, eventually became the editor of the newspaper, and by the time I graduated, I had a collection of work that, though I would never refer to it again or try to use it, would be a security against despair during the long years before I would be published again.

*

I look through what I have written so far and know how it was a blur at the time, and my recollection teems with very precise misunderstandings that cannot be remedied now. Writing seems to be founded on these felt wounds of self-interpretation, without which it cannot exist. Somewhere was the whole fact as viewed by a dispassionate, all-seeing moon.

*

When I graduated in 1960 at the age of twenty-two, I joined the Ford Motor Company as a trainee. I did a ten-month course of familiarisation in the factories and when asked what department I would like to work in chose personnel. During this time I wrote my first novel. When I read the text after leaving it to cool for a fortnight I recognised all the twentieth-century writers I had responded to: Joyce, Lawrence, Hemingway, et al., all forced into contorted cohesion around a nucleus of nothing. I took the typescript to work with me and

threw it into the blast furnace at Dagenham, which satisfied me.

The experience did have a value, and one I recognised even then. I had proved that I could write sustainedly and actually finish a novel. But the hard truth that I was far from ready to write anything until the yeasts of my intense reading had done their work and died was a more difficult restriction to accept. Yet I obeyed it and paid attention to my job—there was plenty going on in industrial relations in the British motor industry 1960–1963—and my future wife, the girl I had met in my first week at university and returned to. I seem to have had nothing much to say about what I was going through in these days—I had no illusions about industry, but, even so, Ford's empire of the human robot exceeded my worst expectations.

However, during my traineeship I was given a chance to reconcile arts and engineering when a whizz-kid commercial sales manager instructed me to write a play about the virtues of the new 105E Anglia van. This I did—with some self-amazement—and the piece was produced at the Stoll Theatre in front of a thousand main Ford dealers who had all enjoyed a very long lunch.

I am disappointed that I have not turned those strange years in the motor industry to much account in my writing. Except for one short story, "Trogs," published in a small left-wing magazine in 1977, and an early aborted novel, I have not been able to make use of it, lacking, as yet, the perspective to do so.

In 1963 I went to Central Africa to work as a personnel officer on a copper mine. The country was then called Northern Rhodesia, a British colony, but when I arrived there were only a few months before the self-government that would lead to full independence in 1964. I had been recruited along with other young graduates with a few years industrial experience to help modernise the management practices of the giant Anglo-American mining corporation, which had previously fitted into the prevailing racial system and now planned to bend to the new African government before being forced to do so.

This was the stuff of comedy, of course, and my first two novels, a linked pair, *The Raining Tree War* and *African Horse,* deal with the six years I spent in this topsy-turvy world trying to find an equilibrium. The South African and Rhodesian government banned both of these books when they were published in 1974 and 1975 (by then I was back in England), claiming that they were obscene. My only satisfaction with this (I did not enjoy the thought that people were being stopped from reading my work) was that the new Zimbabwean government, when it came to power after the war in Rhodesia, revoked the ban.

During my time at university I had not felt drawn towards the theatre, concentrating on poetry and short stories and journalism. I think, also, that the acting groups repelled me, my boarding school stuffiness having not been completely knocked out of me by then. When I went out to Africa I found myself writing very little at first, there being so much to absorb in the turbulent politics of the mining towns and the changes that confronted me at every turn. Rugby and cricket seemed to have more relevance, somehow (perhaps as a means of holding my English identity together), but when I was injured and took refuge in the local amateur theatre as somewhere to spend my spare time, I quickly found myself writing plays.

This was an almost unconscious response to the social and cultural chaos around me. The guts of the hidebound, colonial setup were being torn out and straw stuffed into the hole in the form of a violent, one-party system that could never work (as far as I was concerned). I was wrong only by twenty years. By then Zambia was a wreck, and Kaunda, who had had himself declared president for *life* (some chance of change!), had been cast out.

These early one-act plays tried to contain the confusion within myths that I understood—European myths that gave shape to the whirlwind of hope, aggression, and change around me. One was set in London, another in Dublin, another in Palestine, but the motor in all of them was Africa as it worked on me. Finally I managed to set a two-hander in the town where I worked, and at the moment of writing. No one would play the lead for some reason, and I was forced to do it myself.

My function within the corporation was to do with the replacement of white workers by Zambians as much as anything else—in work, education, training, housing, everywhere that the old barriers had applied. By 1969 this had advanced to the point where I trained an African to replace myself—which was satisfying enough—and I began to think about returning to England. Before I made the move I decided that I must write a full-length play upon an English model, and I chose Noel Coward.

As We Lie was a comedy about a man who protests against his wife's infidelity by going to live in the garden. The shape, style, and attack were (I hoped) created out of an intelligent discipleship. When the play was produced (I had to direct it because no one else would) it lost any claim to imitate Coward, but it did work for the audience. This was encouragement at a crucial time, and armed with the script, I took ship back to England, working on my first novel while aboard.

My six years in Africa had been successful in terms of a career in personnel management, but now that had to be put aside with all its financial attractions and security. I had believed that I would take on this challenge with equanimity, but I had not realised how addictive a high salary and the material trappings of that life are. The belief (hope?) that I would grow out of my ambition to write for a living was strong in my family—wife, mother, et al.—and taken with the fiscal fears, I had a formidable opposition. What surprised me is that I did not quail. Each time I gave solitary thought to the wisdom of what I was doing, I seemed to encounter a decision made of granite. There was no other life I wanted. Not in the hope of fame or literary success, but simply to do the work and live by it.

I rented a converted barn halfway up a mountain pass in the Lake District (where else, Wordsworth?) for the winter. By the end of it I had been forced into a small compromise. Out of desperation to be with people and not stuck in snowbound isolation, I went along with the suggestion that I should have what was essentially a day job. The one that I negotiated was with a travelling theatre—the Century—that I found on a car park in Windermere. When I offered myself as writer/actor/director/manager, any of these, or any combination, they countered with the question "Do you have a car?" When I said yes, they gave me the job of going around putting up the posters.

This mollified my critics (to be a kept man is a condition worse than leprosy in the north of England), and it was a wise move. I had come to terms with the fact that I am not a solitary reaper, that theatre as a live social art was bread and meat to me, and within a year I had my first professional production which, appropriately enough, was on yet another car park, in Preston this time.

Peter Oyston, the director of Century, and Andrew Leigh, the administrator, looked after me, recognising how little I knew of the business. Initially the on-tour actors were suspicious of me because they understood that I had been working in South Africa, this country having an evil resonance in current left-wing politics. This mistake unleashed various monsters of self-righteousness, and no matter how hard I tried to set the record right, I was thought to be a white supremacist on the run. Gradually I managed to dispel this error, and I found that writing my novel *The Raining Tree War* at the same time as I was working with right-on actors in my farce *How to Grow a Guerilla* had the effect of a comic cross-fertilisation that was very African. There was, however, a bad effect in that for ten years afterwards I did abhor the cruelty of quick moral judgements prompted by political identity-seeking in the arts and was often heard to waste my time railing against it.

My marriage now foundered, having been close to the rocks for some time. The hope had been held that I would acknowledge the futility of trying to write and return to industry, but that was now out of the question. A son, Gareth, had been born in Zambia in 1964. My wife decided to stay in the Lake District where she had a job as a teacher. As I did not want to live far away from my child, I became part of the new company formed by Century Theatre when it opened the new Duke's Playhouse in Lancaster only twenty miles away. With Peter Oyston I bought an 1820s farmhouse, named Well House, on the edge of the moors outside the town and settled there with Mary Ellen Ray, an actress from Missouri who had joined the company.

The years at Well House—from 1972 to 1980—formed the first full phase of my writing life. They were spent surrounded by actors who were working to get a new theatre off the ground in a northern textile town that had a history of economic depression and little feeling for the arts in general. A new university had been founded outside the town in the sixties, and that added a new dimension to the place, but it was essentially a start from rock bottom, though the climate in the theatrical profession then was very optimistic that new audiences could be won back from television.

I wrote every conceivable form of stage work for the new theatre, from large-scale, folk epics to revues, from touring shows for the surrounding villages to pantomimes, anything that would go in front of an audience on any size of stage, or in the street. Much of it I have forgotten or mislaid in the frenzy. These plays and pieces were written for the town and the country around it more than for myself. Meanwhile I continued with novel writing—*God Perkins* being about the Century mobile

theatre and my early days with it (inevitably comic); a collection of short stories, *My Organic Uncle;* and the first of the thirty-plus radio plays that I have now written.

Without private income or family money or even expectations of it—and the severing of what I had into two parts after my divorce—writing for a living meant exactly what it said. I threw myself into all the media hoping to construct an income that would have some claim to steadiness. Much time and effort was wasted in flailing around, but I had found a voice in the novel and short-story form. The amount of theatre that I produced and the hurly-burly of the Duke's Playhouse as a place of work—of which Well House was an extension so that the process never ceased—eventually began to force a style and demeanour into my plays, often informed by the fiction I was writing simultaneously. Balance was vital, of course, and often that was either absent or considered heretical (these were the days when *relevance* and *commitment* were the star qualities); thus I often found my writing self either embattled or so sardonic as to be characterless. Politics infused the simplest vaudeville. Work for children was seen as an initiation into the mysteries of social sympathy. So the demands were great, but I believe that my obstinacy was up to the task, and I emerged, dazed and delighted, in 1975 after all this intense and prolific work, with a full theatre for my new plays.

The first to achieve this 100-percent record was *Lile Jimmy Williamson,* a large-scale play about the linoleum millionaire who had run and virtually owned Lancaster between 1880 and 1930 and had left his step on the town. There are opening nights that one remembers with more poignancy than others, and this play provided me with such a memory spiced by fear. We had often had to fight the town's history and be unpopular, but in the case of Little Jimmy Williamson I was dealing with the living past. His paternalistic power was still in place, and there had already been telephone calls and letters from outraged citizens. Williamson had *built* the town, they claimed, not paralyzed it for nigh on a hundred years as I had claimed.

Applause is difficult to analyse, especially if one is looking for a sincere response to what craft and art there is in the work. I had listened to audiences reacting to what I had put on stage plenty of times by then, but that did not lessen the shock of hearing what poured out of the theatre that night as if a dam had broken. I had enough sense to know that it was not all to do with my skill—or the actors'—but came from a source that had been newly sprung. Self-respect was there, and the strange pleasure that the authority of the stage can give.

Other plays followed: *Buck Ruxton,* based on an extraordinary murder by an Indian doctor in the thirties that has a very contemporary ring to it, and finally a play that was a comedy of the future which attracted the citizens less, and I knew it was time to move on.

Because I had concentrated so exclusively on Lancaster, my work for the stage had only been aired in two other places—Manchester and Cheltenham—in both cases with camped-up revivals of my first two full-length plays. I had taken a one-act play to London to play the Fringe: *The Pro,* written about the making of a song with Stephen Boxer as composer, someone whom I had already worked with on many shows at Lancaster. With the end of my time at the Duke's Playhouse within sight and having no real encouragement to believe that national companies were looking in my direction, I started a company of my own to tour the new plays that I wanted to write. This operated from Well House, and most of the actors lived there: Mary Ellen, Fiona Victory, Harriet Walter, Stephen Boxer, Robert McIntosh, then Eric Richard and Joseph Marcell. The first play was for one actor—a challenge to help him when he was out of work—and I wrote *Crates on Barrels.* The set was an old rum barrel cadged from the brewery next door to the Duke's Playhouse, and the actor Christopher Crooks played Crates, the disciple of Diogenes the great Cynic. This play, which opened at the Edinburgh Festival in 1975, founded what was to become Paines Plough, a company that still features largely on the new drama touring scene in Britain.

Between 1975 and 1980 I wrote seven plays for the new company, fitting the characters to the known talents of the actors. Music always had its part, and I made demands on voice and instrument that made a general use of these plays in other repertoires difficult if multitalented actors were not available. The first production to break into national notice was *Music to Murder By* in 1976, a study in possession using the lives of Gesualdo, the innovative madrigalist, and Peter Warlock, the 1920s composer. The action is set near Naples where Gesualdo liberated his muse by murdering his wife in 1590. This story had been put my way by a friend who was a great influence during my Lancaster days—Julian Leigh, son of the composer Walter, who died in the Second World War, and brother of Andrew, who had first helped me to

find my feet in British theatre upon my arrival from Africa, wet behind the ears.

Julian's status was a strange one: he insisted that he was, in essence, a successful failure. Trained to be a composer, he had thrown this over for the life of an unemployable boozer, his intelligence and erudition still intact and operating but transmitted through others. We became very close friends, and he took up the task of teaching me all I did not know about music and much that I still had yet to discover concerning the perverseness of some self-destructive natures. For all his faults—which he would number greater than I—there was no one who guided and challenged me more than Julian. His best strength was a blend of pedantry and perspicacity liberally mixed with toxic humour that had me creatively defensive and wide open at the same time.

It was natural that I should turn then to look at Lancaster as a novelist both to gain useful distance and to explore it in a way that had not been possible on the stage. *Light on a Honeycomb*

Christopher Crooks as Crates in Crates on Barrels, *1975*

Julian Leigh

was the result, set in the town and its enormous county mental hospitals—a surreal interpretation perhaps, but how else can all the physical, social, and psychic dimensions of a town be explored? After my battle with the place it had taken on a personal, cultural meaning. Another, more directly autobiographical approach was made in *Between Ribble and Lune,* a nonfiction book that I wrote the year after this novel. Together they form a Janus-like unity.

Well House had by now become a meeting place for artists of all kinds—in writing, theatre, dance, and music—as well as booksellers, art dealers, farmers, and photographers. It was the venue of many rolling parties, rehearsals, and roughhouses. It had some of the character of the amateur theatre clubs of the Zambian mining towns where things could happen fast—a play could be written and on the stage in three months, all part of one process. To have had two such experiences—both of equal length, six years each—has been a rare privilege. Even today, at

fifty-five, I often yearn for a return of that intense, hell-for-leather creativity.

In 1977 I had written two plays for Paines Plough that were toured together: *Richard III, Part Two* (on the abuses of history, helped by George Orwell) and *Motocar* (an exploration of the exact moment of African freedom-taking when Rhodesia became Zimbabwe). This pair was taken into the National Theatre by Peter Hall to be performed by Paines Plough. Immediately afterwards I wrote another play with an African subject for the Traverse Theatre in Edinburgh: *Livingstone and Sechele,* the story of the famous missionary's only conversion. This was given a new production at the Lyric, Hammersmith and then at the Quaigh Theatre in New York's Off-Off-Broadway where it ran for six months and was my first production in the States.

Africa was still very much in mind for my next novel, *Beloved Latitudes,* which was my attempt to fuse white and black in a crucible of guilt and friendship based on the Congo of the sixties and the Ugandan tragedy. This emerged at the same time as a new stage play for Greenwich Theatre, *An Audience Called Édouard,* in which Manet's *Le déjeuner sur l'herbe* painting comes to life while Karl Marx is being hunted by the Paris police. He bursts out of the river to join the bourgeois sitters and transform them, though only the painter, who is the audience, can know how. (With Jeremy Irons, Stephanie Beacham, Susan Hampshire, and David Burke in the cast and directed by Alan Strachan, 1978).

In that same year Julian Leigh had lent me a little book, *Musical Uproar in Moscow,* which was an edited version of the minutes of the Union of Soviet Musicians Conference in 1948 when Stalin launched a direct attack upon Shostakovich and Prokofiev and demanded a new music for his postwar empire. When I read the book it touched a raw nerve—as Julian had known it would—because the Arts Council had refused to subsidise my play *Music to Murder By* when it was produced because it was *elitist,* its subject being two obscure composers whom the man in the street would not waste his time on. This decision had been the work of my peers on an advisory panel—directors, writers, and theatre people—so I had been doubly incensed and not mollified by the reversal of the *diktat* when the play became a success. Julian's shaft had been well aimed.

I went to Moscow to find out everything I could and visited the Kremlin in the depth of winter. No one was prepared to discuss Stalin, but the places and the system were still intact. What I was looking for was a key as to how I might present the story of the conference—which had been vast—in the microcosm of the theatre. I met an old, English diplomat on the plane home, and he told me a few stories about the postwar period. One of them was what I had been looking for. It was simple enough: there had been a rumour in Moscow in 1948 that Stalin had offered to give Prokofiev piano lessons. Suddenly I saw a room, a piano, two men, then a third (Shostakovich), then a fourth (Zhdanov, the soldier turned culture supremo who had purged the arts in the USSR).

Although the insight was swift, it lay dormant for two years while I wrote other things. When I tried to approach it, the upheaval of moving from Well House and Lancaster to London often got in the way. The decision to make this change had come out of apparent family needs, the future of children now moving on to university, and Mary Ellen's career, which had flourished with Paines Plough, now needed the metropolis.

Fiona Victory (center), Anne Haydn, and Garrett Keogh in Beef, *1981*

Timothy West as Stalin and David Bamber as Shostakovich in Master Class, *1983*

It was an ill-considered move on my part. To leave so much behind required a surgical style that I imagined I might have somewhere, but I was quite wrong. Nonetheless, I ended up in Writerland, north London's Muswell Hill, with *Master Class* (the play about Stalin and the composers) half completed. It was written for Paines Plough—four men and a piano would go into a van, one of the principal requirements of the theatre of poverty—but the company suddenly ran out of money, and Justin Green, the young director for whom I had written it, offered it to other theatres but first to Timothy West, a powerful, distinguished, British actor who could help us get it off the ground. Timothy West put his weight behind the play, and it was first produced at Leicester's Haymarket Theatre, then transferred to the Old Vic, and then on again to Wyndham's in the West End (1983–1984). Since then it has appeared all over the world, including Moscow itself, acting as a flying machine for me.

It may be the case that to write novels one needs a secure sense of home or, at least, some

Well House, Lancaster

rapport with an environment. London could not replace the hills and rivers of the northwest, and I had to face up to a grave mistake. Tom, my son with Mary Ellen, had been dropped into the chaos of London's education system, and the city was no more benevolent to my eldest son, Gareth, who was at King's College, Cambridge, and mourned the loss of Well House and everything that went with it.

I had produced a book every year since 1973, but now the will to write fiction went into limbo, and I was only interested in the artifice of the theatre, an acknowledged unreality. Whenever the opportunity came, I returned to my old haunts in the north, and inevitably a tension grew out of this division. One of the early results was a play drawn from a reading of the Irish, eleventh-century classic *The Cattle Raid of Cooley,* whereby four mythical heroes step out of their own time and place to save the sanity of today but by means of blood sacrifice. *Beef* was set in a slaughterhouse in Dublin (did I mean London?), and the heroes waited for two bulls to be driven down from the north. The hindsight interpretations of one's past plays are untrustworthy, but at some level they must accord with the life being lived at the time.

Beef was the last play that I wrote for Paines Plough, and, like all the others, it was directed by John Adams, with whom I had started the company. We had done eight plays together, and the moment had come for us to go our separate ways. It would be ten years before we worked together again at Birmingham Rep where he had become artistic director and produced *My Father's House,* a play about the Chamberlain political dynasty. John's intelligence, good taste, love of music, and generosity in always giving me room to rethink and rewrite up to the last minute have been of such importance to me that the influence is difficult to calculate. His preferences are part of my view of theatre, and we share many distastes. What we shared in Paines Plough was a need to break out of the encircling political dogmatization that began in the late sixties, the power of which we did not underestimate as it came to dominate new British theatre for the period 1970–1990.

In 1982, perturbed by absence of any desire to write another novel and in deep argument with myself over a love affair, I went to Spain and walked the last two hundred twenty-five miles of the old pilgrim road to Santiago de Compostella. For a hike that lasted only eleven days it had an extraordinary effect, but this was slowly released. Five years later the novel that it generated was published—*The White Cutter,* the story of a thirteenth-century Albigensian stonemason—and I had made a return to the northwest, buying a cottage close to where I had once lived. Within this return to the novel and one landscape I had come truly to love was the influence of two women: my mother, who died at that time, and Alex, she whom I had tried to drive out of my mind during that long, hot walk. My struggle with London had produced a strange splaying out of horizons, a many-coloured universe among three points: Guildford, where Alex lived; the writing retreat in Cumbria; and Muswell Hill. I shuttled among these three for five years during which I wrote three novels: *The Gardener* (a story of adolescent love), *Stagg and His Mother* (my farewell to the reality of mine), and *The Sphinx and the Sybarites* (divination and the flawed magic of wealth in sixth-century B.C. Magna Graecia, published March 1993 and under review as I write).

The stage plays I wrote during this triangular time were all brought to me rather than generated from an internal source: *The Viewing* by the presence of builders in my London house; *Black Star* by Joseph Marcell, who believed that he was the reincarnation of the black American Shakespearean actor Ira Aldridge (d. 1864); *Rousseau's Tale* by my eldest son from his studies; and *Death of a Faun* by the dancer Nicholas Johnson, who wanted to bring Nijinsky with his art and madness to the stage. All touched on interior chords, but each play was more to serve the actor (God as performer in *The Viewing*) than provide a window into a clearing confusion within myself.

Clouds still hang around. History still sticks its spires through as landmarks; better minds, awesome insights, collapsing systems, all intrude on open self-exploration. Current work remains within the tradition established in my writing life: a new play for the Royal Shakespeare Company on Elgar the symphonist (composers again!) and a novel that is in the course of being written whereby Kierkegaard (the father of existentialism) is producing a biography of the seventeenth-century Duke of Buckingham, *mignon* to King James and King Charles, and sensual generator of the English Civil War.

Both the play and the novel have been written here in Guildford where I have settled with a new son, Max, and Alex and her daughters. Next month I will be fifty-five. If the digits are added together the sum is ten, which is a Pythagorean magic number, and I wish he was here to explain why. Late fatherhood, economic pressure, increasing enigmas, and the mysteries of change may edge

the eye from where it should be—if that is where it should be—in the middle of the forehead, the centre of the Cyclopean muse. There is still that play about my hated grandfather to give me salvation if I can show *why* . . . that novel about Borodin and the women's causes he gave his life to (more than his music!) . . . and my notebooks seem to be full of poems these days. It's fifteen years since my only book of verse was published. Time for another. . . .

*

It is only fair that reflections should accompany an autobiography. Some sense should be made of the story in case a reader comes by it who needs comfort from the mistakes or encouragement from the successes. Also the time of the life covered needs a span like a rainbow so that it can be seen to begin, arch, and end, and then, perhaps, come again after the next downpour.

War has defined my life, and knowledge has been the active peace which I have been able to make with this. To fulfill my father's life has always been a spur. He had little. What might have sustained him if he had lived was a natural talent with a pencil. Whereas he might have drawn, I have written. Now he has unseen grandsons, one who draws, one who writes, and the energy from his short life is not wasted. I must have loved the man very much, but I cannot remember a thing about him. That can only mean he is everywhere.

What is in the air of childhood, the wounds that are born, seems to have the prior claim on a writer's history. That is where the inclination to untwist a wrong, to re-present a moment long misunderstood begins. But the primary need is to find the form and style that will enable the story to be told in a way that will delight the outsider. The writer may not see the face of that listener or know the true nature that absorbs the tale, but the knowledge that there is a presence willing to give ear and mind is enough. There are many arguments concerning the real identity of those for whom we write, the weakest of which being that it is only oneself.

I believe that the audience is made up of the swirling ghosts of those whom you would knowingly please with your gifts.

BIBLIOGRAPHY

Novels:

The Raining Tree War, Faber, 1974.

African Horse, Faber, 1975.

God Perkins, Faber, 1977.

Light on a Honeycomb, Faber, 1978.

Beloved Latitudes, Gollancz, 1981.

The White Cutter, Gollancz, 1988.

The Gardener, Gollancz, 1990.

Stagg and His Mother, Gollancz, 1991.

The Sphinx and the Sybarites, Sinclair Stevenson, 1993.

Short-story collections:

Introductions 5, Faber, 1974.

My Organic Uncle and Other Stories, Faber, 1976.

Produced plays:

All the World Should Be Taxed, Lancaster, England, 1971.

How to Grow a Guerrilla, Preston, Lancashire, England, 1971.

The Last of the Wizards (for children), London, England, 1972.

Beauty and the Beast, music by Stephen Boxer, Lancaster, England, 1973.

Gaunt, Lancaster, England, 1973.

Lions and Lambs, Lancashire, England, 1973.

The Human Cartoon Show, Lancaster, England, 1974.

Buck Ruxton, Lancaster, England, 1975.

Crates on Barrels, Edinburgh, Scotland, 1975.

Lile Jimmy Williamson, Lancaster, England, 1975.

The Pro, London, England, 1975.

Ladybird, Ladybird, Edinburgh, Scotland, 1976.

A Tale of Two Town Halls, Lancaster, England, 1976.

Livingstone and Sechele, Edinburgh, Scotland, 1978.

Seconds at the Fight for Madrid, Bristol, England, 1978.

Barricade, 1979.

Later, London, England, 1979.

The Hot Hello, Edinburgh, Scotland, 1981.

Pride and Prejudice (adaptation of the novel by Jane Austen), Leicester, England, 1983.

Black Star, Bolton, Lancashire, England, 1987.

The Edge, London, England, 1987.

King John's Jewel, Birmingham, England, 1987.

The Viewing, London, England, 1987.

Rousseau's Tale, London, England, 1991.

Death of a Faun, Edinburgh, Scotland, 1991.

Produced and published plays:

As We Lie, Nkana-Kitwe, 1969, Cheltenham, England, 1973.

The Dream of Chief Crazy Horse (for children), Fleetwood, Lancashire, England, 1973, Faber, 1975.

Music to Murder By, Canterbury, England, 1976, Faber, 1978.

Motocar [and] *Richard III, Part Two* (music by Stephen Boxer), London, England, 1977, Faber, 1979.

An Audience Called Édouard, London, England, 1978, Faber, 1979.

Beef, London, England, 1981, published in *Best Radio Plays of 1981,* Methuen, 1982.

Master Class, Leicester, England, 1983, Faber, 1983.

Ploughboy Monday, 1985, published in *Best Radio Plays of 1985,* Methuen, 1986.

Other:

(With Jack Hill) *An Eagle Each: Poems of the Lakes and Elsewhere,* Arena, 1972.

Another Country (poetry), Harry Chambers/Peterloo Poets, 1978.

(Contributor) *Peterloo Anthology,* Peterloo, 1979.

Between Ribble and Lune: Scenes from the North-West (nonfiction; illustrated with photographs by Arthur Thompson), Gollancz, 1980.

The Bunch from Bananas (for children), illustrated by Frank Fitzgerald, Gollancz, 1980.

(Editor with Gareth Pownall) *The Fisherman's Bedside Book,* Windward, 1980.

Writer of radio plays: "Free Ferry," 1972; "Free House," 1973; "An Old New Year," 1974; "A Place in the Country," 1974; "Fences," 1976; "Under the Wool," 1976; "Back Stop," 1977; "Butterfingers," 1981; "The Mist People," 1981; "Flos," 1982; "Ploughboy Monday," 1985; "Beloved Latitudes" (from his own novel), 1986; "The Bridge at Orbigo," 1987; "A Matter of Style," 1988; "The Glossomaniacs," 1990; "Plato Not Nato," 1990; "Bringing Up Nero," 1991; "Kitty Wilkinson," 1992; and "Dreams and Censorship," 1993.

Author of television plays: "High Tides," 1976;

"Mackerel Sky," 1976; "Return Fare," 1978; "Follow the River Down," 1979; "Room for an Inward Light," 1980; "Love's Labour," 1983; "The Great White Mountain," 1987; and "Something to Remember You By," 1991.

Contributor of short stories to periodicals and anthologies including: *Dandelion Clocks, London Magazine, Penthouse, Shakespeare Stories, Spectator, Stand,* and various others.

Jane Rule

1931-

When I was ten years old, I put on my first pair of glasses and saw individual leaves on trees, the small stones which made up the gravel drive, the letters on street signs. I was so entranced with the bright, distinctive things around me that at first I didn't notice I could also read the expressions on people's faces far down the dining-room table, across a room. From the back of the classroom, to which my height had always relegated me, I could read assignments on the blackboard and judge a teacher's mood by her frown as well as by her tone of voice.

"You mustn't mind having to wear glasses," my mother said.

Mind? Since no one else in the family did wear glasses, I was the only one to understand what a miracle they were. I was the only one who could choose, if I felt like it, to retreat again into that soft, vague world of the nearsighted where other people's concerns and even identities blurred. Or I could look with new eyes and read a world I had only guessed at before.

"Four eyes!" kids shouted on the playground.

"Two better than you," I'd shout back, meaning it.

I was more vulnerable to my grandmother's grief. She could not be stopped from saying in front of me, "As if it isn't bad enough she's going to be so tall, now she's lost those lovely eyes."

I looked in the mirror, and my eyes didn't seem lost to me. In fact, I saw them better. They were brown. My father teased me about being hot-eyed when I was angry, the source of the title of one of my essay collections years later, *A Hot-Eyed Moderate.*

"Guys don't make passes at girls who wear glasses," my twelve-year-old brother taunted.

At ten, I didn't find that a disadvantage. Having been a close companion to an older brother had demystified boys for me. Other girls' attitudes toward boys I found hard to fathom. Girls weren't interested in going fishing or hunting as I did with my brother and father, nor did they listen to "Jack Armstrong, the All-American Boy" on the radio as my brother and I did. In the

Jane Rule

playground at school, girls clustered together giggling while the boys—and I when they let me—played soccer. Yet the girls had begun to talk more and more about boys who were still largely indifferent to them.

For me the only bad thing about glasses was having to take them off for rough sport, at my grandmother's house to keep her from complaining about them, when I had my picture taken as a favor to my father. Well into my thirties, there are few pictures of me wearing glasses.

I stopped growing when I was twelve. I stood a bespectacled six feet tall. My voice from childhood had been unusually deep. At school I wasn't allowed to sing with the others, only to mouth the

Jane at age five

words, until boys' voices began to change and I could sing their parts.

I was left-handed, too, of the last generation of children who were sometimes required to use their right hands. We moved around the country during my school years enough for me to be sometimes in a school system progressive enough to allow me the use of my left hand. When I wasn't allowed, I cheated as often as I could get away with it. To this day I write from the bottom to the top of the page, angled for right hand use.

Moving from New Jersey to California, from California to Illinois and then Missouri taught me at a younger age than a child growing up in one place that values are clearly relative. In California I went to school with black, Japanese and Chinese children, with children of migrant workers. In Missouri, schools were segregated as were movie houses and country clubs. My father came from the South, and, while he didn't approve of segregation, he was used to it.

If there clearly isn't one right way of doing things, any community's values are not a matter

for moral commitment so much as a matter of social survival. You pull up your socks when other people do. You roll them down when other people do. You don't much mind about the socks. You do get tired of how entirely right people think they are.

In a public school in Missouri, wearing glasses, being six feet tall, left-handed, good at math, good at sports were all social liabilities. In a private girls' school in California, to which we returned for the years my father served at sea in the Second World War, these same attributes were accepted and even sometimes admired. I thrived on new respect without ever really trusting it. Though I had wonderful teachers who challenged and encouraged me through high school and college, none of them had a vision of adult life for a woman outside of marriage and child rearing. Even those who lived alone or with other women paid lip service to universal heterosexuality.

Because my younger sister had been very ill during the war, in and out of navy hospitals, I saw a lot of the work of doctors in the epidemics of polio and spinal meningitis, in the long, slow mending of men brought back from the Pacific maimed and blinded. For some time I thought I would be a doctor until I discovered that I was as inept and bored in the chemistry lab as I was in the kitchen.

Though I wasn't much of a reader, preferring more active occupations in my free time, though my spelling was bad and my handwriting worse, I did like to write. Moving about so much had made me a letter writer early, and my grandmother encouraged the habit by sending a dollar every time I wrote to her. My father, sympathetic to the problems of my left-handedness, bought me a typewriter and said, "To hell with them! Use both hands." So I enjoyed the weekly free writing we were required to do, finding topics wherever I looked. I remember one assignment was to write from the quotation "I am a part of all that I have met." It seemed to me that I could go on writing forever. There was so much to question, so much to discover.

I have probably said too often that in college I studied the great liars in order to learn to tell the truth. But the curriculum at a women's college in the late '40s and early '50s offered very little which could give me any insight into my own life or the world I lived in. What I could learn instead was craft, and, since close analysis of the text was the critical bias of the time, I learned a lot that has been useful to me throughout my writing life. I didn't find the writers like Willa Cather, Gertrude Stein, or even George Eliot and Virginia Woolf until I was out of college.

Aside from a few women poets like Emily Dickinson, Edna St. Vincent Millay, and Eleanor Wylie whom I'd found for myself in high school, Shakespeare, Auden, Donne, Herbert, and Hopkins were the only writers who gave me personal nourishment in my college years. Is it significant that at least six of the eight were attracted to their own sex? I didn't know that at the time. It would have been a great revelation to me and no small comfort in those years of denied feeling, of silence.

I was not trained to be a writer. Most of my teachers discouraged me in that ambition. I was trained to teach, to hand on the great patriarchal tradition of literature, the canon in which I and those who might have been my real mentors had little or no place. Only Jessamyn West, who taught the writing course for a couple of years while I was at Mills College, rebuked me when, for one semester, I dropped her course in favor of volunteering to teach two afternoons a week at a school for the handicapped. She thought I hadn't the proper respect for my own talent, one of those rare rebukes which reassures.

I went to England the summer I was nineteen to study Shakespeare at Stratford. I was the youngest student there of a group of mostly postgraduate scholars from all over the world. During the day we had lectures and workshops. In the evening we went to the theatre to watch John Gielgud and Peggy Ashcroft in such plays as *King Lear* and *Measure for Measure*. For the first time in my life I was with a whole group of people who took their work as seriously as I did, who loved it, who intended to make scholarship their lives. Among them, too, were some who hoped to write. Our passionate interest in our work did not have to be left behind when we went out to play. We drank in the pubs, bicycled in the lanes, punted on the river, took weekend excursions into Wales, to Oxford, and all the time we were arguing, reciting, singing our work. Everyone wore glasses, even at the pub.

I spent a year in England after I graduated from Mills College in 1952, writing my first novel in a cold-water flat in London. I was also an occasional student at University College, studying Shakespeare, seventeenth-century literature, and doing my own independent study of the history of religious festival drama in England. London had been cleaned up from the years of bombing, but little rebuilding had begun. Food and clothing were still rationed. All students were poor, always cold, often hungry, but we all managed to buy books, which were inexpensive, to go to the theatre, lining up sometimes all day for cheap seats, to go for weekends at Cumberland Lodge in Windsor Great Park where we met other students from all over the world for academic discussions, long walks in the park, madrigal singing in the evening. I found time, too, to do volunteer work one afternoon a week at Barnardo's Orphanage.

If I had not been an American, unable to get a work permit, I might have stayed on in England for years, but academic jobs paid so poorly I would probably eventually have been lured back to North America where I could earn enough teaching intermittently to make time to write. Lack of funds sent me reluctantly home after only one year, taking my finished but unpublishable novel with me, leaving behind a life and a woman I loved.

I enrolled in the Stanford Writing Department, admitted on the strength of my novel, though Wallace Stegner's question was, "Why is a nice girl like you writing about decadent stuff like this?" I hated the competitive, commercial atmosphere of the school, the condescending attitude toward women students. I lasted only one quarter, glad of the excuse that I was needed at home while my mother recovered from an operation. I had written nothing but long letters to England, and I marked time until the fall of 1954 when I accepted a teaching post at Concord Academy in Concord, Massachusetts, mainly because it was three thousand miles nearer England. I lived in at the school to save money for an English summer.

I loved teaching, but living in a girls' boarding school at everyone's beck and call twenty-four hours a day without time for my own writing, without privacy, turned the year into a prison sentence. By the time I reached England, two years had passed. We were students no longer, all of us facing hard, practical decisions which seemed to marginalize what had been central to our lives before: love and work we loved, both now redefined as youthful indulgence.

The hope that had sustained me through two barren years, held out against increasing stress and fear, was gone, and I was ill with failure by the time I returned to Concord in the fall. Fortunately I had my own apartment, but the attempts I made to write through that teaching year were futile. Badgered by ill health, discouraged by obstacles in a new relationship, I determined to leave Concord and use my savings, supplemented by help my parents offered, to give myself another year for writing.

I had not been comfortable in the States since my first trip to England, and the McCarthy hearings to rid the country of Communists, who had somehow become equated with homosexuals, made the country an increasingly unpleasant and dangerous place for me to be.

I went to Canada in the fall of 1956 after a chance summer trip to Vancouver, British Columbia, a small city on the shore of an inlet with mountains rising abruptly to the north, with gardens as lovely as those in England.

In Vancouver, living in a four-room flat in the house of a longshoreman, who brought home everything from coffee and tea to caviar and rock lobster tails to supplement an otherwise frugal fare, I began a hopeful life again. I worked at an old oak rolltop desk in a room with a view of the sea and the mountains.

In November of that year Helen Sonthoff, with whom I had taught for two years at Concord, joined me for a holiday which is not, even now, over. When money again ran out, we found plenty of work to do. I did free-lance radio broadcasting, TV script reading, paper marking and tutoring for the English department at the University of British Columbia. Helen accepted a full-time teaching position with the English department.

From my contacts with the CBC, I was invited to a meeting set up to explore the possibility of founding an Arts Club in Vancouver, open both to artists and people interested in the arts where we could meet for readings, lectures, shows. I was on the first board of directors. By the time we had found a building and repainted it ourselves, Helen and I had made good friends with a number of artists—John Koerner, Tak Tanabe, Gordon Smith, Jack Shadbolt—whose work we have over the years collected, about whom I have sometimes written. The Arts Club, modestly begun, evolved into the theatre club it is today.

I had by now written another unpublishable novel and a large number of short stories, some of which would be published in the years to come. Without immediate encouragement, I decided again to take a full-time job. For the academic year of 1958–59 I was assistant director at International House at UBC, a job I enjoyed partly because, surrounded by international students, I was reminded of the idyllic summer I had spent at Stratford. It was a job, however, that ate up all my time. I had to deal with moving into a new building and staffing it while also making myself available to students all day, and I was often out in the evening

Jane (second from right) with parents, Arthur R. and Jane Rule; brother, Arthur;
and sister, Libby; at their cabin in the redwoods

for events I had helped to organize both for students and various ethnic communities in the city. I even ran a booking service and employment agency to help students find work.

Not for the first time I felt a rueful regret about the hold writing had on me. Without that obsession, I might have enjoyed working at International House wholeheartedly. Instead, after a year I accepted an offer from the English department to teach full time, for at least I would have the long summers to myself.

In 1959 Helen and I bought our first house, a little stucco bungalow built on the side yard of an old house in West Point Grey. Helen had owned houses before and was enthusiastic about the freedom we'd have to decorate, the increased privacy, a garden of our own. I'd never thought much beyond having a room of my own, somewhere to wash and fix a meal. The financial burden, the responsibility, the permanence all frightened me. But the mortgage we were as women very reluctantly given was less than the rent we had been paying, and the student room, bath, and kitchenette we put in the basement rented for enough to cover our utilities. In hard times, Helen pointed out, we could live in the basement ourselves and rent out the main floor. We were both aware of the fragility of our jobs, from which we could have been fired at any time on a department head's moral whim. That argument persuaded me.

Soon I realized that owning a house gave us greater rather than less freedom. We could go off, leaving our belongings where they were rather than finding some place to store them. We could rent the house in our absence to help pay for a trip.

We traveled a lot in those early years, east to Helen's mother's New Hampshire farm, south to visit my parents in California, back to England finally, and on to Greece, Italy, Austria. We took only one trip in Canada, all around British Columbia, chaperoning the students of the Players' Club as they toured in *Glass Menagerie,* an experience which gave us firsthand knowledge of the mining towns, cattle towns, the deserts, forests, and mountains from which so many of our students came.

. In that little house on Eighth Avenue, I finally finished *Desert of the Heart,* my third novel, in March of 1961, a few days before my thirtieth birthday. After ten years I still hadn't published anything. Three years later, when *Desert of the Heart* was finally published in England and Canada, I had published only a handful of stories in

Jane in 1963

little magazines. In all that time, I certainly thought I had imagined what it would be like to have a novel published. When my six complimentary copies arrived in the mail, I realized for the first time that there would be more than one copy of the book. There were hundreds of them out there in the world. Some days later I went out shyly to see a whole window display of them in a bookstore. I didn't go in. I simply stood across the street and stared.

Macmillan of Canada gave me a book-launching party at the Arts Club. Ethel Wilson, another Macmillan author and the only novelist I knew who used British Columbia as the setting for some of her books, arrived at the party on double canes because of her severe arthritis. I had never met her and was honored by her presence. When I greeted her, she said, "Well, nobody has ever given me a party, and I wanted to see what one was like."

I was very little prepared for the consequences of publishing a book about love between two women. We had lived in Vancouver long enough to have a circle of friends to whom it would come as no surprise, but one or two who were gay themselves dropped us in fear of being found guilty by association. Though the novel certainly didn't enhance my reputation in the English department for whom writers are by definition already dead, I didn't lose my job. My defenders argued that writers of murder mysteries weren't necessarily themselves murderers. Letters began to arrive from all over the English-speaking world from people who thought they had found in me the only other person in the world who might understand them. I could do nothing about those very unhappy, even desperate letters but answer in sympathy. I became for the media the only lesbian in Canada, a role I gradually and very reluctantly accepted and used to educate people as I could.

Desert of the Heart was published in the States in 1965 and disappeared nearly at once. It lingered on in Canada and England for a few years before it was remaindered, the fate of most first novels. It was revived in the States in a library series on homosexual literature, and then Naiad Press reprinted it, as they have gradually all my books. When Donna Deitch's adaptation of the novel was released as the film *Desert Hearts,* in 1985, the book took on a new life, selling thousands of copies in the first months after the film was shown. It has now been translated into German, Dutch, French, and Italian. It took twenty-five years for that book to find its large audience.

Shortly after *Desert of the Heart* was accepted for publication, Helen's mother died. The following summer we drove across Canada to prepare her farm for sale.

As we drove through mile after mile of empty land, through the seemingly endless Ontario forest, I had a new perspective about why one thousand copies of a novel sold in Canada constituted a best-seller. Trees don't read. I was also made more aware of how much my Canada had been one place, Vancouver. I had small firsthand knowledge even of the province of British Columbia. Though I had already made some effort to read Canadian literature, to look at Canadian paintings, and had begun to have a feel for provincial politics, which alternately shocked and amused me, I had very little sense of the history and geography of Canada. I had learned the geography of the United States, and to some extent its history as well, not from schoolbooks so much as from traveling through the country with a father who had a great taste for geography. We always recited with pride the number of states we'd

actually been in and added each new one to the list with a sense of personal treasure. So actually traveling through Canada began to make each province we traveled through, each city we stopped in, newly our own.

I had known Helen's mother's farm since my first Christmas in New England when it lay deep in snow, paths tunneling out to the cow barns and chicken prisons. The core of the house was an early settler's with a central chimney serving fireplaces in three rooms. There were still wooden shutters on the original windows to give protection from Indian attack. Helen's mother, a city woman, had bought the place after her children had grown. She had added wings to the old house so that children and grandchildren could return in welcome and comfort. Dismantling twenty-five years of rich living was a long, hard job in that humid New Hampshire summer. There were barns full of farm equipment, attics full of old clothes, sheet music, furniture, cupboards full of china, enough to invite the whole congregation of the church for a meal. Everything had to be sorted for auction or distribution to various members of the family. In the little village of Lyme where we went for supplies and to pick up the mail, there were many people ready to advise and criticize Helen for the various decisions she had to make. I did not know how well I would live in such a small and intrusive community. But Helen's mother, in many ways a proud and private woman, had thrived there.

In August we routed ourselves back across the United States for the practical purpose of delivering things from the farm to members of Helen's family. We also had friends to visit, and I wanted to see and to show Helen some of the places of my scattered childhood. Concord Academy was not yet in session, but we stopped to see friends we had taught with and to admire again a town so central to Americans' sense of their independence, underlined for me now by Canada's different route to its own nationhood, a process even then not complete.

We stopped in Westfield, New Jersey, to see Wytchwood, the area my grandfather Rule had developed in the 1920s, the big gatehouse where I had spent the first three and a half years of my life, across the street from the little gatehouse where my grandparents had lived and where my grandfather had built a replica of Bobby Burns's cottage for his grandchildren in that tribal time before the depression scattered the family across the country.

In Kentucky we saw my father's twin brother, who showed us the Rule family farm in Goshen on the Ohio River where my grandfather was raised, where I had visited great-uncles in my childhood. It became a trip of farewell of sorts, as we acknowledged the past and distanced ourselves from our ties in the States in preparation for our decision to become Canadian citizens.

When we got home, we began to look for another house. We missed the view we had had of the sea and mountains in our first apartment. We wanted larger rooms for entertaining friends and students, more wall space for the paintings we were collecting, the books we were accumulating, and by that time my own taste for gardening had developed enough for me to feel cramped in our small square patch.

We found an old house on Second Avenue with a wonderful view of the sea, the mountains, and the city. Its garden terraced down to the road, from which we were protected by a fringe of alders, dogwood, and mountain ash trees. The house itself needed work, but I'd been raised by a builder father and liked working with carpenters, plumbers, electricians, and painters. Before we moved in, we had the upstairs converted from a warren of small bedrooms to one large bedroom, a bath, and a study for Helen. We modernized the kitchen, carpeted nearly the whole house, painted and papered the walls. Over the ten years we lived in the house we made other changes, mainly to accommodate students in winter, guests in summer.

There in 1965 I finished *This Is Not for You,* a novel no one was interested in publishing. After two years of submitting it to various publishers, both my English and American agents shelved it. I gave up writing. Only a self-deluding fool would go on after so many years of work and so little to show for it.

For some months teaching distracted me. I gardened a lot. We gave more dinner parties. A friend lent us his old printing press and taught us to use it. I printed bookplates, wine labels, letterheads, other people's poems. But after two years a book began to grow in my head. Instead of taking

"With Helen and our printing press," 1966

notes, as I always had, I ignored it. It seemed to thrive on neglect, there in my imagination as I waited in my office for a student or set type in my basement or weeded the iris bed. Was there anything really wrong with being a self-deluding fool if it made me happy? I had always written primarily for myself anyway.

In 1968 I began to put *Against the Season* on paper. I was in the middle of it when I realized that, for Helen's sake, we should get away for the summer. If we stayed in town, university chores could take up most of her time. Someone from England coming to teach at the summer school was advertising a house exchange. For only the cost of our tickets we could spend the summer in High-gate. Only days before we left I heard from my New York agent that Hy Cohen, senior editor of the new McCall Publishing Company, had asked for *This Is Not for You* to feature among the first books he published, and he hoped I was working on or had completed another. I packed up the manuscript of *Against the Season* and used jet lag to keep me from missing a day's work. It would be the first book I'd written with a publisher waiting to see it.

That summer men landed on the moon. Helen watched it on television. Helen went out to galleries and bookstores. I took only two breaks in my day, one at four in the afternoon to walk to the ladies' only swimming pond on Hampstead Heath for half an hour's swim, one at nine in the evening to close our favorite neighborhood pub. Helen calls it the summer I wasn't there.

That year I was given a Canada Council Grant, renewed a second year, which gave me two years to concentrate on my own work. I finished *Against the Season* and prepared my first collection of short stories for publication. Every time I have sat on a Canada Council jury since then, I remember how crucially important it was for me to have both that time and that encouragement. I was finishing my long apprenticeship with the blessing of my new country and an editor enthusiastic about my work.

When *This Is Not for You* came out, Hy Cohen took a full-page advertisement in the *New York Times* and sent a copy of the book each week for review for three months without response. The reviews the book did receive from the establishment press read it as a morality tale of self-sacrifice and approved of it. Reviewers in the gay press made the same mistake and hated it. Only a few readers recognized the tragic irony with which I intended to expose a false morality hiding a lack of

heart and courage in the main character. I never wrote another long work dependent on irony. I wanted my vision understood, whether it was approved of or not.

Against the Season, when it came out in 1971, presented readers with a different problem. I had grown tired of writing books locked into the point of view of one or two main characters, a technique which encouraged the self-importance of one or two people at the cost of everyone else. We may wish we occupied center stage in our own living, but the fact is that we rarely do. We play out our lives in a series of minor roles in the company of others similarly occupied. In *Against the Season* I wanted to present that sense of community with no central character. Since I had refused to give any greater weight to one character, the reviewers did the job for me and variously reviewed the book as if the main character were a pregnant unwed mother, a dying old woman, a lesbian owner of a used-furniture shop, or a middle-aged banker. It was hard to believe the reviews were concerned with the same book.

Soon after *Against the Season* came out, McCall Publishing Company failed, and I was again without a publisher. I lost the best editor I ever had. I was about to turn forty, an age I had designated as the end of my apprenticeship when I would embark on my mature work. I said to my mother, "I feel as if I have to wake up on my fortieth birthday speaking with the voice of God." "Don't worry," she answered. "You've been doing that since you were six."

I made an unusual number of false starts before I began a book which was alive enough but so bleak in vision that I felt irresponsible writing it and stopped. I went back to teaching. I wrote an occasional short story. I waited. Writing is a peculiar business. Just as it is very difficult to give it up, it can be as difficult to write simply when you have the time and desire to. A failure of nerve can cost months, even years of silence.

I read little fiction while I'm writing novels, turn rather to writers like Loren Eisley or Barbara Tushman. During fallow periods I am addicted to novel reading, finding an affinity with British novelists like Iris Murdock and Margaret Drabble who write classically comic novels focused on community rather than on the tragic fate of an individual. Ann Tyler and Alice Walker are American novelists whose work has resonance for me. I read poetry less often now, but Phyllis Webb in

Canada and Adrienne Rich in the States have written poems of permanent importance to me.

Helen and I were both interested in the developing women's movement, and we helped to organize the first consciousness-raising group at UBC, made up mainly of graduate students, secretaries, and young faculty members. We met each week. Often during those sessions I wondered what we could possibly accomplish with all our free-ranging talk. Then during the week I found myself thinking about what I had heard. I was learning to be aware, as I never had been before, of what it meant to be a woman in an institution where women were a small minority of the faculty, with very few in tenured positions. I saw how quickly women began to drop out of undergraduate programs, until among the graduate students they were a small minority. Yet our women students were as bright and accomplished as the men in our classes. Young women had a more difficult time earning enough money in the summer to finance their education, and their families were less willing to help them than their brothers. They were simply not as comfortable at the university, not as welcomed or as encouraged. Over the year of questioning and challenging our own immediate environment, directions did emerge which would produce first a noncredit and then an academically established women's studies program. Also we made a study comparing men's and women's salaries at a university which claimed to have an equal pay policy. We discovered that women of equal training and experience were paid an average of three thousand dollars less a year than men. When the report was released, the university had to make adjustments to live up to its own stated obligations. Direct political actions of that sort give enormous satisfaction, but I was being increasingly distracted from my own work.

Of the feminist literature we were all reading, Kate Millett's *Sexual Politics* fired my anger and changed my reading habits permanently. I was never able again to ignore the blatant misogyny of so many male writers. I lost some good ones like Patrick White, but it was a loss for my life's sake.

Judith Finlayson, then at Doubleday Canada, had been writing to me for some time about writing a book about lesbians. I protested that I was a fiction writer with no interest in such a project. I only knew what kinds of books should not be written, examples of which were all around. Finally she sent me Alverez's *Savage God,* a book about suicide, and suggested that the same historical and literary approach might be used to exam-

The author in 1975

ine lesbian experience. If I had had a novel to write, I might still not have been lured into the job, but an advance of enough to give me a year free to write was very persuasive for someone who always before had had to buy time for myself.

Just as I was about to embark on this new project, I was complaining about the time it took for me to look after some money we'd invested in the stock market. I proposed that we get our money out and do something with it that we might enjoy, like buying a place on one of the Gulf Islands. The next morning my nephew, up from California to go to UBC, and Helen sat at the breakfast table looking at ads for property on Galiano, an island we had already visited several times. It had the advantage of being the first island reached from the mainland by the Gulf Island ferry, only a fifty-minute trip. It took us only forty-five minutes to drive to the terminal from our house. Within six weeks we had found the house we wanted, potentially larger than we had imagined, set in woods above the shore rather than on the waterfront. We had a wonderful view in

Vancouver. What we needed here was a sense of quiet and seclusion, a weekend getaway from a life that had become too crowded with meetings, openings, dinner parties. We did not imagine then that it would ever be our year-round home.

Working at what became *Lesbian Images* was more like teaching than the writing I had done before. I outlined a chapter, made up a bibliography, and then read until I had the material I needed. Each chapter was like a lecture. In fact, I set up a seminar to have an audience for the work in progress, something I would not think of doing with fiction. Only Helen saw my fiction in progress in order to read chapters aloud to me, but she never commented on it. By the time I was ready to work with an editor, Judith Finlayson had left Doubleday and turned me over to an editor in the New York office who fortunately was sympathetic to the project. *Lesbian Images* came out in 1975 and was a commercial success in the States. It did nothing in Canada or England, where the blatant title was blamed for its failure. I had insisted on the title to be sure readers could easily find it in the library where there were still very few positive books about lesbians and little way of finding them.

That same year Talonbooks in Vancouver finally kept a promise to publish my first collection of short stories, *Theme for Diverse Instruments*, which they have kept in print to this day. The virtue of a good small press is that, while it may not have the staff or money for promotion and distribution, it can have the staying power which keeps a book available years after it would be out of print with a larger publisher.

Though I was invited to the founding meetings of the Writers' Union of Canada in Toronto, I didn't go. Alice Munro did and phoned to report on her way home to Victoria. Then Margaret Atwood, whom I had known since she had her first teaching job at UBC, wrote to say that it was important for western writers to join because the Union must be national from the beginning, not an Ontario power base posing as Canadian. I dutifully paid my dues, but it was several years before I attended an annual meeting in Ottawa in 1975. I rarely missed one after that, and I served on the membership committee and the National Council.

I had found an organization working for the benefit of writers, for the health of Canadian literature in a country only beginning to admit it had a culture worth nourishing. Canadian writers, given the difficulty of earning a living by the pen, wear a lot of other hats as well. We are teachers, lawyers, politicians, farmers, truck drivers, actors, cooks. The range of skills brought to business at hand was impressive, and people worked hard on everything from fairer contracts to more Canadian books in schools and libraries. We picketed chain bookstores illegally selling American editions of Canadian books at cut-rate prices. We petitioned the government for better copyright laws. Wherever writers' interests were involved, a Union member was there to speak for us. The Union gave us all a sense of community, of "tribe" as Margaret Laurence called it. Every annual meeting was a gathering of old friends, and I never came away without having made new ones.

During the academic year of 1974–75, Helen took a year's leave. She had been serving on the university Senate, heading a search committee for a new dean of women, sitting on various English department committees as the only tenured assistant professor who could represent the views of her peers, and teaching a full complement of courses. She wanted a rest and time to read for and plan a new women's studies course and a new Canadian literature course. We decided to rent our Vancouver house and spend the winter on Galiano.

I had gone back to the bleak novel I had set aside several years before. I saw, when I reread my notes and rough drafts of early chapters, that the end I had imagined was really only the middle of the book. The violent judgment of the plot could be overcome by following the survivors into a new life.

We would not have worked as comfortably as we did if my father hadn't offered to finish the lower floor of the house, adding my study and a bedroom and bath which we moved into, leaving our bedroom upstairs, with the addition of a skylight, for Helen's study. We had the basic space if not all the conveniences of home.

We learned that winter what living on a small island is like, and, even through the long power failures when we shivered in front of the fire in my study and cooked inadequate meals, we loved the quiet rhythm of the life, the simplicity of our days. Our phone rarely rang. Often we took a break at lunch time, packed a picnic, and walked out up to the Bluffs and the wonderful view of Active Pass, the islands lying to the south, the Olympic Mountains down in Washington on a really clear day. We studied mushrooms and birds and wild flowers. On weekends we were ready to welcome city friends with whom we explored more of the island and shared simple meals which we ate in the kitchen. Houseguests seemed to us more satisfying than dinner guests. A conversation begun one day can continue the next, and the luxury of time allows for quiet, too, for breaking away and coming back together. Houseguests stay to do the dishes, change the beds, even sometimes work in the garden.

One day we asked ourselves why we would ever want to go back to the city. Helen felt that, since she had taken leave, she owed the university at least one more year of teaching, but after that early retirement sounded lovely to her. She could be back on Galiano for her sixtieth birthday. If we sold the house in town, we could invest that money and be able to live relatively simply, using the windfalls of my writing money for travel and other nonessentials.

It would also be the fulfillment of one of my childhood dreams. Nearly every summer, as I was growing up, we went to my maternal grandmother's two hundred and forty acres of redwoods in northern California, ten miles from the nearest town. There for July and August, I was free to roam the woods, pick berries in the meadows, fruit in the orchard, to swim and fish in the river. When fall came and it was time to go back to whatever suburb we lived in, I envied the country kids who would stay on and know the seasons year round. There is a certain evening light that falls on the valley fields here on Galiano that reminds me of the golden light on the meadows of my childhood, and the deep woods here are as cool and dark as the redwoods. When the ferry carries off all the summer people, I stay behind, an islander through all the seasons.

"On the island of Galiano, British Columbia, with Helen"

Back at UBC Helen refused all committee work and had a lovely last year of teaching. We sold the house in March and prepared to move in May. At the end of March I had my first severe episode of arthritis and was bedridden for the weeks during which I had intended to do most of the sorting and packing up of the house. My nephew and his wife came to help, taking orders from me as I lay on the living room couch. Other friends volunteered. By the end of April, I could walk again. I wore a neck brace and moved about very tentatively. I worried now about life on the island. All the physical chores I had enjoyed I might not be able to do. I worried about being able to write when I couldn't any longer sit at my typewriter for hours at a time. At forty-five I was too young to give up working altogether.

Doubleday accepted *The Young in One Another's Arms,* but the editor made it plain that publishing a novel was a favor they owed me rather than a habit they wanted to get into. Even when the book won Canadian Authors Association's Best Novel of 1978, Doubleday was not impressed. If I ever did write another novel, I would again be looking for a publisher.

Contract with the World began as two different novels, one about people all the same age, another about young artists in a provincial city far from the centers of culture. Only after months of work in notebooks did it occur to me to put the two together for the richness of thematic material I needed. Then I had to teach myself to write a first draft in longhand because I could do that lying on a couch with a board on my lap. At the end of the day I could sit for the short time it took to type what I had written.

Most writers are superstitious and compulsive about how and where they write. I was no exception. At first what I wrote in my cramped hand seemed to me unlike what I had written before. It was awkward and static. Any writing, after a period of silence, is like rust coming out of long unused pipes, but I could recognize my own rust. What I now put on the page seemed not only bad but foreign to me, and the process was so slow I could not imagine writing a whole book.

Because we were now free of any schedule but our own, I could break away from the frustration of my work. We made a habit of going to the desert for up to a month each winter, sometimes visiting Helen's sisters in Arizona, sometimes going to Borrego Springs, just south of Palm Springs in California. While I was in that dry climate, I was nearly free of arthritis, and we swam and walked

every day. I even found I could do some work there.

I had tried swimming in the waters off Galiano, but I got too cold. In 1979 Helen persuaded me that we needed to put in a pool for ourselves. It seemed to me then a crazy extravagance, but for the last thirteen years we've been able to swim daily for up to six months of the year, and each summer afternoon we've opened the pool to the island children. Over the years we've watched numbers of children learn to swim.

I did learn to write again, and I found another publisher. Harcourt, Brace, Jovanovich published *Contract with the World* in 1980.

I had known Barbara Grier of Naiad Press since she'd published stories of mine in the *Ladder,* then the only lesbian magazine in the States. I approached her about publishing a collection of my stories and essays specifically about lesbian experience as a fiftieth birthday present for me to give to my friends. She could sell it as well, of course, but I didn't want review copies sent out to the straight press. I wanted *Outlander* to be a book for lesbians. Barbara was dubious about the commercial wisdom of combining essays and stories, but she agreed to have the book ready by March of 1981.

I, who usually like to celebrate my birthday as quietly as possible, invited women from all over the continent. Mary Meigs and Marie-Claire Blais came from Montreal. Judy Baca and Donna

With Donna Deitch on Jane's fiftieth birthday, 1981

320

"Helen teaching the children to test the pool water"

Deitch, who had by then begun raising the money to make the film, *Desert Hearts,* came from Los Angeles. Ann Saddlemyer and Joan Coldwell came from Toronto. We rented cottages. We reserved the wonderful restaurant, the Pink Geranium, at the north end of the island, and for a weekend eighteen of us gathered, friendships both strengthened and begun that have nourished us all ever since.

The celebration was such a success that we have given similar parties for Helen's seventieth and seventy-fifth, my sixtieth. They have become important rituals in shaping our own world, in making our own meanings, teaching us to be more comfortable and generous about staging those more conventional gatherings, a family reunion and my parents' fiftieth wedding anniversary.

The Canada Council offers mini writer-in-residencies so that universities or libraries or simply groups in a community may invite a writer for a week or two to offer workshops, give lectures, take part in existing programs. Once Helen was free to go with me, we decided it was a very good way to get to know the country we had adopted. We've been to Edmonton, Calgary, Saskatoon, Regina, Winnipeg, and Montreal, and in each place I've made an effort to be available to writers who aren't attached to academic institutions and to local gay communities. In that way I became a better member of the committee that evaluated literary magazines for funding. It was always a pleasure to come across the work of writers who had briefly been my students.

Also in those years I served on the Koerner Foundation in Vancouver which offered grants to all kinds of projects in the arts, education, and social welfare, and I could encourage people I'd met in the women's movement, in the gay community, in writing workshops to apply.

Naiad Press offered to begin reprinting my earlier novels and to keep them in print. Only Talonbooks in Vancouver had done that for *Theme for Diverse Instruments,* and a cheap paperback of *Desert of the Heart.* The large publishers let all but their very best-selling fiction go quickly out of print.

Lester and Orpen Dennys in Canada offered to publish, in cooperation with Naiad Press in the States, a new collection of my short stories, *Inland Passage,* and a collection of essays, *A Hot-Eyed Moderate,* in 1985. Many of the essays came from my writing for the *Body Politic,* one of Canada's national gay papers. But the collection also included profiles and essays on writing.

I was in Toronto to publicize these two books when *Desert Hearts* opened the Toronto Film Festival. There really was a line of people all around the block outside the theatre, and in the audience were both the leading actresses as well as Donna Deitch, the producer and director. The crowd was so jubilant that Toronto felt like my hometown. I didn't really mind that my interviewers were more interested in what I thought of the film than in the two books I was supposed to be selling. They were surprised, too, that I liked the film. Writers are not supposed to.

Artists often provide each other with raw material, and it is a privilege to be part of a community of makers often dependent on each other for inspiration. I was once given a hand-painted smock which was a response to an image in *Contract with the World,* "a day as hot as zinnias." I wear it with great pleasure.

Memory Board had a gestation period of five years before it was clear to me what needed to be told of the twin brother and sister who had been in my mind so long. In 1987 the novel was published by Pandora, Naiad, and Macmillan of Canada. I finally again had publishers in all three countries. In October of that year I was invited to England to help launch the book.

October is the time of year my parents usually visit us; so I asked them if they would like to join us in England instead. They are as fond of the country as I am, but we'd never been there together. My father suggested that we be their guests. He rented a large apartment for all of us just north of Marble Arch in London for a month.

Sara/Van Gennep, a Dutch publisher bringing out a translation of *Desert of the Heart,* heard I was to be in London and invited me to Holland to help with promotion there. When I told Rob Van Gennep there would be four of us, he was undaunted. We had just time to settle into the London apartment before we flew to Amsterdam for four days of remarkable welcome and hospitality for us all. We had a tour of the countryside, a trip on the canals, a visit to the Van Gogh museum. There were dinner parties every night. The Canadian Embassy helped to host the launching party.

My English publisher, not to be outdone, sent theatre tickets for us all when we got back to London. Canada House put on a wine-and-cheese party for the launching of *Memory Board* and hired a Canadian actress to read since I never give readings of my own work. It was an elegant party to which some of my English friends came. To my great surprise, our next-door neighbor on Galiano, a flight attendant for Air Canada, turned up with her daughter. What might have been a hard social chore turned into a real celebration to share with Helen and my parents. We ended the evening with a late dinner at Rule's.

Pandora spread my publicity chores over the month we were there, and I was never away from London longer than overnight, returning to the apartment with a case full of treats from my hotel room, small bottles of wine, boxes of candy, fresh fruit. On days I wasn't working, we occasionally hired a car and driver to take us into the country, often to loved places we had all seen before but had never shared—Chartwell, Knoll, the Cotswolds. We left London just hours before the great storm struck which laid waste to much of the countryside we'd seen.

Helen and I flew to Montreal where I was scheduled to speak at McGill University, to autograph copies of *Memory Board* in bookstores, and to deal with a film crew from the *Journal,* Canada's national magazine on television.

From there we flew to Toronto where I was interviewed on stage by June Callwood for the Harbour Front Festival. As I had at the film opening, I felt a great personal welcome from the audience. One reviewer, intending a mild put-down, called it "a gay love-in" to account for the size as well as the enthusiasm of the crowd. Gay communities all across the English-speaking world are generously supportive of anyone working in any way on their behalf. It is a loyalty grudgingly envied by people who recognize no such constituency for themselves. I write for the widest audience I can, but I survived to reach it by the courage of presses like Naiad and Pandora, notice in small magazines and newspapers, and the word of mouth of readers who cared.

After five days of interviews in Toronto, I was exhausted. I was already scheduled to go to Ottawa, and the publicity agent at Macmillan told me the media in Winnipeg and Edmonton were eager for me to visit both cities. I thought of the good friends I might be able to see briefly, but I was too tired to extend myself any further. There are very good interviewers in Canada like Peter

Gzowski, but for every one of him there are many who haven't time to do their homework and so ask irrelevant and silly questions like, "Is feminism dead in the '90s?" or quizzically hostile questions like, "Why do all the people on the dust jacket look so unhappy?" Taking gentle control of such interviews is what finally saps energy and patience. From Ottawa we flew home, and I didn't do any local publicity until I was much better rested.

In the spring of 1988, I was invited with Anne Cameron and Joy Kagawa to represent Canada at England's Feminist Book Fortnight, a program so successful that it has begun to rival the Christmas season for sales. Originally only the independent bookstores participated, but now the chain stores are also involved. In no other country has feminist book publishing been so successful, and I saw my books displayed in every kind of bookstore all over the country. In Canada and the United States I can count on finding my books only in gay and women's bookstores.

Again we took advantage of the trip and extended our time a week on either side of the event so that we could also go the theatre, the galleries, and visit friends. Just after we arrived, the government passed a bill making it illegal for any agency funded by the government to present homosexuality as a viable alternative life-style. I was scheduled to speak in libraries, on the BBC's "Woman's Hour," and other similarly vulnerable places. One head librarian considered canceling my appearance. I had some real sympathy for the confusion and fear people were feeling. I explained that I hadn't been sent by the Canadian government to promote homosexuality in England. I had been sent to promote Canadian books written by women, and that is what I intended to do. If the subject came up, however, I would address it. Everywhere we went, this new censorship was the concern of people in the audience. While most argued that it was a law which couldn't be enforced, everyone feared the self-censorship it would encourage.

Helen had never been to Westminster Abbey. We went to look at the plaques of artists honored there, W. H. Auden, Benjamin Britten, Peter Pears, Gerard Manley Hopkins, to name a few of the homosexuals who have contributed to England's greatness. The moral hypocrisy of the present government seemed the greater irony as we stood there where obviously all is mortal vanity. I had once longed to live in England. I didn't any longer. I doubted after that trip if I'd ever go back.

I was grateful to be at home that summer, entertaining visitors, lifeguarding for the children at the pool. People we very much enjoy are also attracted to summer life on Galiano. Margaret Atwood, Graeme Gibson, and their daughter, Jess, spent a summer here, protected by the locals from idle tourists as we have always been. Marian Engel spent two summers here when her twins were young. For many writers crossing the country on hard publicity tours, we are the end of the road, offering respite from the too public world. We are sometimes asked to meet visitors from New Zealand and Australia to give them a few days to recover from jet lag before they cross this large country doing a variety of cultural chores.

For some time I'd been thinking of a novel about people living alone. It might seem an odd topic for someone who has never lived alone for more than a few days at a time. Quite a number of people on this island, both young and old, do live alone, some but not all by choice, and the ways they go about making community are different from the arrangements couples or families make. As I worked in my notebooks, my cast of characters grew much too large for the relatively small book I had in mind, and I decided to limit myself to women. The book is set on Galiano, though the island isn't named. People who live here are reluctant to have their home so much publicized that the tourist invasion gets out of hand.

I did not know while I was writing it that *After the Fire*, which was published in 1989, would be my last book. I'm glad I didn't, for that knowledge would have introduced a self-consciousness from which any novel would suffer.

In 1989, while in Portland, Oregon, for me to give a talk on our way to our winter break in Borrego Springs, Helen fell and broke her arm. She couldn't do very much for herself while it healed, and the fall had made her uncertain about walking out on her own. The weather that winter was stormy, and I didn't experience the relief from arthritis I had in previous years. For the first time I had to take anti-inflammatory drugs in order to be able to keep moving at all. They are said sometimes to cause confusion in elderly people. What I have noticed is not confusion so much as a slowing down of mental processes and a lack of obsessive interest in anything.

I do need to keep as mobile as I can for the simple convenience of our living. If I go off medication, I can't manage. Quite gradually I began to accept the fact that I am not any longer

Jane with Judy Baca at Helen's seventy-fifth birthday, 1991

driven to write. I have been extraordinarily lucky to have had the time intermittently in my life to write much of what has been on my mind to say. Twelve books are a generous allotment of trees for one writer on this suffering planet. When I was asked what I was working on, I didn't want to pretend either that I was writing or suffering writer's block; so I announced my retirement.

I've been bemused by people's reaction to my choosing to fall silent. Most people apparently assume that artists must be artists to the lip of the grave, and they are incensed that anyone could be free to neglect a talent. It is probably perverse of me to take comfort in such indignation, but, since what I have had to say has often caused outrage, it is reassuring to find that my silence can be unsettling, too.

My books are all in print, and they are being translated into more and more languages. There are new film options. After so many hard years of working without any recognition or financial return, I now in idleness make a modest living. Like the moving around I did as a child, the discrepancy between my valuing of my work and the world's

judgment has reinforced my independence from any system of values but my own. How could it not when I have been paid the same amount for an advance on a novel that took me years to write and one short-short story I wrote in an afternoon? And now the library pays more for my scrap paper than I've received for a completed manuscript.

I do, mostly on invitation, write occasional short pieces if the topic interests me, if it is not a matter of repeating what I have already said too many times. In the only other attempt I made to write autobiography some years ago, I discovered that I had dined out on my life for so many years that, lacking an immediate audience to amuse, I was quickly bored with those old stories. I was tempted to write this essay only because the word limit and the literary focus suggested useful restrictions which have allowed me to look with new old eyes at my writing life as I did with new young eyes at the leaves on trees, the expressions on faces, when I first put on glasses over fifty years ago.

BIBLIOGRAPHY

Fiction:

Desert of the Heart, Macmillan (Toronto), 1964, Secker and Warburg (London), 1964, World, 1965, Naiad Press, 1983.

This Is Not for You, McCall, 1970, Naiad Press, 1984, Pandora (London), 1987.

Against the Season, McCall, 1971, Naiad Press, 1984, Pandora, 1988.

Theme for Diverse Instruments (short stories), Talonbooks (Vancouver), 1975, Naiad Press, 1990.

The Young in One Another's Arms, Doubleday, 1977, Naiad Press, 1984, Pandora, 1990.

Contract with the World, Harcourt, 1980, Naiad Press, 1982, Pandora, 1990.

Outlander (short stories and essays), Naiad Press, 1981.

Inland Passage and Other Stories, Lester & Orpen Dennys (Toronto), 1985, Naiad Press, 1985.

Memory Board, Macmillan, 1987, Naiad Press, 1987, Pandora, 1987.

After the Fire, Macmillan, 1989, Naiad Press, 1989, Pandora, 1989.

Nonfiction:

Lesbian Images, Doubleday, 1975, Pluto Press (London), 1989.

A Hot-Eyed Moderate, Lester & Orpen Dennys, 1985, Naiad Press, 1985.

Work represented in such anthologies as *Best Short Stories of 1972,* Oberon, 1972; *Contemporary Voices,* Prentice-Hall, 1972; *New Canadian Short Stories,* Oberon, 1975; *Stories from Pacific and Arctic Canada,* Macmillan, 1975; *After You're Out,* Links Books, 1975; Bob Weaver, editor, *Small Wonders,* CBC, 1982; Ed Jackson and Stan Persky, editors, *Flaunting It,* Pink Triangle Press, 1982. Author of column "So's Your Grandmother," in *Body Politic.* Contributor of reviews and articles to literature journals and other periodicals, including *Canadian Literature, Chatelaine, Globe and Mail, Housewife, Queen's Quarterly, Redbook,* and *San Francisco Review. Desert of the Heart,* adapted by Donna Deitch, was released as the film *Desert Hearts* in 1985.

Pamela Sargent

1948-

Pamela Sargent, while traveling in Moscow, "with part of the Kremlin wall in the background," summer, 1988

Space is transparent. We can see through space, but not through time, except with fallible memory.

As it happened, I couldn't see through space all that clearly in the beginning. I was nearsighted, squinting my way through first grade and part of second before anyone noticed that there might be a problem with my eyes. At close range, the world was discernible and understandable; beyond the limits of my vision, it was chaotic and uncertain. Adults, who towered over me, had faces that were usually too far away for me to be able to read their expressions, so I often missed early warning signs that they might be impatient or angry.

My father, who was athletic, started taking my brother Scott and me to an empty lot near our apartment almost as soon as we could walk. There, we struggled to master the arts of pitching, swinging a bat, and catching pop flies. Scott caught on fast, showing a skill that would bring him, much later in life, to consider a career as a baseball player.

I didn't do so well. My arms weren't strong enough to throw pitches, and at bat I almost never saw the ball until it was past me. In the outfield, the only warning I had that a fly ball might be heading toward me was the crack of the distant bat swung by the blurred figure of my father or brother. I would squint up at the sky as I ran, searching for the hurtling white orb and hoping that I was headed in the right direction. Often, I barely had time to glimpse the ball before being struck in the head, arm, or shoulder; only by accident would the baseball actually find its way to my mitt.

That was the world, an unpredictable place where you could get beaned by a baseball you never saw coming.

Books were different. My mother often read to us; later, after my sister Connie and brother Craig were born, I read to them. Reading, unlike baseball, was something I could master. The words made orderly patterns on the page, ones I could learn to interpret. By holding a book close to my face, I could see what was there. Through stories, I could make sense of the world. I took to books almost immediately and was reading before I started school.

This probably explains a lot about my subsequent life.

*

I was born after my parents had been married for a few years, but still feel as if I've seen their early lives. Are those images in my mind of their past drawn from family stories, or from hundreds of movies about the World War II years and their aftermath? Sometimes it's hard to tell.

Their story might have been good source material for a movie about coming-of-age in the early 1940s. They met in college, at Cornell University. My mother was a New York City girl on a scholarship, working her way through; my father was barely maintaining grades high enough to keep from flunking out. Despite having almost nothing in common except an interest in music (my father sang, and my mother played the piano), they were engaged about a month after they met.

Their courtship had some opposition. My grandfather wasn't at all sure that he approved of my father as a prospective son-in-law; a house-mother in charge of one Cornell dormitory, a

"On the right, my parents, Edward H. Sargent, Jr., and Shirley Richards, on June 27, 1941, their wedding day, with college classmates Edwin Pesnel and Betty Bourne"

woman apparently infected with both anti-Semitism and class prejudice, didn't much approve of my mother. My parents got married anyway, sooner than they might have otherwise, because it seemed the country might soon be at war. The attack on Pearl Harbor came less than six months after their wedding; by the beginning of 1942, my father was in the Marine Corps.

He could have avoided military service altogether. The army, noting his history of having had rheumatic fever as a child, suspected a weak heart and turned him down. He went to the marine recruiters, who said they would take him if he could get through boot camp. He did, and ended up in the South Pacific, in some of the worst fighting of the war. Just before the invasion of Iwo Jima, he suffered a heart attack; that and other injuries landed him stateside, in a California hospital.

It took him a while to recover. He was still in his twenties but doubted he would live very long. My mother joined him in Los Angeles while he tried to decide what to do with what was left of his life. He had always wanted to sing professionally, and eventually landed a contract with Fred Waring and NBC Radio; there was talk of solo performances, of work in motion pictures. There were also warnings from doctors that his heart might not be able to take the strain of a musical career with its erratic hours and physical demands. My father ignored this medical advice. If he didn't have much time left, he would at least use it doing what he loved.

At about this time, my mother became pregnant with me.

If my father had bitter regrets that he was now going to be a father, he never mentioned them to me—although he did admit, not long before his death, that having children had not been one of his youthful ambitions. A career in show business seemed more impractical than ever with a child on the way; my mother, used to having a job, would not be able to work for a while. The pressure was on my father from family members to come back East, settle down, use the GI Bill to get more education, and then find work that would not tax his heart.

My parents moved to Ithaca, New York, where they had met; my father went back to Cornell. My brother Scott was born about a year and a half after I was, and Connie and Craig, who were twins, about three years after Scott.

Our family had made its contribution to the post-war baby boom.

"My father, the Marine in shorts, at a base on Guadalcanal during World War II. The man with him is his friend Art Tatlock, who was later killed in combat."

*

Scott and I were on a train with my mother, going to visit her parents, who had moved to Indiana from New York. My father stood on the platform behind a veil of falling snow, waving to us as the train pulled away. I'm not sure who was helping him look after Connie and Craig, who were about a year old, or if anyone was—not that I was worrying too much about the twins. I had looked forward to their birth, often trying to hold conversations with them when they were still inside my mother, still blissfully ignorant of how much trouble two small children could be.

This wasn't the first time I had been on a train or traveled to Indiana, but it was the first such journey I can remember. My mother's younger brother was going to get married; that was the official reason for the trip to my grandparents' house. The unspoken reason might have been that my mother needed to get away for a while.

Sometime before this trip, my parents had moved out of our most recent apartment into their first house. There was no garage; my father eventually built a carport. I loved that house; it had a second story, which meant I had my own room. There was a backyard, with rosebushes growing near a fence. We had so much space that it seemed unlikely we would ever have to move again.

Years later, when I visited that house again and was invited inside by the people who lived there, the house took on its true dimensions—a small house, with low ceilings, cramped quarters, and a postage-stamp–sized yard. But the house I still see in memory is the spacious one I inhabited as a child.

Whatever dissatisfactions my father had about the life he was now living, he had not given up his music. He continued to sing, both as an amateur and professionally; for a few years he was a paid soloist or member of a professional quartet for a local synagogue, a Catholic church, a Methodist church, and a congregation of Christian Scientists, a schedule that took up most of his weekends.

My mother, with four small children, somehow managed to keep order. She had taught herself to sew during the Depression; the only way she could afford stylish clothes was to make them herself. Food got to the table on a fairly regular basis, clothes got washed, and if our closets, shelves, and dresser drawers were in a chaotic state, well, nobody was going to see them. On the surface, at least, we looked organized.

*

Audrey was the person who first showed me why, in late afternoon, I could often see tiny silhouettes of cars and trucks moving across my bedroom wall. Apparently the metallic roof outside my window caught the light in such a way as to create these images. This optical effect, to my delight, usually coincided with the rush hour, when the traffic on the busy street outside was heaviest.

Audrey was a student at Cornell; she rented a room from my parents and sometimes baby-sat for them. She was planning to be an architect. Since one of my favorite pursuits was building structures with blocks and plastic logs, I understood Audrey's ambitions. There were hints others weren't quite so sympathetic. Her parents, who wrote to her fairly often, apparently disapproved. There were days when I overheard her complaining to my mother about some of her professors, who found the notion of a female architect ludicrous. Audrey eventually became the first woman to get a degree from Cornell's School of Architecture and has been a professional architect ever since.

My parents couldn't have picked a better role model for me if they had tried.

*

Bobby Swayze, a boy a year older than I, was the first person to reveal the science-fictional world to me. He and his mother, a widow who had lost her husband in Korea, moved into the apartment building next door to our house just before I was to start school.

Bobby was addicted to "Captain Video." When his mother was at work, we would watch "Captain Video," then go down to his building's dark and creepy basement, where Bobby had his laboratory, so he could show off his latest experiment. Most of the experiments involved either exotic-looking machines made of tubes and spare parts or chemical compounds that smelled disgusting.

Bobby was also fascinated by hypnosis. He had built a large box, open on one side, out of scraps of wood and hung a crude pendulum made of string and a small iron weight in the opening. This apparatus, he was convinced, could put someone into a trance, but we needed an experimental subject. I immediately thought of my brother Scott.

We would make Scott our slave, powerless to resist any commands. That was Bobby's idea, anyway. We finally got Scott to sit still long enough to watch the swinging pendulum while Bobby chanted, "You're getting sleepy, you're getting sleepier and sleepier," and I gave the pendulum an occasional nudge. Scott did fall asleep, but before we could plant any post-hypnotic suggestions, Bobby's mother had come home from work and was yelling at us for being in the basement again, thus saving Scott from the humiliations of slavery.

I was not surprised to find out years later that Bobby had gone to MIT.

*

I started school at an earlier age than most kids do. Since I had learned how to read by the age of four, my parents figured that I was ready to attend; the school authorities, for reasons of their own, decided to put me in first grade instead of kindergarten. Years lay ahead in which I was destined to be a big disappointment to a lot of my teachers. They mistakenly assumed, since I was so much younger than most of my classmates, that I had exceptional intelligence.

But this ambiguous academic career was in the future. Nothing in my three years at my first school, the Henry St. John Elementary School in Ithaca, prepared me for the scholastic miseries and failures that lay ahead.

The Henry St. John school was a large, imposing, almost sinister-looking brick structure, but schools were supposed to look that way, so its appearance didn't bother me. It was about two blocks from downtown Ithaca and one block from our house, which meant I could take a shortcut through my best friend Adrienne Carlyon's yard (she lived right behind us) and get to school in about three minutes. This had its advantages, since I was already taking after my father, who suffered from insomnia and an inability to get up on time in the morning.

Most of the time, I actually looked forward to going to that school, a feeling I rarely had since.

Miss Mancuso was my first grade teacher. She had curly black hair, wore Chanel No. 5 perfume, and drove a red convertible; she made being a teacher seem glamorous. I must have seemed an unpromising student; for one thing, disgusted by the inanities of the stories in our readers, I refused to respond when asked to read out loud. Soon I was assigned to the group for slow readers, where I might have languished permanently had Miss Mancuso not kept me after school one day.

What was my problem? she asked. I think I mumbled something about how boring the readers were and how I was used to more interesting reading. There was a newspaper on her desk; she handed it to me, perhaps expecting me to decipher one of the simpler headlines to prove my contention that I could read. I did, then started on the story below it until she stopped me.

I won a promotion to the advanced reading group and thrived after that. If there were times when I wanted to be somewhere other than at school, at least I didn't dread going. That dread came later.

*

I became part of a scientific study during my second year at school. The Salk polio vaccine was being tested; some children would get the actual vaccine and others, in the control group, a placebo. My classmates and I lined up in the gym to get our shots. Years later, I was told that I had been given the actual vaccine, which saved me the torment of going through a series of shots again, but this news didn't come as much of a surprise. My reaction to these early polio shots was pronounced; I vomited, collapsed, got taken to the school nurse's office, and was sent home with a high fever. For a while, there were fears that I might have contracted the disease.

Down the street from our house was a home for children with polio, a large old house that was next to a playground. I often went to the playground, and usually a few kids from the home were there, too. That they had braces on their legs or were confined to wheelchairs seemed about as significant to me at first as the fact that my friend Adrienne had freckles. It was a while before I realized how profoundly different their lives were from mine and that there were children even worse off, immobilized in iron lungs.

We were all afraid of polio, which could strike at any time without warning. Our parents were probably a lot more fearful than we were, given that they had a much clearer idea of what damage the disease could do, but we all knew that anyone could be a victim. I could become one of those kids in the home down the street. I'd had my share of serious illness by then, including pneumonia, but polio was different. Having friends who considered it a good day when they could take a few steps without their crutches made it impossible for me to feel childishly invulnerable.

*

Ithaca was child-sized, meaning that I could wander around most of it by myself without getting lost. We were a block from downtown, and I could take a bus to the hills of the Cornell campus. I learned how to swim in Cayuga Lake and often took walks with my father up hillsides and along Ithaca's gorges. Ithaca had the virtues of a small town while, thanks to Cornell's presence, being almost as cosmopolitan as a larger city.

My best friends, Adrienne Carlyon, Leslie Pfaff, and Renée Weber, all lived within walking distance. We would watch television together ("The Roy Rogers Show" was a particular favorite since Dale Evans was one of the few women on TV who wasn't wimpy), go to movie matinees downtown, or head over to the school playground. Leslie, who wanted to be a dancer, often talked us into helping her put on backyard performances in which she would star, prancing around in her

"Our house in Ithaca, with the carport my father built," years later in the early 1980s

ballet slippers. During Cornell's Homecoming Week in the fall and Reunion Weekend in early June, we would marvel at all the raucous old people who suddenly took over the town, roaming around drunk in their red-and-white Cornell jackets and sweaters, pretending that they were still in college.

When we thought about the future at all, which was only in passing, we all assumed we would spend it in Ithaca. We would go to Ithaca High, a relatively exciting prospect since a lot of girls there led a worldly life of dating Cornell guys and going to frat parties. When we graduated, we would go to Cornell—or, if our grades weren't so good, Ithaca College. We would get married and bring up our own families there, although my personal goal was to spend a few years exploring Africa before settling down to rear the six children I planned to have.

None of this came to pass. When I was finishing third grade, my parents decided to move to Albany, New York.

I wrote and directed my first full-scale dramatic productions in sixth grade, basing them on our history lessons. The first was a story about a slave in classical Athens, and the second dealt with life in a medieval monastery, although I introduced a mildly racy subplot about a knight and lady contemplating an affair. We made our own props and costumes; my scripts were run off on the school's mimeograph machine. I cast my classmates in various roles and directed them, rehearsing the plays for a couple of weeks before we put them on for the school.

These creative efforts were partly the result of desperation. I was trying to convince my teacher, Mrs. Tabor, that I wasn't completely hopeless, and that was going to take some doing.

Since moving to Albany, my grades had dropped precipitously. My fifth grade teacher had even become convinced that I had been put in her class solely to make her life a misery. She kept me inside when the other kids were out at recess, forcing me to go over multiplication tables again and again. She told me that I daydreamed too much and would never amount to anything. She gave me extra assignments, which I refused to do or would hand in only under extreme duress. We were soon trapped in one of those vicious circles where her escalating threats only made me more stubborn in my resistance.

My grades were barely high enough to get me promoted to sixth grade. I sometimes think I escaped being held back only because my teacher was dying to get rid of me by then.

Unlike my fourth grade teacher, who bored me, and my fifth grade teacher, who persecuted me, Mrs. Tabor actually seemed to enjoy the classroom. My grades improved; never one of her best students, I was still far from being the worst.

But even Mrs. Tabor could not completely reconcile me to that school, or the even more wretched junior high school I attended afterward. It would probably not be fair to mention these schools by name. I hated them myself but can't honestly say they were bad schools; other students, including my brothers and sister, managed to learn something in them. It might have been the pressure to conform, to fit into a certain acceptable pattern, that made me loathe these schools. Most schools, after all, are in the business of turning out a particular product, one that will fit· into its designated place in life.

Something was definitely odd about my grade school in Albany; I felt that right away, during my first day in fourth grade. It was years before I realized what had made me feel so disoriented. Every student in that fourth grade class was white, a far cry from Henry St. John, where children of Cornell's foreign graduate students and Ithaca's middle-class black community were among my classmates. This was, I suppose, the outward sign of this new elementary school's true purpose. There would be little diversity in its classrooms, only the molding of a largely homogeneous group of children into good workers and citizens.

No one around me seemed especially disturbed by this state of affairs.

*

Not long after we moved to Albany, my paternal grandfather died. Other people, including my mother, had found him an intimidating man, but I always looked forward to his intermittent visits. He was tall (well over six feet), wore hand-tailored suits and expensive shirts, smoked his cigarettes from an ivory holder, spoke perfect French, and had a perpetual tan from sitting under a sun lamp for a few minutes every day. He was also an MIT graduate and an engineer; Stalin had invited him to come to the Soviet Union and work on water projects there, an offer my grandfather, perhaps wisely, refused. Eventually, he became the chief engineer on a flood control project in the Adirondack Mountains of northern New York. He refused to have the reservoir that he designed named after him; instead, it was called Sacandaga Lake, after the indigenous people of the region.

My grandfather, during his last illness, was a patient at the Albany Medical Center, and we often drove over to see him. Young children weren't allowed to visit patients, but my grandfather's room overlooked the parking lot, so we could wave to him from there. Hospital food wasn't to his taste, so he had meals brought in from one of Albany's best restaurants; my father and my aunt smuggled in his martinis.

My parents must have known that he was dying. I kept waiting for him to get better.

A woman named Alice often visited at our house. I grew close enough to her to regard her as a third grandmother, a more accurate role in which to cast her than I realized, because she and my grandfather were in love. We kids didn't know that, although my mother had made it very clear that we were never to mention Alice and her visits to my grandmother.

As it happened, my grandparents' marriage had been over for years. My grandfather, with the help of a housekeeper, had brought up my father and his two sisters largely by himself. My grandmother, judging by a couple of photos taken when

she was a young woman, had perfect skin, thick black hair piled up on her head, and large dark mournful eyes. She suffered from manic-depression and spent much of her adulthood in such places as the Menninger Clinic, Austen Riggs, and other expensive asylums; when she was feeling well, she stayed with her parents or sisters, not my grandfather. One story I heard only after she had died was that she and one of her physicians had fallen in love and lived together for several years, unable to marry because neither of them could get a divorce.

Perhaps, with my grandfather dying, my grandmother was hoping for a reconciliation. Maybe she was determined that she, and not Alice, would be cast in the role of widow. I don't know; I do remember making sure that I hid all of Alice's gifts before my grandmother's visits.

I had been looking forward to the day my grandfather would leave the hospital. Instead, early one morning, my father came upstairs, gathered us all together, and told us our grandfather had died the night before. I didn't believe him. Grandpa Sargent was going to get well, wasn't he? That was what we had been led to believe. I didn't accept the truth for a while. Maybe, on some level, I still haven't.

This was when I first became aware of how irrevocable and final death is.

About a year after my grandfather's death, my mother and I went over to Alice's apartment. My mother was more secretive than usual, sending Scott off to play with his friends and Connie and Craig to a neighbor's house before she told me where we were going. I didn't know that my father, feeling his mother had first claim on his loyalties, thought we shouldn't see Alice anymore.

Alice served us tea and cookies. We were there for a long time, not leaving until it was almost dark. I think my mother thanked her for the mass cards she had sent after my grandfather's death. Alice hugged me before we left, and I told her how much I missed her. My mother was wiping at her eyes when we got downstairs. "Don't say anything to your father," she said as we walked to the car.

*

Grandmother Sargent lived in the Adirondacks, in a cottage in a small town not far from where her parents once had their home. She and her sister, whose husband had fled to Canada with their children after their divorce, shared a small house. A short walk down the road led to a lake and a rocky beach, where we often went swimming.

My father told me almost nothing about his mother's family. My grandmother told me a few tales, and I had to piece together the rest from stories that were sometimes inconsistent.

My grandmother's parents, my great-grandparents, were Mohawks who left a reservation outside Montreal to go south. One story is that my great-grandfather's luck at cards brought him enough cash to make this move. He made a lot of money in lumber, bought a big house, and set about rearing a houseful of children—there were nine of them by then. When his daughters didn't behave, he would threaten them with the most dire fate he could imagine—a stint at Holy Names, a convent and girls' school with the reputation of a prison. He eventually made good on his threat; that's where my grandmother and one of her sisters were educated. They retaliated, though, and got themselves expelled before graduating.

In addition to his house, my great-grandfather also had a camp, a large compound with several buildings along the shores of an Adirondack lake. It's said that he won this camp in a card game; another story has it that he traded a big piece of land farther north for ownership of the compound, but cards are a feature of both stories.

I visited this compound not long ago. It's a children's summer camp now, accessible only by a long, dirt road winding through a pine forest. The original buildings, still there, are large wooden structures that remind me of Iroquois longhouses; each one could easily house a family. My great-grandfather's dream was to house his children, their husbands and wives, and their children in each of these longhouses during the summer and to have them near him during the rest of the year. My grandmother loved that camp and went there as often as she could; my grandfather stayed away. One of my grandmother's brothers eventually sold the place for a ridiculously low price; by then, all of the family's money was gone.

Scott and I lived with our grandmother for a while and visited fairly often after that. I remember those times with fondness, but Scott was miserable.

My grandmother was the first person who really understood me, or so it seemed. Almost alone among the adults I knew, she sympathized with me when I felt depressed and understood my longing for solitude. She told me stories, among

"Emma Sargent, my grandmother on my father's side, at Canada Lake in the Adirondacks," 1962

them a Mohawk folktale of how the Great Bear was taken to the sky. Often, we would sit on her porch or in her living room to read; she had accumulated a lot of books, including several Mika Waltari historical novels. She had a television, but we never watched it unless a baseball game was on. The priests lived next door, between Grandma Sargent's house and the church, and on Sundays, we went to the porch to watch the crowds parking their cars and going into mass. My grandmother, who never went to mass herself, still had enough sense of propriety to tell us to behave ourselves until the masses were over and the churchgoers gone.

This was much too tranquil a life for Scott, and my grandmother would be all over him for the slightest infraction as well. I finally had a defender! My grandmother's home was one place where he wouldn't be able to pick on me.

In the mornings, I sometimes went to my grandmother's room to visit with her while her sister made breakfast. (In our lack of domestic skills, my grandmother and I were much alike.) She would comb her silver hair, a time-consuming process since it fell nearly to her waist, then pin it up. She usually wore a silk robe, and the room smelled of perfume and cigarettes. My grandmother smoked a lot, and the house was filled with ashtrays of all kinds—crystal, cloisonné, china, and glass, but never tacky plastic. I would think: What a great way to live, getting up whenever you feel like it, reading, taking walks, visiting your friends and writing letters, going for a swim, or, if it was winter, building a snow fort.

I think my grandmother was content by then. Given what her earlier life was like, it must have been a hard-won contentment.

When I was ten, my father developed back pain so severe that he was to spend the next few years going from doctor to doctor looking for relief and a diagnosis before he finally had successful surgery and recovered. For a while, he couldn't work; my mother found a job. Our house, which was normally full of visitors—my father was gregarious and could make friends of total strangers in a few minutes—became a dark, silent place.

I left grade school during the era of Sputnik, when we were all being told how much more Russian schoolchildren had to master than we did and how hard we'd have to work to keep up with those paragons. The junior high was even worse than elementary school. Its large, red-brick building struck me as much uglier than Henry St. John, which it superficially resembled; to enter this junior high school was to know dread and utter hopelessness.

By then, thanks to the torments of fifth grade, I had acquired the ability to vomit almost on cue in the mornings in order to convince my mother that I was too sick for school. I was also susceptible to colds, flu, stomach viruses, bronchitis, pneumonia, and almost any contagious illness that came my way, which meant more school days when I could stay home and read, an activity I much preferred to classes. When I was older, I occasionally ditched school entirely and went into downtown Albany, spending the day in the public library, the state library near the capitol, the Albany Institute of History and Art, and poking around in the bookstores that were often fronts for bookies. I looked older than my age, which kept me from being accosted by adults who might want to know why I wasn't in school. My attendance record in junior high may have been one of the worst in the school's history.

My grades plummeted. The only things saving me from complete academic failure were a good memory, an ability to cram at the last minute, and a lust for reading. A few accomplished teachers managed to salvage good work from me—Mr.

Cohen, who temporarily made me an *A* student in math; Mr. Ketchum, who taught English; Mrs. Pock, another English teacher, who greatly admired the actress Vivien Leigh; and Mr. Feldman, who was advisor to the school's drama club. They were the exceptions.

During the lunch period, some of my classmates and I would go across the street to enjoy the cigarettes we weren't allowed to smoke on school grounds. The guys wore leather jackets and talked about cars and shop class; we girls, in Cleopatra eye makeup and beehive hairdos (I had to put on my makeup at school, knowing my father would never allow me out of the house wearing it), pretended to be fascinated by such discussions. All of us were, according to the school authorities, going nowhere fast.

The most significant event of those years was cutting school with a friend so that we could go downtown and see John F. Kennedy in a motorcade, the first time I had ever seen a presidential candidate. His hair, I recall, looked a lot redder in person.

*

I soon had a nervous breakdown. There were plenty of early warning signs—I had run away from home twice and regularly sneaked out of the house at night to see a guy I wasn't supposed to be seeing. I ended up in a place with a lot of other troubled kids and eventually got sane enough to think of putting my life back together. I was fourteen by then and have written more about this time in my life in an essay called "The Writer as Nomad." It was much worse than I care to mention here.

Before the breakdown, I had confronted my parents about the horrors of the high school I seemed doomed to attend. Fortunately, they were willing to let me go to another school, provided I could get admitted. The Albany Academy for Girls, a private day school, took a chance on me and gave me a full scholarship, for which I shall always be grateful. Maybe good scores on their entrance exams were what earned me admission, since little in my academic record showed any promise.

The curriculum was rigorous at the Academy, with lots of required courses in Latin, French, history, English, science, and math. The classes were small, with no more than fifteen girls and sometimes fewer students than that, which meant a lot of individual attention. Makeup wasn't allowed, and the only earrings we could wear were the tiniest and most discreet of posts. Our green uniforms were less than flattering, and our required brown shoes made our feet look like gunboats. In spite of myself, I responded to all of this and actually did well in my classes.

For the first time since my years in Ithaca, I didn't dread going to school.

My main extracurricular interest at the Academy was the literary magazine. I started off on its art board, doing sketches and illustrations, then moved to its literary board during my junior year. I also wrote stories for it, the most notable being one entitled "The Fink," which took place in a school playground and owed something to *Lord of the Flies*.

Among my friends were Debbie Mitchell, who often sneaked off with me to have a cigarette during the lunch hour, and Jane Grumbach, whose mother was the writer Doris Grumbach. In fact, Mrs. Grumbach had once taught at the Academy and was considered something of a scandal since her early novel *The Spoil of the Flowers* was supposedly based on her experiences at the school.

Writing had been partly an escape for me in childhood and partly a way to make some sense of a world that seemed bewildering at best. Until I had overcome a persistent stammer, writing was also my way of communicating and often the only means I had of convincing my teachers that I had learned anything at all. Now, for the first time, I began to feel that it might be a possible profession, an ambition my English teachers, Mrs. Thorstensen and Mrs. Collins, encouraged.

Not, of course, that I had any delusions about ever being able to make a living at it.

In the 1964 Academy yearbook, the *Academe*, my classmate Betty Klingaman wrote the following passage about me:

> Pam entered our class Sophomore year . . . destined to have an impact not only on our class, but also on the whole school. The winter *Academe* published Pam's treatise on the physical fitness tests, "Flabbies of the World, Arise!", and all those uncoordinated or merely happily flabby individuals in the school found that they had a public voice. Since then Pam has continued to present expositions, both verbally and literarily. She can frequently be heard defending her opinions over the babble of the lunchroom, and she has contributed more impartial critical viewpoints to the literary board of the *Academe*. Pam has consider-

able creative talent as a writer and as a designer. Her creative sensitivity, supplemented by her intellectual ability (Pam has received both a National Merit Letter of Commendation and a Regents Scholarship) ensures Pam a successful career wherever she is.

All of which is more flattering than I deserved, since Betty left out any mention of my abysmal and badly accented conversational French, all the cigarettes I covertly smoked in lavatories across New England during our senior class trip, and my efforts with Debbie to disrupt the school's annual gym meet, when the members of all the upper school classes had to compete on various pieces of gymnastic apparatus, on which most of us were as graceful as cattle. Betty even left out my contribution to the school's dress code. Miss Harris, the headmistress, had hauled me into her office during my junior year to criticize my monumentally teased and heavily sprayed hair. Academy girls, she told me, were not supposed to wear "exotic" hairdos. I correctly pointed out that the official dress code said nothing about hair. By my senior year, there were new regulations covering that subject.

That Regents Scholarship was significant, though. I used it to go to college.

Back in the sixties, a New York State Regents Scholarship provided full tuition to any college or university in the state but didn't cover room, board, and a lot of other expenses. This meant that a public college or university was really my only practical choice. My father had recovered from a series of operations on his back, was well and working, and my mother had her job, but they were still getting back on their feet and would have all four of their children in college before long.

Luckily, there was a place that appealed to me—Harpur College in Binghamton, part of the state university system and a school known then as "the public Swarthmore." At the time, Harpur was on a trimester system, with classes starting in the beginning of July. I arrived at college less than a month after graduating from the Academy. ·

My roommate was Ruth Olsen, a worldly Manhattanite who knew a lot about art and literature (more than I did, anyway) and eventually taught me how to make *hamantaschen*, pastries traditionally eaten during Purim. We were both very briefly under the illusion that we might get through the required pre-med courses. Ruth smoked even more than I did and was about as reluctant to get up in the morning, which meant we missed a lot of morning classes. The dorm was usually noisy, so pretty soon I was doing a lot of studying at a bar in Binghamton, which was usually quiet until evenings when more students arrived. Eventually the bartender found out I was underage and threw me out.

The most significant event of that summer, other than realizing that I might want to change my major from biology to philosophy, was meeting George Zebrowski.

George was another freshman, having come to Harpur after graduating from a high school in the Bronx. Unlike some of us, George knew exactly what he wanted to do. He was going to be a writer. Furthermore, he was going to write science fiction. In fact, he and a few friends had already published their own small magazine of book reviews and critical pieces about science-fiction authors, and he had met many of the writers he admired, including Arthur C. Clarke, James Blish, and Isaac Asimov.

He had even started to write a piece of science fiction that would eventually become the novel *Macrolife.*

I was more mystified than impressed by these ambitions. What was science fiction anyway? I had read a little science fiction (mostly the novels of H. G. Wells) and had seen "The Twilight Zone," but there was a lot I didn't know. George set about to remedy my ignorance.

Our first date was not auspicious; we went to see Ingmar Bergman's film *The Seventh Seal.* We broke up a few times before realizing that we wanted to be together for a good long while. We were engaged about a year after we met and were living together by the time I was in graduate school, both of us vaguely assuming that eventually circumstances would compel us to get married.

We never did marry, but we are still living together. Whenever I mention the admittedly slim possibility of marriage to my mother, she tells me, "Better not—you might spoil the whole relationship."

"The Binghamton, New York, apartment in which George Zebrowski (in kitchen) and I (in front) first lived together. This apartment building was the setting for my 1983 novel The Alien Upstairs," *1971*

George Zebrowski, downtown Miami, Florida, 1977

*

Just before my junior year at Harpur, I dropped out, partly to earn needed money and partly because I still had no real idea of what I wanted to do. Having been granted a leave on my Regents Scholarship, I moved into a run-down but roomy off-campus apartment, shared with a succession of roommates and strangers crashing there temporarily, and found a job as an assembly-line solderer. The job was tedious, my Saturdays usually ruined by having to put in overtime, and I soon needed some diversion. One of my favorite activities was going to George's equally run-down apartment, which he shared with his friend Mike Orgill, to read his science-fiction books.

Perhaps without that boring job and the subsequent need for diversion, I would never have read enough science fiction to acquire the background necessary to write it.

The soldering job was followed by one as a sales clerk and then a position as a typist in the Harpur library. Harpur by then was beginning the

transformation that would turn it into the State University of New York at Binghamton, which meant lots of construction as new dormitories rose to house students. The faculty, whose offices were once scattered around the campus in various dorms and classroom buildings, now had an office tower. The public Swarthmore, with its small classes and empty stretches of land, was soon only a memory.

I became a student again about a year after dropping out. I took a lot of philosophy and history, figuring that I might as well study what I enjoyed while I had the chance. I also took a course in astronomy and met a student named Jack Dann in the lectures.

As it happened, Jack wanted to be a writer, too.

This was the sixties, so I went to a couple of Vietnam protests in Washington, D.C., and New York, hung around with some of the students who had founded our SDS (Students for a Democratic Society) chapter, and did drugs. The drugs, politically incorrect as it may be to say so now, didn't really do me any harm, but that may be because my intake was largely limited to marijuana, hashish, and the very occasional trip on acid. By then, I knew I wanted to study philosophy in graduate school and needed to keep my grades high enough to get a fellowship to pay for that. I was also taking Greek, since classical philosophy was my main interest, and studying it without knowing Greek seemed akin to trying to learn physics without knowing math. The Greek professors, unlike others at Harpur, were not tolerant of students who cut classes, which meant that you had to show up no matter how you were feeling.

It may be that the rigidity of these professors and their demands were the only barriers standing between me and a totally drug-sodden, crazed sixties existence.

I had also sold my first published science-fiction story during my senior year in college. This was almost accidental; I had started a story, partly out of exasperation with George and Jack Dann, who had actually had a story of theirs accepted by a little magazine. I threw away my story before it was finished; George fished it out of the wastebasket and told me to complete it and send it out. Edward L. Ferman, then editor of the *Magazine of Fantasy and Science Fiction,* bought this story, which was eventually published in 1970; its title was "Landed Minority." Appropriately, the story took place largely on a college campus.

That was my first sale, which was soon followed by a second, that of my story "Oasis" to David Gerrold for his anthology *Protostars*.

Officially, I spent the next two-and-a-half years as a graduate student in philosophy at the State University of New York at Binghamton. The school had given me a fellowship, and I taught students in introductory philosophy courses while taking my own courses and working on my master's thesis, which was about the ethical theories of Plato and Aristotle.

Unofficially, that fellowship was also subsidizing my fiction writing.

*

I watched the first moon landing, in 1969, at a bar in Paducah, Kentucky. What I remember is that everyone in this bar—the construction workers, the GIs on leave, and a couple of mean-looking, middle-aged truckers—all went absolutely silent when Neil Armstrong made his way down the Lunar Module's ladder to the moon's surface. We were rapt; nobody ordered any drinks for at least an hour. A church wouldn't have been any quieter.

I was in Kentucky because my mother's parents, who had moved from Indiana to western Kentucky when my grandfather retired, were celebrating their fiftieth wedding anniversary. So many relatives had shown up for this event that we took all the motel rooms there were in the small town where my grandparents lived.

Fifty years! How had they managed it? I once ventured the opinion, in my grandmother's presence, that maybe more people had better marriages long ago. "No, they didn't," she told me. "They were unhappy, a lot of them. Most of them just didn't have any way out."

In fact, my grandfather's parents were divorced, and his early life hadn't been easy. He had left school at fourteen, although he went to night school and continued to educate himself after that. He had been drafted and sent to France during World War I. For most of his life, he worked for a brush company, a job he didn't much like; during the thirties, when there was some violence at his plant in Brooklyn, he often had to carry a gun to work to protect himself. In spite of these circumstances, he was one of the calmest, most serene people I have ever met. Never once did I see him lose his temper or betray any unhappiness. My mother told me that, while she was growing up, she never once heard her father raise his voice.

Grandmother Richards had her disappointments in life as well. She suffered from migraines when young, a tendency I inherited, and was often in bed for days at a stretch. She played the violin, but not well enough to be a soloist (or so she thought), and no orchestra then would hire a woman musician. My grandmother settled for teaching children the violin in her home, sending the more gifted ones to other teachers when she had taught them all that she could.

How had my grandparents stayed together? Part of it must have been that they simply assumed that they would, that only the worst sort of betrayal could separate them. Part of it may have been that my grandfather, who never spoke of the father who had abandoned him, was determined never to hurt his own wife and children in that way. But my grandparents were also an extremely affectionate and devoted couple; well into their eighties (they lived to celebrate a sixtieth anniversary and missed their seventieth by only a couple of years), they would hold hands and hug each other whenever the opportunity presented itself. They were perfectly happy spending time by themselves; indeed, their marriage was probably their refuge from the outside.

Watching them, I didn't have to assume that everything was over when you got old.

"In Hermosa Beach, California, near the home of my brother Scott," 1984

"My mother, Shirley Sargent, and her mother, Mildred Richards," 1990

*

It's said that the Vietnam War was one of the most formative events for people my age, and this is true. The war permeated our lives and dominated almost every decision most of us made, whether we were directly affected by it or not. When George dropped out of college for a while to work for the *Binghamton Press,* his draft board in New York City was quick to haul him in for a physical; luckily, he got a 1-Y rating. By the late sixties, more guys we knew had been swept up in the draft. A few became exiles; we had friends who regularly drove young men about to be drafted up to Canada.

Maybe the Vietnam War officially ended in 1973, but it seemed to go on a lot longer than that. By then, more men I knew had come back, and some of them had a lot of physical and mental scars. My brother-in-law became convinced, with good reason, that he had been exposed to Agent Orange during his hitch.

In the town I live in now, we've had various waves of recent Southeast Asian immigrants brought here by the war. In the late seventies, some of the families who had escaped at the last minute were settled in this upstate New York region. They were soon followed by their relatives. In the nineties, we got some new neighbors, Amerasian children of U.S. servicemen.

All of which demonstrates a truth I learned from my father: for those who experience a war, it's never over.

By the time I left graduate school, deciding that I didn't want a Ph.D. after all, I had sold a few more stories. The word was already out that there would be a shortage of academic positions in philosophy departments for a long time to come, so embarking on a career as a free-lance writer made as much sense as struggling at Columbia, where I had been accepted, to get a useless degree. I was also feeling burned-out by the academic world, in which pettiness and departmental warfare among the professors seemed a way of life.

The early seventies were a time—now long past, perhaps forever—when less than a hundred dollars a month could secure an apartment, and a few more extra dollars a week could feed a couple. George and I had an apartment near downtown Binghamton and could survive even if only one of us sold a story each month. In the summers, George brought in extra money by going down to New York to work as a swimming pool filtration plant operator for the Parks Department. I spent a summer up in Albany employed by a paper company while working on my first novel at night. This book never saw print, nor was it ever shown to an editor; I threw it away, thus saving myself a lot of embarrassment and shame, but I had to finish it first to see how truly bad it was.

George and I wrote. Occasionally, we went to New York to see editors and got in what travel we could; a couple of trips were to science-fiction conventions in Philadelphia and Toronto, since we could justify that as business. We had our share of adventures and endured personal problems of the sort that might interest those looking for sensational revelations, but our lives were largely bound up with our work. Whatever else happened to us, it was the writing that really mattered. I suspect that this is true of most writers, in spite of countless biographies, novels, and movies in which you can be left wondering how the writers featured in them ever got any writing done. Most of the time, you're sitting alone in a room or at a desk writing, which doesn't make for a lot of drama, so it's not surprising that the image many have of writers involves more dramatic pursuits that are often incidental to the work.

We also assumed that, if we just kept writing, eventually things would work out, a delusion we might not have had if we had been older and wiser in the ways of the world. I often tell aspiring writers, "Start when you're young, before you know any better. By the time you find out how impossible a profession it is, it'll be too late."

My first novel was written by stealth. I crept up on it by writing a few stories about a family of cloned people, selling one of them to Joseph Elder, who was doing an anthology of science-fiction stories about sex called *Eros in Orbit* for Simon and Schuster. It occurred to me, sometime around 1973 or so, that I might write a novel about the Swensons, the characters in these stories. Joseph Elder, as it happened, was an editor at Fawcett, so it made sense to offer him the novel.

He bought the book, after a couple of months of agonizing on my part, since I was going against the odds by trying to sell a first novel before finishing it. Eventually, I received a contract, a document exactly one legal-sized page in length, written in comprehensible language.

Those days are gone forever, too. My most recent book contract runs five pages, in tiny type—considerably shorter than a lot of recent book contracts—and I still have trouble figuring out what some of the clauses mean.

That first novel, *Cloned Lives,* came out in 1976, at about the same time as my anthology *Bio-Futures,* which I edited for Vintage/Random House.

Before selling *Cloned Lives* to Fawcett, I had sold an anthology called *Women of Wonder* to Vintage and can only assume, looking back on it now, that this happened almost by accident. My colleague Vonda McIntyre, after reading a Vintage science-fiction anthology in which all the stories were by men, had written to an editor to protest. This Vintage editor, Janet Kafka, wrote back to Vonda, suggesting that she do a book of stories by women. Vonda, knowing that I had been trying to sell just such an anthology for a couple of years, called me up and told me to try Janet.

I had no agent at the time and was operating in almost total ignorance of publishing. An unknown writer with a few published stories, I was trying to sell an anthology to one of the most demanding houses in the business. I had a title for the book—thanks to George and our good friend

Jack Dann, who had sat around brainstorming with me until "women of wonder" popped out of our mouths simultaneously—and also a rough idea of what the contents might be, but little else.

Janet Kafka bought the book and, thanks to my total inexperience, Vintage gave me an advance that was larger than I expected. This happened because when Janet called me to ask how much money I needed to secure permissions for the stories I would buy, I misunderstood and thought she was asking how much I needed *in toto* to do the book. I gave her a figure that I knew other anthologists were getting, figuring Vintage might give me a bit less; instead, I got twice the amount I requested.

This kind of luck almost never happens, and I have never again been so lucky.

Women of Wonder came out in 1975—although Janet gave me an early copy at a party for editors and writers held in New York in late 1974—the first book ever published with my name on it. In a way, it wasn't really mine, since I was only the editor, but I remember staring at it for some time, not certain it was quite real.

In many ways, *Women of Wonder* was an education; I learned much about the contributions women had made to science fiction while editing that book. Working on it was also strenuous; George and I moved to a larger apartment while I was reading for the anthology, and I did a lot of my research crawling from box to box in our new place, pulling out books and lying on the floor to make notes. I felt compelled to do my best with that book; to fail would only be letting down other women who wrote science fiction. Often, I have felt that this particular anthology was about due—or overdue—and that I was only a tool it used to get itself published.

Vintage did two more *Women of Wonder* anthologies during the seventies, and Joe Elder bought my second novel, *The Sudden Star,* for Fawcett. Selling that novel hadn't been easy. Joe had his doubts about the proposal I had sent him; I pitched the book to him over the phone in New York, wheezing and coughing with bronchitis as I answered his questions about my proposal. It dawned on me then that this novel, with its multiple points of view, was going to require more technical skill than I had yet demonstrated; its complicated plot, which I did not plan in advance, developed during the writing. Joe left Fawcett before *The Sudden Star* came out to become a literary agent—my first agent, in fact, since I became his client right after learning of his plans.

Joe still represents me. In a profession where most of us are like gypsies, wandering from publisher to publisher and, it seems, losing editors almost as soon as we find them, the relationship between writer and agent is about the most continuity any of us has.

Not all of my novels were sold before I wrote them. *Watchstar* was written before it was offered to David Hartwell at Pocket Books, who published it in 1980. I wrote *The Alien Upstairs* while recovering from surgery, scrawling it in a notebook with cardboard covers; Pat LoBrutto at Doubleday bought that book. My 1986 novel *The Shore of Women* started out as a piece of short fiction; after reaching page two hundred, it finally dawned on me that it was going to be a novel. Lisa Healy at Crown bought *Shore,* but I did a lot of revising and rewriting for her. Luckily, Lisa gave me the space and time to do that rewriting, correctly seeing that my earlier draft left out much of the real story, that of my characters Arvil and Birana.

When I began writing this book, all I had was a vision of a young man making his way to a mysterious city. I knew he was living in a society made up entirely of males but didn't know what he would find during his journey until another character began to speak to me, a young woman who lived in that city. Writing it was largely an unconscious process, at least in the first draft; I had to follow the characters and discover their world along with them.

The Shore of Women has probably been my most successful novel to date. The book was sold to British and French publishers before coming out in the U.S. and brought a lot of mail from readers, many of whom admitted that they had never read a science-fiction book before. The editor who bought *Shore* in England, Carmen Callil, was Managing Director of Chatto and Windus and also Angela Carter's editor; in a letter to me about my book, she admitted to finding my novel "a delightful surprise." Part of the reason *Shore* was a surprise was that Carmen had never heard of me and my work, even though I had been writing for almost seventeen years by then.

A lot of science-fiction readers had never heard of me, either—or, if they had, they associated me with the *Women of Wonder* anthologies and assumed that I was primarily an editor.

There were good reasons for this obscurity.

In 1972, I made my first appearance as a public speaker, at a conference of the New York State English Council, an organization of teachers. Nervousness kept me from sleeping the night before the speech; terror made me grateful there was a podium on the stage for me to lean against, since my legs were shaking. The speech was a disaster. I vowed never to make a speech again, a promise I pretty much kept for the next thirteen years.

During my early years as a writer, I went to various science-fiction conventions, large gatherings of writers and fans, but had stopped attending them altogether by the mid-seventies. Crowds were making me increasingly nervous, and often I was too much in awe of the accomplished writers around me to do much more than gape at them from a corner. My health got worse, not improving until the eighties. Finances played a role; those times when little more than a hundred dollars could pay for a weekend at a convention had receded into history. I wanted to spend what little I had on traveling to places I hadn't yet seen and where I wouldn't have to impress editors, readers, or other writers.

But part of my reason for growing more solitary was a feeling that a lot of this activity was distracting. I had avoided the workshops popular among many of the writers I knew for fear that I'd lose the ability to hear my own voice. Going to a lot of gatherings meant taking more time away from work that required extended periods of concentration. I had to get my work done. Then I could worry about public appearances.

I've gotten over most of these earlier fears, although that may be largely a matter of getting too old to care about such things anymore—after a while, you don't have time to worry about them. It may be that I would have done myself more good earlier by making the rounds of parties, conventions, and editors' offices, by making more of a noise.

But maybe not.

Recently, much to my surprise, I found myself scheduled at a conference to speak on the subject of self-promotion to newer writers. My fellow writers were offering various suggestions about how to handle bookstore autograph sessions and the like, and finally I said, "Look, unless you do your work, none of that's going to matter. You've got to follow your own instincts anyway—that's the only way you can find out what sort of writer you really are. So if you don't want to give speeches or go around advertising yourself in various ways, don't do it."

This goes completely against a lot of accepted wisdom, usually phrased as "the squeaky wheel gets the grease." It probably also goes against a lot of current publishing practice, in which the writer—a more accurate term in some cases might be "alleged author"—is the commodity or brand name the publisher is actually promoting, rather than a book or body of work.

But I still think my counsel is good advice, even if it means remaining more obscure than you might otherwise. By the time you do go public, you may actually have something to say.

When I began writing, it helped that I was living with another writer, namely George, who understood the demands writing can make. Our friend Jack Dann had moved back to Binghamton after dropping out of law school—in a fit of ecstasy, he had sold all his law books after selling a story to *Orbit,* Damon Knight's influential anthology series. In 1972, each of us managed to get a story into the same volume of Michael Moorcock's anthology series *New Worlds.*

I met Terry Carr, the editor who was most supportive of my early short-fiction efforts, when he came up from New York to give a speech at a science-fiction course George was teaching, the first full-credit course in the subject ever offered by SUNY (State University of New York) at Binghamton. (Naturally, as soon as the course was successful and wildly popular, the English department took it over, put it into the hands of professors and graduate students, and got rid of George.) Terry had rejected the first two stories I sent him, but with such wonderful letters that I almost didn't mind the rejections. In 1973, at a party in Toronto, Terry asked if I had a new story to show him. I replied that I did but had doubts about it. "Send it to me," he said. "Probably isn't any good," I replied. "Send it to me," he said in a very firm voice, "and let me decide." He must have been amused by the spectacle of a writer trying to talk him *out* of considering a story.

The editor who bought my first short-story collection was Pat LoBrutto, who was then at Ace. I wasn't at all sure I deserved a short-story collection, but Pat took it anyway. It didn't sell many copies but got some nice reviews.

*

By the time *The Sudden Star* was published in 1979, I had sold three novels to Pocket Books, where David Hartwell was launching an ambitious science-fiction publishing program, eventually to be called Timescape Books. One of my novels was the already completed *Watchstar.* The second, *The Golden Space,* a story of immortal human beings, was another novel I sneaked up on by writing it in sections. The third was to be an epic called *Venus of Dreams.*

Watchstar was beautifully produced and became a Science Fiction Book Club selection, but didn't do all that well. *The Golden Space* had an ugly cover, little promotion, and bombed, although it got some reviews and comments I still cherish. *Venus of Dreams* was never published by Timescape, because by then that entire publishing program had collapsed, despite having had in its line important novels by Gregory Benford, Suzy McKee Charnas, Michael Bishop, Lisa Goldstein, and Norman Spinrad, to name only a few.

By the end of 1982, my career seemed over. Except for Harper and Row and my editor there, Antonia Markiet, who bought my young adult novels, I had no science-fiction publisher, and the remaining editors in the field seemed uninterested in my work.

I would have to start all over again.

My father had been ill, off and on, for a couple of years, and by the summer of 1983 he was so thin and frail that he resembled an El Greco painting. I went home to help take care of him. At the time, I was working with a couple of musicians on what we hoped would be a science-fiction rock musical. Nothing came of this project in the end, although my father, with his musical interests, enjoyed hearing about it.

He was dying, but everyone in the family was in denial about that. He would get well; after all, he wasn't that old. Even when he went into the hospital for what would turn out to be the last time, we kept telling ourselves that he would be all right in the end.

We took turns keeping watch at his bedside; someone had to be there to control and question the bureaucracy of oncologists, nurses, technicians, and other specialists who never seemed aware of what anyone else was doing. One of my jobs was to keep away any hospital clergy trying to bring spiritual solace; another was to dial telephone numbers when my father wanted to call one of his political cronies. He had been a county legislator for several years by then, managing to be independent enough to irritate members of both parties, and an election was coming up that fall.

Sometime during that summer, word reached me from my agent that an editor at Bantam Books, Lou Aronica, had bought *Venus of Dreams* and two sequels. I passed this news along to my father during my next stint of hospital duty. "It's going to be a trilogy," I told him, "because the editor thinks it's too big a story to be just one book, and he's probably right. It does naturally divide into three sections anyway."

My father had his doubts. "Don't do a god-damn trilogy," he said. "You'll just end up repeating yourself." I told him that I would be careful to avoid that. "Then it'll take you a while to finish it," he said, "if you don't want to do the same damned thing over and over again." This turned out to be true.

He died in August. His memorial service was so crowded with friends that many people had to stand. We took his ashes to the Adirondacks and buried them there. One of his favorite sayings was "Know when to get off the stage," and he had always feared dying too late, when there might be no one left to remember him. He avoided that. Lots of people mourned him.

As one person at the memorial service put it, looking around at the mob of mourners gathered there, "Ed always did like a crowd."

*

History was one of the subjects I studied in college, and this probably had an effect on my writing, whether that's obvious or not. In my novels *Venus of Dreams* and *Venus of Shadows,* I tried to write as if I were looking back on the events in those books, which take place about six hundred years from now, from a point even further in the future.

How do we get from where we are now to a particular imagined future? I couldn't see how it was possible to write a convincing science-fiction novel without working that out in some detail, and with some sense of historical development. It's probably no accident that Malik Haddad of *Venus of Shadows* and Laissa of *The Shore of Women,* crucial characters in those novels, are both historians.

It may also be indicative that the *Venus* novels are about several generations of a family. My original inspiration for them was Thomas Mann's *Buddenbrooks;* it occurred to me that the generations of a family would reflect and deepen the impact of the changes in the society around them. Perhaps my own family's experiences influenced me as well.

"Jack Dann (right), George, and I at the first Local Author Brunch in Binghamton, held in our honor by the Women's National Book Association and the Binghamton Press & Sun-Bulletin," *June 16, 1985*

Much as I enjoyed science fiction, I hoped to write other kinds of books and proposed a historical novel to Antonia Markiet, my Harper and Row editor. I wanted to do a young adult novel about Genghis Khan, a figure who had long fascinated me, thinking that his adventurous early life might make a good story for young readers. Toni had her doubts about this idea and turned me down; she didn't say so, but maybe a teenaged Genghis Khan didn't seem a suitable role model for young adults. I didn't mind, because by then I wanted to do a different story, that of the Mongol women about whom history says so little.

Lisa Healy of Crown eventually bought *Ruler of the Sky,* my Genghis Khan novel; Carmen Callil and Alison Samuel at Chatto and Windus secured the British rights before the book was written. Gary Jennings, the author of *Aztec* and other historical novels, praised *Ruler of the Sky* highly and called it the "definitive" novel on the subject; Elizabeth Marshall Thomas, author of *Reindeer Moon,* loved the book and called it "fascinating." I immodestly mention this only because I was overjoyed that these two fine writers admired my novel. Five years of intensive work had gone into that book, during which I often woke up in the middle of the night in terror, fearing that I had taken on much too ambitious a task and would fail completely. Research, work, and travel had taken such a toll on my physical strength that I finally forced myself to give up smoking, something I didn't dare do while I was writing *Ruler* and in need of my nicotine crutch.

Ruler of the Sky came out at the beginning of 1993, ready to make its way, like Genghis Khan himself, in an increasingly uncertain world.

*

I traveled in what was then the Soviet Union during the summer of 1988, for no better reason than that it seemed like the time to go. The people I met there sometimes seemed optimistic and at other times convinced that things were only going to get worse. A few of them spoke openly about getting rid of the worst aspects of the old system but worried about what might take its place. The signs of commerce were everywhere—boys trading handcrafted articles for American jeans and cigarettes, black marketeers offering to change money, open-air markets selling produce unavailable in stores, prostitutes loitering in bars and around hotels where Westerners stayed. Official establishments—banks, stores, hotels—were rife with inefficiency.

I didn't know then that I was seeing the last days of that political system, and supposed that it might actually reform itself instead of collapsing. Surely I had read enough Russian history to know better.

In Yaroslavl, I met a young woman who had become an avid reader of Vladimir Nabokov, now that she was finally able to get his books. She bombarded me with questions about a writer's life in the West. Was it true that we actually had no union to protect our interests? Did we actually have to negotiate our own contracts for each book instead of simply assuming a publishing house would bring them out once they were turned in? How did we live, anyway?

A question that I, along with what must be many bewildered formerly Soviet writers, have been asking myself more often lately.

*

"I'm a writer," I said to George not long ago, "so I'm used to working without a safety net. But now they're taking away my trapeze."

This was in late 1992, when I learned that my editor at Bantam, Betsy Mitchell, had spoken to my agent, Joe Elder. Her message for me, reduced to its essentials, was this: We no longer want your third *Venus* novel. We don't want to publish your books anymore. Get lost.

I had no warning this message was coming, no word that anything was wrong. It didn't seem to matter that my books had all done pretty well and that I had been encouraged to believe that I had a future at Bantam. Downsizing had come to publishing, and if that meant breaking contracts, dumping writers unceremoniously, and destroying what is left of the traditional author/editor relationship, so be it. We live in a more brutal world these days.

On the heels of this news came word that, twenty-three years after publishing my first story, I was on the final ballot for a Nebula Award, given annually by the Science Fiction Writers of America for outstanding novels and stories in the field. This was the first time I had ever been in the running for this award. I'm not sure what this proves—maybe that patience and persistence pay off, or maybe only that if you hang around long enough, people will eventually notice you're there. In the wake of my dismissal from Bantam's list, news of

"One of the too few times when my brothers, sister, and I were all in the same place, in this case Craig's backyard in the summer of 1987. In back: Scott, Pamela, Connie, and Craig Sargent; in the front, my sisters-in-law, Virginia Sargent and Barbara Sargent."

the Nebula nomination and the subsequent news that I had to my shock and delight won the award, gave me a renewed appreciation of the sense of irony that is one of a writer's essential tools.

Ten years after resuscitating my writing career, I'm starting over again. Maybe a better way to put this is that I am in a period of transition, with my first historical novel out, plans for another I hope to write, new *Women of Wonder* anthologies to edit for Harcourt Brace and Company, and hopes of finding a new home for the last volume of the *Venus* trilogy. One part of my life is past, but another is beginning. I try to keep in mind what I rediscovered during the eighties, namely, the joy to be found in the work itself.

Do the writing, and the rest will follow, even if it takes a while. Writers have to hold to that article of faith, whether it's true or not. The good happens side by side with the bad.

BIBLIOGRAPHY

Fiction:

Cloned Lives, Fawcett (New York), 1976, Fontana (London), 1981.

Starshadows (short stories), Ace Books, 1977.

The Sudden Star, Fawcett, 1979, published as *The White Death,* Fontana, 1980.

Watchstar (Earthminds series), Pocket Books, 1980.

The Golden Space, Simon & Schuster/Timescape, 1982.

The Alien Upstairs, Doubleday, 1983.

Earthseed, Harper (New York), 1983, Collins (London), 1984.

Eye of the Comet (Earthminds series), Harper, 1984.

Homesmind (Earthminds series), Harper, 1984.

Venus of Dreams (Venus series), Bantam (New York), 1986, Bantam (London), 1989.

The Shore of Women, Crown (New York), 1986, Chatto & Windus (London), 1987.

Martin H. Greenberg, editor, *The Best of Pamela Sargent,* Academy Chicago, 1987.

Alien Child, Harper, 1988.

Venus of Shadows (Venus series), Doubleday, 1988.

Ruler of the Sky: A Novel of Genghis Khan, Crown (New York), 1993, Chatto & Windus (London), 1993.

Editor:

(And contributor) *Women of Wonder: Science Fiction Stories by Women about Women,* Random House/ Vintage (New York), 1975, Penguin (London), 1978.

(And contributor) *Bio-Futures: Science Fiction Stories about Biological Metamorphosis,* Random House/ Vintage, 1976.

(And contributor) *More Women of Wonder: Science Fiction Novelettes by Women about Women,* Random House/Vintage, 1976, Penguin, 1979.

(And contributor) *The New Women of Wonder: Recent Science Fiction Stories by Women about Women,* Random House/Vintage, 1978.

(With Ian Watson) *Afterlives: Stories about Life after Death,* Random House/Vintage, 1986.

Contributor to numerous anthologies, including David Gerrold, editor, *Protostars,* Ballantine, 1971; Michael Moorcock, editor, *New Worlds Quarterly Three,* Berkley Books, 1972; Terry Carr, editor, *Universe Two,* Ace Books, 1972; Jack Dann, editor, *Wandering Stars,* Harper, 1972; Joseph Elder, editor, *Eros in Orbit,* Trident, 1973; Thomas N. Scortia and Chelsea Quinn Yarbro, editors, *Two Views of Wonder,* Ballantine, 1973; Carr, editor, *Universe Four,* Random House, 1974; Damon Knight, editor, *Orbit 20,* Harper, 1978; Dann, editor, *Immortal,* Harper, 1978; Michael Bishop, editor, *Light Years and Dark: Science Fiction and Fantasy of and for Our Time,* Berkley, 1984; Carr, editor, *Best Science Fiction of the Year,* Tor, 1985; Martin H. Greenberg, editor, *Foundation's Friends,* Tor, 1989; Gregory Benford and Greenberg, editors, *What Might Have Been: Alternate Americas,* Bantam, 1992. Also contributor to science fiction and fantasy magazines. A collection of Sargent's works and papers is in the David Paskow Science Fiction Collection, Temple University, Philadelphia.

Cumulative Index

CUMULATIVE INDEX

The names of essayists who appear in the series are in boldface type. Subject references are followed by volume and page number(s). When a subject reference appears in more than one essay, names of the essayists are also provided.